SMERSH
STALIN'S SECRET WEAPON

ALSO BY THE AUTHOR

The Perversion of Knowledge: The True
Story of Soviet Science

VADIM J. BIRSTEIN

FOREWORD BY NIGEL WEST

НЕ БОЛТАЙ!

SMERSH

STALIN'S SECRET WEAPON

Biteback Publishing

This paperback edition published in Great Britain in 2013 by
Biteback Publishing Ltd
Westminster Tower
3 Albert Embankment
London SE1 7SP
Copyright © Vadim J. Birstein 2011

ISBN 978-1-84954-567-9

10 9 8 7 6 5 4 3 2 1

A CIP catalogue record for this book is available from the British Library.

Set in Garamond
Cover design by Namkwan Cho

MIX
Paper from
responsible sources
FSC
www.fsc.org   FSC® C020471

CONTENTS

Contents (continued)

Extra web content located on http://www.smershbook.com:

Appendix I. Red Army and Navy Officers Arrested During WWII
Appendix II. Foreign Diplomats Arrested by SMERSH from 1944 to 1945
Appendix III. Finnish Persons Arrested by SMERSH in April, 1945

Foreword

Ian Fleming purported in his first James Bond book, *Casino Royale,* published in April 1953, to report factually about SMERSH, described as part of the 'MWD', the successor to the NKVD, and headed by Lavrenti Beria. This particular passage is a curious overlap of error and accuracy, a confusion of the MGB, the *Ministerstvo Gosudarstvennoy Bezopasnosti,* being the Ministry of State Security, and the MVD, the *Ministerstvo Vnutrennikh Del,* which was the Soviet Ministry of Interior Affairs that had emerged from the old NKVD prior to the establishment of the KGB in 1954, following the death of Stalin the previous March, the same year that *Casino Royale* was published.

Fleming's dossier, supposedly prepared by Section S to brief Bond's Chief M, gives an account of SMERSH, an organization concerned, as he correctly mentioned, with counter intelligence and executions which really had existed between April 1943 and March 1946. Although SMERSH had been disbanded and absorbed in the MGB's Third Main Directorate by the time Fleming wrote about it, very few outside of the international intelligence community had any knowledge of the agency which had been created by Stalin to liquidate counter revolutionaries and those suspected of collaboration with the Nazis.

That Fleming lacked any detailed understanding of the real SMERSH is suggested by his assertion that it had been responsible for the murder of Leon Trotsky in August 1940, at a time when it had not yet been created. In fact Trotsky's assassination had been carried out by the NKVD, as is now well-documented, particularly by General Pavel Sudoplatov who had supervised the operation from Moscow, even if at the time the Kremlin publicly had professed innocence of the crime. Fleming's mistake was entirely understandable because by April 1953 very little had been published openly about Soviet wartime or postwar intelligence activities. Indeed, the first book dedicated to the subject, David Dallin's *Soviet Espionage,* would not be released in New York until 1955, so Fleming's slightly inaccurate version almost certainly would have had to have come from official sources. Much information about the structure of Soviet intelligence and its activities would be revealed in 1954 upon the defections of Yuri Rastvorov, Piotr Deriabin, Nikolai Khokhlov and Evdokia and Vladimir Petrov, but when Fleming was writing *Casino Royale,* none of that was available. Certainly word had spread to Russian émigré communities, especially from postwar refugees, about SMERSH's operations, but Fleming's analysis, of only 'a few hundred operatives of very high quality divided into five departments', has a definite air of authenticity, as doubtless was intended. Although his breakdown of SMERSH's five departments, being counter intelligence, operations, administration and finance, investigations and prosecutions, was not strictly accurate, it was close enough. In fact SMERSH was divided into five 'administrations', being personnel, operations, intelligence, investigations and prosecutions.

In 1953, when 007 first was introduced, there was a widespread perception that intelligence agencies routinely murdered their adversaries, and there was good reason for people to believe the worst. Particularly during the period of the quadripartite occupation of Germany and Austria, the Soviets became notorious for abducting their victims, never to be seen again. Although the existence of SMERSH was not widely acknowledged, just such an organization had existed during the latter part of World War II to eliminate collaborators who had acted for the Nazis in 'stay-behind' networks. SMERSH, the Russian acronym for 'death to spies', consisted of killers trained by the NKVD who moved into newly-liberated areas directly behind the front-line troops to mop up enemy spy-rings. Their tactics were deadly but effective, and although SMERSH had been disbanded soon after the war, the Soviets retained a group of experienced assassins who were deployed overseas to liquidate opponents of the state. Details of the NKVD's 9th Section would emerge through the testimony of Nikolai Khokhlov in February 1954 when he confessed to having been commissioned to shoot the Ukrainian nationalist leader, George Okolovich, in Frankfurt, with an ingenious cyanide gas-gun concealed inside a pack of cigarettes. Khokhlov's shocking revelations, of state-sponsored, institutionalized assassination, were given widespread publicity, so Fleming's adoption of SMERSH as a sinister adversary in his fiction is unsurprising.

Later, in the 1957 *From Russia with Love*, Fleming would insert an Author's Note, insisting that SMERSH was still in existence, based at 13 Sretenka Ulitsa in Moscow, and employing 40,000 personnel. He claimed SMERSH was 'the murder apparat of the MGB', thereby introducing a further complication for between 1946 and 1953, the MGB had run the Soviet Union's foreign intelligence operations.

In his *Thunderball*, published in March 1961, Fleming would acknowledge that SMERSH 'had been disbanded on the orders of Khruschev [sic] in 1958' but then, inexplicably, assert that it had been 'replaced by the Special Executive Department of the MWD', thus repeating his original error in *Casino Royale* which the author had corrected in *From Russia with Love*.

The first eye-witness account of SMERSH from the inside emerged in 1972 when Captain Boris Baklanov published his memoirs, *The Nights Are Longest There*, under the pseudonym A. I. Romanov. He had defected in

Vienna in November 1947 and had been resettled in England as 'Boris Haddon' but news of the event was suppressed for more than two decades. In his autobiography Baklanov described how he had served in an NKVD demolition battalion during the war before attending an intelligence school in Babushkin and then being transferred to SMERSH.

Whether Fleming was granted access by the security authorities to Baklanov is unknown, but much of his information did come from privileged sources, as can be seen by his brief reference in *From Russia with Love* to Grigory Tokaev, a Soviet aeronautical expert and a GRU military intelligence officer who had sought political asylum in England in 1947. The author referred to Tokaev's defection as a major setback for the Soviets, but in 1961 Tokaev, who had by then begun a new career as an academic in London and a rocket guidance system designer in Texas, was hardly a household name even if his *Betrayal of an Ideal* had attracted considerable attention when it had been promoted in 1954 with covert support from the Foreign Office's propaganda branch.

During the Cold War denigration of the Kremlin's policies was part of the West's strategy, and both Baklanov and Tokaev were willing to collaborate by exposing SMERSH. Moscow continued to assassinate political opponents, as confirmed by two further defectors, Bogdan Stashinsky in 1961 and Oleg Lyalin in 1971. Indeed, the poisoning in November 2006 of Alexander Litvinenko in a London hotel with polonium-210, a rare radioactive compound, suggests that the topic of Russian governments resorting to extra-legal liquidation remains highly relevant more than two decades after the collapse of the Soviet bloc.

Accordingly, it would appear in retrospect that thanks to Fleming's imagination, and his access to certain Soviet defectors, SMERSH became one of the world's best-known, and notorious, intelligence agencies. However, the truth is even more remarkable.

Nigel West
June 2011

Acknowledgments

I am very grateful to all my colleagues and friends who provided me with information, identified sources, made critical notes, discussed or edited the text and found materials and photos in Moscow archives:

Dr. Vadim Altskan (United States Holocaust Memorial Museum, Washington, DC, USA), Professor John Q. Barrett (St. John's University in New York City, USA), Ms. Susanne Berger (Washington, USA), Professor Jeffrey Burds (Northeastern University, Boston, USA), Professor Emil Draitser (Hunter College, New York, USA), Dr. Hildrun Glass (Ludwig-Maximilian University, Munich, Germany), Dr. Andreas Hilger (Helmut-Schmidt-University of the Federal Armed Forces, Hamburg, Germany), Mr. Sergei Gitman (Moscow, Russia), Mr. Tony Hiss (New York, USA), Dr. Amy Knight (Summit, New Jersey, USA), Dr. Craig G. McKay (Uppsala, Sweden), Dr. Michael Parrish (Indiana University, Indiana, USA), Dr. Nikita Petrov and Mr. Arsenii Roginsky (Memorial Society, Moscow, Russia), and, finally, Ms. Lovice Ullein-Reviczky (Antal Ullein-Reviczky Foundation, Hungary).

I am also grateful to Dr. Karl Spalcke (Bonn, Germany) for sharing with me some details of his terrifying experience of growing up in a Lefortovo Prison cell in Moscow, where he was put together with his mother and spent 6 years of his life, from 13 through 19 years old.

I am also very thankful to my cousin, Anna Birstein (Moscow, Russia), for her permission to use the famous Soviet poster created by my aunt, Nina Vatolina, in June 1941, just after the Nazi invasion. The design of the cover of this book is based on a famous WWII poster depicting a Russian woman's head with a finger at her lips emblazoned with the motto "Don't chatter!"

Finally, I am extremely indebted to my wife, Kathryn Birstein, for her constant support and interest in my research work as well as her extensive editorial assistance. Without her, this book would not have been possible.

NOTES ON TRANSLITERATION AND ARCHIVAL MATERIALS

In transliterating from Russian to English a modified version of the Standard Library of Congress system for the Russian vowels was used, especially in the initial positions:

E = Ye (Yezhov, not Ezhov),

Ia = Ya (Yagoda, not Iagoda),

Iu = Yu (Yurii, not Iurii).

In the final position of last names 'ii' becomes 'y' (Trotsky, not Trotskii), and 'iia' is usually given as 'ia' (Izvestia, not Izvestiia).

On first usage, the names of institutions are given in transliterated Russian (in italics) followed by the English translation.

The majority of documents translated and cited in this book come from the following Russian archives:

APRF	*Arkhiv Prezidenta Rossiskoi Federatsii* [Presidential Archive]
FSB Archive	*Tsentral'nyi arkhiv FSB Rossii* [FSB Central Archive; FSB = *Federal'naya sluzhba bezopasnosti* or Federal Security Service]
RGVA	*Rossiiskii gosudarstvennyi voennyi arkhiv* [Russian State Military Archive]
TsAMO	*Tsentral'nyi arkhiv Ministerstva Oborony Rossiskoi Federatsii* [Defense Ministry Central Archive]
GARF	*Gosudarstvennyi arkhiv Rossiiskoi Federatsii* [State Archive of the Russian Federation]

If a document was published in a Russian book that includes a compilation of documents and could be found in many libraries, a reference to the document in this book is given, and the archival reference can be found in the book. For the documents published or cited in the Russian periodicals and found by the author, the complete reference to the document is given. Russian archival documents are cited and numbered by collection (Fond), inventory (Opis'), file (Delo), and page (List' or L., or in plural, Ll.)

Original documents were found in the RGVA (Moscow), GARF (Moscow), the archive of Vladimir Prison (Vladimir, Russia), the U.S. National Archives and Records Administration (NARA, Washington) and the Archives Branch of the U.S. Holocaust Memorial Museum (USHMM, Washington). Additionally, I used documents connected with the Raoul Wallenberg case available on the website of the Swedish Foreign Office and some documents available on the website of the British National Archives (Kew, Surrey).

The work in the RGVA in Moscow needs a comment. In 1990–91, when I had access to the files of the former foreign prisoners kept in the RGVA (Fond 451), it was called the Special Archive, and only researchers cleared by the KGB (*Komitet gosudarstvennoi bezopasnosti* or State Security Committee) could study documents there. I did not have security clearance and worked there as a representative of the International Commission on the Fate and Whereabouts of Raoul Wallenberg. I had no access to the catalogues of the Special Archive and simply submitted to the head of the archive lists of names of foreigners who had been in Soviet captivity, in whom I was interested in connection with the Wallenberg case. After a while this man brought me archival personal files of most (but not all) of the listed people and I studied the files in his office. As a result, since I did not see catalogues, I do not have archival numbers for all files, and in the text I refer to the file of a particular person without a file number.

There was a similar situation with the Vladimir Prison Archive. In the autumn of 1990, members of the International Wallenberg Commission were allowed to study archival prisoner cards (each prisoner had a special card filled in when he or she was brought to the prison). From a file (*kartoteka* in Russian) of about 60–70,000 cards a few hundred cards of political prisoners kept in Vladimir Prison in the 1940–50s were selected and filmed. Later a computer database was created and a printout of the card records is kept in the Memorial Society Archive in Moscow, which I used in this book.

INTRODUCTION

O, this fatal word SMERSH! ...Everyone froze from fear when he heard it.
—Nikolai Nikoulin, WWII veteran, 2007

We fought not for the Motherland and not for Stalin. We had no choice: the Germans were in front of us, and SMERSH was behind.
—Yelena Bonner, WWII veteran, widow of
Academician Andrei Sakharov, 2010

This book chronicles the activities of Soviet military counterintelligence just before and during World War II, with special emphasis on the origins, structure, and activities of SMERSH—an acronym for the Russian words 'Death to Spies'—which was the Soviet military counterintelligence organization from April 1943 to May 1946. In the Soviet Union, before and after these years, military counterintelligence was part of secret services generally known under the acronyms NKVD (*Narodnyi komissariat vnutrennikh del* or the Internal Affairs Commissariat), and, after the war until the death of Soviet dictator Joseph Stalin in 1953, the MGB (*Ministerstvo gosudarstvennoi bezopasnosti* or State Security Ministry). Formed right after the all-important Soviet victory in Stalingrad, SMERSH was part of the Defense Commissariat (NKO, *Narodnyi komissariat oborony*). Its head, Viktor Abakumov, reported directly to the Soviet dictator Joseph Stalin, at the time NKO Commissar.

In Russia, the first archival information about SMERSH was released in 2003.[1] While not mentioning SMERSH's size directly, this data reveals that this organization was enormous for a counterintelligence service. SMERSH's headquarters in Moscow consisted of 646 officers (at the same time, the HQ of the German military counterintelligence, Abwehr III, was comprised of 48 officers), while in the field there were at least 18–20,000 officers. In 1943, there were 12 fronts (army groups) and four military districts (army groups on the Soviet territory not involved in military actions) with their SMERSH directorates of 112–193 officers each; each front/military district consisted of between two and five armies with their SMERSH departments of 57 officers. Altogether, there were 680 divisions within all fronts with their departments of 57 SMERSH members; and five SMERSH officers were attached to each corps.[2] Taking into consideration that the work of each SMERSH officer in the field was based on reports from several secret informers, the number of servicemen involved in SMERSH activity was several times higher than the number of SMERSH officers.

SMERSH spied on its own servicemen, investigated and arrested even senior officers on Stalin's orders and tirelessly vetted Soviet POWs. From June 1941 to May 1945, forty-seven Red Army generals arrested by military counterintelligence during the war were executed, or died in labor camps or in special investigation prisons while awaiting trial.[3] Later, after Stalin's death in March 1953, these generals were politically rehabilitated— in other words, it was officially admitted that they were innocent; the number of real collaborators with the Nazis among the high Soviet military, like General Andrei Vlasov, was very small. Overall, from 1941 to 1945, military tribunals sentenced 472,000 servicemen whose cases were investigated by military counterintelligence and of them, 217,000 were shot. About 5.4 million Soviet POWs and civilians sent by the Nazis to Germany as slave laborers went through SMERSH's hands, and 600,000 of them ended up as convicts in the GULAG.[4] In Eastern Europe, SMERSH cleansed newly-acquired land of any potential threat to Sovietization. Former Russian émigrés in these countries were specially targeted by SMERSH.

SMERSH successfully fought against and outwitted many operations of the German secret services, the Abwehr and SD (the foreign branch of the German State Security). These results were not only because of the overwhelming number of SMESRH officers compared to the German intelligence services, but were also due to the sophistication of SMERSH's organization. During its three years of existence, SMERSH operatives captured or killed 9,500 German agents and saboteurs and successfully carried out more than 180 deception operations. In August–September 1945, during a short military campaign against Japan, thirty-five SMERSH operational groups dropped from planes to arrest approximately 800 intelligence and military Japanese leaders and at least 400 former White Russian and Russian fascist collaborators with the Japanese. Later, during vetting of the Japanese POWs, SMERSH operatives arrested up to 50,000 alleged Japanese agents. According to General Aleksandr Bezverkhny, head of the current Russian military counterintelligence, ten million POWs, Soviet and foreign, were vetted by SMERSH.[5]

SMERSH was created on Stalin's secret orders. This is not surprising, since SMERSH existed during a time when Stalin was juggling many competing security agencies, constantly changing their structure, responsibilities, and leaders. In addition, Stalin took steps to ensure that SMERSH personnel would be difficult to identify, even by the Red Army personnel they worked among. For instance, SMERSH officers wore standard Red Army uniforms and had standard Red Army ranks, since they were formally part of the Defense Commissariat, but they did not report to the military hierarchy—only to higher-level SMERSH officers. SMERSH officers could be identified only by their special IDs.

Due to the complete secrecy that surrounded SMERSH during and just after the war, its activities are almost unknown in the West. If the name 'SMERSH' is familiar to English readers, it is probably because of its use in the spy novels of Ian Fleming. A Royal Navy intelligence man during World War II, Fleming must have run across the name during his work and decided to use SMERSH as the name of his fictional Soviet spy agency, perhaps because the acronym sounds vaguely absurd in English. In the second chapter of his debut novel, *Casino Royale*, SMERSH is introduced in a fictional 'Dossier to M,' which is a curious combination of fact and fiction.[6] Fleming states correctly that 'SMERSH is a conjunction of two Russian words: "Smyert Shpionam", meaning roughly: "Death to Spies"', but he incorrectly identifies the head of SMERSH as Lavrentii Beria (in fact, NKVD Commissar) and locates its headquarters in Leningrad, while SMERSH headquarters, like all important Soviet agencies, was actually in Moscow. In his second novel, *From Russia with Love*, Fleming places SMERSH's HQ in Moscow on the Sretenka Street, not far from its real location on Lubyanka (Dzerzhinsky) Square, but writes that SMERSH was 'the murder apparat of the MGB', which is not accurate.[7]

Even among Western historians and the many avid readers of World War II history, SMERSH is almost unknown. For instance, the impressive 982-page *The Library of Congress World War Companion*, published in 2007, does not mention SMERSH at all.[8] Similarly, the British historian Chris Bellamy mentions SMERSH only twice in his encyclopedic 813-page study, *Absolute War*, even though this book about the Great Patriotic War analyses, among other topics, the role of the troops of the Soviet security services.[9] Obviously, these omissions have occurred because of the secrecy and lack of archival information until the 2000s. Christopher Andrew and Oleg Gordievsky devote only three paragraphs to SMERSH in their comprehensive book on the history of Soviet security services, *KGB: The Inside Story*, which was published in 1990; this is not nearly enough coverage of such an important organization and its role during World War II.[10] In *The Lesser Terror*, Michael Parrish gives an accurate short account of what was known in the early 1990s about SMERSH's activities and its leader, Abakumov, but the few other English-language books that do mention SMERSH mostly give inaccurate information.[11]

The most important works in English about SMERSH are two little-known memoirs by defectors: *SMERSH* by Nicola Sinevirsky (a pseudonym of Mikhail Mondich, a young man from Carpathian Ruthenia who worked for SMERSH as a translator), and *Nights Are Longest There: A Memoir of the Soviet Security Services* by A. I. Romanov (a pseudonym for the only known SMERSH defector, Captain Boris Baklanov).[12] I have found the information in both of these memoirs to be quite accurate. The detailed descriptions of SMERSH interrogations, during which Sinevirsky acted as translator, are particularly revealing.

If you talk to Russian war veterans about the World War (which they call the Great Patriotic War), most of them still recall the fear of the *osobisty*, as military counterintelligence officers were generally known, and of *smershevtsy* (plural for officers of SMERSH; the singular is *smershevets*). The word *osobist* (singular) comes from the name *Osobyi otdel* (Special Department or OO) of counterintelligence departments in the Red Army until April 1943. For instance, Vladimir Nikolaev, a Russian writer and veteran of World War II, recalled:

> The so-called SMERSH ('Death to Spies') was the most horrible organization within the army and the fleet... Day and night, its countless fattened impudent officers watched every serviceman, from privates up to generals and marshals. Everyone was afraid of SMERSH... Its officers frequently invented criminal cases to demonstrate their necessity and usefulness, but mainly to avoid being sent to the front line. They lived very well and escaped the bullets and bombs.[13]

Aleksandr Solzhenitsyn, who described his arrest by SMERSH operatives at the front in February 1945 in his famous book, *The Gulag Archipelago*, tells us that 'the counterintelligence men used to love that tastelessly concocted word "SMERSH"... They felt that it intimidated people.'[14]

Until recently, many Russians knew of the activities of *smershevtsy* mainly through a popular novel, *In August 1944*, by Vladimir Bogomolov, published in 1974.[15] Bogomolov, a former military intelligence officer, based the novel on his own experience during the war. The KGB (*Komitet gosudarstvennoi bezopasnosti* or State Security Committee) and Defense Ministry were amazed that Bogomolov had managed to recreate the events so accurately without using documents. They tried to prevent the publication of two chapters of the novel, but Bogomolov, who was not a member of the Communist Party or the Writers Union, refused to compromise with the authorities, and the novel was finally published without censorship.[16] The novel describes SMERSH's actions against Ukrainian nationalists and became an icon of the Great Patriotic War among many Soviet war veterans.

The roles of *osobisty* and *smershevtsy* were always controversial in Russia because most of the war veterans who had fought at the front line could not forget—or forgive—the brutality of military counterintelligence. The writer Vasil' Bykov may have given the most powerful descriptions of *osobisty* in his novels *The Trap* (1964) and *The Dead Do Not Feel Pain* (1966). Before *The Trap* was published, a Soviet censor forced Bykov to change the ending of his story in which a lieutenant who had just escaped from the Germans was shot by an *osobist*. In the new ending, the lieutenant was sent into an attack after the *osobist* had threatened to shoot him. The *Dead Do*

Not Feel Pain was banned in the Soviet Union from 1966 till 1982 because of Bykov's portrayals of cruel commanders, a ruthless *osobist*, and a brutal chairman of the military tribunal. As functionaries of the Party's Central Committee indignantly wrote, Bykov depicted the *osobist* called Sakhno 'as a villain and a murderer. Sakhno takes justice in his hands and kills soldiers and officers, and shoots the wounded to death.'[17]

Obviously, the Party bureaucrats would have been more comfortable with the glorious 'truth of generals' celebrated in the memoirs of high commanders. Later Bykov responded to Marshal Ivan Konev, one such memoirist, who criticized Bykov's novel on the grounds that the Soviet leader Joseph Stalin had awarded him the highest Order of Lenin for the Kirovograd Operation in January 1944, which Bykov described. Bykov explained: 'In his [Konev's] and Stalin's opinion, this was a successful operation. Possibly, seen from the Kremlin's perspective, it was. But there was also a different point of view: that of a soldier who was lying on a snowy field covered with blood and trampled down with tank tracks, where our regiment was almost completely destroyed.'[18]

Bykov described his own experience with the OO in *A Long Road Home*, an autobiographical work published after his death in 2003. He recalled how in 1941, when he was a 17-year-old soldier, an *osobist* ordered him to be executed as a traitor because he had become separated from his military unit while trying to buy some food (soldiers were not provided with any rations). An aged Red Army private, not an NKVD executioner, fired a shot over Bykov's head, and he was able to run away. The other unfortunate servicemen detained by the same *osobist* were shot to death.

But it was not until 2003 that a special exhibition at the Central Military Museum in Moscow revealed for the first time the organizational structure and activities of SMERSH.[19] A part of the sixtieth-anniversary celebration of SMERSH's birth, the exhibition presented a flattering portrait of SMERSH and highlighted its success in fighting German spies. However, the exhibition made little mention of SMERSH's more sinister activities, such as the vetting camps (*fil'tratsionnye lagerya*) where hundreds of thousands of innocent repatriated Russian POWs, unfairly suspected of treason and espionage, were subjected to brutal interrogations by SMERSH investigators.[20] Many of the same exhibits, along with some additions, were presented at the exhibition 90 Years of Military Counterintelligence, which opened in December 2008 at the same museum.[21]

The present Russian security service, the FSB (*Federal'naya sluzhba bezopasnosti* or Federal Security Service, the main successor of the Soviet KGB that includes the current military counterintelligence), produced both exhibitions in conjunction with the Central Military Museum. The FSB even published a glossy 'coffee-table' companion book to the 2003 exhibition that is highly complimentary of Abakumov, although he, as an enforcer of

Stalin's will at the highest level, personally arrested and often participated in brutal interrogations of many innocent people.[22] Viktor Stepakov, an FSB-affiliated author, went so far as to raise the question of rehabilitation, i.e., official recognition that Abakumov was not guilty of any crime, in his recent biography of Abakumov. Stepakov cites the opinion of Ivan Krauze, a secret service veteran: 'Viktor Semyonovich Abakumov was a good man… If during an interrogation he beat somebody up, these were enemies of the people since he did not touch innocent [arrestees]… A monument must be erected to him as an innocent victim killed by the libertarian [Nikita] Khrushchev.'[23]

The controversy continues on the Russian TV. In November 2004, a Russian TV documentary, *People's Commissar of SMERSH: The Fall* portrayed Abakumov as a devoted, talented serviceman, inspired by Communist ideals, who was executed on the order of traitors. On May 6, 2009, the Russian government-controlled TV channel Rossiya showed a new 'documentary' movie (actually a work of fiction) called *To Kill Comrade Stalin*, in which Abakumov and SMERSH operatives are shown saving Stalin's life by arresting a Nazi assassin sent by the German secret services. Contrary to this, on December 30, 2010 the Russian historian Nikolai Svanidze broadcasted his TV documentary *Historical Chronicle of 1950. Viktor Abakumov* in which he presented Abakumov quite adequately. Soon after this broadcast Svanidze's TV program was closed.

Many war veterans felt that the *osobisty* would survive because they were in the barrage detachments placed behind the fighting troops, and would end up creating myths about the war. For instance, a former private described the feeling of the servicemen on the front line: 'We [soldiers], dressed in cold greatcoats, will perish at the front line, while *osobisty* in sheepskin coats behind our backs and armed with heavy machine guns, will survive. And later they will tell stories about how they defeated Hitler.'[24] This is exactly what happened.

Recently a number of memoirs written by security veterans who served in SMERSH and military counterintelligence just after the war have become publicly available. Unfortunately, these memoirs provide little information about military counterintelligence history. However, they are a source of details about everyday counterintelligence work, and they also allow the reader to better understand the psychology of these brutal people. Even 65 years after the war the security-service veterans remain mostly staunch Stalinists, extremely anti-Western and anti-American, and they still believe that they made no mistakes in their glorious work of finding traitors within the Red Army.

Here is an example from former SMERSH officer Leonid Ivanov, who wrote in 2009: 'I consider rightful the decision made by J. Stalin [in 1944] to exile the Crimean Tatars [executed by the NKVD, NKGB (State Security

Commissariat) and SMERSH] for their numerous crimes from such an [important] strategic region…as the Crimean Peninsula… The eviction of the Tatars from the Crimea was an act of historic justice. There is no sense in saying that the whole Tatar people in the Crimea were not guilty. And were the Russian people guilty when they were killed and burned alive during the Tatar-Mongolian invasion [in the 13th–15th centuries]?'[25]

Fortunately, material that goes beyond FSB-controlled information has recently become available, enabling me to write this book. In the past ten years, independent Russian archivists and historians from the Alexander Yakovlev International Democracy Foundation and Memorial Society (both in Moscow) have published numerous compilations of original documents released from important archives, including the Presidential Archive of the Russian Federation (APRF), the FSB Central Archive, the State Archive of the Russian Federation (GARF), the Russian State Military Archive (RGVA), and a few others, all located in Moscow. Perhaps most important, the Memorial Society, which is devoted to the commemoration of Stalin's victims, has published a series of books in Russian on the history and structure of the security services and the biographies of many of their key personnel. When I cite documents from these books, I give the number of the document in the book, while all archival details are available in the book. Additionally, many important archival documents were published in the Russian press.

Unfortunately, all these materials were published only in Russian, and so the English-reading audience interested in Soviet and World War II history, as well as many historians who work only with documents translated into English, are not aware of them.

In addition to these materials, my sources for this volume include a number of personal files of foreign prisoners that I studied at the RGVA in 1990–91; some documents that I discovered in the GARF; several incomplete SMERSH/MGB (State Security Ministry) investigation files in the United States Holocaust Memorial Museum (Washington, DC) that the Museum's archive received from the FSB Central Archive in Moscow; numerous memoirs; NKVD history sources published primarily in Russian; and copies of prisoner cards from the Vladimir Prison Archive. Also I used documents from the archive of the Swedish Ministry for Foreign Affairs—the collection of documents on Raoul Wallenberg posted on the website of this Ministry. In the Nuremberg chapter, I cite several documents that I found in the U.S. National Archive (NARA) in Washington, DC.

I even used documents published as photos in the FSB's coffee-table book *SMERSH*, reading the documents with the help of a magnifying glass. Finally, I found a great deal of useful information on several Russian websites that provide access to an enormous number of books in Russian on such topics as military history, World War II, the memoirs of GULAG survivors, and hundreds of interviews with World War II veterans collected from 2007 on.[27] Almost all the materials and documents that I used in this book are available only in Russian and are new to the English-speaking audience.

If my description of SMERSH's activities in this book seems a bit fragmentary, it is because I was only able to reconstruct so much. The SMERSH orders and reports I found are scattered throughout hundreds of sources, and it took years to find and collect them. I have translated extensive excerpts from the most important sources and included them throughout the book. I recreated the organization and work of military tribunals, the Military Collegium of the Soviet Supreme Court, and military prosecutors mostly on the basis of the recently published memoirs. Only during my work on this book were the first statistics on the activity of military tribunals during the war published.[28]

Regrettably, many details are still unknown. For instance, the organizational structure of the NKVD Troops Guarding the Red Army Rear, created in May 1943 partly to support SMERSH's activities, is still a mystery. And only the general structure of the NKGB—that is, the number and names of directorates and departments—is known. This information is important for a complete understanding of SMERSH, because NKGB officers, primarily from the 1st (intelligence) and 2nd (domestic counterintelligence) directorates, replaced SMERSH field officers in newly occupied territory, continuing arrests and interrogations while SMERSH units moved ahead with the advancing Red Army. This NKGB activity was described only in the memoirs of Anatolii Granovsky, an NKVD/NKGB officer who defected to the West in 1946.[29]

While talking about World War II, it is necessary to keep in mind the enormous number of Soviet servicemen killed in that war, especially during the chaotic period that followed the German invasion in June 1941. Officially, Stalin declared that seven million Soviet citizens perished during the war, but according to some memoirs, in his inner circle he used to say that '30 million of our people have been killed, and of them, 20 million were [ethnic] Russians.'[30] In 2010, the General Staff of the Russian Armed Forces claimed that 8,668,000 servicemen were killed during the war, while the total losses were 26.6 million people.[31] The Russian historian Boris Sokolov writes that between 26.3 and 26.9 million servicemen were killed.[32]

Although this number might be an overestimate, it is obvious that the number given by the General Staff was underestimated—possibly, with the intention of making the Soviet and German losses appear equal. In fact, the Germans and their allies lost between 3 and 3.6 million servicemen at the Eastern (Russian) Front, and between 1 and 1.5 million at the Western Front, in addition to approximately 2 million civilians. In 2008, the

Military-Memorial Center of the Russian Armed Forces listed the names of 16.5 million servicemen killed and about 2.4 million men missing in action.[33] Comparing these figures to the 416,000 Americans killed during World War II highlights the enormity of this tragedy.

It is likely that the real extent of Soviet losses will never be known. Even 65 years after the war ended, approximately 80 per cent of archival documents about the war were still classified in Russia and, therefore, it was hard to make an independent estimation of losses.[34] Also, unlike American soldiers, Russian soldiers did not have 'dog tags'. Before the war, in March 1941, special lockets were introduced in which privates were supposed to put a note with their personal data.[35] These lockets were abandoned in November 1942 because of their inefficiency. In October 1941, privates and low-level commanders began to receive special IDs similar to a passport without a photo (the high-level commanders had had such IDs from the beginning of the war) but issuing of these IDs at the fronts was not completed until July 1942. Therefore, during the first year of the war, most servicemen had no identification papers.

And even when sophisticated forensic methods of identification did become available, the Soviet—now, the Russian—state has shown little interest in identifying all the dead. As late as 2005, it was reported that at least a half a million unidentified soldiers killed during 1941–42 were thought to still be lying either unburied or buried in unmarked graves in Russian forests.[36]

The publication of this book is especially timely now, because the present Russian government seems intent on whitewashing Stalin's atrocities and the history of the Soviet security services. Since Vladimir Putin (a former KGB lieutenant colonel and then FSB head before becoming Russian president) came to power in 2000, *siloviki* ('men of power') with mostly KGB backgrounds have taken over key positions in government and business. They call themselves 'Chekists'—followers of the first Bolshevik security service, the CheKa (*Chrezvychainaya komissiya* or Extraordinary Commission), created in 1918 under Felix Dzerzhinsky's command, to unleash the first wave of Soviet repression and persecution, the Red Terror. This group is also known today as the *Corporation* or *Brotherhood*. In February 2009, Andrei Illarionov, a former Putin adviser and now the leading Russian-opposition economist, testified before the American House Committee on Foreign Affairs: 'The members of the Corporation do share strong allegiance to their respective organizations, strict codes of conduct and of honor, basic principles of behavior, including among others the principle of mutual support to each other in any circumstances and the principle of *omerta*.'[37] These people see themselves as the descendants of the NKVD/SMERSH/MGB and are proud of those agencies. *The Economist* dubbed the current Russian regime the 'spookocracy'.[38]

To burnish their image, the current secret services have begun to connect themselves with Russia's imperial past.[39] This process has coincided with an enormous increase in the number of new books glorifying Stalin and his epoch. For instance, during 2010 and early 2011, about 60 books praising Stalin and his administration, compared to 21 serious history books about Stalin's time, were published in Russia.[40] In the spring of 2007, Russian TV (NTV channel) showed a forty-episode series, *Stalin Alive*, in which Stalin is depicted as a repentant intellectual. Even the sinister Beria, NKVD Commissar from 1938 until 1946, whose name was synonymous with terror in the Soviet Union, is portrayed as 'the best manager of the 20th century'. There is nothing about his cruel atrocities in his official biography given on the FSB website.[41]

Putin has ordered textbooks rewritten. One of them called Stalin 'one of the most successful USSR leaders' and used the euphemism 'Stalin's psychological peculiarities' to describe Stalin's mass repressions.[42] The intensive pro-Stalin propaganda has already resulted in the brainwashing of the Russian younger generation. In a poll conducted in October 2009, more than half of respondents over 55, and more than a quarter of 18- to 24-year-olds, said that they felt positively about Stalin.[43]

The current Chekist attempts to whitewash Stalin and his methods must be strongly rebuffed. I hope the present book will help ensure that the atrocities of Stalin's regime will not be forgotten.

For me, the topic of World War II has a personal dimension as well. While researching material for the chapter about the International Nuremberg Trial, I found out that the name of my great-uncle, Dr. Meer D. Birstein, was on a list of victims killed by the Nazis in 1941–42, which was presented by the Soviet Prosecutor Lev Smirnov on February 26, 1946 (Exhibit USSR 279).[44] My great-uncle was a surgeon at a hospital in the town of Vyazma, and he chose to stay with his patients despite the rapid German advance and his own awareness of the German attitude toward Jews.

Also, like everyone born in Moscow during that war, in my childhood I heard stories about the disastrous year 1941, when the Soviet leadership was not prepared for the German advance and about the panic in Moscow on 16 October 1941, when German tanks showed up in Moscow's suburbs. My mother, a doctor who was promoted in 1941 to the rank of Captain of Medical Service, served in a military field hospital from June 1941 until the end of 1943, and witnessed many horrifying events. For thousands of civilian volunteers called *opolchentsy* sent out to defend Moscow, there was only one rifle for every three soldiers.[45] In Leningrad there was only one rifle per thirty volunteers, and there were no munitions. Soviet pilots dropped scrap metal during the night instead of bombs, hoping at least to disturb the Germans' sleep. Since practically all modern planes had been destroyed by the Germans, pilots used old two-man planes made of plywood. The number of Soviet defenders killed during that period, among them many of my parents' friends, is simply unknown. Even more horrifying were stories about the everyday life of servicemen at the front later—arrests of officers by *osobisty* for no discernible reason, punishment battalion (*shtrafbat*) attacks through minefields, and so forth.

The poverty of most of my classmates in the early 1950s was profound. Many were raised by mothers because their fathers had been killed during the war or were imprisoned in the GULAG. And I cannot forget the thousands of human stumps—young men who had lost their legs and sometimes also one or both hands—who were seen after the war in the streets everywhere throughout the country. They had wooden discs instead of legs and they moved by propelling themselves with their hands (if they had them). Many of these 'stumps' had the highest military awards attached to their chests, and most of them begged for money. Their pension was 150 rubles a month, at a time when a loaf of bread cost 100 rubles at the market.

In July 1951, these people disappeared from the streets of Moscow. Following a secret decree, the militia (Soviet police) collected them and placed them in specially organized invalid reservations under squalid conditions, and the government reduced their pensions.[46] From time to time you would see an escapee from one of the reservations, singing patriotic war songs on a suburban train and begging for money.

All these memories will remain with me for the rest of my life.

One more issue is haunting me: the enormous scale of atrocities committed by Soviet soldiers in Eastern Europe and China in 1944–45. This topic was taboo during all the Soviet years, and many of Russia's official historians and nationalists are still furiously denying the facts.[47] But I personally knew two Red Army officers who tried to stop rapes and reported to their superiors about the atrocities they had witnessed. Both were punished for 'slandering the Red Army' and spent years in the GULAG. However, the scale of the atrocities, especially in Hungary and Germany, became clear only from recent publications in Russian.[48] It is scary that even now, 65 years after the war, according to the interviews on the website http://www.iremember.ru, many war veterans recall the atrocities without remorse and consider the mass rapes of women and killings of children and old people to be justified by the atrocities the German troops committed in the Soviet territory in 1941–42.

I would like to end with a citation from the very thoughtful memoirs by Nikolai Nikoulin, a war veteran who became a prominent, internationally known art historian at the Leningrad Hermitage. In November 1941 Nikoulin volunteered for the army, just after he graduated from high school in Leningrad. He wrote his memoirs in the 1970s, not even hoping that they would ever appear in print; they were published in 2008. As he states in the introduction, the memoirs were written 'from the point of view of a soldier who is crawling through the mud of the front lines'. Nikoulin was very strong in accusing the Soviet regime of an inhuman attitude toward its own people:

> The war especially strongly exposed the meanness of the Bolshevik government...
>
> An order comes from above: 'You must seize a certain height.' The regiment storms it week after week, each day losing a large number of men. The replacements for casualties keep coming without interruption; there is no shortage of men. Among them there are men swollen with dystrophy from Leningrad [in the Nazi blockade], for whom doctors had just prescribed intensive feeding and staying in bed for three weeks; there are also 14-year-old kids...who should not have been drafted at all...
>
> The only command is 'Forward!!!' Finally, a soldier or a lieutenant—a platoon commander—or even, infrequently, a captain—a company commander—says, while witnessing this outrageous nonsense: 'Stop wasting the men! There is a concrete-enforced pillbox on the top! And we have only the 76-mm cannon! It cannot destroy it!!!'
>
> Immediately a politruk [political officer], a SMERSH officer, and a military tribunal start to work. One of the informers, plenty of whom are present in every unit, testifies: 'Yes, in the presence of privates he [the officer] questioned our victory!' After this a special printed form, where there is a space for a name, is filled in. Now everything is ready. The decision is: 'Shoot him in front of formation!' or 'Send him to a punishment company!'—which is practically the same thing.
>
> This is how the most honest and responsible people perished...
>
> It was a stupid, senseless killing of our own servicemen. I think this [artificial] selection among the Russian people is a time bomb that will explode in a few generations, in the 21st or 22nd century, when the numerous scoundrels selected and raised by the Bolsheviks will give rise to new generations of those who are like them.[49]

Nikoulin died in 2009. Unfortunately, he lived to see his prediction coming true in the twenty-first century.

For me, writing this book was like talking to the people of my parents' generation, such as Nikolai Nikoulin, Vasil' Bykov, and many, many others. Our 'conversations' were very painful, and like my harrowing postwar memories, they will stay with me forever.

Part I. The Big Picture

CHAPTER 1

Soviet Military Counterintelligence: An Overview

The history of SMERSH is so intimately intertwined with the many skeins of Soviet political and secret service history I decided to start out this volume with a short overview of Soviet military counterintelligence and its place in the larger landscape of the Soviet Union. Hopefully this will serve to keep the reader oriented in the chapters that follow, where detailed explanations of the many byzantine cabals of Stalin and other political and secret service figures are necessary to illuminate the dark history of SMERSH. And as an aid to keeping track of the many confusing transformations and personnel changes in the secret services, I have provided a listing of the various organizations (Table 1-1).

It all began on November 7, 1917 when the Bolshevik Party organized a coup known as the October Revolution and took over political power in Russia. The Party was small, consisting of about 400,000 members in a country with a population of over 100 million.[1] Soon the Bolshevik government was on the verge of collapse. The troops of the Cossack Ataman (Leader) Pyotr Krasnov and the White Army of General Anton Denikin were threatening the new Russian Republic from the South, Ukraine and the Baltic States were occupied by the Germans, and Siberia was in the hands of anti-Soviet Czechoslovak WWI POWs.

But the numerous peasant revolts that erupted throughout Bolshevik-controlled territory were even more dangerous for them. In these circumstances Vladimir Lenin, the Bolshevik leader, unleashed terror to hang onto power. On December 20, 1917, the first Soviet secret service, the VChe-Ka (*Vserossiiskaya Chrezvychainaya Komissiya po bor'be s kontrrevolyutsiei i sabotazhem* or All-Russian Extraordinary Commission for Combating Counterrevolution and Sabotage), attached to the SNK (*Sovet Narodnykh Komissarov* or Council of People's Commissars, i.e. the Bolshevik government) was created.[2] The VCheKa's task was 'to stop and liquidate counter-revolutionary and diversion activity' and 'to put on trial in the Revolutionary tribunal those who had committed sabotage acts and the counterrevolutionaries, and to develop methods for fighting them'. Since this time and to the end of the Soviet Union in 1991, through the VCheKa and its successors, a comparatively small Bolshevik (later Communist) Party controlled

TABLE 1-1. SOVIET SECURITY SERVICES AND THEIR HEADS

Name[1]	Acronym	Dates of Existence	Head	Dates
Vserossiiskaya chrezvychainaya komissiya (All-Russian Extraordinary Commission)	VCheKa	Mar 1918–Feb 1922	F. E. Dzerzhinsky	Mar 1918–Feb 1922
Gosudarstvennoe politicheskoe upravlenie (State Political Directorate)	GPU	Feb 1922–Nov 1923	F. E. Dzerzhinsky	Feb 1922–Nov 1923
Ob'edinennoe gosudarstvennoe politicheskoe upravlenie (Joint State Political Directorate)	OGPU	Nov 1923–Jul 1934	F. E. Dzerzhinsky V. R. Menzhinsky	Nov 1923–Jul 1926 Jul 1926–May 1934
Narodnyi komissariat vnutrennikh del (People's Internal Affairs Commissariat)	NKVD	Jul 1934–Feb 1941	G. G. Yagoda N. N. Yezhov L. P. Beria	Jul 1934–Sep 1936 Sep 1936–Nov 1938 Nov 1938–Feb 1941
Narodnyi komissariat vnutrennikh del (People's Internal Affairs Commissariat) (after the division into the NKVD, NKGB and 3rd NKO Directorate)	NKVD	Feb 1941–Jul 1941	L. P. Beria	Feb 1941–Jul 1941
Narodnyi komissariat gosudarstvennoi bezopasnosti (People's State Security Commissariat)	NKGB	Feb 1941–Jul 1941	V. N. Merkulov	Feb 1941–Jul 1941
Narodnyi komissariat vnutrennikh del (People's Internal Affairs Commissariat) (after the merger of the NKVD, NKGB and 3rd NKO Directorate)	NKVD	Jul 1941–Apr 1943	L. P. Beria	Jul 1941–Apr 1943
Narodnyi komissariat vnutrennikh del (People's Internal Affairs Commissariat) (after the division into the NKVD, NKGB and SMERSH)	NKVD	Apr 1943–Mar 1946	L. P. Beria S. N. Kruglov	Apr 1943–Dec 1945 Jan–Mar 1946
Narodnyi komissariat gosudarstvennoi bezopasnosti (People's State Security Commissariat)	NKGB	Apr 1943–Mar 1946	V. N. Merkulov	Apr 1943–Mar 1946

Name[1]	Acronym	Dates of Existence	Head	Dates
Ministerstvo vnutrennikh del (Internal Affairs Ministry)	MVD	Mar 1946–Mar 1953	S. N. Kruglov	Mar 1946–Mar 1953
Ministerstvo gosudarstvennoi bezopasnosti (State Security Ministry)	MGB	Mar 1946–Mar 1953	V. N. Merkulov V. S. Abakumov S. D. Ignatiev	Mar 1946–May 1946 May 1946–Jul 1951 Aug 1951–Mar 1953
Ministerstvo vnutrennikh del (Internal Affairs Ministry) (after the merger of the MGB and MVD into the new MVD)	MVD	Mar 1953–Mar 1954	L. P. Beria S. N. Kruglov	Mar 1953–Jun 1953 Jun 1953–Mar 1954
Komitet gosudarstvennoi bezopasnosti (State Security Committee) attached to the Council of Ministers (created as a small version of the former MGB)	KGB	Mar 1954–Jul 1978	I. A. Serov A. N. Shelepin V. Ye. Semichastnyi Yu. V. Andropov	Mar 1954–Dec 1958 Dec 1958–Nov 1961 Nov 1961–May 1967 May 1967–Jul 1978
Komitet gosudarstvennoi bezopasnosti (State Security Committee) of the USSR[2]	KGB (USSR)	Jul 1978–Oct 1991	Yu. V. Andropov V. V. Fedorchuk V. M. Chebrikov V. A. Kryuchkov V. V. Bakatin	Jul 1978–May 1982 May 1982–Dec 1982 Dec 1982–Oct 1988 Oct 1988–Aug 1991 Aug 1991–Oct 1991
Mezhrespublikanskaya sluzhba bezopasnoti (Interrepublican Security Service)	MSB (USSR)	Nov–Dec 1991	V. V. Bakatin	Nov 1991–Dec 1991

1. Data from A. I. Kokurin and N. V. Petrov, *Lubyanka: Organy VCheKa-OGPU-NKVD-NKGB-MGB-MVD-KGB,1917–1991. Spravochnik* (Moscow: Demokratiya, 2003) (in Russian).

2. On July 5, 1978, the KGB attached to the Council of Ministers was promoted to the KGB of the USSR and included in the Council of Ministers.

the large population of Russia (later the Soviet Union) through intimidation and terror. In Lenin's terminology, this method of control was called
'the dictatorship of the proletariat'.[3] But, in fact, the Bolshevik's tactics were
the same as those of any organized criminal or fascist group, such as the
Italian Mafia and the Nazi Party in Germany.[4]

The VCheKa, headed by Felix Dzerzhinsky, a Bolshevik from a family of minor Polish nobility, who as a teenager dreamed of becoming a
Catholic priest, consisted of only 12 members. On September 2, 1918, the
VCheKa issued 'The Red Terror Order' to arrest and imprison members
of socialist non-Bolshevik parties.[5] Additionally, all big industrialists, busi-
nessmen, merchants, noble-landowners, 'counterrevolutionary priests', and
'officers hostile to the Soviet government' were to be placed into concentration camps and forced to work there. Any attempt to resist was punished
by immediate execution.

Three days later the SNK issued an additional decree, entitled 'On the
Red Terror'.[6] It ordered an increase in VCheKa staff (known from then on
as the *Chekisty*) culled from the ranks of devoted Bolsheviks. Within a year
the VCheKa became an organization with a headquarters in Moscow and
branches throughout the whole country. The SNK decree also ordered 'to
isolate the class enemies in concentration camps; to shoot to death every person close to the organizations of White Guardists [members of the White
armies], plots and revolts; to publish the names of the executed, as well as
an explanation why they had been executed'. The Red Terror was in full
swing, and during its first two months alone, at least 10,000–15,000 victims were executed.[7] Very soon Dzerzhinsky, a brutal workaholic with an
ascetic lifestyle, earned his nickname 'Iron Felix'.[8]

The first decrees set up the objectives, rules, and even phraseology for
the future Soviet security services. Any real or potential threat to Bolshevik power became a 'counterrevolutionary crime', and later, in Joseph Stalin's Criminal Code of 1926, these 'crimes' comprised fourteen paragraphs
(treason, espionage, subversion, assistance to the world bourgeoisie, etc.) of
the infamous Article 58. The perpetrators of such crimes, soon called 'enemies of the working people', were found mostly among former bourgeoisie, nobles, and any professional or educated person. However, there were
also numerous workers and peasants among the victims of the Red Terror.
Relatives of persons sought for counterrevolutionary crimes were also often
arrested. This practice was formalized in Stalin's time, when legal convictions of relatives of 'enemies of the people' became a standard practice. It's
important to note that only the VCheKa and its successor organizations
were allowed investigate 'counterrevolutionary crimes'.

Already in these first decrees there was a category of enemies called
'the hostile officers', which was the beginning of Lenin's and then Stalin's
suspicious attitude to the professional military. In fact, detachments of

revolutionary soldiers and sailors (as the navy privates are called in Russia) played a critical role in the Bolshevik coup. Very few high army and navy officers joined these detachments or supported the Bolsheviks.

On January 28, 1918, the SNK declared the creation of the Red Army and by February 23, which was later announced as the Red Army's birthday, some detachments of the new army had been formed.[9] On December 19, 1918, the first military counterintelligence organization, the VO (*Voennyi otdel* or Military Department), was established within the VCheKa (Table 1-2).[10] It included previous counterintelligence organizations that existed in the armies in the field.[11] On January 1, 1919, the VO was renamed *Osobyi otdel* (Special Department) or the OO. This name was definitely reminiscent of the political police of the czarist time, when *Osobyi otdel* within *Departament politsii* or the Police Department investigated crimes against the state such as the activities of revolutionary parties, foreign espionage, and treason.[12]

The word 'osobyi' is translated as 'special', but the English definition does not give the full sense of its Russian usage. In the Soviet secret services, *osobyi* (the singular of *osobye*) was used to describe a department whose specific functions required concealment. However, in the Soviet security services the acronym 'OO' was never used for anything but military counterintelligence. In addition to the OO in the VCheKa headquarters in Moscow, there were OOs of fronts (as the army groups are called in Russia in wartime), OOs in the armies, and Special Sections in divisions. The regional VCheKa branches, the so-called GubCheKas, also had OOs.[13]

The task of the OOs was 'fighting counterrevolution and espionage within the army and fleet'.[14] In other words, the Bolsheviks were more concerned about finding enemies of the regime among its own military than about catching enemy agents. This attitude explains why, during the whole of the Soviet era, military counterintelligence was part of security services, and was within the armed forces only during SMERSH's three-year existence and for one other very brief period, and then only formally.

During the Civil War (1918–22) that followed the October Revolution, the Bolsheviks had no choice but to draft czarist officers into the Red Army.[15] Although the loyalty of these officers was obviously an issue, their military training and experience were critical during that war. But with the success of the Red Army in the war, the czarist officers became less dangerous to Stalin than the young Red Army commanders who adored his archenemy Leon Trotsky.

From 1918 till 1925, Trotsky was Commissar for Military (and Naval) Affairs; later this post was called the Defense Commissar. A talented orator (contrary to Stalin, who spoke Russian with a heavy Georgian accent; Stalin's real last name was Dzhugashvili), Trotsky was extremely popular among the Red Army commanders. Taking into consideration that in

Table 1-2. Soviet and Russian Federation Military Counterintelligence Organizations

Creation Date[1]	Military Counterintelligence Unit Name	Acronym	Organization Acronym	Head of the Military Counterintelligence Unit Name and Period of Activity	Birth/Death[2]
Dec 19, 1918	Voennyi otdel (Military Department)	VO	VCheKa	M. S. Kedrov (1918)	1878–1941*
Feb 6, 1919	Osobyi otdel (Special Department)	OO	VCheKa, VCheKa, VCheKa-GPU-OGPU, OGPU	M. S. Kedrov (1919)	1878–1941*
				F. E. Dzerzhinsky (Aug 1919–Jul 1920)	1877–1926
				V. R. Menzhinsky (Jul 20, 1920–May 1, 1922)	1874–1934
				G. G. Yagoda (Jun 1, 1922–Oct 26, 1929)	1891–1938*
				Y. K. Olsky (Oct 27, 1929–Aug 5, 1931)	1891–1937*
				G. Ye. Prokofiev (Aug 6, 1931–Oct 25, 1931)	1895–1937*
				I. M. Leplevsky (Nov 17, 1931–Feb 20, 1933)	1896–1938*
				M. I. Gai (Jun 1, 1933–Jul 10, 1934)	1897–1937*
Jul 10, 1934	Osobyi otdel GUGB (Special Department of the Main State Security Directorate)	OO GUGB	NKVD	M. I. Gai (Jul 10, 1934–Nov 28, 1936)	1897–1937*
Dec 25, 1936	5 otdel GUGB (5th GUGB Department)		NKVD	I. M. Leplevsky (Nov 28, 1936–Jun 14, 1937)	1896–1938*
				N. G. Nikolaev-Zhurid (Jun 14, 1937–Mar 28, 1938)	1897–1940*
Mar 28, 1938	2 upravlenie or Upravlenie osobykh otdelov (2nd Directorate)	UOO	NKVD	L. M. Zakovsky (Mar 28, 1938–Apr 20, 1938)	1894–1938*
				N. N. Fedorov (Apr 20, 1938–Sep 29, 1938)	1900–1940*
Sep 29, 1938	4 otdel GUGB (4th GUGB Department)		NKVD	N. N. Fedorov (Sept 29, 1938–Nov 20, 1938)	1900–1940*
				V. M. Bochkov (Dec 28, 1938–Aug 23, 1940)	1900–1981
				A. N. Mikheev (Aug 23, 1940–Feb 8, 1941)	1911–1941

Creation Date[1]	Military Counterintelligence Unit		Organization Acronym	Head of the Military Counterintelligence Unit	
	Name	Acronym		Name and Period of Activity	Birth/Death[2]
Feb 3, 1941	3 Upravlenie (3rd NKO Directorate)		NKO	A. N. Mikheev (Feb 3, 1941–Jul 19, 1941)	1911–1941**
	3 Upravlenie (3rd NKVMF Directorate)		NKVMF	A. I. Petrov (Feb 3, 1941–Jan 10, 1942)	1902–?
	3 Otdel (3rd NKVD Department)		NKVD	A. M. Belyanov (Feb 3, 1941–Jul 19, 1941)	1903–1994
Jul 17, 1941	Upravlenie osobykh otdelov (Special Departments Directorate)	UOO	NKVD	V. S. Abakumov (Jul 19, 1941–Apr 14, 1943)	1908–1954
Apr 19, 1943	Glavnoe upravlenie kontrrazvedki SMERSH (Main Counterintelligence Directorate SMERSH)	GUKR SMERSH	NKO	V. S. Abakumov (Apr 19, 1943–Apr 27, 1946)	1908–1954*
Apr 19, 1943	Upravlenie kontrrazvedki SMERSH (Counterintelligence Directorate SMERSH)	UKR SMERSH	NKVMF	P. A. Gladkov (Apr 19, 1943–Feb 25, 1946)	1902–?
Apr 19, 1943	Otdel kontrrazvedki SMERSH (Counterintelligence Department SMERSH)	OKR SMERSH	NKVD NKVD/MVD	S. P. Yukhimovich (Apr 19, 1943–Jul 1944) V. I. Smirnov (Jul 1944–Mar 19, 1946)	1900–? 1895–1972
May 4, 1946–Mar 14, 1953	3 Glavnoe upravlenie (3rd Main Directorate)	3 GU	MGB	N. N. Selivanovsky (May 1946–Nov 1947) N. A. Korolev (Nov 1947–Dec 31, 1950) Ya. A. Yedunov (Jan 3, 1951–Feb 19, 1952) S. A. Goglidze (Feb 19, 1952–Mar 5, 1953)	1901–1997 1907–1986 1896–1985 1901–1953
May 4, 1946–Mar 14, 1953	Otdel kontrrazvedki (Counterintelligence Department)	OKR	MVD	V. I. Smirnov (Mar 19, 1946–Apr 23, 1947) A. N. Asmolov (Apr 23, 1947–Dec 20, 1950) P. I. Okunev (Dec 20, 1950–Jun 14, 1951) I. Ye. Klimenko (acting head; head, Dec 13, 1952–Mar 1953)	1895–1972 1906–1981 1906–? 1908–?

Table 1-2 (continued)

Creation Date[1]	Military Counterintelligence Unit		Organization Acronym	Head of the Military Counterintelligence Unit	
	Name	Acronym		Name and Period of Activity	Birth/Death[2]
Mar 14, 1953	3 *Upravlenie* (3rd Directorate)	3 U	MVD	S. A. Goglidze (Mar 12–Jun 29, 1953)	1901–1953*
				D. S. Leonov (Jul 8, 1953–Mar 18, 1954)	1899–1981
Mar 18, 1954	3 *Glavnoe upravlenie* (3rd Main Directorate)	3 GU	KGB (under the Council of Ministers)	D. S. Leonov (Mar 18, 1954–Jun 12, 1959)	1899–1981
				A. M. Gus'kov (Jun 12, 1959–Feb 11, 1960)	1914–2005
Feb 11, 1960	3 *Upravlenie* (3rd Directorate)	3 U	KGB (under the Council of Ministers)	A. M. Gus'kov (Feb 11, 1960–Feb 19, 1963)	1914–2005
				I. A. Fadeikin (Feb 19, 1963–Feb 23, 1966)	1917–1979
				G. K. Tsinev (Feb 23, 1966–Jul 24, 1967)	1907–1996
				V. V. Fedorchuk (Jul 24, 1967–Jul 16, 1970)	1908–2008
				I. L. Ustinov (Sep 4, 1970–Nov 1973)	1920–?
				Vacancy (Nov 1973–Feb 1974)	
				N. A. Dushin (Feb 1974–Jun 1978)	1920–2001
Jun 7, 1978	3 *Upravlenie* (3rd Directorate)	3 U	KGB (USSR)	N. A. Dushin (Jun 1978–May 1982)	1920–2001
May 25, 1982	3 *Glavnoe upravlenie* (3rd Main Directorate)	3 GU	KGB (USSR)	N. A. Dushin (May 1982–Jul 14, 1987)	1920–2001
				V. S. Sergeev (Jul 14, 1987–Nov 1990)	1927–?
				A. V. Zhardetsky (Nov 1990–Aug 1991)	1931–2005
				Yu. Ye. Bulygin (acting head, Aug–Oct 1991)	1934–?
Oct 22, 1991	*Glavnoe upravlenie voennoi kontrrazvedki* (Main military counterintelligence directorate)	GUVKR	MSB (USSR)	Yu. Ye. Bulygin (Nov 1991)	1934–?

1. Data from A. I. Kokurin and N. V. Petrov, *Lubyanka: Organy VCheKa–OGPU–NKVD–NKGB–MGB–MVD–KGB, 1917–1991. Spravochnik* (Moscow: Demokratiya, 2003) (in Russian). 2. (*), executed persons; (**), killed in action.

November 1920, the Red Army and Navy had 5,430,000 servicemen, and even after a partial demobilization in January 1922 numbered 1,350,000, the number of enthusiastic Trotsky supporters was very high.[16] Also, Stalin's failure as a military commander during the Civil War made him especially jealous of Trotsky's popularity.[17]

In the meantime, in 1922, due to Lenin's illness (he suffered from a progressive paralysis), the Politburo, the Party's governing group, elected Stalin General Secretary, i.e. leader of the Bolshevik Party.[18] Trotsky formed an opposition group which resulted in a long struggle between Stalin and Trotsky. In 1927, Trotsky lost all his posts, and two years later he was expelled from the Soviet Union. Finally, on Stalin's order, he was assassinated in 1940 by an NKVD (*Narodnyi komissariat vnutrennikh del* or People's Internal Affairs Commissariat) killing squad.

Stalin never forgot Trotsky's supporters, the 'Trotskyists', especially among the armed forces. They were constantly persecuted, even after World War II.[19] Possibly, Stalin's fear that the officers who served under Trotsky remained his secret supporters despite Trotsky's political defeat was behind Stalin's distrust of the military and his expectation that it would organize plots against him. In fact, there were no military plots; if alleged 'plots' were discovered by the OO, they were OO fabrications to please Stalin.

During the Civil War the OO was considered so important that from August 1919 to July 1920, Dzerzhinsky, chairman of the VCheKa, and from July 1920 to May 1922, his deputy Vyacheslav Menzhinsky, headed the OO in Moscow (Table 1-2).[20] However, from the beginning, the special OO departments were involved in campaigns that were not strictly military. The first OO chief, Mikhail Kedrov, executed civilians, including children, who were suspected of counterrevolutionary activity during the civil war. Military counterintelligence also participated in the creation of phony anti-Soviet underground organizations aimed at misleading White Russians who were living abroad, often trapping emissaries sent to the Soviet Union by those Russian émigrés. In the late 1920s to early 1930s, it was also involved in rounding up and sending into exile independent farming families known as *kulaks* during the organization of the *kolkhozy* (collective farms).[21]

In the 1920s–early 1930s, the OO played a special role in the VCheKa/NKVD. Almost all its leaders (Table 1-2) were later appointed to leading positions in other branches of the security services. Menzhinsky succeeded Dzerzhinsky after the latter died in 1926, and Genrikh Yagoda, once Menzhinsky's deputy and OO head from 1922–29, became the first NKVD Commissar in 1934.[22] On December 20, 1920, foreign intelligence, part of the OO, became a separate *Inostrannyi otdel* or INO (Foreign Department; later the all-powerful First Directorate, and currently, *Sluzhba vneshnei razvedki*, SVR or Foreign Intelligence Service). On July 7, 1922, the OO was divided in two parts, the OO (counterintelligence in the armed forces) and *Kontrrazvedyvatel'nyi otdel* or KRO (Counterintelligence Department; later the Second Directorate) in charge of internal counterintelligence, i.e. capturing spies and White Guard agents.

Artur Artuzov (born Frauchi), a long-time officer of the OO, was appointed head of the KRO.[23] Vasilii Ulrikh, also an OO officer and the future chairman of the Military Collegium of the USSR Supreme Court, became his deputy.[24] However, from 1927 to 1931, the OO and KRO existed as a united structure with a joint secretariat. It was headed by Yan Olsky, who headed army OO departments during the Civil War and then became Artuzov's deputy in the KRO (Table 1-2).[25]

Through the beginning of World War II the OOs were part of the VCheKa's successors, first the OGPU and then the NKVD, and military counterintelligence was focused on the destruction of military professionals whom Stalin did not trust or hated. In 1927, he ordered Menzhinsky, the OGPU chairman, 'to pay special attention to espionage in the army, aviation, and the fleet'.[26]

In 1928, the OGPU prepared the first show trial, the so-called *Shakhtinskoe delo* (Mining Case) against top-level mining engineers in the Donbass Region (currently, Ukraine) and foreigners working in the coal-mining industry.[27] Yefim Yevdokimov, OGPU Plenipotentiary (representative) in the Donbass Region, persuaded Stalin that the numerous accidents in the Donbass coal mines were the result of sabotage. Allegedly, the accidents were organized by a group of engineers, who had worked in the mining industry in pre-revolutionary times, and foreign specialists.[28] According to Yevdokimov, these *vrediteli* (from the Russian verb *vredit'* or to spoil; in English the word *vrediteli* is usually translated as 'wreckers') followed orders from the former owners of the mines who now lived abroad. The idea of sabotage conducted by wreckers played an important role in Soviet ideology and propaganda and was usually applied to members of the technical intelligentsia and other professionals. Stalin ordered arrests, and 53 engineers and managers were duly apprehended.

During the investigation, the OGPU worked out principles that were followed for all subsequent political cases until Stalin's death. Before making the arrests, investigators invented a plot based on operational materials received from secret informers. This was not difficult because, beginning in the VCheKa's time, the Chekists' work, especially that of military counterintelligence, was based on reports from numerous secret informers. Thus the OGPU and its successors always had a lot of information about an enormous number of people and could easily fabricate any kind of 'counterrevolutionary' group. After the alleged perpetrators were arrested, the investigators' job was to force the arrestees to 'confess' and sign the concocted 'testimonies'. Since during interrogations new individuals were drawn in (during interrogations, people were forced to name their friends and co-workers), the case could snowball.

During the investigation of the *Shakhtinskoe delo*, OGPU interrogators applied primarily psychological methods to the arrestees, not the physical torture they widely used during the Red Terror and later. The arrestees were deprived of sleep for days, as the investigators repeatedly read the concocted 'testimonies' and continually threatened to persecute family members. A special Politburo commission, with Stalin's participation, controlled the OGPU investigation. Two months before the end of the investigation the official Communist Party daily newspapers *Pravda* (Truth) and *Izvestia* started to publish articles condemning members of the 'counterrevolutionary organization' in the Donbass Region and the 'bourgeois specialists' guilty of sabotage. Stalin made the same accusations in his speeches.

An open session of the Military Collegium of the Supreme Court began on May 18, 1928 and continued for 41 days. Andrei Vyshinsky, Stalin's main legal theorist, presided. 23 defendants of 53 pleaded not guilty, and 10 admitted to partial guilt. Eleven defendants were sentenced to death (of them, only six were executed). Most of the others were given terms of imprisonment from one to ten years, while eight defendants were acquitted. Yevdokimov was promoted to head of the OGPU's Secret Operations Directorate that included the OO and KRO; in other words, for the next few years he supervised the OO's activity.

The *Shakhtinskoe delo* became a model for the trials that followed in the late 1920s–early 1930s, of which the *Prompartiya* (Industrial Party) show trial in November–December 1930 was the most important.[29] During the investigation, Stalin not only read transcripts of interrogations of the arrestees, but personally suggested questions for additional interrogations. At the trial Nikolai Krylenko, RSFSR (Russian Federation) Prosecutor, declared that in political cases a confession from perpetrators prevails over the proof of their guilt: 'In all circumstances the defendants' confession is the best evidence.'[30] Krylenko referred to the old Roman principle *Confessio est regina probatum* or 'Confession is the Queen of evidence', commonly used by the Inquisition in the Middle Ages. Later Vyshinsky, USSR Prosecutor from 1935 to 1939, supported this thesis.[31] This gave a legal basis for the Chekists to apply every means to force confessions.

All these trials created a mass hysteria among the Soviet population. People became afraid of plots organized from abroad and of numerous foreign spies who supposedly wanted to destroy 'the first proletarian state'. The OGPU successfully promoted a belief that the 'Organs' (as security services were generally called) 'never make a mistake', meaning that if a person was arrested on political charges his or her arrest was justified without proof.

It wasn't long before the military was targeted. Between 1930 and 1932 the OOs prepared the first purge against Red Army officers, charging them with treason and espionage. It became known as the *Vesna* (Spring) Case.[32] From 1924 onwards, the OOs collected materials about czarist officers who served in the Red Army. Known under the operational name *Genshtabisty* (General Staff Members), in 1930 these materials were used to create the *Vesna* Case. Up to 10,000 officers were arrested throughout the country on false charges and many were sentenced and imprisoned, while 31 high-level former czarist officers were executed.

In early 1931, 38 Navy commanding officers were arrested as 'wreckers' in the Baltic Fleet alone.[33] Interestingly, Olsky and Yevdokimov were against the *Vesna* Case and were dismissed. Izrail Leplevsky, who had started the *Vesna* Case in Ukraine, replaced Olsky.[34] Stalin personally wrote a draft of the Politburo decision that accused Olsky, Yevdokimov and some other OGPU functionaries of disseminating 'demoralizing rumors that the case of wreckers among the military was supposedly falsified [in the original, Stalin used a colloquial Russian expression "*dutoe delo*"].'[35]

These actions triggered a flight of servicemen from the country. From October 1932 to June 1933 alone, twenty Red Army commanders and privates crossed the border and escaped to Poland.[36] But the *Vesna* Case was only a rehearsal for the actions brought against the military elite, such as the well-known Mikhail Tukhachevsky case a few years later, during the Great Terror (1936–38).[37] According to the official statistics, from 1937–38 1,344,929 persons were sentenced for 'counterrevolutionary' crimes and 681,692 of them were executed; other sources mention 750,000 executed. During this time physical torture for extracting the necessary 'confessions' became routine during NKVD investigations.[38]

Military commanders were persecuted in several stages, and after each wave the military counterintelligence heads and interrogators most actively involved in the purges were, in turn, arrested, tried, and executed (Table 1-2). Although unquestionably loyal, they—along with high-level NKVD personnel—simply knew too much about Stalin's methods. For instance, Stalin found it necessary to fabricate accusations against Genrikh Yagoda (a long-time head of the OO and OGPU who was also the first NKVD Commissar) and his team, accusing them of organizing a plot within the security services.[39]

Stalin's purges of the military peaked during the years of the Great Terror, when 40,000 members of the military elite were persecuted, including approximately 500 high-ranking officers; of them, 412 were shot and 29 died under interrogation.[40] This number is astonishing considering that only 410 generals and marshals died during the whole of World War II.[41] As usual, Stalin read the interrogation transcripts of the main arrestees and directed investigations. Even during the desperate days of late 1941 Stalin continued to order the arrests of generals, blaming them for the disasters of the first months of the war—disasters that were largely a result of his own mistakes and miscalculations.

Olga Freidenberg, a cousin of the internationally-famous poet and Nobel laureate Boris Pasternak, noted a macabre practice in her memoirs. In those years radio news about show trials and announcements of death sentences for 'enemies of the people' were followed by broadcasts of the Russian folk melody 'Kamarinskaya' or the Ukrainian Cossack dance tune 'Gopak'.[42] In the Kremlin-controlled media of those times, the broadcast of these dances—the Kamarinskaya, traditionally performed by a drunken, joyful peasant, and the Gopak, a victory dance performed with sabers—conveyed a clear, and chilling, message.

Many American authors describe Stalin's actions during the purges as symptomatic of a developing paranoia.[43] In my opinion, Stalin was not mentally ill. Rather, his behavior can be likened to the actions of a Mafia boss who maintains his power and position in the criminal world by killing off all possible opposition. *Chistki* or purges and 'unmasking' enemies in the armed forces and the NKVD obviously played an important role for Stalin—most of the officers who had served prior to the Revolution or were active during the October Revolution and the Civil War had perished and were replaced by recruits from a young generation of devoted Communist and Komsomol (Communist Youth Union) members. These people grew up in Stalin's Soviet Union and were personally devoted to the Leader and Teacher, as Stalin was called in the newspapers. The OO/SMERSH functionaries, including Viktor Abakumov, SMERSH's head, who operated during World War II, belonged to this younger generation.

Between autumn 1939 and summer 1940, Stalin acquired a part of Poland, three Baltic States, and a portion of Romania by making opportunistic use of the secret appendices of the Ribbentrop—Molotov Non-Aggression Pact of 1939. The security services, including the OO, actively participated in the Soviet occupation of the new territory, purging former national and military leaders, politicians, intelligentsia, and industry owners—that is, everyone who could potentially oppose the Sovietization that followed.

In February 1941, Stalin reorganized the security services in response to the new circumstances. The huge, unwieldy NKVD was divided into three parts. Military counterintelligence was transferred to the NKO (Defense Commissariat); a new organization, the NKGB (State Security Commissariat), became responsible for foreign intelligence; and the KRO ran domestic counterintelligence, among other things. Possibly, if not for the war, the NKGB would have continued the mass arrests of the Red Terror period since by March 1941, it had a cardfile for 1,263,000 'anti-Soviet elements' who potentially could have been arrested.[44] The NKVD was left to manage the slave labor in the camps and provide special troops to support NKGB actions in the newly occupied territory. It was also tasked with creating a separate system of camps for foreign prisoners of war.

Stalin was now ready to order his troops to continue their march to the West, but the unexpected invasion of Russia by Adolf Hitler's troops on June 22, 1941 scuttled all his plans. During the disastrous and chaotic first months of World War II, the focus of the state security services returned to controlling the Soviet Union's own citizens, many of whom at first greeted the Germans as liberators. Stalin undid his February changes, and recreated a huge NKVD.

Military counterintelligence was transferred back to the NKVD in the form of the OO Directorate, or the UOO (the 'U' means 'Directorate', which indicated that the OO had become a larger organization), and was given a new chief, the rising star Viktor Abakumov. Abakumov had already demonstrated his efficiency early in 1941, when he participated in the purging of the Baltic States. During this first period of World War II, the main goal of military counterintelligence was to prevent desertions and to vet the vast numbers of servicemen who had been surrounded or captured by the fast-advancing Germans.

In the spring of 1943, with the success of the Red Army in Stalingrad, it became clear that the war was finally becoming an offensive one. The Red Army began to liberate Nazi-occupied Soviet territory and prepared to advance into Europe. At this point, Stalin returned to the tripartite organization of the secret services of early 1941, with the military counterintelligence directorate now rechristened SMERSH and formally made a part of the NKO. In essence, SMERSH was simply the UOO, renamed and made independent of the main body of secret services. Abakumov, the UOO's head, became head of SMERSH, and most of the UOO's personnel were also transferred. SMERSH's staff was considerably larger than the UOO's.

SMERSH differed from the UOO in another extremely important aspect—Abakumov reported directly to Stalin, because Stalin had special plans for SMERSH. The Soviet dictator needed an organization he personally controlled to help him politically consolidate the territorial gains he expected the Red Army to make in Eastern Europe and Germany. Therefore, SMERSH was truly Stalin's secret weapon—a weapon that was even more effective than tanks and bombs in conquering new territory in the West.

By the time of SMERSH's creation, Stalin was the all-powerful dictator of the Soviet Union. He was general secretary of the Communist Party, chairman of the Council of Commissars, chairman of the wartime GKO (State Defense Committee), Defense Commissar, and commander in chief of the armed forces.

The order from Stalin that created SMERSH on April 19, 1943 was marked 'ss' (two small Russian 's' letters, an acronym for *sovershenno sekretno* or Top Secret).[45] A quotation from the order detailing SMERSH's responsibilities conveys a deep distrust of the Red Army, and its last point makes clear that SMERSH was to play a special role:

> The 'SMERSH' organs are charged with the following:
>
> a) combating spy, diversion, terrorist, and other subversive activity of foreign intelligence in the units and organizations of the Red Army;
>
> b) combating anti-Soviet elements that have penetrated into the units and organizations of the Red Army;
>
> c) taking the necessary agent-operational [i.e., through informers] and other (through commanding officers) measures for creating conditions at the fronts to prevent enemy agents from crossing the front line and to make the front line impenetrable to spies and anti-Soviet elements;
>
> d) combating traitors of the Motherland in the units and organizations of the Red Army (those who have gone over to the enemy side, who hide spies or provide any help to spies);
>
> e) combating desertion and self-mutilation at the fronts;
>
> f) investigating servicemen and other persons who have been taken prisoner of war or have been surrounded by the enemy;
>
> g) conducting special tasks for the People's Commissar of Defense.[46]

Due to the secrecy surrounding SMERSH, at first even officers in the field did not know SMERSH's real name. Daniil Fibikh, a journalist working for a military newspaper at the Northwestern Front, wrote in his diary: 'Special detachments SSSh—"*Smert', smert' shpionam*" ["Death, death to spies"] (!) [an exclamation mark in the original] attached to the Special Departments have been organized.'[47] In June 1943 Fibikh found out what this organization was about. SMERSH operatives arrested him for 'disseminating anti-Soviet propaganda' (Article 58-10 of the Criminal Code) after a secret informer reported on Fibikh's critical remarks regarding the Red Army. Fibikh was sentenced to a ten-year imprisonment in the labor camps.

Soon the ruthlessness of SMERSH interrogators became legendary. The investigative officers, known as '*smershevtsy*', tortured and killed thousands of people whether they were guilty of intelligence activity or not. Two Soviet defectors who served in SMERSH published little-known English-language memoirs in which they described the horrific interrogation methods.[48] In one of these books, Nicola Sinevirsky, a military translator, wrote how he was forced to witness a brutal beating by a female SMERSH officer:

> The Pole did not answer. Galya moved closer to him. She moved the rubber hose slowly back and forth in front of his face. 'Don't make yourself a bigger fool than you are already. Is that clear?'

The Pole looked around helplessly and said, 'I don't understand you.'

I translated Galya's words to the prisoner. As I did so, Galya broke in, 'He lies! The son of a bitch! He understands, all right! There is more cunning in him than in all of Poland. Listen to me, you Polish pig!' Galya screamed, raising the rubber hose above her head…

Galya beat the Pole across the face unceasingly. 'I'll beat you bloody. I'll beat you until you confess or you die on this spot!' A torrent of coarse oaths burst from Galya's lips…

The Pole's face was beaten into a formless mass of flesh and blood. Blood dripped in thin streaks over his chest and on his shirt. His badly bruised eyes showed no spark of life…

The work on him was resumed where she had left off before our short break for dinner. It was four o'clock in the morning before the sentries finally carried away the broken body of the dying Pole…

Like a drunken man, I stumbled to my quarters and collapsed on my bed without undressing. In a matter of seconds, it seemed that I had slipped quietly into a heavy coma.

It took days for me to recover from the bloody apparition.[49]

Each front had its own SMERSH directorate stationed at the front line with the Red Army troops, and SMERSH made wide use of informers on all levels of the Red Army and among former prisoners of war.[50] SMERSH's chain of command was completely independent of the military hierarchy, so a SMERSH officer was subordinate only to a higher-level SMERSH officer. Constant communication between SMERSH front-line units and Moscow headquarters was maintained, with Abakumov preparing daily reports for Stalin.

Becoming head of SMERSH was a big promotion for Abakumov. As the chief of SMERSH's predecessor, the UOO, he had been a subordinate of Lavrentii Beria, the notorious NKVD head. Now he was Beria's equal, and his relationship with Stalin was a direct challenge to Beria.

Abakumov soon proved his worth, scoring impressive victories against the Germans. SMERSH had hundreds of double agents working among the Germans, especially in Abwehr intelligence schools. Many German agents therefore were known to SMERSH even before they crossed the front line, and were immediately identified and arrested. SMERSH also identified high-ranking intelligence and counterintelligence officers among German POWs and sent them to Moscow for interrogation. The level of intelligence about the enemy thus increased enormously. Deceptive 'radio games' or 'playbacks', in which captured German intelligence men and radio operators created fake German military broadcasts, were also a great success. However, the screening (fil'tratsiya) of Soviet servicemen who had been in German captivity, and the identification of spies, mostly imagined, among Soviet servicemen remained an important part of SMERSH's job.

The Red Army's advances into Eastern Europe meant that there were whole new classes of people to arrest: active members of political parties, local officials, diplomats, and so forth. Numerous Russian-émigré and White Guard organizations that had dispersed throughout Europe after the end of the Russian Civil War in 1922 were also a target. SMERSH arrested members of these organizations in Bulgaria, Romania, Czechoslovakia, Yugoslavia, and later in the Chinese provinces freed from Japanese occupation. But the group that SMERSH pursued most passionately was the Russian Liberation Army (ROA), which was formed from Soviet POWs in German captivity under the leadership of the former Soviet general Andrei Vlasov and his staff. Following the Yalta agreements with Stalin, British and American Allies forcibly handed over many units of the ROA and other anti-Soviet Russian troops, some of whom were even British citizens, to SMERSH.[51]

People arrested by SMERSH were dealt with in a number of ways. Soviet servicemen were tried by military tribunals and then sent to punishment battalions or executed. Enemy agents of low importance were put in NKVD prisoner-of-war camps, while important prisoners were sent to SMERSH headquarters in Moscow, where they were intensively interrogated both during and after World War II. Among them were former leaders of European governments such as Count István Bethlen, the Hungarian prime minister from 1921 to 1930, and Ion Antonescu, the Romanian fascist dictator from 1941 to 1944, whose wife was also brought to Moscow.[52]

Among SMERSH's actions was the arrest of numerous diplomats. Some of them were guilty of crimes, like the Germans Gustav Richter and Adolf-Heinz Beckerle, both of whom played a crucial role in the Holocaust in Romania and Bulgaria. However, SMERSH also arrested completely innocent Swiss and Swedish diplomats, who were representing neutral governments. This was particularly galling to the Swedes, who had represented Soviet interests in Nazi Germany and Hungary for several years.

Perhaps SMERSH's most infamous arrest was that of the Swedish diplomat Raoul Wallenberg, who saved many thousands of Jews in Budapest at the end of World War II by providing them with fake documents, establishing safe houses, pulling people off trains bound for extermination camps, and so forth.[53] Named a Righteous Gentile by the Israeli government for his heroic actions, the truth of what happened to Wallenberg after his arrest by SMERSH is one of the deepest mysteries of World War II. It seems likely that he died in the Soviet investigation prison Lubyanka in 1947.[54] An even deeper mystery is why he was never repatriated to Sweden, despite the fact that he was a member of the powerful Wallenberg family and worked for the family corporation. The Wallenbergs, whose wholly family-owned interests during World War II amounted to perhaps half the gross national product of Sweden, had also been involved in mutually beneficial financial dealings with the Soviet Union since the 1920s.

High-level Abwehr and SD (the foreign branch of the Nazi State Security) officers also became prisoners of SMERSH. Among them were Lieutenant General Hans Piekenbrock, head of Abwehr Abteilung (Department) I (foreign intelligence) from 1937 to 1943; Colonel Erwin Stolze, deputy head of Abwehr Department II (sabotage and subversion) from 1937 to 1944, who was known as Saboteur No. 2; and Lieutenant General Franz-Eccard von Bentivegni, head of Abwehr Department III (counterintelligence) from 1943 to 1944.[55]

SMERSH also arrested and interrogated SS-Oberführer (Major General) Friedrich Panzinger, former head of the Gestapo's Department A, which specialized in combating Communism and other opposition in Nazi Germany. He was well-known as the head of the Gestapo commissions that investigated both the famous Soviet spy network the Red Orchestra in 1942, and the anti-Hitler plotters in 1944. Between these two investigations, from September 1943 to May 1944, Panzinger headed the Gestapo branch in Riga, the capital of Latvia, and simultaneously commanded Einsatzgruppe A, a Latvia-based SS killing squad. After his release from Soviet imprisonment in October 1955, Major General Panzinger committed suicide while awaiting arrest in West Germany.

SS-Hauptsturmführer (Captain) Heinz Pannwitz, who headed the Gestapo's investigation of the Red Orchestra in France, also fell into SMERSH's hands. After his release, the CIA interrogated Pannwitz concerning his Red Orchestra investigation and his interrogations by SMERSH, and used the resulting information in its 1979 report, *The Rote Kapelle*.[56]

Numerous high-ranking German military generals were also taken prisoner by SMERSH.[57] Among them was the ruthless Lieutenant General Reiner Stahel, who was military commandant of Warsaw during the 1944 Uprising. He was arrested by SMERSH in Romania, where Hitler had sent him in a last-ditch effort to save the German troops stationed there. Stahel died in November 1955 in a transit POW camp, on his way to Germany as part of a large repatriation of German officers. Another SMERSH prisoner was SS Major General Wilhelm Mohnke. The Americans and Canadians mounted a ten-year search for him due to his order to kill Canadian POWs during the Normandy invasion in June 1944. It was only upon Mohnke's release in 1956 that it became known that the Soviets had him all along.[58]

SMERSH operatives also arrested a group of people who witnessed the death of Hitler. In fact, there were two groups of such witnesses in Soviet captivity, and there were two completely separate investigations into the circumstances of Hitler's demise. These were conducted independently by

SMERSH under Abakumov's personal supervision and by the Main Directorate for POWs (GUPVI), which was part of the NKVD, under the supervision of the head of the GUPVI, Amayak Kobulov.[59] The NKVD and SMERSH competed to find out the truth in order to curry favor with Stalin, who was fascinated with the Führer. Stalin suspected that Hitler had somehow survived the bunker, and therefore wanted convincing proof of his death. One of the witnesses investigated by SMERSH, SS-Gruppenführer (Lieutenant General) Hans Rattenhuber, head of Hitler's bodyguards, was, possibly, the person closest to Hitler while he was alive.

Japanese military prisoners were investigated by SMERSH as well. They included General Otozo Yamada, commander in chief of the Kwantung Army, and the American-educated Senior Lieutenant Prince Fumitaka Konoe, who attended Princeton University before World War II. The young prince belonged to a 1,200-year-old family of Japanese rulers, and SMERSH considered him an important prisoner because he was a son and the personal secretary of Prince Fumimaro Konoe, the two-time former Japanese prime minister (1937–39 and 1940–41). In addition, Fumikata Konoe was related to Emperor Hirohito through his wife, Masako, a cousin of the emperor. Konoe, who had never been seriously ill, died suddenly in October 1956 in a transit POW camp on the way back to Japan. His death, like Raoul Wallenberg's, remains a great mystery.

General Yamada was more fortunate; he survived imprisonment and returned to Japan. Hiroki Nohara, deputy head of the Intelligence Department of Yamada's army, was sentenced to death in February 1947 as a spy and executed.[60] The Japanese Consul General in Harbin, Kimio Miyagawa, died in Lefortovo Prison in Moscow before he was tried, while General Shun Akifusa, head of the Japanese Military Mission in Harbin, was convicted of being a spy in December 1948 and sentenced to a 25-year imprisonment. Four months later he died in Vladimir Prison.[61]

To the disappointment of the SMERSH leadership, in August 1945 the last Manchurian Emperor Pu Yi was captured by an NKVD, not a SMERSH, operational group. Although the commander in chief in the Soviet Far East, Marshal Aleksandr Vasilevsky, ordered the transfer of Pu Yi to SMERSH, NKVD Commissar Beria only allowed SMERSH officers to interrogate Pu Yi; he remained in NKVD hands.[62]

Since SMERSH officers wore Red Army uniforms, people arrested by SMERSH operatives frequently did not know that they were in the hands of a separate secret service. Even Soviet POWs used to think that the NKVD or NKGB had arrested them. For instance, Lev Mishchenko, a Moscow physicist who volunteered in 1941 for the *opolchenie* (detachments of civilian volunteers) and was then captured by the Germans, wrote in the 2000s: 'In June 1945, I was arrested by the counterintelligence department SMERSH of the 8th Guard Army. SMERSH...was the name of the NKGB departments within the army.'[63] This misunderstanding led to confusing mistakes regarding SMERSH in the memoirs of many foreign former prisoners of SMERSH.

One of SMERSH's last important tasks was its involvement in the International Nuremberg Trial.[64] Abakumov's investigators proposed five prisoners as possible defendants at Nuremberg. However, the Politburo chose only one of the people on SMERSH's list: the relatively unimportant Hans Fritzsche, an official of Paul Joseph Goebbels's Propaganda Ministry, who was ultimately acquitted. It's possible that Stalin settled on Fritzsche because he did not want his former allies to know that important generals such as Mohnke were in his hands.

The NKVD also brought one defendant from its POW camps, Grand Admiral Erich Raeder, commander of the German Navy until 1943. He was sentenced to life in prison. The main testimony presented by Soviet prosecutors consisted of excerpts from the recorded interrogations of many SMERSH prisoners, but the prisoners themselves were not produced.

Colonel Sergei Kartashov, head of the 2nd Department of SMERSH, which was in charge of the interrogation of important German POWs and Soviet servicemen who had been in German captivity, was the first to arrive in Nuremberg. His assignment was to do an initial evaluation of the situation. Then a special team of three SMERSH officers headed by Mikhail Likhachev, a deputy head of SMERSH Investigation Department, brought Fritzsche to Nuremberg. However, the main task of this team was to monitor the Soviet delegation—the prosecutors, judges, translators, and so forth. They were also tasked with preventing any discussion at the trial of the Molotov–Ribbentrop Pact or of Soviet responsibility for the massacre of 22,000 captured Polish officers executed in 1940 in the Katyn Forest and two other places.[65]

After one of the Soviet military prosecutors, General Nikolai Zorya, was found dead with a gunshot wound to his head in his hotel room during the trial, it became evident that problems existed within the Soviet delegation. The official Soviet statement claimed that the death was due to 'the incautious usage of a fire-arm by General Zorya'.[66] But according to Zorya's son, Likhachev or one of his men killed Prosecutor Zorya to prevent a discussion of the Katyn Forest massacre.

At the same time, in early 1946, SMERSH prepared a series of trials in Moscow against a number of old White Russian generals who had been captured in Europe and Manchuria, including former Soviet General Andrei Vlasov. The most important defendants were tried in closed sessions of the Military Collegium of the Soviet Supreme Court. Only a few short sentences announcing the generals' executions were published in the press. However, these trials took place after the end of SMERSH and will be discussed in another book.

The formal end of SMERSH came in May 1946, when it was merged with the former NKGB, which was now renamed the MGB (State Security Ministry). Abakumov became head of the MGB, and key personnel from SMERSH headquarters in Moscow and from the front directorates took over the key positions in the MGB. As MGB minister, Abakumov supervised not only military counterintelligence but also foreign intelligence and civilian domestic counterintelligence within the USSR, which were the main functions of the former NKGB. He continued to report directly to Stalin, and the MGB became the primary tool for carrying out Stalin's purges and repressions from 1946 until 1951, when Abakumov himself was arrested. The famous Leningrad Case and the Jewish Anti-Fascist Committee Case were only two of the important prosecutions prepared by Abakumov and the MGB in the late 1940s.

In Eastern Europe, the former SMERSH front directorates were converted into the MGB directorates of the Soviet occupation armies. Their function remained the same as during the war—finding spies and traitors within Soviet troops and purging local areas of Soviet political enemies. Hundreds of people were arrested or kidnapped and sent to the Soviet Union. Many times they were simply grabbed off the streets, and their family and friends never knew what had happened to them. Abakumov's first deputy, Nikolai Selivanovsky, supervised the purges in Poland. One of Abakumov's assistants, Pyotr Timofeev, controlled the situation in Romania. The former head of one of SMERSH's front directorates, Mikhail Belkin, oversaw events in Hungary.[67] In Western Europe, SMERSH operatives worked under the cover of the staff of the Plenipotentiary on Repatriation, Colonel General Fyodor Golikov.

Former SMERSH officers also worked in Eastern Europe as MGB advisers to the local, newly organized pro-Soviet state security services and participated in the preparation of East European show trials. Belkin and Kartashov were responsible for arrests and trials in Budapest, while Likhachev interrogated prisoners in Bulgaria, Hungary, and Czechoslovakia. Since these officers reported directly to Abakumov, and Abakumov reported to Stalin, Stalin's control over these trials was assured.

The majority of the important SMERSH prisoners captured during and just after the war were kept and interrogated in Moscow investigation prisons until 1948, when they were sentenced. The rest remained in these prisons until 1950–52, when they were finally tried. Many of them, including former foreign diplomats, were accused of spying; the bizarre paragraph 4 of Article 58, 'assistance to the world bourgeoisie', was also frequently used. The luckiest spies and traitors were tried between May 26, 1947 and January 12, 1950, during a period when the death sentence was replaced by 25-year imprisonment in labor camps. There was a practical, not a humane, reason behind this abolition: with the loss of many millions of men during the war, Stalin needed unpaid workers to help restore industry.

In February–March 1948, special labor camps (at first six, later four more) with especially harsh conditions of life and work were created for 'especially dangerous prisoners', i.e. prisoners sentenced under Article 58.[68] The political prisoners were separated from criminals and moved to these special camps, while the most important political prisoners, especially with 25-year terms, were put in three special prisons—Vladimir, Verkhne-Uralsk and Aleksandrovsk. New convicts convicted under Article 58 were assigned to these special labor camps and prisons exclusively. As in the Nazi concentration camps, prisoners in special camps had numbers attached to their clothes.[69] Therefore, most of the important SMERSH prisoners ended up in this special penal system. In January 1953, there were 221,727 political prisoners in special camps, and 1,313 prisoners in special prisons.[70]

Although SMERSH existed for only three years, from 1943 to 1946, the two years prior to its formal organization (when Abakumov was chief of its direct predecessor, the UOO), and the five years after its demise (when Abakumov was head of the MGB), must be considered as part of its history. There is a continuous thread, during those ten years, of Abakumov's special relationship with Stalin.

Until now, there has been a lack of understanding, in the historical literature, of the part played by Abakumov. Abakumov's role as head of the UOO, SMERSH, and then the MGB was shrouded in secrecy. He was not a member of the Communist Party or Soviet government leadership, and portraits of him were not publicly displayed anywhere in the Soviet Union. Until recently, even the Russian State Archive of Film and Photo Documents, which keeps all documentary films and numerous photos of the Soviet period, did not have Abakumov's picture. There are perhaps only seven or eight photographs of him in existence, and I know of only one occasion, in March 1946, when the newspaper *Pravda* published a photograph of him—sitting next to Marshal Georgii Zhukov, the conqueror of Berlin. Even in the Soviet Union, very few people knew that the MGB, the most feared security service, was headed by Abakumov and not by Beria.[71]

In contrast, two books have been published in English about Lavrentii Beria, who was quite famous during his time in Moscow.[72] Every Soviet citizen was familiar with Beria's appearance because photographs of him were frequently published in newspapers. Also, his portraits, along with those of the other Politburo members, were posted on buildings in every city and town during official Soviet holidays—the 1st of May (International Labor Day) and the 7th of November (Bolshevik Revolution Day). Yet the period during which Beria was head of all the security services only lasted for five years, from 1938 until 1943. After the creation of SMERSH, Beria had to compete with Abakumov for influence.

From 1943 on, as NKVD Commissar, Beria was formally in charge of managing the NKVD labor camps and prisons, but through his close associate, Vsevolod Merkulov, Beria also effectively controlled the NKGB, which was responsible for foreign intelligence and internal counterintelligence. However, after 1943 he was never again, during Stalin's life, the all-powerful security chief he had once been.

On December 29, 1945, Beria, who was still a deputy chairman of the Council of Commissars, was appointed head of the Soviet Atomic Project, while Sergei Kruglov, his devoted and rather colorless deputy, became the head of the MVD (Internal Affairs Ministry, the successor to the NKVD). Therefore, contrary to what is generally believed, from the beginning of 1946 until Stalin's death on March 5, 1953, Beria did not head any of the Soviet secret services. As a member of the Politburo, each of which was assigned a group of ministries to supervise, for the next year Beria oversaw the work of the MGB and MVD, as well as that of ten other ministries, although this supervision was primarily administrative. In February 1947 even this supervisory role was taken away. In July 1947 Abakumov refused to follow Beria's orders regarding the construction of facilities by the MGB for the atomic project.[73]

By September 1947 it was clear that Beria had lost all control over the state security services. Abakumov, on the contrary, continued to amass power, managing to get several MVD directorates incorporated into his MGB. In terms of his control over state security, Abakumov was far more powerful from 1946 to 1951 than Beria had been from 1938 to 1943.

In 1947, Abakumov's MGB lost responsibility for foreign intelligence (its 1st Main Directorate) when Stalin merged it, along with military intelligence (GRU or the Main Intelligence Directorate) and diplomatic and Party intelligence services, into a new organization called the Committee on Information. Undaunted, in October 1949, Abakumov established a new 1st Directorate, charged with counterintelligence on foreigners and on Soviet personnel abroad. It was headed by Colonel Georgii Utekhin, who had headed departments in SMERSH headquarters that were in charge of capturing enemy agents in the Red Army rear and sending SMERSH agents to the German intelligence schools.

As he had done to so many people before, Stalin decided to purge Abakumov, and on July 12, 1951, he was arrested. Many high-ranking SMERSH officers, including Selivanovsky, Likhachev, Belkin, and Utekhin, were also detained. By the beginning of 1953 Stalin pretended that he had nothing to do with the appointment of Abakumov as MGB minister. Stalin told those investigating Abakumov's case that in 1946 Beria had insisted on Abakumov's appointment and that was why he 'did not like Beria and did not trust him'.[74] Apparently, Stalin was preparing to use the Abakumov case as a tool against Beria.

Nikita Khrushchev, who emerged as the Soviet leader soon after Stalin's death in March 1953, played a big part in concealing Abakumov's real role. During the de-Stalinization campaign that started with Khrushchev's secret speech at the Twentieth Soviet Communist Party Congress in 1956 and continued at the Twenty-second Congress in 1961, as well as in a series of speeches at other Party meetings, Khrushchev repeatedly mentioned Abakumov as 'an accomplice' of Beria. Apparently, Khrushchev wanted to make Beria the primary villain of the Stalin period in order to expedite Beria's speedy trial and execution at the end of 1953. By the way, the text of Khrushchev's speech of 1956, published in many languages that same year, appeared in press in the Soviet Union only in 1989.

After Stalin's death on March 5, 1953, Beria was appointed first deputy chairman of the Council of Ministers and Minister of Interior Affairs (MVD). This was a new MVD that included both previous ministries, the MGB and the MVD. In other words, Beria restored the monolithic NKVD structure that had been in effect from 1941–43. However, the new MVD was much bigger than the NKVD of 1941–43, and Beria acquired enormous power.

To counter this threat, Georgii Malenkov, Vyacheslav Molotov and Khrushchev united, and on June 26, 1953, with the help of Georgii Zhukov, first deputy Defense Minister, Beria was arrested as an alleged spy and enemy of the people. On December 23, 1953, the Special Session of the USSR Supreme Court sentenced Beria to death and he was executed. Beria's longtime colleagues—Vsevolod Merkulov, Vladimir Dekanozov, Bogdan Kobulov, and Sergei Goglidze, whom he brought from the Caucasus in 1938, as well as Pavel Meshik and Lev Vlodzimersky, who became his trusted men in Moscow—were also convicted and shot.

The investigation of Abakumov continued for a year after Beria's execution. When Roman Rudenko, the newly appointed Soviet chief prosecutor, was interrogating Abakumov in 1953–54, he tried in vain to connect Abakumov with Beria. Abakumov firmly stated: 'I've never visited Beria's apartment or his dacha. We had a strictly official, working relationship, and nothing else.'[75]

Abakumov and his devoted men—Aleksandr Leonov, former head of the SMERSH Investigation Department, and two of his deputies, Likhachev and Vladimir Komarov, as well as Ivan Chernov, former head of SMERSH's Secretariat, and his deputy Yakov Broverman—were tried by a special session of the Military Collegium of the Supreme Court in Leningrad from 12–19 December, 1954.[76] As 'a member of Beria's gang', Abakumov was accused of treason against the Motherland, terrorism, counter revolutionary acts, and so forth. None of these accusations made any sense. Abakumov pleaded not guilty, stating that 'Stalin gave instructions, and I only followed them'.[77] This was true. As Chernov recalled, during the announcement of the death verdict 'not a muscle moved in Abakumov's face, as if the announcement did not concern him'.[78] Abakumov, Leonov, Likhachev, and Komarov were executed on December 19, 1954, immediately after the trial. Chernov and Broverman were sentenced to imprisonment in labor camps, for 15 and 25 years respectively.

At that time, Khrushchev was first secretary of the Communist Party and, no doubt, approved the indictments and outcome of the trial. Having been a member of Stalin's inner circle, Khrushchev had, of course, signed off on many of Stalin's orders between 1937 and 1953. According to some sources, when Khrushchev came to power, he also ordered the destruction of archival documents pertaining to his role in the Great Terror, during which, as first Party secretary of Moscow and the Moscow Province (*oblast*), he sanctioned thousands of arrests and executions.

Abakumov was one of the few people who, because of his close relationship with Stalin in 1943–51, knew the intimate details of how decisions were made by Stalin and the Politburo, including Khrushchev. Also, Abakumov and his leading investigators received personal instructions from Stalin and Politburo members regarding whom to arrest and what torture to apply. Obviously, Abakumov was a man who knew too much. After his trial, he was determined to share his knowledge. According to the memoirs of the executioner, he shot Abakumov in the back of the head while Abakumov was screaming, 'I will write about everything to the Politburo.' He was dead before he finished pronouncing the word 'Politburo'.[79]

But even before Beria was arrested, soon after Stalin's death political prisoners who had managed to survive the purges began to be released from labor camps and prisons.[80] This process continued for a few years. However, in order to receive a residency permit to live in Moscow or Leningrad, or obtain a professional job, former prisoners needed to be 'rehabilitated'.

Being rehabilitated constituted an official recognition that the political prisoner had been convicted unlawfully and restored the person's civil rights.[81] By April 1, 1954, 448,344 prisoners sentenced for committing 'counterrevolutionary crimes' were still in the labor camps and prisons.[82] In May 1954 the specially created Central Commission for reconsidering the cases of those sentenced for 'counterrevolutionary crimes' started work, and the Military Collegium also began to reconsider many political cases even before Khrushchev's historical speech about Stalin's crimes in February 1956. Soon it appeared that in thousands of cases, including military ones, there was no family member to whom the Military Collegium could report the rehabilitation, since the whole family had perished in purges.[83] As for imprisoned foreigners, they were released and repatriated, mostly in 1954–56.

The following statistics cast light on the enormous work of rehabilitation: from 1918 to 1958, 6,100,000 arrestees were convicted in the Soviet

Union of committing anti-Soviet (political) crimes, of whom 1,650,000 were executed.[84] Of the total number, approximately 1,400,000 political convicts had in fact committed the alleged crimes (for instance, those who joined the Nazi troops and security services during the war), and 4,700,000 were absolutely innocent. Additionally, there were between 2.5 and 7.0 million people, *spetspereselentsy* (special deportees), sent into exile before and during the war.

In 1960 the infamous 'political' Article 58 was abolished, but it did not disappear completely. The new, 'Khrushchev' Criminal Code included separate articles on treason, espionage, terrorism, sabotage, and wrecking. But paragraph 58-10 (anti-Soviet propaganda) was transformed into Article 70: 'Anti-Soviet agitation and propaganda being carried out in order to undermine or weaken the Soviet power...and dissemination, production or keeping works of the same content in the written, printed or other form for the same purpose is punished by imprisonment from six months to seven years and an additional exile from one to five years.' Article 72 stipulated the same punishment for being a member of an anti-Soviet organization. As before, the NKVD/MGB, now the KGB (*Komitet gosudarstvennoi bezopasnosti* or State Security Committee; Table 1-1), investigated such crimes.

In 1966, after Leonid Brezhnev (Communist Party leader from 1964–82) replaced Khrushchev, Article 190-1 was additionally introduced in the code. It stated that 'a systematic dissemination of undoubtedly false fabrications that slander the Soviet power...is punished by imprisonment up to three years'. Since the 1960s, Soviet political dissidents were sentenced mostly under Article 70 or 190-1. However, some writers and poets were tried as 'social parasites' (*tuneyadtsy*).

In 1983–84, during the short tenure of Yurii Andropov, a long-time KGB chairman before he became general (first) Party secretary (Table 1-1), a new paragraph was included in Article 70 that made financial support of political prisoners and their families from abroad a crime, and Paragraph 3 was additionally introduced in Article 188, stating that 'intentional disobedience' to the camp's administration—which could be, for instance, an undone button on the prisoner's shirt—was punished by up to five years' imprisonment. Potentially this article meant that a political prisoner would not ever be released.

Of course, the number of prisoners sentenced in the 1960s–80s for committing 'anti-Soviet crimes' was small compared with the political convicts of Stalin's time, but political charges existed until 1989, when Articles 70 and 190-1 were finally abolished. For example, in 1976 there were 851 political prisoners in labor camps and Vladimir Prison, and of those, 261 were sentenced for anti-Soviet propaganda (Article 70).[85] Additionally, the

KGB warned up to 36,000 potential perpetrators whom it suspected of anti-Soviet activity.

The rehabilitation process stopped for a few years during Brezhnev's time, but then it continued. By January 1, 2002, more than 4,000,000 former political prisoners had been rehabilitated. Except for a small group of Nazi collaborators like General Andrei Vlasov and his confidants, some White Russians, leaders of Soviet security services and real Nazis, all Soviet and many foreign prisoners mentioned in this book were rehabilitated. In other words, almost every serviceman, as well as most of the foreigners arrested by Soviet military counterintelligence during World War II and just after it, were innocent.

In the 1990s–2000s, there were even attempts to rehabilitate Beria and Abakumov. In May 2000, the Military Collegium of the Supreme Court of the Russian Federation refused an application by the members of Beria's family to overturn the 1953 conviction.[86] The court ruled that Beria and his accomplices could not be politically rehabilitated because of their crimes against the Soviet people. But the court found Dekanozov, Meshik, and Vlodzimersky guilty of abuse of authority, rather than of crimes against the state covered by Article 58 of Stalin's time, and the sentence for them was posthumously changed from death to 25 years' imprisonment.

A few years later, following the trend of security services-affiliated historians toward glorifying Stalin and his men, a 798-page book entitled *Beria: The Best Manager of the 20th Century* was published in Russia.[87] It not only glorifies Beria, but also tries to persuade the reader that the crimes Beria committed were necessary for the progress of the Soviet economy, winning the war against Hitler, and successfully fighting the Cold War.

During the 1990s, the Supreme Court of the Russian Federation twice considered Abakumov and his co-defendants' political rehabilitation.[88] In July 1997, the Military Collegium of the Supreme Court found Abakumov, Leonov, Likhachev, Komarov, and Broverman guilty of abuse of authority, but not of political crimes. In December 1997, the Presidium of the Russian Federation Supreme Court posthumously changed the death sentence for these four to 25 years imprisonment in labor camps, and rescinded confiscation of property for all defendants. Chernov was totally rehabilitated in 1992.

The historians and officers of the current FSB (*Federal'naya sluzhba bezopasnosti* or the Federal Security Service) are fond of Viktor Abakumov. One of his biographers, Oleg Smyslov, called him in the press 'a Knight of State Security', while the politician and former KGB Major General, Aleksei Kondaurov, maintains that Abakumov was 'one of the KGB's most democratic leaders'.[89]

The legacy of SMERSH continued with the notorious KGB, which was created in 1954. Until the collapse of the Soviet Union in 1991, military counterintelligence remained within the KGB. Pyotr Ivashutin, former head of one of the SMERSH field directorates, was a KGB deputy chairman between 1954 and 1956, and then, until 1963, its first deputy chairman. Sergei Bannikov, who began his career in the OO of the Baltic Fleet and then served in the SMERSH Directorate of the Navy Commissariat, headed the 2nd KGB Main Directorate (counterintelligence) from 1964 to 1967.[90] Grigorii Grigorenko, one of the radio-games organizers in the 3rd SMERSH Department (he participated in 181 games), headed the same 2nd KGB Main Directorate from 1970 to 1978, and then became KGB deputy chairman, from 1978 to 1983. When Grigorenko died in 2007, an obituary in the FSB-connected newspaper *Argumenty nedeli* (Arguments of the Week) identified fourteen foreign spies discovered and arrested under Grigorenko's supervision, and called him 'a genius of Russian counterintelligence'.[91]

The sinister Filipp Bobkov, head of the notorious 5th KGB Directorate from 1969 to 1984, which was in charge of persecuting political dissidents, graduated from SMERSH's Leningrad School in 1946.[92] Bobkov served as a deputy, then as first deputy KGB chairman, until the end of the KGB in 1991.

During the transition of the Soviet KGB into the Russian Federation Security Ministry, the Federal Security Committee and, finally, the FSB (Table 1-1), military counterintelligence did not change much.[93] In 1997, Colonel General Aleksei Molyakov, head of the FSB Military Counterintelligence Department (UVKR), told the press: 'The situation in the Russian Federation Armed Forces is under our strong control… Military counterintelligence…has clear orders to uncover and prevent extremist and other dangerous tendencies in time…[Its] staff consists of 6,000 officers.'[94] After resigning from the service, Molyakov and Lieutenant General Vladimir Petrishchev, who succeeded him as head of the UVKR in 1997 and served until 2002, joined the *siloviki* ('men of power')—a group of former high-level KGB and military officers who became part of President Vladimir Putin's ruling elite. Molyakov presided over the National Military Fund, which assists retired KGB/FSB and military officers, and is personally supported by Putin.

In 2005, Petrishchev was elected a member of the Highest Council of Officers or VOS.[95] This eleven-member council represents the mostly retired ultra-nationalist high-ranking military, FSB, Foreign Intelligence Service, and MVD (Interior Affairs Ministry) officer community, as well as leaders of the Cossacks. Most probably, Petrishchev, a military counterintelligence professional, is not a genuine member of VOS but is just keeping an eye on its activities from the inside. He is also a member of the thinktank Fund for

Development of Regions, which helps the government with economic and political decisions and the distribution of governmental funds.[96]

There is a representative of military counterintelligence in the Administration of the current Russian President Dmitrii Medvedev: Colonel General Vladimir Osipov, who made his career in various KGB military counterintelligence directorates, including the Moscow Military District.[97] From 1991 till 1998, Osipov worked at the Federal Agency for Governmental Communication and Information (formerly part of the KGB), mostly as head of its Personnel Directorate. From 1998, Osipov headed the Personnel Directorate of the administrations of all three Russian presidents: Boris Yeltsin, Vladimir Putin, and, finally, Dmitrii Medvedev. In other words, from 1998 onwards, the selection of administration staff members was controlled by the *siloviki*, a group of former high-level KGB officers currently in power in Russia, with Vladimir Putin at their forefront. In 2009, while restructuring his administration, President Medvedev appointed Osipov head of the Administration's Directorate for Governmental Awards, which had previously been part of the Personnel Directorate.

In 2008, Russian President Medvedev appointed a new FSB Director: Army General Aleksandr Bortnikov, a former KGB man (from 2003 to 2004, he headed St. Petersburg's FSB branch) who was closely connected to Putin. However, the new director did not make any serious changes in the FSB, and by 2011, Colonel General Aleksandr Bezverkhny still continued to head the Military Counterintelligence Department of the FSB, as the UKVR has been called since 2001. On May 25, 2005, Bezverkhny unveiled a monument entitled 'The Glory of Military Counterintelligence' in the yard of a mansion occupied by the Military Counterintelligence Directorate of the Moscow Military District, at 7 Prechistenka Street in central Moscow.[98] There is also a small, private military counterintelligence history museum in this building. According to the press, most of its exhibition is devoted to SMERSH. Obviously, the Russian security services are proud to claim SMERSH and its brutal activities as part of their history.

Part II. The Roots of SMERSH

CHAPTER 2

Stalin's Ruling Mechanism

The years 1938 through 1941, during which Stalin consolidated his power and gained new territory in Europe, are critical to an understanding of Soviet military counterintelligence and particularly SMERSH. In order to gain total control of the Soviet Union, Stalin made sophisticated and extra-legal use of the Communist Party structure, the secret services, the judicial system, and the legislative system on all levels.

The Politburo: Stalin and His Confidants

By late 1938, with the purges of the Great Terror over, the situation within the Party leadership stabilized. By 1939 the Politburo, the Communist Party ruling body, was Stalin's 'instrument of personal rule'.[1] From March 1939 to March 1946, it consisted of the same nine full members and at first two, then five candidate (non-voting) members:

Members	Candidates
Joseph Stalin	Lavrentii Beria
Vyacheslav Molotov	Nikolai Shvernik
Andrei Andreev	Georgii Malenkov (after Feb.1941)
Lazar Kaganovich	Aleksandr Shcherbakov (after Feb. 1941)
Mikhail Kalinin	Nikolai Voznesensky (after Feb. 1941)
Nikita Khrushchev	
Anastas Mikoyan	
Kliment Voroshilov	
Andrei Zhdanov	

The real Politburo was a small group of five or six of Stalin's most trusted confidants.[2] He called them 'the five' or 'the six', and together they usually worked late into the night. However, Stalin carefully kept up the fiction of a functioning government, officially publishing Politburo decisions as decisions of either the entire Central Committee (CC) of the Communist Party, the Presidium of the Supreme Soviet (the highest legislative body in the Soviet Union), or the Council of Commissars (known after 1946 as the Council of Ministers). Politburo meetings often continued after working hours at Stalin's 'nearby' dacha in the Moscow suburbs. Stalin, especially at his dacha, 'liked to use foul language (*matershchina*). And all members of his circle followed his example'.[3]

At meetings in Stalin's office on the second floor of the triangular eighteenth-century Yellow Palace in the Kremlin, he guided the discussion of matters prepared by the Politburo's secretariat. Non-members like Viktor Abakumov were invited to present important issues. The Politburo voted on each question discussed, and Stalin's secretariat head Aleksandr Poskrebyshev telephoned absent members to record their votes.[4] As did most Soviet people, those in Stalin's inner circle called him 'Khozyain', meaning 'Boss' or 'Master', and stood at attention even while talking to him on the phone.[5] Or they said 'HE', making it clear the significance of 'HE', as Lev Mekhlis, a secretary of Stalin, did: 'It's always pleasant to hear how HE speaks.'[6]

Stalin decided many important questions, especially regarding the NKVD and the Red Army, alone or only with Molotov, and he frequently gave orders orally rather than in writing. For instance, Stalin didn't put his signature on the General Staff plans he approved, even when changes were made.[7] This allowed him to place blame on the generals when things went wrong.

Total Secrecy

Most Politburo decisions were distributed in secrecy, and the details of how the system worked were discovered only in the late 1990s. Stalin's secretariat, known also as 'Stalin's cabinet', was originally called the Secret Department, and then, from 1934 on, the Special (*Osobyi*) Sector of the CC.[8] It was a relatively large organization—in 1930, there were 103 members, while the whole CC staff comprised 375 people.

The Special Sector consisted of seven sections, including the Secret Archive of the CC, which later became known as the Presidential Archive. Assistants to CC secretaries (in 1941, Stalin, Andreev, Malenkov, Zhdanov, and Aleksandr Shcherbakov) and their staffs constituted the first section. Of this group, Stalin's assistant Poskrebyshev was extremely powerful. He prepared all documents for Stalin and controlled his calendar. According to a contemporary, Poskrebyshev was 'a short, stout man...very clever and had a phenomenal memory. He never forgot anything, remembering every detail'.[9] Poskrebyshev headed the Special Sector from 1934 until 1952, despite the fact that in 1940 the NKVD, apparently with Stalin's approval, arrested his first wife, most likely because of a distant family relationship to Trotsky. She was executed in October 1941. In early 1953, Stalin accused Poskrebyshev of losing secret documents and replaced him with his deputy.[10] But after Stalin's death on March 5, 1953, Poskrebyshev was released, and he immediately retired.

A ciphering section, supervised by the NKVD Special (*Spetsial'nyi*) Department, was in charge of sending and receiving cables. However, the most secret letters, including written Politburo decisions, were sent with secret couriers from the NKVD Courier Department (Administration

Directorate). Clearly, Stalin thought the Communist Party was a conspiratorial organization. In 1924, when Party rule was first firmly established, he signed a directive declaring which Party documents should be considered secret.[11] All lower levels of the Party structure—republic (a republican CC), province (*obkom*), city (*gorkom*), and regional (*raikom*) committees—had their own secret Special Sectors that communicated with the Special Sector in Moscow. Of all fifteen Soviet republics, only the Russian Federation did not have its own capital and a national Communist Party with its Central Committee because Stalin did not want to have a competing governmental structure within the Russian Federation. Only the lowest level, the *partkom* (a Party committee) of every institution, received instructions from its regional committee. Stalin liked to compare this structure to the army: 'There are three or four thousand high-level members within our party...I would call them generals of the party. Then there are thirty to forty thousand middle leaders; these are our officers of the party. Then there are between a hundred thousand and a hundred and fifty thousand lower-level party commanders. They are...our noncommissioned officers.'[12]

Stalin's system of making decisions through the Politburo and distributing them secretly through the Party pyramid was technically illegal. Neither Lenin's constitution of 1924 nor Stalin's Soviet Constitution of December 1936 even mentioned the Politburo as a decision-making body. But the Party leaders did not care about legal issues. One of Stalin's cronies, Lazar Kaganovich, bluntly declared in 1934: 'Our Politburo...is the organ of leadership of all branches of socialist construction.'[13]

The Politburo either appointed or approved the appointments of almost all high- and mid-level Party and Soviet government functionaries such as leaders of the NKVD, including heads and their deputies of the Special Department (OO). These appointees, known collectively as the *nomenklatura*, often moved among positions. This policy resulted in some absurd situations.

In 1938, Semyon Dukelsky, a veteran of the OO, was appointed chairman of the Committee on Cinematography. Stalin used to say that 'each film is of great public and political importance'.[14] Therefore, the post of this committee's chairman required a strong Party or NKVD controller. But in the film industry, Dukelsky became known as 'a man of anecdotal stupidity and incompetence...He gave numbers to all film directors and playwrights, from No. 1 to No. 100. Dukelsky thought that movies should be made according to the following principle: Director No. 1 should use a script written by Playwright No. 1, Director No. 2 should use a script by Writer No. 2, No. 5 should work with No. 5, and so on'.[15] Incompetence was no barrier to Dukelsky's next appointments. In 1939, he became Merchant Marine Commissar, then from 1942 to 1943 he headed the ammunition production in the Chelyabinsk Region with its big tank plant, and from 1943 to 1948, he was Justice Commissar/Minister of the Russian Federation.

By 1939, having gained absolute control of the Soviet Union, it was time for Stalin to embark on his long-cherished dream: westward expansion of the Soviet empire. Some historians still believe that Stalin had no intention of attacking the West, but recent comprehensive analyses of old sources and newly discovered archival documents reveal the truth—from the autumn of 1939 on, Soviet military leadership was organizing a strategic plan to conquer Europe.[16] At the end of December 1940, Stalin wrote: 'Defense is especially beneficial if one thinks of it as a measure to organize our offense, and not as an end in itself.'[17]

To accomplish this, Stalin would have to maintain an iron grip on the Red Army and control the opposition he would face in the newly acquired territory. For achieving these two goals, Stalin had to put devoted people in charge of the secret services. His first move in this direction was to bring in Lavrentii Beria, a man from his own southern homeland of Georgia.

Men from the Caucasus

In August 1938, 39-year-old Lavrentii Beria, first Communist Party secretary of Georgia, relocated to Moscow and within a few days was appointed first deputy NKVD Commissar. Stalin had known Beria for some time, and had personally recommended him for the first secretary position. In addition, Beria's previous position as head of the Georgian GPU (and therefore head of the local OO) meant that he had significant secret service experience. Beria was careful to cultivate his personal relationship with Stalin, supplying him with wine from the vineyards of their southern homeland and installing his wife's cousin as Stalin's housekeeper.[18] Stalin had used Beria's predecessor, Nikolai Yezhov, to carry out mass persecutions during the Great Terror, but in April 1939 Yezhov was arrested and tried, and was subsequently executed on February 4, 1940. By November 1939, Beria was NKVD Commissar.

Stalin was in total control of the security services because since 1922, the GPU and its successors, the OGPU and NKVD, had reported directly to the Politburo. But now for the first time Stalin had someone he trusted completely heading the security service. SMERSH officer Romanov said of Beria: 'He spoke Russian well, with far less of a Caucasian accent than, for example, Stalin had.'[19] The brutal and extremely proficient Beria was well prepared for his position as head Chekist. As former head of the GPU in Georgia, he routinely ordered that prisoners be tortured during investigation and even after they had received death sentences.[20] Beria's brutality continued in Moscow. In 1953, his deputy Vsevolod Merkulov testified: 'In my presence a few times Beria beat up arrestees in his office, as well as in prison, with his fists or a rubber truncheon.'[21]

Soon Beria had a well-deserved reputation as the face of political repression. In 1948, the American *Time* magazine wrote: 'Beria seems to be a sane, well-balanced man. In that fact lays the deepening horror of Russia. For Beria, without shrieks or dark yearnings, plods along, like the efficient bureaucrat he is, in the bloody footsteps of [the founder of the CheKa, Felix] Dzerzhinsky.'[22]

To extend his power, Beria brought his own devoted team from the local NKVD branch in Tbilisi—Sergei Goglidze, Vladimir Dekanozov, Bogdan and Amayak Kobulov, Stepan Mamulov, Merkulov, Solomon Milshtein, and Lavrentii Tsanava, among others.[23] Having known each other and worked together for years, they remained in key Moscow positions in the security service until after Stalin's death. Beria affectionately called his cronies by nicknames such as 'Merkulich' (Merkulov), 'Kobulich' (Bogdan Kobulov), and 'Mamulich' (Mamulov); the 'ich' ending makes the last name sound like a patronymic, and therefore more intimate. This affectionate nicknaming seems especially incongruous in the case of Kobulov, Beria's main torturer, who weighed over 300 pounds and covered his fat fingers with gold rings.

Of this group, Merkulov was the most educated.[24] He was 'a man with an athletic figure and a splendid head of thick dark hair flecked with grey'.[25] Born in 1895 in Tbilisi (then Tiflis) to the family of a small nobleman and a czar's army captain, he was four years older than Beria. Merkulov graduated from high school (gymnasium) with a gold medal and then attended the Department of Physics and Math of Petrograd University for three years. After serving in the army until 1918, in 1921 he joined the Georgian CheKa. Here Beria noticed Merkulov in 1923 after the latter published an article about the CheKa; since then, their careers were connected. In 1931, Stalin appointed Beria first secretary of Georgia, and Beria transferred Merkulov as his assistant to the staff of the Georgian Communist Party CC. Later Merkulov headed the Special (Secret) Sector (see above) and other departments of this committee. Merkulov helped Beria to write his official reports and published Beria's glorifying biography in the Small Soviet Encyclopedia. In 1940, already in Moscow, Merkulov additionally published a 64-page-long even more glorifying book about Beria entitled *Vernyi syn partii Lenina-Stalina* (*True Son of Lenin-Stalin's Party*).

In September 1938, the Politburo modified the NKVD structure, no doubt according to Beria's suggestions.[26] Beria restored the GUGB (Main State Security Directorate), the elite intelligence/counterintelligence unit that Yezhov had recently eliminated, as a separate entity, placing his men in the top positions. The brain trust of the NKVD, the GUGB consisted of seven departments, of which the Secret Political, Counterintelligence, Military Counterintelligence (OO), and Foreign Intelligence were the most important. Soon an unnumbered Investigation Unit, traditionally called *Sledchast'*, was added (Figure 2-1). NKVD officers had their own rank names (Table 2-1).

Figure 2-1

THE STRUCTURE OF THE GUGB WITHIN THE NKVD DECEMBER 1939 TO FEBRUARY 1941

GUGB

Vsevolod Merkulov, Head
(also First Deputy NKVD Commissar)
Dec 17, 1938–Feb 3, 1941

Deputies

Bogdan Kobulov,
Dec 17, 1938–Sep 4, 1939;
Vladimir Dekanozov,
Dec 17, 1938–May 13, 1939;
Ivan Serov,
Jul 29–Sep 2, 1939

1st Department

Party Leader Guards
N. S. Vlasik
Nov 19, 1938–Feb 26, 1941

2nd Department

Secret Political
B. Z. Kobulov
Sep 29, 1938–Jul 29, 1939;
I. A. Serov, Jul 29–Sep 2, 1939
P. V. Fedotov, Sep 4, 1939–Feb 26, 1941

3rd Department

Counterintelligence (domestic)
V. G. Dekanozov
Dec 17, 1938–May 13, 1939;
T. N. Kornienko
Jun 25, 1939–Sep 26, 1940;
P. V. Fedotov
Sep 29, 1940–Feb 26, 1941

4th Department

Special Department
V. M. Bochkov
Dec 28, 1938–Aug 23, 1940;
A. N. Mikheev,
Aug 23, 1940–Feb 8, 1941

5th Department

Foreign Intelligence
V. G. Dekanozov
Dec 2, 1938–May 13, 1939;
P. M. Fitin
May 13, 1939–Feb 26, 1941

7th Department*

Ciphers
A. D. Balamutov,
Sep 29, 1938–Apr 8, 1939;
A. I. Kopytsev
Apr 8, 1939–Feb 26, 1941

Investigation Unit

V. T. Sergienko
Sep 4, 1939–Feb 26, 1940;
A. A. Esaulov
Feb 26, 1940–Feb 26, 1941

1st Section *General Staff*	2nd Section *Military Intelligence*	3rd Section *Aviation*	4th Section *Technical Troops*	5th Section *Motorized Infantry*	6th Section *Artillery and Cavalry*	7th Section *Infantry*	8th Section *Political Units*	9th Section *Supply Units*
10th Section *Navy*	11th Section *NKVD Troops*			12th Section *Mobilization Unit*				

Investigation Unit

*The 6th Department in charge of militia (police), firemen, etc. was disbanded on Dec 28, 1938 and merged into the 7th Department.

TABLE 2-1. OFFICER RANKS DURING WORLD WAR II

NKVD/NKGB, 1936–43[1]	Red Army, 1935–43	NKVD/NKGB, 1943–45	Red Army, 1943–46	Wehrmacht (German Army)[2]	SS	American Army
None	None	None	Generalissimo Joseph Stalin (1945)	Oberste Führer (Adolf Hitler)	Oberste Führer (Adolf Hitler)	[President and Commander-in-Chief]
None	None	None	None	Reichsmarschall (Hermann Goering)	None	None
General Commissar of State Security	Marshal of the Soviet Union	General Commissar of State Security	Marshal of the Soviet Union	Fieldmarshal (Feldmarschall) or General-Fieldmarshal	SS-Reichsführer (Heinrich Himmler, 1929–45; Karl Hanke, 1945)	General of the Army
State Security Commissar of the 1st Rank	Army General (1940–43)	State Security Commissar of the 1st Rank	Marshal [of a particular type of troops] or Army General	Colonel General (Generaloberst)	SS-Obergruppenführer	General
State Security Commissar of the 2nd Rank	Komandarm of the 1st Rank or Commissar of the 1st Rank; Colonel General (1940–43)	State Security Commissar of the 2nd Rank	Colonel General	General [of a particular type of troops]	SS-Obergruppenführer	Lt. General
State Security Commissar of the 3rd Rank	Komandarm of the 2nd Rank or Commissar of the 2nd Rank; Lt. General (1940–43)	State Security Commissar of the 3rd Rank	Lt. General	Lt. General (Generalleutnant)	SS-Gruppenführer	Major General
State Security Senior Major	Major General (1940–43)	State Security Commissar	Major General	Major General (Generalmajor)	SS-Brigadeführer	Brigadier General

Table 2-1 (continued)

NKVD/NKGB, 1936–43[1]	Red Army, 1935–43	NKVD/NKGB, 1943–45	Red Army, 1943–46	Wehrmacht (German Army)[2]	SS	American Army
	Komkor (1935–40)	State Security Colonel	None	None	None	None
	Komdiv (1935–40)	State Security Lt. Colonel	None	None	None	None
	Kombrig (1935–40)		None	None	SS-Oberführer	None
State Security Major	Colonel	State Security Major	Colonel	Colonel (Oberst)	SS-Standartenführer	Colonel
State Security Captain	Lt. Colonel	State Security Captain	Lt. Colonel	Lt. Colonel (Oberstleutenant)	SS-Obersturmbannführer	Lt. Colonel
Senior State Security Lt.	Major	Senior State Security Lt.	Major	Major	SS-Sturmbannführer	Major
State Security Lt.	Captain	State Security Lt.	Captain	Captain (Hauptmann)	SS-Hauptsturmführer	Captain
Junior State Security Lt.	Senior Lt.	Junior State Security Lt.	Senior Lt.	Senior Lt. (Oberleutnant)	SS-Obersturmführer	1st Lt.
State Security Sergeant	Lt.	State Security Sergeant	Lt.	Lt. (Leutnant)	SS-Untersturmführer	2nd Lt.

1. A detailed description of the NKVD uniforms and insignias in V. Voronov and A. Shishkin, *NKVD SSSR: Struktura, rukovodyashchii sostav, forma odezhdy, znaki razlichiya 1934–1937* (Moscow: Russkaya razvedka, 2005).

2. There were also ranks for civilians who had non-commanding officer positions: Sonderführer R corresponded to a colonel (Oberst); Sonderführer B, to a major; Sonderführer K, to a captain (Hauptmann); Sonderführer Z, to a Lt. (Leutnant); and Sonderführer G, to a non-commissioned officer.

Military counterintelligence became the fourth GUGB Department, although everyone in the secret services still called it the OO as long as it remained in the NKVD (and I will follow that convention). Each of its twelve sections (Figure 2-1) was in charge of monitoring a particular branch of the army and navy, or, as it was known in Russian, the Military-Marine Fleet. A separate Commissariat for the Military-Marine Fleet, or NKVMF, existed from 1937 until 1946. (I will call it the Navy Commissariat from now on.) The 11th Section monitored the various NKVD troops—the Border Guards, Industrial Facility Guards, Convoy Troops, and Railroad Construction Guards. It's important to note that all NKVD troops were regular military forces, like Waffen SS, and not paramilitary forces, as some historians have stated.[27] In fact, even today when a young man is drafted he does not know whether he will be sent to the regular Russian Army or to MVD (Internal Affairs Ministry) troops. There was also an unnumbered *sledchast'*. OO officers in the Moscow headquarters wore NKVD uniforms, while in the field units they wore the uniforms of the units they were attached to (infantry, artillery, etc.), with insignia showing their NKVD rank—small metal rectangles or squares on the collars, depending on the rank. Political officers wore additional insignia: red stars on the sleeves.

In July 1938, just before Beria's arrival, two important changes were made in the OO structure: (1) local OOs were now embedded in the various army and fleet formations, and were no longer part of the local NKVD office as in the old system; and (2) OO officers now reported only to higher OO officers, not to the head of the local NKVD branch.[28] Now each military district, army and fleet had its OO, while a corps, a division and a brigade had a Special Division. By 1941, there were 16 military districts in the country. This new vertical structure gave Moscow OO headquarters more direct control over the armed forces. By January 1940, the OO headquarters consisted of 394 officers, the GUGB staff totaled 1,484 members, and the NKVD headquarters staff numbered an astonishing 32,642 people.[29]

In December 1938 Viktor Bochkov was appointed the new OO head—a surprising choice, since he had no experience in investigative work.[30] With only a month of service at NKVD headquarters, where he was head of the Prison Directorate, he had worked mainly as a commander for various units of OGPU/NKVD troops. Even more surprising was his appointment on August 7, 1940 as chief USSR prosecutor, despite his complete lack of legal training. Making Bochkov chief prosecutor was clearly part of the effort by Stalin and Beria to extend secret service control over every aspect of a case, from arrest to final sentencing. Later, during the first two years of World War II, Bochkov even held simultaneous positions as chief USSR prosecutor and head of the OO at the Northwestern Front.

The 29-year-old head of the Kiev Military District OO, Anatolii Mikheev, replaced Bochkov as OO head.[31] Amazingly, Mikheev's NKVD career had begun only six months before. However, Mikheev proved up to the task. Only a year later, just before the war with Nazi Germany, Mikheev successfully unleashed a broad program of persecution targeting high-level Red Army officers.

To understand the mechanism of arrests by military counterintelligence and following persecutions it is necessary to know Soviet legal procedures and the work of military tribunals. These issues have never been detailed in historical sources that described Stalin's regime.

CHAPTER 3

Laws and Tribunals

The OO and later SMERSH cases were primarily based on Article 58 (and, in part, 59), the special section of the Russian Federation (RSFSR) Criminal Code adopted in December 1926, which described various 'counter revolutionary' or 'state' crimes.[1] These were 'political crimes' that existed only in the Soviet legal system and were the only type that the NKVD investigated. Another unique character of the Soviet legal system was that not only a perpetrator of political crimes was punished, but also members of his/her family, especially if it was an OO/SMERSH case. The trials of OO/SMERSH cases were also unique. Military tribunals tried only cases of low-ranking servicemen, while high-ranking military officers were tried by the highest military tribunal, the Military Collegium of the USSR Supreme Court or, if there was no real proof of the crime, by the NKVD Special Board which was an extra-judicial court consisting of the NKVD Commissar and his deputies.

Counter revolutionary Crimes

Article 58 begins with a definition of counter revolutionary crimes, unique to Soviet law:

1. Counter revolutionary Crimes

58.1. Shall be considered counter revolutionary any act directed to the overthrow, subversion, or weakening of the worker-peasant soviets or of governments elected by them on the basis of the Constitution of the USSR and constitutions of the union republics, as well as any act intended to subversion or weakening of the internal security of the USSR and of the basic economic, political, and national gains of the proletarian revolution.

By virtue of the international solidarity of the interests of all toiling masses, such actions are considered counter revolutionary also when directed against any other state of the toiling masses, albeit not a part of the USSR.[2]

Paragraph 58-2 states that 'a military revolt or taking power by force' is punished by death or by declaring the perpetrator 'an enemy of working people', depriving him of Soviet citizenship, and confiscating his property. Additionally, riots were punished by imprisonment or death under Article 59, paragraphs 2 and 3. Paragraph 58-6 covers espionage, 'i.e., transmission, theft, and collection for the purpose of transmission of information that in content is a specially protected state secret to foreign states, to counter revolutionary organizations or to individuals'. Paragraph 58-8 states that 'committing terrorist acts against representatives of the government or organizations of workers and peasants [in other words, the Communist Party], and participation in such acts' is punishable by death. Paragraph 58-10 prohibits 'propaganda and agitation aimed to overthrow, undermine or weaken the Soviet government'. This crime was punishable by death during wartime, and in 1941–42, at the beginning of the Great Patriotic War (as World War II is known in Russia), the number of sentences for 'anti-Soviet propaganda' (96,741) reached almost 50 per cent of all convictions for 'counterrevolutionary' crimes (199,817).[3] However, 'anti-Soviet propaganda' in a written form was punished under Article 59-7.

Paragraph 58-11 allows the investigator to consider 'any organizational activity' or 'participation in an organization created to prepare or commit' crimes covered by Article 58 as a plot, which led to the discovery of numerous supposed 'military plots' before and during the Great Patriotic War. Finally, paragraph 58-14 introduces punishment for sabotage, described as 'conscious negligence of duties aimed to weaken the government's power'. On the whole, there were 14 paragraphs in Article 58 and five paragraphs in Article 59 that described 'counterrevolutionary' or 'political' crimes. Later, in 1951, four more paragraphs were included in Article 58.

In July 1934, simultaneously with the creation of the NKVD, paragraph 58-1 (treason against the Motherland) was divided into four parts, 58-1a–d, which were widely used until Stalin's death in 1953.[4] Paragraph 58-1a detailed the crime of treason: 'Actions USSR citizens commit to the detriment of the military might of the USSR...to wit: espionage, disclosure of a military or state secret, going over to the enemy, flight, or crossing the border.' While paragraph 58-1b declared: 'Commission of the same crimes by servicemen is punishable by the highest measure of criminal punishment—shooting, with confiscation of all property.' Paragraph 58-1b was most frequently used by military counterintelligence just before and during the war because it covers a wide spectrum of vaguely described 'political crimes', including espionage and 'going over to the enemy'. Although paragraph 6 in Article 58 already covered espionage, from 1934 onwards, paragraph 58-1b was applied to military 'spies', while 58-6 was used for charging civilians (58-6/I) and foreigners (58-6/II). Paragraph 58-1d stated that a serviceman who did not report to the authorities upon learning of a treasonous plan or the fact of treason was punished by ten years of imprisonment in labor camps.

Paragraph 58-1c was the most outrageous. It legalized the practice of using family members as hostages to prevent servicemen from becoming traitors. Now family members who knew about a treasonous plan were punished by a 5-to-10-year imprisonment and confiscation of property, and even adult family members who knew nothing of any alleged plan (i.e., who were completely innocent), were punished by exile into distant areas and were deprived of the right to vote. Following the text of this paragraph, such family members started to be called *chsiry*, an abbreviation from *chleny sem'i izmennika Rodiny* or 'family members of a traitor against the Motherland'.

Although the total number of persecuted *chsiry* remains unknown, one of the NKVD reports to Stalin mentions that in 1937–38, 'according to the incomplete data, more than 18,000 wives of the arrested traitors were repressed [i.e., arrested and sentenced], including more than 3,000 in Moscow and approximately 1,500 in Leningrad'.[5] Small children classified as *chsiry* were kept in specially organized orphanages.[6] Conditions in these orphanages were terrible. Anna Belova, arrested as a *chsir* (her husband, Komandarm Ivan Belov, commander of the Belorussian Military District, was executed in 1938), recalled that when her mother tried to find her three-year-old granddaughter in an NKVD orphanage, she was told: 'Klementina had died of hunger…We do not bury enemies' offspring…Do you see that trench? Go there, there are many of them. Dig out the bones; possibly, you'll identify those of your kid.'[7] In 1937–38, the NKVD sent 22,427 children of the 'enemies of the people' younger than fifteen years to orphanages.[8]

After the child-survivors reached fifteen, they were tried and usually sentenced to imprisonment in labor camps or even executed. Legally this became possible due to the decree issued just before the war, on May 31, 1941.[9] It stated that children could be criminally charged after they reached fourteen years. However, in December 1941 deputy USSR chief prosecutor Grigorii Safonov suggested that children sentenced as spies or terrorists be executed after they reached sixteen years.[10]

For instance, on July 6, 1941, the Military Collegium under Ulrikh's chairmanship sentenced four teenagers to death (the future executions had been pre-approved by the Politburo). The teenagers were a son and nephews of Nestor Lakoba, Chairman of the government of the Autonomous Republic of Abkhazia (part of Georgia), poisoned in December 1936 by Lavrentii Beria, at the time first secretary of the Georgian Communist Party's Central Committee. From 1937 until 1941, they were kept in Moscow prisons. On July 27–28, 1941, they were shot.[11]

Adult children of traitors and other 'enemies of the people' were also frequently imprisoned as 'socially dangerous elements' or SOE (an acronym of the Russian term), defined as 'persons connected with the especially important criminals' (Articles 7 and 35); in other words, people who did not commit any crime at all, although their relatives supposedly did. In August 1940, the Politburo ordered the Military Collegium to send materials on relatives of military defectors to other countries for their immediate arrest and punishment.[12] The new draconian measures against the family members of military traitors were introduced in June 1941 and July 1942.

If a person was arrested under Article 58, but there were no incriminating materials apart from reports from secret informers about that person's anti-Soviet conversations, Article 19 of the Criminal Code allowed the investigator to still apply Article 58. Article 19 stated that 'an intent [sic] to commit a crime…is punished as the crime itself'. As a result, the arrestee was accused 'through Article 19', as the phrasing went, of the intent to commit a counter revolutionary crime. Some Chekists even considered themselves more sophisticated than their German analogue, the Gestapo. In 1944, Lev Vlodzimersky, head of the NKGB Investigation Department, bragged to a prisoner: 'The Gestapo men are poor imitators of us.'[13]

The Soviets had big plans for Article 58. In 1940, an NKVD interrogator told Menachem Begin, the arrested Polish citizen and the future prime minister of Israel: 'Section 58 applies to everyone in the world…It is only a question of when he will get to us, or we to him.'[14] After the Red Army entered Eastern Europe in 1944, SMERSH began to make wide use of Article 58 against foreign citizens. Mostly they were accused of espionage (58-6) or 'assisting the world bourgeoisie' (58-4).

Military Tribunals

OO/SMERSH cases were tried under Articles 58 and 59 by military tribunals, which existed within the Red Army at the district (in the wartime, a military district was called a front), corps, brigade, and divisional levels, and within the NKVD troops.[15] In the Red Navy there were fleet, flotilla and base tribunals. Tribunals were part of, to use the awkward official term, 'the three-element system of the punishment organs'—OO/SMERSH, a military prosecutor, and a military tribunal.[16] From 1926 to June 1939, military tribunals were subordinated to the Military Collegium only, and from June 1939–1946, to both the Military Collegium and the USSR Justice Commissariat.[17]

The Military Collegium, which had oversight over all military tribunals, was one of three collegia (Civil, Criminal and Miltary) of the USSR Supreme Court.[18] The Supreme Court's chairman, I. T. Golyakov, served from 1938 to 1948, a long term of service in those days. However, V. V. Ulrikh, who played an important role during the Great Terror, served as head of the Military Collegium from 1926–1948, one of the very few high level Communist officials to enjoy such a long tenure. The Military

Collegium consisted of the following departments between 1939 and 1946:

> First Department, Oversight of Trials (evaluation of death sentences from lower tribunals)
> Second Department, Military Tribunals of the Red Army
> Third Department, Military Tribunals of the NKVD Troops[19]
> Fourth Department, Military Tribunals of the Navy
> Appellate Section (appeals from the districts/fronts)
> Archival-Statistics Section
> Secret Ciphering Section
> General Section
> Commandant's Office (Komendatura), in charge of prisoners and executions.

The Directorate of Military Tribunals, which was responsible for the day-to-day operations of the military tribunals, was part of the Justice Commissariat (headed by N. M. Rychkov from 1938–1948).[20] This directorate was also responsible for the education of military jurists through their Military-Judicial Academy. Yevlampii Zeidin headed the Directorate from 1940-1948, which, during this time, was comprised of the following departments:

> Personnel Department
> Department of Military Tribunals of the Red Army
> Department of Military Tribunals of the Navy
> Department of Military Tribunals of the NKVD Troops
> Section of Military Tribunals of Transportation
> Statistics Section
> Military-Judicial Academy (from 1939), education of military jurists for Military Tribunals and prosecutors' offices.

From January 1940 till the German invasion, the NKVD district military tribunals heard all political cases investigated by the OOs.[21] After the beginning of the Great Patriotic War, the divisional tribunals attached to the fighting troops heard most of the cases. Tribunals at the army level heard cases of commanders with the rank of major and above, as well as of battalion commanders and officers of the regimental or battalion staffs. Front tribunals considered cases of high-ranking commanders and generals, as well as the most important cases of low-ranking perpetrators.

Each military tribunal consisted of three officers and a secretary who recorded the minutes of the hearing. The chairman was always a military jurist, and until 1942, two members of divisional tribunals were also military jurists, but later, the members were chosen from officers of the same division.[22] Therefore, the chair was, in fact, a judge.

Typically, a hearing was conducted with numerous violations of the Criminal-Procedure Code of the Russian Federation. M. Delagrammatik, former secretary of a corps tribunal at the Southern Front, describes:

Commonly, a copy of the indictment was not given to the defendant 24 hours before the trial as it should have been done according to law, but the indictment was simply read to him, usually during the day of the court trial. The defendant was shown and not given, according to law, a printed form that stated: 'The indictment was announced to me' (a date). This was a flagrant violation of the law. Most frequently, witnesses were not called up to the hearing because they supposedly were in fighting detachments, and only their testimonies were read.[23]

According to Soviet legal procedure, the defendant had the right not to testify against himself. However, the judges usually asked the defendant to testify because sincere admission of guilt by the defendant would supposedly help him. In fact, the judges needed this admission to pronounce the defendant being guilty.

The defendant was not told that there was no time restriction for his final statement. Deceptively, when giving the defendant his last chance to speak, the judge only said: 'What do you ask from the court?' This was a clear violation of the defendant's rights.

The presence of a jurist as a chairman did not guarantee a fair court procedure. Delagrammatik explains: 'Military judges had poor legal knowledge; they were poorly educated or even lacked education. The judges and prosecutors with the background of party functionaries were especially ignorant and semi-literate. This affected the quality of the pre-trial investigation and of a court trial, and as a result, justice suffered.'

Dual Function of Prosecutors

The role of Soviet prosecutors differed from that in the common law system of Britain and the United States. In general, the Soviet legal system followed continental criminal procedures in which prosecutors are not actively involved in prosecuting cases in courts. Prosecutors and defense representatives were not present at hearings in military tribunals. The military prosecutors' role was investigation of criminal cases in the army, navy, and NKVD troops, and legal oversight of the OOs. The crimes they investigated were mostly covered by Article 193, the military part of the Criminal Code.

In 1941, Article 193 included 31 paragraphs.[24] For instance, 193-7 described desertion as 'an unauthorized leaving of a position for more than 24 hours', while 193-10a introduced a one-year imprisonment for escaping draft during the wartime, and 193-12 covered self-inflicted injury. Four paragraphs, 193-17b (negligence or abuse of power by a commander), 193-20a (surrender of troops or a destruction of fortifications or a battleship by a commander), 193-21a (not following orders from superiors by a commander), and 193-22 (intentional leaving of a battlefield), required the death penalty. Paragraph 193-23, which also required the death penalty, applied specifically to the navy: 'A commander leaving a sinking military vessel, who has not fulfilled his duties to the end, is punished by the highest measure of social defense [death].' To such crimes as rape or embezzlement, prosecutors applied the 'usual', not military, articles of the Criminal Code.

Military prosecutor offices were attached to military tribunals. During the war, an Army Prosecutor had two assistants, two military investigators and several technical office workers.[25] At the divisional level, there was a prosecutor and an investigator. A platoon of Red Army men was attached to each prosecutor's office at the divisional and army levels to guard the arrestees and people under investigation.

Military prosecutors had their own vertical structure. District (front) military prosecutors reported to the Chief Military Prosecutor, who reported to the chief USSR Prosecutor, Bochkov (after November 1943, that position was filled by Konstantin Gorshenin), and needed his approval to appoint military prosecutors. The USSR Prosecutor appointed all front level prosecutors. Therefore, from 1940 to 1943 Bochkov oversaw the whole system of military prosecution and, through him, the NKVD maintained control.

The Chief Military Prosecutor's office in Moscow consisted of the following departments:

> Department of the Chief Prosecutor for the Red Army
> Department of the Navy Prosecutor[26]
> Department of the Prosecutor for NKVD Troops
> Department of the Military Prosecutor for Railroad Transportation (from 1943)
> Department of the Military Prosecutor for Marine and River Navigation (from 1943).[27]

It was headed by the following individuals:

> N. F. Rozovsky, 1935–1939 (arrested)
> P. F. Gavrilov, 1939–May 1940 (acting)
> P. F. Gavrilov, May 1940–February 1941
> N. I. Nosov, March 1941–March 1945
> N. P. Afanasiev, March 1945–July 1950

In an Army Prosecutor's Office cases were usually opened on the order of a member of the Military Council of the Army. Military councils (not to be confused with military tribunals) were unique Soviet institutions of shared command and responsibility in the Red Army. Lieutenant General Konstantin Telegin, a long-time member of such councils during the war, described their role:

> Fronts (as well as armies, except an air force army) were directed by a Military Council…[A military council] consisted of the military commander, two members, chief of staff, artillery and air force commanders…
>
> To implement a commander's decision, an agreement with [the senior] military council member was necessary. All directive documents issued by

the front command were signed by the commander and [the senior] military council member with their names on the same line, while the chief of staff put his signature below, on the next line. This was done to emphasize the equal responsibility of the commander and the military council member for the realization of the decision.[28]

The senior of the two military council members was a high-ranking Party functionary like Nikolai Bulganin or even Politburo member Nikita Khrushchev. The senior member usually had no military training or experience; his role was essentially to be the Politburo's eyes and ears in the field and directly control the activity of high commanders. Stalin frequently changed commanders at the fronts on the basis of reports from these members. The other member was usually a military supply commander. Besides their main duties, military councils were involved in the punishment of servicemen.

The total number of servicemen investigated and sentenced under Article 193 during the war was higher than the number investigated by OO/SMERSH under Article 58. On the whole, all military tribunals, including those in the Navy and NKVD, convicted 2,530,683 servicemen and of them, 471,988 were sentenced for 'counter revolutionary crimes' and 792,192 were convicted of military crimes. About 8 and a half percent, or 217,080, were sentenced to death and executed.[29]

Another count of persons convicted by the Red Army military tribunals only gives a more detailed picture. Of the total number of 994,300 servicemen convicted 422,700, or 42 per cent, served their sentences in their units (usually officers were demoted to privates) or, after July 1942, in special punishment troops called *shtrafbaty* and *shtrafnye roty*. However, this option was generally only available to those who committed military and real (bandits, rapists, embezzlers, etc.), not political, crimes. Most of the 436,600 convicts who ended up in labor camps (45 per cent of the total), were convicted of counter revolutionary crimes. The rest, 135,000, were sentenced to death and executed. One third, 376,300, were convicted of desertion.[30] An NKVD report dated January 1, 1945, which gives a detailed breakdown of the sentences of all the prisoners in NKVD labor camps at that time, indicates that 28.3 per cent were incarcerated for counter revolutionary crimes and only 6.5 per cent were convicted of military crimes (Table 3-1).[31]

Overseeing political cases opened by the OO/SMERSH investigators was the second main duty of military prosecutors.[32] For instance, before the war, in order to arrest a serviceman on counter revolutionary charges, both the OO head and a military prosecutor of the local district were required to sign an arrest warrant, which had to be authorized by a military commander. Additionally, the NKO Commissar had to approve arrests of all officers from platoon commander up, but usually no objections were raised.[33]

TABLE 3-1. PRISONERS IN NKVD LABOR CAMPS ON JANUARY 1, 1945[1]

Type of Crime	Article/Paragraph of the Criminal Code[2]	No. of Prisoners	% of Total
Counterrevolutionary Crimes (investigated by the OOs and other NKVD branches and after April 1943, by SMERSH and NKGB)			
Treason against the Motherland	58-1a, 1b	77,067	19.6
Espionage	58-1a, 1b; 58-6; 193-24	16,014	4.1
Terror acts and terrorist intentions	58-8	10,245	2.6
Diversions	58-9	3,206	0.8
Wreckers	58-7	8,175	2.1
Counterrevolutionary sabotage	58-14	24,567	6.3
Anti-Soviet plots and organizations	58-2; 58-3; 58-4; 58-11	31,298	8.0
Anti-Soviet propaganda	58-10; 59-7	130,969	33.4
Political bandits and participants in riots	58-2; 59-2; 59-3	7,563	1.9
Illegal crossing the border	59-10	5,585	1.4
Smuggling	59-9	1,266	0.3
Family members of traitors (*chsiry*)	58-1c; 58-12	6,449	1.7
Socially dangerous elements (SOE)	7-35	13,112	3.3
Others	No data	57,093	14.5
Total		392,609	100.0
Military Crimes (investigated by military prosecutors)			
Deserters	193-7, 9, 10	49,771	55.4
Self-inflictors	193-12	5,010	5.6
Marauders	193-27	1,743	1.9
Others	193	33,330	37.1
Total		89,854	100.0
Real Crimes (investigated by *militsiya* [Soviet police] and civilian prosecutors)			
Real crimes (bandits, thieves, etc.)	Various Articles	636,736	70.6
Special Laws and Decrees	Not in the Code	254,107	28.1
Violation of the Passport Law	192a	11,945	1.3
Total		902,788	100.0
Grand Total for All Crimes		1,385,271	100.0

1. NKVD report, dated January 1, 1945; quoted in Nikita Petrov, *Istoriya imperiiy 'GULAG.' Glava 12* (in Russian), http://www.pseudology.org/GULAG/Glava12.htm, retrieved September 15, 2011.
2. Classification of paragraphs according to the NKVD report on prisoners in the Correction-Labor Colonies, dated January 1, 1943. Document No. 96 in A. I. Kokurin and N. V. Petrov, *GULAG (Glavnoe upravlenie lagerei) 1917–1960* (Moscow: Materik, 2000), 426–28 (in Russian).

NKVD requests for Kliment Voroshilov's (NKO Commissar from 1926 to 1940) approval of persecutions comprise 60 thick archival volumes. Semyon Timoshenko, who replaced Voroshilov, approved the arrests of generals just before the German attack on the Soviet Union in June 1941.

During the war, the arresting procedure of OO/SMERSH operatives changed.[34] The arrest of a private or a low-ranking officer required a military prosecutor's approval; the arrest of a mid-ranking commander, the approval of the commander and prosecutor of the unit; and the arrest of a high-ranking officer, the approval of the Military Council of the Army. The highest commanders, as before, could be arrested only with the approval of the NKO Commissar—in other words, of Stalin himself.

To arrest a serviceman, an OO/SMERSH investigator wrote the arrest warrant (*Postanovlenie na arrest*) and decision (on the selection of a measure of restraint) (*Postanovlenie ob izbranii mery presecheniya)* which substantiated the necessity of keeping the arrestee in custody. Both documents were also signed by the investigator's superiors and a prosecutor. Copies of these documents were included in the investigation file (*Sledstvennoe delo*), which contained mostly transcripts called *protokoly* of the interrogations that followed.

While concluding the case, the OO/SMERSH investigator summarized the results of his investigation in an indictment (*Obvinitel'noe zaklyuchenie*). This document was also signed by the investigator's superiors, and a copy was sent to a prosecutor. The prosecutor was obliged to ask the accused if he agreed to the indictment and if he had complaints about, for instance, torture during the investigation. Commonly, the final verdict of the tribunal at the end of the hearing simply repeated the indictment.

The relationship between OO/SMERSH investigators and military prosecutors, as well as with military tribunal chairs and members, was uneasy. Prosecutors had legal training, while the majority of OO/SMERSH officers were uneducated and sometimes almost illiterate. Also, as a rule, OO/SMERSH investigators presented cases based on accusations provided by unreliable informers and confessions obtained under duress. Beyond that, the OO investigators used to try to influence the chair's decision. Delagrammatik recalled: 'Frequently the *osobisty* [OO/SMERSH officers] attached a sealed envelope with an inscription "For the Eyes of the Chair of MT [military tribunal] Only" to the case file received by our tribunal. It contained data about the defendant obtained from informers… Sometimes the *seksoty* [secret informers] testified as witnesses (or pseudo-witnesses, if necessary) at the hearing.'[35]

Many honest prosecutors rejected these falsified cases, insisting on a new investigation or even closing such cases entirely. These closures led Aleksei Sidnev, head of the OO of the Leningrad Military District (LVO), to send a report entitled 'On the Anti-Soviet Practice of the Military Prosecutor's Office of the LVO' to Bochkov (an insubordinate act, since Sidnev should have sent the report through his superior, OO head Mikheev) in March 1941.[36] Bochkov forwarded Sidnev's report to his deputy and chief military prosecutor, Vladimir Nosov, who determined that Sidnev had slandered the prosecutors. However, no measures were taken against Sidnev, who later became a high-level SMERSH and then MGB functionary.

The independence shown by military prosecutors was rare and potentially dangerous. During Bochkov's tenure as OO head, dossiers (or, in secret-service jargon, 'operational files') were collected on many military prosecutors, as well as members of military tribunals.[37]

Death Sentences

During the war, the Commander of the Front could disaffirm any decision of tribunals within his front, even a death sentence.[38] In any case, the Front Military Council needed to approve or disapprove the death sentence of a high-ranking officer. In theory, a serviceman condemned to death had the right to appeal; in practice, appealing was useless. As Delagrammatik notes, 'I recall no occasion when the commander of a unit did not approve the death sentence.'[39]

After the summer of 1942, military tribunals usually replaced death sentences in criminal cases with sending the condemned to a punishment unit fighting at the front. Delagrammatik gives an example: 'Two servicemen from the Marine Brigade were convicted of self-inflicted injury "by shooting at each other from behind a tree in order not to be drafted"... Instead of the death penalty, the military tribunal...condemned each of them to 10 years of imprisonment in labor camps. The punishment was commuted to sending them to a punishment platoon. Only "espionage" [i.e., 58-1b] was inevitably punished by death.' Delagrammatik gives more detail about an 'espionage' case of Olga Serdyuk, a woman from Kiev:

> This large young woman, who was a medical nurse, was tried. She was charged with the worst crime—Article 58-1b, treason against the Motherland committed by a military person...
>
> While writing down a transcript [of the hearing], I could not find any espionage activity in her testimony. She admitted that, while a prisoner of the Germans she signed a collaboration agreement with the German intelligence. That was all, but the fact of this recruitment, even in the absence of any espionage activity, was enough for the military tribunal. Even though she herself had told the court about the recruitment and there was no independent proof of it.
>
> A guilty verdict and speedy execution followed.[40]

During the war, military tribunals sentenced more than 2.5 million Soviet military men and women.[41] Of these, 472,000 men were sentenced for counter revolutionary activity, i.e. under Article 58, and a total of 217,000 were shot; of those, 135,000 were sentenced by military tribunals of the Red Army. Death sentences were usually executed by an OO (later SMERSH) officer or a Red Army platoon attached to the OO/SMERSH Department, before the eyes of the formation.

The enormity of these executions becomes evident from a comparison with death sentences in foreign armies. British military tribunals sentenced 40 servicemen, while French tribunals sentenced 102, and American tribunals sentenced 146 servicemen to death.[42] The German field military tribunals sentenced 30,000 servicemen to death, and approximately the same number of German deserters was shot at the end of the war without trial, mostly by the SS blocking units and military gendarmes.

CHAPTER 4

Highest Courts

The Military Collegium of the USSR Supreme Court (*Voennaya kollegiya Verkhovnogo suda SSSR,* called *voenka* by prisoners) and the NKVD Special Board (*Osoboe soveshchanie* or OSO) made decisions in the most important political cases, including those of the OOs and SMERSH. Both were unique in Stalin's Soviet Union.

Military Collegium and Its Chairman

The Military Collegium was the highest military tribunal. It was one of three Supreme Court collegia, and had several functions. From 1934 on, it heard cases of 'treason against the Motherland, espionage, terror, explosions, arson and other kinds of diversion' (Article 58-1, 6, 8 and 9) that had been investigated by the NKVD and later by SMERSH, NKGB and MGB.[1] In 80 to 90 per cent of these cases, which involved high-level commanders, Party functionaries, and intelligentsia, defendants received death sentences. The rest were sentenced to 8 to 25 years of imprisonment in labor camps.[2] The Military Collegium's decisions were approved by the Politburo, usually by Stalin himself.[3]

The Military Collegium also considered appeals from district military tribunals, and evaluated death sentences issued by lower military tribunals.[4] The procedure was as follows: After a military tribunal pronounced a death sentence, it cabled the decision and a description of the case to the Military Collegium. The latter was obliged to respond to the tribunal within 72 hours, by either approving the death sentence or changing it to long-term imprisonment. However, from September 1937 onwards, in death sentences for sabotage and diversion (Article 58-7 and 9) appeals were not allowed and the prisoners were immediately executed.[5] In addition, from 1926 to 1939, the Military Collegium administered the activities of all subordinate military tribunals, appointing chairs and members of tribunals, and so forth.

The Military Collegium's staff was small: at the beginning of the Great Patriotic War there were 66 members, while toward the end, the number increased to 72 members plus six people supervising the activity of NKVD tribunals.[6] From 1926 through 1948, Vasilii Ulrikh chaired the Military Collegium.[7] Although he formally reported to the chairman of the Supreme Court, in a letter to Stalin he made it clear that he understood who was really in charge: 'Although formally the Military Collegium is part of the Supreme Court, in fact it acts as an independent court... While hearing the cases on treason against the Motherland, preparation of terrorist acts, espionage, and diversions, the Military Collegium has been and still is working under the *direct* [italics in the original] guidance of the highest directive organs.'[8] The 'highest directive organs' was one of the Party's euphemisms for Stalin and the Politburo.

Ulrikh's biography is among the strangest of senior Soviet officials. Like Bochkov, Ulrikh had no legal education, graduating in 1914 from the Polytechnic (general engineering) College in Riga. In 1910 he joined the Bolshevik Party and in 1918, the VCheKa. Ulrikh's early career was boosted by the fact that his wife, Anna Kassel, worked in Vladimir Lenin's secretariat. From 1920 to 1922, Ulrikh headed the OO of the Black and Azov seas fleet, and in 1922 he became famous as a supervisor of the extremely ruthless executions-without-trial of thousands of White Guard officers who surrendered to the Red Army in the Crimea. From July 1922 to October 1923, Ulrikh worked as deputy head of the Counterintelligence Department in Moscow, and then he was transferred to the Military Collegium. Although his father was German, Ulrikh was not persecuted in 1937 or 1941, unlike most other Soviet Germans.

Boris Yefimov, the main Soviet political caricaturist for *Pravda* and *Izvestia*, recalled visiting Ulrikh in March 1940 to inquire what happened to Yefimov's brother Mikhail Koltsov (their birth name was Friedland), the famous *Pravda* journalist who was arrested in 1938. Koltsov, who appears in Ernest Hemingway's *For Whom the Bell Tolls* as Karkov, was the chief Soviet political adviser to the Republicans during the Spanish Civil War.[9] Yefimov wrote: 'A small bold man with a red face and precisely trimmed moustache stood at a desk inside a huge office covered with a rug...He received me with ostentatious good nature, clearly posing as an "easygoing" and polite guy.'[10]

Ulrikh did not conceal from Yefimov that he had chaired the Military Collegium session that sentenced Koltsov to a 'ten-year imprisonment without the right to write letters'. Ulrikh added that Koltsov was probably being kept 'in the new [labor] camps behind the Ural mountains'. In fact Koltsov had been executed a month earlier.[11] It wasn't until the 1990s that it became known that the phrase 'ten-year imprisonment without the right to write letters', widely used by the NKVD and later KGB, as well as by the Military Collegium in official answers to the inquiries of relatives, actually meant that a person had been sentenced to death and shot. Apparently Koltsov, who Hemingway said 'was the most intelligent man he had ever met' and 'one of the three most important men in Spain [in March 1937]' knew too much as a Soviet chief adviser about the NKVD's activity during the Spanish Civil War.[12]

Despite the strong secrecy maintained around the Military Collegium's work, Ulrikh allowed his wife to interfere in court decisions and even permitted his lover to be present during official briefings in his office.[13] Also, Ulrikh did not live in a typical apartment building for Soviet officials, but rather in a hotel for foreigners, the Metropol, which was a three-minute walk from the Military Collegium building. Collecting butterflies and beetles was Ulrikh's true passion. Yet during the Great Terror, under the chairmanship of this amateur entomologist, the Military Collegium sentenced 25,355 individuals to death and 11,651 defendants to lengthy prison terms.

Due to the enormous number of death sentences they pronounced, Soviet jurists called Ulrikh and his deputy, Ivan Matulevich, 'Executioners No. 1 and 2'.[14] This sobriquet became literally true on July 28, 1938 when Ulrikh personally shot Yan Berzin, former head of the Red Army's Intelligence Directorate.[15]

Just before the war, Ulrikh—along with Andrei Vyshinsky, the former chief USSR prosecutor notorious for his speeches at Moscow show trials in the late 1930s—insisted on the creation of three separate high military courts for the army, navy, and NKVD.[16] Stalin did not agree. Apparently, he wanted the Military Collegium to remain in the civilian-government structure so it could continue to be used for show-trial sessions, which received wide publicity throughout the Soviet Union and abroad. Show trials took place before specially selected audiences and were the only military tribunal sessions to include a prosecutor and defense counsel (they were excluded entirely during closed sessions), although the defense counsel had no access to the defendant outside of the session. The March 1938 trial of Nikolai Bukharin, an old Bolshevik who was one of the most important Soviet theorists, is the most famous example.

In 1938 a new law introduced a complicated and confusing system of two-institution supervision of military tribunals by the Military Collegium and Justice Commissariat, which continued until Stalin's post-war reorganization in 1946.[17] The Military Collegium continued to be the highest military court, approving death sentences, considering appeals from tribunals, and overseeing the decisions of lower tribunals, but the Justice Commissariat took over the administration of military tribunals and the education of military jurists. By mid-1940, the departmental structure within the Justice Commissariat's Directorate of Military Tribunals nearly replicated that of the Military Collegium. Its head,

Yevlampii Zeidin, 'was a clever and experienced, but also a cautious and slightly dryish man'.[18] Joint orders of the Justice and NKO commissariats appointed members of military tribunals.

During the war, the Military Collegium supervised the activity of front tribunals directly. Ulrikh personally inspected the tribunals of the Western Front four times in 1942, while his deputy Matulevich chaired the Military Tribunal of the Southern Front, and collegium member Leonid Dmitriev chaired the Military Tribunal of the Bryansk Front.[19]

Exterminating the Enemies

From 1939 to 1941, Stalin and the Politburo approved all death sentences. There were several procedures for this. First, the Politburo approved Beria's 'death lists' with the names of those prisoners whose cases had been concluded and for whom the NKVD recommended the death sentence without appeal.[20] These prisoners were condemned by the Military Collegium and executed immediately after the Collegium's session. For instance, in September 1941, at the beginning of the war, Beria sent Stalin a proposal that 170 prisoners, mostly former high-ranking Party functionaries, be executed. The Politburo decision stated: 'Capital punishment should be applied to 170 prisoners who have been convicted of terrorism, spying, sabotage, and other counter revolutionary activity, and they should be shot. The Military Collegium of the Supreme Court should hear the materials of their cases.'[21] Of course, the Collegium sentenced all the listed prisoners to death.

Similar lists of NKVD officers destined for execution were signed by Stalin alone, and then sent to Ulrikh. Ulrikh then wrote an order by hand for an immediate execution without having the cases heard by the Military Collegium.

The rest of the death sentence cases, including the decisions of military tribunals and appeals by the condemned, were considered by the special Politburo Commission on Court (Political) Cases before they were sent to the Military Collegium.[22] Chaired by Mikhail Kalinin, a Politburo member and Chairman of the Supreme Soviet, the Commission included Matvei Shkiryatov, head of the Central Committee's Commission of Party Control (a sort of watchdog commission within the Central Committee), NKVD Commissar Beria or his deputy, and USSR Prosecutor Bochkov. However, the Politburo approved decisions of the Commission and recommended the cases to be considered by the Military Collegium. At the beginning of the war, the Commission was reduced to three members: Kalinin, Shkiryatov, and Merkulov (Beria's deputy and from 1943, NKGB Commissar). The number of death sentences considered by the Military Collegium during the war was very high. In 1944 and the first six months of 1945 alone, the Collegium considered more than 43,000 cases, 13,000 of which were death sentences pronounced by military tribunals.[23]

Stalin also controlled a person's right to appeal a death sentence. Ulrikh or Beria coordinated these appeals with Stalin before the Military Collegium sessions. If he allowed the appeal, the condemned wrote to the Presidium of the Supreme Soviet, but in fact it was Stalin, Politburo members Kalinin, Kaganovich, and Malenkov, and their close associates Semyon Budennyi and Shkiryatov, who decided whether the death sentence should stand or be changed to 20 (later 25) years of imprisonment in labor camps.[24]

The Collegium Procedure

From the 1930s until 1950, the Military Collegium heard most cases in closed sessions in the building at 23 October (now Nikol'skaya) Street, which still exists in the center of Moscow, between the Kremlin and Lubyanka Square. Each case generally took only ten to fifteen minutes. During the 1930s and 1940s, Marshal Mikhail Tukhachevsky and his seven co-defendants; 25 USSR commissars; 19 republic commissars; 131 brigade, corps, and army commanders; more than 100 professors from various universities and institutes; and over 300 directors of the most important industrial plants, among others, were sentenced to death and shot in the basement by the Collegium's own team of executioners. A. V. Snegov, a former high-level Party functionary and a rare survivor (the Military Collegium sentenced him to 18 years in labor camps), described the procedure:

> A prisoner used to be called from his cell and taken to the yard of the Interior [Lubyanka] Prison, where he was put in a bus called 'Black Raven'. Usually several prisoners were transported together. The vehicle left through the iron gates at the back of the complex of the GUGB NKVD buildings and…moved backward into the closed narrow yard of the Military Collegium…
>
> The accused were taken from the vehicle one by one, and brought, using the back stairs, to the second floor, where the Military Collegium was sitting. Usually the Army Jurist Vasilii Vasilievich Ulrikh presided during the 'trial'.
>
> The hearing was short, ten minutes per person. The verdicts—usually a sentence of death by shooting for everyone—were prepared in advance. After the announcement of the verdict, the condemned was brought to the deep basement by the same stairs, and was shot in the back of the head. The executioner was the commandant on duty at the Military Collegium.
>
> The body was dragged to the corner of the basement, where a shoe was taken off the right foot [of the corpse], and a tag made of plywood was attached to the toe. The Investigation File number was written on the tag with a pencil. From this moment on the name of the person was never mentioned again.[25]

At the end of the day, the corpses of the executed were concealed in cartridge boxes and transported to the Moscow Crematorium at Donskoe Cemetery. They were burned during the following night in the presence of the commandant on duty. He also controlled the proper placement of ashes in a secret deep pit with brick walls. Detailed reports about the cremations were sent to Aleksandr Poskrebyshev, head of Stalin's secretariat, who informed Stalin. Executions were also carried out in the basement of the building across the street from the Military Collegium.[26] Currently the mass graves at Donskoe Cemetery, which contain the ashes of thousands of victims, are maintained as a memorial.

At present, the Military Collegium building belongs to one of the oil companies and it is almost ruined. The Russian human-rights Memorial Society has appealed unsuccessfully to the Moscow city government to turn the building into a museum of repressions, but it is unclear if the building survives or it will be demolished.[27]

From September 1937 till 1940, because of the large number of death sentences pronounced by the Military Collegium and other Moscow military courts, condemned prisoners were also executed at the country house built for Genrikh Yagoda, former first NKVD Commissar.[28] A team of NKVD executioners headed by Vasilii Blokhin, who served for 30 years as chief NKVD and then MGB (State Security Ministry) executioner, shot the condemned prisoners in the back of their heads and then buried the bodies. This site is now a memorial known as Kommunarka.

There was also a special room for Military Collegium sessions in Lefortovo Prison in Moscow. Defendants sentenced to death at such sessions were shot in this prison. In some special cases, such as the February 1940 trial of former NKVD Commissar Nikolai Yezhov, a session took place in Sukhanovo Prison, which in 1938 became the most secret of Moscow's investigation prisons.[29] It even had its own small crematorium. Some Military Collegium trials were also conducted in Lubyanka Prison in Moscow and in various military districts.

NKVD Special Board

Appointing Viktor Bochkov chief prosecutor in August 1940 was not the regime's only new lever of control over the legal system. Immediately Bochkov and USSR Justice Commissar Nikolai Rychkov signed two joint instructions giving the NKVD the final say over military tribunal decisions.[30] Accordingly, if by chance a tribunal acquitted the defendant, he was returned to prison until the court secured NKVD approval for his release, which typically resulted in the opening of a new investigation against him and sentencing, usually to 5–10 years in a labor camp, by the OSO (Special Board) of the NKVD.[31]

The OSO procedure was a particularly Kafkaesque invention of the Soviet system. Created in 1934, the OSO was an extra-judicial court within the NKVD not mentioned in the Soviet Constitution.[32] It consisted of the NKVD Commissar and two of his deputies. The chief USSR prosecutor or his deputy attended the hearings, which were conducted without the defendant being present. The OSO considered cases investigated by the NKVD under Articles 58 and 59 that could not be heard in civilian or military courts 'because of operational reasons'. This meant that the cases were so poorly supported that they could not stand in an open trial and the NKVD did not want to identify the secret informers who had been used in the case. Also, the OSO automatically sentenced the family members (*chsiry*) of those who had been condemned to death by the Military Collegium as 'traitors', 'spies', etc.

Before the sessions, the OSO secretariat typed the decisions, based on pre-approved indictments written by NKVD investigators. Until the beginning of the war the OSO did not have the right to confer the death penalty, giving primarily 5–10 year sentences. It met twice a week, hearing about 200–300—later as many as 980—cases per session. No appeal of OSO decisions was possible.

In November 1941, six months after the beginning of the war, Beria reported to Stalin that 10,645 prisoners sentenced to death, mostly by military tribunals, were still in NKVD investigation prisons throughout the country waiting for the Military Collegium and Party leaders to approve their sentences.[33] To help clear this backlog, Stalin approved Beria's proposal that the OSO be given the right to sentence to death political arrestees investigated under Articles 58 and 59.[34] In addition, Beria ordered all finished cases investigated under Article 58 by the central NKVD and its local branches to be sent to the OSO.[35]

Now Viktor Abakumov, head of military counterintelligence (at the time called the UOO), or his representative presented the OO cases at OSO hearings. Since Beria was too overwhelmed with various other duties, during the war his deputies Merkulov, Sergei Kruglov, Ivan Serov, and Bogdan Kobulov chaired the OSO meetings.

The memoirs of Nikolai Mesyatsev, who worked from 1942–43 as an investigator at the Investigation Department of the UOO, include a unique description of the OSO bureaucratic procedure:

> At the Secretariat of the Investigation Department...I was ordered to fill in on a typewriter a special form of the Special Board, which had several columns.
>
> In the first column I typed in the biographical data of the accused, whom I'll call 'N': his last name, first name, patronymic name; year and place of birth; nationality; matrimonial status; last place of work; date of arrest.
>
> In the next column, I wrote the charges as they were described in the indictment that I'd signed, which was also signed by the head of the Investigation Department [Boris Pavlovsky], and approved by the head of the NKVD Special Departments Directorate [Viktor Abakumov] and a prosecutor.

In this particular case, [it was said that] the accused 'N' conducted espionage activity in the Red Army's rear for German intelligence in such-and-such form, which is punishable under Article 58-6. In the next column I wrote that the accused pleaded guilty to espionage activity and his testimony was confirmed by operational data, documents, testimonies of witnesses, and so on.

Each of such forms (the others were written by investigators from other NKVD departments) was given a number and approximately 250–300 of the filled-in forms were stitched together in a file.[36]

Mesyatsev also described the OSO meeting:

The meeting of the Special Board took place in an office on the so-called Narkoms' Floor [i.e., where Commissar Beria's huge office was located]. The office was small, and the walls were painted a deep crimson color. Curtains on the windows were closed.

To the left from the window, there were two desks positioned perpendicular to each other; on them were desk lamps, turned on. [Sergei] Kruglov, deputy NKVD Commissar, was sitting behind one of the desks, and [Viktor] Bochkov, USSR Chief Prosecutor, was behind the other…

There was a row of chairs in front of the desks occupied by investigators who would make presentations of their cases…Each of them held a sheet of paper (some had several sheets) with a number that corresponded to the number in the files that were lying in front of the two members of the Special Board.

After the Deputy Commissar called my number, I (as well as the other investigators in their turn), was obliged to say the following: '"N" is accused under Article 58-6 of the Russian Federation Criminal Code of espionage for German intelligence. He pleaded guilty, which is confirmed by such-and-such investigation materials.'

My presentation took no more than a minute. The Deputy Commissar suggested sentencing 'N' to a 10-year imprisonment. The prosecutor agreed, and the fate of the accused 'N' was sealed. I left the room.

The cases for OSO meetings were prepared not only by the central NKVD in Moscow, but also sent to Moscow by the NKVD heads (commissars) of the republics, heads of regional UNKVD branches and heads of military district OOs. The decisions were short and were typed on a special form. Here, in the original formatting, is an example of a decision from the Archival Investigation File of the American Communist Isai (Isaiah) Oggins sentenced as a spy in 1940:

Excerpt from the Protocol [transcript] No. 1
of the Special Board under the People's Internal Affairs Commissar,
January 5, 1940

Heard: Case No. 85 of the GUGB Investigation Department of the NKVD,
on the accusation of OGGINS Isai Samoilovich, b. 1898 in Massachusetts
(USA), an American citizen.

Decided: To sentence OGGINS Isai Samoilovich to EIGHT-year imprisonment as a spy. The term begins from February 20, 1939 [the date of Oggins's arrest]. The [Investigation] File is to be sent to the [NKVD] archive.

Head of the Secretariat of the Special Board under
the People's Internal Affairs Commissar.

(IVANOV)

NKVD's seal.[37]

In fact, since 1928 Oggins spied not against, but for the Soviets—at first
for the Comintern (Communist International, the international organization of Communist parties with its headquarters in Moscow), then for
NKVD foreign intelligence—in Europe, the United States, and China.[38]
As for Vladimir Ivanov, who signed the excerpt, he headed the OSO Secretariat of the NKVD/MVD from 1939 until 1946, the OSO Secretariat
of the MGB in 1946–47, and then the OSO Secretariat of the new Beria's
MVD from July to November 1953.

A prison official announced the OSO decision to a prisoner while he
was still in an investigation prison. The prisoner was obliged to sign a copy
of the decision, but it made no difference if he refused to do so. Then the
prisoner was transferred to a transit prison, and from there he was sent to
a labor camp. As for death sentences, they were carried out within twenty-
four hours, with the prisoner learning of his impending execution only a
few minutes before it was to take place.

According to the MVD report to Nikita Khrushchev, dated December
1953, in 1940 the OSO convicted 42,912 people under Article 58, and
during the war, this number varied.[39] For comparison, numbers convicted
of Article 58 crimes by the Military Collegium for the same years are given:

Year	OSO	Military Collegium[40]
1941	26, 534	28,732
1942	77,548	112,973
1943	25,134	95,802
1944	10,611	99,425
1945	14,652	135,056
Total	**243,954**	**471,988**

In fact, the number of the convicted by the OSO, especially during the
war, might have been from two to three times higher. The other archival

records show that in 1943 alone, SMERSH, NKGB, and NKVD submitted 51,396 cases to the OSO, and 681 of the accused were sentenced to death, while in 1944 the OSO convicted a total of 27,456 prisoners.[41] For unknown reason the 1953 MVD report mentions only 10,611 convicted in 1944, and not 27,456. Similarly, the report gives the number 14,652 for 1945, while the historian Nikita Petrov gives the number 26,518 for that year.[42]

The following numbers, which are for 1945 only, illustrate the enormity of the persecution endured by the Russian populace:

899,613 defendants were sentenced by civilian courts and military tribunals

357,007 were sentenced by military tribunals only (of these, 134,956 were sentenced on counter revolutionary charges)

297 were sentenced by the Military Collegium

26,581 were sentenced by the OSO.[43]

Like the death sentences pronounced by the Military Collegium in closed sessions, the death sentences pronounced by the OSO remained a state secret. On September 29, 1945 Beria signed an instruction on how to answer inquiries regarding the whereabouts of those who had been convicted by the OSO to death and executed during the war. He ordered the continuation of claims that the prisoner 'was sentenced to 10 years of imprisonment and deprivation of the right to write letters and receive parcels'.[44]

The OSO within the NKVD/MVD existed until July 1950. However, in November 1946 on Abakumov's order a second OSO was created within the MGB, which considered political cases from 1947 to 1953.[45] It was reorganized after Stalin's death and finally disbanded in September 1953.

Nikolai Mesyatsev, who had legal training, wrote in 2005: 'The Special Board…was a mockery of the natural right of every individual to openly defend his innocence and publicly participate in the procedure of establishing the extent of his guilt.'[46] Archival materials of the OSO have never been declassified, and the lists of the names of the convicted and the number of sentenced *chsiry* and foreigners remains unknown. But even if the OSO records are eventually declassified, it will not be easy to examine them: recently all OSO records were moved from the FSB Central Archive in Moscow to its archival branch in the city of Omsk in Siberia.

CHAPTER 5

Division of Europe

The period from mid-1939 to mid-1941 was the time of mutual understanding between two dictators, Stalin and Adolf Hitler, and their division of Europe. As a result, Germany acquired part of Poland and most of Western Europe, while the Soviet Union included another part of Poland and occupied the Baltic States, part of Romania and tried to conquer Finland. Soviet propaganda called the Soviet annexations 'the acts of assistance' to the supposedly oppressed Ukrainians, Belorussians and other working people. Even now most of the Russians do not consider these occupations part of World War II and think that the war began only on June 22, 1941, the day of the German attack against the Soviet Union.

During this period of Soviet expansion, military counterintelligence in general and Viktor Abakumov in particular gained valuable experience. Techniques developed by the NKVD and its Special Department (OO) to eliminate all opposition in the new territories were later continued and refined by SMERSH.

Secret Agreement

In May 1939 Stalin replaced Maxim Litvinov, the Jewish, pro-British Foreign Affairs Commissar, with Vyacheslav Molotov.[1] Beria's man Vladimir Dekanozov became deputy Commissar. These were steps toward making a deal with Hitler.

On August 23, 1939, the infamous Molotov–Ribbentrop Non-Aggression Pact, containing a secret agreement to divide Eastern Europe between Germany and the Soviet Union, was signed in Moscow.[2] Poland was divided between the two countries, and Germany agreed that Finland, Estonia, and Latvia were in the sphere of Soviet interests. The division of Poland was like the final word in Stalin's old dispute with now dead Marshal Tukhachevsky: Hitler received Warsaw, which was almost taken over by Tukhachevsky's troops in 1920, while Stalin got Lvov, which he unsuccessfully tried to conquer during that time.

The pact with the fascist Nazis, the deadly enemy of German Communists, did what even the Great Terror could not—it caused millions of dedicated but naive Communists worldwide to finally drop their support for Stalin's Soviet Union. *Time* magazine voiced the outrage of many worldwide when it referred to the agreement as the 'Communazi Pact' and called the signatories 'communazis'.[3] Two weeks after the signing, Stalin explained to Georgi Dimitrov, head of the Comintern, his Machiavellian reasons for signing the covenant (a division into paragraphs is added):

> A war is on between two groups of capitalist countries…for redividing the world, for the domination of the world! We see nothing wrong in their having a good hard fight and weakening each other. It would be fine if at the hands of Germany the position of the richest capitalist countries (especially England) were shaken. Hitler, without understanding it or desiring it, is shaking and undermining the capitalist system…

We can maneuver, pit one side against the other to set them fighting with each other as fiercely as possible. The non-aggression pact is to a certain degree helping Germany. Next time we'll urge on the other side…

Now [Poland] is a fascist state…The annihilation of that state under current conditions would mean one fewer bourgeois fascist state to contend with! What would be the harm if as a result of the rout of Poland we were to extend the socialist system on the new territories and populations?[4]

This explanation clearly reveals Stalin's long-term plan for the Sovietizing of Europe, beginning with the division of Poland and continuing after World War II with the creation of the Soviet bloc.

Strictly speaking, the division of Europe was a step within Stalin's doctrine of the offensive war, i.e., the need to rapidly carry the war into enemy territory and achieve a victory at 'little cost', which was repeated in the Red Army's Field Regulations (*Ustav*) from 1929 onwards.[5] In vain Valentin Trifonov—one of the Red Army organizers and the first Military Collegium's Chairman (before Vasilii Ulrikh)—tried to call Stalin's attention to the strategy of defense. On June 17, 1937, four years before Hitler's attack, Trifonov wrote to Stalin: 'Most probably, Germany will be our mighty enemy in the future war and [the Germans] will have the serious advantage of a sudden attack. This advantage can be neutralized only by creating a system of efficient defense along the border…Defense is the strongest method of carrying out a war and, therefore, a plan for defending our state borders will be less costly than a plan for an offensive war.'[6] Five days later, Trifonov was arrested, and he was executed on March 15, 1938. The *Ustav* of 1939 repeated the doctrine of the offensive war.

Poland

On September 1, 1939, German troops invaded Poland, and World War II began. A week later, nine days before the Red Army advanced into Poland, Beria ordered the creation of two NKVD operational groups in Kiev and Minsk, each of which would consist of 300 hand-picked Ukrainian and Belorussian NKVD officers and NKVD operatives from Moscow and Leningrad. Their goal was simple: to purge all opposition in Poland to the Soviet military takeover. They were under the command of NKVD commissars Ivan Serov of Ukraine and Lavrentii Tsanava of Belorussia, who specialized in purging Soviet-occupied territories from this time until the end of World War II.[7] The groups had additional operational support from units of NKVD Border Guard Troops.

To coordinate NKVD actions in the newly acquired territories, Beria's first deputy Vsevolod Merkulov was sent to Kiev and Viktor Bochkov (at the time, still OO head), to Minsk. Official documents referred obliquely to this operation as 'measures in connection with ongoing military training'.

Beria's dispatch of September 15, 1939, clarified the plan: 'Following our troops after the occupation of towns, provisional administrative groups… will be created; heads of the NKVD operational groups will be included.'[8]

By September 16, 1939, the Germans occupied most of their part of Polish territory, as defined in the Non-Aggression Pact, although Warsaw put up a brave defense. The next day, the Red Army invaded Poland on the flimsy pretext of protecting Belorussians and Ukrainians living in Polish territory.[9] German and Soviet troops met near Lvov, Lublin, and Bialystok at the end of September, and even held a joint parade in the city of Brest.[10] The parade inspectors, the German General of Tank Troops Heinz Guderian and the Soviet Kombrig (Brigade Commander) Semyon Krivoshein (a famous tank commander during the Spanish Civil War who, ironically, was a Jew), chatted in French. They had met before, in 1929, when Guderian inspected the Kazan Tank School in the Soviet Union. Two years later, during the German invasion, Guderian used Lev Tolstoy's Yasnaya Polyana mansion as his headquarters.

On September 28, 1939, Warsaw surrendered. On the same day Merkulov reported to Moscow that NKVD Operational Group No. 1 had arrested 923 Polish officers, policemen, landowners, 'representatives of the bourgeoisie', Ukrainian nationalists, and so forth, in the newly acquired territory.[11] A second NKVD operational group arrested an additional 533 men. Mass arrests and exiles of Polish citizens continued through 1940.[12] A new organization, the UPVI (NKVD Directorate for POWs and Interned Persons), was created two days after the Soviet invasion of Poland to manage the new prisoners. It had its own system of concentration camps.

On March 3, 1940, Stalin and five Politburo members, along with Beria himself, approved Beria's proposal to execute Polish officers interned in POW camps as well as officers and members of 'various spy and diversion organizations of the former land and factory owners' held in NKVD prisons.[13] The result was the infamous Katyn Forest massacre: the execution, in April 1940, of approximately 22,500 Polish officers and prisoners in the Katyn forest near Smolensk and in prisons in Kharkov and Kalinin (currently, Tver). Merkulov, Bogdan Kobulov, and Leonid Bashtakov, head of the 1st NKVD Special Department (registration and statistics), were in charge of organizing the executions. The local OOs actively participated in the preparation of the executions.[14] Altogether, the NKVD killed almost half the Polish officer corps and many members of the Polish intelligentsia, including medical doctors. Only 395 men were spared, mostly those of interest to the foreign intelligence department (Pavel Sudoplatov, the notorious organizer of terrorist acts, compiled the list of names).

On March 20, 1940 Beria ordered eleven NKVD killing squads to be sent to the newly acquired parts of Ukraine and Belorussia.[15] Thirty-year-old Pavel Meshik, one of Beria's most devoted men, headed the group dispatched to Lvov, where the main atrocities took place. In December Beria reported to Stalin that from September to December 1940 in these parts of Ukraine and Belorussia 'up to 407,000 people were arrested…and [additionally] 275,784 people were sent to Kazakhstan and the northern regions of the USSR'.[16]

The massacre continued in June and July of 1941. As the Germans advanced and the Soviets retreated from the former Polish territories, NKVD guards executed at least 10,000 local prisoners who were being held without trial.[17] In the callous NKVD jargon, these were known as 'losses of the first category'.

On August 12, 1941, the Politburo amnestied Polish prisoners and ordered their release, as well as that of the deported Polish citizens.[18] By October 1, the NKVD was ready to release 51,257 of the convicted Poles and the arrested Poles who were awaiting trial, and 254,473 of the deportees.[19] Soon many of these people joined the Anders Army commanded by the released General Wladislaw Anders. Until the German attack on June 22, 1941, Anders was kept in Lubyanka Prison in Moscow after he had refused to join the Red Army.[20] However, 12,817 of the Polish prisoners and 33,252 of their family members remained in the NKVD camps and in exile in the Soviet Union. The Anders Army moved to Iran, at the time occupied by Soviet and British troops.

The Invasion of Finland

On September 28, 1939, Joachim von Ribbentrop, Hitler's foreign minister, made a second visit to Moscow. In a rushed early meeting at 5 a.m., he signed the German–Soviet Boundary and Friendship Treaty, which contained a secret protocol that finalized the division of Poland and ceded Lithuania to Stalin. Stalin's translator Valentin Berezhkov recalled: 'When a map with the just agreed upon border between the German possessions and the Soviet Union was brought in, Stalin put it on the desk, took one of his big blue pencils and, allowing his emotions to come out, wrote his signature with a flourish in gigantic letters that covered the newly acquired territories of Western Belorussia and Western Ukraine.'[21] Now all three Baltic States, plus Finland and eastern Poland, would be under Soviet control. Two days later, in a long speech supporting the German war against Britain and France, Molotov blamed the Allies: 'It is senseless and criminal to conduct such a war, a war "to destroy Hitlerism."'[22]

Like the Nazi invasion of Poland, which began on the German–Polish border with a provocation organized by the German secret services, the Soviet war with Finland began with the NKVD's artillery shelling of its own Soviet troops, which was then blamed on the Finns.[23] Aleksandr Shcherbakov, the Party propaganda chief, explained the Soviet aggression: 'Lenin's theory teaches us that in favorable international circumstances a Socialist country must—and is obliged to—initiate a military offensive against the surrounding capitalist countries for the purpose of widening the front of Socialism.'[24]

Stalin was so confident that he would win a fast victory over Finland that he did not even inform Marshal Boris Shaposhnikov, Chief of the General Staff, who was on vacation, about the beginning of military actions.[25] According to Soviet plans, the whole operation would take twelve days.[26] To Stalin's chagrin, Finland was able to withstand his appetite for 'widening the front of Socialism'. This was not surprising. In early 1940 General Konstantin Pyadyshev courageously wrote to his wife from the front: 'Our commanding officers are extremely poorly trained, many are not even able to use maps. They are incapable of commanding, and they have no authority among privates. The Red Army men are also poorly trained and many of them do not want to fight. This is why the desertion is so high.'[27] This and other letters to his wife ended up in the general's OO file, but he was arrested later, in September 1941, at the beginning of the Great Patriotic War.

The morale of the troops and the coordination of fighting units were so bad that during the first ten days of January 1940 alone, the OOs of these Red Army units sent Stalin 22 reports complaining about the poor efficiency of the troops.[28] As for discipline, NKVD *zagradotryady* (*zagraditel'nye otryady*, literally 'fence detachments' or barrage units) were created for the first time in Red Army history. The joint order of the NKO and NKVD commissars stated:

To prevent the desertion and to purge the rear of the fighting army of enemy elements, we order:

1. To form control-barrage detachments from the operational NKVD regiments…and put them under the command of Special Departments.

2. The task of control-barrage detachments should be to organize covering force, raids in the rear of the fighting army, checking documents of single servicemen and civilians going to the rear, and capturing deserters.

3. The detainees should be sent to the Special Departments…

4. Each control-barrage detachment should consist of 100 men and include three rifle platoons, as well as an operational group of the Special Department of 3–5 men…

5. The best personnel of the Special Departments should be mobilized [for these detachments]…

6. … The deserters should be immediately transferred under military tribunals and tried within 24 hours.[29]

From January to March 1940, *zagradotryady* arrested 6,724 Red Army men.[30] Of them, 5,934 were sent back to the fighting units, and 790 were tried by military tribunals. Of the latter number, only six servicemen were acquitted. Later, during the war with Germany, the barrage units became one of the main tools of the NKVD and SMERSH.

During the five months of the Winter War, from November 1939 to March 1940, the Finns' preparation, tactics, and determination were far superior to those of the Soviets, who suffered 131,500 casualties to the Finns' 21,400.[31] Stalin was so outraged by the unprofessional performance of Kliment Voroshilov as NKO Commissar that in May 1940 he replaced Voroshilov with Semyon Timoshenko.

Nikita Khrushchev recalled a quarrel between Stalin and Voroshilov just after the war:

> One day Stalin angrily criticized Voroshilov in our [Politburo members'] presence at the nearby dacha. He was very nervous, and viciously attacked Voroshilov. Voroshilov also became angry; he stood up with a red face and snapped at Stalin: 'You are to blame. You have exterminated the military [during the Great Terror].' Stalin shot back an angry reply. Then Voroshilov picked up a platter with a small boiled pig on it and smashed it on the floor. This was the only time that I witnessed such a situation. Stalin definitely felt elements of defeat in our victory over the Finns in 1940.[32]

But the new appointment was not a demotion for Voroshilov. Despite Voroshilov's unprofessionalism, Stalin promoted him Defense Committee head (in this capacity, Voroshilov supervised both the new Defense Commissar Timoshenko and the Navy Commissar Nikolai Kuznetsov) as well as deputy chairman of Sovnarkom in charge of military industry. Contrary to the physically short Voroshilov and Semyon Budennyi, two of Stalin's pals from the Civil War, Timoshenko, whom Stalin called a *muzhik* (literally, a real man), was very big and tall. As Timoshenko used to say, 'Stalin…liked huge guys'.[33] Later, in 1945, Stalin forced his son Vasilii to marry Timoshenko's daughter.

The terms of the March 12, 1940 peace agreement stipulated that Finland would lose a small but densely populated part of its territory along with important nickel mines, but would maintain its sovereignty and independence.[34] The aggression against Finland caused the Soviet Union's expulsion from the League of Nations.

Of more than 6,000 Soviet POWs taken by Finnish troops, about 100 refused to return to the Soviet Union.[35] Those who returned were vetted in the Yuzhskii NKVD Camp by NKVD—most likely OO—investigators. On June 29, 1940, Beria presented Stalin with a list of 232 repatriated servicemen, proposing that the Military Collegium of the Supreme Court sentence them to death.[36] In many cases this was unnecessary, since 158 had already been executed. It is possible that these were the Soviet POWs who volunteered for Boris Bazhanov's small anti-Soviet Russian People's Army in Finland during the Winter War.[37]

Punishment of commanders arrested by the OOs continued after the war. In July 1940 Beria reported to Stalin:

> On March 3, 1940, KONDRASHOV Grigorii Fyodorovich, commander of the 18th Rifle Division…was arrested for treason…

The investigation by the NKVD Special Department established that because of KONDRASHOV's negligent actions his division was encircled by the enemy...KONDRASHOV left the column and ran away...

The NKVD considers it is necessary for KONDRASHOV Grigorii Fyodorovich, who has admitted his guilt, to be tried by the Military Collegium of the USSR Supreme Court for treacherous actions...

I await your instructions.[38]

Stalin wrote on the first page of the report: 'He should be tried, and harshly. St[alin].' On August 12, the Military Collegium sentenced Kondrashov to death, and on August 29, he was executed.

The Baltic States, Bessarabia, and Western Ukraine

The Baltic States were the next victims of Soviet expansion. In June 1940, the Red Army invaded Latvia, Estonia, and Lithuania under the ruse of 'mutual assistance pacts'.[39] Again, NKVD troops played a special role in the occupation. On June 17, 1940, with Soviet troops still on the march, NKO Commissar Timoshenko described the steps to be taken:

1. Our border guards should immediately occupy the border with Eastern Prussia and the Baltic coast to prevent spying and diversion activity from our western neighbor.

2. (Initially), one regiment of NKVD troops should be moved to each of the occupied republics to keep order.

3. The question of the 'government' of the occupied republics should be decided as soon as possible.

4. The disarmament and disbanding of the armies of the occupied republics should begin. The population, police, and military organizations should be disarmed.[40]

Some details of the annexation became publicly known fifty years later. In January 1991, on the order of Mikhail Gorbachev's government, Soviet tanks fired at civilians in Vilnius, the Lithuanian capital. Fourteen civilians were killed and 600 wounded. After this, first the government-independent radio station *Ekho Moskvy* (Echo of Moscow) transmitted a speech by Georgii Fedorov, who had served in the Red Army troops which had occupied Lithuania in 1940 and later became a prominent historian. Fedorov appealed to the tank crews, asking them not to follow further criminal orders from Moscow. He compared the situation with the events in 1940:

Before we crossed the border [in 1940], our political officers told us that we would see all the horrors of capitalist slavery in Lithuania: poor peasants, terribly exploited workers weak from hunger, and a small group of rich people exploiting the poor.

Instead, we saw a blooming, abundant country…

Our people in power—criminals and scoundrels—robbed Lithuania… Executioners called…'officers of the People's Commissariat for Internal Affairs'…acted with enormous brutality…And we, soldiers of the Red Army, covered this revelry of robbery, violence, and killings that was cynically called 'acts of will of the Lithuanian people'.[41]

In 1940, Stalin sent three special watchdogs, officially plenipotentiaries for the Soviet government, to supervise events in the Baltics: Party ideologue Andrei Zhdanov to Estonia; infamous former USSR prosecutor Andrei Vyshinsky to Latvia; and Beria's man, Vladimir Dekanozov, to Lithuania. Later Merkulov, Abakumov, and Serov went to Lithuania, Estonia, and Latvia, respectively, to organize and supervise the arrests and deportations.

Irena Baruch Wiley, the wife of the American Envoy Extraordinary and Minister Plenipotentiary to Latvia and Estonia, witnessed the deportation: 'The long trains with curtained windows left every night for Russia. I had thought that in the unspeakable brutality of the Nazi invasion of Austria I had witnessed the depths of horror, but there was something even more nightmarish, more terrifying in watching, weary and helpless, this silent nightly exodus. The Nazis committed their atrocities night and day; the Russians, more surreptitious, only under cover of darkness.'[42] Here then, in 1940, was a template for taking over a foreign state, a template that was expanded upon and used successfully, with SMERSH's help, in the East European countries at the end of the war.

By July 21, 1940, Soviet-controlled governments had taken power in the three republics. Members of the Baltic governments were taken to the Soviet Union. A year later, after the beginning of war with Germany, former Latvian and Estonian officials and their wives were jailed without trial and held in solitary confinement. They were not sentenced until 1952, when they became nameless secret political prisoners, held in strict isolation in the infamously inhuman Vladimir Prison, identified only by numbers.[43]

The arrests continued through 1941. On May 16, 1941, Merkulov sent Stalin the final deportation plan for the former Baltic States.[44] The plan stipulated the arrests of prominent members of 'counter revolutionary' parties; members of Russian emigrant organizations; all policemen, landowners, and owners of industrial plants; army officers; and so on. The arrestees 'should be placed in [labor] camps for five to eight years and after their release they should be exiled to distant areas of the Soviet Union for twenty years'. In addition, their family members were to be banished to distant parts of the Soviet Union for twenty years. Incredibly, in 2009 Viktor Stepakov, the FSB-connected historian, wrote: 'This document…was *an example of true humanism* [emphasis added]. During that complicated time, enemies…could [simply] be shot to death.'[45]

But for many, this was a death sentence. For instance, during June–September 1942, 9,080 Lithuanian deportees, plus ethnic Finns and Germans exiled from Leningrad, were relocated to Yakutia (currently the Sakha Republic within Russia), a Siberian area with an extremely severe climate, as 'fishermen'. Of these, only 48 per cent could work and 36 per cent were children under 16. The deportees were provided with no housing, food, boats or fishing-gear and were forced to live in dug-outs, each for 60 deportees. Only 30 per cent of them survived.[46] By June 1941 Merkulov was able to report to the Central Committee that almost all the members of the intelligentsia of these small countries were in Soviet labor camps, and the number of the arrested and deported was about 66,000.[47] However, the current Baltic States consider this number to have been underestimated:

Country	Total population	Deportees Russian sources[48]	Baltic sources[49]
Lithuania	2,879,000	28,533	35,000
Latvia	1,951,000	24,407	35,000
Estonia	1,133,000	12,819	15,000

Simultaneously, mass purges were organized in the other territories occupied by the Red Army. May 1941 saw the deportations of approximately 12,000 family members of 'counter revolutionaries and nationalists' from Western Ukraine, formerly a part of Poland.[50] Purges also took place in Bessarabia, previously a part of Romania, now renamed the Soviet Republic of Moldavia. There were deportations from several other areas of Romania and Belorussia as well. On the whole, the number of the deported during 1940-41 was approximately 380,000–390,000, and of them, 309,000–325,000 were former Polish citizens.[51]

The Soviets had a different attitude toward ethnic Germans in the same states. Special Soviet–German agreements allowed ethnic Germans to move from the Baltic States to Germany, while ethnic Lithuanians, Russians, and Belorussians living in the Polish territory now occupied by Germany were forced to move to Soviet-occupied Lithuania.[52] The Soviets even paid substantial sums of money to the Baltic Germans for property losses.

On June 26, 1940, during the Baltic campaign, the Presidium of the Supreme Soviet introduced new working rules, apparently in connection with the preparations for a big war. The Presidium's decree established a seven-day working week and an eight-hour instead of seven-hour working day.[53] Now quitting a job without permission of the administration or being late for work by 20 minutes were punished by imprisonment for two to six months. This meant that people became attached to particular working places and could not change jobs. On December 26, 1942 an additional decree increased the punishment to two to five years. Before the war, 2,664,472 perpetrators were sentenced under the June 26 decree, and during the war, their number was 7,747,405.[54]

In 1941–42, five more decrees introduced additional restrictions. The number of people who fell foul of the working rules during the war reached 8,550,799; of these, 2,080,189 served terms in labor camps, making these convicts a majority among all prisoners. Probably, the feeling of slavery had an impact in the low morale of just-drafted soldiers during the first disastrous period of the war with Germany. The June 26 decree was abolished only in 1956, three years after Stalin's death; overall, from 1940 to 1956, 14,845,144 perpetrators were convicted under it.[55]

Three Security Services

After the expansion, Stalin tried to maintain a good relationship with Hitler. In November 1940, Molotov, Merkulov, and Dekanozov arrived in Berlin for economic and political negotiations with the Nazis.[56] Not everything went smoothly, but Dekanozov stayed in Berlin as Soviet Plenipotentiary and Bogdan Kobulov's brother Amayak, who had no experience in intelligence, became NKVD chief *rezident* (head of a spy network) in the Soviet Legation. These appointments gave Beria and the NKVD a great deal of control over diplomats, especially those who were stationed in Berlin.

With the new workload occasioned by the western expansion, it became clear that the NKVD was too monolithic to function efficiently. In January 1941, Beria proposed separating the intelligence and counterintelligence functions from the more mundane domestic terror organs by removing the GUGB from the NKVD and turning it into the State Security Commissariat, or NKGB.[57] The NKGB would include three important directorates: foreign intelligence, domestic counterintelligence, and secret political directorate. From this time onwards, during almost all of the many subsequent reorganizations of the Soviet security services, foreign intelligence was called the 1st (or 1st Main) Directorate, and interior counterintelligence the 2nd (or 2nd Main) Directorate.

GUGB head Merkulov became head of the new NKGB, with Beria remaining head of the now smaller NKVD, whose main function was to manage the countless Soviet labor camps and prisons with a population of 2,417,000 prisoners and an additional population of 1,500,000 people in labor and special settlements, including those transported from the Baltic States and other occupied territories.[58] Although not the direct head of the NKGB, Beria still controlled it through Merkulov. On January 30, 1941, with Beria's promotion to the rank of State Security General Commissar, speculation was rife that he would eventually succeed Stalin.[59]

The OO, the 4th GUGB Department, was not incorporated into the new NKGB, but instead was split into three parts.[60] One part, which handled military counterintelligence in the border guards and other NKVD troops, remained within the NKVD and became its 3rd department.[61] In his first affiliation with military counterintelligence, on February 25, 1941

Abakumov became NKVD deputy Commissar in charge of supervising this and several other departments. The second and most significant part went to the Defense Commissariat (the NKO), becoming its 3rd Directorate.[62] Now every military district (called fronts in wartime), army, corps, and division had a 3rd department whose heads reported jointly to a 3rd department superior and to their unit's military commander.[63] The third part of the OO became the Navy Commissariat's (the NKVMF) 3rd Directorate.

But even though two parts of military counterintelligence were formally moved to the NKO and NKMF, Beria still controlled all secret services. The staff of the new 3rd directorates remained on the sixth floor of the NKVD Lubyanka building, and a special Central Council consisting of the NKGB and NKVD commissars, along with heads of the two 3rd directorates and the NKVD 3rd department, coordinated all military counterintelligence. Additionally, new deputy head positions were created within the 3rd directorates and their subordinate departments, which Merkulov filled with members of his staff.[64] Finally, the NKGB had the right to transfer any investigation conducted by the 3rd directorates to its own investigation unit. In addition, the NKVD maintained a central archive through which it was able to keep detailed tabs on whatever happened in the other secret services.[65]

The three-part organization of security services—the 3rd NKO Directorate, NKGB and NKVD—from February to July 1941 is remarkably similar to that Stalin established in April 1943, when for the Soviets the war started to turn from the defensive to offensive. In fact, this three-part structure made sense only if the Red Army was on the offensive. Military counterintelligence was moving with the front line and made the first arrests of real and potential anti-Soviet enemies in the new territories. Then the NKGB continued this job in the occupied territories, while the NKVD was primarily in charge of policing and keeping the arrested enemies and POWs. Most probably, the change in the year 1941 was part of Stalin's general preparation for moving Soviet troops westward beyond the newly acquired territories.

CHAPTER 6

On the Verge of the War

Apparently, with the acquisition of new territories and having implemented a new structure of security services aimed at better ruling the enlarged country, Stalin did not expect that the war with Germany would come soon. He initiated a new wave of purges against the military, especially those officers who recently fought in Spain and showed independence from Moscow in their professional decisions. At the same time, Stalin made preparations for a future offensive war by making himself head of the government (Chairman of the Council of Commissars), which would allow him to declare and lead a war if necessary.

New Mass Purges

Just two months before the war, the NKO 3rd Directorate began to uncover a new military 'plot', this time in the air force and the armaments industry. The investigation was triggered by an extraordinary event. On April 9, 1941, thirty-year-old Pavel Rychagov, head of the Air Force Directorate and a deputy Defense Commissar, dared to confront Stalin at a Politburo meeting. Rychagov, a flying ace who had fought in both Spain and China, was distraught about a spate of plane crashes caused by mechanical problems. At the meeting, he blurted out: 'The accident rate is high and will continue to be so because you force us to fly in coffins!'[1] After a pause, the dictator responded: 'You should not have said that.' Rychagov was dismissed instantly, but, in keeping with the usual ritual, not immediately arrested.[2]

Two days later came the arrest of the first 'plotter', and more arrests continued until the beginning of the war with Germany (Appendix I, see http://www.smershbook.com).[3] As head of military counterintelligence, Mikheev was in charge of the arrests. Among the sixteen leading air force generals and officials arrested between April and June 1941 was Aleksandr Loktionov, recent commander of the successful Soviet military occupation of the Baltic States.[4] Yakov Smushkevich, deputy head of the General Staff in charge of the Air Force, who was awarded the Star of the Hero twice— for his service in Spain (where his nom de guerre was 'General Douglas') and later for commanding the air force group during a short military action against Japanese troops in 1939 near the Khalka River—was arrested in a military hospital after a serious operation and brought to Lubyanka Prison on a stretcher. Because almost all those arrested were Spanish Civil War heroes, the operational name for the case was 'The Plot of Heroes'.

Rychagov was finally arrested on June 24, 1941 two days after the Nazis began their invasion.[5] Arrested on the same day were his wife, Maria Nesterenko, a legendary female pilot and deputy commander of a special aviation corps, and afterwards, five more commanders. Arrests continued through July 1941.

After severe beatings, almost all of those arrested 'confessed' to having been plotters.[6] The only ones who did not sign confessions were Loktionov and Nesterenko. Investigative journalist Arkadii Vaksberg, who had access to the investigation files, later wrote: 'I do not have the strength to describe the kinds of torture the investigators applied to this remarkable woman [Nesterenko].'[7]

As usual, Stalin personally supervised the investigation and read the interrogation transcripts.[8] The senselessness of arresting experienced air force officers at this time underscores Stalin's extreme fear of any military challenge to his power. The investigation was interrupted only by the lightning advance of German troops toward Moscow.

Just Before the War

On May 4, 1941, the Politburo appointed Stalin chairman of the Council of Commissars (Sovnarkom or SNK), demoting Molotov to Stalin's deputy.[9] Previously, Stalin was only a Party secretary—officially not a governmental position. As Sovnarkom chairman, Stalin merged the work of the Sovnarkom with that of the Politburo. He created the Bureau of Sovnarkom in which he included all Politburo members (except Kalinin), and the Bureau made all major decisions regarding industry, agriculture, and the economy. From this time onwards, Politburo meetings in Stalin's office began as Bureau of Sovnarkom meetings and then continued as Politburo meetings. Nikolai Voznesensky became Stalin's deputy in charge of Sovnarkom questions, and Georgii Malenkov was in charge of the Party questions. However, Stalin made all decisions. Yakov Chadaev, Sovnarkom's Secretary who wrote down transcripts of Bureau of Sovnarkom meetings, recalled in his memoirs: 'Stalin's comrades-in-arms had a great reverential attitude toward him and had never contradicted him.'[10]

Now, as head of the government, Stalin could lead the war, if necessary.[11] The day after his appointment as Sovnarkom chairman, Stalin indirectly mentioned a plan to 'fight for our land on foreign soil' at a Kremlin banquet following a graduation ceremony for Military Academy students. He proposed a toast: 'Only a war against Fascist Germany, and winning that war, can save our country. I want to drink to the war, to offensive efforts in that war, and to our victory in that war!'[12]

But Hitler ruined all of Stalin's plans. In the early hours of June 22, 1941, German troops invaded Soviet territory, and the Great Patriotic War, as World War II is known in Russia, began.[13] The Germans claimed it was a preemptive measure: 'Due to the enormous threat to the eastern German border created by the massive concentration and preparation of all kinds of Red Army troops, the German government has been forced to take immediate military counter measures.'[14] Though Hitler had planned the invasion of the Soviet Union for some time, his fears of a Soviet military build-up were not unfounded. At the time of the German attack, the Red Army had 5.4 million servicemen, and the Soviet Union was clearly superior in manpower and weaponry.[15]

Soon after the attack, 550 million copies of detailed Soviet maps held in military warehouses became German trophies.[16] Interestingly, these maps showed only the area bordered by the cities of Petrozavodsk–Vitebsk–

Kiev–Odessa on the East, and Berlin–Prague–Vienna–Budapest–Bucharest on the West. According to Stalin's prewar plans, these would be the areas of future battles, to the west of Soviet territory. Military maps of Soviet regions to the east of the Petrozavodsk–Vitebsk–Kiev–Odessa line were not produced before the war, and a few days after the German attack Soviet commanders found themselves in regions for which they had no maps at all.[17] Only in early 1942, after gigantic efforts, did the Soviet troops begin to receive newly printed maps.

Preparations on June 21, 1941

A day before the German invasion, Stalin was still denying the possibility of an attack. On June 21, 1941, the Soviet military attaché to France, Major General Ivan Sousloparov, reported that the Germans would attack the next day.[18] Stalin replied: 'This information is an English provocation. Find out who the author is, and punish him.' Fortunately for Sousloparov, as he had predicted, the war began the next day.

By the evening of June 21, Stalin could no longer hide from the truth. The Soviet naval attaché to Germany, Mikhail Vorontsov, who had just arrived from Berlin, was summoned to the Politburo meeting at 7:05 p.m.[19] According to the Navy Commissar Nikolai Kuznetsov, Vorontsov spent fifty minutes describing the imminent German attack.[20] Apparently, after his report, Stalin and the Politburo finally realized that the country was on the verge of a military catastrophe.

The Politburo immediately ordered the organization of two new fronts, the Southern and the Northern.[21] The usage of the word 'fronts' in the Politburo decision, as during the war, instead of 'military districts', as it should be in peacetime, means that Politburo members understood that war had become inevitable. Georgii Zhukov, who had replaced Shaposhnikov as Chief of the General Staff, was appointed commander of both the Southwestern and Southern fronts, while deputy defense Commissar Kirill Meretskov became commander of the Northern Front. After this Timoshenko, the NKO Commissar, and Zhukov sent a directive to the Leningrad, Baltic, Western, Kiev, and Odessa military districts to be on alert for a German attack.[22]

Additionally, the Politburo reinstated Lev Mekhlis as head of the Main Political Directorate of the Red Army, the GlavPURKKA.[23] The GlavPURKKA was a directorate within the Party Central Committee responsible for ideology and morale within the armed forces, while Mekhlis was one of Stalin's most loyal men, having served as his personal assistant from 1924 to 1930. Later, during the 1937–38 purges, Mekhlis monitored the Red Army through GlavPURKKA's network of political commissars. His predecessor at this post, Yan Gamarnik, shot himself in 1937 while expecting to be arrested. Despite Mekhlis's devotion, Stalin liked to play jokes on him, and Mekhlis told his friends: 'He is a cruel man. Once I told him straight: "I've never heard a good word from you."' In this new crisis, Stalin turned to Mekhlis again.

CHAPTER 7

The Scapegoats: Hunting for Generals

The German attack on June 22, 1941 provoked total chaos in Red Army troops at the Soviet–German border. The Red Army appeared not to be ready for defense. Soon Stalin ordered that some generals be considered traitors, making them scapegoats for the defeat.

The War Begins

The Politburo meeting on June 21, 1941 ended at 11:00 p.m., but even after all preparations had been made Stalin was not psychologically ready for the German attack. Four and a half hours later, at 3:25 a.m., Zhukov woke Stalin up with a phone call and told him about the German invasion. As Zhukov recalled in 1956, 'Stalin was breathing heavily into the receiver, but for a few minutes he couldn't say a word. To our [Zhukov and Timoshenko's] repeated questions he answered: "This is a provocation of the German military. Do not open fire to avoid giving them an opportunity to widen their activity."…He did not give permission to open fire until 6:30 am.'[1] Interestingly, this episode disappeared from Zhukov's later published, refined and smoothed memoirs.

Three German army groups invaded the Soviet Union. Army Group North went through the Baltic region toward Leningrad, Army Group Center advanced toward Moscow, and Army Group South moved through Ukraine toward Kiev. The Soviet Union's difficulty in the Winter War had convinced Hitler that the Soviet Union could be quickly conquered, and at first it seemed to be true. The German invaders moved rapidly forward, causing mass fear and chaos among the Soviet troops.

The German attack and the Soviet military disaster that followed deeply shocked the Soviet population. Almost all Soviet citizens had seen the propaganda movie *If War Begins Tomorrow*, filmed in 1938 at parades and military training exercises. In the movie, the Red Army destroys a military aggressor in four hours on the enemy's soil by using all kinds of weapons, including poisonous gas, and the war triggers a rebellion of the proletariat at the enemy's rear. The lyrics of an extremely popular song from the movie—'We'll destroy the enemy on the enemy's soil / Shedding little of our blood, using a mighty blow'—gave voice to the widely held Soviet opinion that they would win a quick and relatively painless victory against Germany.

Stalin was a big fan of this movie; he watched it during and after World War II, even inviting foreign guests to join him in the screening room.

On June 29, Stalin visited the general staff twice. Beria, Anastas Mikoyan, and Georgii Malenkov accompanied him. These visits were an unpleasant surprise for Georgii Zhukov, head of the General Staff, and Timoshenko, the Defense Commissar. After listening to Zhukov's report, Stalin yelled at him: 'What kind of a general staff is this? How is it that a head of the general staff has lost all self-control during the first day of the war, has no communication with the troops, doesn't represent anybody, and doesn't command anybody?'[2] Stalin spent the next day at his dacha in what was generally believed to be a state of extreme frustration.

On June 30, the GKO, or State Defense Committee, was created to coordinate Soviet war efforts.[3] It consisted of only five people: Stalin (chairman), Molotov (deputy chairman), Voroshilov, Malenkov, and Beria.[4] This group, for all intents and purposes, replaced the Politburo during World War II and made all crucial defense-related decisions. Each GKO member was responsible for a particular group of industries or army supplies.

Additionally, the Stavka (Supreme High Command) was formed to co-ordinate the military planning of the Red Army, the Navy Commissariat, the NKVD border and interior troops, and the partisan movement.[5] It was chaired by NKO Commissar Timoshenko, later Stalin, and included Chief of the General Staff Zhukov, Molotov, marshals Voroshilov and Budennyi, and Navy Commissar Kuznetsov; there was also a board of advisers.[6] Formally, all military campaigns designed by the General Staff were approved by the Stavka. However, until mid-1942, Stalin actually made all military decisions alone.

On July 3, Stalin opened a radio address to the nation with the words: 'Comrades! Citizens! Brothers and Sisters!'[7] This was the first time he had ever used the expression 'brothers and sisters'. As a contemporary wrote, Stalin 'may have been ill because he talked indistinctly and frequently drank water. It was terrifying to hear his hand trembling and the decanter hitting the edge of the glass'.[8]

Immediately after the German attack, martial law was declared in the country.[9] Military tribunals were charged with hearing not only cases of servicemen, but also of civilians, if they involved threats to the defense of the Soviet Union or state security. Cases were prosecuted within twenty-four hours after the perpetrator was charged. Initially, tribunals were obliged to get Moscow's approval for every death sentence, but on June 27, 1941, this requirement was abolished. By September 1941, commanders and political commissars of divisions were also given the right to confer the death sentence.[10] Executions were carried out immediately.

The security services also reacted quickly to the German attack. On June 28, Abakumov, Merkulov, and Bochkov, representing the NKVD, NKGB, and the chief Prosecutor's Office, signed a top-secret joint order putting the NKGB (civilian cases) and the two military counterintelligence directorates and the NKVD 3rd department (military cases) in charge of investigating traitors (Article 58-1) who went over to the German side and civilians who crossed the border in the hope of escaping the Soviet Union.[11] The three military counterintelligence organizations were also responsible for arresting and investigating the family members of these traitors (*chsiry*) under Article 19-58-1a (intention of committing an act of treason). The cases were heard by military tribunals or the OSO.

Boris Yefimov, a political caricaturist for *Pravda* and *Izvestia*, recalled the summer of 1941 in his memoirs: 'Of course, Stalin did not think that the drastically worsening situation at the fronts was a result of his own mistakes and errors. His own infallible wisdom and categorical opinion were axiomatic. Only others could make mistakes.'[12] The hunt for scapegoats had begun.

The Meretskov Case

On June 24, 1941, only two days after the German attack, the 3rd NKO Directorate arrested deputy defense Commissar Army General Kirill Meretskov. This arrest seems particularly bizarre because Meretskov had been appointed commander of the Northern Front and military adviser to the Stavka only three days earlier, but it makes more sense if you consider a story told by Vasilii Novobranets, at the time a member of the Razvedupr or RU (Intelligence Directorate) of the General Staff. According to Novobranets, in January 1941 Meretskov 'was demoted to deputy NKO Commissar after telling Stalin that Germany was preparing for war and the Soviet Union should urgently begin defense preparations'.[13] If this is true, the arrest was Stalin's revenge for Meretskov's accurate prediction.

Meretskov was accused of being a member of the alleged Rychagov air force plot, probably because he had also fought in the Spanish Civil War under the alias 'Volunteer Petrovich'. Lev Schwartzman, deputy head of the NKGB Investigation Unit, testified in 1955 that investigators 'beat [Meretskov] with rubber truncheons. Before Meretskov's arrest, testimonies were extracted from forty witnesses attesting to his participation in a military plot...I had orders from the highest level, and one could not violate such orders'.[14] Apparently even after Stalin's death Schwartzman was afraid to name him as the one who had ordered the beatings.

Another former investigator added that Meretskov 'confessed' to 'participating in a spy group and preparing a military coup against Stalin'.[15] As yet another investigator recalled, Colonel General Aleksandr Loktionov, arrested just before the war, was mercilessly beaten in front of Meretskov, but refused to cooperate: 'Loktionov was...covered with blood, and Meretskov could not stand seeing him because he had testified against [Loktionov].

Loktionov...roared in pain, rolled on the floor, but refused to sign [a confession].' Merkulov also participated in beatings, which, astonishingly, he did not consider torture: 'During interrogations, with or without my involvement, interrogators punched the faces of Meretskov and [Boris] Vannikov [Armaments Commissar, arrested on June 7, 1941] and beat their backs and buttocks with rubber truncheons, but these beatings did not turn into torture. I also beat up Meretskov and Vannikov, as well as the other arrestees, but did not torture them.'[16]

In September 1941, Stalin suddenly ordered the release of Meretskov, Vannikov, two of his deputies, and several subordinates who had been arrested before the war.[17] However, many others arrested in connection with the Rychagov and Vannikov cases were soon executed (Appendix I, see http://www.smershbook.com). In Lefortovo Prison, Meretskov was given a new military uniform and immediately brought to Stalin's office in the Kremlin, where Stalin cynically asked him about his health (after three months of torture!).[18] Then he ordered Meretskov to catch up with the Seventh Independent Army, his new command.

Stalin offered the following apology to Vannikov: 'We made a mistake... Some scoundrels slandered you!'[19] Vannikov, appointed deputy Armaments Commissar and later Munitions Commissar, was a ruthless manager who liked to tell his subordinates: 'Once when I was the Munitions Commissar, my chief engineer changed a [technical] decision on his own to a more economical one. I ordered that he be shot.'[20] And then, to illustrate his point, he would take a gun from his pocket and put it in front of him.

In Stalin's circle, Vannikov was considered 'an outstanding organizer of the armament industry, a good friend, an easy and responsive man', as well as a mischievous joker.[21] Even if Vannikov thought of his trick with the handgun as a joke, his subordinates took the threat seriously.

General Dmitrii Pavlov

Colonel General Dmitrii Pavlov had the misfortune of commanding the embattled Western Front while Meretskov was in prison. On July 4, 1941, Pavlov was arrested by an NKVD special group and brought to Moscow. Two days later Lev Mekhlis, the Politburo-appointed member of the Military Council of Pavlov's front and, in fact, Stalin's representative, cabled Stalin that Pavlov's six closest subordinates, all generals, should also be arrested. Stalin agreed.[22] Mekhlis also reported that an additional number of low-level commanders had already been arrested and detained. Stalin was so impressed by Mekhlis's activity that on July 10 the GKO appointed Mekhlis deputy NKO Commissar.

Pavlov and three other generals under his command (Appendix I, see http://www.smershbook.com) were accused of failing to follow Stalin's orders to attack the Germans.[23] They were unable to do so simply because their own troops had already been virtually wiped out by the advancing Germans after a previous order from Moscow to resist them. Pavlov was also accused of being a plotter: 'While part of an anti-Soviet plot and a commander of the troops of the Western Front, [Pavlov] betrayed the interests of the Motherland by opening the front to the fascists.' Pavlov was interrogated about Meretskov, and Meretskov was interrogated about him.[24] Evidently, the investigators were trying to connect the Pavlov and Meretskov cases.

The investigation of the 3rd NKO Directorate proceeded with lightning speed. In two weeks a draft verdict was on Stalin's desk. Stalin ordered that the charge of 'an anti-Soviet military conspiracy' be dropped; no doubt he had reconsidered the wisdom of publicizing such a conspiracy at a time when the Party most needed the Red Army.[25] The charges instead emphasized the generals' alleged cowardice.

During the night of July 22, 1941, at a session of the Military Collegium in Lefortovo Prison in Moscow, Pavlov explained that the new Soviet western border established after the acquisition of Polish territory in 1939 was not properly fortified: 'At the time of military actions, of 600 artillery fortifications planned, only 169 were equipped with cannons, but even they were not in working condition.'[26] Pavlov also stated that 'the basic reason for the rapid movement of the German troops…was the enemy's obvious superiority in aviation and tanks. Besides that, Lithuanian troops…
did not want to fight… The Lithuanian units shot their commanders. That gave German tank units the possibility of striking us.'[27] Given their country's recent takeover by the Soviets, it is no surprise that some Lithuanian divisions revolted.

Pavlov's last words were: 'There was no treason at the Special Western Front… We are defendants…because we failed to prepare sufficiently for this war during peacetime.'[28] Following Stalin's pretrial instructions, the Military Collegium sentenced the generals to death for cowardice and they were executed immediately after the trial.[29] Of course, Stalin knew very well that the poorly trained troops were not psychologically ready for a defensive war. For instance, the deputy artillery commander of the Red Army, Colonel General (later Marshal) Nikolai Voronov, reported to Stalin on August 15, 1941: 'Our infantry reacts painfully to the appearance of enemy airplanes, to shelling by enemy artillery, and to the explosions of enemy shells and mines, even in small numbers. Soldiers are convinced that we have the right to shoot and throw bombs, but the enemy doesn't have the right to shoot at and bomb us.'[30]

But Stalin needed scapegoats. Six days after Pavlov's execution Stalin warned:

I urge everyone to understand that in the future anyone who violates the military oath and forgets his duty toward the Motherland, who discredits the high rank of a Red Army military man, every coward and panicking person who leaves his position without an order and surrenders his arms to the enemy without a fight, will be punished without mercy according to the wartime law.

All commanders…of regiments and above should be aware of this order.

Defense Commissar of the USSR

J. Stalin.[31]

Members of the generals' families were also persecuted.[32] Sewage worker was the only employment permitted to General Pavlov's widow in exile in Siberia. The case foreshadowed later purges of high-ranking officers.[33]

After Pavlov's dismissal, Stalin appointed Lieutenant General Andrei Yeremenko Commander of the Western Front, but Yeremenko soon became commander of the newly created Bryansk Front. This general was infamous for his outrageous behavior. Kombrig Ivan Ganenko, a secretary of the Central Committee of Belorussia and a member of the Military Council of the 13th Army of the Bryansk Front, cabled to Stalin:

Yeremenko, without asking me about anything [Ganenko had just come from the front line], began accusing the Military Council of cowardice and treason against the Motherland. After I said that one must not lodge such strong accusations [without a reason], Yeremenko attacked me with his fists and hit me in the face a few times, and also threatened to execute me. I told him that he could shoot me, but he had no right to humiliate my dignity as a communist…

Yeremenko pulled out his Mauser, but [Lt. Gen. Mikhail] Yefremov [Yeremenko's deputy] prevented him from shooting. Then Yeremenko began to threaten Yefremov. During this disgusting scene, Yeremenko was using foul language hysterically the entire time.

After cooling off a little bit, Yeremenko began to boast that, supposedly with Stalin's support, he had beaten up a few corps commanders and had smashed one commander's head.[34]

In fact, Yeremenko's behavior was not unique. Beating of subordinates became so common in the troops that in October 1941 Stalin even signed a special order trying to stop this practice.[35]

Stalin did not respond to Ganenko's telegram. Interestingly, when Yeremenko and his troops were surrounded near Moscow, Stalin sent a special plane to save him. Yefremov, on the other hand, fought in encirclement in April 1942 until he was wounded, then shot himself in order to avoid being taken a prisoner. Later Yeremenko became one of the key commanders during the Stalingrad Battle. After the war and Stalin's death he was even promoted to the rank of marshal.

Background of the Pavlov Case

The accusations directed at Pavlov were totally false. Stalin and his pre war military leaders were responsible for the complete disorganization of the army. In an interview given in the 1990s, Vladimir Novikov, former deputy Armaments Commissar, described the situation of June 1941:

Within two weeks after the Fascists attacked the Soviet Union it appeared that there were no guns [in the Red Army]…This was…because stocks of guns were kept in the regions near the [Western] border. According to the Armaments Commissariat's information, there was a reserve of approximately 8 million guns, but I think there were as many as 10 million guns. However, almost all the guns were kept in storage facilities in the territory that was soon taken by the enemy. In addition, the loss of guns by our retreating army was also enormous.

The absence of anti-tank weapons was also unexpected. As a result, usually only bottles filled with inflammatory liquid were used against enemy tanks during the first months of war. In peacetime, we produced an enormous quantity of anti-tank weaponry, including anti-tank rifles, but on the insistence of the Main Artillery Directorate of the Defense Commissariat (headed by Marshal G. I. Kulik, who was not a professional in this field), a year before the war the production of anti-tank rifles and 45- and 76-millimeter anti-tank cannons was terminated…

The number of produced anti-aircraft guns was also very low.[36]

Another reason Stalin may have decided to target Pavlov is that he had challenged Stalin's authority three years before, and Stalin never forgot such personal offenses. In 1956 Pavlov's wife, Aleksandra, wrote to Nikita Khrushchev requesting that he rehabilitate her dead husband. She mentioned an episode that clarifies Pavlov's arrest:

In the summer of 1938, D. G. Pavlov, Pavel Sergeevich Alliluev (Commander of the Armored Vehicle Directorate), and G. I. Kulik (Commander of the Artillery Directorate) personally petitioned Comrade Stalin. They asked him to stop the arrests of the old cadre commanders. I do not know whether, of the three men, G. I. Kulik is still alive. As for Alliluev, he died suddenly the same year, a day after he returned from a resort. Possibly, K. Ye. Voroshilov is aware that the petition had been handed over to Stalin himself.[37]

It seems that Pavlov's wife forgot that Kulik's deputy, Grigorii Savchenko, had also signed the petition.[38] The petitioners even prepared a draft decision for Stalin's signature that would have put an end to the arrests.

Stalin did not forget this challenge to his authority and eventually all four signatories vanished.

Pavel Alliluev was first. He was Stalin's brother-in-law, the beloved brother of Stalin's wife, Nadezhda, who had committed suicide six years earlier, on November 9, 1932. Alliluev died mysteriously 'of a heart attack' in his office on November 2, 1938, after he found out that literally all of his subordinates had been arrested. His daughter, son, and nephew suspect he was poisoned by the NKVD.[39] Later, in 1946, after her arrest and conviction, Pavel's wife Yevgenia spent ten years in Vladimir Prison in solitary confinement.[40] The following year, their daughter Kira was arrested and then exiled for many years.

Possibly, Pavlov was next, because during interrogations in February–May 1939, investigators forced Mikhail Koltsov to testify that in Spain (where Pavlov commanded the tank forces of the Republican Army) Pavlov had been a defeatist, swindler, and drunkard.[41] At that time Stalin did not give the order to pursue the issue of Pavlov's conduct in Spain, but now, in 1941, he decided to get rid of Pavlov.

General Savchenko had also already been targeted. He was arrested three days before the war, in connection with the Rychagov Case (Appendix I, see http://www.smershbook.com).[42] On October 28, 1941, he was shot without trial.

In November 1941 Stalin went after Grigorii Kulik, who had been one of his trusted generals since the Civil War. In Spain his nom de guerre was 'General Cooper', and in 1940 he received a promotion to marshal. However, he did not entirely escape the Great Terror. In May 1939, his wife, Kira Simonich-Kulik, disappeared without a trace.[43] Shortly before her disappearance, Stalin told Kulik that his wife was an Italian spy and said that he should divorce her, which Kulik declined to do. Stalin's suspicion of Simonich-Kulik was likely prompted by her foreign contacts: one of her sisters was married to an Italian military attaché, and their mother also lived in Italy.

In 1953, the details of Simonich-Kulik's murder came to light during the investigation of Beria and his accomplices, but this bizarre story was published only in the 1990s.[44] Apparently, Beria ordered Merkulov and a group of NKVD operatives to kidnap Kulik's wife on a Moscow street. After Beria and Merkulov interrogated her in the NKVD, she was executed without trial. During interrogations Beria and the others claimed that the operation was ordered 'from above', meaning by Stalin.

In November 1941 Stalin ordered Stavka member and deputy NKO Commissar Kulik to restore order in the Crimea—an impossible mission at the time.[45] After Kulik's predictable defeat in the Crimea, he reported to Stalin: 'The army had turned into a gang! All they did was drink and rape women. I had no chance of defending Kerch with such an army. I arrived too late; it was impossible to save the situation.'[46] Kulik was tried by a special session of the Supreme Court and demoted to major general, dismissed from the post of deputy NKO Commissar, and deprived of all military awards. In vain he appealed to Stalin in a long letter, saying: 'If I am a wrecker [as accused under Article 58-7] and conducting underground work, I should be shot. If I am not, I ask you to punish the slanderers.'[47] Stalin did not answer. Later Kulik commanded various formations and was promoted to lieutenant general, but then demoted to major general again. Finally, in 1947, after being arrested for anti-Soviet conversations, he was sentenced to death and executed in August 1950.

Other 1941 Cases

After the Pavlov Case, military counterintelligence seems to have gone somewhat out of control. Numerous arrests of commanders of all ranks, including generals, followed at the Western and other fronts. Many of them were sentenced under paragraphs 193-17b (abuse of power) and 193-20a (surrender of troops), and executed (Appendix I, see http://www.smershbook.com). In Moscow, Mikheev's deputy, A. N. Klykov, reported to Beria about one of Stalin's favorites, Marshal Semyon Budennyi, commander of the Southwestern Front and Timoshenko's deputy.[48] The report accused Budennyi of spying simultaneously for British, Polish, Italian, and German intelligence. These accusations were so obviously ridiculous that the report went no further. However, two months later Timoshenko was dismissed as deputy Commissar and appointed commander of the Southwestern Front instead of Budennyi, while Budennyi became commander of the Reserve Front (in existence only until October 1941).

Incredibly, on July 16, 1941, Mikheev even denounced NKO Commissar Timoshenko, pointing to Timoshenko's connection with the previously executed military leaders.[49] Timoshenko was not arrested, but on July 19, 1941, Stalin himself became NKO Commissar, while Timoshenko was demoted to a post as Stalin's deputy. The same day Mikheev was made head of the 3rd Department of the Southwestern Front, and two months later he was killed in action while trying to break through a Nazi encirclement. He was one of 3,725 *osobisty* killed and 3,092 missing in action between June 22, 1941 and March 1, 1943.[50]

Later Abakumov's investigators continued to collect compromising materials on Timoshenko. In 1953, General Boris Teplinsky wrote a letter from a labor camp to Marshal Aleksandr Vasilevsky: 'While having been in prison [in Moscow]…[the investigators] offered me the chance to play a role of a provocateur against Marshal Timoshenko because I was a cell mate of his former deputy, Major General F. S. Ivanov [arrested in 1942, released in 1946]…After I refused, the investigation of my case stopped…For the next 9 years I had no idea about my future fate.'[51]

CHAPTER 8

Directorate of Special Departments (UOO)

With the Soviet Union now defending its own ground rather than taking new territory, Stalin decided to merge the recently created NKGB and the three military counterintelligence services back into the NKVD. The thought was that a monolithic NKVD could better control the retreating army and keep order more efficiently than three separate services.

UOO Structure and Activities

On July 17, 1941, the GKO issued an order to transfer the 3rd NKO Directorate back to the NKVD as its Special Departments Directorate, or UOO (Figure 8-1).[1] An NKVD instruction explained: 'The goal of the reorganization of the 3rd directorates into special departments within the NKVD is to conduct a merciless fight against spies, traitors, saboteurs, deserters, and various kinds of panic-stricken persons and disorganizers.'[2] Viktor Abakumov, retaining his position as deputy NKVD head, was now appointed head of the UOO, an important position because military counterintelligence became so critical. Solomon Milshtein, who was involved in the extermination of Polish officers in the Katyn Forest massacre, became his deputy.[3] Six months later, in January 1942, the 3rd Navy Commissariat Directorate was also transferred to the UOO.[4]

Five days after the reorganization in the NKO and NKVD, the NKVD and NKGB were again merged into one Commissariat, the NKVD.[5] Operational directorates, largely repeating the GUGB structure, were created within the new NKVD, and the UOO became one of six operational directorates (Figure 8-1). Beria remained NKVD Commissar and Merkulov was once again his first deputy.

By the end of 1941, Abakumov's UOO headquarters consisted of eight departments, and Abakumov acquired three more deputies: Fyodor Tutushkin, Nikolai Osetrov, and Lavrentii Tsanava. Later, both Tutushkin and Osetrov headed SMERSH front directorates. By July 1942, after additional changes, the UOO headquarters in Moscow increased to twelve main departments (Figure 8-2), and had a staff of 225 people.[6]

Field operations were carried out by OO directorates at each of the six fronts created in July 1941, which reported to the UOO, the Main Directorate, in Moscow (Table 8-1). Later, in August—December 1941, additionally six, and in January 1942—August 1942, five more fronts with their OO directorates were organized. There were department-level OOs in all armies, corps, divisions, and independent brigades but not at regimental and battalion levels. OO functions at this level were performed by a single

Figure 8-1   THE RECONSOLIDATION OF MILITARY COUNTERINTELLIGENCE INTO THE NKVD'S UOO
JULY 1941 TO APRIL 1943

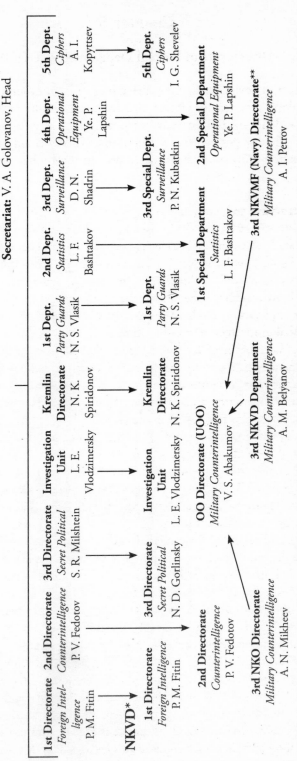

NKGB
Vsevolod Merkulov, Commissar

First Deputy Commissar: I. A. Serov
Deputies: B. Z. Kobulov, M. V. Gribov
Secretariat: V. A. Golovanov, Head

1st Directorate
Foreign Intelligence
P. M. Fitin

2nd Directorate
Counterintelligence
P. V. Fedotov

3rd Directorate
Secret Political
S. R. Milshtein

Investigation Unit
L. E. Vlodzimersky

Kremlin Directorate
N. K. Spiridonov

1st Dept.
Party Guards
N. S. Vlasik

2nd Dept.
Statistics
L. F. Bashtakov

3rd Dept.
Surveillance
D. N. Shadrin

4th Dept.
Operational Equipment
Ye. P. Lapshin

5th Dept.
Ciphers
A. I. Kopyttsev

NKVD*

1st Directorate
Foreign Intelligence
P. M. Fitin

2nd Directorate
Counterintelligence
P. V. Fedotov

3rd Directorate
Secret Political
N. D. Gorlinsky

Investigation Unit
L. E. Vlodzimersky

Kremlin Directorate
N. K. Spiridonov

1st Dept.
Party Guards
N. S. Vlasik

1st Special Department
Statistics
L. F. Bashtakov

3rd Special Dept.
Surveillance
P. N. Kubatkin

2nd Special Department
Operational Equipment
Ye. P. Lapshin

5th Dept.
Ciphers
I. G. Shevelev

2nd Directorate
Counterintelligence
P. V. Fedotov

3rd NKO Directorate
Military Counterintelligence
A. N. Mikheev

OO Directorate (UOO)
Military Counterintelligence
V. S. Abakumov

3rd NKVD Department
Military Counterintelligence
A. M. Belyanov

3rd NKVMF (Navy) Directorate**
Military Counterintelligence
A. I. Petrov

*The following operational NKVD units are not shown: Transportation Directorate: N. I. Sinegubov, Head; Economic Directorate: P. Ya. Meshik, Head; 4th Special Dept. (*Governmental Communications*): V. A. Kravchenko, Head; 6th Special Dept. (*State Depository of Valuables*): V. N. Vladimirov, Head. Also not shown are numerous nonoperational NKVD units (e.g., the GULAG).
** Incorporated in the UOO on January 11, 1942.

Figure 8-2

THE STRUCTURE OF THE UOO WITHIN THE NKVD
JULY 1941 TO APRIL 1943

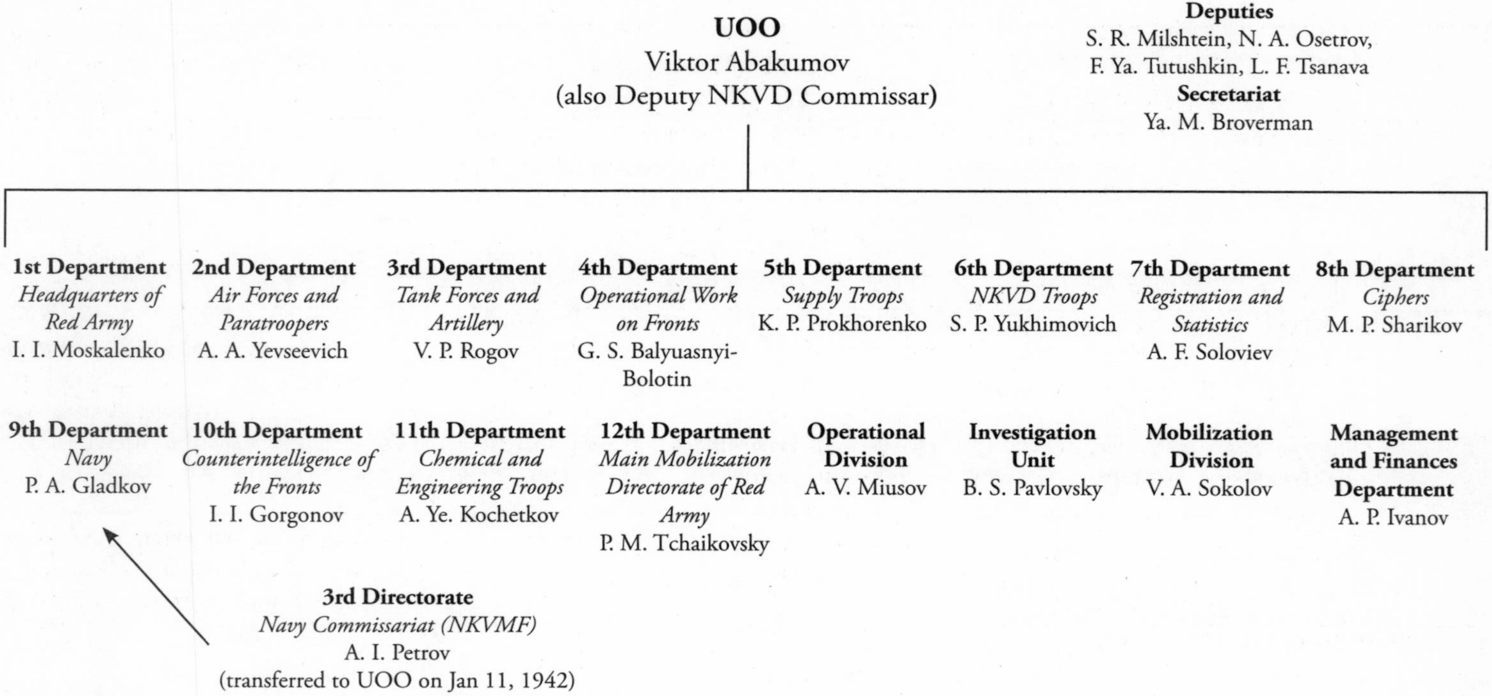

UOO
Viktor Abakumov
(also Deputy NKVD Commissar)

Deputies
S. R. Milshtein, N. A. Osetrov,
F. Ya. Tutushkin, L. F. Tsanava
Secretariat
Ya. M. Broverman

1st Department
Headquarters of Red Army
I. I. Moskalenko

2nd Department
Air Forces and Paratroopers
A. A. Yevseevich

3rd Department
Tank Forces and Artillery
V. P. Rogov

4th Department
Operational Work on Fronts
G. S. Balyuasnyi-Bolotin

5th Department
Supply Troops
K. P. Prokhorenko

6th Department
NKVD Troops
S. P. Yukhimovich

7th Department
Registration and Statistics
A. F. Soloviev

8th Department
Ciphers
M. P. Sharikov

9th Department
Navy
P. A. Gladkov

10th Department
Counterintelligence of the Fronts
I. I. Gorgonov

11th Department
Chemical and Engineering Troops
A. Ye. Kochetkov

12th Department
Main Mobilization Directorate of Red Army
P. M. Tchaikovsky

Operational Division
A. V. Miusov

Investigation Unit
B. S. Pavlovsky

Mobilization Division
V. A. Sokolov

Management and Finances Department
A. P. Ivanov

3rd Directorate
Navy Commissariat (NKVMF)
A. I. Petrov
(transferred to UOO on Jan 11, 1942)

TABLE 8-1. OO DIRECTORATE HEADS AS OF JULY 1941[1]

Front	Military Commander[2]	Head of the OO Directorate[3]
Northern, then **Leningrad Front** (from Aug 1941; some troops were included in the **Karelian** and **Volkhov** fronts)	Lt. Gen. M. M. Popov, Jun–Sep 1941 Marshal K. Ye. Voroshilov, Sep 1941 Army Gen. G. K. Zhukov, Sep–Oct 1941 Maj. Gen. I. I. Fedyuninsky, Oct 1941 Lt. Gen. M. S. Khozin, Oct 1941–Jun 1942 Marshal L. A. Govorov, Jun 1942–Jul 1945	P. T. Kuprin, Jul–Aug 1942 D. I. Mel'nikov, May–Jun 1942 A. S. Bystrov, Jun 1942–Jun 1945
Northwestern Front (disbanded in November 1943; later became **1st Belorussian Front**)	Col. Gen. F. I. Kuznetsov, Jun–Jul 1941 Maj. Gen. P. P. Sobennikov, Jul–Aug 1941 Lt. Gen. P. A. Kurochkin, Sep 1941–Oct 1942 Marshal S. K. Timoshenko, Oct 1942–Mar 1943	I. Ya. Babich, Jun–Jul 1941 V. M. Bochkov, Jul–Dec 1941 N. A. Korolev, Jan–May 1942 I. Ya. Babich, May 1942–May 1943
Western Front (in Apr 1944, divided into the **2nd and 3rd Belorussian fronts**)	Army Gen. D. G. Pavlov, Jun 1941 Marshal S. K. Timoshenko, Jul–Sep 1941 Col. Gen. I. S. Konev, Sep–Oct 1941 Army Gen. G. K. Zhukov, Oct 1941–Aug 1942 Col. Gen. I. S. Konev, Aug 1942–Feb 1943 Army Gen. V. D. Sokolovsky, Feb1943–Apr 1944	L. F. Tsanava, Jul–Oct 1941 A. M. Belyanov, Oct 1941–Jan 1942 L. F. Tsanava, Jan 1942–Mar 1943
Central Front (disbanded in Aug 1941, troops moved to the **Bryansk Front**)	Col. Gen. F. I. Kuznetsov, Jul–Aug 1941 Lt. Gen. M. G. Yefremov, Aug 1941	P. G. Begma, Jul–Aug 1941

Table 8-1 (continued)

Front	Military Commander[2]	Head of the OO Directorate[3]
Southwestern Front (disbanded in Jul 1942; created again in Oct 1942 as the **3rd Ukrainian Front**)	Col. Gen. M. P. Kirponos, Jun–Jul 1941 Marshal S. M. Budennyi, Jul–Sep 1941 Marshal S. K. Timoshenko, Sep–Dec 1941 Lt. Gen. F. Ya. Kostenko, Dec 1941–Apr 1942 Marshal S. K. Timoshenko, Apr–Jul 1942 Col. Gen. N. F. Vatutin, Oct 1942–Mar 1943	A. N. Mikheev, Jul–Sep 1941 N. N. Selivanovsky, Oct 1941–Aug 1942 A. F. Frolov, Oct–Dec 1942 P. V. Zelenin, Dec 1942–Apr 1943
Southern Front (disbanded in Jul 1942; troops transferred to the **Northern Caucasian Front**)	Army Gen. I. V. Tyulenev, Jun–Aug 1941 Lt. Gen D. I. Ryabyshev, Aug–Oct 1941 Col. Gen. Ya. T. Chernichenko, Oct–Dec 1941 Lt. Gen. R. Ya. Malinovsky, Dec–Jul 1942	N. S. Sazykin, Jul–Sep 1941 P. V. Zelenin, Oct 1941–Jul 1942
Front of Reserve Armies (on Oct 10, 1941, merged with the **Western Front**; later **2nd Ukrainian Front**)	Army Gen. G. K. Zhukov, Jul–Sep 1941 Marshal S. M. Budennyi, Sep–Oct 1941	A. M. Belyanov, Jul–Oct 1941

1. From August–December 1941, six more fronts were added.
2. Dates from K. A. Zalessky, *Imperiya Stalina. Biograficheskii entsiklopedicheski slovar'* (Moscow: Veche, 2000), 558–62 (in Russian). Short biographies of these commanders in ibid. and Michael Parrish, *Sacrifice of the Generals: Soviet Senior Officer Losses, 1939–1953* (Lanham, MD: The Scarecrow Press, Inc, 2004).
3. OO directorate heads were assigned on Jul 17, 1941. See N. V. Petrov, *Kto rukovodil organami gosbezopasnosti 1941–1954. Spravochnik* (Moscow: Zven'ya, 2010), 111–5 (in Russian).

OO officer (*osobist*) attached to these units. The chain of command within the OO directorates at the fronts was hierarchical. A typical OO unit at the division level consisted of about twenty-five people:

Position[7]	Equivalent State Security Rank	Military Rank[8]
Head	Captain	Lt. Colonel
Assistant head	Senior Lieutenant	Major
Two operational officers	Lieutenants	Captains
Secretary (usually a woman)	Junior Lieutenant	Senior Lieutenant
Executive officer	Junior Lieutenant	Senior Lieutenant
A platoon of 15–20 riflemen	—	Privates

In the field, the OO assistant heads and operational officers of OO departments conducted the actual investigations of political cases. In addition to clerical duties, the secretary was in charge of ciphers and coded messages. The head of each OO sometimes carried out executions personally. From July 1942 onwards, OOs had 'the right to arrest deserters and, when necessary, shoot them to death' without trial.[9]

The OO head recruited informers commonly called *seksoty* (secret workers) or *stukachi* (this word comes from the Russian word *stuchat'* or to 'knock', and carried the meaning of secretly knocking at the door of the NKVD office) among officers of the military staff. A classified KGB textbook explains how this worked: 'Operational workers recruited agents and informers in all military units of the front line forces, despite the presence or absence of hostile elements [in the units]. The number of agents of special departments also grew due to recruitments of secret informers in reserve units, from where they were sent to the front line forces.'[10]

The OO officers met secretly with their informers in offices apart from the regular military facilities, often located in separate buildings. *Seksoty* were sworn to secrecy. Pyotr Pirogov, a former Soviet officer and later a defector to the West, recalled the document that an OO officer ordered him to sign after recruiting him, which read: 'I, Pirogov, had a conference with a member of the Special Section and undertake to tell no one of this meeting. I am aware that in the contrary case I shall be subject to prosecution under Article 58 of the Criminal Code.'[11] Each *seksot* or *stukach* was given a code name that he used for signing his reports.

Seksoty (the plural) were also recruited among the privates. An infantryman recalled in 2009: 'I remember one night the *osobist* of our regiment called me [from the wet trenches] up to the battalion headquarters in a dry dug-out. He kept me for an hour and a half, trying to recruit me to be a *stukach*, but I refused. What could he do to me? I was a machine-gunner, not an informer. The *osobist* got mad and I remember how he screamed at me: "If you want to live, don't you dare tell anybody about our conversation!"'[12] Another infantryman remembered the same: 'Our *osobisty*…talked to me…and even gave me a pseudonym, "Leonov", derived from the name of my place of birth—Leonovo. Later they continually rebuked me: "Why don't you want to share what you know with us? Why don't you write a report for us?" What would I write in a report if there weren't traitors among us? Should I write some fiction?'[13]

From the structure of the UOO and its field branches it is obvious that during the first period of the war, the main objective of military counter-intelligence was spying on the Red Army and Red Navy in order to keep them in line. For instance, on July 22, 1941 Viktor Bochkov, OO head of the Northwestern Front, issued the following directive:

> There were numerous cases when formation commanders and privates left positions without an order, ran away in panic, and left all military equipment behind. The most dangerous is…that some special departments did not even investigate such cases and did not arrest the guilty servicemen, and they were not tried. All secret agents should be instructed to identify such persons…
>
> The fight against the deserters, panic-mongers and cowards is the main task of our organs [i.e., OOs], along with the fight against spies and traitors…
>
> Special departments must introduce strong discipline and order in the rear of divisions, corps, and armies so the desertion and panic should be terminated in the next few days.[14]

According to the reports of the OOs of the Western, Northwestern, Southern, Southwestern and Leningrad fronts, from July to December 1941, 102 large groups of Soviet servicemen defected to the enemy. In addition, the OOs prevented the crossing over of 159 additional groups and 2,773 individual servicemen.[15]

Self-injured servicemen, nicknamed *samostreltsy*, were one more OO problem. On August 2, 1941, the GKO ordered the OOs to arrest 'self-injured' servicemen and, if necessary, to shoot them on the spot as deserters.[16] A mortar man recalled in 2006:

> There was a good guy in our company, a sharp-sighted observer, a Kazakh by origin.[17] I was thunderstruck when it came to light that he put a bullet through his own arm. It was easily recognized. That's all—military tribunal and death by shooting. As a rule, the execution was performed in front of the regiment's formation.
>
> There was another episode in the regiment. Several soldiers formed a circle and one of them threw a grenade in the center to wound everyone in the leg…

I heard about one more way to evade participating in combats—to raise your hand over the parapet of the trench [soldiers facetiously called this method of self-inflicted injury *golosovanie*, or 'voting']…

The special group in our regiment that prevented desertion and exposed the *samostreltsy*…was [called] *Osobyi otdel* and its staff numbered some five men… Everybody tried to keep their distance from them. We also knew that there were secret *Osobyi otdel* informers in all of the regimental detachments.[18]

Most of the Red Army men hated the *osobisty*. Here is a song written by members of an unknown tank crew (my translation):

The first shell ignited fuel
And I escaped from the tank not remembering how
Then I was questioned in the *Osobyi otdel:*
'Son of a bitch, why didn't you burn along with the tank?'
And I answered, and I said:
'In the next attack I'll certainly be dead.'[19]

Zyama Ioffe, a member of a military tribunal during almost the whole war who dealt with the *osobisty* on a daily basis, explicitly stated in 2009:

Every *osobist* looked at the surrounding people with the arrogant and impudent conviction that he could send any soldier or officer, despite rank and file, to a penal detachment or 'make him knuckle under', or shoot him to death, or 'grind him into the dust of labor camps' [Beria's favorite expression], or organize a special vetting for him, etc…

The power over people and complete impunity, especially when the 'worker of the organs' [as the NKVD/MGB officers called themselves] was constantly told [by his superiors] that potential enemies and traitors existed everywhere while he was the only specially trusted person, used to turn him into a real piece of shit…

Very few had guts to withstand the *osobisty*.[20]

Another veteran, Izo Adamsky, an artillery officer, recalled that at the front line the hatred of the *osobisty* (who became SMERSH officers) continued until the end of the war:

On the Oder River [near Berlin, in May 1945], a drunken *osobist* slept in my dug-out all the time because he was afraid of going out alone and getting a bullet in his back. The *osobisty* even had an order about 'self-guarding' that forbade them to move around without guards at any time.

This was because many wanted to get even with the *osobisty* when they had an opportunity. I remember such occasions very well.[21]

In the numerous memoirs of the NKVD/SMERSH veterans published in the late 2000s, military counterintelligence officers typically wrote about themselves that 'our authority was very high' among servicemen.[22] Obviously, even more than 65 years after the war they were not ready to face the real attitude of fighting soldiers toward them. As Ioffe put it, 'almost everyone hated the *osobisty*'.

Only once did Ioffe see an *osobist* who was fighting the enemy. During a disastrous retreat from the Northern Caucasus in the autumn of 1942, Goldberg, head of the Army's OO, 'grabbed a machine gun from the hands of a guard soldier of the tribunal, and rushed to head off the running crowd. He stopped the retreating soldiers, turned them around, and led them back to the positions they had just left'.[23]

Stalin's Order No. 270

The high number of Red Army servicemen who were taken prisoner (POWs), especially in Belorussia and Ukraine, was unprecedented. The German Army Group South, supported by several Italian, Hungarian and Slovak divisions, occupied Belorussia and most of Ukraine, while Romanian troops occupied the former Bessarabia and the region near Odessa. By the end of September 1941, in the area around Kiev (the capital of Ukraine) alone, 665,000 Soviet servicemen had been encircled and taken prisoner. The POWs became the main focus of Stalin's anger and a target of military counterintelligence.

According to current Russian data, from June to December 1941, between 2 million and 3.8 million servicemen were taken prisoner.[24] At the end of 1941 only about eight percent of the servicemen listed on June 22, 1941 remained in uniform.[25] The Germans recorded higher numbers for 1941–43 than the Russian sources typically give. On December 11, 1941, Hitler declared that the German troops had captured 3,806,865 prisoners.[26] In February 1942 Alfred Rosenberg, the German minister for the Occupied Eastern Territories and the main ideologist of Nazi racial theory, wrote: 'Currently, of 3.6 million POWs, only a few hundred thousand are capable of work. Most of them died of hunger and bad weather. Thousands are sick with typhus. In most camps the commandants...consider death to be the best solution for them.'[27]

In mid-1942, the number of prisoners continued to grow. By May 1942, the German and Romanian forces jointly conquered the Crimea, and 150,000 Red Army men were captured in the Crimea; 240,000 were taken the same May near Kharkov; 80,000 men were captured in June during the battle on the North Donets River; and about 95,000 men were taken in July near Sevastopol. Here is the number of Russian servicemen taken prisoner for the years 1941 to 1945 from both Russian and German sources:

Year	Russian sources[28]	German sources[29]
1941	Approx. 2,000,000	3,355,000
1942	1,339,000	1,653,000
1943	487,000	565,000
1944	203,000	147,000
1945	40,600	34,000
Total	4,069,000	5,754,000

At the end, only about 1.7 million Soviet POWs were still alive in German hands.[30]

Not all prisoners were taken because of military defeat or encirclement. In the autumn of 1941, changing sides and going over to the enemy occurred on a large scale. To prevent this, the heads of OOs attached to troops defending Moscow took measures even against their own subordinates. One order from the 16th Army's OO head stated: 'I warn all operational workers [the word "officer" was not used until early 1943] of Special Departments that if the acts of treason against the Motherland continue, the operational worker who is responsible for the unit in which such an act took place, as well as the OO head and deputy head of this unit, will be court-martialed.'[31]

Stalin's harsh personal attitude toward Soviet POWs is evident in his infamous Order No. 270, dated August 16, 1941. Four days before that, NKO Commissar Timoshenko brought a draft of the order to Stalin and Stalin substantially edited it. The order included examples of three generals—Vladimir Kachalov, Commander of the 28th Army (Western Front), Nikolai Kirillov, Commander of the 13th Rifle Corps, and Pavel Ponedelin, Commander of the 12th Army (both at the Southern Front)—who supposedly panicked and deserted. It introduced the slogan 'Cowards and deserters must be liquidated!' The order concluded:

> I order that:
>
> 1. Anyone who removes his insignia during battle and surrenders should be regarded as a malicious deserter, whose family is to be arrested as the family of a breaker of the oath and betrayer of the Motherland. Such deserters are to be shot on the spot.
>
> 2. Those who find themselves surrounded are to fight to the last and try to reach their own lines. And those who prefer to surrender are to be destroyed by any available means, and their families deprived of all state allowances and assistance.
>
> 3. Bold and brave people are to be more actively promoted.
>
> 4. This order is to be read to all companies, squadrons, [and] batteries.[32]

Although Stalin wrote in the text 'I order', Molotov (GKO's deputy chairman), four marshals (Semyon Budennyi, Kliment Voroshilov, Semyon

Timoshenko, and Boris Shaposhnikov), and Army General Georgii Zhukov signed the order as well.

Soviet propaganda never mentioned that generals Nikolai Kirillov and Pavel Ponedelin were taken prisoner along with 103,000 servicemen (according to the German data) in one of the most devastating defeats of the Red Army in 1941, near the Ukrainian town of Uman.[33] Hitler, on the contrary, widely publicized this victory and even invited Benito Mussolini, the Italian Duce, to visit the troops in the Uman pocket. On August 26, 1941, the two dictators boarded a plane at Hitler's HQ Wolfschantze in East Prussia, and flew to Uman. In Uman, they inspected an Italian division that was fighting alongside the Germans.[34] Not until 2010 did a Russian author finally publish a book about the Uman disaster.[35]

The Military Collegium condemned Generals Kachalov, Kirillov, and Ponedelin in absentia to death as traitors (paragraph 58-1b), not being aware that one of them, Kachalov, had already been killed in action. But Stalin, apparently, did not forget the humiliating visit of the two fascist leaders. In May 1945, SMERSH arrested Kirillov and Ponedelin, who had survived Nazi imprisonment, and in August 1950 the Military Collegium sentenced them to death for the second time and they were executed. Stalin personally approved the executions.

The Fallout from Order No. 270

After Order No. 270, Stalin signed an additional order that required commanders, commissars, and OOs of corps and divisions to report the names of all servicemen taken prisoner, as well as the names of their family members.[36] The wives of Kachanov, Kirillov, and Ponedelin were arrested and sentenced to exile (Appendix I, see http://www.smershbook.com).

Essentially, Order No. 270 was just the continuation of Stalin's long-standing policy toward POWs. For instance, in 1938, most of the Russian soldiers who had been in German or Austrian captivity during World War I were persecuted, despite the passage of twenty years. In March 1938, Stalin made a note on an NKVD report concerning the arrest of former POWs: 'Former Russian [underlined in the original] prisoners of war should be counted and examined. J. St[alin].'[37] A prisoner recalled: 'In 1938, workers and simple *kolkhoz* [Communist collective-farm] peasants started appearing in the prison cells [of NKVD investigation prisons], all utterly unable to imagine why they had been arrested. It turned out that they had been prisoners of war.'[38]

A new word began to be used, *okruzhenets*, meaning a serviceman who had been encircled (*okruzhenie* in Russian) by Germans. On September 6, 1941, the Red Army newspaper *Krasnaya Zvezda* published for the first time an editorial article about POWs, but without a reference to Order

No. 270. David Ortenberg, the newspaper's editor-in-chief, later recalled the main statement of the article: 'It is a shame to be taken prisoner by the German-fascist scoundrels, a shame toward the people, comrades, families, children, and it is a crime against the Motherland.'[39] Following this trend, the Leningrad Front commander, Georgii Zhukov, went even further than Stalin. In a ciphered cable of September 28, 1941, he ordered: 'All servicemen should know that the families of anyone who has surrendered to the enemy will be shot, and all survivors of the surrender will be shot upon their return from captivity.'[40]

Following the directives of Order No. 270, in autumn 1941, field OOs focused their arrests on both low-level personnel and high-ranking officers.[41] Additionally, the order was used for the execution of an enormous number of mid-level commanders, as well as privates, without trial, on the order of the army military council or a front commander. Lev Mekhlis personally ordered executions although he wasn't even a member of a military council. After he and Kirill Meretskov arrived at the headquarters of the Northwestern Front as Stavka representatives in September 1941, Mekhlis simply wrote an order to execute General Vasilii Goncharov, Artillery Commander of the 34th Army, without trial.[42] Goncharov was shot in front of the staff formation. Viktor Bochkov, OO head of the front, reported to Mekhlis on those officers who dared to complain about this execution. Then Mekhlis ordered the front tribunal to sentence Major General Kuz'ma Kachanov, Commander of the 34th Army, to death. Kachanov was executed in Mekhlis's presence.

Though preoccupied with executions, Mekhlis did not forget that he, as head of the GlavPURKKA, was also in charge of troop morale. The commander of the 163rd Rifle Division of the same front received a cable from Mekhlis: 'I'm sending a good military band to join [your] division...The enemy must tremble at the sound of the Soviet march.'[43]

In these complicated circumstances some military prosecutors tried unsuccessfully to remind commanders and heads of OOs about the law. For example, in October 1941 Boris Alekseev, Prosecutor of the 43rd Army (Western Front), found out that 30 commanders and privates had been executed in a few days without trial, only on the order of the Military Council of this army. He immediately ordered the divisional prosecutors to increase their supervision over such cases. Additionally, he told Major General Stepan Akimov, Commander of the 43rd Army, that he would not tolerate executions without trial, and reported to the Chief Military Prosecutor Nosov, 'I've pointed out to the Army high command and the OO head that it is necessary to follow proper regulations.'[44] But Georgii Zhukov, Commander of the Western Front, continued ordering executions without trial. In November 1941, on Zhukov's order Lieutenant Colonel A. G. Gerasimov and Commissar G. F. Shabalov were shot in front of formation.[303]

As for Mekhlis, in May 1942, after the defeat of the Red Army in the Crimea (where he represented the Stavka), he lost his posts of deputy NKO Commissar and head of the GlavPURKKA and was demoted to Corps Commissar, two ranks lower. However, Mekhlis remained a member of military councils until the end of the war. With Stalin's approval, he moved among nine fronts, denouncing commanders and HQ members to Stalin. After visiting the Bryansk Front in 1943, a correspondent for the military newspaper *Krasnaya zvezda* (Red Star) described Mekhlis: 'He is feared, disliked, and even hated.'[304]

Part III. Military Counterintelligence: July 1941–April 1943

CHAPTER 9

At the Moscow Gates

By August 1941, the German Army Group Center took Smolensk. On September 27, the GKO issued the disastrous 'Directive to Organize a Strategic Defense'.[1] Because of this confusing, incompetent directive, thirty-seven divisions near Vyazma and twenty-five divisions near Bryansk were encircled. In the region to the west of Moscow the Red Army lost almost a million servicemen, of whom 673,000 were taken prisoner.

Panic in Moscow

On October 2, the Germans began Operation Typhoon, their advance on Moscow.[2] Viktor Kravchenko, a witness to this event who later defected to the West, remembered the widespread alarm of those days: 'Day and night smoke belched from the chimneys of the NKVD, the Supreme Court, the Commissariat of Foreign Affairs, various other institutions and Party headquarters. Our leaders were hastily destroying records, wiping out the clues to their decades of official crimes. The government, evidently under orders from the top, was covering up its traces. The first snows of October were sooty with burnt paper.'[3] Another witness, an African-American who worked in Moscow, also recalled: 'Many Communist party members were throwing away their party credentials, some tearing them up and stuffing the pieces down the toilet, others simply tossing their party tickets with their names and pictures rubbed out, into the street. I saw scores of these passes strewn along sidewalks.'[4]

Nikolai Sbytov, head of the Air Force Fighter Command, remembered that during those days he was the only professional military commander in Moscow.[5] On October 5, his fighters noticed a German tank column within about fifty kilometers of the capital. Sbytov reported this threat to brigade Commissar Konstantin Telegin, a member of the Military Council of the Moscow District. Instead of ordering a bombardment of the column as Sbytov recommended, Telegin apparently reported Sbytov to the UOO, because suddenly Abakumov telephoned Sbytov and ordered him to come immediately to NKVD headquarters. There Abakumov interrogated Sbytov in the presence of Merkulov and Aleksandr Avseevich, head of the UOO department responsible for the air force. Abakumov was convinced that the tank sighting was false and that Sbytov was guilty of disseminating rumors aimed at starting a panic in Moscow, but he could not order Sbytov's arrest without Stalin's approval. Fortunately, Stalin believed Sbytov, and the GKO approved an attack on the very real column of German tanks.

Abakumov stayed in Moscow during the entire October crisis. However, after the war, Ivan Serov, one of his main enemies, accused him of planning a cowardly escape from Moscow.[6]

The Nazi troops were so close to Moscow that on October 15, 1941, the GKO ordered the evacuation of the main commissariats, including the NKVD, and foreign legations to Kuibyshev (currently, Samara) on the Volga River.[7] All important buildings were mined and the UOO camouflaged buildings in the Kremlin.

The next day the Germans reached the suburbs of Moscow and fearful chaos set in. A subsequent report stated: 'On October 16–18, according to incomplete data, 779 leading administrators from 438 industrial facilities fled.'[8] Approximately two million Muscovites left the city on foot. Kravchenko recalled that on October 16:

> The most hysterical rumors spread everywhere. It was said that a *coup d'état* had occurred in the Kremlin, that Stalin was under arrest, that the Germans were already…on the edge of the city… Crowds surged from street to street, then back again in sudden waves of panic.
>
> Already riots and looting had begun. Stores and warehouses were being emptied by frenzied mobs…
>
> At Sovnarkom headquarters…high officials rounded up the younger women employees for a drunken debauch that went on for hours. In hundreds of other government offices people behaved as if the end of the world had come. Aerial bombardment and rumors whipped the panic into frenzy.[9]

Another witness, the writer Arkadii Perventsev, a Communist, wrote: 'If the Germans had known what was going on in Moscow, 500 of their paratroopers could have taken over Moscow.'[10] The Germans bombarded Moscow five or six times a day, and the bombings continued through November.[11]

At the October 19 GKO meeting, Beria advised: 'We should leave Moscow or they will strangle us like chickens.'[12] Stalin strongly objected. Still, he ordered all Politburo members, except Malenkov and Beria, to move to Kuibyshev. Later he ordered Molotov and Mikoyan to come back. The GKO appointed Major General Kouzma Sinilov, former commander of the NKVD Border Guard Troops of the Murmansk Military District, as military commandant of Moscow.[13] General Sinilov's measures were harsh.

Kravchenko remembered: 'The military tribunals worked around the clock. Though many thousands were arrested and shot, it was not terror which quenched the panic. It was the news…that the Germans were withdrawing under blows from the newly arrived Siberian and Far Eastern troops.'[14]

On November 7, 1941, the anniversary of the Bolshevik revolution, Stalin ordered a traditional military parade at Red Square in Moscow. It was organized cautiously, in secrecy, and was an important statement of resistance at a time when Hitler had planned his own victorious parade in Moscow. 28,500 men, 140 cannons, 160 tanks, and 232 vehicles took part in the parade. Additionally, there were military parades in the cities of Kuibyshev, where the main governmental organizations and foreign diplomats had been evacuated, and Voronezh, where many Ukrainian organizations had been evacuated from Kiev.

In Moscow it was a very cold, snowy day. Stalin was standing on Lenin's Mausoleum in a fur cap with the earflaps turned down and knotted in front, while Marshal Semyon Budennyi inspected the parade. In a speech that was transmitted on the radio, Stalin said, in particular: 'The German-Fascist aggressors are facing a catastrophe. Currently, hunger and poverty are rampant in Germany, and during the first four months of the war Germany lost four and a half million soldiers… The German invaders are down to their last resources… A few months more—half a year, maybe a year—and Hitler's Germany will explode due to its own crimes.'[15]

If Stalin believed what he said, he was completely out of touch with reality. The troops standing in front of the Mausoleum were skeptical. Mark Ivanikhin, one of the few participants in the parade who survived the war, recalled in 2010: 'I was only eighteen, without any military experience, but even I understood that it wouldn't be possible to push the Germans out in such a short period of time.'[16] In the United States, the Soviet documentary *Moscow Strikes Back*, which featured Stalin's speech, was among four winners for Best Documentary at the 15th Annual Academy Awards in 1942. It also won the National Board of Review Award and the New York Film Critics Circle Award for Best War Fact Film. American audiences did not know that due to the bad weather Stalin's speech in the documentary was not filmed during the parade, but afterwards, in one of the Kremlin palaces, where Stalin repeated his speech in front of cameras.[17]

The fierce Soviet defense, combined with a crumbling German supply line, finally halted the German advance on November 21, 1941.[18] The German troops were stopped only 40 miles from Moscow. After regrouping, the Red Army began advancing west on December 5. Amazingly, Berlin received information about the chaos in Moscow much later, and then only from the intelligence services of other countries.[19] In the Soviet Union, discussing what happened in Moscow in October 1941 was taboo until the first detailed description was published in 1995.[20]

Executions Continue

Incredibly, the sentencing and execution of 'political enemies' continued in Moscow through October 1941.[21] A huge group of Latvian military leaders, arrested in Latvia in May–June 1941 (plus one who was arrested earlier), were sentenced to death in July 1941 as members of an anti-Soviet plot; they were executed en masse on October 16, 1941, during the height of the frenzy of fear (Appendix I, see http://www.smershbook.com). On the same day, the wives of Tukhachevsky, Uborevich, and some other executed Soviet officials were also shot. On October 28, Ulrikh and six members of the Military Collegium left Moscow for Chkalov (currently Orenburg), where the main part of the Military Collegium's staff had moved in August, but on December 19, Ulrikh was back and the Collegium continued its work in Moscow.

Ironically, the fate of the generals arrested as members of Rychagov's 'plot' was decided precisely when the need for experienced officers was the greatest. On the night of October 15, 1941, the prisoners in Moscow's Lubyanka Prison were transferred to prisons in Kuibyshev and Saratov. Three days later Beria ordered, with Stalin's approval, the execution without trial of Rychagov, his wife, 18 other 'plotters', and an additional five prisoners, including Mikhail Kedrov, the Old Bolshevik who was the first OO head.[22] A team of executioners arrived from Moscow, and on October 28 most of the prisoners were shot near the village of Barbysh, not far from Kuibyshev. The others were shot a few days later in Saratov.

On February 13, 1942, the OSO sentenced to death the rest of 'Rychagov's plotters' and a few other 'military plotters and spies', including Ivan Sergeev, former Munitions Commissar, and three of his deputies, as well as a number of other industrial managers and designers arrested in May–June 1941. They had appeared two weeks earlier on Beria's execution list of 46 people, on which Stalin wrote in blue pencil: 'Shoot to death all those listed. J. Stalin.'[23] This was the last time Beria provided Stalin with such a list. The listed were executed on February 23, 1942 (Appendix I, see http://www.smershbook.com). Now all the Rychagov-connected 'plotters' were dead, and their family members were sentenced to many years of imprisonment in labor camps or exile in Central Asia.

The Aftermath

Although the counteroffensive had started, many Red Army detachments that fought near Moscow experienced serious problems. Field OOs and Abakumov personally informed Beria about numerous problems.

In November 1941, the just-formed 1st Shock Army began its successful attack against German troops. On December 9, Abakumov reported to Beria: 'Bad organization of rear services hampers the fast advancement of the 1st [Shock] Army [at the Western Front]. Sometimes servicemen do not receive hot food for 5–6 days... On November 25, the 18th Ski Battalion did not have food at all... The army does not have the necessary number of vehicles. For instance, the 71st Rifle Brigade has only 20 trucks instead of 162.'[24]

In general, losses in the military equipment were enormous. By July 9, 1941, the Red Army lost 11,700 tanks, and by the end of 1941, it lost 6.29 million rifles and 11,000 planes.[25] But the real problem was not even the losses, but the devil-may-care attitude of Soviet servicemen to the military equipment. In February 1942, the OO head of the above-mentioned 1st Shock Army reported to Beria:

> From December 1, 1941 to January 20, 1942, total of 77 tanks were lost. Of them, 33 were destroyed by the enemy, 4 tanks drowned while crossing rivers and in swamps, and 42 tanks were disabled due to mechanical problems...
>
> From November 20 [1941] to January 21, 1942, 230 vehicles were lost. Of them, 70 trucks were lost or abandoned, 91 trucks were disabled due to mechanical problems, and the enemy destroyed 69 vehicles...
>
> Of the total number of 363 tanks taken from the enemy no tanks were repaired, and of 1,882 [enemy] vehicles only 59 have been repaired and are used now.[26]

In fact, the situation with vehicles was catastrophic. Of 272,600 that the Red Army had before the war and 206,000 that were taken for the army from civilian organizations, 271,400 were lost in battles before August 1941.[27] This considerably restricted the speed and efficiency of the Soviet offense.

There were other problems. The OO of the 20th Army of the same Western Front reported to Abakumov: 'Even during the defense...communication between the army detachments is frequently broken. As a rule, after the telephone connection has disrupted, radio transmitters are rarely used. Our men do not like transmitters and do not know how to use them... All detachments have good radio transmitters, but in insufficient numbers. There is a lack of radio operators, and some of them are poorly trained.'[28]

Soon the Western Allies helped to solve these and other problems. Two weeks before the frenzied confusion in Moscow, on October 1, 1941, the First Moscow Protocol of the lend-lease aid program was signed by American, British and Soviet representatives.[29] In fact, the first British convoy arrived in the northern Russian port of Archangel even before that, on August 31. It delivered British Valentine and Mathilda medium-sized tanks, American Bantam jeeps and Studebaker US6 trucks that Britain had received from the United States. In the summer of 1942, Studebaker trucks and radio transmitters reached the Red Army on a massive scale. Overall, the Soviets received about 400,000 Studebaker and other trucks, 422,000 field telephones, and 35,800 radio transmitters.[30] The Red Army servicemen called the trucks 'Studery', and those vehicles, along with the American military jeeps known as 'Willis', became icons of Allied aid.

Despite all the setbacks, the Red Army continued its counteroffensive until April 1942, pushing the German Army Group Center 175 miles west of Moscow.

Combat Losses, End of 1941–Early 1942

In general, Soviet combat losses from the autumn of 1941 through the spring of 1942 were enormous. The situation near Leningrad (currently St. Petersburg) is a good example.

By September 1941, Army Group North had encircled Leningrad and the 900-day siege of Leningrad had begun. On June 25, 1941, Finland started the 'Continuation War', trying to get back the part of the country lost to the Soviets in 1940, and the Finns were also shelling Leningrad. Nikolai Nikoulin, whose unit fought at the Sinyavin Heights not far from Leningrad during the winter of 1941–1942, described what the servicemen witnessed in the spring of 1942:

> Piles of corpses at the railroad looked like small hills of snow, and only the bodies that were on the top were visible. Later in the spring, when the snow melted, the whole picture became exposed, down to the bottom.
>
> On the ground there were bodies dressed in summer outfits, in soldier's blouses and boots. These were the victims of the autumn 1941 battles.
>
> On top of them, there were layers of bodies of marines in peacoats and wide black trousers.
>
> On top of the marines lay the bodies of soldiers from Siberia, dressed in sheepskin coats and Russian felt boots [*valenki*], who were killed in January–February 1942.
>
> On top of them, there was a layer of bodies of political officers dressed in quilted jackets and hats made of fabric; such hats were distributed in Leningrad during the blockade.
>
> In the next layer, the bodies were dressed in greatcoats and white camouflage gear; some had helmets, while others did not. These were the corpses of soldiers of many divisions that attacked the railroad during the first months of 1942.[31]

Hendrick Viers, who defended this railroad on the German side and whom Nikoulin met in the 1990s, told him about the combat in January 1942: 'At the early dawn, a crowd of Red Army soldiers used to attack us. They repeated the attacks up to eight times a day. The first wave of soldiers was armed, but the second was frequently unarmed, and very few could reach the road.'[32]

Contemporary St. Petersburg officials do not seem to care about those who perished. At the beginning of 2009, the remains of more than 180,000 soldiers killed in the autumn of 1941 still lay in the forest at the Sinyavin Heights. Instead of burying the remains, in 2008 the city administration used this territory as a dump.[33]

CHAPTER 10

More About OOs

Catching German spies was the main duty of OO officers. In 1941–1942, due to the disastrous situation at the front, they worked in close cooperation with the political officers. Because of their privileged position, many OO officers were out of control.

Catching German Spies

There were no special units in the OOs and the UOO that dealt with German spies. Identification of German agents was part of the routine work of the OOs. In November 1941, Pavel Zelenin, OO head of the Southern Front, issued the following order:

> Enemy intelligence agents are trying to infiltrate our military units under the cover of [Soviet] servicemen who supposedly have escaped as POWs from the enemy, or who have gotten through the encirclement or become detached from their formations. Their goals are diversion, espionage, and demoralization [of our troops]...
>
> I suggest conducting all cases against agents in the investigation departments of the OOs of the front and the armies, as well as in the OO of NKVD Troops Guarding the Rear... The divisional and brigade OOs... should conduct preliminary investigations...
>
> As a counterintelligence measure, the OO heads of the armies should introduce a practice of recruiting enemy agents, especially those who previously served in the Red Army... The front OO should approve such recruitments, as well as the dispatching of these double agents behind the enemy's front line.[1]

The NKVD Troops Guarding the Rear of the Red Army (hereinafter 'rear guard troops') that Zelenin mentions belonged to a separate directorate formed in April 1942 within the NKVD Main Directorate of Interior Troops and headed by State Security Senior Major Aleksandr Leontiev.[2] Head of the rear guard troops of a particular front reported to Leontiev and the Military Council of the front. Also, the

Military Council of the front, together with the head of the rear guard troops of the front, decided how deep in the front's rear these troops should operate.

Nikolai Stakhanov, head of the NKVD Main Directorate for Border Guard Troops, described the rear guard troops in his report to Beria about a meeting with the American major generals John R. Deane, head of the U.S. Military Mission in Moscow, and Harold R. Bull, assistant chief of staff (G-3) at Dwight D. Eisenhower's headquarters (SHAEF) in Europe.[3]

Two days before this meeting, on January 15, 1945, a group of American and British military representatives, including Dean and Bull, had a two-hour conversation with Stalin in the Kremlin.[4] The Allied generals thanked Stalin for the Soviet supportive offensive during the ongoing Battle of the Bulge (December 16, 1944–January 25, 1945).[5] In response to the generals, Stalin declared, 'We have no [special] treaty, but we are comrades,' and talked at length about the offensive, stressing the importance of the 'Cheka-type' troops for controlling German espionage in the conquered areas.

The American generals were so interested in the 'Cheka-type' rear guard troops that Beria ordered Stakhanov to provide the generals with basic information on the structure and activities of these troops. According to Stakhanov, the rear guard troops were typically placed 15–25 kilometers behind the front line, at the rear of the combat detachments. Their task was 'to fight individual agents and small intelligence-saboteur groups of the enemy'. The rear guard troops consisted of divisions of 5,000 men each; each division included three regiments, and each regiment consisted of three battalions. These troops did not have tanks or artillery, but they had vehicles for mobility.

Back in 1941, the *osobisty* constantly reported on the capturing of enemy agents. For instance, in December 1941 the OO of the Western Front reported to front commander Zhukov that from the beginning of the war, '505 agents were arrested and identified. Of them, four were recruited before the war; 380 were recruited from the POWs; 76 were civilians recruited in the occupied territories; 43 were from civilians who lived near the front line; and two agents were found among the headquarters staff'.[6] Almost a year later, during August 1942, at the Stalingrad Front '110 agents were arrested and identified...Of them, 97 were arrested at the front line and three in the front's rear, while 10 were unmasked through secret agents...Of those, 12 were commanding officers, 76 were privates, and 13 were women'.[7]

These reports did not mean that all servicemen whom the *osobisty* described as agents were, in fact, real agents. For example, many soldiers were arrested for keeping leaflets the Germans had dropped from planes. Besides the propaganda leaflets, there were also leaflets that a Soviet serviceman could use as a pass if he decided to change sides and to get through the front line to the Germans. But many soldiers kept the leaflets simply as paper for writing letters or making cigarettes. They were supplied only with low-quality tobacco called *makhorka*, and they had to roll their own makeshift cigarettes from *makhorka* and a piece of paper. German leaflets worked well for this purpose, but if an OO informer told the supervising *osobist* that a soldier had an enemy's leaflet, the soldier was usually arrested on suspicion of being an enemy agent or planning to change sides.[8] These cases were so numerous that in November 1942 the head of the Main Directorate of Military Tribunals (Justice Commissariat) and the chief military prosecutor issued a joint directive trying to prevent sentencing 'when the ill intention of the servicemen who possessed leaflets had not been established'.[9]

Here is an example of a typical OO suspect. In September 1942, the 24-year-old officer Yeleazar Meletinsky was arrested by the OO Department of the 56th Army and accused of espionage. He knew German and served in military intelligence. In his memoirs, Meletinsky wrote:

> The arrestees under investigation were kept in a big barn…separately from the sentenced placed in a special dugout. Interrogations were conducted in another semi-dugout…Strangely, only ten years [of imprisonment] were given for treason [instead of the death penalty], but a person could be shot for praising the German technical equipment. The barracks were very dirty, and everybody had lice…Convoy soldiers were extremely rude…
>
> The investigator called me up only once. 'Do you admit your guilt?' 'No.'…'We won't check anything [the investigator said]. I have enough material to shoot you to death. We won't accuse you of espionage, but we'll try you for agitation…'
>
> The military tribunal…sentenced me to 10 years in corrective labor camps plus five years of deprivation of civil rights after that term, as well as confiscation of all my possessions. I was accused of anti-Soviet agitation aimed at demoralizing the Red Army. The verdict said that I praised the Fascist regime and Hitler.
>
> The Red Army soldier who took me [from the tribunal] to the dugout where the sentenced were kept told me on the way that the German books found in my officer's field bag had caused the tribunal's decision. These were a trophy Russian-German phrase book and a book of Lutheran psalms that one of the German prisoners had given to me.[10]

The fact that Meletinsky was a Jew and, therefore, would be extremely unlikely to 'praise the Fascist regime and Hitler' only emphasizes the absurdity of the verdict. The other arrestees, falsely accused of treason, including two teenagers drafted in the nearby village, were sentenced to death and mercilessly shot. Many years later Meletinsky became a distinguished, internationally recognized linguist.

The OOs arrested not only real and imagined enemy agents, but also sent their own agents to the enemy. A report from the Stalingrad Front mentioned the OO's active counterintelligence measures:

> On the whole, 30 agents were sent to the enemy's rear in August [1942]; of them, 22 had counterintelligence duties, and eight had other tasks.
>
> Additionally, during the retreat to the new positions, 46 *rezidents* [heads of spy networks], agents, and liaison people were left at the enemy's rear. They were assigned to penetrate the enemy's intelligence organs and collect counterintelligence information.
>
> Three agents came back from the enemy's rear and brought important information about the enemy's intelligence.
>
> In August…the NKVD Special Department of the Front opened two Agent Files, one under the name '*Reid*' [Raid], about watching the safe apartments used by German intelligence in the city of Stalingrad, and another called '*Lira*' [Lyre], on watching the Yablonskaya [German] Intelligence School…
>
> Also, 10 spies were arrested.[11]

Apparently, there was no contact with the agents in the field except through the liaison people or agents who reported the information when they came back.

OOs and Political Officers

The OO officers worked on a daily basis with the political officers known as *politruki* (the plural of *politicheskii rukovoditel'*, meaning political mentor), who were responsible for enforcing correct political behavior among the servicemen.[12] In the field units, one of the duties of political officers was a distribution among members of the Party and Komsomol (Communist Youth Organization) of the 'correct' slogans that they were obliged to shout during attacks. These included 'For the Motherland!', 'For Stalin!', and 'Death to the German occupiers!'[13] However, war veterans recalled that the slogans had only propaganda value in the military newspapers because nobody would have been able to hear such shouts in a noisy battle.[14]

In July 1941, the Red Army's *politruki* were renamed military commissars (*voennye komissary*) and became independent of the military command, like OO officers.[15] Commissars, important during the Civil War, had been revived in 1937 during the Great Terror, then demoted in 1940 and made subordinate to military command. Now commissars again became very powerful, reporting only to their own headquarters, GlavPURKKA (part of the Central Committee), and not to the military commanders. Until May 1942, the GlavPURKKA was headed by Lev Mekhlis and after June 1942, by Aleksandr Shcherbakov, a Politburo candidate member.

Although commissars remained primarily responsible for troop morale and Party organizations in the army, they also monitored whether unit commanders followed orders and could recommend the arrest of servicemen they suspected of treason. Additionally, until October 1942 political commissars even had some limited oversight of field OO officers, because OO officers in corps and divisions reported not only to their OO superiors but also to the political commissars of their military units.

In October 1942, the role of political commissars was again transformed, perhaps because of improved discipline in the Red Army.[16] Political commissars, now renamed *zampolity* (the plural of *zampolit*, a short form of 'deputy commander for political matters'), began reporting once again to their military unit commanders, as well as to their own superiors.

Each corps, division, and brigade had a *zampolit* appointed by the Glav-PURKKA, and *zampolity* at these levels headed their own political departments. A corps *zampolit* reported to the Army Political Directorate, which reported to the Front Political Directorate.[17] At a regimental level there was a *zampolit* appointed by the Army Political Directorate, as well as a *partorg* (Party secretary responsible for the members of the Communist Party), a *komsorg* (secretary of the Communist Youth Organization) and an *agitator*, in charge of reading newspapers to the privates, while at a battalion level, there were a *zampolit*, a *partorg*, and a *komsorg*. *Partorgi*, *komsorgi*, and *agitatory* were appointed from among servicemen and assisted the *zampolity*. Through these chains of command many Party and Komsomol members reported on their fellow comrades. Finally, there was a company *zampolit* who every three days wrote a bulletin to his superior regarding the political morale of his company. This was an organization that spied on servicemen in addition to the OOs.

Most commanders hated the *zampolity*. Georgii Arbatov, later head of Moscow's Institute of USA and Canadian Studies, recalled:

> We, fighting commanders...secretly despised [*zampolity*] and laughed at them... In trying to justify their privileged position and participation in command decisions without professional knowledge...they made our difficult life at the front line even harder. And they ruined the lives of many good and courageous people, accusing them of "defeatist thoughts" or "enemy propaganda"...or making scapegoats of them for military failures.[18]

However, looking back at the war years, some former privates consider 'political workers' to have been necessary in the army because they were the only source of news. They also regulated the high tension among soldiers of different ethnic origins (according to many memoirs, the level of hidden anti-Semitism was very high among Russian privates).[19] Of course, through political commissars, soldiers 'received just a restricted portion of the actual information. Usually it was vague, as well'.[20]

Even now, however, other veterans still deeply despise the 'political workers' and call them names like 'rear rats and parasites'.[21] The writer Viktor Astafiev, a veteran, wrote: 'I consciously did not join the Party at the front, although in 1944 the political departments...forced almost everyone to join it... But we did not care about Stalin and about screaming "hurrah"; our dream was to drop down and have a little bit of sleep.'[22]

Although the OO head did not interfere in the day-to-day affairs of the unit commander the way a *zampolit* did, the military commander had to submit copies of all his orders to the OO officer. The OO officer could submit written questions that the commander was obligated to answer in writing. OO heads also had a say in the promotion of unit officers.[23]

Censorship was another example of joint activity of the OO and *zampolity*.[24] Servicemen were categorically prohibited from writing diaries or other personal notes, and very few of them dared to violate this prohibition.[25] All letters were severely censored. Using data culled from servicemen's letters, the OO heads reported on troop morale to Abakumov's deputy, Solomon Milshtein.[26] Each report included politically correct and incorrect excerpts from these letters. The politically incorrect letters were confiscated and destroyed, their authors were punished, and the *zampolity* of the offending writers' units were informed. OO officers were urged to remain vigilant: 'All OO heads are instructed to send agents [secret informers] to identify individuals who have voiced anti-Soviet statements and to prevent them from engaging in any anti-Soviet activity.'[27]

The OOs also reported on the work of political officers. The 7th departments of the front political directorates (and the 7th sections within the political departments of the armies) attracted the special attention of the *osobisty*. These political departments and sections were in charge of political propaganda among the enemy troops. Officers of these units interrogated German POWs, used them for writing propaganda leaflets and for radio transmissions to the German troops, and so on. This close relationship with enemy POWs was constantly monitored by the *osobisty*.[28]

In 1941, the OO and political officers were better armed than the infantry. On October 21, 1941 the commander of the armored troops, Colonel General (later Marshal) Yakov Fedorenko, reported to Stalin: "Automatic arms [machine guns]..., designed for the infantry, in fact are given to the rear units of the divisions, armies, and fronts, especially to such institutions as tribunals, prosecutor's offices, and special and political departments, and not to the fighting troops. Most commanders also have these arms... It is necessary to ban having these automatic arms in the rear units."[29] Stalin never issued any such order.

Officers Out of Control

In spite of dual control of the troops through military counterintelligence and political officers, discipline was not ideal and sometimes, even OO officers committed outright murder. On December 12, 1941, Marshal Timoshenko, commander of the Southwestern Front, and Nikita Khrushchev, of the front's Military Council, signed an order stating: 'The Head of the Special Department of the First Tank Brigade, and Assistant to the Technical Department of the Tank Regiment, ordered, without any reason, that the Lieutenant of the 1st Tank Brigade be shot to death.'[30] The order said the officers were to be tried by a military tribunal 'for overreaching their authority, unauthorized shootings, and beatings [of subordinates]'.

There is an additional note in the order: 'All members of this group were drunk.' The problem of drunken officers was serious. In August 1941, Stalin signed a GKO decision: 'Beginning September 1, 1941, every soldier and commander at the front line is to be provided with 100 grams of 40-proof vodka every day.'[31] From June 1942 on, only the front-line troops involved in offensive actions received 100 grams of vodka, while the rest received 50 grams.[32]

Most of the Great Patriotic War veterans always recalled their every-day '100 grams' with warm feeling. However, the distribution of vodka was not well managed: 'Vodka is still given to HQ members, commanders, and units with no right to receive it. Some unit commanders and commanding members of HQs use their positions to get vodka from storage in violation of orders and rules. Military councils of the fronts poorly control the distribution of vodka. The inventory of vodka in the units is not carried out satisfactorily.'[33] Tank crews even invented a method to conceal vodka they had obtained illegally. They dismantled several shells, threw the gunpowder away and replaced it with vodka, then attached projectiles back and made special marks on the shells.[34] Only the crew members could distinguish the usual kind of shells from those filled with vodka. An American POW liberated by Soviet troops from a German concentration camp reported to the American military officials in April 1945: 'Most of the Russian front-line troops, including officers, are intoxicated at all times.'[35]

Drinking was a serious problem even during the Battle of Moscow. On April 5, 1942, Stalin signed an angry order regarding the air defense (PVO) corps of Moscow:

> Discipline in the Moscow Regional PVO Corps is very poor. Drinking parties, especially among the commanding officers, are common. Poor discipline and excessive drinking are not being properly dealt with. The number of discipline violations incurred by Red Army privates, officer cadets, and low- and high-level commanders of the PVO detachments is growing.
>
> This situation must not be tolerated any more.

I order:

1. To arrest and try by military tribunal:

a) The commissar of the Main PVO Directorate, Brigade Commissar Kurganov, for chronic drinking;

b) The commissar of the 745th Anti-Aircraft Artillery Regiment, Corps Commissar Zakharov, for drinking and for not reporting [to his post] during an enemy-air-raid alert;

c) *Politruk* [political officer] of the 3rd Company of the 175th Artillery Regiment, Andreev, and the air force mechanic of the same company, Military Technician of the 2nd Rank Kukin, for a drinking party, riot, and random gunfire that resulted in the fatal shooting of Lieutenant Kazanovsky, the head of the signal company.

2. To dismiss the commander of the PVO Main Directorate, Major General of Artillery [Aleksei] Osipov, for drinking, and to demote him from his position...

[...]

10. To inform all commanding and political officers of the PVO detachments about this order.

Defense Commissar   J. Stalin.[36]

Of the mentioned officers, the fate of General Osipov is known. He was appointed commander of the Gorky Regional PVO Division, while the entire PVO Main Directorate was disbanded and its directorates and departments were placed under the military council of the Air Defense Troops.

Pyotr Todorovsky, a 19-year-old infantry platoon commander in 1944 who became a famous movie director after the war, recalled that drinking caused enormous losses among young soldiers:

Before the attack a sergeant used to bring us half of a bucket of [pure] alcohol and give each of us a cup of it... Usually a newly drafted soldier (we called them '*pervachok*' [first-time participant]) drank a lot—for instance, half of the cup—because of fear. ... After drinking too much the newly drafted soldiers were almost always killed in the first attack. And the *starichki* [old men] didn't drink at all, or only pretended that they were drinking: they touched the alcohol with their lips, but didn't swallow. Drinking a little bit helped a soldier during an attack, but drinking too much [often] resulted in his death.[37]

There were also accidents caused when servicemen stumbled upon a cache of methyl alcohol. An infantryman recalled: 'During the battle for the city of Brest a tank car full of methyl alcohol was discovered at the railroad station... A lot of soldiers...filled their flasks with that alcohol, others drank while repeating: "We'll perish anyway, while fighting."… In the battalion, I think, at least fifty passed away.'[38]

The situation described in the Timoshenko–Khrushchev order was quite typical. The military tribunals of the Don Front reported to Moscow that during the first quarter of 1942 'unauthorized executions of subordinates and crimes due to drunkenness were common among commanders'.[39] When Georgii Malenkov, a GKO member, came to inspect the Volkhov Front, the OO head reported that in March 1942 almost all of the commanding officers of the 59th Army got drunk frequently and had disreputable sexual relationships with servicewomen or so-called 'PPZhs' (an acronym of *pokhodno-polevaya zhena*, or 'campaign wife').[40]

Although the OO and political officers considered PPZhs a problem in terms of morale, marshals like Konstantin Rokossovsky and Georgii Zhukov each lived openly during the war with a PPZh, and it was a common practice for high- and mid-level commanders.[41] A lieutenant-veteran recalled: 'Many servicewomen were officers' PPZhs, but platoon commanders didn't have PPZhs. We slept in the same dugout where our soldiers slept, while a company commander had his individual dugout. So, the company commander and officers of higher posts had more favorable conditions to have a PPZh… Usually a PPZh was decorated with the "For Combat Merits" medal.'[42] High commanders were even more generous. For instance, Lidia Zakharova, Marshal Zhukov's PPZh, received the Red Banner Order, the Red Star Order, five medals, and three foreign military awards. After the Red Army crossed the border with Germany, some officers even picked up girls of 16 or 17 and kept them for a while.[43]

While there is no known record of what happened to the drunken OO men of the 1st Tank Brigade, the episode was not unusual. In 1946 Ivan Serov wrote to Stalin about the behavior of Pavel Zelenin, one of Abakumov's men and later a high-level functionary in SMERSH:

At the beginning of 1942, we [NKVD headquarters] received information that many groups among our soldiers at the Southern Front crossed the lines and went over to the enemy. At the same time, Security Major Zelenin, head of the Special Department of this front, did not prevent these treacherous actions during this difficult time, but became demoralized, lived with female typists, and gave them medals. He also enticed the wife of the head of the Army Political Department to his apartment, where he got her drunk and raped her…

C.[omrade] Abakumov called for Zelenin, but I do not know his decision.[44]

Abakumov constantly received reports from various fronts about the unprofessional behavior, misconduct and illegal actions of OO officers.[45]

During 1942, he issued several orders demanding that the OOs improve the quality of their investigative work.[46]

CHAPTER 11

Alleged New Traitors (Late 1941–Early 1943)

It sounds incredible, but draconian measures against military commanders and their arrests by Abakumov's men continued on a mass scale during the next two years, which were decisive in turning the course of the war.

Typical Accusations

From autumn 1941 to early 1943, the UOO, including Abakumov personally, continued to arrest generals at the fronts. Most of them were charged with treason and espionage (paragraph 58-1b) (Appendix I, see http://www.smershbook.com). On the whole, from 1941 to 1945, field military tribunals sentenced 164,678 so-called traitors: in 1941, 8,976; in 1942, 43,050; in 1943, 52,757; and in 1944, 69,895.[1]

Disseminating lies about the Red Army (paragraph 58-10) was the second common accusation. Any criticism of the Red Army or Party leaders, especially discussions about the disastrous period at the beginning of the war, was considered lies and anti-Soviet propaganda. For example, a former secretary of a military tribunal recalled that a colonel received ten years in a labor camp for telling his fellow officers that Marshal Semyon Budennyi, with whom he had attended military academy, could not understand the principles of fractions.[2] Among generals alone, twenty were arrested and sentenced from 1941 to early 1943 for anti-Soviet propaganda (Appendix I, see http://www.smershbook.com). Overall, at the end of 1944, prisoners sentenced on 58-10 charges constituted a third of all 392,000 political prisoners in the GULAG.[3]

The UOO also discovered new 'plots'. The purported plot of teachers at the Frunze Military Academy (Appendix I, see http://www.smershbook.com) was the most bizarre. Eight teachers (seven generals and a colonel) were arrested in November and December 1941 in the city of Tashkent, to which the Academy was evacuated from Moscow in October. As Abakumov reported to Stalin in 1945, they 'were arrested as active participants in an anti-Soviet group whose goal was to establish contacts with the Germans and to overthrow the Soviet government. During their hostile activity the participants…intended to create conditions favorable for the Germans to enter Moscow'.[4]

It is hard to believe that Abakumov seriously considered it possible that these teachers had contacts with the Germans and tried to help them to conquer Moscow. It was discovered in the late 1950s, during the rehabilitation process, that this nonsense was based on the secret reports of a female informer named Bondarenko who worked at the Political Department of the Frunze Academy.[5] Interestingly, despite the rhetoric, the 'plotters' were charged with paragraph 58-10 (anti-Soviet propaganda), and not accused of treason and plotting (which would be paragraphs 58-1b and 58-11, respectively). The teachers were brought to Moscow and kept in NKGB investigation prisons (the UOO/SMERSH did not have its own prisons), where the investigation was conducted.

As usual, under torture the arrestees were forced to 'confess', and the investigator Mikhail Likhachev, who will be mentioned in this book more than once, was especially successful in extracting these 'confessions'. However, the fates of the teachers, as well as of the other 29 generals kept in NKGB prisons, were decided only after the war, when Abakumov presented Stalin with a list of generals arrested by the UOO/SMERSH and kept in Moscow prisons without trial.

Put on Ice

The generals arrested in 1941 and brought back to Moscow, like the Frunze Academy teachers, or after Moscow prisons were evacuated in October 1941, Konstantin Samoilov and others, as well as those arrested in 1942 (Vladimir Golushkevich, Fyodor Romanov, Aleksandr Turzhansky; Appendix I, see http://www.smershbook.com) were held in solitary confinement or, in the prison's jargon, 'conserved' or 'put on ice', in the most horrifying prison of all, Sukhanovo (or Sukhanovka). In official documents, this facility was called 'Special Object No. 110'.[6] In 1938, under Beria's supervision, this small seventeenth-century monastery in the Moscow suburbs was converted into an especially harsh investigation prison, equipped with tools for torture.[7] Beria had a personal office on the second floor, connected by an elevator with the torture chambers on the first floor. Beria's elevator also reached the basement where the punishment cells, *kartsery*, were located. Later Abakumov used the same office.

Approximately 150–160 prisoners under investigation were kept in this prison. Most of the cells were extremely small—1.56 by 2.09 meters (61.4 by 82.3 inches)—especially for two prisoners.[8] For one prisoner, there was room only for a stool made of iron pipes and a table one meter long and 15.24 centimeters wide, both attached to the floor, and a narrow, but very heavy wooden folding bed (in fact, a board) attached to the wall. In the early morning the prisoner was ordered to lift the bed up and a guard locked it to the wall. In the evening, a guard unlocked the bed, and the prisoner was ordered to let it down. At night, the stool supported the bed. In the cells for two prisoners, there were two folding beds. Frequently an interrogated prisoner was kept with a stool pigeon as a cell mate.

During the day, the bed was up, and a prisoner had no choice but to sit on the iron stool and stare at the iron door of the cell; the door was equipped with a peephole through which a guard watched the prisoner from the corridor. Yevgenii Gnedin, a prisoner at Sukhanovo, recalled:

There was one guard for every three cells. The shade of the peephole was moved up almost every minute. If a prisoner made an incautious movement, the door's lock was immediately opened and a guard stepped in and inspected the prisoner and the cell.[9]

There was a window in the cell furnished with specially made glass that was corrugated, and almost opaque. The same type of glass covered a bulb attached to the ceiling. The window was fortified with bars and mesh. The guard opened a small panel above it for a few minutes every morning.

The walls were painted a depressing light-blue color. A bucket was used as a toilet, and every morning the prisoner was ordered to take the bucket out to a lavatory in the corridor to empty it. Alexander Dolgun, an American prisoner, wrote in his memoirs: 'The toilet was one of eight doors in the short corridor, four on each side [on every floor].'[10]

In Lubyanka and Lefortovo, two guards accompanied a prisoner on the way from his cell to an investigator's office. But in Sukhanovo, two guards held the prisoner's arms and the third pushed the prisoner from behind.[11] According to memoirs, investigators used 52 methods of torture in this prison, such as forcing an interrogated prisoner to sit on a stool upturned so that the stool's leg penetrated the prisoner's rectum; putting an interrogated prisoner in a cell full of cold water up to the knees for a day and a night.[12] These were typical additions to the standard severe beatings. For extra punishment, there were cold *kartsery* without a heating device and hot *kartsery* with overheating, dark *kartsery* without light, and *kartsers* so small that a prisoner could only stand.

Some prisoners (both male and female) were brought from Lubyanka and Lefortovo to Sukhanovo for a short time, to give them a psychological shock, to frighten them, or to briefly torture them. If a prisoner was not interrogated for a long time, his investigator called him once every three months to make sure that he had not gone insane.[13] Some prisoners did end up going insane, but usually they were not sent to a prison mental hospital right away, and terrified their prison neighbors with wild screams. Sometimes a prisoner managed to commit suicide despite the tight surveillance.

During the war, the 'conserved' generals were kept without interrogation. It is hard to imagine how the 'iced' prisoners managed to survive for years in the horrific conditions of Sukhanovo. They were tried only in 1951–52. At the time three of them had already died in Sukhanovo and in Butyrka Prison Hospital (the only hospital in investigation prisons in Moscow). One more general, Fedot Burlachko, died in 1949 in the MVD Kazan Psychiatric Prison Hospital, which was notorious for its inhumane treatment of prisoners.[14]

After Stalin's death Sukhanovka was not used as a prison any more, but it continued to belong to the MVD.[15] In the 1960s–70s, there was a special MVD school, then a training center for MVD troops. Although from 1992 onwards, buildings of the former prison were given step by step to the Orthodox Church, part of the MVD School existed in the monastery until 1995. The church officials completely destroyed Beria–Abakumov's office and torture chambers below it that were intact until the mid-1990s. No research of the buildings by historians, no descriptions by architects, and even no photos were made. Currently, it is a working monastery consisting of newly constructed shining buildings without any reminder of the terrifying past and tortured victims. The FSB Central Archive keeps a register of the prisoners held in Sukhanovo during Stalin's time as one of its main secrets.

Stalin's Approval

It should be remembered that generals were usually arrested with Stalin's personal approval. The case of Major General Ivan Rukhle is an example of a senseless action during a turning point of the war, leading up to the Battle of Stalingrad.

On the Stavka's decision, General Rukhle, head of the Operations Department and deputy chief of the headquarters (HQ) of the Stalingrad Front, was dismissed from his posts at the end of September 1942 and then arrested on October 5.[16] Before that, on the order of Georgii Malenkov, Stavka's representative at the Stalingrad Front, Colonel Yevgenii Polozov, HQ chief of the 4th Tank Army, together with the OO of that army, falsified materials against Rukhle. Malenkov chose Polozov for this purpose because Polozov had hated Rukhle deeply ever since Rukhle fired him from the HQ of the front for poor professional performance. Rukhle was charged with treason (Article 58-1b) during the preparation of the previous operation in Kharkov.

In May 1942, approximately 230,000 Soviet servicemen were taken prisoner near Kharkov and 87,000 were killed while attempting to get through the German encirclement. Marshal Semyon Timoshenko, commander of the Southwestern Front; Nikita Khrushchev, a member of the Military Council; and General Ivan Bagramyan, HQ chief of that front, were responsible for the ill-planned offensive that culminated in this catastrophe. After Rukhle received the plan of their offensive for implementation, he tried to contact Stalin through Nikolai Selivanovsky (head of the front OO) and Abakumov, and with their help to send Stalin a report regarding the weak points of the plan. However, Timoshenko had already declared at the HQ meeting that

'Comrade Stalin, our great friend and teacher, has approved the offensive plans of the front', and, therefore, that Rukhle acted against Stalin's will.[17] Instead of handing Rukhle's report over to Stalin, Abakumov informed Khrushchev that some HQ members were against the plan.

Timoshenko and Khrushchev soon realized that the offensive was poorly prepared and would result in total defeat. Anastas Mikoyan, a Politburo member, recalled:

> I remember well May 18 [1942], when a serious threat of the defeat of our Kharkov offensive operation was coming. Late at night a few Politburo members—Molotov, Beria, Kalinin, Malenkov, probably Andreev, and I—were in Stalin's office. We already knew that Stalin had rejected the request of the military council of the Southwestern Front to stop the offensive because of the danger of [German] encirclement. Suddenly the telephone rang.
>
> Stalin told Malenkov: 'Find out who it is and what he wants.'
>
> [Malenkov] took the receiver and told us that it was Khrushchev...
>
> Stalin said: 'What does he want?'
>
> Malenkov answered: 'On behalf of the high command [of the Southwestern Front] Khrushchev requests stopping the offensive on Kharkov immediately and concentrating the main efforts on the counterattack against the enemy.'
>
> 'Tell him that given orders are not discussed, but followed,' said Stalin. 'And then hang up.'[18]

Later, after a special investigation of the catastrophe by Aleksandr Vasilevsky, acting chief of the general staff, Stalin dismissed Bagramyan from his post, while Timoshenko and Khrushchev were reprimanded. Rukhle was chosen as a scapegoat.

Rukhle was brought to Moscow and kept in Lubyanka Prison for the rest of the war. In August 1944 Polozov, arrested for 'anti-Soviet agitation' and already sentenced, was placed together with Rukhle, apparently as a cell spy, and advised Rukhle to 'confess'. But only in February 1952 did the MGB Department for Investigation of Especially Important Cases conclude the case. Rukhle was charged with a 'criminal attitude toward his duties while being at high positions in the HQ of the Southwestern, and then the Stalingrad Front' under Article 193-17b. The case was so weak that on September 4, 1952, after the hearing, the Military Collegium returned materials to the MGB for an additional investigation.

On March 23, 1953, after Stalin's death, the Military Collegium heard Rukhle's case for the second time. Now he was accused of a 'criminal attitude toward his duties' (Article 193-17a), but only at the Stalingrad Front. Rukhle strongly denied his guilt, but the Collegium sentenced him to a ten-year imprisonment, which he had already spent in Lubyanka. Rukhle was released, and on May 29, 1953, the Plenum of the Supreme Court rehabilitated him. After this his rank was restored and he continued his military career.

One lucky navy commander was released through the intervention of a friend. Investigator Mikhail Likhachev, who has already been mentioned, arrested Admiral Gordei Levchenko, deputy Navy Commissar and commander of the troops in the Crimea, on November 16, 1941, after the Crimea had fallen. Later an important investigator in SMERSH and the MGB, Likhachev, who had never been in battle, cynically asked Levchenko: 'What was your criminal activity in connection with the surrender of most of the territory of the Crimean Peninsula to the enemy?'[19]

On January 25, 1942, Levchenko was sentenced to a prison term of ten years in a labor camp, and promptly the next day a transcript of Levchenko's interrogation was on Stalin's desk. But Navy Commissar Nikolai Kuznetsov courageously defended Levchenko, and a few days later Stalin pardoned Levchenko, who was demoted to captain of the first rank and returned to the fleet. He was appointed commandant of the Leningrad and then the Kronstadt Naval bases. In 1944, he was promoted again to deputy VMF Commissar.

Many other navy commanders were punished and some were executed. On December 1, 1942, Kuznetsov wrote to the Military Council of the Black Sea Fleet: 'The number of those convicted is enormously high compared to the other fleets…Report to me on the reasons for this large number of convictions and on your measures.'[20] Little information is available about most of these cases. Some commanders and pilots were punished if a vessel was blown up by a mine. Others were convicted because they destroyed their vessels to prevent them from being taken by the enemy, an action that tribunals considered treacherous.

The Purges Widen

In June 1942, Beria suggested the GKO would widen the number of crimes for which family members of perpetrators would be persecuted.[21] Espionage was one of his examples. From the beginning of the war, the OOs arrested over 23,000 servicemen on charges of espionage, attempts at treason against the Motherland, and treacherous intention. Additionally, in the non-occupied territories of the USSR 1,220 arrestees were sentenced as spies and 2,917 arrestees accused of spying were under investigation. In Beria's opinion, family members of those sentenced to death for espionage needed to be punished.

Beria also reported to Stalin on another extremely troubling trend: since the beginning of the war, sixteen servicemen had killed their commanders and gone over to the enemy. In fact, there was always tension between privates and commanding officers in the Red Army. As the World War II veteran Vasil' Bykov recalled, the relationships within the army were based on 'the rule of complete obedience to superiors and cruelty without mercy toward subordinates'.[22] He also explained, from his own experience: 'Every serviceman felt fear coming from a threat behind, from superior commanders and all punishment organs [OOs, SMERSH, NKVD troops]…When a commander promises to shoot you on the spot in the morning if you don't take back a farm or a height just captured by the enemy…you do not know who to fear more, the Germans or your commander. A German bullet may miss you, but the bullet of your commander won't, especially if he involves a military tribunal.'[23]

Tension also existed due to the special privileges enjoyed by commanding officers. Unlike privates, commanders received an additional food ration called *doppayok*, which included a can of meat, a piece of butter, a package of sugar, and good quality tobacco or even cigarettes.[24] Privates respected only those officers who shared their additional rations with them. An additional privilege was introduced in April 1942, when commanders from the company level up, as well as their deputies, were ordered to have *ordinartsy* (orderlies or batmen)—privates who were their personal servants.[25] As a result, a disrespected or cruel officer was always at risk because he could be easily shot by his own men in combat, when the killer could not be identified, or else left wounded and unattended on a battlefield.[26] Apparently, the cases Beria singled out were unusual because the perpetrators subsequently deserted to the enemy.

In answer to Beria's suggestions, on June 24, 1942 Stalin signed an extremely strong GKO Decision on the persecution of family members of all traitors, military and civilian, who had been sentenced to death under Article 58-1a (even in absentia) by tribunals or the OSO.[27] The included crimes were: spying for Germany and its allies; changing sides; aiding the German occupiers; participation in the punitive organs or administration established by the Germans in the occupied territories; attempted or intended treason. Now the relatives of the condemned (*chsiry*) were automatically arrested and sent into exile for five years on the decision of the OSO. As for cases of killing commanders, Beria sent a new instruction to the OO heads at the fronts:

> 1. Each terrorist act against commanders and political officers in the Red Army and Military-Marine Fleet committed by a private or a low-level commander must be carefully investigated. Persons who commit a terrorist act must be shot to death in front of their units, like deserters and servicemen with self-inflicted injuries. The decision [to execute] must be authorized by the head of the OO. A special record on the execution of the guilty serviceman should be written.

2. The local NKVD office in the territory where the relatives of the ex-ecuted person live must be informed via a ciphered telegram to take the appropriate legal measures against them.28

No information is available on how many servicemen were executed following this instruction, but these and similar instructions remained in effect after the UOO became SMERSH in 1943.

Chapter 12

Special Tasks of the OOs

In addition to finding traitors and spies among the troops, Abakumov's men were charged with some general tasks such as clearing regions near front lines of the local civilian population, organizing barrage units behind the fighting Soviet troops—the role of *osobisty* and later SMERSH officers most hated by Russian veterans—and vetting former POWs.

Civilian Casualties

In 1941, the OOs were involved in 'cleansing' regions near the front lines—that is, clearing out the local Russian population. Stalin ordered the troops to show no consideration for civilians caught up in military actions. In November 1941, he advised the commanders of the Leningrad Front: 'While moving forward, do not try to take over a particular place…[but instead] raze built-up areas to the ground and burn them down, burying the German staffs and units hiding there. Leave any sentimentality aside and destroy all built-up areas in your path. This is the best course.'[1]

Four days later the Stavka (Stalin and Shaposhnikov) ordered the de-struction of villages in the enemy rear:

1. All built-up areas in the German rear located in a 40–60 kilometer zone from the front line and 20–30 kilometers to the left and right of the roads must be destroyed and burned down.

To destroy the built-up areas in this location, aviation should be sent in immediately; intensive artillery and mortars should also be used…

3. During enforced retreats of our units in various parts [of the front line], the Soviet locals must be taken with the troops, and buildings in all built-up areas must be destroyed, without exception, to prevent the enemy from using them.[2]

A directive of the Military Council of the Western Front ordered the OOs to take charge of enforcing the eviction of civilians: 'All citizens who

resist eviction must be arrested and transferred to the NKVD organs…
This order is to be executed by local officials and Special Departments of
the formations and units.'[3]

Stalin's cable (paragraphs added) to the leaders of the defense of Leningrad illustrates his callous attitude toward his own countrymen:

To: Zhukov, Zhdanov, Kuznetsov, Merkulov

There are rumors that the German scoundrels, while marching to Leningrad, are sending old men and old women, along with younger women
and children, ahead of their troops as civilian delegates from the occupied
regions with a request to the Bolsheviks to surrender LENINGRAD. There
are also rumors that among the Leningrad Bolsheviks are people who think
that arms should not be used against such delegates.

In my opinion, if such people do in fact exist among the Bolsheviks, they
should be the first to be destroyed because they are more dangerous than the
fascists. My advice is: do not be sentimental, kick the enemy and its supporters, whether they volunteered to be human shields or not, in their teeth. War
is implacable, and those who are weak or hesitant are the first to be defeated.

If one among us hesitates, he will be the main person guilty of the downfall of Leningrad. You must destroy the Germans and their delegates, no
matter whether they volunteered or not, and kill the enemies. There should
be no mercy toward the German scoundrels or their delegates.

I ask you to inform the commanders and commissars of all divisions and
corps about this, as well as the Military Council of the Baltic Fleet and
commanders and commissars of ships.

September 21, 1941   J. Stalin[4]

Most of the evicted civilians were doomed to die. In July 1942, the
German Secret Field Police reported from the occupied territory: 'Refugees
from the areas of military actions…frequently eat peculiar bread consisting
of rotten potatoes from the previous season mixed up with moss and gar-
bage… Many times we found the corpses of female refugees who had died
of hunger. It is not surprising that under these circumstances refugees join
partisans or begin stealing and robbing while moving around alone or in
groups.'[5]

Between 15 and 17 million Soviet civilians died during the Great Patriotic War.[6] Apparently, the evicted persons constituted a high percentage
of this number.

Teenagers were special OO targets. In December 1941, Nikolai Selivanovsky, OO head of the Southwestern Front, who would later be Abakumov's first deputy in SMERSH, ordered that 'all teenagers appearing at the
front line and in the rear who do not have parents, or have lost their parents' were to be detained and questioned.[7] These teenagers were suspected

of being German agents. Three weeks later the acting chief USSR prosecutor approved the death sentence for treason and espionage for Soviet citizens aged 16 and older.[8]

Inevitably, the entire population of ethnic Germans living in the Soviet Union became suspects. During 1942, all ethnic German males aged 15 to 55 and females aged 16 to 45 were 'mobilized' (in fact, arrested) for work in the 'labor battalions' supervised by the NKVD.[9] On October 14, 1942, the GKO ordered that the same measures be applied to all nationalities with whom the Soviet Union was in a state of war—Romanians, Hungarians, Italians, and Finns. All such people were considered a potential 'fifth column'.

Barrage Units

The cruelty of Stalin's draconian orders could not prevent soldiers from retreating in 1941, and the OOs and the newly created NKVD barrage units (*zagraditel'nye otryady* or, for short, *zagradotryady*; literally, 'fence detachments'), which belonged to the OOs, were tasked with preventing retreats and desertions. These units are remembered with deepest hatred by literally every war veteran who fought at the front line and survived. As during the war with Finland, the barrage units were usually positioned behind the fighting troops, firing on them until they turned around if they started to retreat. In June 1941, OO barrage detachments also scoured the roads and train stations near the front lines for deserters.[10] From July 19, 1941, barrage units grew until the divisional and corps OOs had NKVD barrage platoons, an army OO had a company, and an OO directorate of the front had a barrage battalion. On October 31, 1941, Abakumov's deputy Milshtein reported to Beria:

> From the beginning of the war until October 10, 1941, the NKVD Special Departments and the NKVD Barrage Units for Guarding the Rear detained 657,364 servicemen who detached from their units or deserted from the front.
>
> Of them…Special Departments captured 249,969 men, and… NKVD Barrage Units…captured 407,395 servicemen.
>
> Of those, 632,486 men were sent back to the front…
>
> By decisions of Special Departments and military tribunals, 10,201 men were shot; of that number, 3,321 men were shot in front of their formations.[11]

By October 1942, 193 NKVD barrage units were operating at all fronts. Grigorii Falkovsky, a former infantryman, recalled in 2008 the death of his friend, Naum Shuster, at the beginning of the Battle of Kursk in July 1943: 'A *zagradotryad* was stationed behind our backs… A few soldiers scrambled out of the first row of our just-destroyed trenches trying to save themselves from the [German] tanks, and rushed toward us. My friend Naum Shuster was among them. He ran straight toward a lieutenant, a member of the *zagradotryad*. And when Naum was within three meters of him, the lieutenant shot Naum point-blank with his handgun, firing directly into Naum's forehead. Naum died instantly. This scoundrel killed my friend!'[12]

In addition to these OO units, Stalin ordered that each rifle division have a barrage unit, 'a battalion of reliable soldiers'.[13] Soldiers called these units 'rear outposts', 'covering forces', or even 'Mekhlis's men'. A survivor from the Western Front recalled: 'They shot everybody who did not have a special permit to leave the front line, and sometimes even those who had the permits, but didn't have time to show them.'[14]

Barrage units were unable to stop the defeat of troops encircled by the enemy. In mid-1942, possibly the worst situation was in the 2nd Shock Army at the Volkhov Front, where the barrage units were formed in April 1942.[15] By June 1942, many detachments of this army were completely cut off from supplies. Later, the head of the front's OO reported to Abakumov that in June 'there were days when servicemen received no food at all and some died of hunger. Zubov, deputy head of the political department of the 46th Division, detained Afinogenov, a private of the 57th Rifle Brigade, who had cut a piece of flesh from the corpse of a dead Soviet soldier for food. Afinogenov died of exhaustion on the way'.[16] More likely, he was shot on the spot because there was no mercy for cannibals. On July 11, 1942, 2nd Shock Army commander Andrei Vlasov was taken prisoner while trying to get through the enemy encirclement. This was the same Lieutenant General Vlasov who soon began the creation of the Russian Liberation Army (ROA) under German control. Contrary to Vlasov, Aleksandr Shashkov, head of the OO of the 2nd Shock Army, committed suicide rather than be taken prisoner.

The NKVD rear guard troops also could not stop the wave of deserters at the Volkhov Front and in nearby areas. In September 1942, the deputy head of the NKVD Directorate of the Leningrad Province complained to Moscow in a report with the long title 'On the Inadequate Supervision of the Barrage Service of Field Units and NKVD Troops Guarding the Rear of the Northwestern and Volkhov Fronts and the 7th Separate Army':

As a result of the decreased attention of the Special Organs [OOs] of the field detachments and headquarters of the NKVD Troops...the number of deserters recently increased in the rear of front units.

The regional NKVD organs and militia [police] arrested 381 deserters in 1942...

Deserters are leaving their units with arms, documents, and horses and they even steal vehicles. In the forests in the rear of the troops, deserters are building comfortable dugouts where they can live for a long time. They are robbing [the local population], and are real bandits. Upon detection and during arrests they are putting up armed resistance.[17]

Nikolai Nikoulin, an infantry veteran, explained in his memoirs how the whole punishment system worked before, during, and after attacks:

> The troops used to attack while being galvanized by fear. Facing the Germans with all their heavy machine guns and tanks, [and enduring the] horrific mincing-machine-like bombing and artillery shelling, was terrifying. But the inexorable threat of being shot to death [by our own side] was no less frightening.
>
> To keep an amorphous crowd of poorly trained soldiers under control, shootings were conducted before a combat. Some weak, almost dying soldiers, or those who had accidentally said something anti-Soviet, or, occasionally, deserters, were used for this purpose. The division was formed into the shape of the [Russian] letter 'П', and the doomed were slaughtered without mercy. As a result of this 'prophylactic political work', the fear of the NKVD and commissars was deeper than the fear of the Germans.
>
> And during the attack, if somebody turned back, he was shot by the barrage detachment. Fear forced soldiers to move forward and be killed. This was exactly what our wise [Communist] Party, [supposedly] the leader and organizer of our victories, was counting on.
>
> Of course, shootings to death also continued after an unsuccessful combat. And if regiments retreated without an order, barrage detachments used heavy machine guns against them.[18]

Barrage units existed until October 1944.

Vetting POWs

In August 1941, Stalin ordered commanders, political commissars, and OOs at the corps and division levels to write up lists of servicemen who 'had surrendered to the enemy', and to send these lists to the General Staff.[19] This was a preparation for the *fil'tratsiya* (vetting; literally, 'filtering') of Soviet servicemen who had been POWs or had been encircled by German troops.

Three months later, in December 1941, the GKO ordered the setting up of special NKVD camps to assist in vetting 'former Red Army servicemen who were captured or surrounded by the enemy'.[20] From 1941 to 1942, twenty-two of these camps were organized, and the officers of the OO, and later SMERSH, conducted the interrogations there. The vetting procedure in the NKVD Podolsk Camp near Moscow in 1944 was described by Junior Lieutenant Roman Lazebnik in a 2008 interview:

During the night we were brought to a camp surrounded by two lines of barbed wire. Immediately…we were given the uniforms of privates without officers' shoulder boards, as well as soldiers' boots, and brought to barracks. Our barrack was for the Red Army commanders who had been taken prisoner or were in the detachments surrounded by the enemy. There were also barracks for privates and sergeants, and separate barracks for civilians. In the barracks, there were iron beds [not wooden bunks, as in labor camps]. We were given 350 grams of bread daily and a bowl of porridge twice a day… Daily newspapers were brought to our barrack… It was forbidden to write letters to relatives.

No officer in the barrack talked about his past, the war or his experiences as a prisoner… The atmosphere was very tense in terms of morale, and some officers could not bear the waiting. One officer threw himself at the camp's fence which was alive with high-voltage electricity… It was terrible torture to wait, and hope…

After vetting, 95 per cent of officers were sent to penal battalions… Interrogations were conducted only during the night, and officers were interrogated every night. There were no beatings, but the *osobisty* had other methods for breaking an interrogated prisoner.

My investigator was calm and behaved quite correctly. He never mentioned his name. He did not beat me up or threaten me while he was methodically asking questions. One night I was surprised by not being taken for an interrogation, and in the morning… I was called up to the camp's *komendatura* [administration office], where they asked me if I had complaints or was beaten during interrogations… They told me that I would be released as a serviceman who had been successfully vetted and would be sent as a private to the army in the field… The *osobisty* advised me not to tell anybody that I had been vetted.[21]

For each prisoner in these special camps, OO/SMERSH investigators opened a *Fil'tratsionnoe delo* or Filtration File, which contained transcripts of interrogations and other materials. As proof that the prisoner had not collaborated with the Germans, confirmation of the interrogation details was required from at least two people who were with the prisoner during his internment.

According to the NKVD report dated October 1944, the total number of Soviet servicemen, who had been German POWs or encircled by the enemy before breaking out, vetted in filtration camps to date was 354,592. Of them, 50,441 were officers.[22] The report stressed that although the camps were administered by the NKVD 'the vetting…is conducted by counterintelligence SMERSH departments' and 11,556 of those vetted had been arrested by OO/SMERSH departments. Among the arrested by SMERSH, 2,083 servicemen were identified as enemy intelligence and counterintelligence agents, and 1,284 were officers.

Of those not arrested, only 60 percent of the officers were sent back to the army to continue their service. The remaining 40 percent were demoted to private and sent to penal assault battalions (*shturmovye batal'ony*) created in the Moscow, Volga, and Stalingrad military districts on Stalin's order.[23] Each assault battalion consisted of 929 demoted officers who were used, in Stalin's words, for 'the most active parts of the fronts', such as attacks through minefields. The chance of survival in an assault battalion was almost zero. The few survivors were recommended for promotion to their previous ranks and positions.

In addition, 30,740 servicemen were sent to the 'labor battalions' to work in the military industry. Although they were not formally convicted, they were treated as prisoners and forced to work in these battalions for a few months to as long as two years. By May 1945, the number of men in the filtration camps had jumped to 160,969 servicemen. They were used as forced labor workers by 23 industrial commissariats while still under investigation.

Aleksandr Pechersky, the famous leader of the 1943 escape from the Sobibor Nazi extermination camp, was among the rare survivors of the assault battalions.[24] After his escape, Pechersky fought in a partisan detachment. Then the detachment joined the Red Army, and Pechersky was vetted and sent to the 15th Separate Assault Rifle Battalion.[25] After he was wounded in battle, Pechersky was released from the assault battalion to continue his service in the regular troops.

Here is an example of a typed certificate for the survivor Luka Petrusev (the formatting of the Russian original is preserved, including the typical two-line levels of signatures following the military hierarchical positions of signatories):

SECRET

EXCERPT from ORDER
No. 0181
to the TROOPS of the WESTERN FRONT
March 6, 1944   Red Army in the Field

The servicemen of the 4th Separate Assault Rifle Battalion who have redeemed their guilt [a special Soviet expression for such cases] in battles with the German occupiers are restored to their rights as officers and are listed:
[Names 1 through 4 are not given]

5. Former commander of the 219th Howitzer Artillery Regiment of the 64th Rifle Division, Lieutenant Luka Kouz'mich PETRUSEV is listed in the reserve of the 2nd Separate Regiment of Reserve Officers of the front.

For the Commander of Troops	Member of the Military Council
of the Western Front	Lieutenant General
Lieutenant General	/L. MEKHLIS/
/POKROVSKY/	

This is true: Chief of the Regimental HQ
Major /POLTAEV/ [signature]
[Stamp][26]

Not everyone survived long enough to be vetted because many had perished earlier at the hands of the *osobisty*. The former secretary of a military tribunal describes a typical scenario: 'The head of the NKVD's OO of the corps was a tall, heavy man. He used to come to the cell that held the servicemen destined for vetting…He would pick a weak or shy serviceman and take him away. Then he would beat him up with his enormous fists until the man confessed to being a spy. After this came a painful investigation and a tribunal meeting, followed by an execution.'[27]

Penal Detachments

By June 1942, the OOs had arrested 23,000 servicemen for spying and treason as well as for 'treacherous intentions' since the beginning of the war.[28] An OO deputy head's report to Abakumov illustrates the scale of arrests made by the OOs at the Stalingrad Front:

> On the whole, from October 1, 1942, to February 1, 1943, according to incomplete data, special organs of the Front [the OOs] arrested 203 cowards and panic-mongers who escaped from the battlefield. Of them:
>
> 49 men were sentenced [by military tribunals] to death, and shot in front of the troops;
>
> 139 men were sentenced to various terms in labor camps and sent to punishment battalions and companies.
>
> Additionally, 120 cowards and panic-mongers were shot in front of the troops on decisions of special organs.[29]

Now, in mid-1942, Stalin decided not to waste the sentenced men with mass executions, but to use most of them in penal detachments. On July 28, 1942 in his infamous Order No. 227 'No Step Back!' Stalin ordered the creation of penal battalions (*shtrafnye batal'ony*) for officers (not to be confused with *shturmovye batal'ony*, where officers were sent after vetting) and penal companies (*shtrafnye roty*) for privates.[30] Tribunals could order the suspension of any sentence, even the death penalty, and send the convicted serviceman to a penal detachment instead. Interestingly, in the order Stalin mentioned similar punishment units in the German army as his reason for creating their Russian counterparts. Information about penal detachments in the Red Army has become available only recently.

Commanders from the brigade level up also had the right to send an officer, with no investigation or trial, to a penal battalion for one to three months. For instance, in April 1944 Georgii Zhukov, the first deputy defense Commissar, sent F. A. Yachmenov, commander of the 342nd Guard Rifle Corps, to a penal battalion for two months for not following orders and for behaving, in Zhukov's opinion, in a cowardly fashion.[31] And from August 1942, commanders at the corps and division level had the authority to send privates and junior officers to penal companies for crimes such as desertion or failure to follow orders.[32] Therefore, it was easy for commanders to dispose of any serviceman they disliked. Criminals released from labor camps (750,000 in 1941 and 157,000 in 1942) were also enlisted in penal companies, although political prisoners were not released.[33]

A penal battalion consisted of 800 former officers called 'penal privates' or 'exchangeable fighters', while a penal company comprised 150–200 privates. One to three penal battalions were formed at each front, and each army had between five and ten penal companies. By 1944, overall the Red Army had 15 penal battalions and 301 penal companies. The commanders and *zampolity* assigned to penal units were trusted, experienced officers. A representative (*operupolnomochennyi*) of the OO directorate of the front was also attached to each penal battalion.

The commander of the penal battalion and his *zampolit* had the right to shoot a penal private instantly if he refused to follow orders. For these officers, a month of service in a penal unit was equivalent to six months in the regular troops. A radio operator attached to a penal battalion in 1944 recalled of the punished officers: 'Most of them were decent men…of high performance of duty and high military morale… Foul language (*maternaya bran*) was considered inappropriate among them [although it was a common language of Red Army officers]… They did not take prisoners. They also did not take German trophies…[including] bottles of schnapps and pure alcohol.'[34]

Chances of survival in a penal unit, as in an assault battalion, were very slim, because these troops were used for forced reconnaissance or attacks through minefields. '*Shtrafbat* [penal battalions] and death were synonymous', according to one military tribunal member.[35] In 1944, monthly losses in the regular military troops totaled 3,685 men, while in the penal units, the figure was 10,506.[336] At least 1.5 million servicemen served in the penal units from 1942 to 1945. It is unknown how many survived. If a serviceman completed his term or was wounded in battle, he was promoted to his former rank and sent back to a regular unit, and he had his military awards returned to him.

German POWs

During the first year of war with Germany, Soviet troops took very few German prisoners. By 1942, only 9,174 captured German and Romanian soldiers were being held in NKVD POW camps.[37] According to OO reports to Abakumov, some German soldiers surrendered voluntarily.

Most German and other foreign prisoners, as well as wounded enemy soldiers, were simply shot on sight or killed after being tortured.[38] Stalin himself issued a direct instruction to General Georgii Zhukov: 'You should not believe in prisoners of war. You should interrogate a prisoner under torture and then shoot him to death.'[39]

After interrogating prisoners, the OO would send only a few of them to the NKVD camps for POWs in the rear. Most were shot. Here is a report on the interrogation of a captured German pilot who refused to answer the questions of the OO officer (the formatting of the Russian original, which has the typical structure found in NKVD/SMERSH documents, is retained):

'I approve'

December 18, 1942
Deputy Head of the NKVD OO of the Western Front,
Major of State Sec.[urity]
/Shilin/

DECISION

Army in the field, December 18, [1942]. I, deputy head of the 6th Section of the NKVD OO of the Western Front, Captain of State Sec.[urity] Gordon, after having examined the materials of the case of a POW of the German Army, a fighter pilot, Lieutenant Justel Martin, b. 1922 in the town of Osterade (East Prussia),

FOUND OUT [that]

Justel was a member of the Hitler youth organization, volunteered for the German Army in 1939, and actively participated in the actions of the German occupation in France and other countries. For this, he was awarded an Iron Cross of the 2nd Class. He did not give testimony on the military equipment of the German Army, saying that he knew nothing about it.
On the basis of the above, I

DECIDED [that]

Justel Martin SHOULD BE SHOT as an uncompromising enemy of the USSR.

Deputy head of the 6th Section of the OO NKVD,
Captain of State Sec.[urity] [signature] /Gordon/

'I agree':
Head of the 6th Section of the OO NKVD of the W[estern] F[ront],
Captain of State Sec.[urity] [signature] /Zaitsev/
December 18, 1942.[40]

The second document, handwritten, reported on the execution of the pilot:

Army in the field, December 19, 1942

We, the undersigned Jr. Lieutenant of State Sec.[urity] Ostreiko and Jr. Lieutenant of State Sec.[urity] Samusev, wrote this document to give notice that today, at 2:00 a.m., we executed the decision of the NKVD OO of the W/f [Western Front] regarding the POW Justel Martin.

We sign after the execution,

[signatures] Samusev, Ostreiko.[41]

Of course, not all POWs refused to answer the counterintelligence officers.[42] If a German prisoner gave important information during his first interrogation, he might be sent to Moscow for further questioning by the head of the 4th Department of the UOO, frequently with colleagues from other departments.

The policy of taking as few enemy POWs as possible continued until the end of World War II. In 1944, 2nd Ukrainian Front commander Marshal Ivan Konev described to Yugoslavian Communist Milovan Djilas the Soviet victory at Korsun'-Shevchenkovsky in January 1944. Djilas recalls:

> Not without exultation, [Konev] sketched a picture of Germany's final catastrophe: refusing to surrender, some eighty, if not even one hundred, thousand Germans were forced into a narrow space, then tanks shattered their heavy equipment and machine-gun nests, while the Cossack cavalry finally finished them off. 'We let the Cossacks cut up as long as they wished. They even hacked off the hands of those who raised them to surrender!' the Marshal recounted with a smile.[43]

However, by 1943 the Soviets had begun to capture significant numbers of POWs. On January 30, 1943, the commander in chief of the German troops that encircled Stalingrad, Field Marshal Friedrich von Paulus, surrendered his army.[44] Of approximately 100,000 German servicemen and 19,000 'hiwis' (Soviet POW volunteers used as noncombatants) who became prisoners, only 5,000 Germans—mostly officers, who were treated better than privates—survived the Soviet camps.[45] From Stalingrad onwards, a huge flow of German, Italian, Spanish, and Hungarian POWs began to populate POW camps inside Russia. Some of the captured intelligence officers ended up in Lubyanka Prison in the hands of the UOO.

In general, Soviet propaganda depicted the Germans as subhuman beings. Here is an example of a 'politically correct' excerpt from a letter written by Private Il'ichev to his relatives, which was included in an official OO report (in translating the letter, I have tried to capture the flavor of the Russian text): 'I was a live witness to the surrender of the Fascist scum on a mass scale not far from the town of Kalinin. I wish you could see the miserable and terrifying shape of these dogs in human appearance… The day is coming when our army will beat up this scum on its own territory. Then no one will have mercy, even toward a three-month-old child. I will personally tear to pieces a degenerate [child] of these dogs.'[46]

The attitude of civilians toward the Germans was similar. Nikolai Gavrilov, a Muscovite who visited the city of Kaluga (only 100 miles from Moscow) just after it was liberated from the German troops on December 30, 1941, witnessed the following scene: 'I saw children sliding down a hill… After I approached them, I realized that they were using [as a sled] the frozen body of a Fritz [a generic name for a German soldier in Russia during World War II]. His boots had been removed and his feet were cut off. Water was poured over the body, and it was covered with dung. The nose was destroyed… The kids pulled the body uphill using a rope with a hook. The 'burden' was very heavy, and they worked hard.'[47]

With the continuation of the war, the morale of the German POWs was changing. Lazar Brontman, a front journalist, wrote in his diary in March 1944: 'Major Shemyakin, former professor of psychology at Moscow University…introduced an interesting taxonomy: a) the Germans taken prisoner in 1941–42 were proud and arrogant; they began talking only after being punched in the ear; b) a German lance corporal captured in 1943, during the Stalingrad battle…typically not only ordered POWs to line up, but also squatted down beside the line, to check and realign; c) the Germans taken in 1943–44 were completely apathetic and indifferent.'[48]

In the meantime, in the summer of 1942, the German Army Group South followed Hitler's order 'to secure the Caucasian oilfields' and moved to the Northern Caucasus. Although on August 21 the German soldiers raised a Nazi flag on Mount Elbrus, the highest peak in Europe, the Red Army quickly pushed the Germans from that area.

By February 1943, after the surrender of Paulus's Sixth Army in Stalingrad, the Soviet troops began to regain what they had lost during the previous two years of war. For almost two years a huge territory of Ukraine, Belorussia and a part of Russia had been controlled by the German occupation military and civilian administration, in which German security services played an important role. Additionally, in this territory various German security services opened numerous spy schools that recruited volunteers from the Soviet POWs and local population. At this turning point it became clear that military counterintelligence needed to focus its attention on the real German intelligence and counterintelligence services, and not on the alleged spies within the Red Army. In the meantime, the structure and activity of the German intelligence and counterintelligence services was very complex.

Part IV. German Intelligence Services at the Eastern Front

CHAPTER 13

German Military Intelligence at the Eastern Front

By 1943, a complex German intelligence network existed at the Eastern Front and in the occupied territories. After the creation of SMERSH, Soviet counterintelligence's main goal became finding and arresting members of German intelligence and counterintelligence. Arrest of Soviet collaborators and vetting of Soviet citizens living in areas that had been occupied by German troops was also an important part of SMERSH's work. Since the German secret services at the Eastern Front have never been described in detail in historical sources in English, their general structure and activities are presented below.

There were two main German intelligence services, the Abwehr, military intelligence and counterintelligence, and the SD (Sicherheitsdienst) or Amt (Office) VI, the foreign intelligence within the State Security Main Office (Reichssicherheitshautamt or RSHA) of the SS (Schutzstaffel, a military organization of the Nazi Party). Abwehr can be described as the Red Army's Intelligence Directorate merged together with the UOO, while the RSHA's function was similar to that of the GUGB in the NKVD or the NKGB in 1941. In addition to their headquarters in Berlin, both services had branches in the field and in the occupied territory.

Abwehr, its Leaders and the RSHA

Abwehr was part of the Nazi military leadership structure. Formally, the High Command of the Armed Forces (Oberkommando der Wehrmacht or OKW) directed operations of the German Armed Forces that included the Army (Heer), Navy (Kriegsmarine), and Air Force (Luftwaffe). Abwehr was one of four OKW branches, and its full name was the Overseas Department/Office in Defense of the Armed Forces High Command (Amt Ausland /Abwehr im Oberkommando der Wehrmacht). The OKW's Operations Branch distributed Abwehr's intelligence information and its summaries to the intelligence evaluation sections of the army, navy, and air force. Admiral Wilhelm Canaris, Abwehr's head, reported to the German High Command, consisting of OKW Chief Wilhelm Keitel, Operations

Branch Chief Alfred Jodl, and his deputy, Walter Warlimont. Canaris was 'a slim man of medium height…possessed of an extraordinary lively intelligence'.[1] Every day the German High Command reported to Hitler about the war situation, but the most important intelligence information Canaris reported to Hitler personally.

Abwehr's structure was established on June 1, 1938, four months before Beria reorganized the NKVD.[2] Abwehr had three operational departments (Abteilungen) of five: I (intelligence), II (sabotage), and III (counterintelligence). Its headquarters in Berlin were small; in March 1943 only sixty-three officers served in Abteilung I, thirty-four in Abteilung II, and forty-three in Abteilung III.[3] Therefore, Abteilung III's HQ in Berlin was 15 times smaller than SMERSH's HQ in Moscow (646 officers) organized the same year with a similar counterintelligence function.[4]

Abwehr's Abteilung I collected intelligence on foreign armies, was in charge of identifying foreign spies in the armed forces (similar to the UOO and partly to the SMERSH mandate), disseminating disinformation among enemies, and guarding military and state secrets.[5] It consisted of twelve groups, organized according to geography and economic principles. Colonel Hans Piekenbrock, 'a Rhinelander who enjoyed life and was always ready for a joke', headed Abteilung I from 1936 until March 1943 and was, possibly, Admiral Canaris's best friend.[6] Admiral Canaris called him 'Pieki', and 'Pieki' 'called Canaris "Excellency", a title to which general officers had a right under the Kaiser'. Piekenbrock was so popular among his colleagues that one of the Abwehr's operations against Britain in 1940 was even called 'Operation Elena' after his wife. Piekenbrock frequently accompanied Canaris on his trips abroad, establishing contacts with foreign intelligence services and organizing and inspecting the work of Abwehr I outposts. Before the war he visited seventeen countries.

In March 1943 Piekenbrock left the Abwehr for the army, and Colonel Georg Hansen succeeded him as head of Abteilung I. He was 38, 'blond, tall, slim, good-looking, who in contrast to the elegant Piekenbrock often buddied up to the enlisted men'.[7] In May 1945, Piekenbrock was taken prisoner by SMERSH.

In the Soviet structure, military intelligence had functions similar to the main function of Abteilung I. From April 18, 1943 onwards, there were two intelligence organizations: *Razvedupr* or RU (an abbreviation from *Razvedyvatel'noe upravlenie* or Intelligence Directorate; headed by Fyodor Kuznetsov) of the Red Army's General Staff (field intelligence) and *Glavnoe razvedyvatel'noe upravlenie* (Main Intelligence Directorate) or GRU (headed by Ivan Il'ichev) of the Defense Commissariat (NKO) (in charge of foreign intelligence).[8] There were three operational departments within RU: the 1st, in charge of field intelligence; the 2nd, in charge of agent intelligence, and the 3rd that analyzed the incoming information. The Investigation Department, along with the 1st and 2nd departments, interrogated the German POWs.

Until the summer of 1943, Colonel Erwin von Lahousen, 'an Austrian officer and a bitter enemy of Hitler', headed the Abwehr's Abteilung II in charge of sabotage.[9] Before the Anschluss, the incorporation of Austria into the Third Reich in 1938, Lahousen served in the Intelligence Department of the Austrian General Staff as a specialist on Czechoslovakia. He was six foot tall, called 'Long L' in the Abwehr and 'gained the complete confidence of his chief', Canaris.[10] In August 1943, von Lahousen was sent to the Eastern Front, and another of Canaris's close associates, Baron Wessel von Freytag-Loringhoven, succeeded him.[11] In 1944, Loringhoven provided the detonator charge and explosives for the assassination attempt against Hitler. On July 26, 1944 he committed suicide after being arrested by the Gestapo.

Von Lahousen's deputy, Colonel Erwin Stolze, called 'Saboteur No. 2', headed Group 2A within Abteilung II, which specialized in diversions and terrorism in the Soviet Union. Until 1936, Stolze served in Abwehr I and was responsible for the intelligence collected in Eastern and Southeastern Europe.[12] He supervised a number of White Russian officers, including General Yevgeny Dostovalov and Colonel Pyotr Durnovo, who conducted analysis of the Soviet press and used other Russian sources to provide Stolze with information. Stolze did not know that General Dostovalov was a double agent. From 1923 on, he worked for Soviet intelligence, and later he even moved to the Soviet Union, where he was arrested and executed in 1938.[13] Therefore, most probably he provided Stolze with disinformation. Colonel Durnovo, on the contrary, became head of Abwehr's agents in Yugoslavia in 1941. In February 1945 he and his family were killed during the infamous bombing of Dresden.[14] Stolze's close relations with the leaders of the Ukrainian emigration community were helpful in Abwehr's preparation for Operation Barbarossa. On May 31, 1945, SMERSH arrested Stolze in Berlin.

The function of Abteilung II was based on the activity of the division Brandenburg-800.[15] This division began in October 1939 as a battalion of Volksdeutsche, Germans living outside of Germany who were fluent in Polish. They were very successful saboteurs during the invasion of Poland, operating in the rear of the Polish troops. The original Brandenburg-800 battalion consisted of four companies, one of which comprised men from the Baltic countries and Russians, mostly emigrants. Later, volunteers from Soviet POWs were added. When the Brandenburg-800 expanded into a division, it included British, Romanian, African, Arab, and other units. From the end of 1942, the division was attached directly to Abteilung II. The men of the division became known as the Brandenburgers.

In action, a Brandenburger unit could be as small as a two-man team or as large as a full 300-man company, depending on the mission. The units operated in the enemy's rear or in the German rear if the troops were in retreat. From the autumn of 1939 onwards, a special group of Brandenburgers watched the Ploesti oil fields in Romania. In 1940, groups of Brandenburgers dressed in the uniforms of the enemy played an important role in the conquest of Norway, Belgium, and the Netherlands. Later they were also active in Afghanistan, Iran, the Middle East, and Africa.

In the Soviet structure the 4th NKVD Directorate headed by the infamous Pavel Sudoplatov was similar to Abteilung II.[16] Originally, this directorate was formed on July 5, 1941 as the Special Group (terrorist and diversionary acts in the enemy's rear) subordinated directly to Commissar Beria. On October 3, 1941 the group was transformed into the 2nd NKVD Department (with the same functions), which on January 18, 1942 became the 4th NKVD Directorate. On April 14, 1943, it was transferred to the NKGB as its 4th Directorate.

The 4th NKVD/NKGB Directorate was almost an independent service with its own intelligence at the enemy's rear and abroad, and its own terrorist troops. The operational troops consisted of 5,000 men, up to 2,000 of whom were foreign Communists who lived in the Soviet Union. The activities of Abwehr's Abteilung II and 4th NKVD/NKGB Directorate were similar to those of the British Special Operations Executive or SOE.[17]

Abwehr's Abteilung III, that is comparable with SMERSH's HQ, consisted of eleven groups, most of which were composed of sections called 'referats'. Colonel Franz Eccard von Bentivegni, known as 'Benti' to insiders, headed it until April 1944. Karl Abshagen, Canaris's biographer, wrote: 'Despite his Italian name, [Bentivegni] came from a Prussian family... He was a typical old-fashioned Prussian officer, most careful about his appearance and never to be seen without an eyeglass in his eye... Bentivegni's personal relations with Canaris did not become as close as those with Piekenbrock.'[18] In May 1944 von Bentivegni left the Abwehr for the army, and in March 1945 he was taken prisoner by SMERSH.

In general, the Abwehr leaders tried not to follow the orders that would involve Abwehr in military atrocities. In April 1942, Colonel Piekenbrock told Canaris: 'Herr Keitel [OKW Chief] should be told once and for all to inform Herr Hitler that we of the Abwehr are not an organization of assassins like the SD or the SS.'[19] With this attitude, Canaris and many other high-level Abwehr officers later joined the anti-Hitler military Resistance.

There was a serious reason why Piekenbrock mentioned the SD: in the spring of 1942, the Abwehr began to lose its positions to the SD, part of the RSHA. Created in September 1939, the RSHA consisted of the SD or Amt VI (foreign intelligence), Gestapo (investigation of political opposition), Kripo (criminal police), interior intelligence and the department for investigation of ideological loyalty.[20] This German organization and the NKVD had a similar function, security of the ruling party. Even the name SS and the NKVD's motto were similar: the SS meant the 'Shield Squadron' of the Nazi Party, while the NKVD was 'the sword and the shield' of the Soviet Communist Party. The title of RSHA head Reinhard Heydrich (and from January 1943 onwards, Ernst Kaltenbrunner), was 'Chief of the Sicherheits-polizei and SD'. Walter Schellenberg headed the SD from autumn 1941 until the end of the war.[21] He had the rank of colonel, and from June 1944 onwards, of brigadier general.

By March 1942, the SD took under its control almost all Abwehr's counterintelligence work. Admiral Canaris signed the following agreement with Heydrich: 'Counterintelligence shall in future be an additional function of the Security Police and SD.'[22]

Abwehr's Branch for Russia 'Stab Walli'

Before the end of 1939, Abwehr had almost no information about the Red Army.[23] After the German and Soviet occupation of Poland in September 1939 and the Soviet annexation of the Baltic States in the summer of 1940, the situation changed. During this period, many thousands of refugees were suddenly on the move. The Abwehr used refugee crowds as an opportunity to send German, Ukrainian, and Polish agents onto the newly occupied Soviet territory. Also, from January 1940 to June 22, 1941, 327 Red Army men, from private to colonel ranks, escaped to the Germans.[24] They brought a lot of documents and maps with them.

As a result, by May 1941, the Abwehr knew the exact location of seventy-seven Soviet Rifle divisions in the former Polish territories that soon became a battleground.[25] Paul Leverkühn, head of the Abwehr station in Turkey, later wrote: 'In June 1941, the distribution, arms and armament of the Russian force and the location of their aerodromes, at least in that portion of Poland which they occupied, were known with comparative exactness.'[26] This information helped to destroy many Soviet planes on the ground within the first hours of the German attack on June 22, 1941.

The German agents collected not only military information, but also information on the NKVD and OOs. In May 1941, Anatolii Mikheev, head of the 3rd NKO Directorate in Moscow, describing the goals of German intelligence, noted:

> Sometimes the Gestapo agents [at the time, the Soviets called all German agents 'the Gestapo agents']...are tasked with collecting intelligence specifically on the NKVD organs and their leadership, for instance with finding out the following:
> 1. What is a Special Department [OO] and to whom does it report?

2. Is there a connection between the NKVD organs and the Special Department and how are they subordinated?

3. What are the names, nationalities, and addresses of the [OO] workers?[27]

In early 1941, an operational organization with the code name 'Stab Walli'—the future main target of SMERSH—was formed from Abteilung I's eastern groups to head up Abwehr's participation in Operation Barbarossa. It was located in the area of Sulejowek outside Warsaw, on the estate of General Jozef Pilsudski, the Polish dictator from 1925 to 1935.[28] Soon Stab Walli was divided into I, II, and III, representing the three Abwehr departments.

Also, schools for training Russian Walli agents were opened. In January 1942, Walli I started to select volunteers for schools from among Soviet POWs. A former attendee of the Central School in Sulejowek recalled:

The 'students' were mostly former Red Army officers or captured young Soviet radio operators who needed to be taught ciphers...

A German Hauptmann (Captain) headed the Warsaw Intelligence School...During World War I he was a POW in Russia, spoke Russian perfectly and liked to repeat that he 'knew the Russian soul well'. Nobody knew his name.

German instructors taught us radio operation and ciphering methods, while former Soviet officers taught other subjects: military, economical, political, and sociological intelligence, topography, working methods of the [NKVD] and counterintelligence, and so on. There was Major General [M. B.] Salikhov (alias Osmanov), a Lieutenant Colonel of the General Staff with the alias [I. P.] Pavlov, a Major with the alias Zorin (he also headed a special laboratory that produced any Soviet document), and a Colonel with the alias Shelgunov...

A course lasted 11 or 6 months, and students spent 10 hours a day in classes... Every week four–five graduates left the school to be dropped in the Red Army rear.[29]

Walli I was responsible for military and economic intelligence at the Soviet–German front.[30] Its head, Lieutenant Colonel Wilhelm Baun, was 'a short, thin, chain-smoking ex-infantryman...who had been born in Odessa in 1897, spoke Ukrainian as well as Russian'.[31] From 1921 to 1937, he worked at the German consulates in Odessa and Kiev. Admiral Canaris used to say that Baun had 'a special gift for intelligence work'.[32]

Five years later, while interrogating the arrested Baun, the American counterintelligence officer Arnold Silver had a low opinion of him: 'It did not take more than a few hours to determine that Baun was alcoholic dependent.'[33] One more American intelligence officer, Captain Eric Waldman, recalled Baun as a dishonest person: 'Gustav Hilger, the former German diplomat…discovered that Baun had stashed away under his bed a large trunk full of U.S. dollars, which should have been spent on operations. Another incident occurred when Baun tried to blackmail [Major Heinz Danko] Herre [also a captured German officer].'[34]

Walli I consisted of five referats:

IX:	intelligence on ground troops;
IL (Luft):	intelligence on the air force;
I Wi:	economics intelligence;
I G:	fabrication of false documents;
I I:	radio transmitters, ciphering, and codes.[35]

Walli II, in charge of sabotage within the Red Army and at its rear, was headed by Major Seeliger, who had great experience in irregular warfare.[36] In summer 1943 Soviet partisans killed him. Senior Lieutenant Müller, and, finally, Captain Becker succeeded him. The OKW's directive to Abteilung II and its Walli II was to have 'agents to promote rivalries and hatred between the various peoples of the Soviet Union'.[37]

Walli III mostly collected information about the NKVD. Its head, Lt. Col., later Col., Heinz Schmalschläger started his Abwehr career in Vienna in 1935 and later claimed that he was the nephew of Admiral Canaris.[38] He was also responsible for Stab Walli as a whole. By 1943, Walli III consisted of five groups:

1. Commanding Group (general administration, planning of operations), Head: Oberstleutnant Heinz Schmalschläger
2. Analytical Group (intelligence analysis, issuing information for field groups and writing reports to Berlin), Head: Hauptmann Krickendt
   Referat I (study and analysis of intelligence data, writing reports)
   Referat IIIF (arrest of the enemy agents, analysis of the work of Soviet intelligence, writing memos)
   Referat of Personnel and Training
3. Military-Topographic Group (preparation of operational maps of Abwehr field groups; maps of the location of Soviet intelligence agents; charts of movements of the German radio operators and Abwehr's agents, etc.), Head: Hauptmann Krickendt
4. Radio Group (joint with Walli I until the end of 1942)
5. Transport (reparation of vehicles of field groups).[39]

Stab Walli received intelligence and counterintelligence materials from operational units in the field. After a preliminary evaluation, materials were sent to Abwehr headquarters in Berlin and to the Fremde Heere Ost or FHO (see below). In the field, during the advance of the three German army groups A (South), B (Center), and C (North) into Soviet territory, the Abteilung I and III reconnaissance detachments working under Walli I and III, respectively, moved with the troops, frequently even ahead of them with the forward tank units.[40]

There were two types of detachments, commando units of 25–60 men assigned to each of the army groups, and squads (gruppen) of 12 men assigned to each army. In all, there were only 500–600 intelligence men in the Abwehr detachments at the Eastern Front. Both commando units and squads included Abwehr officers, translators, radio operators, and others. Commandos and squads were in constant radio contact with Walli I and III. All Abwehr groups reported also to Abwehr officers of the department '1c' responsible for intelligence in the army groups. Within an army, the staff of each German detachment from a divisional level upward consisted of three departments, 1a (operational), 1b (the rear, supplies), and 1c (intelligence).

In the towns abandoned by the retreating Red Army, the commandos and squads searched for documents—orders, cables, and so forth—left behind by the military commanders (the responsibility of Abteilung I) and by the NKVD (the responsibility of Abteilung III). For instance, in the city of Brest-Litovsk, they discovered a large cache of documents in NKVD headquarters, which they sent to Stab Walli in cars and trucks. It included a top-secret telephone book containing all of the Kremlin numbers and home numbers of all members of the Soviet government. In the Belorussian capital of Minsk, Abwehr groups discovered twenty-nine safes filled with secret documents, including lists of all members of the Soviet government and Party elite and their relatives with private addresses and phone numbers.[41] Special Abwehr IIIF squads were in charge of finding spies and terrorists in the rear of the German armies.

Walli I was also active in a wide area behind the front line.[42] Squads were sent into enemy territory for reconnaissance, frequently dressed in Red Army uniforms. They used local informers and interrogated POWs. In December 1941, Walli III began to send its agents to penetrate partisan detachments. However, as Baun admitted to the American interrogator Silver in 1947, 'not one of his wartime operations had been successful…The Soviets had rolled up [the] agents one after another'.[42] In the summer of 1942, the names of the German army groups were changed to South A, South B, and Don, while the attached Abwehr squads and groups received numbers.[44]

Walli II detachments were sent for special sabotage actions. For instance, a Brandenburger group penetrated into Soviet territory a day before the German attack. It took over a bridge and prevented its destruction by the Soviets until the main German troops arrived.[45] During the first days of the war, numerous groups of saboteurs dressed in Red Army or NKVD/NKGB uniforms were parachuted into various locations in Belorussia, frequently before the arrival of the German troops.[46] In Brest, German saboteurs put the telephone and telegraph cables out of commission and cut the electricity and water supplies to the city before it was taken over by the Nazi troops. The Party, the city, and the military authorities were helpless. In the Baltic States, 80 specially trained Estonians were dropped behind the Soviet lines and reported locations, operations, and movements of Soviet troops. To distinguish them from the Soviet servicemen, they had 'a rust-red cloth about the size of a handkerchief with a circular yellow spot in the middle'.[47]

On October 9, 1941, during the German fast advance toward Moscow, a company of Brandenburgers was dropped near the Istra Water Reservoir, about 30 kilometers from Moscow.[48] A detachment of NKVD troops killed all paratroopers before they blew up a dam and destroyed the main Moscow water supply.

In 1941–43, several Brandenburger groups were dropped near Murmansk, a city on the Barents Sea, with orders to destroy the railway from Murmansk to Leningrad.[49] Murmansk had a big port, where in 1941–42 British and American ships brought American supplies sent to the Soviet Union as part of the American lend-lease. Also, this railway was important for moving Soviet troops in the North and supplying the encircled Leningrad. In 1942–43, numerous Brandenburger sabotage groups were dropped into Southern Russia.

Some of the Brandenburg detachments were hard to control.[50] On June 30, 1941, the Gruppe Nachtigall, part of the Brandenburg corps formed of western Ukrainian émigrés, entered the city of Lvov, followed by an SS-Einsatzgruppe. Just before the Soviet troops left the city, the NKVD killed in local prisons at least 3,000 Ukrainians—followers of the nationalist leader Stefan Bandera.[51] The Jews were blamed for these atrocities because they allegedly supported the Soviet invasion in 1939. Using this rumor as an excuse, the Einsatzgruppe, along with the newly formed local Ukrainian police and, apparently, some of the Nachtigall members, slaughtered between 2,000 and 4,000 Jews and Poles.

Bandera, supported by the Nachtigall, proclaimed an independent 'Ukrainian State' in Lvov and formed a government under his deputy, Yaroslav Stetsko. In Berlin Alfred Rosenberg, Minister for Eastern Territories, was outraged since his plans for the area did not include any state independent from Germany. By July 12, the Gestapo arrested Bandera and Stetsko and they spent most of the rest of the war in Sachsenhausen-Zellenbau concentration camp. On Canaris's order, the Nachtigall was transferred from Ukraine to Germany. Later the Ukrainian Insurgent Army (UPA), organized by Ukrainian nationalists in the area of Lvov, became one of the main targets of the NKVD, SMERSH, and the NKGB. The UPA fought against the Germans, the Soviets, and the Polish underground Armija Krajowa (Home Army).[52]

In the autumn of 1941, Walli II formed an additional battalion, Bergman (later Corps Alpinist), for actions in the Caucasus.[53] It consisted of

1,500 volunteers, mostly Soviet POWs of various Caucasian ethnic groups. In 1942 and 1943, this battalion fought in the Caucasus, then in the Crimea, and from April 1944, in Romania and Greece. The Abwehr also used two special groups, Tamara 1 and 2, formed of Georgian emigrants, attached to the Army Group South, for diversion and intelligence collection.

The FHO Takes Over

The RSHA was not the only threat to Abwehr's activity. In December 1941, after the German troops stopped near Moscow, Hitler decided to make decisions in Russia by himself and became Supreme Commander of the Army High Command (Oberkommando des Heeres or OKH). De facto the OKH was responsible for military actions at the Eastern Front, and the OKW, at the Western Front in Europe. With this change, Abwehr remained in the OKW, but the cooperation of Stab Walli with the OKH increased.

The OKH had its own military intelligence department, the FHO (Foreign Armies East), responsible for military affairs in Eastern Europe.[54] It analyzed information received from the Abwehr and other sources and made estimations and predictions. From mid-1942 on, the FHO was directly subordinated to the Chief of the General Staff and to the OKH Operations Department. Colonel Reinhard Gehlen, head of the FHO from April 1942 onwards, was a forty-year-old 'thin man of medium height with dark thinning hair'.[55] General Franz Halder, Chief of the General Staff from 1938 until September 1942, highly praised Gehlen: '[He] combines extraordinary ability and knowledge with unusual assiduity and a soldier's ardour. He is born a leader.'[56]

Gehlen introduced a new three-part structure for the FHO's Russian department.[57] Gruppe (Section) I, headed by Captain Gerhard Wessel, produced a daily enemy situation report, situation maps, and statistics, including numbers of Soviet prisoners.

Gruppe II, under Major Heinz Danko Herre and then Major Horst Hiemenz (Herre eventually became head of the training section of the Vlasov Army consisting of former Red Army servicemen), reported on the economic and military potential of the Soviet Union and evaluated the strategy and operational intentions of the Stavka. It assessed the statements of Soviet POWs, evaluated captured documents and Soviet press items, and maintained the main index of Soviet formations and Soviet high-level personnel.

Gruppe III was responsible for translating captured documents, press articles, radio broadcasts, and propaganda materials. Colonel Alexis Baron von Rönne, fluent in Russian, an FHO liaison with the Abwehr, SD, OKH, and OKW—and later a member of the anti-Hitler plot—headed this section until March 1943, when he was appointed head of the Fremde

Heere West, an equivalent of the FHO at the Western Front. Captain Egon Peterson succeeded him. At a special interrogation center subordinated to Gruppe III and commanded by the former Soviet Major Vasilii Sakharov, selected Soviet POWs were interrogated in detail.

Two signals intelligence offices shared information on reconnaissance with the FHO, *Fremde Luftwaffe Ost*, German Air Force intelligence, and *Leitstelle für Nachrichetenaufklärung Ost*, the OKH signals intelligence organization. The Germans broke a number of Red Army, Soviet Air Force, and NKVD ciphers, and the FHO received a lot of information obtained through radio reconnaissance.

In mid-1942, Walli's sections I and III were placed under the operational control of the FHO.[58] To make the contact more efficient, Walli I moved closer to the location of the FHO. From June 1941 until July 1942, German General Staff and Gehlen's office were in Mauerwald (now Mamerki), while Walli I was stationed nearby. Mauerwald was not far from 'Wolfschanze' (Wolf's Lair), Hitler's headquarters near Rastenburg, a small town in East Prussia (now Ketrzyn, Poland).

From mid-July to October 1942, when Hitler used his other headquarters 'Wehrwolf' (should be 'Werewolf' in English, but Hitler ordered that it be spelled 'Wehr' as the word 'defense' in German) near Vinnitsa in the occupied Ukraine, the OKH and Walli I were stationed in Vinnitsa itself. In November 1942, Hitler went back to the Wolfschanze, and the OKH, to Mauerwald, while Walli I moved to Neuhof (now Timofeevka), again not far from Mauerwald. They stayed there until November 1944. In 1943, Hitler stayed in 'Wehrwolf' twice, in February–March and August–September.

From July 1942 onwards, the FHO was responsible for evaluating information from Walli's sections I and III and for providing an independent estimate of the enemy situation. However, Major Hiemenz, head of FHO Group II, was skeptical regarding the information he received from Walli on Russia: 'All we got from Canaris was rubbish.'[59]

CHAPTER 14

Abwehr's Failures and Successes

In fact, the real problem was the FHO's poor evaluation of information received from Walli. Gehlen's personal great reliance on 'Max' messages from 'Klatt Bureau' in Sofia (Bulgaria), and from 1943, from Budapest (Hungary) became a classic example of the Abwehr's and Gehlen's poor judgment.[1]

Fritz or Richard Klatt was an alias name of Richard Kauder, a converted Jew, born in Vienna, who volunteered for the Abwehr to protect his Jewish mother. His 'Klatt Bureau' reported to Vienna's Abwehr post on two main situations: Soviet troop dispositions on the Eastern Front ('Max' messages) and British dispositions in the Middle East ('Moritz' messages from Turkey). The number of messages received in Vienna from 'Max and Moritz' was enormous: 3,000 in 1942, 3,700 in 1943, and 4,000 in 1944.[2] However, the true source of Klatt's information remains one of the main spy mysteries of World War II.

'Max' and 'Moritz' Cables

The Abwehr's Viennese post Ast XVII (the number means the German military district) that received Klatt's cables was organized after the Anschluss with Austria in 1938, and in 1940 it became Ast Vienna. Therre were two departments in it, I (espionage) and III (counterintelligence), and the Ast was responsible for collecting intelligence in the countries to the South East from the Reich and, after June 1941, in the Soviet Union.[3] Colonel Rudolf Count von Margona-Redwitz, a close friend of Admiral Canaris, headed Ast Vienna until April 1944, when he was transferred to the Army High Command (OKH) in Berlin, and another of Canaris's friends, Colonel Otto Amster, succeeded him in Vienna.

In July 1944, after the unsuccessful assassination attempt on Hitler, the Gestapo arrested both colonels as the Abwehr anti-Hitler plotters. On October 12, 1944 Count Margona-Redwitz was sentenced to death and executed, while Amster escaped from prison in April 1945 and in May SMERSH arrested him. In Vienna, in August 1944 Colonel Otto Wiese succeeded Amster.

In October 1940, Kauder and Ira Longin (or Iliya Lang), a White Russian and a close associate of the White Russian general Anton Turkul, established Dienststelle I or 'Klatt Bureau' in a villa in the central part of Sofia, Bulgaria. Sofia was important for the German intelligence and counterintelligence because Bulgaria was the only German ally country that continued to have diplomatic relationships with the Soviet Union, and the huge staff of the Soviet Embassy in Sofia included NKVD/NKGB and military spies. General Turkul was the leader of a fascist group of White Russian military emigrants in Europe, and in 1938 he moved from France to Berlin. After the Molotov–Ribbentrop Pact was signed, Turkul left Berlin for Rome, where he organized his own intelligence network. Later, in 1944, he joined the Russian Liberation Army under General Andrei Vlasov's command. In 1940, Turkul agreed to supply Sofia's outpost with information gathered by his agents.

David Kahn described Kauder in his book *Hitler's Spies*: '[Kauder] was of middle height, with a round face, well fed and well dressed... He spent his days in his office and on the move, apparently also doing some private business and paying off the Bulgarian police so he would not be bothered. He spent his nights in restaurants and cafes dining well and dating women.'[4] The radio call sign of the 'Klatt Bureau' was 'Schwert', meaning 'Sword'.

Presumably, Kauder's agents, including 'Max', were stationed inside the Soviet Union, even in high positions in Moscow.[5] Kurt Geisler, a former Abwehr officer who worked in the Stab Walli from 1941 to 1943 and was later captured by the Soviets, testified in 1947: '"Max" is a former Czar's Army officer and a colonel in the Red Army signal troops. During the war he was the head or a deputy head of signals at the staff of one of the southern Red Army's fronts located subsequently in Rostov-on-Don, near Baku and in Tbilisi.'[6] Colonel Friedrich Schildknecht, head of the FHO group from October 1941 till September 1942, and captured in 1943 in Stalingrad, was of a similar opinion: '["Max"] was an officer of the Red Army's General Staff or a senior staff officer working at the front or army headquarters of the Soviet Armed Forces.'

Geisler also mentioned that 'BAUN, who was in the town of Nikolaiken (East Prussia) with his Walli I, was making a monthly map, on which he marked information from "Max" reports every day. Each week he reported the data on the map to Colonel [Eberhard] Kintzel [Gehlen's predecessor as FHO head]...I also know that Admiral CANARIS sent a number of the "Max" reports to HITLER'.[7] The *Fremde Luftwaffe Ost* (German Air Force intelligence) also considered Max's reports the best intelligence the Luftwaffe ever had. But, in fact, it is not known if the information was real.

In December 1941, British intelligence began to intercept and decipher Kauder's messages between his bureau in Sofia and the Ast Vienna, and soon MI6 started to suspect the Soviets of being behind Kauder's activity.[8] At the same time, Moscow received some of the British-intercepted materials through John Cairncross and Kim Philby, the Soviet agents in MI6. Additionally, the GRU (Soviet military intelligence) received deciphered 'Moritz' messages through the agent 'Dolly' (presumably, James MacGibbon) and his handler Ivan Sklyarov (alias 'Brion'), Soviet Military Attaché in London.[9] In July 1942, the NKVD also began to intercept and decipher Kauder's messages. However, Kauder's modus operandi remained unknown.

The 'Klatt Bureau' operated independently of the main Abwehr office in Sofia attached to the German Legation and headed by Colonel Otto Wagner (alias 'Dr. Delius'). Colonel Wagner was skeptical regarding Kauder's activity. In 1946, he told the American investigator Arnold Silver: 'One wall of Klatt's office was covered with a map of the USSR west of the Urals, with a small light near each city. Whenever [an] *Abwehr* officer visited Klatt, one or more lights flashed repeatedly, whereupon Klatt would exclaim, for example, "Ah! A report from Kiev has just come in."'[10]

At the end of 1942, Wagner complained to Admiral Canaris and Hans Piekenbrock, suggesting that Kauder might be a Soviet spy, and ordered an investigation of Kauder's activity.[11] It was found that there was no radio station handling Kauder's traffic in Bulgaria. When confronted with this fact, Kauder responded that he received information from Turkey by phone. This coincides with Ira Longin's statement to Arnold Silver, the American investigator, in 1946 that he called from Istanbul to Kauder in Sofia. Also, Geisler told his Soviet interrogators that because of the problem with receiving radio messages from 'Max' in Berlin, in 1942 he met with Longin in Sofia twice and discussed this problem with him. But in 1943 Wagner's investigators also discovered that Kauder and Longin had contacts with the Soviet Legation in Sofia and, possibly, were given information there.

Despite the suspicion, in September 1943 Kauder was allowed to move to Budapest, where he headed his own Abwehr outpost, *Luftmeldekopf Südost* (Air Intelligence Outpost, Southeast).[12] By this time, Kauder's group consisted of 25–30 members, of whom 6–7 were ciphering operators, and 4–5 were radio operators. All Kauder's staff members were Jews or half-Jews, and being employed by the Bureau was crucial for their survival. Until August 1944, cables were sent to Vienna, and after that, to both Vienna and Berlin. For cover, the Bureau's signboard said *Bureau of the Preserve Plant 'Fruits and Vegetables'*.

After August 1944, when Abwehr I was included in Schellenberg's SD as part of the Amt Mil (Military Department), Lieutenant Colonel Werner Ohletz, head of the Branch C (operations in the east), became responsible for Kauder's network.[13] In November 1944, the SD moved the 'Klatt Bureau' to the small town of Csorna in Hungary, while the Ast Vienna was relocated to the village of Obing in Bavaria.[14]

On February 12, 1945, two days before the Red Army took over Budapest, Kauder and his staff members were brought to Vienna. Austrian customs officers interrogated Kauder on suspicion of planning an escape to Switzerland.[15] They confiscated his three metal boxes with cash, as well as an expensive stamp collection and jewelry that belonged to his mother and his mistress, Ivolia Kalman. Besides these valuables, Kauder declared that he had left 252 golden coins and 5,800 Swiss francs in the bank of Csorna.

Finally, Colonel Wiesel, head of Ast Vienna, arrested Kauder on Schellenberg's order.[16] SS-Hauptsturmführer Alfred Klausnitzer, who specially arrived from Berlin, continued interrogations, now about the Bureau. After being imprisoned for two months, Kauder was released because of the approaching Red Army.

Kauder's Channels

While Kauder, Ivolia Kalman, Ira Longin, and General Turkul were caught by the Americans and British in 1945 and then intensely interrogated, SMERSH operatives arrested staff members of the 'Klatt Bureau', including Kauder's wife, Gerda Filitz. This is known from a short description by Nigel

West and Oleg Tsarev of the still secret Soviet archival file 'Klatt' in their book *The Crown Jewels*.[175] The file contains materials from the SMERSH/MGB investigation of the Kauder case conducted in 1945–47. The SD investigator Klausnitzer was also captured and interrogated by SMERSH. Additionally, Franz von Bentivegni, former head of the Abwehr III, and Otto Armster, former head of the Ast Vienna, were questioned about Kauder.

Recently several excerpts from the transcripts of interrogations of these prisoners were published in Russian.[18] On April 19, 1945 Gerda Filitz testified: 'The "Klatt Bureau" was subordinated to the central intelligence organ Luftwaffe-1 Abwehr [Ast] in Vienna. At first Klatt was in contact with Lieutenant Colonel [Roland] von Wahl-[Welskirch] and then with Colonel Wiese…Additionally, "Klatt" had a direct connection with Berlin through SS-Brigadenführer [Walter] Schellenberg.'[19] Von Wahl-Welskirch, whom Filitz mentioned, headed the referat Abwehr I Luft (intelligence on the air force) in the Ast Vienna. He was a friend of Kauder's mother and employed Kauder in the Abwehr in 1939.[20]

According to Filitz, Ira Longin (she called him Langin) played the main role in providing Kauder with information about the Soviet Union:

> The White Russian emigrant Langin Ivan [?], alias 'Longo', a Russian, an officer of the old [Czar's] and White armies, emigrated [from Russia] in 1919 and lived in Budapest… While the Bureau was located in Budapest, Klatt personally involved Langin in its work.
>
> Langin was connected with a counterrevolutionary organization, located in the Soviet Union… At first Langin was in contact [with the organization] through messengers, but from 1942 on, he contacted it by radio.
>
> There was an agent who radioed cables from a military detachment located in the town of Tiflis [Tbilisi, Georgia]. A Russian military counterrevolutionary organization provided him with materials, and he sent the information to the 'Klatt Bureau'. I know that this agent worked with Langin until February 12, 1945, the day when the Gestapo arrested me.[21]

Later Filitz added that 'Klatt didn't know personally Langin's people who provided him with information'.[22] Valentina Deutsch, the arrested Kauder's radio operator, added that Longin was subordinate to General Turkul. She described Kauder's system of cables:

> After receiving intelligence from the Soviet Union, Klatt used to personally look it through and make some changes, mostly editorial. Usually, Klatt took out the details that could have been unfavorable for the German high command. Then he gave the text of the radiogram to ciphering operators…
>
> Klatt always marked Lang's radiograms with the intelligence on the Soviet Union by [the name] 'Max'…

Klatt marked the data about the British troops in the Near East by the name 'Moritz', the data about Turkey he marked 'Anker' or 'Anatol', and about Egypt, by the word 'Ibis'.[23]

However, only Kauder, whom SMERSH interrogators did not have in their hands, could identify the meaning of his marks. Later he described to the British interrogators his system of sorting out cables from Turkey.[24] 'Ibis' was a ship that sailed in the Black and Aegean seas, and Kauder paid the captain of this ship, who was a friend of Ira Longin, for gathering and transmitting the intelligence information. Most of these telegrams were sent to Sofia by the coastal police station in the port of the city of Burgos (Bulgaria).

In Ankara the Spanish pro-German diplomat Pedro Prat y Soutzo, a friend of General Turkul, agreed to use the Spanish Embassy for sending cables to Sofia. His assistant was trained in Sofia as a radio operator. George Romanoff, another of Ira Longin's friends, used to bring the intelligence materials to the Embassy, and the Germans paid him for the information. These telegrams Kauder marked 'Anchor'.

The same Romanoff also provided another of Kauder's agents, his old friend Wilhelm Goetz, with the intelligence information. Goetz was a Jewish businessman from Budapest who had had problems with the Germans. With the help of Colonel Otto Hatz, the Hungarian Military Attaché to Sofia from 1941 and Ankara from 1943, Goetz was employed at the Hungarian Embassy in Ankara and sent cables from there. Kauder marked them 'Islam'. However, in October 1944 Goetz defected to the British.

In his testimony Kauder mentioned that Hatz 'was glad to help me, and he was generously rewarded for the help'. In fact, Hatz, a triple agent, was involved in many affairs. In Turkey he participated in the unsuccessful peace negotiations between Hungary and the Western Allies, about which he also informed 'Dr. Delius' (Wagner) and Adolf Beckerle, the German Ambassador to Sofia.[25] In January 1944, Hatz even had a personal meeting with Admiral Canaris in an attempt to work out a joint strategy of negotiations with the Americans.[26] Allen Dulles, head of the OSS office in Switzerland, reported to Washington: 'Hatz is reliable pro-German. However, he is short in funds and has numerous affairs with women. There is also an unconfirmed report to the effect that he is in touch with Jews who are paid by Hungarian Intelligence and that he shares in the profits which he makes from smuggling currency.'[27] Soviet military intelligence was also well informed about the Hungarian negotiations with the Western Allies in Turkey.

According to Kauder, cables were sent by radio only in urgent situations; more frequently information was delivered to Sofia by couriers who flew once a week by Lufthansa. The Press Attaché at the Spanish Embassy,

Vladimir Velikotny, a White Russian, prepared the reports. They were sent in sealed envelopes from the Hungarian Military Attaché in Turkey to the Hungarian Military Attaché in Sofia, from whom Kauder received the reports. Apparently, Hatz organized this channel, but in October 1944, he was called back to Budapest and transferred to a commanding military post.

On November 7, 1944, Hatz defected to the Soviets by plane and brought with him documents about the Hungarian Army and military fortifications on the Danube River.[28] Most probably, Hatz spoke Russian because in his SMERSH/MGB documents he is mentioned with a patronymic name, Otto Samuilovich Hatz, as was done for foreigners who knew Russian. Hatz wrote four leaflets in Hungarian and made a record addressing the Hungarian troops and asking them to follow his example and to surrender to the Red Army troops that encircled Budapest.[29] In retaliation, the Germans arrested Hatz's parents and brother and sent them to a concentration camp in Germany, where his mother died. After the Red Army took over Budapest, Hatz assisted at the Soviet Military Commandant's Office. In April 1945, SMERSH operatives arrested him and from mid-May 1945, he was kept in Moscow investigation prisons. Interestingly, in October 1946 he was put for a while with Hans Piekenbrock, former head of Abwehr I.[30]

SD officer Klausnitzer, who had questioned Kauder in Vienna, testified during the SMERSH/MGB interrogations: 'Klatt was arrested [in Vienna] on suspicion of playing a double game. He was accused of having been in contact with British intelligence and feeding the German intelligence with British disinformation. Additionally, Kauder was accused of embezzling and taking for himself the money he received from the German intelligence.'[31] Apparently, Klausnitzer was well informed about Kauder's contacts with the British through Bandi (Andor) Grosz (aliases André György, Andreas Greiner, and 'Trillium' in the American Dogwood spy network created by Alfred Schwartz).[32] Grosz was a Czech Jew and a shady triple agent who from January 1942 onwards was a go-between for Jewish organizations in Hungary and other German-occupied territories and Allied intelligence circles in Turkey. As for embezzling, the valuables confiscated by the Austrian customs supported this accusation.

However, Kauder told his British interrogators that Klausnitzer questioned him mostly about the Hungarians, Hatz, and Momotaro Enomoto, a Japanese journalist and spy in Sofia, whom Kauder knew well.[33] Possibly, Klausnitzer also mentioned Hatz and Enomoto during interrogations in SMERSH because later MGB investigators accused Hatz of spy contacts with Kauder and Enomoto. In any case, Klausnitzer insisted that 'based on interrogations, I had an impression that Klatt did not collect intelligence, and the information he sent out was just a creation of his imagination… Klatt frankly said that he would not have been working for the German intelligence if he was not able to make a lot of money. I concluded that Klatt was an adventurer, a swindler and he gambled for getting big money'.[34]

Klausnitzer considered Longin (Lang, as he called him) to have been more important in the spy network than Kauder:

> According to the photo I've seen, Ira Lang has a high forehead, wide face, is snub-nosed, has deeply positioned eyes, wide mouth, he is about 48–50 years old. He should have been an officer. Klatt recruited him in Budapest and brought him to Sofia. Apparently, he sent people equipped with radio transmitters…from there to Russia through Romania…
>
> Lang was the main person, while Klatt was only an impresario…[Lang] received 220 pieces of gold per month. With the help of Turkul's organization he obtained very important information that immediately was sent to Berlin. It was noticed that he got the exceptionally valuable data that influenced the German tactics.[35]

The 'pieces of gold' meant coins. As Kauder told the British, 'beginning in November 1944, Longin refused [to accept] hundred dollar bills. He demanded his salary in gold coins—napoleons. Longin began his spy career at 207 coins a month; the last payment…was 350 gold napoleons'.[36] Therefore, the whole business was quite profitable for Longin.

After interrogating Klausnitzer and the other 'Klatt Bureau' prisoners in 1945, in the spring of 1946 SMERSH operatives tried to kidnap Kauder in Salzburg, in the American occupational zone of Austria, but this attempt failed.[37]

In July 1947, after analyzing all information the investigators collected, the MGB sent a 61-page-long *Memorandum on the KLATT-MAX Case* to Stalin.[38] It included the following main conclusions.

First, only eight percent of all 'Max' messages contained real information, while most of them were far from reality. This was not something new. Already in April 1944 Beria signed a report to Stalin that stated that the analysis of radio messages sent from Sofia to Budapest and from Sofia to Vienna from autumn 1941 until spring 1944, intercepted by the NKVD, NKGB, and SMERSH, demonstrated that most of Klatt's data on the Red Army detachments and their movements were pure fantasies.[39]

Second, according to Soviet counterintelligence radio control, there were no attempts to send radio messages from Soviet territory to Sofia during the war. Additionally, contrary to Wagner's suspicion, the MGB investigators found that Kauder and Longin did not receive information from the Soviet Legation in Sofia.

The MGB investigators suggested that Kauder might have prepared messages by himself, possibly using three main sources. He could receive eight percent of reliable information from the Russian émigrés who interrogated Soviet POWs for the Germans. The émigrés who worked in foreign embassies in Sofia could also have access to information on the Soviet Union. The MGB report mentioned the Swedish Legation as an example. Possibly, Sweden was singled out because at the end of 1943, the Soviet Foreign Affairs Commissariat asked the Swedes to recall their minister and military attaché from Moscow, accusing them of supplying the German Supreme Command with secret information about the Red Army.[40] Finally, Kauder might have bought some information from German intelligence officers. Therefore, the MGB investigators basically concluded that Kauder concocted or invented the texts of his cables to Vienna and Berlin. However, it is hard to believe that one person could create thousands of cables by himself during a short period of time.

Still a Mystery

In the meantime, Kauder, Longin, and General Turkul were investigated by the American and British security services. In 1946 and 1947, the American officer Arnold Silver and the British MI5 officer 'Klop' Ustinov (the father of Peter Ustinov, the actor) interrogated these three individuals. Ustinov's real name was Jona Baron von Ustinov, but for some reason he hated his name so much that he amazingly called himself 'Klop' which means 'a bedbug' in Russian. The two interrogators concluded that the whole of Kauder's network was a creation of Soviet intelligence through which it fed the Abwehr and FHO with sophisticated disinformation.[41] According to Kauder, already in 1941 he suspected that Joseph Schultz, his contact with Turkul and the network that Turkul and Longin supposedly had in the Soviet Union, was a Soviet agent.[42] Kauder claimed that Schultz admitted this himself at the end of the war. However, Schultz disappeared and could not be traced. It is also possible that Schultz was Kauder's invention, a 'red herring' to distract Silver and Ustinov's attention to Longin and Turkul.

Despite the conclusions of the Soviet and Anglo-American investigators, it is still unclear where Kauder's information originated from and what part Kauder played in creating the texts of cables. Apparently, through his people Longin controlled most of the materials that were sent from Ankara to Sofia. As the American investigator Silver characterized him, Longin was capable of any trick: 'Ira Longin was an intelligent liar who could spin off 60 cover stories in as many minutes.'[43] Interestingly, in March 1944 when Turkul came to Budapest, he began to suspect Longin of working for the Soviets.[44] However, there is still no conclusive proof that Soviet intelligence ran Longin.

Finally, the notorious Pavel Sudoplatov, head of the NKVD/NKGB terrorist directorate during the war (its function was similar to the Abwehr II), created more confusion, claiming in his memoir that his Moscow agent Aleksandr Dem'yanov (alias 'Heine') was Kauder's 'Max'.[45] But the memoir of Dem'yanov's wife, who was also a Soviet agent, as well as other Russian recollections, do not support this identity.[46] Additionally, when Germany attacked the Soviet Union, Kauder had already sent 600 'Max' messages to Vienna, and the Abwehr clearly identified two 'Max' agents, referring to 'Heine' as 'Max North', and to Kauder, as 'Max South'.[47] Therefore, Dem'yanov had nothing in common with Kauder's 'Max'.

The Russian security services never mentioned what happened to Kauder's arrested co-workers and Klausnitzer. Usually such prisoners were sentenced to long imprisonment in labor camps, while Klausnitzer might have received a death sentence as an SD officer. As for Otto Hatz, his investigation was concluded at the end of 1951 and on January 29, 1952, a session of the Military Tribunal of the Moscow Military District sentenced him to fifteen years' imprisonment in labor camps as a Hungarian spy. This was a 'lenient' conviction for a spy because usually spies received the death sentence or 25 years of imprisonment; the tribunal took into consideration that Hatz voluntarily joined the Soviets and worked for them in 1944–45. Hatz's verdict mentioned Ast Vienna and Kauder:

> During his spy activity Hatz was connected with military attaches of other countries, in particular, of Finland and Japan, as well as with the German intelligence men from the German intelligence offices 'Abwehrstelle Sofia', 'Abwehrstelle Vienna', and 'Klatt Bureau'. From them, he received intelligence information about the Soviet armed forces and sent it to the [Hungarian] Intelligence Directorate in Budapest.
>
> Additionally, in 1943 Hatz Otto established contact with the representatives of American intelligence and participated in the secret political negotiations of the Americans with the [Hungarian] government of [Miklós] Horthy about a possibility of Hungary quitting the war.[48]

In July 1952, Hatz was sent to the Ozernyi Special Camp for political prisoners in the Krasnoyarsk Province. Four years later he was released and returned to Hungary. He became a trainer of the Hungarian and East German fencing teams and in 1977, 75-year-old Hatz died in Budapest.[49] In mid-1947, the Americans released Kauder, Longin, and General Turkul, coincidently at the same time as the MGB sent its report on Klatt to Stalin. Arnold Silver saw Kauder for the last time in Salzburg in 1952, while in 1964 he heard from his colleagues that Kauder tried to approach the CIA to offer his assistance.

If only eight percent of the 'Max' information was real, as Soviet investigators concluded, Admiral Canaris, the FHO, and Gehlen, as well as Fremde Luftwaffe Ost, look bad for relying upon this source. The two other main Abwehr sources of information on the Soviet Union that the FHO relied on, 'Stex' in Stockholm and German journalist Ivar Lissner in Harbin (China), also worked under Soviet intelligence control.[50]

Successful Operations

The German intelligence failures are unexpected because in general, as Gehlen described to the Americans in June 1945, the FHO had good knowledge of Soviet intelligence and its methods:

> The Russians repeatedly attempted to deceive their enemies by planting specially prepared reports in the international press...ANKARA and STOCKHOLM played an important role in this respect... Sometimes the Russians even succeeded in giving their 'news items' the appearance of coming from different sources and of corroborating one another. Especially numerous were reports planted by the Russians concerning exhaustion within the ranks of Russian troops, low morale, food troubles in the interior, and counter revolutionary trends in the Soviet Union...
>
> Besides these general methods of deception, certain deceptive 'news' might also be spread by agents...
>
> Neutral and friendly foreign correspondents were also used by the Russians to deceive the enemy.[51]

Some intelligence information the Germans received supposedly from Moscow was surprisingly correct. For instance, the story and activity of Vladimir Minishkiy or Agent 438, as E. H. Cookridge (a pen name of Edward Spiro, the British journalist and intelligence officer), Gehlen's biographer, calls him, remains a mystery. The name 'Minishkiy' makes no sense in Russian.

Cookridge writes that according to Minishkiy's statements, before the war he was a high-level Comminist Party functionary in Moscow.[52] However, the Russian historian Boris Sokolov could not find the names Minishkiy or Mishinsky as other sources called him on the lists of staff of the Party's Central Committee, or the Moscow City and Province committees.[53] In October 1941 a Walli I group captured Minishkiy, a political Commissar, near the city of Vyazma. After Hermann Baun, head of Walli I, interrogated him, Minishkiy was transferred to Gehlen's headquarters. Gehlen personally recruited Minishkiy and in May 1942, after training, Minishkiy was smuggled through the front line. The operation was called 'Flamingo'.

According to 'Flamingo' messages from Moscow, Soviet officials believed in Minishkiy's cover story of escaping from the Germans written by Baun's men, and as a reward he was supposedly appointed to a political-military desk at the GKO office. In reality, it was impossible for a Soviet officer who had been in German captivity to be accepted into the GKO staff because he would be vetted in an NKVD filtration camp and, most probably, sent to a *shtrafnoi* battalion. However, judging from Minishkiy's messages to Gehlen, he might have had access to high-level military information. Here is an example.

On July 14, 1942, Gehlen and Heinz Herre, head of the FHO's Gruppe II, presented General Hadler, Chief of the General Staff, with a report based on the message they had just received from Minishkiy.[54] It stated that during the previous night a meeting of 'the war council' took place in Moscow. Marshals Boris Shaposhnikov and Kliment Voroshilov, Commissar for Foreign Affairs Molotov, and 'heads of the British, American, and Chinese military missions' were present. Boris Shaposhnikov reported on future military plans, including preparations for the Stalingrad Battle. The problem of Soviet reserves of manpower, and a redirection—to support British troops in Egypt—of armaments destined for the Soviet Union as part of the lend-lease were also discussed.

Most of the circumstances he mentioned were wrong. This could not be a GKO meeting because the message did not mention Stalin and other GKO members. Most probably, it was a meeting of the representatives of the Red Army (Shaposhnikov and Voroshilov) and Foreign Affairs Commissariat (Molotov) with the Allied military attachés who came to Moscow from Kuibyshev, where foreign embassies moved in June 1941. Heads of military missions could not have attended this meeting because the British and American military missions were organized in Moscow later, in 1943.

But surprisingly, the main details of the message were correct.[55] As it stated, later in July 1942 the Red Army began its retreat to the Volga River, at the same time defending Stalingrad and the Northern Caucasus, and it was on the offensive near Orel and Voronezh. Also, the Soviet government admitted that it had a problem with recruiting new men because of the enormous losses during the first year of the war. And the same July Stalin agreed to redirect a part of the lend-lease military equipment to Egypt to reinforce British troops fighting with Erwin Rommel's Panzer Army Africa.

It remains unknown how Minishkiy acquired information about the agenda of the meeting. Also, he supposedly sent this and other messages through a radio operator 'Aleksander', another Baun agent in Moscow. It is questionable if 'Aleksander' could operate from Moscow, totally controlled by the NKVD counterintelligence. Therefore, the whole of Operation Flamingo looks suspicious, like a Soviet deception. However, there was no sense in Soviet intelligence releasing real information on a number of military plans, a lack of Soviet servicemen in mid-1942, and the help to British troops in Africa.

Cookridge writes that Minishkiy stayed in Moscow for three months, and then Gehlen organized his escape with the help of a Walli I field group that brought him back.[56] Later Minishkiy worked in Group II of the FHO. Presumably, he surrendered to the Americans along with the rest of Gehlen's men and later lived in the United States.

In a number of other cases the FHO was efficient. For instance, it had discovered the existence of SMERSH within three months of its creation.[57]

In July 1943 the FHO captured a secret manual for SMERSH's officers. Gehlen wrote in his memoirs that it described 'how to detect "parachutists, radio operators, saboteurs, and other German espionage agents". It was translated by Group III, and we modified our tactics and forged documents accordingly.'[58] Possibly, this was a copy of the *Instruction for Organizing the Search for Enemy Agents* that SMERSH headquarters sent to every SMERSH officer in the field. A copy of the translated text was immediately sent to Hitler, who attentively read it from cover to cover.

In comparison, SMERSH was able to summarize information on German intelligence only eight months later. In February 1944 Abakumov reported to Stalin and the GKO on the publication of the *Collection of Materials on the German Intelligence Organs Acting at the Soviet–German Front.*[59]

The FHO also conducted the so-called radio games, *Funkspiele*, both with Abwehr III and alone, by using Soviet defectors or captured Soviet radio operators to pass false information to Soviet intelligence and military command. The FHO considered the radio game conducted by Ivan Yassinsky, a former Soviet military interpreter captured in August 1943, very successful. Supposedly, Yassinsky managed to receive 'descriptions of Soviet Intelligence schools at Stavropol and Kuibyshev, where SMERSH trained its senior agents'.[60]

In fact, there was no SMERSH school in Stavropol. If this information was not a Soviet deception, most probably Yassinsky had discovered a military intelligence school in Stavropol-on-Volga (currently Toliatti), a town located near Kuibyshev. In October 1941, the Red Army Military Institute (College) for Foreign Languages that trained military translators and agents was evacuated there from Moscow. Ivan Kruzhko, an attendee of the intelligence courses at this institute, later recalled: 'We were taught to become specialists in the German language. There were also special subjects like geography, German political economy, as well as military disciplines: martial arts, shooting skills, long marching in full marching order, orienting, interrogation of prisoners and so forth.'[61]

Secret Field Police (GFP)

In addition to the Abwehr, there was another counterintelligence organization within the Wehrmacht, the Secret Field Police (Geheime Feldpolizei or GFP). Its task was similar to that of the UOO or the U.S. Army's Counterintelligence Corps (CIC)—the safety and support of the operations of the field army, which mainly consisted of discovering espionage in the German Armed Forces.[62] The GFP was headed by Field Police Chief of the Armed Forces Wilhelm Krichbaum, a close friend of Heydrich, who reported to the OKW Chief Keitel, while Chief of the Army Police Cuno Schmidt was attached to the OKH and reported to Krichbaum.

In reality, the GFP mainly prevented desertion from the German Army, conducted investigation for military tribunals, and fought against partisans. Typically, the GFP worked as a group of approximately 50 men attached to an army and its field operations were coordinated with the Abwehr department 1c.[63] Overall, there were 24 such groups at the Eastern Front. Although in the Wehrmacht, GFP personnel were selected from SS, Gestapo and Kripo (criminal police) men and cooperated with the SS-Einsatzgurppen. Also, field Abwehr III detachments frequently used the GFP for executions. In the occupied territories, the GFP established its own network of local agents.

In 1939, the special Reichssicherhetsdienst (RSD) Gruppe was included in the GFP. It was formed in 1933 as Führerschutzkommando (Führer protection command), Hitler's personal guards in Bavaria. The RSD members were both SS officers and Wehrmacht servicemen. In 1942, the RSD participated in killing the local Jews before Hitler's arrival in the Wehrwolf bunker near Vinnitsa.[64] Oberführer Johann Rattenhuber headed this security force from March 1933 until May 1, 1945, when, fleeing from Hitler's bunker after Hitler's suicide, he was captured by SMERSH.

Chapter 15

German Intelligence and Occupation

Unlike Abwehr, the SD was not part of the German army and its representatives followed the troops in the rear within the Einsatzgruppen, the special killing squads, and later became part of the German administration in the occupied territories. In the occupied territories the SD created its own numerous espionage and diversion schools for volunteers from Soviet POWs and the local population.

The SD and Einsatzgruppen

Within the SD, headed by Walter Schellenberg, three referats of its Abteilung (Section) VI C (espionage in the USSR and Japan) were responsible for gathering and analyzing information on the Soviet Union.[1] Dr. Heinz Gräfe, a former lawyer, headed Abteilung VI C until September 1944, when he was killed in a car accident, and Dr. Erich Hengelhaupt, former specialist in theology and a journalist, succeeded him. Both men were experts on Russia and White emigrants. After almost three million Soviet servicemen were taken prisoner during the first months of Operation Barbarossa, the SD formed its network of Aussenkommandos—mostly mobile commands that interrogated POWs captured near the front line. Many of these SD officers were Baltic Germans who knew Russian well.

The SD was deeply involved in the organization and activity of the SS Einsatzgruppen. On Hitler's orders, the SS Einsatzgruppen were created in 1939, just before World War II, with the task of, as SS General Erich von dem Bach-Zelewski put it at the Nuremberg Trials, 'the annihilation of the Jews, Gypsies, and political commissars'.[2]

In June 1941, Einsatzgruppen followed the German troops in the rear. Einsatzgruppe A was attached to Army Group North and operated in the Baltic States, while Einsatzgruppe B was attached to the Army Group Center and operated in Belorussia. The latter included a special detachment for Moscow, but Moscow was never taken. Finally, two Einsatzgruppen were attached to the Army Group South, Einsatzgruppe C that operated in the Northern and Central Ukraine, and D, which operated in Moldavia, Southern Ukraine, the Crimea, and, eventually, the Caucasus.[3] Their functions partly overlapped with the Abwehr I and III squads because Einsatzgruppen also searched for the Communist Party and NKVD documents.

An Einsatzgruppe consisted of at least 600 men and had headquarters and operational smaller groups, Einsatzkommandos, of 120–170 men, of whom 10–15 were officers. Each Einsatzkommando consisted of two or three smaller units called Sonderkommandos. Einsatzgruppen included members of all SS branches. For example, Einsatzgruppe A under the command of Dr. Franz Walter Stahlecker consisted of:

Members of	Number of men[4]
Waffen SS	340
Gestapo	89
SD	35
Order Police (Orpo)	133
Criminal police (Kripo)	41

Leaders of the Einsatzgruppen, usually highly educated men, received orders from Reinhard Heydrich, head of the RSHA, or from Bruno Streckenbach, Heydrich's deputy and head of the RSHA Personnel Department.[5] Streckenbach had personal experience of heading the Ensatzgruppe I in Poland in the autumn of 1939. After this, in 1939–40, as head of the Gestapo and SD in Krakow, he supervised the arrests and persecution of Polish professors as part of the so-called AB Aktion. Like the Katyn Forest massacre in the Soviet Union in April 1940, this German action aimed to destroy the Polish elite and intelligentsia.

During the first months of the war with the Soviet Union, Einsatzgruppen executed Jews, political commissars, and other high-ranking officers selected from Soviet POWs. In many places Einsatzgruppen were extremely efficient. For instance, the city of Brest was taken over on June 22, 1941, at 9:00 a.m., and by 2:00 p.m. the arrests of the Communist Party and Soviet officials, as well as the Jews, began according to the lists of names prepared by German agents before the war.[6]

Einsatzgruppen committed outrageous atrocities in the occupied territories.[7] For example, Einsatzgruppe C (commanded by Dr. Otto Rasch) carried out the well-known massacre of Jews in Kiev's suburb Babi Yar. Kiev was taken by German troops on September 19, 1941. Despite a chaotic Red Army retreat, before leaving big cities like Kiev and Kharkov, the NKVD operatives and engineering troops usually put remote-controlled mines in important buildings.[8] These mines were blown up by radio signals after the cities were occupied by the Nazis. Many civilians were killed in the central part of Kiev by such explosions, which went on for more than a week, and fires destroyed what was left of the buildings. The Germans and local Ukrainians blamed the Jews for the explosions. As SS representatives reported to Berlin, in retaliation 33,771 Jews were rounded up and killed on September 29 and 30, 1941, by Sonderkommando 4a of Einsatzgruppe C, two squads of the Order Police known as Orpo, and the local collaborators, the Ukrainian militia (police).[9] In fact, the SS decided to exterminate the Jewish population of Kiev on September 16, before the fall of the city and the explosions. By December 1941, the four Einsatzgruppen that followed the German troops had exterminated about 300,000 Jews in the newly-occupied territories.

Einsatzgruppen cooperated with the Abwehr III field groups in vetting Soviet POWs. Abwehr III officers made lists of the Jews, Gypsies, and commissars identified among the POWs. Einsatzgruppen or the GFP used these lists for carrying out executions.[10] From July 1941 onwards, the Gestapo and SD operatives were also responsible for screening POWs and carried out executions of the selected POWs. The Orpo had its own Police Battalions that conducted executions and actions against partisans, and its members also participated in Einsatzgruppen.

Operation Zeppelin

In the spring of 1942, Walter Schellenberg, head of the Amt VI, developed the plan for Operation Zeppelin. In 1945, he testified in Nuremberg:

> The purpose of...[Zeppelin] was to choose from a selection of Russian prisoners intelligent and suitable men to be deployed on the eastern front behind the Russian lines... The POWs thus selected were turned over to Commandos in the rear, who trained the prisoners...in assignments of the secret messenger service and in wireless communications. In order to furnish these prisoners with a motive for work, they were treated extremely well. They were shown the best possible kind of Germany.[11]

The SD Referat VI C/Z was responsible for the whole operation.[12] Its staff was located in the Wansee Villa widely known due to the 1942 conference *The Final Solution of the Jewish Question* that took place there. In November 1944, Schellenberg also moved with his staff to this villa after the Prinz-Albrecht-Palais at Wilhelmstrasse 102, the SS headquarters in Berlin, was bombed out.

At first SS-Sturmbannführer Walter Kurreck headed Referat VI C/Z. After he left Berlin in July 1942 to participate in the Einsatzgruppe D in Southern Russia, SS-Obersturmbannführer Rudolf Oebsger-Röder succeeded him. In the field, special Aussenkommandos of up to 50 men attached to Einsatzgruppen selected Soviet POWs who agreed to work for the SD. Radio contact with the field groups was conducted by 'the Havel Institute', a powerful SD radio station (Referat VI F) installed in Wansee near the villa. The Havel Institute also taught radio operators for Operation Zeppelin.

In February 1943, Oebsger-Röder also left Berlin to command the Einsatzkommando Cluj in Hungary, and SS-Standartenführer Heinz Gräfe became head of the Referat VI C/Z. Two main field Hauptkommandos, Russland-Mitte (consisting of four Aussenkommandos, operational area from the Northern Ukraine to the White Sea) and Russland-Süd (from seven to ten Aussenkommandos, operational area from the Northern Ukraine to the Black Sea; later divided into 'Russland-Nord' and 'Ukraine-Süd') were organized. In the summer of the same year, Dr. Erich Hengelhaupt replaced Gräfe. A year later he divided each part of Operation Zeppelin, including the headquarters staff, into two bureaus: one for compiling information, and another for evaluating the collected information and writing reports to the Referat's chief and Schellenberg. In the main headquarters, the second bureau was also in control of field agents.

The headquarters of each Hauptkommando were in charge of controlling agent operations and training, and preliminary evaluation of incoming information. Compilations of information were sent to Wansee by plane or courier. After Hengelhaupt was promoted to Abteilung VI C head, SS-Standartenführer Walter H. Rapp, a career SD-man, headed Referat VI C/Z from November 1944 to April 1945.

At the beginning of the operation, three secret training schools for Zeppelin agents were organized in the concentration camps Buchenwald, Sachsenhausen, and Auschwitz.[13] Later, there were five Zeppelin companies, four of which were formed of volunteers from a particular ethnic group: Georgians, Armenians, Azeri, and other Caucasian people. People from Central Asia were trained in a camp near Warsaw. Russian agents for parachuting near Moscow, Leningrad, and the industrial region in the Ural Mountains were taught at the Hauptlager Jablon school near the city of Lublin in Poland.

A separate group of approximately 200 experts on the Soviet economy was selected from among the POWs and kept in Special Lager L.[14] These experts analyzed intelligence information on the Soviet economy obtained from Soviet sources and the press, as well as from POWs, and prepared maps and charts of Soviet industrial regions and particular objects.

During the first year, about 3,000 agents graduated from the Zeppelin schools.[15] After the German defeat at Stalingrad in February 1943, the number of POW volunteers for schools dropped significantly.

The FHO provided Zeppelin's agents with specific information for each operation on Soviet territory.[16] Most of these operations failed because agents were captured or killed, or immediately surrendered to the NKVD or SMERSH. Despite this, from 1942 to 1943, the German army had from 500 to 800 agents behind Soviet lines at any time.

Opperation Zeppelin unsuccessfully tried to form an auxiliary military unit, the Russian SS troops. In June 1942, the 1st Russian National SS Detachment or *Druzhina* No. 1 was organized under the command of the former Soviet Lieutenant Colonel Vladimir Gil (pseudonym 'I. G. Rodionov').[17] 'Druzhina' is an old word for a military unit of a Middle Ages Russian prince. By March 1943, *Druzhina* No. 1 became the Special 'Druzhina' SD Brigade that included three rifle battalions and other detachments. The brigade's officers were former Red Army commanders or White Russian officers, and the former Soviet Major General Pavel Bogdanov headed the counterintelligence department. However, the brigade's staff was formed of SS officers and SS-Obersturmbannführer Appel supervised the brigade. On August 16, 1943, while stationed in Belorussia, part of the brigade turned against the Germans and about 2,200 members changed sides. It became the 1st Anti-Fascist Partisan Brigade under Gil-Rodionov's command, but on May 14, 1944 Gil was killed in battle.

Jointly with Alfred Rosenberg's Ministry for Eastern Territories, Zeppelin organized the so-called national committees in exile. According to the Nazi plan, the committees represented future governments of independent states that would be formed after the German victory. There were Georgian, Armenian, Azeri, Turkistan, North Caucasian, Volga Tatar, and Kalmyk committees.[18] For these committees, Rosenberg's ministry opened seven of its own schools in Germany and Poland for training agent-propagandists selected from among POWs and workers brought to Germany from the occupied territories. Finally, the Russian Committee headed by General Andrei Vlasov, which later became the Russian Liberation Army (ROA), was formed in 1942 in Berlin. This was a joint effort of the OKW Propaganda Department, Abwehr, and the RSHA.

In the Occupied Territories

The Germans divided the occupied Soviet territories into two zones, A and B. Zone A included a territory of 800–1,000 kilometers in the rear of the fighting troops and was administered by military commandants. Territories far from the front (Zone B) were managed by Reichskommissars appointed by the Ministry for Eastern Territories established in July 1941.[19] Before the war, Hitler planned to organize four Reichskommissariaten in Russia, but only two were established, Reichskommissariat Ostland (Baltic States and Belorussia, Reichskommissar Hinrich Lohse) and Reichskommissariat Ukraine (Ukraine and the neighboring territories, Reichskommissar Erich Koch). Both Abwehr and SS organized local centers within the German civilian administration of Reichskommissars.

In July 1941, Abwehr established its center, Abwehrstelle (or Ast) Ostland, in Riga.[20] It consisted of three departments (intelligence, sabotage, and counterintelligence) and coordinated intelligence and counterintelligence work in the occupied Baltic States and part of Belorussia. Branches (Abwehrnebenstellen or Ansts) were also organized in Tallinn, Kaunas, and Minsk and smaller units in other Baltic towns, as well as mobile detachments in Belorussia. Ast officers could make arrests and carry out investigations. In 1942, Ast Ostland opened two schools for training its own agents. In 1944, the SMERSH Directorate of the 2nd Baltic Front captured lists of the Ast Ostland agents who were sent to the rear of the Red Army.

To combat NKVD agents and partisans in Ukraine, in August 1941 Abwehr III formed a counterintelligence center Ast Ukraine in Rovno (later it moved to Poltava), headed by Colonel Naumann.[21] It consisted of five referats:

III F:combating Soviet intelligence agents

III C:combating the Soviet underground and partisans

III L:counterintelligence in the air force

III Kgf:counterintelligence among POWs

III M:counterintelligence in the Navy in the city of Nikolaev (a port on the Black Sea).

Ast Ukraine had branches (Ansts) in Kiev, Nikolaev, and Vinnitsa as well as smaller units under the cover of military staffs. Many of these units were headed by White Russian émigrés. The work of Ast Ukraine was based on information from local secret agents.

At the beginning of 1943, the Abwehr had 130 intelligence and sabotage centers in the occupied territory. It opened 60 schools in Minsk, Vitebsk, Smolensk, Orel, Poltava, the Crimea, and so forth. According to SMERSH information, the schools trained four categories of agents:

1. Agent-spies, whose task was to gather information about the Red Army and send it back to German intelligence centers;

2. Agent-saboteurs, whose task was to blow up military and industrial facilities;

3. Agent-terrorists, whose task was to assassinate Red Army commanders and government functionaries;

4. Agent-propagandists, whose task was to disseminate false rumors about the Red Army and its inevitable defeat.[22]

After training, the agents were sent into Soviet-controlled territory.

In Zone B, the SS established a chain administered by five SS and Police Leaders (Höhere SS und Polizeiführer or HSSPf).[23] Himmler personally appointed HSSPfs and they reported to him. Higher SS and Police Leaders (Höchste SS und Polizeiführers or HöSSPfs) headed regional SS centers and reported to the HSSPfs.[24] An SS und Polizeiführer (SSPf) commanded a local headquarters staff that represented the Orpo, Gestapo, SD and Waffen SS and was usually formed of Einsatzgruppen personnel who had operated in the region. Additional police forces were recruited from among the locals.

From mid-1943 onwards, finding and arresting members of all the above-mentioned German organizations was the main goal of SMERSH. In addition, SMERSH took on the enormous task of arresting and vetting Soviet collaborators and many Soviet citizens who had the misfortune to have lived in German-occupied territories.

Soviet Collaborators

The relationship between the local population and the German invaders during the occupation was not black and white, but much more complicated. The brief German occupation of Kaluga, a town located 190 kilometers to the southwest of Moscow, was a good example. German troops occupied Kaluga on October 13, 1941, during their fast advance toward Moscow. By November 8, the Germans had organized a Jewish ghetto, ordered the Jews to put on yellow stars, shot some of them, and hanged several partisans.

At the same time, the Germans opened Orthodox churches—an important anti-Soviet propaganda gesture. Most churches had been closed since the 1920s because in the Soviet Union the Church was viewed as a potential ideological rival of Communism. In 1941, Metropolitan Sergei Voskresensky, who lived in Riga, even created the 'Russian Orthodox Mission in the Liberated [i.e. German-occupied] Regions of Russia', with Pskov as the Church administration center.[25] Nikolai Gavrilov, a sculptor drafted by the Red Army to draw illustrations of war scenes, recalled: '[In Kaluga] fifty-two official marriages of Germans with our girls were registered in the churches… During the retreat, the Germans took these women with them and later killed them.'[26] After the Soviet 50th Army took back Kaluga, OO operatives hunted down collaborators—administrators appointed by the occupants, the editor and staff of a Russian newspaper that was published in Kaluga during the two-month occupation, and so forth.

Three days before Kaluga was liberated, the GKO ordered the arrest of the family members of all traitors and German collaborators sentenced by the OSO.[27] In June 1942, a new GKO order defined the family members of the servicemen and civilians who had been sentenced to death for treason, worked for the Germans during the occupation or escaped with the retreating Germans: the father, mother, husband, wife, sons, daughters, brothers and sisters 'if they lived together with the traitor or were at his expense at the time when the crime was committed'. [28]

The scale of Russian collaboration with the Nazis was astonishing.[29] Approximately 10 percent of the whole population in the occupied territory supported the Germans, about 700,000 former Soviet servicemen became 'hiwis' (noncombatant volunteers) and 1.4 million participated in the Nazi-controlled military units. To administer this huge number of volunteers, in December 1942 Lieutenant General Heinz Hellmich was appointed 'General for Eastern Troops' and attached to the Second Section of the OKH General Staff's Organizational Deparment headed by Claus von Stauffenberg, the future leader of the 20th July 1944 Plot.[30] In January 1944, General Ernst Köstring, former Military Attaché in Moscow (1935–41) and in March-June 1943, 'Delegate General for Caucasus Questions' (i.e., military governor of the occupied part of the Caucasus), replaced von Stauffenberg and his title became 'General of Volunteer Formations'.[31] Köstring was born in Russia, spoke perfect Russian and knew the country well.

One can understand a Soviet POW volunteering for an Abwehr or Zeppelin school—it was the only chance for survival in the inhuman conditions of the German POW camps.[32] Many also saw this as an opportunity to return to Soviet territory. However, the creation of Russian troops under German control was another matter. There were the above-mentioned Special 'Druzhina' SD Brigade and the Vlasov Army, as well as the Russian National Liberation Army (RONA) and various Cossack formations. The RONA of 10,000 men was created in the Lokot' Republic, a Russian-administered region in German-occupied territory. It existed from 1941 to 1943 and was supported by Günther von Kluge, Commander of the Army Group Center.[33] The main Cossack formation, the XVth SS Cossack Cavalry Corps, formed in 1943 under the command of the German General Helmuth von Pannwitz, numbered 50,000 men. On the whole, by mid-1944, the Wehrmacht had 200 battalions of troops formed of Russians, Ukrainians, Belorussians and other nationalities.

The memoirs of Soviet POWs mention an important psychological detail of being taken prisoner: 'In a few days all imprisoned Red Army commanders suddenly turned into strong enemies of their own country, the country where they were born, and of the government which they had sworn allegiance to…Those who continued to address "Comrade Commander" were punched in their faces or were even beaten up more seriously, and saying "*Gospodin ofitser*" ["Sir officer", the address used in the Czar's Army] became common.'[34] In Oflag XII-D for officers in Hammelsburg, the imprisoned Soviet major generals Fyodor Trukhin, Dmitrii Zakutnyi and Ivan Blagoveshchensky 'cursed Stalin and the Soviet regime with the worst words and they agreed to the fact that [Mikhail] Tukhachevsky and his accomplices were innocent executed victims'.[35] These three generals soon became among the most enthusiastic supporters of General Andrei Vlasov and his army. These examples show that many servicemen hated the Soviet regime so much that they were ready to fight against it, even on the enemy's side. Not the least important reason for this was Stalin's refusal to admit the existence of Soviet POWs. Soviet servicemen were supposed to commit suicide, not be taken prisoner.

The number of deserters and draft-evading individuals caught by the NKVD Rear Guard Troops was also enormous. According to Beria reports, from June 1941 till mid-1943, it reached 1,666,891 men; of these, 1,210,224 were deserters. Later, in May 1944 alone, 24,898 deserters and 26,300 draft-evading individuals were caught, 285 of whom were officers.[36] Of this number, 9,128 individuals were arrested and transferred for investigation to SMERSH, NKGB, and the Prosecutor's Office. Even at the end of the war, among 27,629 Soviet servicemen captured by the Germans between December 1944 and March 1945, 1,710 men (6 percent) crossed the front line voluntarily.[37] If these figures are accurate, this is a very high number. Possibly, some Soviet POWs who changed lines so late in the war hoped to end up in the hands of the Allies. If so, they did not know that, according to the secret agreements in Yalta, most of them would be handed back to SMERSH and the NKVD.

In many Soviet regions, especially Ukraine, in 1941 the local population greeted the German troops as their liberators from the Soviet regime. The head of a partisan staff in Belorussia reported that the day before the Germans came 'the unstrained anti-Soviet individuals whistled at and unequivocally threatened the evacuating Soviet and Party activists and their families, while some Soviet administrators used every reason to escape the evacuation'.[38] In the Stavropolsky Region, located on the border with the Northern Caucasus and occupied by the Germans in 1942, the population was convinced that German rule would be forever.[40] Soon the German atrocities against Soviet POWs, Jews, and later the whole population (with the German racial attitude toward Slavs as inferior Untermenschen) turned most of the people against the occupiers. But the Soviet regime refused to excuse either open collaborators during the two-year occupation period or the whole population living in the German-occupied territory, since everyone could be considered to have been 'following orders of the German administration' and, therefore, punishable as a traitor.[39]

The population of Belorussian and West Ukrainian territories taken back by the Red Army in 1943–44 immediately experienced Stalin's attitude toward those who were under the German occupation. All men were mobilized. A witness wrote: 'The lack in men [in the troops] was so considerable that mobilization, in fact, turned into hunting people, like slave traders hunted Negros in Africa in the past…At dawn we encircled a village. We were ordered to shoot every person after the first notification who would try to escape from the village. A special commando group entered every house in the village, forcing all men to come out, irrespective of age and health, and to gather in the square. Then they were convoyed to special camps. There they were checked by doctors, while the politically unreliable were taken away.'[41]

Regular soldiers called the mobilized locals *chernorubashechniki* (black shirts) or *sumochnye divizii* (divisions with bags) because these peasants were not given uniforms and many of them had self-made bags with food.[42] Commonly they were not provided even with rifles because they were supposed to get trophy guns after a battle. Most of these unarmed people were wiped out in the first skirmish with the Germans.

The suspicion of collaboration continued until the end of the Soviet Union. Every Soviet citizen, even born after World War II, needed to mention in their biography form if he or she, or his or her relatives, had lived in the occupied territory during the war. If they did, this could prevent a person from being hired for a job connected with the military or secret issues, or from being allowed to travel abroad because for going abroad, each Soviet citizen needed the approval of the Communist Party and KGB officials.

Part V. The Birth of SMERSH

CHAPTER 16

The Birth of SMERSH

At the beginning of 1943, the situation at the fronts started to change. After the success in Stalingrad, Soviet troops began advancing into the southern part of Russia. With the tide of war now turned in the Soviets' favor, desertions among their troops decreased considerably. Stalin's attitude toward the army, especially toward officers, also started to change.

The Turning Point: Spring 1943

To increase patriotism among the troops, in January 1943 Stalin opened a propaganda campaign to remind servicemen of Russia's past military glory during the imperial period. At first, shoulder boards similar to those used by the czar's army officers and soldiers were introduced.[1] Now the color, insignia, number, and size of the stars on the shoulder boards identified the troop type and rank.

On January 28, 1943, Marshal Georgii Zhukov and 22 generals were awarded the newly introduced Order of Suvorov of the 1st Class for the victory in Stalingrad. This was one of three orders named after the historical Russian military heroes, Generalissimo Aleksandr Suvorov (1730–1800), General Mikhail Kutuzov (1747–1813), and Prince Aleksandr Nevsky (1221–1263). The movie *Aleksandr Nevsky* had already attracted public attention to this Russian hero who fought German knights in the thirteenth century. Filmed by the famous director Sergei Eisenstein, it was a blockbuster in 1938 and became even more popular in 1941, when on Stalin's order it was shown again after the German invasion. Later Stalin personally edited film scripts that glorified Suvorov as a great warrior and Kutuzov as a savior of Russia from Napoleon's troops. Stalin gave a copy of the film *Kutuzov* to Winston Churchill, who courteously wrote him back: 'I must tell you that in my view this is one of the most masterly film productions I have ever seen.'[2]

The Order of Suvorov was given to commanders for a successful offensive, the Order of Kutuzov for the successful planning of an operation by staff members, and the Order of Nevsky for personal courage. They were established on July 29, 1942, the day after Stalin signed the infamous Order No. 227 'No Step Back!'—apparently, to show that commanders would be not only punished, but also awarded.[3] However, the first orders were given only at the end of December 1942–January 1943. The Order of Nevsky directly appealed to the czar's time, when the Order of Saint Aleksandr Nevsky had been given since 1725. No historical image of Prince Nevsky existed, and in 1942 the designer depicted on the order a portrait of the actor who played Nevsky in the movie.

In July 1943, the word 'officer' was also introduced.[4] Until then, it was not officially used in the Soviet Union because it immediately created a mental association with White Guard officers. The Red Army officers were called 'commanders' and only after July 1943 did they become 'officers'. In August 1943, a propaganda brochure entitled *The Heroic Past of the Russian People* was published mostly for the army *politruki*. Now Russia was considered the leading nation among the many nations inhabiting the Soviet Union.

In the meantime, by 1943 Soviet intelligence and counterintelligence knew little about the complexity of the German intelligence and security services. This knowledge came later, as a result of the interrogations of numerous captured German intelligence officers, as well as German-trained Russian agents who voluntarily surrendered to the Soviets. Even so, it became evident that military counterintelligence needed to concentrate on fighting against the German enemy rather than focusing its attention on its own servicemen. After realizing this, Stalin ordered the creation of a real counterintelligence service, called SMERSH, which reported personally to him.

Stalin's New Secret Service

In March 1943, the reorganization of security services began. Vsevolod Merkulov, a man with 'an athletic figure and a splendid head of thick dark hair flecked with grey', who Stalin put in charge of the transition, gathered the OO heads of several fronts and armies in Moscow.[5] Abakumov's closest subordinates, Pavel Zelenin, Nikolai Khannikov, Mikhail Belkin, and Isai Babich, were among the participants. Merkulov told the assembled leaders that 'the Central Committee and Comrade Stalin' had asked the OOs to increase their efforts so 'no spy, agent, or terrorist would escape the attention of the special departments'.[6] It is likely the changes were discussed at a late-night meeting of the GKO, which both Merkulov and Abakumov attended on March 31 at 11:30 p.m.[7]

In April, Merkulov presented Stalin with three different drafts for the revival of the early 1941 NKGB.[8] In the first two versions, the new NKGB would include military counterintelligence under the name 'Smerinsh', that is, '*Smert' inostrannym shpionam*' or 'Death to foreign spies'. The third version proposed two separate organizations, the NKGB and Smerinsh, as a directorate within the Defense Commissariat (NKO). This draft and other relevant documents were discussed at a GKO meeting that began at 10:05 p.m. on April 13.[9] Leading NKVD and OO officers were invited—Merkulov, Abakumov, Lavrentii

Tsanava, Nikolai Selivanovsky, Nikolai Korolev, Khannikov, Babich, and Niko-lai Mel'nikov (deputy head of Sudoplatov's 4th NKVD Directorate)—and all of them would end up being affected by the changes. General Filipp Golikov, the newly appointed deputy defense Commissar for Red Army personnel, and Aleksandr Shcherbakov, head of the GlavPURKKA, also attended. By 11:30 p.m. most of the participants had left, although Stalin, Molotov, Beria, and Malenkov continued their discussion until after midnight.

The next day the Politburo ordered the NKVD to be divided into two parts, and the revived NKGB became a super-agency handling foreign intel-ligence, counterintelligence within the USSR, and so forth (Figure 16-1).[10] Merkulov was appointed NKGB Commissar while Beria remained the head of NKVD. The responsibilities that the NKVD was left with—the orga-nization of slave labor, police work, control of the system of POW camps, and NKVD troops—were far less important and glamorous than the in-telligence and counterintelligence work that the NKGB now took on.[11] Although this may seem a huge diminution of Beria's power, in actuality he retained much of it through his control of his close associate Merkulov.

Abakumov was summoned to Stalin's office on April 15 and 18, and the final decision was made on April 19, 1943, at a Politburo meeting attended by Abakumov and Merkulov.[12] As usual, the draft of the Politburo decision said that the decision was made jointly by the Party's Central Committee and Sovnarkom (Council of Commissars). However, Stalin crossed out the words 'the Central Committee' with a blue pencil and signed the document as Sovnarkom's chairman.[13] The document was registered as Sovnarkom Resolution No. 415-138-ss; the two letters 'ss' (*sovershenno sekretno*) mean top secret, although members of the Sovnarkom had not seen it yet. The resolution ordered the NKVD's UOO to be split into three separate mili-tary counterintelligence directorates within the NKO, Navy Commissariat, and NKVD, respectively, as had been done in early 1941.

Two days later Abakumov was called to Stalin's office again and the document finalizing the creation of SMERSH was signed.[14] It had a singu-larly long, awkward title: 'GKO Decision No. 3222-ss/ov [the letters "ov" mean "of special importance"] on the Responsibilities and Structure of the Main Directorate of Counterintelligence (GUKR) SMERSH (Smert' shpi-onam).'[15] Thus, in the final version the name 'Smerinsh' or 'Death to for-eign spies', became 'Smersh', meaning 'Death to spies'. The original, with Stalin's signature, was sent to Abakumov.

On April 29, Abakumov was again in Stalin's office.[16] Apparently, dur-ing this half-hour visit, Stalin signed a document specifying appointments for high-level positions within GUKR SMERSH, including heads of de-partments, which Abakumov had prepared two days earlier.[17] Nikolai Se-livanovsky became Abakumov's first deputy, while Pavel Meshik and Isai Babich became deputies.

Figure 16-1   THE REORGANIZATION OF THE NKGB AND THE NKO'S SMERSH
APRIL 1943 TO MAY 1946

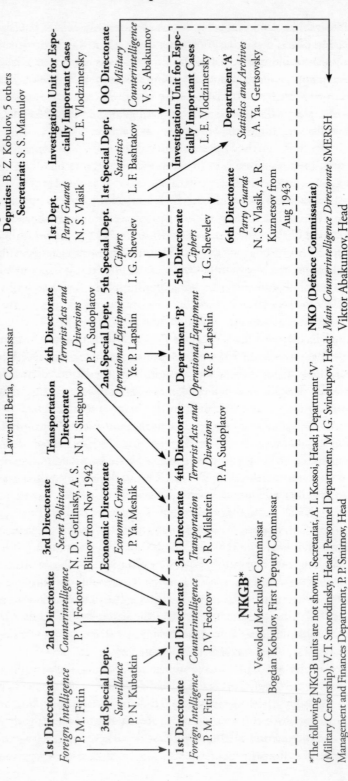

*The following NKGB units are not shown: Secretariat, A. I. Kossoi, Head; Department 'V' (Military Censorship), V. T. Smorodinsky, Head; Personnel Department, M. G. Svinelupov, Head; Management and Finances Department, P. P. Smirnov, Head

Abakumov was appointed deputy Commissar of the NKO, reporting directly to Stalin. Although he was relieved of the NKO post a month later, Abakumov's removal as deputy Commissar was not a slight against him. Stalin simply wanted to reduce the number of NKO deputies. He promoted Marshal Georgii Zhukov to be first deputy, and replaced sixteen deputy commissars, including Abakumov, with only one, Marshal Aleksandr Vasilevsky, head of the General Staff.[18] In any case, as head of GUKR SMERSH, Abakumov continued 'to be subordinated directly to the People's Commissar of Defense [Stalin] and to follow only his orders', as Decision 3222-ss/ov mandated.

On May 4, the Directorate of the NKVD Troops for Guarding the Rear of the Red Army ('rear guard troops') was promoted to a separate Main Directorate and given the responsibility of providing support for SMERSH's activities.[19] On December 1, 1944, Lt. General Ivan Gorbatyuk replaced Leontiev as head of this Main Directorate. These troops, now numbering 163,000 men, continued to capture German soldiers, spies, and paratroopers in the rear of Soviet combat units. The rear guard troops existed until October 13, 1945.

The same order that created GUKR SMERSH within the NKO created a parallel organization within the Navy Commissariat, the NKVMF, which was simply a reorganization of the 9th Department of the UOO that dealt with the navy.[20] This organization was known as the Navy UKR SMERSH. A month later the 6th Department of the UOO, in charge of monitoring NKVD troops such as the Border Guards and rear guard troops, was reorganized into a third counterintelligence unit, the OKR Smersh, which remained within the NKVD.[21] At the time, the NKVD troops grew into a separate army: in 1942, the number of servicemen in these troops was 420,000, and by January 1945, it reached 800,000.[22]

The Navy and NKVD counterintelligence units were smaller and therefore less significant than the NKO's SMERSH. This is evident from the fact that they were organized as a UKR and an OKR, respectively. In all Soviet acronyms, 'G' at the beginning means 'Main'; 'U' means 'Directorate'; 'O' means 'Department'; and 'KR' means 'Counterintelligence'. A 'Main Directorate' is a larger organization than a 'Directorate', and a 'Directorate' is bigger than a 'Department'. UKRs were subordinated to the GUKR, and each of the UKRs was comprised of departments. In typed documents of the NKVD's OKR Smersh, only the 'S' in 'Smersh' was capitalized, while in NKO and NKVMF documents, SMERSH was spelled in all capital letters. UKRs were always comprised of one or more OKRs.

The Navy UKR SMERSH was headed by Pyotr Gladkov and two of his deputies, Aleksei Lebedev and Sergei Dukhovich. It consisted of four departments, along with an investigation unit, a ciphering section, an operational equipment section, and some miscellaneous units. It was given its own building in a central part of Moscow and moved out of the Lu-byanka building. Besides the main headquarters in Moscow, each of the four fleets—the Baltic, Northern, Black Sea, and Pacific—had its own field OKR or Department of Counterintelligence that reported to the Navy UKR SMERSH in Moscow.

The OKR Smersh consisted of six sections, a special group (used for se-cret operations), a group for the registration of informers, and a Secretariat. Its head reported directly to NKVD Commissar Beria. Besides the Moscow headquarters, there were numerous branches of OKR Smersh: an OKR in the NKVD rear guard troops at each of the twelve fronts; two OKRs in the interior NKVD troops (in Ukraine and on the Northern Caucasus); ten Smersh departments in each of the border guard groups; and a department in the First Motorized NKVD Division and the Special Motorized NKVD Brigade.[23] As with the other two SMERSH organizations, there was a ver-tical, centralized command structure in which each OKR reported to the next higher OKR level. Also, there were OKR Smersh departments in four big industrial cities: Moscow, Kuibyshev (now Samara), Novosibirsk, and Sverdlovsk (now Yekaterinburg).

The work of the NKVD's Smersh was based entirely on reports from informers. During 1943 and 1944, it arrested 293 alleged traitors to the Motherland, 100 espionage suspects, 76 'German supporters', and 356 de-serters among the NKVD troops.[24] Additionally, in 1944 almost 10,000 servicemen, including 450 officers, were transferred from the NKVD troops (which were considered elite units compared to the military) to the Red Army because of 'compromising materials' the OKR Smersh had col-lected on them.

Besides its primary function of spying on NKVD troops, the NKVD OKR also kept an eye on the activities of Abakumov's SMERSH. For example, NKVD counterintelligence reported to Beria on SMERSH officials who had sent looted property from conquered European ter-ritories to the Soviet Union. If arrested, SMERSH officers and their informants were tried by military tribunals of NKVD troops, not of the Red Army.[25]

Similarly, SMERSH officers reported to Abakumov on the false infor-mation that investigators of the rear guard troops extracted from arrested locals by beatings and torture. At the same time, there was also cooperation between the NKVD's Smersh and Abakumov's SMERSH. If the NKVD's Smersh captured German paratroopers dropped behind Soviet lines, they were transferred to Abakumov's SMERSH for full investigation.

Of the three military counterintelligence organizations, the NKO's GUKR SMERSH became the most important and powerful agency by far. For simplicity's sake, from this point on, this organization will be referred to as SMERSH.

The Structure and Function of SMERSH

A separate attachment to GKO Decision No. 3222-ss/ov detailed the organization of SMERSH and its branches in the army:

> The 'Smersh' organs are a centralized organization. At the fronts and military districts the 'Smersh' organs (the NKO 'Smersh' directorates at fronts and NKO 'Smersh' departments at the armies, corps, divisions, brigades, military districts, and other units and organizations of the Red Army) are subordinated only to their higher organs...
>
> The 'Smersh' organs inform Military Councils and commanders of the corresponding units, troops, and organizations of the Red Army on the matters of their work: on the results of their combat with enemy agents, on the penetration of the army units by anti-Soviet elements, and on the results of combat against traitors of the Motherland, deserters, and self-mutilators.[26]

Compared to its predecessor, the UOO, SMERSH was mostly focused on enemy spies, although Red Army servicemen were still under suspicion. The rules for arrests of servicemen were also detailed in the same GKO Decision:

> a) The arrest of a private or a junior officer should be approved by a prosecutor;
> b) [The arrest] of a mid-level commander should be approved by the commander and prosecutor of the military unit;
> c) [The arrest] of a high-level commander should be approved by the Military Council [of the front] and a prosecutor;
> d) [The arrest] of a commander of the highest level should be authorized by the People's Commissar of Defense [Stalin].[27]

Abakumov kept Stalin updated on all high-ranking commanders, and according to Merkulov, Abakumov reported to Stalin almost every day 'on the behavior of a number of leading military officers'.[28]

In general, the organization of SMERSH repeated the structure of the UOO within the NKVD. The headquarters, GUKR SMERSH, was located on the fourth and sixth floors of the NKVD/NKGB building in the center of Moscow at No. 2 Dzerzhinsky (Lubyanka) Square with the entrance from Kuznetsky Most Street. Abakumov's huge office was on the fourth floor.

GUKR SMERSH directed the work of the field directorates assigned to the fronts, which hereinafter will be referred to as UKRs SMERSH to distinguish them from the GUKR SMERSH in Moscow. Whenever both organizations are meant, they will be referred to simply as SMERSH.

On the whole, fifteen UKRs were established at the fronts in April 1943 (Table 16-1). All heads of front UKRs remained at their posts until the end of the war or until the front was disbanded.

In the GUKR, thirteen assistants to Abakumov with their staffs were responsible for the UKRs:

Name[29]	Front Responsibility	Dates
A. A. Avseevich	Northwestern	Apr 29, 1943–Jul 9, 1943
G. S. Bolotin-Balyasnyi	Volkhov/3rd Belorussian	Apr 29, 1943–May 22, 1946
I. P. Konovalov	Southern/4th Ukrainian	Apr 29, 1943–May 27, 1946
S. F. Kozhevnikov	Leningrad	Apr 29, 1943–Jun 4, 1946
N. G. Kravchenko	Bryansk/2nd Baltic	May 26, 1943–Jul 1944
A. P. Misyurev	Kalinin/1st Baltic	Apr 29, 1943–May 27, 1946
F. G. Petrov	Southwestern/3rd Ukrainian	May 26, 1943–Dec 28, 1943
K. L. Prokhorenko	Voronezh/1st Ukrainian	Apr 29, 1943–Oct 4, 1944
V. P. Rogov	Western/3rd Belorussian	Apr 29, 1943–May 27, 1946
N. A. Rozanov	Northwestern/2nd Belorussian	Oct 10, 1943–May 4, 1946
I. T. Rusak	Karelian	Apr 29, 1943–May 27, 1946
V. T. Shirmanov	Central/1st Belorussian	May 26, 1943–Mar 23, 1944
P. P. Timofeev	Steppe/2nd Ukrainian	Sep 23, 1943-May 22, 1946

They were not only in constant contact with the front UKR staffs, but also personally visited the front UKRs, bringing orders and instructions from the GUKR. Another assistant, Major General Ivan Moskalenko, was responsible for general matters and personnel. One of the assistants, Vyacheslav Rogov, became very close to Abakumov, and after the war Abakumov appointed him head of the 4th MGB Directorate (specializing in searching for suspects).

Colonel Ivan Chernov, former head of a section in the UOO, was appointed head of the GUKR SMERSH Secretariat, while Yakov Broverman, former head of the UOO Secretariat, became Chernov's deputy.

GUKR in Moscow consisted of eleven operational and three non-operational departments (Figure 16-2), a total of 646 men (for comparison, in 1942 the UOO staff in Moscow consisted of 225 men). Not all departments corresponded to their UOO predecessors. With the new focus on the Germans and other foreign enemies, two departments, the 3rd and 4th, were transferred from the NKVD/NKGB. The 3rd Department was in charge of capturing German spies in the rear and organizing 'radio games'

TABLE 16-1. HEADS OF UKR SMERSH DIRECTORATES IN APRIL 1943[1]

Front or District	Front Military Commander	UKR Head[2]
Karelian Front (disbanded in Nov 1944)	Col. Gen. V. A. Frolov	A. M. Sidney, D. I. Mel'nikov (Mar–Nov 1944)
Leningrad Front	Marshal L. A. Govorov	A. S. Bystrov
Kalinin Front (1st Baltic Front from Oct 1943; Zemland Group from Mar 1945)	Army Gen. A. I. Yeremenko	N. G. Khannikov
Volkhov Front (in Feb 1944 divided between the Leningrad and 2nd Baltic fronts)	Marshal K. A. Meretskov	D. I. Mel'nikov
Northwestern Front (disbanded Nov 1943; 2nd Belorussian Front from Feb 1944))	Col. Gen. I. S. Konev	Ya. A. Yedunov
Western Front (3rd Belorussian Front from April 1944)	Army Gen. V. D. Sokolovsky	P. V. Zelenin
Central Front (1st Belorussian Front from Oct 1943)	Marshal K. K. Rokossovsky	A. A. Vadis
Voronezh Front (1st Ukrainian Front from Oct 1943)	Army Gen. N. F. Vatutin	N. A. Osetrov
Bryansk Front (2nd Baltic Front from Oct 1943)	Col. Gen. M A. Reiter	N. I. Zheleznikov
Southern Front (4th Ukrainian Front from Oct 1943)	Army Gen. F. I. Tolbukhin	N. K. Kovalchuk
Steppe Military District (2nd Ukrainian Front from Oct 1943)	Col. Gen. M. M. Popov	N. A. Korolev
Northern Caucasian Front (Primorsk Army from Nov 1943)	Col. Gen. I. I. Maslennikov; Col. Gen. I. Ye. Petrov from May 1943	M. I. Belkin[3]
Transcaucasian Front	Army Gen. I. V. Tyulenev	N. M. Rukhadze
Transbaikal Front	Col. Gen. M. P. Kovalev	I. T. Saloimsky
Far Eastern Front	Army Gen. M. A. Purkarev	A. N. Chesnokov
Moscow Military District	Col. Gen. P. A. Artemiev	F. Ya. Tutushkin

1. Of six districts, only the Moscow Military District is included, as it was the biggest and most important.
2. From Order of Defence Commissariat No. 4/ssh, dated April 29, 1943.
3. In October 1944, Mikhail Belkin was appointed head of the UKR of the 3rd Baltic Front under the command of Army General I. I. Maslennikov. From July 1945 to June 1946, Belkin headed the Inspectorate (a branch of SMERSH) at the Allied Control Commission in Hungary.

Figure 16-2

The structure of **SMERSH** within the Defence Commissariat
April 1943 to May 1946

Main Counterintelligence Directorate
SMERSH

Viktor S. Abakumov, Head
(subordinated to I. V. Stalin,
Defence Commissar)

Deputies
N. N. Selivanovsky, P. Ya. Meshik,
I. Ya. Babich, I. I. Vradii
plus 16 assistants
Secretariat
I. A. Chernov, Head;
Ya. M. Broverman, Deputy Head

1st Department
*Counterintelligence in
the Staff of the Defence
Commissariat and the
Red Army Commanders*
Major General
I. I. Gorgonov

2nd Department
*Filtering Enemy
POWs, Vetting Soviet
POWs*
Colonel
S. N. Kartashov

3rd Department
*Capturing Spies
in the Red Army Rear,
Radio Games*
Col. G. V. Utekhin
Apr 1943–Sep 1943;
Col. V. Ya. Baryshnikov
Sep 1943–May 1946

4th Department
*Counterintelligence
behind the Front Line*
Col. P. P. Timofeev
Apr1943–Sep 1943;
Col. G. V. Utekhin
Sep 1943–May 1946

5th Department
*Guidance of SMERSH
Directorates of Fronts*
Col. D. S. Zenichev

6th Department
Investigation
Colonel
A. G. Leonov

7th Department
*Registration and
Statistics*
Colonel
A. Ye. Sidorov

8th Department
Ciphering
Colonel
M. P. Sharikov

9th Department
*Operational Techni-
cal Equipment*
Lt. Colonel
A. Ye. Kochetkov

10th Department
*Searches, Arrests,
Surveillance*
Major
A. M. Zbrailov

11th Department
Special Operations
Col. I. A. Chertov

Personnel Department
Major General
I. I. Vradii

**Management
and Finances**
Lt. Colonel
S. A. Polovnev
Apr 1943–Nov 1944;
Col. M. K. Kochegarov
Nov 1944–May 1946

Political Department
Col. N. M. Siden'kov

with their help, and the 4th Department was in charge of counterintelligence measures behind the front line. Five of the departments, the 1st, 2nd, 3rd, 4th and 6th, were involved directly in investigation.

The UKR SMERSH of a front directed the subordinated SMERSH departments (OKRs) within the armies and units. Three SMERSH officers were attached to each rifle regiment, while the OKR at the division level consisted of 21 men, including a head, his deputy, a ciphering officer, investigators, a commandant, and a platoon of guards.[30] The OKR of each army included 57 men, while the size of a front UKR depended on how many armies the front was comprised of. If the front consisted of five armies, its UKR included 130 officers; if there were fewer armies, the UKR had 112 officers.[31] The UKRs of military districts, of which the Moscow Military District was the biggest, consisted of 102–193 officers. For operational work, such as guarding prisoners, the Red Army provided SMERSH with field formations made up of regular servicemen. SMERSH front directorates were provided with a battalion, SMERSH army departments, a company, and SMERSH departments at the regiment, division, or brigade level, a platoon.

The positions and responsibilities of the personnel and departments in the UKR SMERSH and OKR SMERSH were very similar. Here is the typical structure of a UKR SMERSH:

Position/Unit	Duties
Head	Commanding
Secretariat	Secretarial work
Personnel Department	In charge of the cadres
1st Department	Overseeing the staff of the headquarters
2nd Department	Counterintelligence in the rear, catching German agents, interrogation of German POWs, vetting Soviet POWs
3rd Department	Guidance of subordinated units and combating enemy agents, anti-Soviet elements, traitors to the motherland, military criminals
4th Department	Investigation
Komendatura	Guarding prisoners; executions
Records Section	Making and keeping records

The only difference was the that OKR SMERSH organizations had 'sections' instead of 'departments' and the responsibilities of the 3rd Department in UKR SMERSH units was divided between the 3rd and 4th sections in OKR SMERSH units with investigations being carried out by a separate Investigative Section.

The 1st Department of the GUKR SMERSH was in charge of counterintelligence within the Red Army command. Operational officers were assigned to all military units from the battalion level upward.[32] The 1st Department coordinated all the information from secret informers and also controlled the political officers within the Red Army. Colonel Ivan Gorgonov, head of the 1st Department, previously headed the 10th UOO Department, which administrated the work of the front OOs.

The 2nd Department was in charge of working with foreign POWs and of 'filtering' Soviet servicemen who had been POWs.[33] Its head, Colonel Sergei Kartashov, who had been working in military counterintelligence since 1937, was extremely efficient; he had a phenomenal memory and remembered hundreds of detainees' names and all the details of their cases. The department was also responsible for collecting intelligence and sending SMERSH agents to areas immediately behind enemy lines.

To identify important people among prisoners, especially intelligence officers among German POWs, operatives of the 2nd departments depended on German informers. Nicola Sinevirsky wrote that 'the Germans informed on one another very willingly. In our work with POWs we learned that even by offering them cigarettes and promising them liberty, one in ten would do a job for us'.[34] Sinevirsky gives an example: 'Hans had been a driver in the Abwehr of the Middle Group Army Headquarters. He could identify a number of German spies, which explained why SMERSH had dragged him from one stockade to another... The first day, he recognized and identified seven spies. By SMERSH standards, he did an excellent job and was rewarded with generous rations of tinned meat, white bread, and chocolate.'

In January 1945, Abakumov proudly wrote to Beria:

> From September 1, 1943, to January 1, 1945, the SMERSH organs of the fronts and military districts recruited 697 former enemy agents and used them to search for German spies and saboteurs. They helped to arrest 703 German spies and saboteurs.
>
> At present, the SMERSH organs are using 396 agent-identifiers to find enemy agents... I have already reported to Comrade Stalin on the matter described above.[35]

Information about the capture and interrogation of important prisoners was cabled to Moscow. Abakumov or his deputy would review the information and decide whether the prisoner should be sent to the capital. These prisoners were investigated by the 2nd Department's Investigation Unit, but sometimes the 4th Department became involved too. If the case was significant enough for prosecution, the 6th Department would also become involved. Some prisoners were considered so important that they were kept in Moscow investigation prisons until 1951–52, when they were finally sentenced.

In the field, the 2nd departments, which were also known as operations departments, worked in cooperation with the units of the NKVD rear guard troops. They also did the work of the NKGB in liberated Soviet territory before the NKGB staff members arrived. In large formations, these detachments were known as the SMERSH Military Police. 'The first step always taken by the Operations Department of SMERSH was to arrest all the organized enemies of the Soviet Union,' wrote Sinevirsky, who worked as a translator in the 3rd Section of the 2nd Department of the UKR SMERSH of the 4th Ukrainian Front.[36] 'This included every leading member of any political party opposing communism...SMERSH men had been ordered also to arrest all active elements in any democratic parties.'

The 3rd Department of GUKR SMERSH was in charge both of identifying German agents working behind the Red Army's front, and of radio games. In the field, officers or branches of the 3rd Department were assigned to all military units from the corps and higher.[37] To find German agents, field officers cooperated with the 2nd departments of UKRs of the fronts and the 4th sections of OKRs of the armies.[38] To search for an important German agent, an operational 'Search File' was created by the 1st Section of the 3rd GUKR Department in Moscow and sent to field branches.

Colonel Georgii Utekhin, who before the war headed the Counter-intelligence Department in the NKGB Leningrad Branch, ran the 3rd GUKR SMERSH Department until late September 1943, when he was appointed head of the 4th Department. Colonel Vladimir Baryshnikov, former head of the 2nd Section in charge of radio games in the 3rd Department, replaced Utekhin. Dmitrii Tarasov, a member of the radio games team, vividly described Vladimir Baryshnikov in his memoirs:

Vladimir Yakovlevich [Baryshnikov] was an example of an armchair analyst or scientist. He was short and...solidly built. However...he was a little bit pudgy and always had a round-shouldered posture. While sitting at the desk, his face appeared to be drowning in papers because he was extremely short-sighted but refused to use eyeglasses. He had a soft and complaisant temper, was benevolent and intelligent, had tact, and doubtless was a man of high principle.[39]

The 4th Department of GUKR SMERSH was charged with 'finding the channels of penetration of enemy agents into the units and institutions of the Red Army'[40] and sending Soviet agents into German territory to collect counterintelligence on training schools for German agents. It consisted of only twenty-five men, divided into two sections. The first section trained agents to be sent behind the front lines and coordinated their work.[41] Its deputy head, Major S. V. Chestneishy, wrote cover stories—'legends' in

Chekist jargon—for Soviet agents. The second section, headed by Captain Andrei Okunev, collected and analyzed information about Nazi intelligence activity and German schools for intelligence agents. Baryshnikov's and Okunev's sections frequently cooperated in conducting radio games.

Colonel Pyotr Timofeev, former head of the 1st Department (capturing German spies) of the 2nd NKVD Directorate (counterintelligence), headed up the 4th GUKR SMERSH Department until late September 1943. Tarasov described Timofeev: 'Pyotr Petrovich, called "PP" among his subordinates, was a man of medium height, stocky, with a massive shaved-bare head and big features in a long face. He was cheerful and energetic. He was considered an indisputable authority.'[42] In September 1943, Utekhin replaced Timofeev, who became one of Abakumov's assistants.

Branches of the 4th Department in the field were responsible for interrogating and investigating newly captured Germans. Their officers, junior and senior investigators, were assigned to all formations from the corps level and above. They also investigated cases of Russian servicemen and repatriated POWs arrested on suspicion of anti-Soviet activity. With the advance of the Soviet army to the West, branches of the 4th Department interrogated more and more German and other foreign prisoners.

The 3rd and 4th GUKR SMERSH departments also collaborated with the 1st (Foreign Intelligence, headed by Pavel Fitin) and 4th (Terror and Sabotage, headed by Pavel Sudoplatov) Directorates of the NKGB. The GUKR SMERSH, the NKVD, the Navy Commissariat, and partisan detachments were obliged to share military intelligence information they obtained in German-occupied territory, as well as information about enemy agents, with the Intelligence Directorate (RU) of the Red Army's General Staff. This agency was organized on April 19, 1943, at the same time as SMERSH, and was headed by Lieutenant General Fyodor Kuznetsov.[43] The RU did not collect foreign intelligence; this remained a function of the Main Intelligence Directorate (GRU) of the Red Army (headed by Ivan Il'ichev), which received it from such sources as the network of Soviet agents in Switzerland (the Rote Drei group, a part of the Red Orchestra). The other GRU *rezidents* (heads of spy networks) sent information from England, Turkey, Sweden, USA, and Japan.

The front and army SMERSH units were responsible for holding German POWs for interrogation by the RU investigators. The RU officers also interrogated SMERSH prisoners in Moscow. In turn, the RU was obliged to provide SMERSH with intelligence information about agents who were being prepared, by the Germans, to infiltrate the Red Army. In order to collect intelligence, between May 1943 and May 1945 the RU sent 1,236 groups of agents and terrorists to the enemy's rear.[44] Just after the war, in June 1945, the RU and GRU were united, and General Kuznetsov became head of this enlarged GRU of the General Staff.

In addition to two military intelligence agencies, in April 1943 a small group headed by Colonel General Filipp Golikov and subordinated directly to Stalin also began analyzing intelligence information. This group did not include a representative of SMERSH. The whole system of intelligence and counterintelligence became exceedingly complicated, but all their branches were controlled by Stalin as Supreme Commander in Chief, Defense Commissar, or GKO Chairman.

The 5th GUKR SMERSH Department headed by Colonel Dmitrii Zenichev—and, from July 1944, by Colonel Andrei Frolov—was in charge of supervising the UKRs of fronts. It also maintained military field courts. These courts were introduced by a secret decree of the Presidium of the Supreme Soviet issued on April 19, 1943; that is, at the same time as SMERSH's creation. As with the other documents in the SMERSH package, Stalin approved the text of this decree after several editorial changes.[45] The decree had a long and awkward title: 'On Measures of Punishment of the German-Fascist Villains Guilty of Killing and Torturing Civilians and Captured Red Army Soldiers, of Spies and Soviet Traitors to the Motherland, and of Their Accomplices', and its text was declassified only in 1997.[46] The possible punishments included death by hanging at a public meeting or being sentenced to ten years of especially hard labor. Separate special hard labor (*katorzhnye*) sections were created in the Vorkuta, Norilsk, and Dal'stroi labor camps for a total 30,000 convicts sentenced by these field courts.[47]

Each court consisted of the chairman of the Military Tribunal, heads of SMERSH and political departments of the unit, and a military prosecutor. The decision of the court had to be approved by the unit commander. The existence of military field courts was kept secret.

The field courts considered cases immediately after taking over territories previously occupied by the enemy. Because the decree was secret, defendants did not know the exact reason for their conviction. The most active military field courts were within the 1st Ukrainian Front. From May 1943 to May 1945, these courts tried 221 cases against 348 defendants, of whom 270 were sentenced to death and hanged.[48] From September 1943, military tribunals could also use the April 19, 1943 decree, and it continued to be used to sentence traitors and German collaborators after World War II. The total number of executed is unknown, but the number of collaborators sentenced to especially hard labor (*katorga*) in 1943–45 was approximately 29,000, of whom 10,000 could not work physically.

Nicola Sinevirsky had an acquaintance who occasionally participated in the field courts:

> Despite the excellent food we were given, Mefodi had lost weight. His lean, pale face made him look years older than when I had first met him...

'My conscience is no longer clear, Nicola,' Mefodi said abruptly. 'Frequently, I have to act as the third judge in a military tribunal and I condemn people to death. You can never understand how disgusting the whole business is. The prosecutor reads his charges, then demands capital punishment. Our triumvirate always confirms that sentence and the prisoner is taken out and shot...Under such conditions, anyone would look sick. It would be an easy thing for me to commit suicide...'

The pupils of his eyes were enlarged and there was a near-insane look in them. It was a ghastly thing to see.[49]

The 6th Department or Investigation Unit existed only in the GUKR SMERSH in Moscow. Its investigators commonly worked in coordination with investigators of the 2nd Department. Later, its head and deputy head, Aleksandr Leonov and Mikhail Likhachev, respectively, played important roles in interrogations of the highest level German POWs, and Likhachev headed a group of SMERSH officers sent to the Military International Trial in Nuremberg.

Cases prepared by the 6th Department were tried by the Military Collegium or the OSO of the NKVD. As already mentioned, in May 1943, Abakumov and Merkulov joined the OSO board.[50] They or their representatives presented cases investigated by SMERSH or the NKGB, respectively.

The 7th GUKR SMERSH Department was in charge of statistics and archival data. It was also responsible for surveillance of high-level military personnel in the Central Committee and the Defense and the Navy Commissariats, as well as those involved in secret work who were sent abroad. Colonel Aleksandr Sidorov, who previously worked at a similar 1st NKVD Special Department, was appointed head of this department. After the war he continued heading the 7th Department (statistics and archival data) of military counterintelligence.

The 8th Department was responsible for ciphering. Later, after 1946, its head Colonel Mikhail Sharikov continued the same work in the MGB.

The 9th Department was in charge of operational equipment.Earlier, in the UOO, its head, Lieutenant Colonel Aleksandr Kochetkov, had overseen the 11th Department that was in charge of surveillance of the engineering, chemical, and signals troops. After the war, in 1946–49, Kochetkov headed the MGB's Department 'B', which was in charge of the use of technical equipment, including the surveillance of phone calls. The 10th Department carried out arrests, searches and surveillance.

Little is known about the activity of the 11th GUKR Department 'S', i.e. Special Operations, headed by Colonel Ivan Chertov. According to the recollection of a member of this department, it was responsible for sending intelligence and terrorist groups, similar to those created by Sudoplatov's 4th NKGB Directorate (terrorism), to the rear of the German troops.[51] Sudoplatov used groups of 15–20 trained saboteurs, many of whom were foreign Communists who had participated in the Spanish Civil War and knew the German language well. Members of the groups formed by the 11th Department were selected from among physically strong men, usually former sportsmen who knew martial arts and were able to use various types of firearms. These intelligence and terrorist groups were sent to the enemy's rear during the massive Red Army offensive actions. In other words, this was SMERSH's version of the Abwehr's Brandenburger saboteurs.

Finally, there was a Political Department in Moscow consisting of only two people: its head, Colonel Nikifor Siden'kov, and a typist.[52] Later, in the MGB, Abakumov promoted Siden'kov to an important position as deputy head of the Main Directorate for the MGB Interior Troops (former NKVD/MVD Interior Troops).

Of course, SMERSH also had purely administrative personnel, and administration and finance Departments. Ivan Vradii, one of Abakumov's deputies, headed the Personnel Department. The Administration and Finance Department was headed at first by Lieutenant Colonel Sergei Polovnev, then, from August 1943, by Lieutenant Colonel Maksim Kochegarov, former head of the 1st Moscow GUKR SMERSH School. After the war, Kochegarov was a deputy, and then, from November 1947 till mid-1951, head of the MGB Administration Department.

CHAPTER 17

Leaders of SMERSH

While appointing Viktor Abakumov and his deputies Nikolai Selivanovsky, Pavel Meshik, and Isai Babich leaders of SMERSH, Stalin, obviously, had serious reasons. He needed a secret service that would fight enemy intelligence, control the enormous Soviet army, and be loyal and subordinated only to him. Apparently, Abakumov and his deputes' backgrounds and careers fit Stalin's expectations.

Abakumov the Man

Abakumov was tall and well built, with a square face, high forehead, brown eyes, big nose and mouth, thick lips, and brown hair.[1] He was considered quite handsome by men and women alike. 'Romanov', the pseudonym of a SMERSH officer who later defected, was impressed with Abakumov: 'There was no doubt that the chief of GUKR Smersh was a very handsome man. He had an athletic build, just a shade overweight... He had...one eyebrow just a shade higher than the other. His thick, dark hair was brushed back.'[2]

In a three-page, handwritten autobiography that Abakumov prepared for the NKVD in December 1939, he claimed he was born in 1908 in Moscow.[3] However, some mystery surrounds his real age, place of birth, and early career. In 1952, after he was arrested, investigators checked a church register of births in a small village in the Moscow Region. A record of Abakumov's birth was not found.[4] But the investigators apparently believed that Abakumov was not born in Moscow, as he claimed, but somewhere near Moscow.

Abakumov claims that his father received a salary so low that 'our family of five people—a brother, a sister, and me—was always poor.' He says that before the October Revolution his father was a worker who was sometimes employed in a small pharmaceutical plant in Moscow. These details helped establish Abakumov's 'class origin' as proletariat, which was important for his NKVD career. It is possible that Abakumov concealed his father's real position; this was common practice, because even as innocuous a position as store manager would place one in the ideologically undesirable bourgeoisie class.[5] After the October Revolution, Abakumov's father was a maintenance man in a hospital. He died in 1922 when Abakumov was fourteen. Abakumov also states that before the revolution his mother was a seamstress, and after the revolution she was a charwoman in the same hospital where her husband worked.

According to Abakumov, he attended only four years of grade school. Amazingly, he was very literate, often editing documents written by his barely literate subordinates. 'Romanov' stresses in his memoirs that Abakumov's orders 'were very different from army orders...[They] were always absolutely clear, and never had any kind of introduction.'[6]

Abakumov also claims to have volunteered for the army in 1921. This is odd, since even under the Soviet standards of the time a thirteen-year-old boy would not have been accepted. This and the above-mentioned inconsistencies in Abakumov's biography led Boris Sokolov, a knowledgeable Russian historian, to hypothesize that Abakumov might have been three or four years older and better educated than he claimed.[7] It is also possible that somebody helped Abakumov join the army at such a young age so that he could at least eat—there was famine throughout the country in those years. Another mystery is that no sources give any information about Abakumov's brother and sister.

In any case, Abakumov served as a medical orderly in the 2nd Moscow Special Brigade until the end of 1923. This brigade was part of the Formations for Special Tasks, or ChON—military units consisting mostly of Party and Komsomol (Union of Young Communists) members who were used to back up Chekist actions. They were formed in April 1919 and played an important role in the Civil War.[8] From November 1919 until mid-1921, Nikolai Podvoisky, an Old Bolshevik, who was one of the leaders of the Revolution and the first War Commissar, was its commander.[9]

In August 1920, an anti-Soviet peasant uprising broke out in Tambov Province. In April 1921, the Politburo appointed Mikhail Tukhachevsky, one of the best Red Army military leaders, Commander of the Tambov Military District and put him in charge of suppressing the uprising.[10] Apparently, Vladimir Lenin insisted on Tukhachevsky's appointment after Tukhachevsky commanded a successful repression of the military anti-Bolshevik revolt in the city of Kronstadt in March 1920. As Tukhachevsky's sister Olga recalled, after the appointment to Tambov Tukhachevsky 'went to his room and drank for two days... This was the only occasion during his whole life when he became dead drunk'.[11]

The tactics the thirty-year-old Tukhachevsky used against the peasants were brutal even by Civil War standards. For instance, on June 11, 1921 he signed an order to shoot numerous hostages and anyone who did not give his name. The uprising was finally suppressed only in July–August 1921, after Tukhachevsky's troops used, at least once, chemical weapons against the insurgents and their families who were hiding in the forests.[12]

Abakumov's 2nd Moscow Special Brigade participated in suppressing this and a similar peasant revolt in the Ryazan Province. One can only wonder what effect participating in these events at such a young age may have had on the teenage Abakumov.

In 1924, after the ChON was disbanded, Abakumov returned to Moscow, where he worked at several unimportant jobs. In 1930, after being accepted as a member of the Communist Party, he was appointed head of the Military Department of the Komsomol Zamoskvoretsky Regional Office. In 1932, he joined the OGPU, the NKVD's predecessor, which existed from 1922 to 1934.

First Years in the OGPU/NKVD

For the first year Abakumov worked in the Economic Department (EKO) of the Moscow Regional Branch of the OGPU (Table 17-1). In 1933, he was transferred to the Economic Directorate (EKU) of the central OGPU. Mikhail Shreider (who was, at the time, the head of the 6th Section of the EKO of the OGPU's Moscow Regional Branch), describes Abakumov's transfer:

> [Yakov] Deich, first deputy of the OGPU Plenipotentiary [Representative] of the Moscow Region, called me on the phone and recommended that I take into my section a 'good guy' who had had problems with his previous superior, the head of the 5th Section [Iosif Estrin]. Although he was not 'a very capable guy', some important persons 'asked for him very much'.

TABLE 17-1. VIKTOR ABAKUMOV'S POSITIONS FROM 1932 TO 1943

Position	Organization	Department/Directorate[1]	Section	Dates[2]
Plenipotentiary[3]	OGPU	Economic Department, PP (Moscow Regional branch)	5th	1932–1933
Plenipotentiary	OGPU	Economic Directorate	1st (?)	1933–Jul 10, 1934
Plenipotentiary	NKVD	Economic Department, GUGB	1st	Jul 10, 1934–Aug 1, 1934
Plenipotentiary	NKVD	GULAG	3rd	Aug 1, 1934–Aug 16, 1935
Operational Plenipotentiary	NKVD	Department of Guards, GULAG		Aug 17, 1935–Nov 11, 1936
	NKVD	Department of Guards of Camps and Places of Imprisonment, GULAG		Nov 11, 1936–Apr 15, 1937
Operational Plenipotentiary	NKVD	4th Department (Secret-Political), GUGB		Apr 15, 1937–Mar 1938
Asst. to a Section Head	NKVD	4th Department (Secret-Political), 1st Directorate	2nd	Mar 1938–Sep 29, 1938
Asst. to a Section Head	NKVD	2nd Department (Secret-Political), GUGB	2nd	Sep 29, 1938–Nov 1, 1938
Head of a Section	NKVD	2nd Department (Secret-Political), GUGB	2nd	Nov 1, 1938–Dec 5, 1938
Acting Head of Directorate	UNKVD	Rostov Province		Dec 5, 1938–Apr 27, 1939
Head of a Directorate	UNKVD	Rostov Province		Apr 27, 1939–Feb 25, 1941
Deputy Commissar	NKVD			Feb 25, 1941–May 20, 1943
Head of Directorate	NKVD	OO Directorate		Jul 19, 1941–Apr 14, 1943

1. PP, *Polnomochnoe predstavitelstvo* or (here) Representation of the Central Economic Department of the OGPU within the Moscow Regional Branch of the OGPU; GULAG, *Glavnoe upravlenie lagerei* or Main Directorate of Camps within the NKVD. Biographies of all persons, in N. V. Petrov and K. V. Skorkin, *Kto rukovodil NKVD. 1934–1941. Spravochnik* (Moscow: Zven'ya, 1999) (in Russian).

2. From Abakumov's biography in ibid., 80–81.

3. A special title of an OGPU/NKVD investigator.

Deich did not tell me who was asking for Abakumov, but, from the tone of his voice, they were very high-ranking people, and most probably, their wives were behind it [Abakumov was a ladies' man]… Deich added that Abakumov was supposedly an adopted son of one of the October Uprising leaders, [Nikolai] Podvoisky.[13]

Shreider's recollection is not quite accurate. In fact, in 1933, Abakumov was transferred to the OGPU Economic Directorate or EKU. Moving from the regional office to the Moscow headquarters after only a few months was a big promotion, which seems to confirm Shreider's statement that Abakumov had a patron. The information that Abakumov was supposedly Nikolai Podvoisky's adopted son is interesting since Podvoisky was the commander of Abakumov's unit until 1921. However, after being blamed for a military disaster in Ukraine during the Civil War, his military career took a nosedive. From September 1921, Podvoisky presided over the Council of Sportsmen (*Sportintern*) and later held other Party posts. As Boris Bazhanov, one of Stalin's secretaries and an individual well versed in Party intrigues once wrote, 'In government circles his [Podvoisky's] name was usually accompanied by the epithet "old fool."'[14]

There is no documentary evidence that Podvoisky adopted Abakumov; in fact, he did adopt two sons, but Abakumov wasn't one of them. The adoption of children, especially those of other Party colleagues, was common among the Old Bolsheviks. For instance, Mikhail Kedrov, the first head of the OO and Podvoisky's brother-in-law, raised Iogan (Ivan) Tubala, a son of friends of Kedrov's wife.[15] However, if Abakumov was Podvoisky's protégé, this would have given him extraordinary opportunities.

Although Podvoisky did not serve in the VCheKa/OGPU, he was connected with the leaders of that organization. Through his marriage to Nina Didrikil, Podvoisky was related to the members of the OGPU/NKVD elite. One of her sisters, Olga, was married to Mikhail Kedrov.[16] Another, Augusta, was married to Christian Frauchi. Their son, Artur Artuzov (surname at birth: Frauchi), became one of the most important leaders of the OO, Counterintelligence Department (KRO), Foreign Intelligence (INO), and Military Intelligence (RU).[17] Podvoisky was also well acquainted with Genrikh Yagoda, OGPU head, and then the first NKVD Commissar. In 1918–19, before Yagoda was transferred to the OO in the VCheKa, he was Podvoisky's secretary (*upravlyayushchii delami*).

The EKU controlled all branches of industry, agriculture, and foreign trade, and it constantly discovered 'spies and saboteurs' among the foreign specialists working in the Soviet Union and among members of the pre-revolutionary intelligentsia.[18] While serving in the EKU, Abakumov met Pavel Meshik, who was working as an assistant investigator in the 1st

Section of the EKU. Later, from mid-1943, Meshik was one of Abakumov's three deputies in SMERSH.

In 1934, Abakumov was involved in EKU general operational activities, such as supervising informers. However, his superiors had a problem with his character: 'Sometimes he does not think over the possible consequences of his [secret] agents' work. Although he is disciplined, he needs moral guidance.'[19] These notes evidently refer to Abakumov's reputation as a playboy.

Among his colleagues, Viktor Abakumov was known as being quite gregarious and a keen dancer, earning the nickname *Vitya-fokstrotochnik* ('Vik-foxtrot dancer'; Vitya is a diminutive of Viktor).[20] This detail is interesting because in 1924, OGPU head Yagoda sent an order to all regional OOs and other OGPU departments banning the foxtrot, shimmy, and other new Western dances in public places.[21] They were considered 'bourgeois society's imitations of a sex act' and in 1930, the dances were officially prohibited in the Soviet Union. However, big bands became popular again in the Soviet Union in 1944, after the Western Allies opened the Second Front in Europe. Even the Dzerzhinsky NKVD Club in the city of Kuibyshev (currently, Samara), where the main Moscow organizations, including embassies, were evacuated, had its professional 'NKVD Jazz Orchestra'.[22] In 1948, the word 'jazz' was prohibited as part of a campaign against the 'bourgeois culture' and 'rootless cosmopolitans' [a euphemism for the Jewish intelligentsia] and many jazz musicians were persecuted. The NKVD Jazz Orchestra was reduced to a small group called the 'MVD Variety Orchestra'.

Shreider describes another incident that also sheds light on Abakumov's character. Showing up one day at a 'safe' apartment used by NKVD officers for meetings with their informers (in secret-service jargon, such apartments were called *kukushki,* or 'cuckoos', referring to the fact that a cuckoo leaves its eggs in other birds' nests), Shreider found Abakumov in the company of a young woman, who was supposedly one of his informers. She did not conceal the fact that she had an intimate relationship with Abakumov and that Abakumov wrote 'her' reports to the NKVD by himself, and she only signed them. Later Shreider found out that Abakumov's other female informers did the same.

Womanizing was very common behavior within the NKVD, especially as the powerful secret service officers could easily blackmail their female informers with threats of arrest. Some NKVD leaders did not bother with seduction and simply raped female informers or women they picked up or arrested.[23] The most infamous example was Beria. Every Muscovite (including myself, when I was a child) was aware of the special Beria team headed by Colonel Rafael Sarkisov, head of Beria's bodyguards, who would simply snatch attractive women and girls off the street and bring them to Beria.[242]

Beria was also brazen enough to attack women among the *nomenklatura*. According to Abakumov's former deputy, Abakumov stopped gathering secret reports on Beria's affairs after it became clear that 'the wives of so many high-level functionaries were mentioned in the reports that the leak of this information would have made Abakumov an enemy not only of Beria, but of half of the party and country leaders'.[25] The list of hundreds of women whom Beria raped became evidence at his trial in 1953.

Womanizing even ended the successful career of one of the cronies Beria brought from the Caucasus—Vladimir Dekanozov. In contrast with the physically big Abakumov, Dekanozov was 'short, almost a dwarf, stocky, with a barrel-like chest, nearly bald head and bushy red eyebrows'.[26] In 1953, his driver testified: 'Dekanozov used women in the car. Trips with women occurred almost daily. Sometimes Dekanozov, traveling in the car day and night, picked up several women.'[27] On March 19, 1947, the Politburo discharged Dekanozov from the post of deputy foreign minister because of a sex scandal: he had seduced a daughter of Molotov's close co-worker.[28]

As for Abakumov, after he became MGB Minister in 1946, he ordered the arrest of the popular Soviet movie star, Tatyana Okunevskaya, after she rejected his advances.[29] It is possible that Abakumov was particularly interested in her because his rival, Beria, had previously drugged and raped her. In Abakumov's investigation file there is an undated letter from his common-law wife, Tatyana Smirnova, saying that sometimes Abakumov beat her up and that he had had a love affair with a female co-worker, who later became his legal wife.[30]

Abakumov's dalliances were also well known in the NKVD/MGB: 'Abakumov was a regular nighttime visitor to the [NKVD/MGB] club, playing snooker with his cronies and having sex with his numerous mistresses in a private room, which he kept stocked with a great variety of imported liqueurs and French perfumes.'[31] Although prostitution was outlawed in the Soviet Union, Abakumov may also have patronized prostitutes. Ivan Serov, a Beria associate who feuded with Abakumov for years, reported to Stalin in 1948 that 'during the difficult days of war [Abakumov] used to stroll along the city streets [in Moscow], searching for easy girls [prostitutes] and taking them to the Hotel Moscow'.[32] According to Peter Deryabin, a former MGB officer, Abakumov 'maintained a string of private brothels'.[33]

However, in 1933, Abakumov was not yet powerful enough to get away with such flagrant womanizing. A furious Shreider wrote a report about Abakumov's behavior to the EKO head, and the next day Abakumov was fired. Somebody's 'strong hand' (possibly Deich or Podvoisky) helped him again, and he was appointed, as Mikhail Shreider put it, 'an inspector at the Main Directorate of [Labor] Camps'—that is, the GULAG, the NKVD directorate headed by Matvei Berman that administered the slave labor of convicted prisoners in camps and prisons.[34] The 3rd section of the GU-LAG, where Abakumov worked, managed camp guards. It was reorganized twice (Table 17-1, middle column) and in August 1935, when the section was renamed the Department of Guards, Abakumov was promoted to Operational Investigator. On December 20, 1936, he was also promoted to State Security Junior Lieutenant, which was quite a high rank for a 28-year-old Chekist. It is possible that Deich was instrumental in this promotion because at the time he held the high position of Yezhov's secretary.[35]

In the GUGB

On April 15, 1937, while still listed on the organizational chart of the GULAG in the Secret-Operational Section, Abakumov was transferred to a much more prestigious job in the Secret-Political Department (SPO) of the GUGB, the predecessor of the NKGB.[36] It's possible that this promotion, too, was achieved with someone's protection. The SPO was in charge of fighting anti-Soviet elements and members of political parties, and Abakumov arrived at a very important time. The Great Terror was in full swing and the SPO was investigating the case of Genrikh Yagoda, the first NKVD Commissar, working to connect him to old Chekists and Party functionaries.

Abakumov was personally involved in the investigation of at least three Great Terror cases. On June 21, 1937, Valentin Trifonov, who supervised the activity of foreign concessions in the USSR, was arrested. An Old Bolshevik, from December 1917 to January 1918 Trifonov was a VCheKa member, at a time when the VCheKa consisted of only eleven people.[37] Later he worked under Podvoisky, and during the Civil War he commanded a Special Expeditionary Corps that conducted punitive operations against the Don Cossacks. Then from 1924 to 1925, Trifonov was first chairman of the Military Collegium. Abakumov interrogated Trifonov from June to September 1937.[38] On March 5, 1938, Stalin and four other Politburo members signed a list of names (a 'death list') of individuals, including Trifonov, who the NKVD had suggested should be executed.[39] Ten days later the Military Collegium sentenced Trifonov to death and he was shot.

Another case involved Semyon Korytnyi, a secretary of the Moscow City Party Committee, who was arrested on June 26, 1937. His main 'crime' was that his wife, Izabella Yakir-Belaya, was Iona Yakir's sister. A high-ranking military leader, Yakir was arrested a month before Korytnyi, and was tried and executed with Tukhachevsky on June 11, 1937. Nikita Khrushchev recalled the Korytnyi couple in his memoirs: 'Korytnyi was a Jew, a very efficient man, a good organizer and orator. He was married to Yakir's sister, who was also a devoted Party member. She spent the whole Civil War at Yakir's side, and was a Party functionary [in the Red Army].'[40] Khrushchev did not mention that, as first Party secretary of Moscow, he was required to approve the arrest of Korytnyi and his wife. He also didn't mention that after Korytnyi's daughter Stella was released from a labor camp in 1956, he cried in her presence and repeatedly claimed that he was unable to do anything to help when the Korytnyis were arrested.[41]

In 1954, Roman Rudenko, the USSR Chief Prosecutor, wrote in his rehabilitation request to the Central Committee:

> During the two months after his arrest, Korytnyi did not admit his guilt. On August 21, 1937, Abakumov...received Korytnyi's personal testimony that, since 1934, Korytnyi had been one of the leaders of the Moscow Regional Center of a counterrevolutionary Trotskyist organization [i.e., supporters of Leon Trotsky]...
>
> During the subsequent interrogations conducted by Abakumov, Korytnyi gave detailed testimony about the counterrevolutionary activity of the Trotskyist organization and its members.
>
> During the session of the Military Collegium of the USSR Supreme Court, Korytnyi pleaded not guilty and stated that during the preliminary investigation, the investigators had forced him to give invented testimony and to make false statements about other persons.[42]

Despite his plea, in August 1939 the Military Collegium sentenced Korytnyi to death and on September 1, 1939, he was executed.

The third case Abakumov worked on involved Nathan Margolin, a Moscow City Party functionary arrested in November 1937. In 1955, Rudenko's successor, Pyotr Baranov, wrote:

> After investigation, it was concluded that the accusation against Margolin was falsified by former NKVD workers—Abakumov, Vlodzimersky, and Glebov-Yufa (all of whom have been convicted)...
>
> During the investigation, unlawful methods and force were applied to Margolin. As a result, on November 27, 1937, he attempted to commit suicide in his cell by trying to suffocate himself by pulling with his hands a loop [around his neck] made of two handkerchiefs.[43]

The expression 'unlawful methods' is a euphemism for 'torture'. In February 1938, the Military Collegium sentenced Margolin to death and two days later he was executed.

An official evaluation of Abakumov's performance at the time of the three investigations stated: 'He mercilessly fights spies and wreckers, as well as fascist agents.'[44] In March 1938, Abakumov was promoted to assistant head of a section, apparently in recognition of his investigative work. Two months later he also received his first award, the Honored VCheKa-GPU Worker medal.

In September 1938, Abakumov was promoted again, this time to head of the 2nd Section, after Bogdan Kobulov, Beria's closest man, was appointed head of the SPO (Table 17-1). Abakumov became involved in the even more important case of Yakov Serebryansky, a legendary figure in the OGPU/NKVD, who created NKVD killing squads throughout the whole of Europe. After inspecting the transcript of Serebryansky's first interrogation on November 12, 1938, Beria wrote on the first page: 'Comrade Abakumov! He [Serebryansky] should be strenuously interrogated.'[45] Then Abakumov, Kobulov, and Beria himself interrogated Serebryansky on November 16. As Serebryansky later stated, he was mercilessly beaten and, as usual, forced to sign testimony that the interrogators had prepared for him.

In his memoir Pavel Sudoplatov mentions one more arrested foreign intelligence officer, Pyotr Zubov, in whose investigation Abakumov participated.[46] As a result of torture, Zubov became an invalid. Like Serebryansky, at the beginning of the war, on Sudoplatov's request to Beria, Zubov was released from imprisonment and became part of Sudoplatov's terrorist department.

In the Rostov Province NKVD

In December 1938, as Abakumov wrote in his biography, 'the leaders of the NKVD promoted me to the high Chekist post of UNKVD Head of the Rostov Province'.[47] Interestingly, a year before that, Abakumov's protector Yakov Deich had been appointed to that post, which he held for five months. For Deich, contrary to Abakumov, this appointment was not a promotion, but rather the beginning of his downfall after his career had peaked as head of Yezhov's NKVD Secretariat. Deich was arrested in March 1938 and six months later he died in prison while still under investigation; most probably, he was killed during an interrogation. Abakumov's appointment was perhaps the first time Stalin became aware of the capable young Chekist, since this level of appointment was approved by the Politburo. The Rostov Province, populated by Don Cossacks, was so politically important that before Abakumov's appointment, Stalin sent one of his own secretaries, Boris Dvinsky, to head the Party organization there. The Don Cossacks were one of the main anti-Bolshevik forces during the Civil War, and they strongly resisted collectivization (the organization of collective farms called *kolkhozy*) in the 1930s.

From 1930 to 1937, Dvinsky, a Party functionary, was deputy head of the Secret Sector of the Central Committee, as Stalin's secretariat was called.[48] He was also Stalin's personal secretary. While working in Rostov, Dvinsky remained very influential in Party circles: he was a Central Committee member and was still in direct contact with Stalin. In 1938, along with Abakumov's predecessor German Lupekin, Dvinsky asked for the Politburo's approval to execute 3,500 people and to sentence an additional 1,500 to ten or more years in labor camps. Earlier the Politburo had already ordered the execution of 5,000 people in the province as well as the sentencing of 8,000 to long-term imprisonment.[49]

In 1939, Dvinsky and Aleksandr Poskrebyshev, head of Stalin's secretariat and Stalin's personal secretary, wrote an obsequious article entitled *The Teacher and Friend of Mankind* for a book honoring Stalin's sixtieth birthday.[50] Therefore, in Rostov, Abakumov was working with one of Stalin's most devoted personal confidants.

As usual, at first Abakumov was working as acting head of the Rostov Province NKVD branch. Three weeks after his appointment, on December 28, 1938, he was promoted to State Security Captain, two ranks above his previous rank of state security lieutenant.[51] It was quite unusual to skip a rank, and this promotion meant that the NKVD leaders wanted to encourage the young appointee.

Five months later, in April 1939, Abakumov finally became head of the Rostov Province NKVD Directorate. Almost nothing is known about Abakumov's activity in Rostov. During the Soviet–Finnish Winter War (December 1939–March 1940), Abakumov's directorate managed to arrest a group of sixteen alleged Finnish spies, supposedly led by a local Gypsy.[52] The case was obviously phony since Rostov-on-Don is nowhere near Finland and Finnish spies would hardly consent to being led by a Gypsy. It is difficult to imagine how NKVD investigators explained what these Finnish spies were doing in this southern area of Russia. Most likely they were arrested simply because they were of Finnish and Karelian ethnicity. From 1937–38, the NKVD arrested 11,066 Finns throughout the whole country, and of these, 9,078 were executed.

In his biography Abakumov proudly wrote: 'While heading the Rostov UNKVD, I was elected a delegate of the 18th VKP(b) [Communist Party] Congress [in 1939].'[53] To be a delegate of a Party Congress, the highest organ of the Communist Party, was considered extremely prestigious in Soviet society and Abakumov's election could have happened only if Dvinsky was supporting him.

On March 14, 1940, the 31-year-old Abakumov was promoted to State Security Senior Major, equivalent to Major General in the army, in recognition of his 'service eagerness and industriousness'—once again skipping a rank. This promotion is especially surprising because he had just been investigated in connection with the allegations of an informer. According to a secret report, in the late 1920s, before he joined the NKVD, Abakumov 'was observed using anti-Semitic expressions'.[54] But the report included even a more incriminating detail: in 1936 Abakumov had supposedly had an affair with the wife of a German citizen named Nauschitz, an alleged German spy.

Abakumov denied the affair. However, he admitted that 'he was acquainted with a citizen-woman MATISON [names were always typed in caps in NKVD documents], whom he met twice at a business club in Moscow'.[55] The NKVD investigation found that the woman's first husband had been executed for counter revolutionary activity, and her second husband lived abroad. In fact, someone named Abram Matison, a former Soviet trade representative in Persia, was arrested in Moscow in June 1939. In February 1940, he was sentenced to death and executed.[56]

The investigation had no repercussions for Abakumov. On the contrary, soon after his promotion Abakumov received an important military award, the Order of the Red Banner.

Deputy NKVD Commissar

After the NKVD was divided into the NKVD and NKGB in February 1941, Beria called Abakumov back to Moscow. At this point it appears that Abakumov was in Beria's favor, because on February 25, 1941, Abakumov was appointed deputy NKVD Commissar. This was quite a promotion for an NKVD officer whose previous position was as head of an important but provincial NKVD directorate. Abakumov was soon given an important assignment: to participate in the cleansing of the Baltic states in the spring of 1941.

After the NKVD/NKGB merger in July, Abakumov became head of the UOO. He was also promoted to state security Commissar of the third rank, equivalent to lieutenant general in the army. For the next two years Abakumov remained one of the most powerful men under Beria.

Many military counterintelligence officers admired Abakumov. Nikolai Mesyatsev, a former OO/SMERSH investigator, recalled in his memoirs:

> Abakumov kept the members of the Central Apparatus of Special Departments [in Moscow] firmly in his hands. He was greatly feared. As the [OO] veterans said, he was tough and willful. He worked a lot and forced others to work a lot. I liked his appearance, it gained everyone's favor.[57]

In another interview, Mesyatsev added: '[Abakumov] always talked about business calmly. He did not order anyone to stand at attention in front of him and invited [a visitor] to sit down.[58]

Sergei Fedoseev, another NKVD man, had a similar opinion: 'It was easy to talk to him. Despite his high position and the authority he had at the highest level of power, he was an open person, and any worker in the NKVD could approach him, regardless of any disparity in rank. He could create a relaxed feeling during a conversation and, most important, give good professional advice and support you if necessary.'[59]

Abakumov differed from the other NKVD leaders in other ways as well. Unlike Beria, he had interests besides power and women. A contemporary wrote:

[Abakumov] liked, for instance, to walk on foot through Moscow (!) [all other Soviet leaders used heavily guarded cars]. He rarely used a car, and if he went by car, he usually drove it himself. One could see him at the skating rink at 28 Petrovka Street skating or, more frequently, standing in a crowd of 'regular' people and watching the skaters. At a stadium, where he used to go to support the *Dinamo* team [an NKVD soccer team], he also sat among ordinary people. Besides sport, he was interested in theatre... Interestingly, he liked classical music and used to go to concerts of symphonic and chamber orchestras.[60]

Another contemporary wrote more skeptically about Abakumov after the war:

He was very pushy and insistent, with abrupt and demanding manners toward subordinates. He liked to 'mix' with common people and to give money to poor old women. He also liked spicy Caucasian *shashlik* [a type of kebab] and Georgian wines, despite his kidney stones. He was...very well dressed...[and] was also an excellent driver and frequently drove a trophy white Fiat sports car.[61]

In February 1943, Abakumov was promoted to State Security Commissar of the 2nd Rank, an equivalent to Colonel General in the army. With his subsequent appointment as head of SMERSH in April that year, Abakumov became Beria's equal. Maksim Kochegarov, a SMERSH subordinate close to Abakumov, later described his style of administration as SMERSH's head:

In SMERSH ABAKUMOV kept everyone in fear. This allowed him to dictate his will in all cases...

ABAKUMOV developed a special, deliberately elaborate system of intimidation and persecution of his subordinates.

By using foul language with or without a reason, ABAKUMOV suppressed any shy attempt of a subordinate to contradict him. Any word said against his opinion always provoked a flood of ABAKUMOV's verbal abuses mixed with threats to punish the subordinate, to 'send him to Siberia', or to imprison him.

After the frightened and stunned victim of ABAKUMOV's abuse left his office, ABAKUMOV's adherents—[Ivan] CHERNOV, head of [SMERSH] Secretariat, and [Yakov] BROVERMAN, his deputy—continued working on the subordinate. They tried to persuade him that to contradict ABAKUMOV was, in fact, to do harm to himself...

ABAKUMOV did not restrict himself to frightening people. By the same token he wanted to show that he was a boss who cared about his subordinates. Frequently he was quite generous, but for this purpose he used governmental funds. Therefore, he used a stick and a carrot method, and at the same time he went around the law.[62]

Apparently, while working with Beria as UOO head, Abakumov learned something from Beria's style of command and administration.

Abakumov's Deputies

Much less is known about Abakumov's new deputies. Two of them, Nikolai Selivanovsky and Isai Babich, came from OOs. The third, Pavel Meshik, was an old colleague of Abakumov and a Beria man.

Nikolai Selivanovsky

In 1923, after graduating from a GPU school in Moscow, the 21-year-old Nikolai Nikolaevich Selivanovsky joined the OO of the Central Asian Military District.[63] From 1930 to 1941, he served in various sections of the OO in Moscow. He was definitely successful because in July 1937 he received his first award, the Order of the Badge of Honor.

Interestingly, in July-October 1937 Selivanovsky made trips to Prague and Paris, two centers of the Russian emigration in Europe. Although the goals of these trips are unknown, during that year the NKVD organized a series of provocations and terrorist acts in both cities in which Selivanovsky might have participated. In the spring of 1937, on Stalin's order, NKVD agents planted (with the help of the Czech police) falsified documents among the belongings of Anton Grylewicz, a German émigré who lived in Czechoslovakia.[64] Grylewicz, a former German Communist leader, was very close to Leon Trotsky and Stalin hoped that the Czech authorities would organize a trial against Grylewicz, which would be, in fact, an anti-Trotsky trial. Most probably, this plan emerged due to the close relationship between the Soviet and Czech intelligence services from 1936–38, when they even had a joint intelligence center (Vonano, located in Prague) that worked against the Germans and Austrians.[65] Grylewicz was arrested in Prague in June 1937, just after the Tukhachevsky trial in Moscow, but in November he was released after he had proven that he was not the owner of the incriminating documents.

In Paris, a group of NKVD agents headed by Yakov Serebryansky was preparing to kidnap Trotsky's son, Lev Sedov, and Selivanovsky's trip might have been connected with these preparations. However, Sedov mysteriously died in February 1938 after a surgical operation, and the kidnapping became unnecessary. The same year Serebryansky and the members of his group were arrested upon their return to Moscow, and, on Beria's order, Abakumov tortured Serebryansky in Lubyanka.

Selivanovsky could also have participated in preparations for the assassination of the NKVD defector Ignatii Reiss, who was killed on September

2, 1937 in Switzerland (however, the preparations were made in Paris), or in the successful kidnapping of General Yevgenii Miller, chairman of the Russian émigré military organization ROVS.[66] On September 22, 1937, a group of NKVD agents abducted Miller in Paris. The general was brought to Lubyanka Prison in Moscow, where he was kept at first as Prisoner No. 110 and then as 'Pyotr Ivanov'. On May 11, 1939, he was finally shot without trial.

Most of the participants in these terrorist acts were liquidated. Sergei Shpigelglas, deputy head of the NKVD's foreign intelligence who organized Reiss's and Miller's operations in Paris, was arrested in November 1938, and in January 1940 the Military Collegium sentenced him to death and he was executed. Former Russian émigrés who assisted Shpigelglas in Paris and then escaped to Moscow were also executed. But Selivanovsky's career continued to be successful.

Back in Moscow, in 1938, Selivanovsky fabricated a case against Eduard Lepin, a military attaché to China and former military attaché to Finland and Poland.[67] As a military attaché, Lepin represented military intelligence. At the end of 1937, he was called back to Moscow and arrested as an alleged member of a Latvian nationalistic group within the Red Army; Selivanovsky headed the investigation. On August 20, 1938, the Military Collegium sentenced Lepin to death, and he was shot.

In 1939, Selivanovsky became head of the 7th Section (responsible for infantry), then from 1939 to 1940, he headed the 9th Section (supply units), and, finally, from 1940 to 1941, the 5th Section (motorized infantry) of the OO. He continued to head this section after the OO was transferred to the NKO in February 1941. In November of that year, Selivanovsky succeeded Mikheev as head of the OO of the Southwestern Front after Mikheev was killed in action.

On July 25, 1942, Selivanovsky, now head of the OO of the Stalingrad Front, sent a ciphered telegram directly to Stalin, trying, as he said, 'to save Stalingrad, to save the country'.[68] Two days earlier Lieutenant General Vasilii Gordov replaced Marshal Timoshenko as commander of the Stalingrad Front. At the same time, the Germans began a successful offensive and by July 25, three divisions of the front were surrounded by the enemy. In his telegram Selivanovsky accused Gordov of mistakes that resulted in the defeat and stated that Gordov was not respected by his subordinates.

It was a serious military insubordination to address Stalin over Abakumov and Beria, Selivanovsky's direct superiors, and immediately Beria ordered Selivanovsky to come to Moscow. Later Selivanovsky recalled: 'In Moscow, Beria cursed me for a long time. He said that the appointment of a front commander should not be my business because it is a prerogative of the Supreme High Command.'[69] But Stalin, apparently, considered the telegram important. It arrived just after the Red Army left the city of

Rostov-on-Don, and the telegram informed Stalin about a potentially even bigger disaster at the Stalingrad Front. At the time, Stalin was preparing his infamous NKO Order No. 227 ('No Step Back!') that introduced penal battalions and companies into the army, as well as barrage units consisting of Red Army, and not NKVD, servicemen.

On July 27, Stalin signed this order, and almost immediately he ordered Abakumov to personally evaluate the situation at the Stalingrad Front. In the meantime, on August 1, Gordov and Nikita Khrushchev, a member of the Military Council of the front, ordered, following Stalin's Order No. 227, the creation of two penal battalions for officers, penal companies for privates, and 36 barrage detachments.

Abakumov and a huge group of his high-level subordinates spent five days inspecting the situation at the front line in Stalingrad, questioning commanders and checking the NKVD and Red Army barrage detachments in the rear.[70] Firstly, Abakumov briefed Gordov and Khrushchev. Then he divided his subordinates into three groups and sent them to different detachments of the front. Abakumov, accompanied by Selivanovsky, led one of the groups. It was attacked by German aircraft several times on the way to and at the front line.

On August 6, the groups were back at the front HQ to discuss the results of their inspection trips, and the next day Abakumov sent a report to Stalin. Gordov was dismissed and later appointed commander of the 33rd Army at the Western Front, while Colonel General Andrei Yeremenko replaced him as commander of the Stalingrad Front. However, after the war, in 1947, Gordov was arrested on charges of treason; in fact, the MGB secretly recorded his critical talks about Stalin.[71] On August 24, 1950 the Military Collegium sentenced Gordov to death and he was executed.

At the end of August 1942, after Abakumov left, Selivanovsky reported to Moscow on the activity of his OO that month:

On the whole, 110 German spies have been arrested and unmasked. Among them...there were 12 commanding officers and 76 servicemen, and 13 women-spies...

On the whole, 30 of our agents were sent in August [1942] to the enemy's rear. Also, 26 *rezidents* [heads of spy networks] and agents were left in the enemy's rear during the withdrawal of our troops tasked with becoming members of the enemy's intelligence and collecting counterintelligence information.

Three agents returned from the enemy's rear. They provided our military intelligence with important information.[72]

It is not clear whether Selivanovsky was talking about two crucial pieces of intelligence his department received in August 1942—about the structure of the 6th German Army under the command of Field–Marshal Friedrich von Paulus, and the German plans for taking Stalingrad.

In SMERSH, Selivanovsky, Abakumov's deputy, was responsible for collecting and analyzing intelligence data. Of the three SMERSH deputies, he was the closest to Abakumov, continuing as his deputy after the war when Abakumov became State Security Minister. After Selivanovsky was arrested in 1951 as 'Abakumov's accomplice', he became mentally ill and was sent to a special psychiatric hospital for examination. Possibly, this saved him from being tried and executed along with Abakumov. After his release in 1953, Selivanovsky was discharged from the MVD 'due to health problems'. Selivanovsky outlived Abakumov by 43 years (he died in 1997), and he never released any secrets about his work in SMERSH/MGB, including information about the fate of Raoul Wallenberg, in whose case he was involved.

Pavel Meshik

Abakumov's second deputy, Pavel Yakovlevich Meshik, was, according to his son Charles, 'a tall, handsome man. He had a beautiful voice and a very self-confident style of behavior'.[73] Interestingly, Meshik was so fascinated by Charles Darwin's *Origin of Species* that he named one of his three sons after Darwin.

In March 1932, at the age of twenty-one, Meshik began his work in the EKU of the OGPU, where he met Abakumov.[74] In 1937, he moved to the GUGB Counterintelligence Department. In December of the same year he received the Order of the Badge of Honor, most likely for his participation in fabricating the case of Moisei Rukhimovich, Defense Industry Commissar.[75] In July 1938, the Military Collegium sentenced Rukhimovich to death and he was shot.

In January 1939, Meshik was appointed assistant to Bogdan Kobulov, head of the NKVD Investigation Unit. Sergei Mironov-Korol', arrested on January 6, 1939, was Meshik's first victim in this unit. He was a prominent old Chekist—he began his career as head of OOs during the Civil War, and later occupied many important posts.[76] In 1937, Mironov was appointed Minister to Mongolia, and from April 1938 onwards, he headed the 2nd Eastern Department within the Foreign Affairs Commissariat. For almost a year Meshik used to call Mironov's wife Agnessa to his NKVD office to give her short notes written by Mironov, asking her to write brief replies. She was never arrested for being the wife of an 'enemy of the people', and for the rest of her life Agnessa tried to figure out why Meshik organized the exchange of letters.[77]

She didn't know that this was a common method used by NKVD interrogators to blackmail the investigated prisoner. To force the prisoner to write or sign false testimonies, especially if other people were mentioned, an investigator would tell the prisoner that his wife would not be arrested as long as he was 'cooperating', and as proof that she was still free, the investigator used the exchange of notes. In February 1940, the Military Collegium sentenced Mironov to death and he was executed. Interestingly, Mironov has never been rehabilitated, which usually means that he had tortured the arrestees when he worked in the OGPU/NKVD.

Ironically, Mikhail Kedrov, the first head of the OO (Table 1-2), was among the victims whose cases Meshik helped to fabricate. Kedrov, arrested in April 1939, was accused of having been an agent of the czar's secret police (*okhranka*) in the past, of connections with the NKVD's fake 'Yagoda plot' of old Chekists, and of being an American spy. In his appeal to the Politburo, Kedrov described in detail how Meshik tortured him. On July 9, 1941, the Military Collegium miraculously acquitted Kedrov.[78] However, following USSR Prosecutor Bochkov's instruction about acquittals, Kedrov was not released from prison. With the Germans marching on Moscow, he was moved to Saratov and shot on October 18, along with twenty-two other prisoners.

Meshik personally tortured other arrested Chekists, including Kedrov's son Igor and Ivan Miroshnikov.[79] Miroshnikov, who survived long imprisonment in labor camps, testified in 1953 that Meshik was especially brutal when he used to arrive in Sukhanovo Prison completely drunk and beat up prisoners. Miroshnikov added that 'generally, Meshik was extremely cynical. He used to show his fist to me while saying, "Here is the Soviet government," then come up to me and hit me with the fist with terrible force'.[80] However, Igor Kedrov was not as lucky as Miroshnikov. On January 24, 1940, the Military Collegium sentenced him to death and the next day he was executed.

One more survivor, Aleksandr Mil'chakov, former General Secretary of Komsomol (Communist Youth Organization) and then head of Glavzoloto (the company that managed the state gold mines), who was arrested in May 1939, also recalled Meshik as a cynical investigator and person:

> Lieutenant Meshik, comfortably leaning in a chair, puts his legs on the desk. There is a rubber truncheon brought from Berlin near the inkwell on it. Recently an NKVD delegation visited Berlin, apparently to 'exchange experiences' [with the Germans]. From time to time Meshik takes the truncheon in his hands and plays with it...
>
> After Meshik sniffed a small flask, his eyes began to glitter and he laughed loudly. Today Meshik is 'philosophizing': 'The Chekists are Stalin's new vanguard. And we will destroy everybody who is in our way... We, the Chekists, are a party within the party... You are saying that you are not guilty of anything... But you must be destroyed because you are useless for us... Stalin himself blessed your arrest.'[81]

In September 1939, Meshik was appointed head of the Investigation Unit of the NKVD Main Economic Directorate. At his trial in December

1953, Meshik claimed that he was not responsible for the interrogation methods he used (note that he talks about himself in the third person): 'I think the problem is not how many prisoners Kobulov and Meshik have beaten up, but that they did beat them up... I think that Beria's low trick and disgusting crime was that he persuaded interrogators that the Instantsiya allowed and approved the beatings [of course, Stalin did approve the torture]... Interrogators, including myself, used beatings and torture thinking it was the right thing to do.'[82] The word 'Instantsiya' that Meshik used was an important term in the Party jargon of Stalin's bureaucrats. As Stalin's biographer Simon Sebag Montefiore noted, Instantsiya was 'an almost magical euphemism for the Highest Authority'.[83] It was used in official documents and speeches to indicate Stalin or, sometimes, the Politburo. In other words, NKVD/MGB officials never said that Stalin gave them an order; they said the Instantsiya did.

As previously mentioned, in March 1940 Meshik headed an operational NKVD group that arrived in the just-occupied Lvov Province.[84] This was one of eleven NKVD groups sent to the former Polish territory to 'cleanse' (an NKVD term) it of 'anti-Soviet elements'. A month later Meshik was decorated with the military Red Star Order, possibly for this action.

In February 1941, Meshik was appointed NKGB Commissar of Ukraine even though, like Abakumov, he was only thirty-one years old. Meshik reported to Moscow on the nationalistic underground Ukrainian movement in the newly acquired former Polish territories and on the movements of German troops in the Nazi-occupied part of Poland.[85] Apparently, Moscow was impressed by Meshik's activity because in May 1941, he received the Honored NKVD Worker medal.

The day after Operation Barbarossa began, Meshik was able to give Nikita Khrushchev, then Ukrainian first Party secretary, detailed information from secret informers regarding the local reaction to the invasion.[86] A few days later, the Ukrainian NKGB began to arrest people who had criticized the response of Soviet leaders to the German invasion. During the first days of the war, 473 political prisoners, whose executions Merkulov approved in Moscow on Meshik's request, were shot to death in Kiev's prisons.[87]

In July 1941, in the middle of the battle for Kiev, Meshik went back to Moscow, where he was appointed head of the Economic Directorate (EKU) of the new NKVD.[88] In February 1943, he was promoted to State Security Commissar of the 3rd Rank and, finally, on April 19, 1943, he became deputy head of SMERSH.

It is possible that Abakumov was forced to choose Meshik as a deputy since a difficult relationship developed almost immediately between them. Much later, in August 1948, Ivan Serov, first deputy MVD minister, reported to Stalin that 'in 1943, Abakumov told me that he would eventually shoot Meshik, no matter what'.[89] No doubt Abakumov considered Meshik to be Beria's spy. In turn, Meshik despised Abakumov. After Abakumov was arrested in 1951, Meshik called him 'an adventurer'.[90]

In December 1953, Meshik was tried along with Beria and five of his men, including Merkulov and Kobulov. All of them were sentenced to death and executed on December 23, 1953.

Isai Babich

Abakumov's third deputy, Isai Yakovlevich Babich, was born in 1902 to a Jewish family in the small Ukrainian town of Borislav.[91] Although Babich was the only person of Jewish origin close to Abakumov, in the 1990s the German historian Joachim Hoffmann mistakenly wrote that Abakumov 'surrounded himself with a whole group of Jewish collaborators'.[92]

In 1920, Babich joined the local branch of the CheKa in the city of Nikolaev and made a slow but steady advance within the CheKa, and then the NKVD of Ukraine. From December 1936 till August 1937, he headed the OO of the NKVD Directorate of Kiev Province, and in January 1938, Babich was promoted to acting head of this directorate. In other words, Babich supervised all arrests of military personnel during the Great Terror in Kiev Province, and in December 1937 he was awarded the Red Banner Order—apparently for this activity. In February 1938, he was transferred to the OO in Moscow, where he headed several sections.

Finally, in September 1940, Babich was appointed head of the OO of the Baltic Military District, which was created from the territory of the three just-annexed Baltic States: Latvia, Estonia, and Lithuania. As head of military counterintelligence, he was in charge of the numerous arrests of high-ranking officers of the former armies of these states.

At the beginning of the war, Babich was a deputy head, and from May 1942 onwards, head of the OO of the Northwestern Front. In February 1943, he was promoted to State Security Commissar of the 3rd Rank (Major General). As Abakumov's deputy, Babich was responsible for SMERSH operations that sent agents behind enemy lines. The summer and autumn of 1945, when he headed SMERSH units in the Russian Far East during the short military campaign against Japan, were the highest point in his SMERSH career. After the war Babich became deputy head of the 3rd MGB Main Directorate (as SMERSH was called after it became part of the MGB in 1946), and he held that position until his death in 1948.

Besides the three operational deputies, Stalin appointed a fourth deputy, Lieutenant Colonel Ivan Vradii, to head the SMERSH Personnel Department.[93] In Abakumov's MGB, Vradii also headed the Personnel Directorate. After Abakumov's arrest in 1951, Vradii was demoted to head of the labor department in the Ukhto-Izhemsk Labor Camp Directorate attached to the USSR Justice Ministry. In 1954, Vradii was accused of embezzling 26,000 rubles for the renovation of his apartment and transferred to the reserve.

On May 26, 1943 the newspapers *Pravda* and *Izvestia* published an order signed by Stalin assigning all SMERSH leaders actual military ranks.[94] Selivanovsky, Meshik, Babich, and Pavel Zelenin became lieutenant generals, while Vradii and thirty-four of Abakumov's assistants, along with the heads and deputy heads of SMERSH front directorates, became major generals.[95] Curiously, only Abakumov was not given military rank during the war, even though he often wore a Red Army uniform. He remained State Security Commissar of the 2nd Rank, equivalent to Colonel General in the army.

The Personnel

Many officers of the GUKR SMERSH, especially investigators, were former mid-level OO officers. They had participated in the fabrication of cases during the Great Terror and survived the purges of that period, which wiped out the OO leadership. For instance, almost all low-level members of Izrail Leplevsky's investigation team of about thirty officers, who created the 1937 Tukhachevsky case, continued their service.[96] Two of Abakumov's deputies, Selivanovsky and Babich, were veterans of the old OO.

The career of Vladimir Kazakevich, who from 1943 to 1945 was deputy head of the UKR SMERSH of the 2nd Belorussian and then of the 4th Ukrainian fronts, was typical of mid-level SMERSH officers.[97] Nicola Sinevirsky recalled Kazakevich at the end of the war: 'He was a tall man, heavyset of frame. His twisted nose gave his face a fierce look, and made almost everybody afraid of him. He was a severe and exacting officer.'[98] In 1928, Kazakevich started working for the Ukrainian GPU as a secret agent, reporting on his fellow students at the Kharkov Institute of People's Industry. As he wrote in 1948, 'they were imprisoned due to my reports as an agent'.[99] Later he joined the Ukrainian NKVD, but in 1937 he was transferred to Moscow, to the 4th GUGB (secret-political) Department. Then, in 1938, he was moved to the 5th GUGB (OO) Department.[100]

Before long, Kazakevich became known in Beria's NKVD as one of the most efficient and ruthless investigators.[101] Over a short period, he falsified at least eleven cases against high-level military men, including Marshal Aleksandr Yegorov and Komandarm Ivan Belov, who were sentenced to death. One of them, Komdiv N. F. Sevastiyanov, described Kazakevich's methods in a letter to Stalin: 'Captain Kazakevich used to hit me in the face so badly that I flew through the room. He punched me in the chin, under my ribs, and hit my knees with the heels of his boots... He forced me to lie down on a chair and then beat me with a rubber truncheon while knowing well that I had an inflamed liver... Also he beat me up with a truncheon while I was lying on the floor... During the three months that I was in Lefortovo Prison, I slept not more than an hour a day.'[102] Other victims also made statements about the torture Kazakevich inflicted on them. The arrested Corps Commissar A. I. Zabirko wrote: 'Kazakevich told me that he would beat me up until my ribs were broken or I became insane.'[103] Most probably, Kazakevich used these torture methods later, in SMERSH.

The Military Collegium sentenced Sevastiyanov to death in July 1941, after the war had begun. At the time, Kazakevich was deputy head of the 3rd NKVD Department and then deputy head of OOs and, later, UKRs of various fronts. In November 1944, Kazakevich, together with Abakumov, cleansed the Bialystok region of Poland of members of the underground Armija Krajowa. For his activity, he received twenty-four military awards. Kazakevich retired in 1948.

In 1956, while being asked in the Chief Military Prosecutor's Office about Sevastiyanov, Kazakevich refused to admit that he had tortured him. As a result of the prosecutor's reinvestigation of the Sevastiyanov case, Kazakevich was expelled from the Party, and two years later, his military pension was reduced by half as a punishment for his falsification of cases, although he had never been criminally charged.

This was quite typical. Kazakevich's superior, Nikolai Kovalchuk, head of the UKR SMERSH of the 4th Ukrainian front, was also a brutal torturer. In 1937, in Tbilisi, Aslamazov, the arrested Komsomol secretary, jumped out a window during terrible beatings by Kovalchuk, a member of the Secret-Political Department in the Georgian NKVD.[104] Soon Kovalchuk continued his successful career in Moscow, then in the UOO and SMERSH. After the war he even rose to deputy state security minister. Only in 1954 was Kovalchuk forced to retire and deprived of his lieutenant general rank for the 'activity of discrediting an officer', a Party euphemism that described torture used by a high-ranking security officer.

To prepare the new personnel, special schools for teaching SMERSH officers were opened in 1943: two in Moscow, for 600 and 200 students respectively, and four more in the cities of Tashkent (300 students); Sverdlovsk (now Yekaterinburg; 200 students); and one each in the Siberian cities of Novosibirsk and Khabarovsk (200 and 250 students, respectively).[105] These schools were established by GKO order and may have represented Stalin's solution to the problem of unprofessional investigators.[106] Later, special military counterintelligence courses in Leningrad and Saratov were also reorganized into schools. Depending on the school, the training lasted from four to nine months. Reserve groups of 50–100 graduates were created at each field SMERSH directorate and at the GUKR in Moscow. Despite these efforts, SMERSH officers remained poorly educated. Nikolai Mesyatsev, one of the SMERSH investigators, recalled in 2005 that 'investigators were usually recruited from among poorly educated, uncultured people'.[107] Everyone who worked in SMERSH was sworn to secrecy. Sinevirsky recalled that before he was allowed to work as a translator in the UKR SMERSH of the 4th Ukrainian Front, he was forced to sign three copies of this pledge:

I hereby promise that never and at no place, even under the threat of capital punishment, will I mention anything of my work in the headquarters of the counterintelligence SMERSH of the Fourth Ukrainian Front. I am aware that should I fail to carry out this promise I will become subject to the severest penalties including the highest measure of punishment—shooting.[108]

Since SMERSH was formally part of the army, SMERSH officers had the ranks and uniforms of military officers.[109] Romanov, a former SMERSH officer, wrote that 'this was a camouflage measure to make it impossible to distinguish them from the rest of the armed forces'.[110] In contrast, the ranks of NKGB and NKVD officers and their special insignias differed from those of the military. Therefore, NKGB and NKVD officers could be identified by their uniforms during World War II but SMERSH officers could not. What made it more confusing was that NKVD troops transported SMERSH prisoners. Typically, foreign POWs did not understand that they were being investigated by SMERSH, a special military counterintelligence service. The only secret service group known at that time in the West was the NKVD, and this has led to a lot of misidentification of SMERSH investigators as NKVD operatives in the memoirs of former POWs.

Part VI. SMERSH in Action: 1943–44

CHAPTER 18

General Activity

Although SMERSH continued working on identifying real and imagined Soviet military traitors and deserters, as the UOO had done before, its primary focus now shifted to countering German intelligence and counterintelligence. All operational SMERSH officers in the field were provided with a long instruction entitled *Organization of Search for and Liquidation of Enemy Agents*.[1] Since German agents generally possessed forged Soviet documents and military awards, GUKR also published secret reference booklets for verifying military documents (*Materials for Identification of Forged Documents*, May 1943) and awards (*Materials for Identification of Forged USSR Awards and Medals*, September 1943). Additionally, it became easier to identify German agents with false documents because in December 1943 a unified system of officer IDs was introduced in the Red Army.[2] Now the IDs were created at special printing houses and had numbers that could be checked.

Near the front line, SMERSH initiated new tactics for capturing German agents, using operational groups of three members who constantly checked the documents of all suspicious-looking individuals.[3] Two members of each group were SMERSH officers, and the third was a recruited former German agent who could identify other agents. But with the transformation of the UOO into SMERSH, Abakumov failed to take control of counterintelligence in the partisan (guerrilla) movement in the rear of the German troops.

In Partisan Detachments

With the creation of SMERSH it became unclear which organization was in charge of the Special Departments (OOs) within the partisan movement. While Panteleimon Ponomarenko, the influential first Party secretary of Belorussia, headed the partisan movement, the NKVD—under Lavrentii Beria—supervised the OOs in the partisan detachments created in 1942.[4]

The Soviet partisan movement had a long history. In the 1920s and 1930s, special schools attached to the OO trained terrorists and saboteurs for future war, and similar schools in the Red Army were part of the 5th

Department of the General Staff.[5] During the Great Terror of 1937–38, most of the sabotage specialists were arrested, convicted, and executed. They were considered unnecessary because of Stalin's doctrine that future military actions would take place in the enemy's territory.

On June 29, 1941, a week after the German invasion, the Council of Commissars (Sovnarkom) and the Central Committee ordered the creation of partisan detachments in the German-occupied territories.[6] On July 5, the NKVD formed its own special sabotage group, which reported directly to Beria.[7] Pavel Sudoplatov, who had successfully overseen the 1940 assassination of Leon Trotsky, was appointed its head. This group later became the 4th NKVD Directorate in charge of terror and sabotage in enemy-occupied territory. In April 1943, Sudoplatov's directorate was transferred to the NKGB (State Security Commissariat), and its activities now partly overlapped those of SMERSH.

Paralleling the measures in Moscow, in 1941, local NKVD, NKGB, and Party functionaries in the German-occupied territories of Ukraine and Belorussia, as well as the OOs, political and military intelligence departments of the armies and fronts created their own partisan detachments.[8] At the end of the summer of 1941, Ponomarenko sent Stalin a detailed plan for centralizing control over all partisan groups. The following December, Stalin summoned Ponomarenko to the Kremlin, where, after a two-hour discussion, he approved the establishment of the Central Headquarters of the Partisan Movement (TsShPD).[9]

It was not until May 30, 1942, that the State Defense Committee (GKO) ordered that the TsShPD should be attached to the Stavka—in other words, directly subordinated to Stalin, with Ponomarenko appointed as its head.[10] Beria tried to oppose this decision, believing that Sudoplatov's department in Moscow should control all partisans. In a compromise move, Vasilii Sergienko, NKVD Commissar of Ukraine and Beria's protégé, was made Ponomarenko's deputy, thus essentially leaving Beria in charge of the partisans.

The fighting unit of the partisan movement called *otryad* (a detachment) consisted of varying numbers of men. By January 1942, NKVD operational groups that had OO functions were created within all *otryady*.[11] Official reports attest to their efficiency: for example, from 1942 to 1944, counterintelligence in the Ukrainian partisan detachments exposed and arrested 9,883 spies and traitors, of whom 1,998 were Gestapo spies.[12]

Not all of those arrested were real German spies. For example, there was a bizarre but widespread belief among partisan commanders and heads of the partisan OOs that many local Jews who, having escaped Nazi extermination efforts, tried to join the partisans, were Gestapo spies. On August 10, 1943, the commander of the Osipich partisan detachment reported to Moscow: 'Recently, the Gestapo has started to use Jews as spies. The

Gestapo offices in Minsk and Borisovo have established a nine-month course for the Jews. Spies have been sent to apartments in the city and to partisan detachments, and supplied with poison to kill their commanders and other partisans. Several of these spies were unmasked near Minsk.'[13]

Based on this belief, many Jewish escapees were arrested and executed as spies in partisan detachments.[14] The truth was that the Abwehr had opened numerous schools to train local Belorussian, Ukrainian, and Russian volunteers as saboteurs, propagandists, and translators, while the Jews were hunted down by the Gestapo and SS-Einsatzgruppen, and had nothing to do with these schools.[15]

But anti-Semitism was not the only reason for false accusations. Another report reads: 'In August 1943, the head of the Special Department of the Chkalov Brigade of the Baranovichi Partisan Detachment (Belorussia) personally shot to death nineteen-year-old Yelena Stankevich, a scout in this brigade's "For the Soviet Motherland" unit, accusing her of being a Gestapo spy. In fact, she simply refused to be his lover.'[16] Such executions were quite common. In the same year, Ivan Belik, head of the OO of the 'Assault' Partisan Brigade in Belorussia, shot a woman partisan, Verkhovod'ko, who was pregnant by Boris Lunin, commander of the brigade, on the false charge that she was a German spy.[17] The real reason for her execution was that Lunin, who had a small harem in the brigade, did not want to deal with a pregnant girlfriend. In 1957 Belik and Lunin were sentenced to seven years in labor camps for this crime.

Some of the 'spies' captured by partisans ended up in the GUKR's Moscow headquarters. On March 18, 1943, Henri Czaplinski (in Russian documents, Genrikh Maksimovich Chaplinsky), a 53-year-old Polish Jew and professor at the Krakow and Lvov conservatories, joined the Donukalov Partisan Brigade near Minsk.[18] As an internationally known violinist, he had performed in many countries before the war, and also spoke several languages. From 1922 to 1923, he was a professor at the Hamburg Conservatory in Toronto, and from 1925 to 1927, he was first violinist with the Philadelphia Symphony Orchestra.

Czaplinski told his OO interrogators that in 1940 he was arrested by the NKVD in Lvov and spent seven months in the Byelostok NKVD prison, from which he escaped during a German bombardment. On July 13, 1941, *The New York Times* published information about Czaplinski's successful escape.[19] After his escape, the multilingual Czaplinski worked as a translator at the headquarters of various Luftwaffe units stationed in Belorussia, which caused the OO officers of the partisan brigade to conclude that Czaplinski was an important German spy. Czaplinski was sent to Moscow, and on May 15, 1943, Ponomarenko and Lavrentii Tsanava, NKGB Commissar of Belorussia, reported to Stalin:

Preliminary interrogations of Czaplinski suggest that he might have been a German intelligence agent sent to the Donukalov partisan detachment with the task of getting to the rear of Soviet troops. He may also have worked in various countries as a longtime German intelligence agent. Czaplinski has already been transferred to the Main Directorate of SMERSH to Comrade Abakumov.[20]

Unfortunately, I have no information about what happened to Czaplinski at the hands of Abakumov's subordinates.

In the autumn of 1943, Ponomarenko and Tsanava, and not GUKR SMERSH, still controlled the OOs in partisan detachments. On August 20, 1943, Abakumov sent a strong missive to Ponomarenko:

The organs of counterintelligence ('SMERSH') are charged with fighting against enemy agents penetrating headquarters and detachments of partisans. However, in many cases the unmasked spies, saboteurs, terrorists, members of the so-called Russian Liberation Army and other detachments created by the Germans, who have given themselves up to partisan detachments, are transferred to our [Soviet] territory, but the organs of counterintelligence 'SMERSH' are not informed. They are interrogated by members of the headquarters of the partisan movement who are incapable of investigating such cases. Documents brought from the partisan detachments and protocols of interrogations of the unmasked spies are copied and sent to various addresses. As a result, a wide circle of persons has knowledge of serious [secret] operational measures.[2]

Ponomarenko reacted swiftly and sternly, writing:

Believing that it is expedient to continue transferring to you captured enemy agents and materials in which your Directorate might be interested, we are extremely surprised by your claims... A question arises: Why, since the time 'SMERSH' was formed, has no worker from this Directorate told us what measures they were planning against enemy agents?... Why are no workers from your agency present in partisan detachments?[22]

Abakumov and Ponomarenko did not reach an agreement, and SMERSH did not take control of the partisan OOs. This question soon became unimportant when the Red Army began advancing to the West and liberating Soviet territory from the Germans. On January 13, 1944, seven months after SMERSH was created, the TsShPD was disbanded. Local headquarters, not Moscow, were now responsible for partisan detachments. Ponomarenko returned to Belorussia to supervise partisan activity there.

Ponomarenko never forgot his skirmish with Abakumov. After Abakumov was arrested in July 1951, Ponomarenko, then a Central Committee secretary, used to boast to his Party colleagues that he had helped to get rid of Abakumov.[23] He was probably among those who made sure that Stalin received the report denouncing Abakumov, who was subsequently dismissed and arrested on Stalin's orders.

Abakumov had much more success in taking control of the radio games from Beria's subordinates.

The 'Radio Games' Rivalry

In addition to counterintelligence work in the rear of the Soviet troops, the 3rd Department of GUKR in Moscow was also in charge of radio games—also known as playbacks—which were intended to deceive the enemy.[24] As already mentioned, German intelligence also widely used radio games against the Soviets. For instance, two arrested leaders of the famous Soviet spy network 'Red Orchestra', Leopold Trepper (alias 'Director') and Anatolii Gurevich (alias 'Kent', 'Sukolov', and 'Barcza'), agreed to send radio messages for the Gestapo hoping that Moscow would think that they were working under Nazi control. Soviet radio games operated by using German agents captured from various German intelligence services.

Soviet radio operations started in 1942 in two NKVD directorates, the 2nd (counterintelligence) headed by Pyotr Fedotov (like Abakumov, he was Yakov Deich's protégé), and the 4th (terrorism) headed by Pavel Sudoplatov.[25] As the UOO head, Abakumov also personally controlled some of the radio games, especially in the Moscow Province. He presented written scenarios of the planned games to Stalin, who made editorial notes in blue pencil.[26] Within the 2nd NKVD Directorate, a section headed by Vladimir Baryshnikov in the 1st (German) Department (headed by Pyotr Timofeev) was responsible for the games. In April 1943, this section was transferred to SMESRH, and Dmitrii Tarasov, head of the radio operations team, recalled the transfer in his memoirs: 'V. Ya. Baryshnikov was appointed head of the [3rd] Department of the GUKR SMERSH, while the radio operations group became a separate section within this department… Its staff reached eight members, and I was promoted to the head of the [2nd] section.'[27]

In July 1943, before the Kursk Battle, Abakumov issued UKRs with the secret *Instruction on the Organization and Conduction of Radio Games with the Enemy*.[28] It stated the goal of the games: 'To paralyze the activity of the enemy's intelligence services.' Each radio game was carefully prepared. At first Baryshnikov, after interrogating and recruiting captured German agents, sent Abakumov a proposal for a game. For instance, on June 25, 1943 Baryshnikov wrote:

The [captured German] group [of two agents, one of whom was a Soviet double agent] has a very interesting task [i.e., recruiting an agent inside the Soviet Union for the assassination of Lazar Kaganovich, a GKO member and Commissar for Transportation]. That could allow us to conduct a serious counterintelligence action (for example, to call for the arrival of qualified [German] specialists in recruiting agents). Therefore, this group should be engaged in a radio game. The first radio communication should be transmitted on June 26 [1943].[29]

Abakumov wrote on the report: 'I agree.'

In Tarasov's section, Majors Sergei Yelin and Vladimir Frolov, and Captains Grigorii Grigorenko and Ivan Lebedev (Tarasov's deputy) were the main developers and conductors of the games.[30] Tarasov describes the preparation of messages: 'The counterintelligence members wrote texts of radiograms that contained military disinformation for a transmission to the enemy based on the General Staff's recommendations. The style of writing by a particular operator and a legend [story] given to him were also taken into consideration. In the most important cases consultants from the General Staff participated in this work.'[31]

Tarasov details the contacts with the General Staff and military intelligence (RU):

[We] were in constant contact with A. I. Antonov, deputy head of the General Staff, and S. M. Shtemenko, head of the Operational Directorate of the General Staff, as well as with F. F. Kuznetsov, deputy head of the General Staff and, simultaneously, head of the RU. Meetings with the first two took place in the General Staff's building or the Stavka mansion at Kirov Street [not far from the Kremlin], while we met with Comrade F. F. Kuznetsov in the USSR Defense [Commissariat] at Frunzenskaya Embankment.[32]

Usually the former German radio operators—Germans or Russians who had graduated from German intelligence schools and agreed to work for Baryshnikov's section—were placed in Lubyanka Prison and brought to SMERSH's headquarters (another part of the same huge building) when there was a need for them or for radio transmission sessions. If radio sessions were conducted from a particular territory where the controlling German intelligence supervisors expected the agents to be located at the time, Tarasov's men brought the operators to this area.

During the reorganization of security services in April 1943, Sudoplatov's 4th NKVD Directorate was transferred to the NKGB and became its 4th Directorate. This directorate continued to control some important radio games. According to Sudoplatov's memoirs, the NKGB's success with radio game Operation *Monastyr'* (Monastery) sparked Abakumov's jealousy. This was the game in which Aleksandr Demiyanov, or 'Max'—wrongly identified in Sudoplatov's memoirs as Abwehr's 'Max' from the 'Max and Moritz' operation—participated. Allegedly, when Abakumov came to Sudoplatov's office demanding the transfer of all radio games to GUKR, Sudoplatov agreed to do so if ordered. The order came within one day, but it excluded Monastery and Couriers, another deception game. Abakumov was displeased, knowing that the results of these two operations were reported directly to Stalin.'[33]

Sudoplatov's interpretation makes little sense—the results of all important radio games were reported directly to the Stavka, which meant that Stalin was already supervising all the most significant ones. For example, in September 1943, on Meshik's report about one of the games, Abakumov wrote: 'Such disinformation materials must not be sent without Com. [rade] Stalin's approval.'[34] However, the mere fact that information about two of the supposedly most successful games had been held back was apparently enough to anger Abakumov.[35] The clash surrounding the radio games illustrates the tension and developing rivalry between Abakumov and the Beria–Merkulov duo after the creation of SMERSH.

Despite Abakumov's opposition, the operations *Monastyr'* and *Berezino* (which followed in 1944) remained in Sudoplatov's hands. During the latter, twenty-two German intelligence men sent by the famous Otto Skorzeny into Soviet territory in response to false radio messages were caught, and thirteen radio transmitters and 225 packages of equipment and weapons were seized.[36] Later Skorzeny wrote: 'None of…my own men ever got back. I wondered whether the Russians were having a game with us all the time.'[37] Apparently, Sudoplatov hoped to lure Skorzeny himself with this game, but this did not happen.

As of spring 1943, SMERSH was responsible for most of the other radio games. Scores of deceptive operations were organized, and through them SMERSH collected a great deal of military information, especially about the transportation of German troops, terrorist acts in the rear of the Soviet troops and on German-occupied Soviet territory, and so forth. Operation *Ariitsy* (Aryans), a particularly successful joint SMERSH–NKGB–NKVD game, demonstrated that the Germans had very inadequate intelligence about the Soviet situation.

In May 1944, the Walli I (Abwehr's center for Russia) flew twenty-four agents, under the command of Captain Eberhard von Scheller (alias 'Quast') into Kalmykia—an autonomous republic on the shore of the Caspian Sea in southern Russia.[38] Von Scheller, a WWI hero who was awarded two Iron Crosses for bravery during that war, had worked in the Abwehr since 1938. Being sent to Kalmykia was punishment for a crime that he did not describe to SMERSH officers. Kalmykia was populated by the small nation of Kalmyks, a nomadic group professing Lamaism that settled in the lower reaches of the Volga River at the beginning of the eighteenth century. Incidentally, Vladimir Lenin's father was a Kalmyk who had risen to the status of a minor nobleman.

Von Scheller's group was supposed to prepare a base for the future arrival of the so-called 'Kalmyk Corps of Dr. Otto Doll' (many heads of Abwehr groups had aliases with the title of 'doctor'), consisting of 3,458 horsemen (36 squadrons), that the Abwehr Group 103 organized during 1942–43. Dr. Doll's real name was Sonderführer Otmar Rudolph Werva, and he was a German academic and Abwehr officer.[39] During the Russian Civil War, he served in the Ukrainian nationalistic troops that fought for the independence of Ukraine. The German plan was for this corps to initiate an uprising against the Soviet regime, among the Kalmyks. Amazingly, German intelligence was apparently unaware that by then there were no Kalmyks left in Kalmykia.

In December 1943, the Politburo ordered the liquidation of the Kalmyk ASSR and renamed it the Astrakhan Region within the Russian Federation.[40] This was Stalin's retaliation for Kalmyk collaboration with the Germans during the occupation of a part of Kalmykia near its capital, Elista, from August 1942 to mid-1943. The Germans wooed the Kalmyks with the promise of an independent Great Kalmyk State with territory from the Black Sea to the Caspian Sea. During the occupation, a Kalmyk Cavalry Corps was formed, consisting of four divisions with five squadrons each, to fight against the Red Army.[41]

Following the Politburo decision, the NKVD executed an operation under the code name 'Ulusy' (*ulus* means region in the Kalmyk language), for which Beria and his deputy Vasilii Chernyshev were responsible. The NKVD troops rounded up the Kalmyks in Kalmykia (more than 93,000), put them on 46 trains, and deported them to the Altai, Novosibirsk, and Omsk provinces in Siberia. Sixteen thousand Kalmyks died during this operation.[42] In March and June 1944, the remaining Kalmyks were deported from the Rostov and Stalingrad provinces; thus, no Kalmyks remained by the time German agents landed in Kalmykia.

During a clash between the NKVD and NKGB operational groups of the Astrakhan region and the German agents who were parachuted in, twelve German agents, including von Scheller, were taken prisoner, and the rest were either killed or managed to escape. SMERSH and the NKVD quickly developed a joint plan for a new radio game, Aryans, with the involvement of captured agents. On May 26, 1944, Abakumov and Aleksandr Leontiev, head of the NKVD Department for Combating Bandits, signed the plan, which Beria approved the next day. In the GUKR, Abakumov's deputy Meshik and Baryshnikov, head of the 3rd Department, were responsible for implementing the plan.

Von Scheller volunteered for Soviet counterintelligence, and Hans Hansen, the radio operator of the downed German plane, agreed to work with von Scheller. The two were given the aliases '*Boroda*' (Beard) and '*Kolonist*' (Colonizer). In response to the disinformation transmitted, another German plane loaded with supplies for von Scheller's agents landed in Kalmykia, where it was destroyed and five newly arrived agents were captured. After this von Scheller wrote to Abakumov:

Sir General!
I've volunteered for the Russian counterintelligence and I have worked honestly and hard for the implementation of a secret task. Our joint efforts succeeded in shooting down a gigantic German U-290 transport airplane and its passengers, including four German agents, were captured by the Russian counterintelligence service. Therefore, I ask for your approval to include me into the Soviet counterintelligence network. I pledge to keep secrets of the service for which I, probably, will end up working, even if I'd be working against German intelligence. In this case I ask for your approval of giving me the alias 'Lor'.
E. von Scheller.[43]

Although further details of the ongoing operation are unknown, SMERSH sent a total of forty-two radio messages to the Germans and received twenty-three responses. In August 1944, the 3rd GUKR Department decided to end the game, and the last cable was sent to Germany, claiming that everyone in the second group had been killed and that the Kalmyks had refused to help von Scheller's group. Von Scheller was supposedly going to the Western Caucasus, and would move from there to Romania. As a result of the game two planes were destroyed, twelve agents and members of German air crews were killed, and twenty-one German saboteurs were taken prisoner.

Baryshnikov's team did not trust von Scheller. During detailed interrogations it appeared that von Scheller had tried to force Hansen to send a coded message to their German handlers that would reveal that they were operating under SMERSH's control. Hansen refused and made a statement to SMERSH officers: 'I've become acquainted with the honest and just people [meaning Baryshnikov's men] who had been described to us [by Nazi propaganda] in a completely different way... If I'm impressed by the country in general as much as the officers and soldiers impressed me, I'll conclude that any nation would be honored to be a friend of the Soviet Union.'[44] Because of this, von Scheller and Hansen were dealt with differently by SMERSH. On October 20, 1945, the OSO sentenced von Scheller to death and two weeks later he was executed, while Hansen was sentenced to imprisonment in labor camps. He survived and was repatriated to Germany after Stalin's death.

On April 21, 1945, at the end of the war, Abakumov received one of the highest military awards, the Kutuzov Order of the 1st Class, for the successful conclusion of a radio game code named '*Tuman*' (Fog).[45] It remains a mystery why only Abakumov was awarded for this effort because many participants, including Merkulov, were involved in it. The game concerned a German agent, a Russian named Pyotr Tavrin, who was sent by German intelligence to Soviet territory, and his wife. There are two main versions about how and when this happened.

The first is based on the documents of Gehlen's FHO, studied by E. H. Cookridge, the author of a book about Gehlen and his German intelligence men. He wrote that Pyotr Ivanovich Tavrin 'had been captured [by the Soviets] on May 30, 1942, in the Rzhev area. He informed his captors that he had been awarded the Orders of the Red Banner and of Alexander Nevsky…and displayed these medals with pride; but after the usual indoctrination he was prepared to go back as a spy'.[46]

However, Tavrin could not have had the Aleksandr Nevsky Order because this award was established on July 29, 1942, after Tavrin had been captured. The first Aleksandr Nevsky Order was bestowed in November 1942, after (according to Cookridge) Tavrin was smuggled back through the front line in September 1942. Even more questionable is the claim that Tavrin 'was given a succession of important appointments, first at the ministry of defense, then on the staff of the supreme headquarters and eventually, with the rank of colonel, at the headquarters of Marshal Ivan Chernyakhovsky', as well as the claim that on October 17, 1943 he was awarded 'the gold badge of a Hero of the Soviet Union'.[47] In August 1944, 'Tavrin sent a signal saying that he had fallen under suspicion. Gehlen decided to withdraw him and asked Zeppelin [the SD spy organization] to collect him in a Messerschmitt'. At the end, Cookridge cites the supposedly Soviet information that on September 5, 1944 Tavrin, a German spy in the uniform of a Soviet colonel, and his wife were arrested near Smolensk and later executed.

The KGB/FSB version begins from the arrest on September 5, 1944 of a Zeppelin agent with false documents in the name of Pyotr Ivanovich Tavrin (his real last name was Shilo), and a woman, his wife, with false documents for Lidia Shilova (her real last name was Bobrik).[48] Surprisingly, in his memoirs Tarasov, who participated in Operation Fog, refers to the couple as the Pokrovskys [sic] and not the Tavrins.[49] Over the years the FSB has changed its version of the circumstances of their arrest four or five times, so I will only address the published documents.[50]

On September 30, 1945 Merkulov reported to the GKO that on May 30, 1942, Tavrin-Pokrovsky crossed the front line and went to the Germans after the OO officer of his unit questioned him about his past. Tavrin had something to hide because from 1931 to 1938, he was arrested three times for embezzlement, and each time he managed to escape. Then he received a new passport under the name Tavrin instead of Shilo. While being held prisoner in German POW camps, in July 1943 he volunteered for German intelligence. Merkulov wrote:

> From September 1943 till August 1944, [Tavrin] was personally trained as a terrorist for committing terrorist acts against the USSR leaders. [Heinz] Gräfe, head of the SD Eastern Department, [Otto] Skorzeny, SD member who took part in kidnapping [Benito] Mussolini [in September 1943], and SS Major [Otto] Kraus of the SD post [Russland-Nord] in Riga supervised the training. Additionally, G. N. Zhilenkov, former [Party] secretary of the Rostokinsky Regional Committee in Moscow, who has betrayed the Motherland and currently lives in Germany, guided Tavrin for a long time.
>
> On the night of September 4 to 5 [1944] [Tavrin] was sent over the front line by a four-motor German plane from Riga Airport… The German intelligence organ, the Riga SD branch known as Zeppelin, organized his transportation.
>
> The goal of sending [Tavrin] is to organize and conduct a terrorist act against C.[omrade] Stalin, as well as, if possible, acts against the other members of the government: Beria, [Commissar for Railroad Transportation Lazar] Kaganovich and Molotov… For discovering further intentions of German intelligence, a radio game has been started… Tavrin's wife, Shilova Lidia Yakovlevna (arrested), who graduated from German courses for radio operators and was sent together with Tavrin, is used as an operator [in the game].[51]

The details Merkulov described became known from the interrogation of Tavrin conducted in Lubyanka, where the Tavrins were brought after their arrest near Smolensk, by Baryshnikov, head of the 3rd GUKR Department; Aleksandr Leontiev, head of the NKVD Department for Combating Bandits; and Leonid Raikhman, deputy head of the 2nd NKGB Directorate (interior counterintelligence).[52] Interestingly, Merkulov stressed Tavrin's connection to Georgii Zhilenkov, the highest Party official captured by the Germans, who became one of the leaders of the anti-Soviet movement and the Vlasov Army. Before the war, Zhilenkov was a secretary of Moscow's Rostokinsky Regional Party Committee and a member of the Moscow City Party Committee. After the end of the war Zhilenkov surrendered to the Americans, but on May 1, 1946 they handed him over to the Soviets. On August 1, 1946 the Military Collegium sentenced Zhilenkov, along with General Vlasov and his other close collaborators, to death and they were executed.[53]

Tavrin-Pokrovsky's testimony corroborated the words of a captured high-level RSHA officer whom Tarasov identified as 'John':

> In Zeppelin circles, Pokrovsky [Tavrin] was discussed a lot. He was considered a 'big bird' that would bring Zeppelin glory, awards and more power in intelligence activity. In their conversations Hauptsturmführer [Alfred] Backhaus [of the Zeppelin headquarters in Berlin], [Otto] Kraus, and Untersturmführer [Heinz] Gräfe used to repeat: 'Imagine the consequences if Pokrovsky succeeds in fulfilling his assignment.'[54]

If this testimony is true, it shows that Walter Schellenberg's men in the Zeppelin branch had no idea about real life in the Soviet Union and the impossibility of Tavrin's task.

Tavrin described how after leaving the plane, which had crashed while landing, the couple started out for Moscow by motorcycle. Tavrin was dressed in the uniform of a Soviet Major and Shilova, in that of a Junior Lieutenant. Tavrin had false documents of a deputy head of the OKR SMERSH of the 39th Army of the 1st Baltic Front and a fake typewritten order to come to the GUKR in Moscow.

Soon a group of NKVD operatives stopped them to check their papers. One of the officers noticed that the high military awards on Tavrin's chest were attached incorrectly. The awards included the Gold Star of a Hero and the Aleksandr Nevsky Order that have already been mentioned, citing Cookridge's story. Tavrin even had a fake newspaper clipping saying that he received the Gold Star on October 9, 1943. In fact, the star apparently belonged to Major General Ivan Shepetov, who was captured by the Germans on May 26, 1942 and executed in the Flossenberg Camp on May 21, 1943 after he tried to escape from the camp.

Interestingly, Tavrin did not try to fight or escape. A head of the local NKVD unit quickly established that there had never been a Major Tavrin in the 39th Army. The NKVD officers also found Tavrin's sophisticated diversion equipment hidden in the motorcycle. Tavrin and Shilova were sent to the GUKR in Moscow. Three NKVD and one huge SMERSH search groups also arrested the pilot, navigator, radio operator, and two gunners of the German plane. All of them were sent to Moscow.

The Tavrins agreed to participate in a SMERSH radio game called first 'A Couple', then 'Fog'. Most probably, SMERSH officers promised the couple that their lives would be spared if they collaborated. SMERSH's task was to persuade the Zeppelin agents to come to Soviet territory, where they would be caught. Baryshnikov supervised the writing of false radio messages by Majors Frolov and Grigorenko (the future KGB colonel general), and then Abakumov or his deputy Isai Babich approved the texts. Pavel Fedotov, head of the 2nd NKGB Directorate, and Leontiev, head of the NKVD Department for Combating Bandits, were informed about each message because they supervised the investigation of the Tavrin case. Tavrin and his wife were kept in Lubyanka Prison as prisoners 35 and 22 (corresponding, apparently, to the numbers of their cells), and were taken to a secret dacha outside Moscow for radio transmission sessions.

Tarasov mentions that 'the contact with the enemy was made with a delay because Pokrovsky [Tavrin] was not honest during the investigation and it took a long time for the Soviet counterintelligence to find out all the necessary details. To explain the long delay in communication, it was decided to create the impression that Pokrovskaya [Shilova] had tried to establish contact but was unable to do so due to her poor training'.[55] Finally, in September 1944, Shilova sent her first message to Zeppelin under SMERSH's control: 'We have arrived successfully, and started the work.'[56]

The Germans were completely fooled. Later 'John' testified to SMERSH that 'the radio contacts [with Shilova] were conducted with difficulty because Pokrovsky's wife was poorly trained'.[57] According to the messages, Tavrin was trying to penetrate the Kremlin circle. Strangely, some messages were addressed to Gräfe, although Tavrin was aware of Gräfe's death on January 1, 1944. On April 9, 1945, Shilova sent the last message, to which Berlin did not respond.

Soon after the war, in August 1945, the OSO sentenced members of the plane crew to death and they were executed. For some time SMERSH and, later, the MGB, hoped that German agents might visit the Tavrins, and the couple was kept alive. On February 1, 1952, the Military Collegium sentenced them to death. Tavrin admitted that he was guilty of treason, but rejected the accusation of being a terrorist: 'I have never been determined to follow the German order to conduct a terrorist act in the center [Moscow].'[58] His wife stated the same: 'I was dreaming about the Motherland and my people. I do not regret that I flew back. If it is necessary, I'll die...I ask for one thing: I'd like to share my fate with my husband... I believe that from the moment he stepped on our native ground he would not do anything against the Motherland.'[59] Tavrin was executed on March 28, 1952, and his wife, four days later. In May 2002 the Chief Military Prosecutor's Office refused to rehabilitate them.

It remains unclear why Cookridge gave an erroneous account of the Tavrin story. It's possible that the documents he used were a red herring to conceal the fact that for two years Tavrin was being trained for a special assignment and was not successfully serving in the Red Army. Unfortunately, in his recent book about Nazi espionage Christer Jörgensen repeated Cookridge's version of Tavrin's story without any changes.[60]

However, not everything is clear in Tavrin's 'true' story, which is now known due to the publications of FSB historians who had access to three volumes of the Tavrin investigation file. For instance, Aleksandr Mikhailov,

FSB Major General, describes how in the 1930s, Tavrin successfully escaped from arrest three times, managed to attend law school, and even worked as a senior investigator at a Prosecutor's Office in Voronezh.[61] It would have been almost impossible to do this in the 1930s, when people's backgrounds were constantly checked. The first escape, when some arrested criminals supposedly dismantled a wall and fled together with Shilo, is especially suspicious. This is one of the typical methods that the NKVD used for legalizing their secret informers.[62]

During interrogations in Moscow, Zhilenkov stated that in the German camp Tavrin told him that before the war he 'lived in Voronezh and worked in the local NKVD directorate as head of the personal guards of the first secretary of the Voronezh Province Party Committee', Iosif Vareikis.[63] Zhilenkov added that he did not believe Tavrin's stories, especially because 'soon after Tavrin arrived in the camp, he was accused of stealing 130 rubles, and then prisoners beat him up for cheating while playing cards'. Anyway, it is possible that Shilo-Tavrin was recruited as an OGPU-NKVD agent after his first arrest and then luckily managed to 'escape'. If so, most probably he went to the Germans as an NKVD (i.e., Sudoplatov's) agent. This explains why he surrendered to the NKVD operatives practically voluntarily. If this scenario is accurate, it is a mystery why he was finally shot.

But perhaps the most complicated and least-known radio game was organized in December 1944 in collaboration with the General Staff's Intelligence Directorate (RU).[64] A month earlier, Soviet agents had reported from Germany that the Nazis were preparing an attack against American and British troops in the Ardennes. To get the Germans to move some of their troops from the Eastern Front to the Ardennes, Stalin ordered that a deception game be devised to persuade the Germans that the Red Army was exhausted and would temporarily discontinue its offensive.

Tarasov and Fyodor Kuznetsov, head of the RU, were responsible for the operation. They devised a very complicated radio game involving twenty-four transmitters located in a number of Soviet cities, from Kuibyshev to Leningrad. They transmitted reports, supposedly from various sources, but all containing the same basic information: part of the Soviet troops had been called back from the fronts for reorganization and training. RU agents disseminated similar disinformation among the population in the war zone.

The operation worked perfectly. The German command completely trusted the false information, and, on December 16, 1944, the Germans began their attack in the Ardennes, which involved not only the last reserves of the German army but also several tank divisions transferred from the Eastern Front. While the Western Allies were fighting in the Ardennes, the Soviet troops were preparing a new assault. On January 12, 1945, at the request of the Allies, the 1st Ukrainian Front and then the 1st Belorussian

Front began their attack on Poland, and on January 13 and 14, the 2nd and 3rd Belorussian fronts attacked Eastern Prussia. The German defense in these areas was weakened because of radio game disinformation.

From 1943 to 1945, SMERSH and the NKGB conducted 183 radio games, some of which continued for years.[65] Local SMERSH departments also organized radio games. Overall, approximately 400 German intelligence officers and agents were arrested and participated in the games. When the games ended, most of them were shot. For example, in March 1944 SD officer Alois Galfe, who had specialized in training the Russian POWs recruited for Operation Zeppelin, was captured by SMERSH operatives not far from Moscow as part of the '*Zagadka*' (Puzzle) game.[66] This game was jointly conducted by the 3rd and 4th GUKR SMERSH departments and continued after the arrest of Galfe. Galfe was taken to Lubyanka Prison, where Abakumov interrogated him for six hours. On January 27, 1945, the OSO sentenced Galfe to death as a German spy and he was executed.

Kirill Stolyarov, a Russian historian, concluded: 'SMERSH outfoxed the Abwehr… Stalin, who made replacements in the cadres quickly at the slightest indication of incompetence, kept Abakumov in his position during the whole war.'[67] However, success was incomplete. Until the end of the war, 389 unidentified German agents continued to send radio messages from the territory liberated by the Red Army.[68]

Although the details remain unknown, radio games continued long after the war, apparently, with British and American intelligence. On November 15, 1952, MGB Minister Semyon Ignatiev reported to Stalin: 'A plan of the cancellation of radio games advantageous for us and conducted from the territories of the Baltic Soviet Republics, will be presented to you on November 20.'[69]

In the Abwehr Schools

From the UOO, SMERSH inherited the practice of sending agents to the enemy's rear. Some of these military counterintelligence officers successfully joined German intelligence organizations and also schools, where they collected information on the schools, their staffs, and students. On the Eastern Front there were more than 130 intelligence and counterintelligence SD and Abwehr organizations and 60 schools.[70] Information gathered by Soviet agents allowed SMERSH operatives to arrest German agents when they entered Soviet territory.

Frequently, SMERSH agents had already attended the Abwehr schools. While many civilians and Soviet POWs volunteered for these schools ostensibly as German agents, they really intended to use the opportunity to return to Soviet territory and join the Red Army. After graduation, when Abwehr centers sent them to Soviet territory to work as German spies, these individuals found SMERSH units and gave them detailed information about the Abwehr schools and the tasks assigned to them by the German intelligence. In Chekist jargon, this was a situation in which a person 'has admitted his/her guilt and testified about himself/herself'. These people were, of course, highly valuable to SMERSH, and when they were sent back as double agents, their special knowledge yielded much greater success at collecting intelligence than the results attained by other SMERSH agents.

In Moscow, the 4th GUKR Department controlled the sending of agents and double agents to the enemy. In the UKRs at the fronts, the 2nd departments handled these operations. From April 1943 to February 1944, 75 SMERSH officers were introduced into German intelligence organs and schools, and 38 of them managed to return.[71] SMERSH agents collected information on 359 Abwehr officers and 978 intelligence school graduates; as a result, SMERSH operatives arrested 176 saboteurs operating in the Red Army's rear. From September 1943 to October 1944, SMERSH sent ten groups of parachutists (78 officers) into the enemy's rear at various fronts.[72] Of these, six groups managed to join German intelligence as Soviet spies, recruiting 142 Soviet agents and unmasking 15 enemy agents.

On June 24, 1944, Maj. Gen. Pyotr Ivashutin, head of the UKR of the 3rd Ukrainian Front, sent a report to Abakumov describing the UKR's success:

To: Head of the Main Counterintelligence Directorate SMERSH,
        Security Commissar of the 2nd Rank V. Abakumov

June 24, 1944

Report

On the work of the Directorate of Counterintelligence SMERSH
of the 3rd Ukrainian Front in the enemy's rear
from October 1, 1943 to June 15, 1944

During this period, the work in the enemy's rear included the penetration of our agents into the intelligence and counterintelligence organs of the enemy that were acting against our front. Until the end of 1943, Abwehr-groups 103, 203, and 303 were active against us. To penetrate these organs, the following agents were sent to the enemy's rear [the names are omitted in the published document]. At the time, three of our agents—Rastorguev, Mikhail Aleksandrovich; Turusin, Georgii Dmitrievich; and Robak, Nadezhda Petrovna—had already joined Abwehrgroup-203.

Turusin, after being sent by the enemy to our rear, came to us to acknowledge his guilt and gave detailed testimony about himself and the other agents. Then, following our order, he recruited three agents of

Abwehrgroup-203 to work for us. Later, when they were sent to our territory, they voluntarily gave themselves up to us. He helped us to arrest three more saboteurs who were parachuted in with him, and gathered valuable information about the staff and agents of the Abwehrgroup.

Rastorguev, another former agent of the Abwehrgroup-203, came to us to acknowledge his guilt. With Turusin and with GUKR SMERSH's sanction, in September of last year he was sent to the enemy's rear with the task of recruiting a member of the German intelligence staff. He fulfilled our task and recruited this officer and three more agents. After he was sent to the enemy for the second time, he personally brought three agent-members of his intelligence team back to us. Based on his information, the SMERSH Directorate of the 2nd Ukrainian Front arrested two agents of Abwehrgroup-204. He also collected full information on fourteen agents and ten staff members of Abwehrgroups 203 and 204.

Robak, Nadezhda Petrovna, an agent of Abwehrgroup-203, along with two other women agents, was parachuted into the rear of our front at the end of July 1943. She voluntarily came to us to acknowledge her guilt and gave detailed information about her connections with the German intelligence and about other agents. In 1943, based on her information, we arrested four women agents of Abwehrgroup-203, who were left in the Donbass [the coal mining area between Russia and Ukraine] to collect intelligence and to penetrate the Red Army. Like Rastorguev, with the sanction of the GUKR SMERSH, on September 22, 1943, she was sent to the enemy's rear with the task of recruiting a staff member of the German intelligence. She fulfilled the task, and the recruited intelligence officer has already sent agents of Abwehrgroup-203 into the hands of Soviet counterintelligence.

Head of the SMERSH Directorate of the 3rd Ukrainian Front,
Major General   IVASHUTIN.[73]

For some reason, Ivashutin's report did not mention the name of Afanasii Polozov, the German intelligence officer recruited by Nadezhda Robak. As was common among Russian teachers in the Abwehr schools, he worked under the alias of 'Vladimir Krakov' or 'Dontsov'.[74] A young Cossack, he served as a veterinarian in the 38th Cavalry Division of the Red Army, and on May 12, 1942, he was taken prisoner by the Germans. After training in German intelligence schools, in April 1943 Krakov was appointed head of the Abwehrgroup-203 school for saboteurs attached to the 1st German Tank Army then stationed in the Ukraine. Soon he started searching for contact with Soviet military counterintelligence and sent some of his agents, including Nadezhda Robak, to find SMERSH officials.

Although it doesn't mention Polozov by name, Ivashutin's report presents the recruiting of Polozov and his work for SMERSH as a success.

However, Polozov's work for Ivashutin ended tragically. Later he testified: 'When it became impossible [i.e., too dangerous] to continue my work [for SMERSH], in March 1944, I crossed the front line near the town of Yampol, and came to the head of counterintelligence of the Soviet Tank Army [of the 2nd Ukrainian Front] Shevchenko, who knew about my work.'[75] To Polozov's complete surprise, Shevchenko said that he had never known Polozov and that Polozov had never worked for Soviet counterintelligence.

On March 30, 1944, Polozov was arrested and sent to the GUKR SMERSH in Moscow for investigation. On November 1, 1944, the OSO sentenced Polozov to twenty years in labor camps as a military traitor who worked for the Germans. In fact, as was established during the re-evaluation of Polozov's case, his achievements were impressive: 'According to the information of the 4th Department of the GUKR SMERSH… Polozov released from [POW] camps, recruited, and persuaded to give themselves up to the Soviet counterintelligence…more than forty people.'[76] After Stalin's death (1953), Polozov was pardoned in September 1955.

Some other unlucky Soviet agents were simply shot to death on the spot by rabid officers and servicemen who indiscriminately killed anybody who crossed the line. On January 12, 1945, the troops of the 1st Ukrainian, 1st and 2nd Belorussian fronts assumed the offensive. Coded orders to move toward the Soviet troops were radioed to Soviet agents working in the enemy's rear. Military intelligence and counterintelligence officers of the regiments, divisions, and corps of these fronts received the following instruction: 'Intelligence officers who come out of the enemy's territory should be provided with good food, medical help (if necessary), and clothing. It is categorically forbidden to take personal belongings, documents, weapons, and radio transmitters from them.'[77]

Four days later Soviet agents began to approach the Soviet troops. However, not all commanders welcomed them. Marshal Konstantin Rokossovsky, Commander of the 2nd Belorussian Front, issued the following order:

> On January 19, 1945, in the town of Mlave, Engineer-Captain Ch-ov [the name was shortened to conceal his identity], commander of the group of agents, approached the servicemen of the 717th Rifle Regiment of the 137th Rifle Division and asked them to show him the way to the intelligence headquarters of the front. They did not help Comrade Ch-ov, but instead, brutally killed him…
>
> On January 18, 1945, a group of operational agents commanded by Lieutenant G-ov approached the servicemen of the 66th Mechanical Brigade near the town of Zechaune. The group was sent to Lt. Col. L-o, Commander of the 66th Mechanical Brigade. Instead of determining that the group consisted of intelligence officers, L-o called them 'Vlasovites' [i.e., solders of General Vlasov's Army of Soviet POWs formed by the Germans],

and ordered that they be shot. Luckily, they were not shot and, therefore, saved from death...

I have ordered the [Military] Prosecutor of the Front to investigate incidents of executions.[78]

The number of Soviet secret agents who were executed on the spot in similar incidents is unknown.

In 1943, the Abwehr opened special schools (Abwehr-209 and others) to train thirteen- to sixteen-year-old teenagers as agents; boys were selected from the German-occupied Soviet territories. On November 1, 1943, Abakumov forwarded to Stalin a report from Vladimir Baryshnikov, head of the 3rd GUKR SMERSH Department, concerning the arrest of twenty-nine such agents dropped mostly at the Kalinin and Western fronts.[79] The young saboteurs were supplied with explosives disguised as pieces of coal. All of the teenage agents immediately found SMERSH or NKGB operatives and gave themselves up. Despite this, all of them were imprisoned in labor camps.

CHAPTER 19

Against Our Own People

In addition to its new responsibilities, SMERSH remained in charge of spying and reporting on Soviet servicemen. In the field, SMERSH used all kinds of measures to prevent Red Army servicemen from changing sides. For instance, in July 1943 UKRs of the Bryansk and Central fronts conducted the operation 'Pretense "The Treason of the Motherland"' in preparation for the Battle of Kursk.[1] Groups of SMERSH-trained soldiers came up close to the enemy trenches, pretending that they wanted to cross the lines, and then threw grenades into the trenches. SMERSH operatives hoped that after this the Germans would shoot at any Red Army serviceman who appeared near their trenches.

The number of servicemen sentenced as traitors by military tribunals increased considerably after the OOs became SMERSH: in 1941, the tribunals convicted 8,976 traitors; in 1942, 43,050; in 1943, 52,757; and in 1944, 69,895.[2] The investigations conducted by SMERSH officers were usually unprofessional and cases were generally falsified. A 1943 incident sheds light on the quality of investigation in the SMERSH field branches.

A Report on SMERSH

In May 1943, Aleksandr Shcherbakov, deputy NKO Commissar and head of the Army's Main Political Directorate (GlavPURKKA, a directorate of the Central Committee), reported to Stalin on his and Abakumov's inspection of SMERSH activity within the 7th Independent Army at the Karelian Front not far from Leningrad.[3] This inspection was prompted by a complaint from the army's commander, Major General Aleksei Krutikov, who reported to Moscow that most of the espionage cases prepared by the SMERSH department of his army were fabricated.

Shcherbakov wrote that their inspection revealed many falsified cases. Several paragraphs of the letter demonstrate the common work methods of SMERSH field investigators:

> During inspection it was found that in a number of cases the Special Departments [it was the time of SMERSH, but many still referred to the SMERSH units by their previous name] used unlawful methods and violated the law. In particular, the Special Departments used as cell informers individuals who had already been sentenced to VMN [death] for espionage…[Later] head of the Special Department of the [7th] Army, Colonel Com.[rade] Dobrovolsky, appealed to the Military Council of the Army asking that VMN be replaced by imprisonment for individuals who helped [the investigators] to incriminate others.[4]

Yakov Aizenstadt, a member of a military tribunal, also recalled this practice: 'Soon I discovered that "*nasedki*" [stool pigeons] and "*stukachi*" [informants], charged with getting confessions from prisoners under investigation, were put in each cell… Each "*nasedka*" and "*stukach*" had his pseudonym or alias, and each secret report contained the cell number.'[5] Interestingly, when referring to cell informants, Shcherbakov used the term '*kamernyi svidetel*' (cell witness) instead of '*vnutrikamernik*' (cell insider), which was common in NKVD–SMERSH jargon. Perhaps, Shcherbakov considered the last word too explicit—that is, clearly indicative of the fact that the 'witnesses' were planted.

Shcherbakov continued: 'An additional practice was the presence of investigators of the Special Departments at the trial [to intimidate the defendants], which was not necessary.'[6] In the 1930s, NKVD investigators routinely rehearsed defendants before the open court trials, telling them what they should say during the trial and threatening to beat them severely after the trial if they did not follow instructions. Obviously, SMERSH investigators used similar methods, and their presence at the military tribunal sessions was meant to remind the defendants of their threats. Shcherbakov also emphasized that 'another defect in the work of the punishment organs of the 7th Army was the complete lack of supervision by the prosecutor during the investigation'.[7]

Stalin immediately reacted to these points in Shcherbakov's report. On May 31, 1943, he signed Order of the NKO Commissar No. 0089ss, handing down various punishments for SMERSH officers and prosecutors of the 7th Independent Army.[8] The head of the SMERSH Department, Dobrovolsky, and the Military Prosecutor of the army received strict Party reprimands, while one of the investigators was to be tried and sentenced to five years in the labor camps. Three other investigators were to be discharged and sent to a punishment battalion. Finally, the Deputy Prosecutor of the Army responsible for supervising SMERSH Department work was demoted in rank.

However, it is unlikely that these fairly mild measures affecting one army represented a serious attempt to change SMERSH's conduct. Besides, Stalin's order did not address the general conclusions Shcherbakov placed at the end of his letter: 'There are many inexperienced and semiliterate officers in the Special (currently, SMERSH) Departments. This defect should be corrected by transferring a few thousand political officers to [military] counterintelligence.'[9]

The last recommendation was clearly Shcherbakov's attempt to place his own people, political officers, in Abakumov's SMERSH. Political officers constantly complained about SMERSH operatives and commanding officers.

Transferring thousands of political officers who had no legal training would not have made SMERSH departments more professional, but would have increased GlavPURKKA's influence within SMERSH, which Stalin definitely did not want. He needed SMERSH to remain under Abakumov's sole control, thus ensuring that, through Abakumov, SMERSH would be under his own exclusive control.

Denouncing High Commanders

In 1943, 60 percent of trials in the tribunals of the Leningrad Front involved charges of 'anti-Soviet propaganda' (Article 58-10).[10] For most of convicts terms of five to ten years in the labor camps were commuted to service in punishment battalions and companies. For convicted officers, three months in a penal battalion was equivalent to a ten-year prison term. Even generals were arrested at the front for 'anti-Soviet propaganda' or treason (Appendix I, see http://www.smershbook.com). Here are a few examples.

In May 1943, SMERSH arrested Lieutenant General Vladimir Tamruchi, commander of tank troops at the Southwest Front, just after he left hospital. He was charged with treason and spent the next seven years in the inhuman Sukhanovo Prison in solitary confinement.[11] In October 1950 he died, still awaiting trial.

Before long, another general became a long-term prisoner of Sukhanovo. In December 1943, Lieutenant General Ivan Laskin arrived in Moscow, ostensibly to be appointed to a new position. Head of the HQ of the Northern Caucasian Front, Laskin was an internationally known figure.

On January 31, 1943, he headed the military operational group that took prisoner the staff members of Field Marshal von Paulus's 6th Army in Stalingrad, and Paulus himself surrendered personally to Laskin.[12] In Moscow, Aleksei Antonov, head of the General Staff, informed Laskin about his new appointment as HQ head of the 4th Ukrainian Front. Before going to this front, Laskin was sent to the sanatorium Arkhangelskoe near Moscow, supposedly to rest and relax for a few days. However, the very next day a major came to Laskin's room, saying that he had been sent to bring Laskin to the Military Intelligence (RU) HQ in Moscow. This was a lie: the major and two other officers who accompanied him were actually SMERSH operatives, and a car brought Laskin and the officers not to the RU, but to Lubyanka Prison. In his memoirs, Laskin recalled what happened next:

> The officers took my handgun away from me and searched my pockets… I was brought to a huge room without windows, where my general's shoulder boards were pulled off, then military orders were removed from my chest. Two guards, after grabbing my wrists, pulled me along an iron stair to… Colonel General Abakumov.
>
> [Abakumov] looked at me from my feet up to my face and demanded in a fierce voice:
>
> 'Tell me about your crimes.'
>
> I strongly answered that I had never committed or even thought about committing any crime against the Motherland…
>
> He continued to shout at me:
>
> 'Already in 1938 we wanted to arrest you…and it's a pity that we didn't. And since then you have tried to escape our organs. Now you'll find out who we are!'[13]

The 'organs' was a typical way the Chekists referred to themselves. Laskin was charged with treason (Article 58-1b) and kept in Sukhanovo Prison. Ironically, on December 31, 1943 the American government awarded him the Distinguished Service Cross 'for extraordinary heroism in connection with military operations against an armed enemy, an action against our common enemy, Germany, in World War II'.[14] Clearly, the Western Allies highly valued the capture of Field Marshal Paulus.

It wasn't until December 1952 that the Military Collegium sentenced Laskin, now charged with not following his military duty (Article 193-1a), to ten years' imprisonment. Allegedly, he violated his military oath in 1941, when, while he and his unit were surrounded by the Germans, he destroyed his Communist Party ID, got rid of his gun and exchanged his uniform for civilian clothes. Obviously, these ridiculous charges were trumped up to conceal the fact that Laskin had already spent almost ten years in Moscow investigation prisons without having committed any crime. The same December, Laskin was released.

Soon after Stalin's death, during the process of rehabilitation, it was discovered what lay behind Laskin's case: Mikhail Belkin, head of the UKR of the Northern Caucasian Front, denounced Laskin to Abakumov. Belkin greatly desired the Order of Lenin, and he asked Laskin to officially recommend him for that award. Laskin refused because he did not know Belkin well enough. Laskin's arrest and the whole 'case' were a direct result of Belkin's vengeance. In 1953 Laskin was rehabilitated, but only in 1966 did Soviet authorities present him with his Distinguished Service Cross.

The case of Major General Boris Teplinsky, head of the Operational Department of the Air Force of the Siberian Military District, was more personal for Abakumov. General Teplinsky was arrested in connection with his friend, high-ranking NKVD/NKGB official Viktor Il'in. According to some memoirs, Il'in confronted Abakumov with compromising information about one of Abakumov's love affairs.[15] However, Sudoplatov claimed that Il'in was arrested because he had notified Teplinsky about the preparations for his arrest in the GUKR SMERSH, and Abakumov used this as a reason for complaining about Merkulov and Beria and their subordinates to Stalin. Most probably, both events took place.

Anyway, on April 28, 1943 Abakumov personally arrested Teplinsky, and on May 3, 1943, Il'in was arrested in Merkulov's office. Teplinsky and Il'in were accused of treason, conspiracy, and anti-Soviet propaganda. This was one of the cases that were without movement for years. During interrogations Teplinsky was tortured, and on eleven separate occasions he declared a hunger strike.[16] It wasn't until February 1952 that the OSO MGB sentenced Il'in to eight years of imprisonment for anti-Soviet propaganda, and he was then released because he had already spent this term under investigation. In March 1952, the Military Collegium sentenced Teplinsky to a 10-year imprisonment; he was released after Stalin's death. Both were soon rehabilitated due to the lack of evidence that they had committed any crime.

On April 1, 1944, Abakumov presented Stalin with a long summary of reports from his subordinates concerning the Western Front headed by Vasilii Sokolovsky:

> I report to you that agents of the Main Directorate SMERSH and the Counterintelligence Directorate of the Western Front reported to me that recently generals and officers of the Red Army General Staff and the Western Front have repeatedly stated that the Commander of the Western Front, Army General Sokolovsky, and his Head of Staff, Lieutenant General [Aleksandr] Pokrovsky, have not guided military operations appropriately.

For instance, Lieutenant General [A. I.] Shimonaev…said: 'From 1942 to the present, the Western Front has been using two to three times more ammunition than any other front, but it has not achieved any result… Sokolovsky and Pokrovsky organized intelligence poorly. They did not have a clear understanding of the enemy or its fortifications—knowledge that is crucial in deciding where to break through the enemy's defense…'

Col. Alekseev said: 'On Pokrovsky's order, Colonel Il'initsky, head of the Front's Intelligence Department…falsifies estimates of the enemy's force…'

In January of this year [1944], based on our information, Comrade [Fyodor] Kuznetsov, head of the Red Army Intelligence Directorate, sent a commission to inspect the Intelligence Department of the Western Front. [Deputy USSR Prosecutor] Lieutenant General [Afanasii] Vavilov headed the commission, which included Major Krylovsky. The commission discovered outrageous facts concerning the work of the Intelligence Directorate…

Il'initsky, with Pokrovsky's approval, tried to compromise this Commission and even accused Krylovsky of drinking vodka instead of working. However, the Military Council of the Western Front did not take necessary measures based on the facts revealed [by the Commission].

On March 25…rocket launchers fired on our own troops, causing enormous losses in the 352nd Rifle Division… Pokrovsky asked that these significant casualties not be revealed to anyone…

In a conversation with Lieutenant General [Pavel] Zelenin, head of the Counterintelligence Directorate [of the Western Front], [Lev] Mekhlis, a member of the Military Council of the Western Front, said that Sokolovsky…was not happy with some members of the Red Army General Staff, calling them idlers. He was also sarcastic about some of their orders, which he criticized.[17]

Stalin ordered a new special commission headed by Malenkov to investigate the situation at the Western Front. Mekhlis handed over an anonymous letter to Malenkov from one of the commanders who complained about Abakumov's subordinates. Apparently, Mekhlis wanted to clear himself of Abakumov's accusations that he had not done enough against Sokolovsky and his accomplices. This anonymous letter was written with great passion:

I ask you, Comrade Stalin, not to judge me harshly.

The situation…at the Western Front is outrageous… Commanders are not trusted, and, in fact, counterintelligence representatives became the real heads of the military units. Frequently they undermine the authority of the commander…

They are spying on commanders, secretly watching their every step. If a commander summons someone, after leaving the commander this person is ordered to appear at the counterintelligence department, where he is interrogated about the purpose of the commander's call and what the commander said...

All rights and initiative were taken from commanders. A commander cannot make any decision without the approval of the counterintelligence representative. Even women [PPZhs] were taken from commanders, while each counterintelligence officer lives with one or two women.

Commanders are threatened by the actions of Mekhlis against them, while the majority of the commanders have defended the Motherland, not caring about their own lives...

Why is this going on? Did the years 1937–38 come back again?

I do not sign this letter because if I put my name, I will be destroyed.[18]

In its long report to Stalin dated April 11, 1944, the Malenkov Commission described facts even more outrageous than those Abakumov had reported. Eleven military operations attempted at the Western Front during that period failed. The losses were enormous: 'From October 12, 1943, to April 1, 1944, at the site of active military operations alone, 62,326 men were killed, and 219,419 men were wounded... In all...the Western Front lost 330,587 men. In addition, hospitals admitted 53,283 servicemen who needed medical attention.'[19] During the same period, German losses at that front totaled approximately 13,000: that is, about five times fewer casualties than the Russian forces sustained.

The commission concluded: 'Unsuccessful actions at the Western Front during the past six months, heavy losses, and significant utilization of ammunition were...due...only to the poor leadership of the Front commanders.' It also recommended the dismissals of Sokolovsky, Pokrovsky, Il'initsky, and some others. It blamed Nikolai Bulganin, a member of the Military Council before Mekhlis, and Mekhlis for not reporting the trouble at the Western Front to the Stavka, and recommended that Bulganin be reprimanded. On April 12, 1944, Stalin signed a Stavka directive to rename the unfortunate Western Front the '3rd Belorussian Front'.[20] Three armies of the former Western Front were transferred to the newly created 2nd Belorussian Front.

Despite strong accusations in the Abakumov and Malenkov reports, this time Stalin's punishment of the Western Front commanders was extremely lenient. Sokolovsky was dismissed, but appointed to the high position of chief of staff of the 1st Ukrainian Front. Pokrovsky continued as head of the Staff of the 3rd Belorussian Front. Only Il'initsky lost his post. Mekhlis became a member of the Military Council of the 2nd Belorussian Front, and Bulganin, a member of the Military Council of the 1st Belorussian Front.

Soon, in November 1944, Bulganin received an enormous promotion to deputy defense Commissar, and inclusion in the GKO. Now the heads of the NKO main directorates reported first to Bulganin, and he reported to Stalin.[21] Abakumov and Shcherbakov continued reporting directly to Stalin.

The reasons behind Stalin's support and promotion of Bulganin remain unclear. According to some memoirs, Bulganin's drunkenness and the fact that he kept on staff a harem of young women were legendary among the military at the fronts.[22] In addition, while on military councils, he had five adjutants, two telephone operators, a personal cook, and a servant. Among those in Stalin's circle, Bulganin was considered the military officer with the least amount of professional education.[23] Incredibly, during the entire time he held military appointments during the war, Bulganin remained chairman of the Soviet State Bank.

POW Vetting Continues

In addition to army investigations, SMERSH continued vetting servicemen who had been taken prisoner or were in detachments encircled by the enemy—previously a task of the OO officers. Such servicemen were collected in the specially organized Collection-Transit Posts (SPP) in the rear of armies or Vetting-Filtration Posts (PFP) of fronts. Here the detainees were kept for five to ten days. From December 1943 on, special commissions that included a SMERSH officer and four army representatives conducted the investigations.

Generally, it was the same as the previous vetting by OO officers. At first, a detainee gave written testimony, which the SMERSH officers studied carefully. Then the person was interrogated in detail and his answers compared with the testimony. Finally, SMERSH investigators decided the person's future fate, and a written investigator's decision was filed. Various decisions were possible: a person could be drafted into the army for a second time; sent to work in the military industry; sent (in the case of a demoted officer) to serve in an assault battalion; or discharged as an invalid or dead person. If SMERSH officers suspected they were dealing with a German agent, a special Record File (*Delo-formulyar*) was opened for that person.

Frequently the German agents were caught because their soldier's passport-sized IDs were made too perfectly. The staples in Soviet soldier IDs were made of iron and rusted spots would appear on the pages of the IDs around the staples. Although the printing work and paper in the forged German-made IDs were almost identical to those in the real IDs, staples in the forged IDs were made of stainless steel and the IDs did not have the rusted spots, and this feature was immediately recognized by SMERSH officers.

After the initial vetting, the person was transferred to a Front Screening-Filtration Camp (called NKVD Special Camps before 1944), where vetting continued for the next two months and the preliminary decision was checked more carefully. There were fifteen such camps in the rear of the 2nd Belorussian Front; thirty each, in the rear of the 1st Belorussian and 1st Ukrainian fronts; ten each, in the rear of the 2nd and 3rd Ukrainian fronts; and five in the rear of the 4th Ukrainian Front. Up to 10,000 people were kept in each camp; 58,686 were vetted from February 1 to May 4, 1945 in the camps of the 3rd Ukrainian Front alone, and of these, 376 were arrested. The vetting camps continued operating after the war in Soviet territory and in Eastern Europe, and the last of them were closed only after Stalin's death in 1953.

As previously in the OOs, SMERSH officers did not send all those returning from captivity to filtration camps. Some were executed on the spot. Mikhail Shmulev recalled: 'I ran from the Germans twice. The first time I was unlucky—I was caught and punished. The second time I managed to get to our advancing troops. I was stopped twice by drunken officers who wanted to execute me on the spot as a spy or a Vlasovite before I got to the military *komendatura* [commandant's office]. Then I was kept in a SMERSH cell for convicts sentenced to death. For fifteen days I shared a cell with those unfortunates who had failed to convince investigators they had not served the enemy and were not traitors of the Motherland. They were shot.'[24]

The story of a woman pilot, Anna Timofeeva-Yegorova, is even more shocking. At the end of 1944, her attack aircraft was shot down near Warsaw and fell to the ground, engulfed in flames. At the last moment she managed to parachute out, but she was taken prisoner and placed in Küstrin (Kostrzyn in Polish), the concentration camp for Allied soldiers (Stalag III-C Alt-Drewitz). Timofeeva had serious burns that were treated by doctor-prisoners in a camp hospital. Bravely, the fellow prisoners managed to salvage her numerous awards (two Red Banner orders, the Red Star Order, the medal 'For Bravery', and the medal 'For Taking over the Caucasus'), as well as her Party ID, risking their lives to do so.

On January 31, 1945, the Red Army liberated the camp, and prisoners were ordered to the town of Landsberg for vetting. Timofeeva put on a coat given to her by fellow British prisoners, attached her military awards to it, and started on her way, hardly able to walk. Soon SMERSH operatives picked her up and brought her to their headquarters. She recalled:

> During the first night, two soldiers with machine guns took me to the second floor for interrogation. I could hardly move my legs because with every motion the thin skin that had just developed over the burned areas cracked and blood oozed when I bent my arms and legs. Every time I stopped, a soldier pushed me in the back with the butt of his machine gun.
>
> They brought me into a bright room with pictures on the walls and a big rug on the floor. A major sat at the table. He looked friendly. But first, he

took my awards and my party ID away from me and studied them with a magnifying glass. For a long time he did not allow me to sit down. I thought I would fall to the floor, but I managed to keep myself conscious and begged for permission to be seated. Finally, he allowed me to sit down. I thought I wouldn't be able to rise from the chair by any means. Suddenly the 'friendly' major yelled at me, 'Stand up!' and I jumped up from the chair. Then he shouted at me:

'Where did you get the awards and the party ID?'

'Why did you allow yourself to be taken prisoner?'

'What [German] task did you have?'

'Who gave you the task?'

'Where were you born?'

'Whom were you ordered to contact?'

The major continued to ask these and similar questions until dawn. To all my answers, he shouted: 'You are lying, Alsatian dog!'

This continued for many nights... They insulted me with every unprintable word... My name was not used anymore. Now I was 'a fascist Alsatian dog...'

On the tenth day in SMERSH I lost my patience. I stood up from the trestle bed and, without saying a word, walked to the exit and up the stairs, right to the major on the second floor.

'Stay still, you whore! I'll shoot!' shouted the guard, rushing toward me. But I continued to walk, I almost ran upstairs...

I opened the door quickly and shouted, or I only thought that I shouted: 'When will you stop your insults? You can kill me, but I won't let you insult me anymore!'[25]

Timofeeva was lucky. Finally, Major Fedotov released her. However, only in 1965 did she receive the highest military award for bravery, the Hero of the Soviet Union Star.

Timofeeva's story was quite typical because air forces were especially targeted by SMERSH. Technically ignorant themselves, *osobisty* considered any technical failure as sabotage, and commanders frequently hid pilots from SMERSH officers while accident investigations were in progress. From 1943 till the end of the war, at least 10,941 pilots and crew members were taken prisoner by the Germans or were missing in action.[26] Many wounded pilots who escaped from the enemy experienced beatings at the hands of SMERSH; in addition, investigators crushed their fingers with boots, staged executions, and so forth, not to mention that SMERSH prisoners were not fed or allowed to use a bathroom.[27]

Sometimes pilots used force to free their fellows from the clutches of *osobisty*. When Aleksandr Pokryshkin, commander of the 9th Guard Air Division and the most famous Soviet flying ace, saw what SMERSH

БУДЬ НА ЧЕКУ,
В ТАКИЕ ДНИ
ПОДСЛУШИВАЮТ СТЕНЫ.
НЕДАЛЕКО ОТ БОЛТОВНИ
И СПЛЕТНИ
ДО ИЗМЕНЫ.

НЕ БОЛТАЙ!

The famous poster 'Don't Chatter' created during the first days of the Great Patriotic War. By Nina Vatolina (the author's aunt). © ANNA BIRSTEIN, MOSCOW

LEFT: Aerial view of Stalingrad from a German bomber, September 1942. © BUNDESARCHIV

RIGHT: Kiev is recaptured, November 1943. The centre of the city was destroyed by fighting and bombs left by the NKVD sabotage groups. © RGAKFD/ROSINFORM, KRASNOGORSK

Stalingrad, February 1943. German prisoners of war. © RGAKFD/ROSINFORM, KRASNOGORSK

LEFT: Viktor Abakumov, head of SMERSH, at the Front, March 1945.
© PHOTO ITAR-TASS, MOSCOW

RIGHT: Vienna is taken, April 1945. It will soon become a centre of SMERSH activity in Europe. © RGAKFD/ROSINFORM, KRASNOGORSK

Stalin and the GKO members at the Trophy German Equipment Exhibition in Gorky Park, Moscow, 1944 © RGAKFD/ROSINFORM, KRASNOGORSK

A SMERSH Arrest Order. Text says: 'Order No. 786, July 31, 1944. To Deputy Head of the 4th Section of the SMERSH Counterintelligence Department (OKR) of the 7th Army, Captain Com.[rade] [name blanked out] for the arrest and search of Abudikhin Nikolai Semenovich. Head of the Special Department Colonel [signature; name blanked out]. Head of the Operational Registration Section [signature]. Arrest was sanctioned by the Military Prosecutor of the 7th Army [the name is blanked out].' Although the name of the SMERSH Department's head was blanked out, according to the signature, this was, in fact, A. A. Isakov, who headed the OKR SMERSH of the 7th Army from April 1944 to January 1945. Note that an old NKVD form was used instead of an NKO form.

General Helmuth Weidling and other German officers captured by SMERSH. In front of the German Chancellery, May 2, 1945. © RGAKFD/ROSINFORM, KRASNOGORSK

Other prisoners of war taken in Berlin, May 1945. © RGAKFD/ROSINFORM, KRASNOGORSK

Russian women working as forced labourers in Germany waiting to be sent home, May 1945. They are unaware they will be vetted by SMERSH and the NKVD on their return.
© RGAKFD/ROSINFORM, KRASNOGORSK

Nuremberg, Soviet prosecutor Yurii Pokrovsky. Boris Solovov, a member of the SMERSH team, sits to the left. © RGAKFD/ROSINFORM, KRASNOGORSK

Soviet prosecutor Nikolai Zorya addressing the Nuremberg tribunal (he would soon die of a gunshot wound to the head under mysterious circumstances). © RGAKFD/ROSINFORM, KRASNOGORSK

Nuremberg. Defendant Hans
Fritzsche (he was brought from
Moscow by a SMERSH team).
© OFFICE OF THE US CHIEF OF
COUNSEL/HARRY S. TRUMAN LIBRARY

Victors in the Kremlin, 1945. Stalin is in the front; behind him, left to right: Anastas
Mikoyan, Nikita Khrushchev, Georgii Malenkov, Lavrentii Beria, and Vyacheslav Molotov.
© RGAKFD/ROSINFORM, KRASNOGORSK

SMERSH ID card of Major Anatolii Nikolaevich Fetisov. © MUSEUM OF WWII, NATICK, MA

officers did in a vetting camp to Ivan Babak, he almost shot to death the camp's commandant.[28] During the war, Babak shot down 37 enemy planes before he was shot down himself in April 1945. In the vetting camp, he was terribly tortured, and *osobisty* refused to believe that he was a Hero of the Soviet Union. Pokryshkin took Babak with him and Babak returned to his corps. However, military counterintelligence did not forget about him, and he was arrested after the war, in 1947. Again Pokryshkin's intervention saved Babak, but Babak was forced to resign from the air force.

According to FSB historian Stepakov, 5,416,000 Soviet servicemen and civilians went through SMERSH's vetting, and of these, 600,000 were selected and tried as war criminals and collaborators.[29] General Aleksandr Bezverkhny, head of the current Russian military counterintelligence, believes that on the whole, SMERSH dealt with more than ten million people.[30]

Operations at Home: Deportations

On March 4, 1944 Abakumov was awarded the Order of Suvorov of the 2nd Class, along with Beria and Merkulov, who received the Order of Suvorov of the 1st Class and Order of Kutuzov of the 1st Class, respectively.[31] Beria's deputies Kruglov, Serov, and Arkadii Apollonov, and Merkulov's first deputy, Bogdan Kobulov, also received awards. It is ironic that these security leaders received the highest Soviet military awards for their nonmilitary actions against Soviet civilians—organizing the deportations of four ethnic groups, or 'nations' in Soviet terminology, into exile. Besides the above-mentioned Kalmyks, the Karacharovs, Chechens, and Ingush were transported from the Caucasus to Central Asia and Siberia. In Stalin's opinion, these small nations were Germany's collaborators and traitors to the Soviet Motherland.

The deportations were Stalin's reprisals for actions by insurgents of these nations in mid-1942 to early 1943 in the rear of the Red Army as it fought the Germans in the foothills of the Caucasus. With access to oil posing a constant problem for them, the Germans were determined to seize the oil fields in Azerbaijan and Chechnya. Furthermore, the Germans considered the conquest of this area the first step toward conquering the Middle East. With the German success in 1941, many people in the Northern Caucasus saw an opportunity to free themselves of their traditional enemies, the Russians.[32] Russia had waged a war of conquest against the mainly Muslim Northern Caucasians from 1816 to 1865. In 1936, more than 1,000 families of the *kulaks* (prosperous peasants) were deported from the Northern Caucasus and most mosques were closed.[33] In answer, a guerrilla war began. In some form this terrible conflict continues today.

In November 1941, insurgents in that area totaled approximately 5,000, and in the summer of 1942, this figure increased by 300 percent.[34] In

February 1942, there were 6,540 anti-Soviet fighters in only twenty Chechen villages. Many Chechens and Ingush left the Red Army to join the insurgents in the mountains. In January 1942, most of the insurgents joined the Special Party of Brothers of the Caucasus (OPKB) with the goal of fighting for the defeat of Russia in the war with Germany and later creating a Muslim state.[35] This party established contacts with the Germans and from July 1942 to July 1943, the Germans parachuted numerous groups of Caucasian saboteurs, mostly Soviet POW volunteers, into Chechnya and Dagestan.[36]

Groups of insurgents also appeared in Armenia, Georgia, and Azerbaijan. The Abwehr helped anti-Soviet emigrants to cross the Soviet border to join the insurgents. Pro-German sentiments ran high among the population of the German-occupied areas of the Northern Caucasus because they were under the control of General Ernst Köstring, the former German attaché in Moscow from 1931–33 and 1935–41. Köstring and most of his HQ officers belonged to the military resistance group that hated Hitler and tried hard to ameliorate the Nazi racial policy in those areas.[37] In February 1943, the Red Army counteroffensive began, and in October 1943 the Germans were defeated in the Caucasus.

Beria was sent to the Caucasus as a Stavka representative twice, in August–September 1942 and March 1943.[38] Of course, he brought Merkulov and other cronies with him. Beria created a formation of NKVD troops consisting of 121,000 men, separate from the Red Army units. However, most of these troops were not involved in the fight against the Germans. During his trial in 1953, Beria testified: 'I didn't allow the NKVD troops to participate in the defense of the Caucasus…[because] the deportation of the Chechens and Ingush was planned.'[39]

Stalin's reprisal for the insurgency was truly terrible.[40] On January 31, 1944, the GKO issued two top secret orders to deport the Chechen and Ingush populations to Kazakhstan and Kirgizia.[41] In total, about 650,000 men, women, and children were deported by 19,000 SMERSH, NKVD, and NKGB operative officers backed up by 100,000 NKVD troops, and 714 officers were given military awards. As an NKVD officer recalled, during professional training the security officers were shown an educational documentary film about the arrests and deportations of the *kulaks* and their family members from Russia in the late 1920s–early 1930s.[42] Therefore, the NKVD and SMERSH were well trained for such actions.

The deportations were executed with extreme cruelty. People who could not be transported, such as patients in hospitals, were burned, buried alive, or drowned in lakes.[43] Mikhail Gvishiani, former head of Beria's guards whom Beria brought to Moscow, supervised the burning alive of 700 inhabitants in the village of Khaitoba.[44] Like Abakumov, he received the Order of Suvorov of the 2nd Rank for the operation.

Similarly, in March 1944 the Kabardins and Balkars were deported from the neighboring regions of the Caucasus; Beria personally commanded the action.[45] Then, in May–June 1944, the Crimean Tatars (a population of 180,000), Greeks, Bulgarians, and Armenians were deported from the Crimea to Central Asia.[46] Interestingly, Hitler had the same idea as Stalin, to completely evacuate the population of the Crimea, which Hitler wanted to turn into a German Gibraltar.[47] At the end of 1944, the Turks-Meskhetians and Kurds living in Georgia were also deported to Central Asia.[48]

Chapter 20

First Trials of War Criminals

With the retaking of Soviet territory by the Red Army, SMERSH also undertook the arrest and investigation of German war criminals and Russian collaborators who had committed atrocities during the occupation. The public trials continued after the war.

First Public Trial

On July 5, 1943, Abakumov reported to Stalin on the investigation by the UKR SMERSH of the North Caucasian Front into the atrocities committed by Sonderkommando SS 10a (SK10a) in the city of Krasnodar during the German occupation.

The SK10a, a sub-unit of Einsatzgruppe D commanded by Otto Ohlendorf, consisted of about 120 men. From June 1941 to August 1942, it operated under SS-Standartenführer Heintz Seetzen, first in the Ukraine, where it exterminated the Jewish population in the towns of Berdyansk, Melitopol, Mariupol, and Odessa, and then in the cities of Taganrog on the Sea of Azov and Rostov-on-Don.[1] In August 1942, SS-Obersturmbannführer Dr. Kurt Christmann succeeded Seetzen, who received the War Service Cross (first class) with Swords for his extermination activity. The SK10a continued operations until July 1943, when the German troops began to retreat. According to Abakumov's report, under Christmann's command the unit exterminated 4,000 inhabitants of Krasnodar. The SK10a killed its victims using the gas van known as the *dushegubka* (soul-killing machine) in Russia.

Abakumov described how, after the Red Army had liberated Krasnodar, seven inhabitants had come forward claiming they had been members of an underground Communist organization fighting against the occupation. However, they related so many details of the German atrocities that SMERSH operatives began to suspect that these individuals had participated in the executions. The investigation revealed that, in fact, they were Soviet members of the SK10a unit. With the help of local witnesses, the UKR

SMERSH arrested eleven former SK members and investigated their crimes. Abakumov suggested putting these individuals on open trial in Krasnodar.

Georgii Malenkov ordered that the Krasnodar report be considered by a commission consisting of Nikolai Shvernik, Chairman of the Extraordinary State Commission for Ascertaining and Investigating Atrocities Perpetrated by the German Fascist Invaders and Their Accomplices (ChGK); Andrei Vyshinsky, deputy foreign Commissar; Nikolai Rychkov, USSR Justice Commissar; Viktor Bochkov, USSR Prosecutor; and Abakumov.[2] The ChGK was created after Stalin declined participation in the United Nations Commission for the Investigation of War Crimes proposed in October 1942 by the British and U.S. governments.

The Malenkov Commission decided that the Military Tribunal of the North Caucasian Front would try eleven defendants in an open trial, which was held in Krasnodar on July 14–17, 1943, and presided over by Judiciary Major N. Y. Mayorov, Chairman of the Military Tribunal of the North Caucasian Front.[3] Eleven Soviet collaborators, charged with treason under Article 58-1a (civilians) and 58-1b (Soviet servicemen), were accused of assisting Colonel Christmann's SK unit in the killing of 7,000 people—patients in the municipal hospital, a convalescent home, and a children's hospital—in Krasnodar in 1942–43.[4] The court appointed three counselors to defend the accused. However, Soviet legal procedures allowed the counselors to meet with their clients only in the court and they were not permitted to cross-examine eyewitnesses.

During the trial, two defendants, N. Pushkarev and V. Tishchenko, described in detail the gas vans used by Einsatzkommando 10a for killing Jews and other victims. Until then, the existence of these vehicles was a Nazi secret. A witness named Ivan Kotov, who had been loaded into a gas van but survived, also testified:

> On 22 August [1942] I went to Municipal Hospital No. 3... As I entered the courtyard I saw a large truck with a dark-gray body. Before I had taken two steps a German officer seized me by the collar and pushed me into the vehicle. The interior of the van was crammed full of people, some of them completely naked, some of them in their underclothes. The door was closed. I noticed that the van started to move. Minutes later I began to feel sick. I was losing consciousness. I had previously taken an anti-air raid course, and I immediately understood that we were being poisoned by some kind of gas. I tore off my shirt, wet it with urine, and pressed it to my mouth and nose. My breathing became easier, but I finally lost consciousness. When I came to, I was lying in a ditch with several dozen corpses. With great effort I managed to climb out and drag myself.[5]

Eight defendants were sentenced to death and publicly hanged.[6] The rest were convicted to twenty years in special hard labor camps. Alexander

Werth, a British journalist, referred to the trial as 'first-rate hate propaganda' aimed at emphasizing the suffering of the Soviet people under the German occupation.[7] The German SK10a members were not caught and only a few German officers of this unit were ever put on trial. Otto Ohlendorf was the main defendant at the Nuremberg trial of Einsatzgruppen leaders (September 1947–April 1948).[8] He was sentenced to death and hanged on June 7, 1951. SK commander Seetzen went into hiding near Hamburg after the war under the false name 'Michael Gollwitzer'. After his arrest by the British authorities in September 1945, he committed suicide.

In 1972, three former SK10a officers tried in West Germany received lenient four-year sentences for the 1941 massacre of 200 Jews in the city of Taganrog and the 1942 massacre of 214 children in the town of Yeisk. In 1973, three more officers were convicted and given from two to four and a half years for shooting hundreds of Jews and other civilians in Ukraine in 1941.

Finally, in 1980, Kurt Christmann was tried in Munich.[9] From 1946 to 1948, he was interned in the British occupation zone under the false name 'Dr. Ronda', after which he successfully fled to Argentina. He returned to West Germany in 1956 and was arrested by West German police in November 1979 on charges of participating in the murders of 105 persons in Krasnodar in 1942–43. On December 19, 1980, a court sentenced Christmann to ten years in prison. He died in 1987.

The last SK10a case—of Helmut Oberlander, who had served in SK10a as an interpreter—ended in November 2009.[10] In February 1942, the seventeen-year-old Oberlander, an ethnic German and Soviet citizen, was conscripted to the occupation troops. In 1954 he arrived in Canada and obtained Canadian citizenship in 1960. His citizenship was revoked in 2001 and 2007, but there was no proof that he had participated in the SK10a atrocities. In 2009 the Canadian Federal Court of Appeal reinstated Oberlander's Canadian citizenship.

The Kharkov Trial

On September 2, 1943, Abakumov suggested trying several German officers taken prisoner on January 31, 1943, when the 6th German Army surrendered in Stalingrad. These officers had committed atrocities against Soviet POWs, and were the first Germans anywhere to be tried as war criminals. Abakumov wrote:

> To: Sovnarkom of the USSR, Comrade Vyshinsky
>
> In mid-January 1943, while tightening the encirclement of the 6th [German] Army, our troops took over a transit camp for POWs, the so-called Dulag-205, located near the village of Alekseevka not far from Stalingrad. Thousands of bodies of Red Army soldiers and commanders were found on and near the territory of the camp. All of the prisoners had died of

exhaustion and cold. Also, there were a few hundred extremely exhausted former Red Army servicemen.

The investigation conducted by the Main Directorate 'SMERSH' revealed that the German soldiers and officers, following orders of the German high command, severely mistreated POWs—brutally exterminating them by beating and execution, creating unbearable conditions in the camp, and starving them to death. It was also established that the Germans subjected POWs to the same brutality in the camps in Darnitsa near Kiev, Dergachi near Kharkov, and in the towns of Poltava and Rossoshi.

The following direct perpetrators of the death of Soviet people are currently under investigation in the Main Directorate 'SMERSH':

KÖRPERT, RUDOLF, former commandant of the Dulag-205 camp, colonel of the German Army, born 1886 in the Sudetenland (Germany) to a merchant's family. Taken prisoner on January 31, 1943, in the city of Stalingrad.

VON KUNOWSKI, WERNER, former chief quartermaster of the 6th German Army, lieutenant colonel, born 1907 in Silesia, a noble, son of a major general of the German Army. Taken prisoner on January 31, 1943, in the city of Stalingrad.

LANGHELD, WILHELM, former counterintelligence officer (Abwehr officer) at the Dulag-205 camp, captain of the German Army, born 1891 in the city of Frankfurt-on-Main to a family of bureaucrats, member of the Fascist Party since 1933. Taken prisoner on January 31, 1943, in the city of Stalingrad.

MÄDER, OTTO, former adjutant to the Commandant of the Dulag-205 camp, senior lieutenant of the German Army, born 1895 in the Erfurt Region (Germany), member of the Fascist Party since 1935. Taken prisoner on January 31, 1943, in the city of Stalingrad.

The testimonies of KUNOWSKI, LANGHELD, and MÄDER confirmed a direct order from the highest command of the German Army to exterminate Soviet POWs, both officers and privates, as 'inferiors'...

Thus, approximately 4,000 Soviet POWs were imprisoned in the Alekseevsk camp, although it was built to hold only 1,200 prisoners...

As the German officers KÖRPERT, KUNOWSKI, LANGHELD, and MÄDER testified, Soviet POWs were half-starved in the Dulag-205 camp. Beginning in December 1942, the high command of the 6th German Army represented by Head of Staff, Lt. Gen. [Arthur] SCHMIDT, completely stopped food supplies to the camp...[11] By the time the camp was liberated by the Red Army, approximately 5,000 men had died. The POWs, almost insane from hunger, were hunted down by dogs during the distribution of food, which was prepared from waste products...

LANGHELD testified: 'I usually beat the POWs with a stick 4–5 cm in diameter. This happened...also in the other POW camps...'

During the investigation…former Red Army servicemen…held in the Dulag-205 camp, were identified and interrogated…

Thus, ALEKSEEV, A. A…testified…on August 10, 1943:

'Mortality in the camp was high because…bread and water were not given at all…

'Instead of water, we collected [and drank] dirty snow mixed with blood, which caused mass illness among the POWs…

'We slept on the ground and it was impossible to get warm. Our warm clothes and *valenki* [felt boots] were taken from us, and we were given torn boots and clothes from the dead…

'Many servicemen, unable to withstand the horrific conditions of the camp, went insane. About 150 men died per day, and during one day in the first days of 1943, 216 men died…The German commanders used to set dogs—Alsatians—on the POWs. The dogs knocked down the weak POWs and dragged them across the ground, while the Germans stood around laughing. Public shootings of POWs were common in the camp…'

KÖRPERT, KUNOWSKI, LANGHELD, and MÄDER admitted their guilt.

The case is still under investigation. I have notified the government that an open trial and its detailed description in the media are necessary.

Abakumov.[12]

Perhaps Abakumov had addressed his report to Vyshinsky, and not to Stalin, because the question of war crimes concerned an agreement with the Allies. A month later, from October 18 to November 11, 1943, a conference of Allied foreign ministers was held in Moscow, resulting in the Moscow Declaration signed by the Soviet, American, British, and Chinese leaders. Its section titled *Statement on Atrocities* (signed by Roosevelt, Churchill, and Stalin) dealt with German war criminals: 'Those German officers and men and members of the Nazi party who have been responsible for or have taken a consenting part in the…atrocities, massacres and executions will be sent back to the countries in which their abominable deeds were done in order that they may be judged and punished according to the laws of these liberated countries and of free governments which will be erected therein.'[13]

The trial of the four German officers who participated in atrocities in the Dulag-205 camp did not take place in 1943, probably because SMERSH continued interrogations of Körpert, Mäder, and four other high officials of the camp until the autumn of 1944. However, Wilhelm Langheld, also mentioned in the September 1943 report, was a defendant at a trial that came about because of a new report from Abakumov to the GKO (addressed to Stalin and Molotov) on November 18, 1943. Abakumov suggested launching a new open trial of German war criminals who had participated in the liquidation of Soviet citizens in Kharkov and Smolensk.[14]

Using the April 19, 1943, secret decree of the Presidium, which provided a legal basis for the punishment of German war criminals and collaborators, Abakumov proposed trying three captured German officers, including Langheld, and one Soviet collaborator. Abakumov especially emphasized SMERSH's possession of new proof that the occupiers had used gas vans for mass killings not only in the Krasnodar Region but also in Kharkov and Smolensk, where, in all, 160,000 inhabitants were executed.

Abakumov proposed using eighty-nine witnesses who had testified about German atrocities, materials of the ChGK, and medical reports of exhumations by leading Soviet medical experts, including academician Nikolai Burdenko (who a few months later chaired the commission investigating the exhumed bodies of Polish officers in the Katyn Forest) and Viktor Prozorovsky, USSR chief medical expert.

Abakumov also attached a draft decision to his report, mandating that the trial be held in Kharkov on December 10–12, 1943.[15] The draft proposed that Shcherbakov, a secretary of the Central Committee and head of the GlavPURKKA; Konstantin Gorshenin, the new chief USSR prosecutor (appointed on November 13, 1943); and Abakumov should organize the trial. As events in early December 1943 demonstrate, Abakumov's plan for the Kharkov trial was approved, but the trial proposed in Smolensk was postponed.

The German atrocities in Kharkov began after the city's occupation by the 6th German Army under Field Marshal Walter von Reichenau on October 24, 1941. Before capturing the city, on October 10, von Reichenau, an anti-Semite and supporter of the SS-Einsatzgruppen activity, issued his infamous order to the troops in the Eastern territories:

> The soldier in the Eastern territories is not merely a fighter according to the rules of the art of war but also a bearer of ruthless national ideology...
>
> Therefore the soldier must have full understanding for the necessity of a severe but just revenge on subhuman Jewry. The Army has to aim at another purpose, i.e., the annihilation of revolts in [the] hinterland which, as experience proves, have always been caused by Jews.[16]

The German occupation continued until February 16, 1943, when the Soviet troops of the Voronezh Front liberated the city. But on March 15, 1943, the SS-Panzerkorps recaptured Kharkov.[17] This corps included a group called Leibstandarte SS Adolf Hitler (commanded by SS-Gruppenführer Sepp Dietrich, one of Hitler's closest confidants) and 3.SS-Panzer-Division Totenkopf (commanders: SS-Obergruppenführer Theodor Eicke, killed February 26, 1943, and SS-Obergruppenführer Max Simon), also mentioned as guilty parties in Abakumov's indictment because their military actions had resulted in the massacre of retreating Soviet troops.

Historian Charles Sydnor described the behavior of the Totenkopf division: 'The Russians had abandoned most of their vehicles and equipment and were trying to escape on foot…The SSTK [Totenkopf] First Panzergrenadier Regiment…methodically cut down the panicked herds of stampeding Russians fleeing.'[18]

The other SS-troops were no better. In his memoirs, Curzio Malaparte, an Italian officer, recalled his conversation with Sepp Dietrich, commander of Leibstandarte SS Adolf Hitler, in Berlin in 1942: 'I told [Dietrich] about the Russian prisoners in the Smolensk camp who fed on the corpses of their comrades…Dietrich burst out laughing: *"Haben sie ihnen geschmeckt?—* Did they enjoy eating them?"* he laughed opening his small pink-rooted fish-mouth, showing his crowded sharp fishlike teeth.'[19]

The Nazi leadership considered the recapturing of Kharkov so important that Heinrich Himmler paid a visit to the city, where, on April 23, 1943, he gave a speech to the SS Panzer divisions praising their 'dreadful and terrible reputation'.[20] Finally, on August 23, 1943, the Soviet troops of the Voronezh, Southwestern, and Steppe fronts recaptured Kharkov, and SMERSH started preparing the trial.

On December 3, 1943, the 6th (Investigation) Department of GUKR wrote a draft indictment of four captured German officers and two Russian collaborators being kept in Moscow Lubyanka Prison.[21] From December 5 to 15, Abakumov remained in constant contact with Stalin and other Party leaders, coordinating all details of the future show trial. During the trial he reported to the leadership every day, and, until the end of the trial, the trial documents were routinely altered according to instructions from Moscow.

The trial took place in Kharkov from December 15 to 18, 1943, and was the first trial of German servicemen for war crimes. The Military Tribunal of the 4th Ukrainian Front, presided over by Major General of Justice A. N. Myasnikov, tried four defendants—three Germans and one Russian (for some unknown reason, only three Germans and one Soviet defendant were present at the trial), and accused six high-ranking German military, intelligence, and military police officers of war crimes. As in Krasnodar, the court appointed three defense counselors from Moscow. Renowned Soviet writers and journalists, including Aleksei Tolstoi, Konstantin Simonov, and Ilya Ehrenburg, were present, along with foreign journalists, and the trial was filmed.[22]

The indictment prepared by GUKR pronounced:

> Investigation has established that the atrocities, violence, and plunder in the town and Region of Kharkov were committed by officers and men of the German Army and in particular by: SS Division 'Adolf Hitler', commanded by Obergruppenfuehrer of SS troops Dietrich; SS Division 'Totenkopf', commanded by Gruppenfuehrer of SS troops Simon; the German Punitive

Organs: the Kharkov SD Sonderkommando led by its commander, Sturm-bannfuehrer Hanebitter; the group of German Secret police in the town of Kharkov, headed by Polizei Kommissar Karchan and his deputy—Police Secretary Wulf; the 560th group of Secret Field Police attached to the staff of the 6th German Army—Polizei Kommissar Mehritz; the defendants in the present case: Reinhard Retzlaff [Retzlaw in the Russian documents], official of the 560th Group of the German Secret Field Police; Wilhelm Langheld, Captain of German Military Counter Espionage Service; Hans Rietz [Ritz in the Russian documents], Assistant Commander of the SS Company SD Sonderkommando; Mikhail Bulanov, chauffeur of the Kharkov SD Sonderkommando.

The preliminary examination has established the system followed:

Asphyxiation with carbon monoxide in specially equipped automobile 'murder vans' of many thousands of Soviet people;

Brutal massacres of peaceful Soviet citizens and destruction of towns and villages of temporary occupied territory;

Mass extermination of old people, women, and small children;

Shooting, burning, and brutal treatment of Soviet wounded and prisoners of war.

All this constitutes a flagrant violation of the rules for the conduct of war established by international conventions, and of all generally accepted legal standards.[23]

The prosecutor's interrogation of the defendants Langheld, Retzlaff, Rietz, and Bulanov in the court went smoothly. Basically, they repeated what had already been included in the detailed part of the indictment. Apparently, this was a typical well-rehearsed show trial, albeit, for once, presenting accurate accusations. Evidently, the defendants learned their roles well while they were held in the Lubyanka. One of the Russian courtroom translators, Anna Stesnova, was even an officer of the 1st Section of the 2nd GUKR Department. The prosecution's questions focused mainly on the killing of Soviet citizens in gas vans and by shooting. On December 16, Langheld testified that in May 1942 he had witnessed how German soldiers forced prisoners to enter a gas van:

Among the people being loaded into [the] gas van were old men, children, old and young women. These people would not go into the machine of their own accord and had therefore to be driven into the gas van by SS men with kicks and blows of the butt ends of automatic rifles...

I heard from Captain Beukow that the same kind of gas vans were used in… Kharkov, Poltava, Kiev.[24]

Hans Rietz, a former lawyer and then Assistant SS Company Commander within Sonderkommando 4a, gave similar testimony:

On 31st May, 1943 I arrived in Kharkov and reported to the Chief of the Kharkov Sonderkommando, Hanebitter… The next day…Lt. Jacobi… showed me the vehicle standing in the yard. It was an ordinary closed army transport lorry, only with an airtight body.

Lt. Jacobi opened the doors of the machine and let me look in. Inside the machine was lined with sheet iron, in the floor was a grating through which the exhaust gases of the motor entered, poisoning people inside the van.

Soon afterwards the doors of the prison opened and arrested persons were led out in groups… Those of the prisoners who held back were beaten and kicked.[25] Reinhard Retzlaff, an auxiliary officer of the 560th Group of the Secret Field Police (GFP) attached to the headquarters of the 6th German Army, also mentioned Hanebitter in his testimony about the usage of gas vans in Kharkov in March 1942.[26]

This testimony revealed for the first time that the GFP, like the Einsatzgruppen, had committed atrocities. In Kharkov, Gruppe GFP 560 was active from October 1941 to August 1943. The last defendant, the Soviet collaborator Mikhail Bulanov, driver of a Gestapo truck, also testified to the killing of victims in a gas van.[27] All of the defendants also admitted to personally torturing or executing arrested Soviet prisoners.

Currently, there is no doubt that gas vans were also used by Einsatzgruppen in Poland, Belorussia, Smolensk, Riga, and elsewhere.[28] However, it is puzzling that the name Kranebitter mentioned by Rietz and Retzlaff in their testimonies was written in the official records as Hanebitter. In fact, SS-Sturmbannführer Dr. Fritz Kranebitter, Doctor of Jurisprudence, was the Sipo (Secret Police) and SD commander in Kharkov from March to August 1943.[29] He arrived in Kiev in February 1942, then moved to Kharkov and after that, to Dubno. In November 1943, he was appointed head of Amt IV (Gestapo intelligence and counterintelligence) within the Security Police and SD Staff in Italy and left Ukraine. He was never charged and died in Austria in 1957.

Two of the three additional German witnesses, prisoners who were not defendants in this trial, committed just as many atrocities as those being tried. They were SS-Obersturmbannführer Georg Heinisch, former district Commissar (Gebietskommissar) of Melitopol, Ukraine, and Heinz Jantschi, a sergeant-major and Assistant Abwehr officer at the Dulag-231 transit camp for Soviet POWs. Heinisch testified about his own crimes: 'In the period from 3rd September, 1942, till 14th September, 1943, between 3,000 and 4,000 persons were exterminated in the Melitopol region…During my work in Melitopol, there were three or four mass operations, in particular in December 1942, when 1,300 persons were arrested at once.'[30] Then he added:

[SS-Oberführer Otto] Somann [Chief of Security in the Breslau area] told me about the camp in Auschwitz in Germany where the gassing of prisoners was also carried out… Those who were to be executed first entered a place with a signboard with 'Disinfection' on it and they were undressed—the men separately from women and children. Then they were ordered to proceed to another place with a signboard 'Bath'. While the people were washing themselves special valves were opened to let in the gas which caused their death. Then the dead people were burned in special furnaces in which about 200 bodies could be burned simultaneously.[31]

No foreign correspondent attending the trial recognized the importance of this first public evidence of mass killings in Auschwitz. Possibly, this was because the defendants were obviously forced to give testimonies the court wanted to hear. As Arthur Koestler reported, '[F]or the foreign observer the Kharkov trial (which was filmed and publicly shown in London) gave the same impression of unreality as the Moscow trials, the accused reciting their parts in stilted phrases which they had obviously learned by heart, sometimes taking the wrong cue from State-Prosecutor and then coming back to the same part again'.[32] On December 29, 1943, *Time* magazine wrote only that three German defendants and one Russian defendant were tried and executed.[33]

Tellingly, this trial, like that in Krasnodar, did not mention that most of the victims killed in Kharkov were Jews, although a written report of the local commission on atrocities stated that up to 15,000 Jewish residents of Kharkov were murdered between December 1941 and January 1942.[34] Interestingly, after the troops of the 1st Ukrainian Front liberated Auschwitz in January 1945, the first reports from the field stated that 'the mass extermination of people, and in particular, the Jews brought from all over Europe, was the main purpose of the camps'.[35] However, in the report to the Central Committee in Moscow, the words 'the Jews' had disappeared, and afterwards, the extermination of the Jews in Auschwitz was not mentioned in Soviet documents, only 'millions of citizens from all over Europe'.

Karl Kosch, a professional architect who served as a private in the German Army, also testified about his knowledge of gas vans in Ukraine in 1943. However, the last witness, Jantschi, talked at length mostly about the movement of Soviet POWs and arrested civilians from a camp near the city of Vyazma to a camp in the city of Smolensk, in which he took part.[36] Of 15,000 people who left Vyazma, only 2,000 arrived in Smolensk—the rest died or were exterminated on the way—and of the 10,000 prisoners who were left in Vyazma, 6,000 died. Although this horrific story described the German military authorities' general attitude toward Soviet prisoners, it had little to do with the events in Kharkov. Most probably, Jantschi's testimony was prepared for the Smolensk trial that did not take place. Much later this testimony would have grave consequences for Jantschi.

On December 18, 1943, the chair of the tribunal read the verdict, which had been approved in Moscow. The four defendants were sentenced to death by hanging. The verdict specifically mentioned the military and police involved:

> Violent atrocities against Soviet civilians were carried out on the territory of the city and region of Kharkov by officers and soldiers of:
>
> The SS Adolf Hitler Division, commanded by Obergruppenführer of S. S. Troops Dietrich, the Death's Head Division, under the command of Gruppenführer of SS Troops Simon.
>
> By the German punitive organs.
>
> The Kharkov SD Sonderkommando, commanded by Sturmbannführer Hanebitter.
>
> By the Kharkov group of the German Secret Field Police, commanded by Police Commissar Karchan.[37]

A witness to the execution on the next day later recalled:

> Plenty of people gathered at the Blagoveshchensk Market Square. There were four gallows…The convicts were standing in the body of a truck located under the gallows, with its sides pulled down. The Germans were smoking, while the Russian convict, dressed in a black robe, was standing apart from them…
>
> Several [Soviet] soldiers came up [to the convicts] and tied their hands. The Russian dropped on his knees in front of the Red Army soldiers, but they also tied his hands. Then a noose was placed around the neck of each convict. The truck started to move slowly. I looked at the last German. He moved his legs, and then he hung in the air and jerked. I closed my eyes. When I opened them, he was still jerking. I looked at the crowd. When [the German] hung in the air, a long sound 'Ah-h-h-h' was heard from it [the crowd]. Many took steps backward, and some turned around and ran away.[38]

Apparently, public hanging was so unpopular that in May 1944 it was replaced by nonpublic shooting.[39] However, the public execution of war criminals by hanging was restored after the war.

After the defense counselors were back to Moscow, Beria called them to his Lubyanka office and yelled at the aged Nikolai Kommodov, who had just defended Langheld and Rietz: 'At the trial you acted not as a defense lawyer, but as a prosecutor. This was written in every foreign newspaper!'[40] This was a lie. Most probably, Beria followed Stalin's lead knowing that Stalin had not forgotten Kommodov's defense of Dr. Dmitrii Pletnev, a personal enemy of Stalin's, who was falsely accused of poisoning the writer

Maxim Gorky at the Bukharin Trial in 1938.[41] Kommodov was so frightened by Beria's reprimand that he died of a heart attack a few days later.

The legal outcome of the trial was summarized by one of the leading Soviet jurists Aron Trainin in his book *The Criminal Responsibility of the Hitlerites* published in 1944.[42] Trainin wrote that 'the Hitlerites' should be tried for launching a war of aggression which was a fundamental 'crime against peace'. This and other principles discussed in the book became a basis of statements by Soviet prosecutors at the International Nuremberg Trial.

Soviet filmmakers made a propaganda film named *Sud idet!* (The Court Is In Session!) about the Kharkov Trial, and it was shown throughout the country. The American Office of Strategic Services (OSS) made a shortened version of this film. In July 1944 *Life* magazine published a few stills from this documentary.[43] In June 1945, an American movie 'We Accuse', compiled from the Soviet, British, and German newsreels and focused on the Kharkov Trial, was shown in a number of New York movie theaters, except those owned by the members of the Hays Office, Hollywood's censorship bureau.[44] The office demanded extensive cuts, in particular, of the footage of atrocities. However, soon the U.S. Army Signal Corps released even more horrifying footage of the liberated death camps in Europe.

Later Atrocity Trials

Sepp Dietrich and Max Simon, whom Abakumov connected with atrocities in 1943, were captured and tried by the Allies. On July 16, 1945, the U.S. Military Tribunal at Dachau (Case No. 5–24) sentenced Dietrich to life in prison, commuted to twenty-five years, for the execution of American POWs by his troops in 1944 (the Malmedi massacre). After serving ten years, Dietrich was released. On May 14, 1957, the German court sentenced him to twenty-nine months for his part in the Night of the Long Knives in 1934. In 1966, Dietrich died aged seventy-three of a heart attack.

Max Simon was captured by British troops and sentenced to death in 1947 for his complicity in the September 1944 massacre of civilians in Italy. The sentence was commuted and he was released in 1954. In October 1955, a German court tried him again. Twice acquitted, Simon died on February 1, 1961, before the start of a third trial.

Georg Heinisch, who was a witness at the Kharkov Trial, was among those convicted and sentenced to death at the Kiev trial (December 1945– January 1946).[45] He confessed to his participation in the extermination of 3,000 Jewish children in October 1942. By chance, while working with archival documents, I discovered the fate of the two other Kharkov witnesses, Jantschi and Kosch.

The materials in Jantschi's Personal File clearly reveal that on August 9, 1943, he voluntarily crossed the front line near the town of Sumy.[46] This explains his detailed testimony to GUKR investigators concerning Dulag-231 and the horrible treatment of Soviet POWs, which he repeated in Kharkov. However, he also described his personal discovery of six Jews among the Soviet POWs in the Vyazma Camp and seventeen Jews among prisoners in the Miller Camp, all of whom he handed over to the SD command for execution. Additionally, in September 1941, Jantschi was involved in sending Soviet POWs to Germany for slave labor.

On August 7, 1944, both Jantschi and Karl Kosch, the third witness at the Kharkov Trial, were transferred from a prison in Moscow to the special POW Camp No. 27 in the Moscow suburbs. However, on November 13, 1946, both were returned to Lefortovo Prison in Moscow, where Sergei Kartashov's (now the 4th MGB) department started a new investigation. For at least two years the prisoners were kept together and interrogated from time to time. On May 5, 1948, Jantschi made an unsuccessful suicide attempt.

Extensive interrogations (fifty-two instances) of Jantschi began in December 1949 and continued through July 1951. Finally, on January 12, 1952, the Military Tribunal of the Moscow District sentenced him to twenty-five years in prison as a German spy (Article 58-6) and a war criminal (April 19, 1943, Decree). Interestingly, no documents in his Personal File mention the Kharkov Trial, although the verdict repeated his testimony in Kharkov almost word for word. On January 15, 1952, the same military tribunal sentenced Kosch as a German spy to twenty-five years in prison, with no credit for the time of the Kharkov trial.

On February 16, 1952, the Supreme Court denied Jantschi's appeal, in which he pleaded guilty but asked the court to consider the circumstances under which he committed the crimes. The next day he again attempted suicide by hitting his head against a wall. On March 30, 1952, Jantschi was brought to Vladimir Prison, where he was kept in solitary confinement for some time. Kosch arrived in Vladimir later, on May 16, 1952. Like many other German prisoners in Vladimir, Jantschi and Kosch were released in October 1955.

It remains a mystery why SMERSH/MGB considered these two German prisoners so important that they were held without trial until 1952. Only a few high-level German generals and foreign diplomats were treated similarly. Possibly, Jantschi and Kosch were used as cell spies against their own fellow German prisoners. In any case, it is clear that, at least in 1952, military counterintelligence wanted, for unknown reason, to conceal their involvement in the Kharkov Trial.

On January 22, 1944, Abakumov sent the GKO a new report addressed to Stalin, Molotov, and Beria.[47] The GUKR proposed a new trial in Smolensk for thirteen defendants arrested by SMERSH. The investigation revealed the extermination of 135,000 civilians in the Smolensk region during the German occupation, and also stated that the German authorities had used children for slave labor and forced teenage girls into prostitution. In addition, German intelligence used teenagers as spies in the Red Army's rear. However, the trial was postponed because from January 16 to 23, 1944, academician Nikolai Burdenko's commission was working in the Katyn Forest, examining bodies of dead Polish officers and trying to prove that the Germans, and not the NKVD, had shot the victims—a question that was raised at the Nuremberg trial as well.[48]

The only cases proposed for open trials were those that would create public sympathy for the suffering of the Soviet people. Very few knew about the routine military tribunal trials. For instance, in September 1944, Lieutenant General Mikhail Belkin, head of the SMERSH Directorate of the 3rd Baltic Front, completed the investigation of Rudolf Körpert and Otto Mäder (mentioned in Abakumov's September 1943 letter to Vyshinsky), and four other high-level officers of the Dulag-205 administration.[49] They were accused of 'mass extermination of Soviet citizens' and 'having implemented the policy of German fascism concerning the extermination of the Soviet population'. On October 10, 1944, not in a public trial, as Abakumov suggested, but in a closed military tribunal, all six were sentenced to death by shooting. It remains unclear if and when Werner von Kunowski, the last general on Abakumov's September 1943 list, was executed.

Even less was known about the routine military trials in the field. For example, in December 1944, the military tribunal of the 1st Baltic Front tried nine members of a Lithuanian paramilitary group captured by SMERSH. From 1941 to August 1944, that group had arrested Soviet servicemen and parachutists and handed them over to the Germans. They also fought against the advancing Red Army.[50] The group's leader was sentenced to death and shot, and the others were sentenced to ten years in labor camps. It is not surprising that the Soviets wanted to prevent the world from knowing about those who viewed the German invasion as an opportunity to free themselves from the Soviet regime.

Open public trials continued after the war, but now Beria was put in charge of organizing them. On November 2, 1945, he ordered that a special commission consisting of Merkulov (NKGB), Abakumov, and Sergei Kruglov (NKVD) be set up to evaluate the cases of 105 important war criminals being held in POW camps and prisons.[51] Three days later, the commission forwarded to Molotov a list of 85 potential defendants for future open trials in Leningrad, Smolensk, Velikie Luki, Kiev, Nikolaev, Minsk, Riga, and Bryansk. Defendants were selected and grouped according to their activities and region. The Politburo approved the plan for future trials and ordered that a commission headed by Vyshinsky, and including Abakumov and Kruglov, be responsible for organizing the trials.[52]

The trials took place from December 1945 to February 1946, at the same time as the Nuremberg trials.[53] Surprisingly, the extermination of Jews was discussed at these trials, making it hard to believe that less than two years later Stalin unleashed his own anti-Semitic campaign against the 'cosmopolitans' and the American 'fifth column', the code words for identifying Soviet Jews as enemies of the state and supposedly potential American spies. At the trials, all 85 German defendants, including 18 generals, were sentenced either to death by hanging (66 defendants) or twelve to twenty years in the labor camps.

Oddly, during the first trial (December 28, 1945–January 4, 1946) of eleven Germans accused of atrocities committed in the Leningrad region and the cities of Novgorod and Pskov in 1941–42, a prosecutor asked the defendant Arno Diere (in the Russian records, Duere) about the Katyn massacre.[54] Diere claimed that he had helped to bury the bodies of Polish officers supposedly shot there by the Nazis. However, it became clear that he was lying. Diere stated that the Katyn Forest was in Poland and not in Russia and that the trench used for the burial was 15–20 and not 1.5–2.0 meters deep, and so on. In fact, Diere had participated in mass killings of Soviet civilians, and by cooperating with the Soviet investigators and lying he had saved his own life.

On January 5, 1946, Major General Heinrich Remlinger—the former military commandant of Pskov, who admitted his guilt but insisted that he had followed orders—and seven other convicts were hanged in Leningrad.[55] Diere was sentenced to fifteen years of hard labor in camps. He survived and in 1954, he admitted that he had lied about his involvement in the Katyn Forest massacre.

On September 10, 1947, the Politburo approved nine more open trials of 137 Germans.[56] Stalin personally controlled the decisions of the military tribunals that followed and approved on the phone death sentences for the German generals. Additionally, in October–November 1947, 761 prisoners were sentenced as war criminals in closed sessions of military tribunals.[57]

Part VII. Toward Berlin

CHAPTER 21

Crossing the Border

In late March 1944, troops of the 2nd and 3rd Ukrainian fronts crossed the border with Romania. On May 1, 1944, Stalin explained the Soviet move to the West: 'Our tasks cannot be restricted by pushing the enemy troops out of our Motherland... We must free our brothers from German enslavement—the Poles, Czechoslovaks, and our allied nations of Western Europe who have been conquered by Hitler's Germany.'[1]

During May 1944, new commanders of the 1st–3rd Ukrainian fronts were appointed and the main members of the Stavka, along with the commanders of every front, were given aliases to use in communications between Moscow and the fronts. Stalin's alias was 'Semenov', Nikolai Bulganin became 'Balashov', while Georgii Zhukov was called 'Zharov' (Table 21-1). Evidently military leaders became more careful in messages that could potentially be intercepted by the enemy.

The work of SMERSH UKRs of the 2nd and 3rd Ukrainian fronts and of the 2nd (foreign POWs and Soviet servicemen who had been POWs) and 6th (investigation) GUKR departments significantly increased. SMERSH operatives in the field were searching for members of General Vlasov's Russian Liberation Army (ROA), as well as for any local politicians, activists, and White Russian émigrés who could potentially create problems for the Soviet-controlled regimes Stalin planned to set up. Nicola Sinevirsky, who worked for SMERSH, wrote later that SMERSH's 'mission was to wipe out the segment of Europe that still thought differently and did not accept the Soviet system'.[2]

Romania

On August 30, 1944, troops of the 2nd Ukrainian Front took over Ploesti (the oil-rich region of Romania, which was of utmost importance for the Nazi war machine), and then reached Bucharest the next day. The front included a Romanian division formed in the Soviet Union.

A week earlier, on August 23, Romania's 23-year-old King Mihai I had ordered his guards to arrest the dictator Marshal Ion Antonescu and other leaders of the Romanian fascist regime.[3] King Mihai was a great-great-grandson of the British Queen Victoria by both of his parents; he was also

Table 21-1. Alias Names Used for Soviet Military Leaders in 1944–45[1]

Name	Position in May 1944	Alias Name
Stalin I. S.	Defence Commissar, GKO Head and Supreme Commander	Semenov
Zhukov G. K.	Deputy Defence Commissar, Deputy Supreme Commander	Zharov
Vasilevsky A. M.	Deputy Defence Commissar, Head of the General Staff	Vladimirov
Voroshilov K. Ye.	GKO and Stavka Member	Volgin
Timoshenko S. K.	Stavka's Plenipotentiary, coordinator of the 2nd and 3rd Baltic fronts	Tikhonov
Meretskov K. A.	Commander of the Karelian Front (*Belomorsk*) [name of a city]	Maksimov
Govorov L. A.	Commander of the Leningrad Front (*Leningrad*)	Gavrilov
Zhdanov A.A.	Member of the Front Military Council, Leningrad Front	Zhigulev
Maslennikov I. I.	Commander of the 3rd Baltic Front (*Kavkaz* [the Caucasus])	Mironov
Yeremenko A. I.	Commander of the 2nd Baltic Front (*Sosna* [Pine Tree])	Yegorov
Bagramyan I. Kh.	Commander of the 1st Baltic Front (*Utes Slava* [Cliff Glory])	Baturin
Chernyakhovsky I. D.	Commander of the 3rd Belorussian Front (*Stal'* [Steel])	Chernov
Petrov I. Ye.	Commander of the 2nd Belorussian Front (*Pobeda* [Victory])	Platov
Mekhlis L. Z.	Member of the Front Military Council, 2nd Belorussian Front	Malakhov
Rokossovsky K. K.	Commander of the 1st Belorussian Front (*Molot* [Hammer])	Rumyantsev
Bulganin N. A.	Member of the Front Military Council, 1st Belorussian Front	Balashov
Konev I. S.	Commander of the 1st Ukrainian Front (*Zarya* [Dawn])	Kievsky
Khrushchev N. S.	Member of the Front Military Council, 1st Ukrainian Front	Khmelev
Malinovsky R. Ya.	Commander of the 2nd Ukrainian Front (*Priboi* [Surf])	Morozov
Susaikov I. Z.	Member of the Front Military Council, 2nd Ukrainian Front	Savin
Zakharov M. V.	Head of HQ, Member of the Front Military Council, 2nd Ukrainian Front	Zolotov
Tolbukhin F. I.	Commander of the 3rd Ukrainian Front (*Vulkan* [Volcano])	Trofimov
Zheltov A. S.	Member of the Front Military Council, 3rd Ukrainian Front	Zhilin
Biryuzov S. S.	Head of HQ, Member of the Front Military Council, 3rd Ukrainian Front	Belyaev
Mel'nik K. S.	Commander of the Separate Maritime Army	Markov

1. Document No. 96 in "Voina. 1941–1945," *Vestnik Arkhiva Presidenta Rossiiskoi Federatsii* (Moscow, 2010), 208–9 (in Russian). Although the document is dated 1943 in the publication, in fact the date should be May 1944.

a third cousin of the future Queen Elizabeth II as well. The king's action was preceded by lengthy secret negotiations with the Western Allies and the Soviets.

On August 17, the Romanian opposition to Ion Antonescu had signed an armistice, which the King announced to his people on the radio. On August 26, in response to the Romanian 'betrayal', the Germans, under Lieutenant General Reiner Stahel's command, attacked Bucharest. Stahel was one of the Führer's most loyal and ruthless generals, and on July 27, 1944 Hitler personally awarded him the Iron Cross for successfully bringing out a group of German troops encircled by the Red Army near Vilnius, the capital of Lithuania. After this, Hitler appointed Stahel Military Commander of Warsaw and then ordered Stahel's transfer to Romania during the German suppression of the Warsaw Uprising, which took place between August 1 and October 2, 1944.[4]

The German efforts failed. On September 2, 1944, Minister Manfred von Killinger shot his secretary and himself, just after the Romanians burst into the German Legation.[5] Colonel Traian Borcescu, former deputy head of the Romanian Special Intelligence Service, recalled in 1994: 'I ran to stop [Killinger], and I saw him fall right next to his secretary. "Don't panic," said Karl Clodius, Germany's representative for economic affairs in Bucharest, "the captain of a ship never leaves it when it's sinking."'[6] As *Time* wrote, 'Fat, scarfaced Dr. Karl Clodius has long been Adolf Hitler's successful advance man in the Balkans.'[7] All other members of the legation and most of the German colony (about 350 people) were detained by the Romanian security service in a concentration camp.

During these dramatic events, on September 29, a 21-man team from the Office of Strategic Service (OSS, the American intelligence service during World War II and the CIA's predecessor), headed by Lieutenant Commander Frank Wisner, was dropped into Bucharest.[8] Wisner's code-name was 'Typhoid', while the operation was called 'Bughouse'. Before this, Wisner was stationed at the OSS office in Istanbul and then in Cairo.[9] With King Mihai's permission the team immediately organized an evacuation of 1,888 Allied flyers captured by the Germans in Romania, Bulgaria, and Yugoslavia.

The team sent a huge number of Romanian diplomatic documents to the State Department in Washington.[10] It also acquired about ten thousand dossiers in the buildings of the former Gestapo and German Legation. The reports and letters by SS-Hauptsturmführer Gustav Richter, 'adviser on the Jewish question' at the legation, were among the most valuable.[11] From 1941–1943, Richter was Eichmann's representative in Romania, and after that, he served as police attaché at the German Legation—i.e., the SD chief in Romania.

After analyzing all these materials, the OSS counterintelligence branch X-2 identified over 4,000 Axis intelligence officials and agents, over a hundred subversive organizations, and about two hundred commercial firms used as cover for espionage activity.[12] A two-hundred-page file of this data was forwarded to Soviet foreign intelligence. The NKGB handed the American file over to the GRU (military intelligence), but it is unknown whether SMERSH received this information.

Until November, Wisner and his team were the only Americans in Bucharest, and Wisner established contacts with both the Romanian General Staff and Soviet military authorities. The team exchanged some information with the Soviets and even obtained the right to interrogate German military prisoners in Soviet custody. Wisner was on such good terms with the HQ of the 2nd Ukrainian Front that he was offered assistance in setting up an OSS outpost in Budapest.[13] However, Wisner obviously remembered Bill Donovan's (OSS head's) oral instruction 'to change [the German] targets to Russian intelligence targets in the Balkans'.[14]

There were also teams of British intelligence (SOE) agents in Romania.[15] The cooperation of British intelligence and Soviet foreign intelligence began in Moscow in September 1941, when Lieutenant Colonel Robert Guinness signed the first agreement with the Soviet representative, 'General Nikolaev' (who was actually the prominent intelligence operative Colonel Vasilii Zarubin).[16] However, from the beginning the Soviets suspected the British of spying and in October 1945, British specialists discovered Soviet secret listening devices throughout the British Intelligence Mission's building in Moscow.[17] On December 10, 1944, the Soviet Foreign Commissariat sent a diplomatic note to the British Embassy in Moscow that stated: 'The presence of the other intelligence groups in addition to those [of SMERSH] that are already in existence does not seem expedient.'[18] From this time onwards, the Soviets pushed all the British and, eventually, the American intelligence teams out of Romania and Bulgaria.

On August 30, 1944 Stalin ordered the troops of the 2nd Ukrainian Front to continue on the move, while part of the troops of the 3rd Ukrainian Front stayed in the city. In Bucharest, the Romanians handed the German diplomats-detainees over to operatives of the UKR SMERSH of the 3rd Ukrainian Front, while the Swedish ambassador, Patrik Reuterswärd, who took over German interests in Romania, ceded the building of the German mission to the Soviet military representatives.[19] Interestingly, in 1943, he offered himself to the German Ambassador Killinger as a go-between in the proposed secret negotiations between the British and German representatives on a separate peace agreement.

Additionally, SMERSH operatives arrested all German military diplomats on September 2, 1944, including General Erik Hansen (head of the mission), Admiral Werner Tillessen (head of the navy mission), and General Alfred Gerstenberg (head of the air force mission) (Appendix II, see http://www.smershbook.com).[20] General Stahel was also taken prisoner. Stalin considered the capture of the

German military diplomats and generals a great success of the 2nd Ukrainian Front's high command.[21] The arrested German diplomats, along with Stahel, were sent to Moscow. This varied group included the above-mentioned Gustav Richter and Willy Roedel, a devoted Nazi and Killinger's assistant on intelligence matters. Later both became cell mates of the Swede Raoul Wallenberg.

General Karl Spalcke, German military attaché to Romania from 1942 to 1944, was also among those arrested. SMERSH was especially interested in him because in the 1920s–30s, Spalcke was involved in the joint Soviet–German military program and personally knew Marshal Mikhail Tukhachevsky who was executed in 1937. Spalcke, a specialist in modern Russian history, hated the Nazi Party and despised both Richter and Roedel. Max Braun, Spalcke's assistant, later told the MGB interrogators:

> After Stauffenberg's assassination attempt on Hitler [on July 20, 1944], Killinger cursed Stauffenberg at the meeting of the Legation's staff. He called Stauffenberg 'a pig' and said that he would personally shoot to death any member of the Legation who was involved in Stauffenberg's affair.
>
> General Spalcke had the courage to tell Killinger, in the presence of members of the Legation, that Stauffenberg is not a pig, but he is a courageous officer of the General Staff who had proven that in a battle...
>
> Killinger and the staff members were stunned by Spalcke's speech, but Killinger did nothing against Spalcke because Spalcke was not involved in the assassination attempt.[22]

Later in March 1945, SMERSH operatives arrested Spalcke's wife and 13-year old son in East Prussia and took them to Moscow. Until April 1950 they were kept together in a Lefortovo Prison cell. In 1951 they were convicted as 'socially dangerous elements' to eight and five years of imprisonment respectively. They were released in December 1953. General Spalcke, who was imprisoned in Vladimir Prison, was released in October 1955. I am happy to report that I found General Spalcke's son on the internet and contacted him through a German colleague of mine. Despite his terrible experience during his teenage and young adult years, he became a prominent West German diplomat.

There was also Josias von Rantzau, an anti-Nazi (although in 1938 he joined the NSDAP) and a friend of Adam von Trott and Ulrich von Hassell, anti-Hitler resistance members in the German Foreign Ministry.[23] Kurt Welkisch, press attaché of the German legation, was also sent to Moscow. He was a secret Soviet agent of the Red Orchestra network with the alias 'ABC'.[24] Welkisch's reports to Moscow's military intelligence HQ during 1940 and 1941 kept Soviet intelligence well informed about the staff of the German Legation in Bucharest.

On September 7, 1944, the last transport of the detained German diplomats arrived in Moscow. It consisted of fifteen people, including Counsel

Gerhard Stelzer, who replaced von Killinger for a short time as head of the legation.[25] Stelzer was important for SMERSH because in the 1930s, he had served at the German Embassy in Moscow. His wife, Renata, was also arrested and arrived with him at Moscow prison.

A similar Soviet attempt to arrest the Hungarian diplomats failed. Lieutenant General Sergei Shtemenko, head of the operational directorate of the general staff, wrote in his memoirs: 'There was a signboard on the door of the Hungarian Embassy: "Swedish Embassy." Later it became known that this protective sign was installed with the approval of the Swedish Ambassador.'[26] However, SMERSH operatives managed to arrest Alfons Medyadohy-Schwartz, Hungarian chargé d'affaires (Appendix II, see http://www.smershbook.com).

On August 31, a group of Romanian Communists, who had been keeping in custody the eight high Romanian officials arrested on King Mihai's order, handed them over to the commanders of the 2nd Ukrainian Front.[27] Three days later Marshal Malinovsky, commander of this front, reported to Moscow that the Romanian prisoners had been sent to Moscow via special train.

The group included Ion Antonescu and his wife Maria; Mihai Antonescu, the Romanian foreign minister; General Kristia Pantasi, Defense Minister; General Konstantin Vasiliu, Inspector of Gendarmes; Eugen Kristesku, general director of the Special Information Service; Gheorghe Alexianu, governor of the Romanian-occupied Soviet territory; Radu Lekka, general Commissar on Jewish affairs; and some others. A special team of SMERSH operatives was in charge of guarding the prisoners and bringing them to Lubyanka.[28] The prisoners were told that they were being taken to Moscow for negotiations regarding the conditions of the armistice.

This was a lie. All these people were intensively interrogated in the 2nd, 3rd, and 6th GUKR SMERSH departments.[29] Abakumov considered Kristesku's information about British intelligence in Romania so important that he ordered Sergei Kartashov, head of the 2nd GUKR department, to prepare a special report for Stalin.[30]

Apparently, it was planned to try these Romanians for the atrocities committed by the Romanian troops against Soviet civilians in 1941–43. On October 16, 1941, Romanian troops occupied the city of Odessa in Ukraine. Four days later the building that housed the Romanian military command was blown up and 60 Romanian officers and soldiers died. The explosion was caused by a radio-operated mine left by an NKVD diversion group. In retaliation, Ion Antonescu ordered the execution of 200 hostages for every dead Romanian officer, and 100 hostages for every dead soldier. About 5,000 hostages, mostly Jews, were hanged and shot in the streets of Odessa. Additionally, on October 23–25, approximately 20,000 Jewish men, women and children were burned alive, and from

5,000 to 10,000 Jews were shot. In Transistria, the area near Odessa, about 250,000 Jews were exterminated in concentration camps during the Romanian occupation.[31] But SMERSH's plan for a trial was never implemented.

On April 9, 1946, Ion and Mihai Antonescu and Generals Pantasi and Vasiliu were handed over to the Romanian secret police to stand trial in Bucharest.[32] Later Alexianu was also transferred to Romania. These five were sentenced to death along with another eighteen defendants, and they were all accused of betraying the Romanian people on behalf of Nazi Germany, supporting the German invasion of the Soviet Union, murdering political opponents and civilians, and other crimes. Ion and Mihai Antonescu, Vasiliu, and Alexianu were executed on June 1, 1946; for the others, the death sentence was commuted to imprisonment. In December 2006, the Bucharest Court of Appeals overturned Ion Antonescu's conviction for certain crimes.[33] It decreed that the war against the USSR to free Bessarabia (Moldavia) and northern Bukovina (taken by the Soviets in 1939) was legitimate.

In the meantime, SMERSH operatives continued to arrest high-ranking Romanian and German intelligence officers and numerous Russian émigrés. On November 22, 1944, Abakumov reported to Beria on SMERSH activities in Romania:

On the whole, by November 15 [1944], 794 enemy intelligence and counterintelligence officers were arrested, including:

Officers of Romanian and German intelligence	47
Rezidents of Romanian and German intelligence	12
Agents of German intelligence	180
Agents of Romanian intelligence and counterintelligence	546
Agents of Hungarian intelligence	9

Among the arrestees are: BATESATU, Head of the Romanian intelligence center 'N' of the 2nd Section of the Romanian General Staff; SERBANESCU, Deputy Head of the Intelligence Center No. 2 of the 'special information service' of Romania; a German, STELLER, *rezident* [head of a spy network] of German intelligence; ZARANU, *rezident* of the German intelligence organ 'Abwehrstelle-Vienna', and others.

The investigation has found that German and Romanian intelligence services actively used White Guardists and members of various anti-Soviet émigré organizations for espionage against the Red Army.

'SMERSH' organs have arrested 99 members of such organizations, who have admitted that they spied for the Germans and Romanians.

For instance, the following active White Guardists were arrested in the city of Bucharest: POROKHOVSKY, I. Ye., General Secretary of the Main Ukrainian Military Organization in Europe; KRENKE, V. V., Doctor of

Economics; DELVIG, S. N., Lieutenant General of the Czar's Army.[34]
They confessed to their contacts with the enemy intelligence services...

   I have already reported on all of this to Comrade STALIN.[35]

The last phrase was a reminder to Beria that although Abakumov was obliged to report to Beria, he, in fact, reported directly to Stalin.

Interestingly, on September 26, 1944 Stalin had already signed a cable to the commanders of both the 2nd and 3rd Ukrainian fronts: 'The Stavka...prohibits the making of arrests in Bulgaria and Romania... From now on, nobody should be arrested without the permission of the Stavka.'[36] Therefore, it is possible that Stalin personally approved most of the above-mentioned arrests.

A few months later, an arrested Finn, Unto Parvilahti, met Romanian intelligence officer Theodor Batesatu, who was mentioned by Abakumov, in Lefortovo Prison. Parvilahti wrote in his memoirs: 'A black patch covered his [Batesatu's] right eye-socket; the eye was missing and he told me that he himself had shot it away when trying to blow his brains out on capture..."Now *they're* going to do the firing," he said with grim humor.'[37]

Soviet military leaders also urged the arrest of the Romanian king and his court, but Stalin decided to use Romanian Communists to get rid of the king later. General Shtemenko recalled:

> In late August and the beginning of September 1944...while reporting to the Stavka on the military situation, many times A. I. Antonov [first deputy head of the General Staff] and I...suggested taking decisive measures against [i.e., arresting] the king's court. As usual, the Supreme Commander [Stalin] listened to us attentively, lit his pipe unhurriedly, smoothed out his smoky moustache with the pipe's mouthpiece, and said approximately the following: 'The foreign king is not our concern. Our tolerance toward him will be advantageous for our relationships with the Allies. The Romanian people...will make their own decision regarding the real meaning of the monarchy. And it's reasonable to think that the Romanian Communists... will help their people to understand the situation.'[38]

In the meantime, on July 6, 1945, Stalin gave the king the highest Soviet military award, the Order of Victory, made of platinum, gold, silver, rubies, and diamonds. The other recipients of this order were fifteen of the highest military leaders of the war; Stalin and Marshals Georgii Zhukov and Aleksandr Vasilevsky received it twice.[39] Among the five foreign recipients, including the Supreme Commander of the Allied Forces in Europe, Dwight D. Eisenhower, and British Field Marshal Bernard Montgomery, King Mihai was the only civilian.[40]

Apparently, while awarding Mihai supposedly for ordering the arrest of Ion Antonescu and his accomplices, Stalin tried to gloss over the fact that on February 27, 1945, Stalin's watchdog Andrei Vyshinsky, Soviet Deputy Commissar for Foreign Affairs, whom Stalin sent to Bucharest, forced Mihai I to appoint the new government headed by the pro-Soviet Petru Groza as prime minister.

In December 1947, Stalin's secret plan to get rid of Mihai I was implemented. Backed by orders from Moscow, Groza and Gheorghiu-Dej, general secretary of the Romanian Communist Party, forced the king to abdicate. In 2007, King Mihai I recalled: 'It was blackmail... They said, "If you don't sign this immediately we are obliged"—why obliged I don't know—to kill more than 1,000 students that they had in prison.'[41] Outside the palace the king could see soldiers and artillery facing the compound. A few days later he left the country. Only in 1992, after the fall of the Communist regime, did the king visit Romania again.

Bulgaria

On September 7, 1944, the Red Army invaded Bulgaria from Romania. Bulgaria had joined the Axis in 1941, when the Bulgarian King (Tsar) Boris III declared war against England and the United States, but not against the Soviet Union.[42] His father, Ferdinand I, was the founder of the royal dynasty of Bulgaria and a relative of Queen Victoria, as well as of the French, Belgian, Portuguese, and Mexican royal families. Additionally, Boris III was married to Giovanna di Savoia, daughter of Victor Emmanuel III of Italy. During World War II, German Minister Adolf Heinz Beckerle constantly tried to intervene in Bulgaria's internal affairs.[43] Tsar Boris was extremely embarrassed by Beckerle's efforts, especially because Beckerle was not a professional diplomat, but a policeman.

On August 15, 1943, during the ongoing collapse of Italy (on July 10 the Western Allies landed in Sicily, and the armistice was signed on September 3), Tsar Boris visited Hitler and refused to change Bulgaria's neutrality toward Russia. Apparently, this was too much for Hitler. Shortly after his return from Berlin Boris III died mysteriously—most probably, poisoned by the Germans. Boris's son, Simeon II, was only six years old, and his uncle Prince Kyril of Bulgaria, Prime Minister Professor Bogdan Filov, and Lieutenant General Nikola Mihov of the Bulgarian army were appointed regents, while Dobri Bozhilov succeeded Filov as prime minister. All these people were pro-German.

On September 2, 1944, the Soviet Union declared war against Bulgaria and after five and a half hours the Bulgarians called for an armistice. By September 9, the Fatherland Front—a coalition of the Communist Party, the left wing of the Agrarian Union, and a few pro-Soviet politicians who had returned from exile in the Soviet Union—had taken power.[44] Bulgaria became the first Communist-controlled country outside the Soviet Union, and the Bulgarian population in Sofia enthusiastically welcomed Soviet troops.

The new Bulgarian authorities immediately ordered the arrests of the young tsar's regents, former ministers of all cabinets from January 1941 to September 1944, and all members of the parliament during that period.[45] In two days, 160 former politicians on this list were arrested, and their properties were confiscated. Later many of them were executed without trial.[46]

On September 11, Georgi Dimitrov, the famous Bulgarian Communist, ordered from Moscow the creation of 'people's courts' for trying these and other 'traitors'. At the time Dimitrov headed the Department of International Information of the Central Committee, the Comintern's successor. Apparently, Stalin wanted to deal with the most important of the arrested former Bulgarian leaders himself because Prince Kyril, former prime ministers Bozhilov and Petru Gabrovski, two other ministers, and three members of parliament were handed over to the UKR SMERSH operatives of the 3rd Ukrainian Front and were brought to Moscow Lubyanka Prison. In Sofia, Soviet military intelligence also seized the Bulgarian state archive and sent it to Moscow, where most of its documents are still kept at the Military (former Special) Archive.

After a three-month investigation by SMERSH (the details of the interrogations are unknown), Moscow decided that Prince Kyril and other Bulgarian arrestees should be tried in Sofia and not in Moscow, and they were transported back to Bulgaria.[47] On February 1, 1945, the Bulgarian People's Court sentenced the three regents, 22 former ministers, 87 members of parliament, and 47 generals and colonels to death as war criminals who had involved Bulgaria in World War II on the German side, and they were executed.[48]

In September 1946, Simeon II, his sister Maria Louise and their mother Queen Giovanna were sent into exile. Tsar Simeon II, who had never abdicated, returned to Bulgaria in 1996, and served as prime minister from 2001 to 2006.

In the meantime, SMERSH operatives hunted Axis diplomats in Bulgaria. Later, in prison, the Italian diplomat Giovanni Ronchi claimed that while immunity for foreigners was one condition of Germany's capitulation in Sofia, the Soviets immediately violated this agreement.[49] In accordance with the agreement, members of the Italian and German legations were put on a special train that went from Sofia to Turkey.[50] The evacuation was organized by a Swedish diplomat, chargé d'affaires Erland Uddgren, and two representatives of the Swedish Red Cross were on board the train, which was flying the Swedish flag. For some time, the train stayed on the Romanian border with Turkey, while the diplomats waited for Turkish visas.

In Moscow, Stalin ordered the train to be found and the diplomats arrested.[51] An operational group of the NKVD rear guard troops of the 3rd Ukrainian Front located the train and took a number of diplomats, including 32 Germans and a few Italians, into custody. SMERSH operatives of the 3rd Ukrainian Front sent a group of important German and Italian diplomats, including Ronchi, to Moscow (Appendix II, see http://www.smershbook.com), but nothing was ever heard of the rest of the people on the train. However, the two Swedish representatives returned to Sofia. SMERSH operatives also arrested members of the Hungarian Legation in Sofia and sent them to Moscow (Appendix II, see http://www.smershbook.com).

In an operation similar to that which had taken place in Bucharest, in early September a six-man OSS team arrived in Sofia.[52] It organized the evacuation of 335 airmen, mostly Americans, by train to Turkey. This train had better success than the one with German and Italian diplomats on board, and on September 10, it reached Istanbul. On September 26, the American and British intelligence missions left Sofia after Soviet military authorities threatened to arrest them.

SMERSH unleashed mass arrests of Russian émigrés. The Soviets were well informed about White Guard military organizations in Bulgaria. Nikolai Abramov, a son of General Fyodor Abramov, the Russian All-Military Union (ROVS, a Russian émigré military organization) leader in Bulgaria, for many years was an OGPU/NKVD agent. From 1931 to 1937, he sent detailed reports to Moscow about the ROVS' activity in Bulgaria.[53]

In Sofia, SMERSH operatives arrested two former commanders of the White armies, Lieutenant General Nikolai Bredov and Colonel V. P. Kon'kov.[54] The latter was also a commander of the Russian Corps that fought alongside the Germans. Another arrested officer, B. P. Aleksandrov, for years headed special courses at a school in Bulgaria that trained White Russian terrorists who were then sent to the Soviet Union.[55] This and similar schools in Prague and Paris maintained contact with the intelligence services in many countries. Aleksandrov was in touch with Finnish intelligence, and SMERSH investigators accused him of having been a Finnish spy. Several arrested émigrés were shot—for instance, Dmitrii Zavzhalov, editor of the newspaper *Za Rossiyu* [For Russia].[56] But most of them were sent to Moscow, and their fate is unknown. As for Kon'kov, he survived a long-term sentence in the labor camps, and returned to Bulgaria after Stalin's death.

Slovakia

Simultaneously with the events in Romania and Bulgaria, on August 29, 1944, Slovak Defense Minister Ferdinand Čatloš (pronounced Chatlosh) announced on the radio that German troops had occupied Slovakia, and the Slovak National Uprising under the command of General Jan Golian, and then General Rudolf Viest, began.[57] Besides the Slovak troops (about 60,000 men), partisan detachments under the leadership of Soviet commanders were parachuted to Slovakia via an airlift called the 'Main Land—Uprising Slovakia'. About 1,500 Soviet military planes carried Czechoslovak paratroopers, military equipment and supplies from Soviet territory to the insurgent area.[58] Partisan detachments also included the escaped French and Ukrainian POWs, as well as groups of British SOE and American OSS operatives.[59] From September 7, 1944 to February 18, 1945 a Soviet military mission headed by Major Ivan Skripka and a small British–American military mission headed by the British Major John Segmer and American Captain James Holt Green operated at the HQ of the insurgents.

A number of events preceded the uprising. At the end of 1943, General Čatloš ordered two strong divisions to be stationed in the area where he expected the Red Army would enter Slovakia. His plan was to help the Red Army, but he wanted to maintain Slovakian independence. At the beginning of August 1944, Čatloš sent a courier, Karol Šmidke (pronounced Shmidke), a pro-Communist leader who was well known in Moscow, to inform the Red Army high command of his plan.[60] But Šmidke also brought plans of other Slovak political factions, and Moscow refused to deal with Čatloš. Possibly, the Soviets considered him a German collaborator because during the first two weeks of the German invasion in June 1941, Čatloš commanded the Slovak Expeditionary Army Group within the German troops. After the uprising started, Stalin refused to permit the British and Americans to significantly assist the insurgents.[61]

Due to bad coordination of efforts and failures of the troops of the 1st Ukrainian Front at the Polish–Slovak border, by October 27 the German troops and the Slovak units that remained loyal to the pro-German Slovak fascist President Jozef Tiso had defeated the insurgents. Generals Viest and Golian were captured by the Germans and were later executed in the Flossenbürg concentration camp, while General Čatloš, who deserted to the partisans on September 2, ended up in SMERSH's hands together with General Jozef Turanec (pronounced Turanets), who succeeded Čatloš as Slovak Defense Minister after the escape of the latter. Both generals were brought to Moscow and, apparently, were kept in secrecy because SMERSH investigators ordered Jan Loyda, a German POW who was put with Čatloš (and later with Raoul Wallenberg and his cell mate Willy Roedel) obviously as a cell spy, not to tell anybody that he had been his cell mate.[62]

In January 1947, Čatloš and Turanec were brought back to Prague to testify during the trial of Jozef Tiso, who was sentenced to death on April 15, 1947.[63] In December of the same year, Čatloš was tried and sentenced to five years in prison, but the next year he was released. Turanec, who in 1941–42 commanded the Slovak Motorized Division in Soviet territory, was sentenced to death. His death sentence was commuted to a 30-year imprisonment, and in 1957 he died in Leopoldov Prison, where convicted functionaries of the Tiso regime were incarcerated.[64]

One more Slovak officer, Captain František Urban (who during the uprising fought in the Aleksandr Nevsky partisan detachment under the command of a Red Army officer, V. A. Stepanov), was ordered to come to Moscow and join the 1st Czechoslovak Army Corps formed in the Soviet Union and commanded by General Ludvik Svoboda, a personal friend of Marshal Ivan Konev.[65] On September 25, 1944, Captain Urban arrived in Moscow and was immediately arrested. In Lubyanka Prison he shared a cell with the Finn Unto Parvilahti.[66] After a two-year SMERSH investigation, the OSO sentenced him to five years in labor camps, allegedly for treason and collaboration with the Germans. In 1951, he was released to the Czechoslovak military authorities and returned to Slovakia.

Yugoslavia

By October 20, 1944, the troops of the 3rd Ukrainian Front, assisted by partisans of the Yugoslavian Communist leader, Josip Broz Tito, had liberated a considerable part of Yugoslavia, including its capital Belgrade. With the assistance of Yugoslav Communists, SMERSH operatives began making arrests.

In early October, Yugoslav partisans arrested the Russian émigré Mikhail Georgievsky and handed him over to SMERSH. Georgievsky, a professor of ancient languages, was the main ideologist and general secretary of the emigrant anti-Soviet organization, the National Alliance of the New Generation (NSNP) established in 1930 and known since 1936 as the National Alliance of Russian Solidarists (NTS).[67] The goal of the NSNP/NTS was to organize a revolution in Russia, and for years the NTS sent its agents into the Soviet Union to establish contacts and collect information on the political situation inside the country.

In 1941, Georgievsky's plans to move to England were thwarted by the rapid German occupation of Yugoslavia. He refused to serve the Germans, and the Gestapo arrested him in the summer of 1944 along with a great many other NTS members. In Moscow, Georgievsky, after being held in investigation prisons until the autumn of 1950, was finally sentenced to death and executed on September 12, 1950.[68]

On December 24, 1944, in the town of Novi Sad, UKR operatives of the 3rd Ukrainian Front arrested another influential emigrant, 66-year-old Vasilii Shulgin. Shulgin was a Russian monarchist leader who had been a well-known political figure before the 1917 Bolshevik revolution.[69] On March 2, 1917, he accepted the abdication of Nicholas II. During the Civil War, Shulgin actively participated in the White Russian movement, escaping to Romania in 1920, and later living in Bulgaria, Germany, France, and Yugoslavia. In 1925–26, Shulgin secretly visited the Soviet Union, later describing the trip in his 1927 book, *Three Capitals*, published in Berlin. He wrote sympathetically about Soviet Russia. In fact, the 'secret' trip was organized by the OGPU, using the old enemy for propaganda purposes. However, during his time in Yugoslavia Shulgin did not participate in politics. A group of SMERSH arrestees that included Shulgin was sent to Moscow by plane. This was the first flight in Shulgin's life. On January 30, 1945 Shulgin was brought to Lubyanka Prison.[70]

A nineteen-year-old officer, Pavel Kutepov, was arrested in Panchevo, a town near Belgrade. His father, Major General Aleksandr Kutepov, head of ROVS from 1928 to 1930, was kidnapped on January 26, 1930, by an OGPU terrorist group in Paris headed by Yakov Serebryansky.[71] General Kutepov died after his kidnappers injected him with morphine. In the eyes of the Soviet secret services Pavel Kutepov was guilty merely for having such a father. The SMERSH interrogators decided that Pavel intended to kill Stalin. In June 1945, Abakumov reported to Stalin:

> KUTEPOV testified that having been born in emigration, he was raised in an atmosphere of hatred of the Soviet Union and, being on good terms with the terrorist [Boris] KOVERDA, a murderer of the Soviet Envoy [Pyotr] VOIKOV [in Warsaw in 1927], he decided to follow [Koverda's] example and to commit a terrorist act against Comrade *Stalin* [Stalin's name was inserted in handwriting in the original].[72]
>
> To do this, beginning in 1941 KUTEPOV sought a way to enter the USSR. For this purpose, he tried to join the German intelligence in order to be sent to the Soviet Union. When this failed, he decided to change sides and go to the Red Army to obtain the trust of the organs [i.e., secret services] and thus get to Moscow.
>
> Following this plan, KUTEPOV stayed near Belgrade after the Germans were pushed out of Yugoslavia. Here he was arrested. The interrogation of KUTEPOV continues.
>
> ABAKUMOV.[73]

In fact, Pavel Kutepov, a cadet at the Russian Military Cadet Corps in the town of Belaya Tserkov, was a member of a pro-Soviet underground organization in this émigré corps.[74] Oddly, he was convinced that his father had not been kidnapped, but had secretly gone to the Soviet Union on Stalin's invitation. After the Soviet troops took over Yugoslavia, and before his arrest, Kutepov Jr. worked as a translator for the Red Army. This work was no doubt what Abakumov meant by 'he decided to change sides and go to the Red Army to obtain the trust of the organs'.

Apparently, SMERSH/MGB investigators failed to prove Kutepov's alleged intention to kill Stalin, because in 1947 he was sentenced to 20 and not 25 years in prison (that year, the death sentence was replaced by a 25-year imprisonment). After conviction, as of July 25, 1947, Shulgin and Pavel Kutepov were being held in Vladimir Prison, and both survived the imprisonment.[75]

Back in March of 1945, Abakumov had reported to Beria that in all, SMERSH operatives had arrested 169 leaders and active members of anti-Soviet emigrant organizations in Romania, Bulgaria, and Yugoslavia.[76]

Hungary

After Yugoslavia, the troops of the 3rd Ukrainian Front marched into Hungary, where the 2nd Ukrainian Front had already begun encircling Budapest. Although the details are unknown, at the time Abakumov was already involved in Hungarian affairs. On September 23, 1944, a Hungarian delegation headed by Baron Ede Atzel crossed the front line and was captured by SMERSH operatives of the 4th Ukrainian Front.[77] The delegation represented the underground Hungarian Independent Movement and included Joseph Dudas, one of the Hungarian Communist leaders. The Hungarians wanted to discuss the possibility of an armistice.[78]

The delegation was sent to the military intelligence (RU) HQ in Moscow, where it met with General Fyodor Kuznetsov, head of the RU. Then, on Abakumov's demand, the Hungarians were moved to the GUKR SMERSH and, apparently, interrogations followed. On September 29, the Hungarians were sent back to the 4th Ukrainian Front, and two of them were wounded while crossing the front line. It remains unclear why Abakumov wanted to control the Hungarian negotiators.

Abakumov's personal representative also tried to take control of the second (now official) delegation of the Hungarian government, headed by General Gabor Faragho, which crossed the front line on September 28 at the location of the 1st Ukrainian Front. Kuznetsov, acting on Stalin's order, took control of the delegates and brought them to Moscow.

On December 8, 1944, SMERSH operatives of the 2nd Ukrainian Front arrested Gerrit van der Waals (a Dutch lieutenant, who, after having been taken prisoner by the Germans, escaped and worked for British Intelligence SOE in Budapest), and Karl (Karoly) Schandl, a young Hungarian lawyer and a member of an underground resistance organization who accompanied van der Waals.[79] Van der Waals had important military information for British Intelligence SOE and planned to cross the Soviet front line in order to reach his intelligence contact. On December 6, van der Waals and Schandl naively reported to the Soviet troops who had just arrived, and they were taken into custody. As Schandl stated later, on December 12 they were interrogated separately and the interrogator 'asked why they had helped the British and the Americans in Budapest and not the Russians'.[80] On January 2, 1945, van der Waals and Schandl were taken to Bucharest, and two weeks later they arrived in Moscow by way of Kiev. They were put under the jurisdiction of the 2nd GUKR SMERSH Department.

Van der Waals and Schandl became victims of the Allies' general misunderstanding of the Soviet attitude toward agents of the Allies. Nicola Sinevirsky described what a SMERSH officer told him in Prague in May 1945: 'It is quite evident that British Intelligence is slipping,' he said. 'I am really amazed at the British… They instruct their agents very badly. Any agent, regardless of whom he works for, must remember, and remember well all his life, that he dare not, at any time or anywhere, disclose the fact that he is an agent… The answer is obvious. Death to Spies.'[81] In other words, SMERSH arrested everyone who declared himself to be a British agent.

On December 24, 1944, fighting began inside Budapest while SMERSH operatives continued making arrests. On January 23, 1945, a UKR official of the 2nd Ukrainian Front reported on the arrests between January 1 and January 20, 1945:

> On the whole, 48 [agents] were arrested. Of them:
>
> | | |
> |---|---|
> | Agents of German intelligence | 39 |
> | Agents of Hungarian intelligence | 7 |
> | Agents of German Counterintel.[ligence]organs | 2 |
>
> [...]
> In addition, during this period five officials of the Hungarian intelligence service and three representatives of the diplomatic corps were detained. This number includes:
>
> | | |
> |---|---|
> | Employees of the Swedish Embassy in Budapest | 2 |
> | Employees of the Hungarian Consulate in Romania | 1 |
>
> According to their nationalities, they are:
>
> | | |
> |---|---|
> | Hungarians | 6 |
> | Swedes | 1 |
> | Slovak | 1.[82] |

The Swede was the well-known Raoul Wallenberg, while the Slovak was the diplomat Jan Spišjak (pronounced Spishak).

Raoul Wallenberg, a Swedish businessman trained as an architect, arrived in Budapest on July 9, 1944 as Secretary to the Swedish Legation.[83] In this capacity he represented the Utrikesdepartementet (UD), the Swedish Ministry for Foreign Affairs, as well as the War Refugee Board, an American governmental organization established by President Franklin D. Roosevelt in January 1944. That board was a U.S. executive agency created to aid civilian victims of the Nazi and Axis powers, especially the European Jews.[84] Hungary was the last country in Europe where a considerable population of approximately 250,000 Jews still existed, mostly in Budapest. Although on July 6 Admiral Miklos Horthy, the Hungarian regent (really a dictator), ordered the suspension of deportations of the Jews under German supervision to extermination camps in Poland, it was only a matter of time until the deportations resumed. During a short period Wallenberg organized measures that eventually saved the lives of thousands of Budapest Jews, including the printing and distribution of *Schutzpasses*, protective passports recognized by both the Hungarians and the Germans.

Wallenberg's work was facilitated by the fact that he belonged to an extremely powerful family in Sweden. His elder second cousins, the brothers Jacob and Marcus Wallenberg, owned an enormous financial and industrial empire, and were also on familiar terms with the Swedish government. While staying in Budapest, Raoul used the brothers' Stockholms Enskilda Bank as a conduit for funding for his humanitarian work.

However, there was also a negative aspect of this blood relationship. During the whole war, the Svenska Kullagerfabriken AB, a ball-bearing factory that was the main enterprise of the Wallenberg brothers, supplied mostly Germany, but also England and the Soviet Union, with ball bearings that were crucial for the military industry. Because of their continuing supplying of Germany, the relationship of the brothers with the U.S. and England became extremely tense in 1943–44, and this had consequences for the brothers after the war.

As for Jan Spišjak, no doubt he was unpleasantly surprised by the detention. Although he represented the government of the Axis country, before the war, from 1940 to 1941, he had provided Soviet diplomats in Budapest with important intelligence information, and could expect better treatment at the hands of Soviet counterintelligence.[85]

At first Wallenberg and Spišjak were 'detained and guarded', but not arrested.[86] A Soviet military report stated that on January 13, 1945, Wallenberg, along with Vilmos Langfelder, an engineer who was Wallenberg's driver, approached the soldiers of the 7th Guard Army of the 2nd Ukrainian Front fighting in Pest. Wallenberg 'refused to go to the rear because, as he said, he was responsible for about 7,000 Jewish citizens in the eastern part [Budapest consists of the western part Buda and eastern part Pest divided by the Danube River] of the city'.[87] Wallenberg asked to meet with high-level Soviet commanders and to send a telegram to Stockholm to inform the Foreign Office of his whereabouts. The head of the Political Department of the 151st Rifle Division reported Wallenberg's detention to his superior, and the head of the Political Department of the 7th Guard Army issued an order 'to forbid Raoul Wallenberg to have contacts with the outside world'.[88] Later Langfelder told his cell mate in Lubyanka Prison in Moscow that Wallenberg had never reached Marshal Rodion Malinovsky, commander of the 2nd Ukrainian Front, with whom he intended to discuss the 7,000 Jewish survivors in Budapest he was responsible for.

Colonel General Matvei Zakharov, head of HQ of the 2nd Ukrainian Front, reported Wallenberg's detention to Nikolai Bulganin, Stalin's new deputy.[89] From the end of 1944, military commanders reported to Stalin through Bulganin. However, Abakumov still reported directly to Stalin and SMERSH issues, such as the question of Wallenberg's arrest, were decided by Stalin himself.

On January 17, 1945, Bulganin answered Zakharov: 'Raoul Wallenberg should be arrested and brought to Moscow. The necessary orders have been given to counterintelligence "SMERSH."'[90] On January 19, Wallenberg and Langfelder were arrested.[91] Persons like Wallenberg and Langfelder, arrested without arrest warrants and detained, were called the *spetskontingent* or special contingent.

On January 22, Nikolai Korolev, head of the UKR of the 2nd Ukrainian Front, sent a list of addresses of embassies in Budapest to the head of the SMERSH operational group with a footnote stating that the list was 'based on data in the Reference Book received by the Political Directorate of the front from Ambassador of Slovakia SPASHEK [Spišjak], as well as on the basis of [blank, where a word was erased—possibly "interrogations"] of the detained [sic!—not arrested] Secretary of the Swedish Legation in Budapest, Wallenberg.'[92] Most probably, Wallenberg was interrogated at the OKR of the 18th Rifle Corps. On January 25, Wallenberg and Langfelder were put on a train, under guard.[93] After arriving in Moscow on February 6, they were taken to Lubyanka Prison. The events that followed will be described elsewhere.

Interestingly, witnesses in Budapest reported to Stockholm the actual true date of Wallenberg's arrest:

> Mr. Raoul Wallenberg, attaché of the Swedish legation in Hungary, was arrested on January 17th by Russian military authorities. Some letters written in prison have been received from him, but he has now disappeared. In Stockholm it is believed that he has been killed, because he was fearless and would never have refrained from speaking the truth.[94]

On January 27, 1945, Bulganin ordered Spišjak and two Swiss diplomats, Max Meier and Harald Feller, to be arrested and sent back to Moscow.[95] They were transported there as SMERSH prisoners guarded by NKVD convoy troops. Two years later, on January 8, 1947, after interrogations in Moscow, Spišjak was handed over to the Czechoslovak security service, to stand trial in Prague.[96] Meier and Feller were luckier, eventually being exchanged for Soviet citizens arrested in Switzerland.

On February 13, 1945, the troops of the 2nd and 3rd Ukrainian Fronts took the rest of Budapest, and the 102-day siege was over. The former Hungarian minister of finance Nicholas Nyaradi recalled the final battle he witnessed:

The Germans were behind a barricade of ripped-up paving blocks and over-turned trams... A line of Soviet infantrymen simply marched, as though on a parade... Naturally, they were mowed down by German machine guns... I counted a total of twenty such attacking waves of Soviet infantrymen, each new row falling on top of the dead... Then the last waves of the Russians, charging up the stack of corpses, vaulted the barricades and slaughtered the Germans with savage ferocity.

What made my blood run cold was not the way in which the Nazis were exterminated, but the complete indifference with which the Russian officers commanded their men to die, and the complete indifference with which the soldiers obeyed the orders.[97]

Marshal Malinovsky granted his troops three days of 'pillage and free looting,' which turned into a two-week rampage of rape, murder, and drunkenness.[98] Nyaradi wrote: 'Even the women of the Red Army managed to rape Hungarian men, by forcing them into sexual intercourse at the point of tommy guns!'[99] Swiss diplomats presented a detailed description of events in a report they compiled in May 1945, after returning to Switzerland:

During the siege of Budapest and also during the following fateful weeks, Russian troops looted the city freely. They entered practically every habitation, the very poorest as well as the richest. They took away everything they wanted, especially food, clothing, and valuables... There were also small groups which specialized in hunting up valuables using magnetic mine detectors in search of gold, silver, and other metals. Trained dogs were also used... Furniture and larger objects of art, etc. that could not be taken away were frequently simply destroyed. In many cases, after looting, the homes were also put on fire...

Bank safes were emptied without exception—even the British and American safes—and whatever was found was taken... Russian soldiers often arrested passersby, relieving them of the contents of their pockets, especially watches, cash and even papers of identity.

Rapes are causing the greatest suffering to the Hungarian population. Violations are so general—from the age of 10 to 70 years—that few women in Hungary escape this fate. Acts of incredible brutality have been registered... Misery is increased by the sad fact that many of the Russian soldiers are ill and medicines in Hungary are completely missing...

Near the town of Godollo, a large concentration camp has been erected where some forty thousand internees are being held and from where they are being deported for an unknown destination toward the East. It is known that these internees get very little food unless they sign an agreement to engage as volunteers in the Red Army or accept a contract for work in Russia… The population of Germanic origin from the age of two up to the age of seventy is deported en masse to Russia…

Russians have declared that all foreigners who stay in Budapest will be treated exactly as if they were Hungarians… During looting the [Swiss] legation, at one of four occasions, the Russians put a rope around the neck of Mr. Ember, an employee of the legation, in order to force him to hand over the keys of the official safe. As he refused to do so, even in his plight, they pulled the rope around his neck until he lost consciousness. Then they took the keys from his pocket, emptied the safe, and took away all the deposits, amounting to several millions…

A big safe of the Swedish legation which the Nazis had unsuccessfully tried to remove was removed by the Russians with all its contents. This affair will have a diplomatic consequence as the Swedes propose to protest to Russia.[100]

The Swedish press did complain about the last event. Amazingly, Soviet diplomats confirmed that Soviet soldiers had looted the Swedish legation and raped a servant.[101]

Witnesses reported more on Soviet behavior to Stockholm: 'The Russians seemed not to differentiate in their treatment of good or bad Hungarians, Jews or Gentiles, pro Allies or quislings. The Russians did not respect the "protective passports" with which Hungarian Jews had been issued by neutral legations. They qualified these as "interference in Hungarian domestic affairs."'[102]

During this period, SMERSH, as usual, was hunting enemy agents in Budapest. Between January 15 and March 15, 1945, operatives of the UKR SMERSH of the 2nd Ukrainian Front arrested 588 people, including 110 agents of German intelligence services, 20 agents of Hungarian counterintelligence, 56 terrorists, 10 officers of German intelligence and counterintelligence, and 30 officers of Hungarian intelligence and counterintelligence.[103]

All high-ranking officers, diplomats, and other important foreigners were taken to Moscow. Count István Bethlen, Hungarian Prime Minister from 1921 to 1932 and an influential figure in politics, was among them. His main offense, in Soviet eyes, may have been that in 1943, he was among those Hungarian politicians who tried to organize secret, separate peace negotiations with the British and Americans, but not the Soviets. Apparently, the Soviets ignored information received in March 1943 from a Soviet spy ring in Switzerland that Count Bethlen also planned peace negotiations with the Soviet Union.[104]

On December 2, 1944 SMERSH operatives of the 3rd Ukrainian Front detained Bethlen, and at first the Count was kept in Hungary. On February 17, 1945, Deputy Commissar for Foreign Affairs Dekanozov reported to

Foreign Affairs Commissar Molotov: 'Count Bethlen is the most outstanding representative of the Hungarian reaction and a convinced advocate of
pro-British orientation…Bethlen must be…arrested and transported to the
Soviet Union, where he must be kept for a few months, after which the issue must be settled for good.'[105] Molotov wrote on the report: 'Carry out.
March 20, 1945.' After this Bethlen was flown to Moscow, imprisoned and
on April 28, 1945 formally arrested. On October 5, 1946 the 72-year-old
Count died in the Butyrka Prison Hospital in Moscow.

The Armija Krajowa

In late July 1944, the troops of the 1st Belorussian Front under Marshal
Konstantin Rokossovsky began the liberation of Poland; they were followed
by the troops of the 2nd and 3rd Belorussian and the 1st Ukrainian fronts.
Rokossovsky was one of the few Soviet commanders who was arrested in
1937 but later released. Of Polish origin, he was accused of spying for Poland, and was brutally tortured during interrogations by OO investigators.
During World War II, Rokossovsky successfully commanded several fronts.
In 1944, Rokossovsky's 1st Belorussian Front included the 1st Polish Army
under General Zygmund Berling, formed in the Soviet Union. It consisted
of four infantry divisions, one cavalry brigade, and five artillery brigades.
Counterintelligence was called the Informational Department and included SMERSH officers who did not know Polish.[106]

Rokossovsky's troops were in the suburbs of Warsaw on August 1, 1944,
when the Polish underground Armija Krajowa, subordinate to the Polish
Government-in-Exile in London, began its tragic Warsaw Uprising.[107] On
Stalin's order, Rokossovsky's troops stopped advancing until the uprising
was over. There is little doubt that Stalin's reason for holding the Russian
troops back was his desire to have the Germans destroy the Armija Krajowa
for him. On August 25, 1944, the HQ of the NKVD rear guard troops of
the 3rd Belorussian Front explicitly demanded that the troops disarm and
detain every Armija Krajowa unit moving to Warsaw to help the insurgents.[108]

Stalin had his own plans for Poland. In an attempt to co-opt the Polish
emigrant government in London, a Communist provisional government,
the Polish Committee of National Liberation (PCNL), was created in Moscow on July 21, 1944. The PCNL agreed that all military operations in
Poland would be conducted under Stalin's control. The 1st Polish Army
was merged with the Armija Ludowa, a group of pro-Communist partisans
in Nazi-occupied Poland, and became the Ludowe Wojsko Polskie (People's
Army of Poland, or LWP). On August 1, 1944, the PCNL moved to the
liberated city of Lublin.

From August to December 1944, Nikolai Bulganin represented Soviet
interests at the PCNL, organizing local administrations on Soviet-occupied

territory and coordinating the activity of the 1st, 2nd, and 3rd Belorussian fronts and the 1st Ukrainian front.[109] He was also responsible for 'cleansing the rear of the Red Army of various groups representing the emigrant [Polish] "government" and the armed units of the so-called Armija Krajowa... and detaining their officers via "SMERSH" organs.'[110] NKVD troops under Beria's deputy, Ivan Serov, collaborated with SMERSH operational groups to carry out the cleansing. Serov had prior experience, having cleansed the newly acquired Polish territories in 1939.[111]

Another unit was created within the LWP to conduct the cleansing—the Main Informational Directorate under Piotr Kozuszko (Kozhushko in Russian).[112] This military counterintelligence unit at first consisted exclusively of SMERSH and NKVD operatives. On October 17, 1944, Beria reported to Stalin and Molotov: 'To enforce the counterintelligence organs of the Polish Army [LWP], Comrade Abakumov will send 100 "SMERSH" workers. We will also send 15 comrades from the NKVD–NKGB to help the Polish security organs. Comrade Abakumov—"SMERSH"—and Comrade Serov will assist on sites of the Counterintelligence Directorate of the Polish Army and its head, Comrade Kozhushko.'[113] The directorate had its own concentration camps for detaining arrested members of Armija Krajowa (or AK, in Chekist parlance).

On October 26, 1944, Serov reported to Beria:

> Through the agents, operational SMERSH groups on the territory of the Bialystok Voevodstvo [Province] found out that...an 'AK' unit of 17,000 men is in the Bielovezhskaya Pushcha [forest]. Comrade MESHIK [Abakumov's deputy] was sent to check this information. He reported that...the 'SMERSH' operational group of the 2nd Belorussian Front is performing actions against the AK members [i.e., arresting them] ...
>
> The investigation of 20 cases of active members of the 'AK' has been completed and in the near future they will be sentenced by the Military Tribunal.[114]

Investigations were conducted with the usual cruelty. A former member of the Armija Krajowa detachment, a woman partisan named Stanislava Kumor, recalled: 'In the Bialystok Prison, the Chekists broke my arms, burned me with cigarettes, and lashed my face with a whip.'[115]

Apparently, the Armija Krajowa's threat in the Bialystok Region was so serious that Abakumov and Lavrentii Tsanava, one of Beria's men and later NKGB Commissar of Belorussia, were sent to clear up the situation. On October 29, 1944, Beria reported to Stalin:

> To assist Comrades ABAKUMOV and TSANAVA in carrying out the measures, two NKVD regiments are being relocated to the town of Bialystok.

The troops will arrive on the evening of October 31, 1944.

Therefore, a total of three NKVD regiments and up to 4,000 men will be concentrated in Bialystok.

Major General KRIVENKO of the NKVD is being sent to Bialystok to command the NKVD troops.

All comrades being sent have already been instructed.[116]

General Mikhail Krivenko was deputy head of the NKVD Main Directorate of Border Guards. He had already participated in the anti-Polish action in 1940, when, as head of the NKVD Convoy Troops, he organized the transportation of captured Polish officers from the Ostashkov Camp, where they were being held, to the Katyn Forest, where they were massacred. Krivenko and other participants in the execution received high awards.[117] From 1942 to 1943, Krivenko again headed the NKVD Convoy Troops.

Four days after Beria's report to Stalin, Abakumov and Tsanava sent Beria a coded cable reporting on their first measures in Bialystok:

In this operation we are using 200 experienced SMERSH and NKGB operatives, as well as three NKVD regiments.

The operational groups have the following objectives:

To find and arrest: leaders and members of the 'Armija Krajowa'; agents of the Polish emigrant government; leaders and members of other underground organizations undermining the work of the Committee of National Liberation, and, partly, of the Red Army; agents of the German intelligence organs 'Volksdeutsch' and 'Reichsdeutsch'; members of gangs and groups hiding in the underground and forests; and persons opposing measures on the resettlement of the Belorussians, Ukrainians, Russians, and Rusyns [a small Slavic nation in the Carpathians] from Polish territory to the Soviet Union.[118]

Therefore, every Pole who opposed the Sovietization of Poland was arrested. In addition, all Slavs of non-Polish origin were forced to move to the Soviet Union.

Abakumov and Tsanava continued:

The operation to capture [the enemies] is scheduled for November 6 of this year. Until then, we are working to establish who should be arrested...

Up to November 1 [1944], the operational 'SMERSH' groups had arrested...499 persons, of whom 82 were sent under guard to the territory of the Soviet Union [possibly, to GUKR SMERSH in Moscow]. We are preparing to send the remaining 417 persons to the NKVD Ostashkov Camp.

An additional 1,080 men were disarmed and transferred to the reserve of the Polish Army...

We are using the Bialystok City Prison to hold the arrestees until they are transported under guard to the Soviet Union.[119]

This was the same Ostashkov Camp in which the captured Polish officers were held in 1939–40 before they were massacred.

On November 8, 1944, Abakumov and Tsanava sent another cable to Beria:

On November 8 [1944], 1,200 active members of the Armija Krajowa and other underground organizations were arrested. Of them, 1,030 persons were sent to the NKVD Ostashkov Camp by special train No. 84176...

On the night of November 6/7 of the current year, the documents of people living in the city of Bialystok were checked, resulting in the arrest of 41 members of the 'AK' and other criminal elements.

The operation to capture members of the 'Armija Krajowa' and agents of German military intelligence continues.

On November 11, we are planning to send a second train to the Ostashkov Camp.[120]

The first train, carrying 1,030 prisoners identified as 'interned persons,' left Bialystok on November 7, 1944, and arrived in Ostashkov on November 19.[121] Amazingly, 15 prisoners managed to escape on the way to Ostashkov. The last cable to Beria from Abakumov and Tsanava in Bialystok said:

On November 12 [1944], we sent a second train No. 84180 with 1,014 arrested active members of the 'Armija Krajowa'...to the Ostashkov Camp. A total of 2,044 persons were arrested and sent out...

On November 10, the Chief Plenipotentiary for resettlement informed [us] that he had listed 33,702 families to be resettled...196 families have already been sent to the BSSR [Belorussia]...

A total of 341 persons are working on the resettlement...

We consider it expedient to leave small [NKVD] operational groups subordinate to Colonel [Vladimir] KAZAKEVICH, deputy head of the Directorate 'SMERSH' of the 2nd Belorussian Front, who is in charge of the operational work in Bialystok and Bialystok Voevodstvo...

We consider it expedient to return and to continue conducting our usual duties.

We ask for your instructions.[122]

The second train, carrying 1,014 Poles, left Bialystok on November 12, 1944,[123] and arrived eight days later in Ostashkov. Later, on April 14, 1945, 1,516 Poles were transferred to other POW camps, while the rest were sent back to Poland in 1946 and 1947.[124]

Beria considered the operation complete. On November 14, 1944, in a cover letter accompanying copies of Abakumov and Tsanava's last report, he wrote to Stalin, Molotov, and Malenkov: 'During the operation, 2,044 active members of the Armija Krajowa and other underground organizations were arrested. The work preparing the resettlement of the Belorussians and Ukrainians to the Soviet Union has been improved... I think Comrades ABAKUMOV and TSANAVA should be allowed to leave.'[125]

The permission was granted and Abakumov returned to Moscow, while Tsanava went to Belorussia. Two months later Tsanava was back at the 2nd Belorussian Front as NKVD Plenipotentiary. Now the SMERSH Directorate of this front was under his, and not Abakumov's, control.

CHAPTER 22

In the Heart of Europe

Within a year of its creation, SMERSH was more powerful than the NKGB and NKVD. The growing power of Abakumov and SMERSH made Beria determined to restore his own power over all security services. On May 5, 1944, Beria was promoted to deputy chairman of the GKO, which made him Stalin's deputy. He was also chairman of the Operational Bureau of the GKO in charge of routine GKO work. Beria thus became responsible for the work of all branches of the defense industry, the NKVD, the NKGB, and the daily work of the GKO. By 1945, he also received partial control over SMERSH.

Beria Gains Control

On January 11, 1945, the activities of NKVD, NKGB, and SMERSH were newly coordinated under Beria as a system of NKVD plenipotentiaries (*upolnomochennye*, meaning representatives) and their staffs at the fronts.[1] Seven such plenipotentiaries were appointed 'to cleanse the rears of Red Army fronts of enemy elements.' High-level officials from the NKVD, NKGB, and SMERSH were chosen to be the plenipotentiaries (Table 22-1).

Abakumov became NKVD Plenipotentiary to the 3rd Belorussian Front, Abakumov's first deputy, Nikolai Selivanovsky, became Plenipotentiary to the 4th Ukrainian Front, and Pavel Meshik was appointed Plenipotentiary to the 1st Ukrainian Front. Heads of UKRs and of the NKVD rear guard troops at the fronts were automatically made deputy plenipotentiaries. This move subordinated Abakumov, two of his deputies, and the heads of UKRs to Beria. Ivan Serov, Beria's deputy, was appointed Plenipotentiary to the 1st Belorussian Front, and he soon became one of Abakumov's

TABLE 22-1. NKVD PLENIPOTENTIARIES AND THEIR DEPUTIES, JANUARY 11–JULY 4, 1945[1]

Front	Commander	Plenipotentiary	Deputy Plenipotentiaries[2]
1st Baltic Front (transformed into Zemland Operational Group, Feb 25–Apr 2, 1945)	Army Gen. I. Kh. Bagramyan	I. M. Tkachenko, NKVD and NKGB Plenipotentiary within Lithuanian Republic[1]	N. G. Khannikov, SMERSH; B. P. Serebryakov, NKVD (1st Baltic); M. I. Romanov, NKVD (Zemland)
2nd Baltic Front	Army Gen. A. I. Yeremenko; Marshal L. A. Govorov (from Jan 4, 1945)	P. N. Kubatkin, Head, NKGB Leningrad Branch	N. I. Zheleznikov, SMERSH; V. A. Abyzov, NKVD
1st Belorussian Front	Marshal G. K. Zhukov	I. A. Serov, Deputy NKVD Commissar	A. A. Vadis, SMERSH; P. A. Zimin, NKVD
2nd Belorussian Front	Marshal K. K. Rokossovsky	L. F. Tsanava, Head, NKGB of Belorussian Republic	Ya. A. Yedunov, SMERSH; V. T. Rogatin, NKVD
3rd Belorussian Front	Army Gen. I. D. Chernyakhovsky; Marshal A. M. Vasilevsky (Jan 18–Apr 26, 1945); Army Gen. I. Kh. Bagramyan (from April 26, 1945)	V. S. Abakumov, Head, GUKR SMERSH; also, Acting Plenipotentiary in East Prussia (Feb–May 1945)	P. V. Zelenin, SMERSH; I. S. Lyubyi, NKVD
1st Ukrainian Front (later Central Group of Troops stationed in Austria-Hungary)	Marshal I. S. Konev	P. Ya. Meshik, deputy head, GUKR SMERSH	N. A. Osetrov, SMERSH; N. P. Zubarev, NKVD
4th Ukrainian Front	Army Gen. I. Ye. Petrov; Army Gen. A. I. Yeremenko (from Mar 26, 1945)	N. N. Selivanovsky, first deputy head, GUKR SMERSH	K. K. Koval'chuk, SMERSH; S. M. Fadeev, NKVD

1. NKVD Order No. 0016, dated January 11, 1945 and signed by Beria. Document No. 1 in *Spetsial'nye lagerya NKVD/MVD SSSR v Germanii 1945-1950 gg. Sbornik dokumentov i statei*, edited by S. V. Mironenko, 11-14 (Moscow: ROSSPEN, 2001) (in Russian).
2. In each case of a front, deputy plenipotentiaries were heads of the UKR and of NKVD Rear Guard Troops for the front.

principal enemies. Through Serov, Beria controlled events in Poland until April 1945, when Selivanovsky was put in charge of the country.

A Special Operational Group was created in Moscow to coordinate and oversee the activities of the NKVD plenipotentiaries.[2] Boris Lyudvigov, deputy head of the NKVD Secretariat and a devoted Beria man, was appointed as its head.

There were reasons for coordinating the three Soviet security services, beyond Beria's desire to gain control over them. At the beginning of 1945, the activity of groups of German terrorists in the rear of advancing Soviet troops intensified.[3] On February 8, 1945, Aleksandr Vadis, head of the UKR of the 1st Belorussian Front, reported to Moscow that 'of 184 [German] agents discovered by "SMERSH" during January 1945, 124 agents had orders to carry out sabotage and terrorist acts.'[4] According to other SMERSH reports, the German intelligence services had tried unsuccessfully to replicate what the Soviet partisan movement did in the rear of the German armies in the Nazi-occupied Soviet territories. Small SMERSH operational groups became prey for the German terrorists. However, Soviet troops were advancing so fast that the German secret services did not have enough time to organize a widespread partisan movement.

After appointing plenipotentiaries, the NKVD–NKGB–SMERSH joint operations got under way immediately. On January 15, 1945, Abakumov reported to Beria on the organization of special NKVD groups at the 3rd Belorussian Front:

1. Six operational groups were created for Chekist work [i.e., the arrest and screening of Germans] at the areas of each army of [the 3rd Belorussian] Front.

The groups consist of a head, two deputy heads (one in charge of the NKVD troops), twenty operatives, and two translators. Each group is supported by an NKVD regiment.

Additionally, a reserve consisting of operatives [SMERSH officers] and NKVD troops was created for special tasks.

Detailed instructions were given to every member of the group... They were told to find and immediately arrest spies, saboteurs, and terrorists of the intelligence organs of the enemy; members of the bandit-insurgent groups; members of fascist and other organizations; leaders and operational staff of the police, and other suspicious individuals; and also to confiscate depots of weapons, radio transmitters, and technical equipment left by the enemy for [sabotage] work.

The operational groups were instructed to pay special attention to these measures in the towns and big villages, train stations, and industrial plants.

On January 16 of this year, the operational groups, together with the NKVD troops, will be sent to their destination.

Each group received 10 trucks for the transportation of the arrestees and for operational needs...

[...]

Additionally, [I] asked Headquarters to intensify the guarding of water reservoirs and wells to prevent enemy agents from poisoning them...

3. We are preparing a prison to hold the arrestees to be transported from East Prussia.[5]

The activity of such NKVD operational groups (their staffs included NKVD, NKGB and SMERSH officers) was also described in the order by Lavrentii Tsanava, Plenipotentiary to the 2nd Belorussian Front:

January 22, 1945
Top Secret
No. 10 s/s
To: Commanders of all NKVD operational groups
Heads of all OKR SMERSH of the armies
Commanders of all regiments of the NKVD Troops Guarding the Rear of the 2nd Belorussian Front
[...] We suggest:

1. During the movement of Red Army troops an NKVD group should move along with the advancing detachments so, after the troops enter a town or a built-up area, the group would be able to immediately capture [all spies, agents, terrorists, etc., 'despite their nationality or citizenship'][6], weapons, lists, archives and other documents.

An operational group should be led by its commander or his deputy, together with a battalion of the NKVD troops.

2. An operational group that follows the advancing Red Army detachments should be located near SMERSH departments...

3. For cleansing the towns and their suburbs taken over by the Red Army from the enemy elements, it is necessary to leave operational groups supported by the necessary number of troops and to have constant connection with these groups.

The experienced operational officers should be commanders of such groups.

4. Persons arrested by the operation groups and those received from SMERSH organs should be concentrated in specially organized detaining places with reliable military guards which would exclude the opportunity of escape efforts.

The most important prisoners should be [immediately] investigated to discover the underground counterrevolutionary organizations and arrest their participants in time.

5. The most important arrestees—spies, saboteurs, terrorists, leaders of various insurgent or bandit organizations, official members of the intel-

ligence and counterintelligence organizations of the enemy—should be handed over to the Investigation Department of the Counterintelligence Directorate SMERSH of the Front.

[...]

NKVD Plenipotentiary at the 2nd Belorussian Front,

Security Commissar of the 3rd Rank L. Tsanava

Deputy NKVD Plenipotentiary at the 2nd Belorussian Front,

Lieutenant General [Ya.] Yedunov

Deputy NKVD Plenipotentiary at the 2nd Belorussian Front,

Major General [V.] Rogatin.[7]

Actually, the activity of these groups almost repeated what the German Abwehrgroups did in Soviet territory in 1941.

East Prussia

In February 1945, on Stalin's order, Abakumov and his operatives inspected the remains of Hitler's Wolfschanze HQ in Rastenburg in the conquered part of East Prussia.[8] SMERSH operational groups from the 3rd Belorussian Front and the 57th Rifle Division of the NKVD Interior Troops participated in this operation. Although not much was left after the bunkers were blown up following Hitler's departure on November 20, 1944, Abakumov reported to Moscow: 'I think our specialists would be interested in inspecting Hitler's headquarters and seeing these well-organized bunkers.'[9] A few months later Abakumov and a team of SMERSH investigators returned to Rastenburg with a German prisoner, Major Joachim Kuhn, a participant in the military plot against Hitler. With Kuhn's guidance, SMERSH investigators found the plotters' hidden plans to kill Hitler, as well as other documents.

East Prussia was occupied by the troops of the 3rd Belorussian Front under Marshal Aleksandr Vasilevsky's command (which included Abakumov's SMERSH Directorate). Its capital, Koenigsberg, was besieged and finally taken over on April 6–9. Paul Born, a German veteran, described a Soviet attack in East Prussia:

[Our] experienced veterans...knew that after the third whistle the Russians would attack. And as proof, a shouting crowd emerged from the forest and ran toward us...

When there were only 100 meters between us, [our] commander ordered us to open fire...We stood up against the first attack...

The next time two crowds were already rushing at us from the forest after the third whistle. Even after our heavy machine gun opened fire at them at a distance of 100 meters, we could not stop them...

Everyone was firing without interruption and aiming at the middle of a slowly approaching crowd of completely drunk, shouting people.[10]

During the occupation, numerous Red Army units committed unspeakable atrocities against the civilian German population. Soviet Lieutenant Leonid Rabichev, who later became a writer and artist, recalled a typical scene on the Prussian roads:

In carts, cars, and on foot, old men, women, and children—entire huge families—slowly moved along all the roads and highways of the country to the west.

Our tank crews, infantrymen, artillerists, and members of the Signal Corps caught up to them and, to clear the way, threw them into the ditches on the sides... They pushed aside old people and children and, forgetting about honor and dignity and the retreating German troops, assaulted women and girls by the thousands.

Women, mothers and their daughters, lay to the right and left of the highway, and a crowd of laughing men with half-lowered pants stood in front of each of them.

Those who were already bleeding and fainting were pulled aside, and the children who rushed to their aid were shot on the spot. Loud laughter, roars, cries, and moaning were heard. Commanders, majors, and colonels, stood along the highway laughing or directing...each of their soldiers to participate [in the rapes]. This was not revenge on the damned invaders, but hellish deadly gang rape, an opportunity to do anything without punishment or personal responsibility...

The colonel, who at first was just directing, joined the line himself, as the major shot witnesses, children, and old people who were hysterical.[11]

This was a common attitude toward the Germans. The head of a political department of the NKVD border guard corps reported to his superiors: 'The medical doctor of the 1st Rifle Battalion reported that...the servicemen...told her, "It is a pleasure to see a pretty German girl crying in your arms."'[12] Neither Vasilevsky nor Abakumov stopped the atrocities.

Apparently, Stalin did not care what was going on in East Prussia because it was a territory targeted to become part of Russia after being cleansed of the German population. On April 20, 1945, after the troops of the 1st Belorussian (Zhukov, commander in chief) and the 1st Ukrainian (Konev, commander in chief) fronts entered the territory that would become East Germany, Stalin signed a directive to the military councils of these fronts:

The Stavka of the Supreme Command orders:

1. Try to change the attitude [of troops] toward the Germans—toward POWs, as well as civilians. The Germans must be treated better. The cruel treatment of the Germans forces them to fear [the troops], and creates obstinate resistance and a refusal to be taken prisoner. The civilian population

is organizing gangs because it fears [Soviet] revenge. This situation is not in our favor. A more humane attitude toward the Germans will facilitate our military actions in their territory and, undoubtedly, will diminish the persistence of the German defense.

[...]

J. Stalin

Antonov [head of the General Staff].[13]

No such order was issued to the 2nd and 3rd Belorussian fronts that fought in East Prussia and Pomerania—another region of Germany later cleansed of the German population.

To implement the transition of East Prussia into a Russian territory, a special post of NKVD Plenipotentiary for the Zemland Operational Group (former 1st Baltic Front, disbanded on February 24, 1945 and turned into this group, which was now subordinated to the 3rd Belorussian Front) was created (Table 22-1). After February 1945, the title became NKVD Plenipotentiary for East Prussia, and Abakumov was acting Plenipotentiary in addition to his other duties. The HQ of this Plenipotentiary, called *apparat*, consisted of 40 Chekists and included six departments (operational, investigation, archival, administrative, transportation, and supplies departments, secretariat, commandant, and translators). Also, there were 17 regional and eight city groups of 8 to 14 men each, which conducted operational work, and four prisons located in old German prisons.

In East Prussia, SMERSH continued to routinely arrest Soviet field officers. On February 9, 1945, Captain Aleksandr Solzhenitsyn—commander of a battery and later author of *The Gulag Archipelago*—was arrested.[14] The NKGB seized Solzhenitsyn's letters to his friend, Nikolai Vitkevich, along with Vitkevich's replies to Solzhenitsyn. Both officers criticized Stalin and discussed the possibility of creating an organization after the war that would restore 'authentic' Leninism.

Since the case involved a serviceman, the NKGB transferred the documents to the GUKR SMERSH, and on February 2, Abakumov's deputy Babich ordered Solzhenitsyn's immediate arrest. Solzhenitsyn remembered that 'the SMERSH officers at the brigade command point tore off...shoulder boards, and took my belt away and shoved me along to their automobile.'[15] This was the beginning of a long trip to Moscow along with other prisoners. After a four-month investigation by the 2nd NKGB Directorate (counterintelligence) in Moscow, the OSO sentenced Solzhenitsyn to eight years of imprisonment in the labor camps.

Among other responsibilities, NKVD plenipotentiaries supervised the so-called mobilization—that is, the arrest and deportation—of the civilian population of Soviet-occupied German territory.[16] In 1943–44, the academician Ivan Maisky, Soviet Ambassador to England and Molotov's deputy, developed the concept of forced work of the mobilized population as war reparation, and it was widely implemented.[17] On February 3, 1945, the GKO ordered the total mobilization of 'all male Germans from 17 to 50 years old capable of working and serving in the army' on the territories occupied by the 1st, 2nd, and 3rd Belorussian fronts and the 1st Ukrainian Front. The order stated: 'The Germans who had served in the German army or in the "Volkssturm" troops, should be considered prisoners of war and sent to the NKVD camps for POWs. All of the other Germans should be organized into work battalions of 750–1,200 individuals to be used for work in the Soviet Union, primarily in the Ukrainian and Belorussian SSR.'[18]

From February 10, 1945 onwards, plenipotentiaries were obliged to report daily to Moscow on mobilization progress.[19] The results of arrests and mobilization of Germans, especially in East Prussia, were impressive. In March, after taking over Koenigsberg and an additional SMERSH/NKVD operation for mopping up German agents and soldiers in the ruined city on April 11–19, Abakumov reported to Beria:

> The operational groups have arrested 22,534 spies, saboteurs, terrorists, and other hostile elements at the territory occupied by the 3rd Belorussian Front [in East Prussia].
>
> All arrestees were sent by 11 special trains to the Kalinin and Chelyabinsk NKVD camps.
>
> 113 active German terrorists and saboteurs, who tried to kill Red Army commanders and servicemen, were shot on the spot.
>
> After the arrests and operative checking...35,150 persons were left [in 1939, the East Prussian population was 2.49 million inhabitants], mostly old men and women, children, invalids, and sick people. All of these Germans now live in special settlements, where they are under the surveillance of local [Soviet] military commandants.
>
> 1,500 Germans were mobilized in two battalions and all were sent by special trains to the station Yenakkievo [in the Donbass region in Russia] to be used by *Narkomchermet* [the Commissariat for Iron Production] and *Narkomstroi* [the Commissariat for Construction].
>
> The cleansing of the rear from spies, saboteurs, terrorists, and other hostile elements at the territory of the 3rd Belorussian Front has been mainly fulfilled. Arrests have declined sharply because no German population remains within which we can conduct operational work [i.e., make arrests]...
>
> I ask for your permission to return [to Moscow], and to make Comrade ZELENIN, head of the Directorate 'SMERSH' of the 3rd Belorussian Front, or Comrade BABICH, my deputy in the Main Directorate 'SMERSH,' responsible for the current operational work...
>
> I will return to this front again if you deem it necessary.

I await your orders.

ABAKUMOV.[20]

Suicides became common among the arrested East Prussians. On March 11, 1945, Beria forwarded Stalin and Molotov a report from Prussia:

The women arrestees talking among themselves say that they have been collected for sterilization... Many Germans say that all German women left in the rear of the Red Army in East Prussia were raped by servicemen of the Red Army... Previously, a considerable part of the German population had not believed Nazi propaganda about the brutal treatment of the German population by the Red Army, but because of the atrocities committed by some Red Army soldiers, part of the population has committed suicide... Suicides of Germans, especially women, are becoming more and more frequent.[21]

On May 5, 1945, Beria ordered a team of three generals to replace Abakumov in East Prussia.[22] It included Colonel General Arkadii Apollonov, head of the NKVD Main Directorate of Interior Troops and deputy NKVD Commissar, Lieutenant General Ivan Gorbatyuk, head of the Main Directorate of the NKVD rear guard troops, and Lieutenant General Fyodor Tutushkin, head of the SMERSH Directorate of the Moscow Military District. Zelenin was ordered to send 400 SMERSH operatives from his SMERSH Directorate to assist the team. Apollonov and his team were charged with the final cleansing of East Prussia, to eliminate the remaining 'spies, terrorists, and saboteurs acting in the Red Army's rear.' It is likely that the replacement of Abakumov as a Plenipotentiary by Beria's deputy Apollonov meant that Beria wanted to keep this newly conquered country under his control.

As for Abakumov, in March 1945 he went to Moscow and did not participate in the conquest of Berlin. Probably, this was one of the main reasons for Abakumov's hatred of Ivan Serov—Beria's man and Plenipotentiary to the 1st Belorussian Front under Marshal Zhukov's command, that eventually conquered Berlin. It is likely that this was also a reason why after the war Abakumov enthusiastically organized a campaign against Zhukov.

Within the territory occupied by the 1st Belorussian Front, 202 operational SMERSH groups were subordinate to Plenipotentiary Serov, who on February 18, 1945, ordered that every German on Polish territory be found.[23] Using local Poles and Russians as informers to report on the Germans resulted in the arrests of 4,813 suspects, of whom 2,792 were investigated and found to be Germans.

Finally, on April 16, 1945, the mass arrests and deportations of the German population stopped. The next day Beria personally reported to

Stalin on the results of the joint work of the NKVD–NKGB–SMERSH operational groups under the plenipotentiaries. A total of 215,540 individuals were arrested, of whom 138,200 were Germans (8,370 intelligence officers, terrorists, etc.), 38,660 were Poles, and the rest were Soviet citizens (of these, 17,495 were considered traitors). Five thousand arrestees died 'in the course of operations and on the way to the [concentration] camps.'[24]

Two days later Beria sent new instructions to the plenipotentiaries of the 1st, 2nd, and 3rd Belorussian, and the 1st and 4th Ukrainian fronts.[25] All captured servicemen of the German Army; members of the Volkssturm, SS, and SA; and staff members of German prisons, concentration camps, and so forth, were to be sent to the new concentration camps set up for this contingent, while former members of the Russian Liberation Army were detained in the vetting camps.[26] By September 1945, nine new camps had opened for the arrestees in Germany. Three were old Nazi concentration camps—Buchenwald, Sachsenhausen, and Jamlitz.[27] Additionally, Beria ordered the setting up of camps for those interned in Poland (1st Belorussian and 4th Ukrainian fronts) and Germany (2nd and 3rd Belorussian and 1st Ukrainian fronts).[28]

Beria also tried to establish NKVD control over prisoners who potentially had intelligence information and were important to SMERSH: 'Arrestees who may be interesting in operational terms can be transported only with NKVD approval.'[29] But Abakumov's men did not follow this order. All important people arrested by SMERSH operatives continued to be sent to Moscow upon the approval of Abakumov or his deputy.

Officers of SMERSH, NKVD, and NKGB received awards for their work on the plenipotentiary staff. Three plenipotentiaries, Abakumov, Serov, and Tsanava, were awarded the Order of Kutuzov of the 1st Class, one of the highest Soviet military awards.

For unknown reasons, Beria did not send plenipotentiaries to the 2nd and 3rd Ukrainian fronts (Table 22-1). Possibly, he had decided that the countries liberated by these fronts were less important than Germany and Poland. The UKRs of these fronts continued to report directly to the GUKR. On April 4, 1945, the troops of the 2nd Ukrainian Front took Bratislava, the capital of Slovakia, and on March 31, 1945, troops of both fronts took Vienna. After the war, Vienna became the location of the UKR of the Central Group of Soviet troops in Europe that controlled the Soviet occupational zone in Austria, Hungary, and Czechoslovakia.

Operation in Helsinki

In the meantime, one of the oddest SMERSH operations was taking place in formally independent Finland. From June 26, 1941 onwards, Finland was at war with the Soviet Union. On September 4, 1944, an armistice ended the conflict, and on September 19, 1944, a Finnish delegation signed a temporary peace agreement in Moscow.

Politburo member Andrei Zhdanov was sent to Helsinki to head the Soviet part of the Allied Control Commission (ACC) in Finland.[30] Although officially the ACC consisted of 150 Soviet and 60 British staffers, in fact Zhdanov's staff reached 1,000 men and he used this enormous Soviet presence in Helsinki to intervene in Finnish internal affairs. On September 27, 1944, Finland declared war against Germany. A few days before the end of this war, on April 27, 1945, a group of SMERSH operatives transported twenty Finnish and former Russian citizens from Helsinki to Lubyanka Prison in Moscow.

On the evening of April 20, 1945, Yrjö Leino, the newly appointed Finnish Home Secretary, was called to Hotel Torni in Helsinki, where Zhdanov's office was located. Zhdanov's deputy, Lieutenant General Grigorii Savonenkov, handed Leino a letter, signed by Zhdanov, containing a demand to arrest twenty-two persons and hand them over to SMERSH representatives.[31] These twenty-two individuals were allegedly 'guilty of war crimes, espionage for Germany, and terrorist acts against the Soviet Union.' Leino, a devoted Communist and son-in-law of Otto Kuusinen, a leader of the Finnish Communists and member of the Central Committee of the Soviet Communist Party, followed Moscow's order without consulting the Finnish government. Abakumov's report to Beria makes it clear that the Soviet Union operated with impunity in the supposedly sovereign state of Finland:

> I am reporting that, following the instruction of Comrade STALIN, a special group of the Main Directorate 'SMERSH' under the Soviet Control Commission in Finland, through the Finnish police arrested 20 White Guardists and agents of German and Finnish intelligence services, who have been conducting hostile activity against the Soviet Union.
>
> The arrests of these persons, according to the plan approved by the Stavka, were made as follows:
>
> The Head of the Operational Group of SMERSH in Finland, Major General KOLESNIKOV [possibly, Kozhevnikov],[32] reported to Comrade ZHDANOV the evidence against those targeted for arrest. On behalf of the Soviet government, he made a statement to the Finnish government demanding that they be arrested and handed over to us.
>
> After this the Finnish police, under the control of our [military] counterintelligence, arrested these persons and handed them over to us.
>
> On April 21 [1945], the arrestees were brought to the Main Directorate 'SMERSH.'
>
> Information on the arrest of the White Guardists and intelligence operatives (along with their testimonies at the preliminary interrogations) has been reported to Comrade STALIN.[33]

On Leino's order, the Finnish State Police arrested twenty people from the list, but two managed to escape. Ten of those arrested were Finnish citizens, nine had Nansen passports, and one was a Soviet citizen (Appendix III, see http://www.smershbook.com for details of arrestees). Nansen passports, the internationally recognized identity cards, were given by the League of Nations (the predecessor of the United Nations) to refugees after World War I, and Fridtjof Nansen—a famous explorer and the Nobel Peace Prize winner in 1933—was High Commissioner of the League until his death in 1930.

One of those holding a Nansen passport, Vladimir Bastamov, was a member of the ROVS branch in Finland.[34] In January 1940, he volunteered for the Russian People's Army (created on the initiative of Boris Bazhanov, a former member of Stalin's secretariat, who in 1928 defected to the West). This army included about 300 volunteers recruited in POW camps. At the end of the Winter War, the 1st Detachment of this army, in which Bastamov served, participated in a military operation against Soviet troops near Lake Ladoga. Therefore, Bastamov was a real enemy. But another Russian detainee, Vasilii Maksimov, was arrested by mistake because a person with the same name, who had left Finland at the time, was on the Soviet list. Maksimov was sent back to Finland only after spending ten years in a Soviet prison.

Another arrestee, Stepan Petrichenko, had just been released from a Finnish prison when Zhdanov requested his rearrest. Born in 1892, he was drafted into the Russian Navy in 1913.[35] In 1917, Petrichenko joined the Bolshevik Party, but in March 1921, he became one of the leaders of the military uprising of approximately 27,000 sailors and soldiers in the town of Kronstadt near Petrograd (as St. Petersburg was called from 1914 to 1924). The main demand of the insurgents was to abolish Bolshevik political departments in the fleet and army and to give real power to the newly elected councils, without Bolshevik control. The uprising was suppressed by 45,000 Red Army troops under Mikhail Tukhachevsky's command, and during the fight 130 commanders and 3,013 Red Army servicemen were killed. Petrichenko, along with 8,000 insurgents, escaped to Finland. By the summer of 1921, 2,103 of those who had been captured by the Red Army were sentenced to death, and 6,459 were imprisoned.

In August 1927, Petrichenko reported to the Soviet Legation that he would like to restore his Soviet citizenship. He also described in detail the Kronstadt Uprising and the activity of the Russian emigrant community in Finland. Stalin ordered Petrichenko to work as a Soviet agent and from that time on, Petrichenko was, possibly, the main agent reporting on Russians living in Finland. In 1941, the Finnish authorities arrested him, and he was imprisoned until September 25, 1944. Apparently, since Petrichenko had been exposed in Finland as a Soviet agent, he was no longer useful as a spy and SMERSH probably arrested him for his part in the Kronstadt Uprising.

The Finnish police handed over the arrestees and their personal files to a group of SMERSH operatives. Zhdanov personally supervised the loading of the arrestees, handcuffed in pairs, onto two planes at the Helsinki-Malmi Airport. Unto Boman-Parvilahti, a Finnish businessman and former Finnish Liaison Officer in Berlin, recalled later that inside the plane 'soldiers with machine pistols were now sitting in the airplane like sphinxes, with the barrels of the pistols pointed at us and their fingers on the triggers.'[36] In Moscow, the arrestees were taken from the airport straight to Lubyanka Prison.

Leino told Marshal Carl Mannerheim, the Finnish president, about the SMERSH operation only after it had already been completed.[37] Mannerheim was outraged, but it was too late to do anything about it. The Russian émigré colony was in a panic. The architect I. N. Kudryavtsev wrote in his memoirs:

Alarming rumors started circulating that an arrest list for the second group had been prepared. The news that Soviet agents had visited several Russian families was especially depressing. During interrogations, the agents demanded information in written form on the behavior and activity of certain persons over several of the past years. This resulted in the flight of many Russians to Sweden, just in case.[38]

At the end of 1945, SMERSH finished investigating the 'Finns' as they became known among prisoners in Russia; in Finland, they were called 'Leino's Prisoners.' On November 17, the OSO of the NKVD sentenced Petrichenko to ten years in labor camps 'for participating in a counter-revolutionary organization and as a member of the Finnish intelligence service.'[39] He was sent to the Solikamsk Labor Camp, where he died on June 2, 1947. The OSO also sentenced the other 'Finns' as spies and 'assistants to the international bourgeoisie' to various terms in labor camps (Appendix III, see http://wwwsmershbook.com).

The fate of the 64-year-old White Major General Severin Dobrovolsky was different. During the Russian Civil War, Dobrovolsky was a military prosecutor in General Yevgenii Miller's army in the Archangel Province.[40] In Finland, Dobrovolsky worked as an editor of a Russian émigré newspaper and he headed a group of Russian fascists. He also organized a channel for ROVS terrorists to cross the Soviet–Finnish border. But General Nikolai Skoblin, a contact person between Finland and the ROVS headquarters in Paris, compromised this channel. From 1930 onwards, he served as an OGPU/NKVD secret agent and reported to Moscow about the coming terrorists. In 1935, Dobrovolsky warned General Miller, at the time head of ROVS, that Skoblin might be a Soviet agent, but General Miller disagreed.[41] Miller's trust in Skoblin cost him his life. On September 22,

1937, with Skoblin's participation, a team of NKVD agents kidnapped Miller in Paris and brought him to Moscow. As already mentioned, Miller was secretly executed in May 1939.

On November 27, 1945 the Military Tribunal of the Moscow Military District sentenced Dobrovolsky under Article 58-4 (participation in a counter revolutionary organization) to death. On January 26, 1946 he was executed.

On July 26, 1947, after inquiries regarding the fate of the arrestees were made in the Finnish Parliament, the OSO of the MGB changed imprisonment of the 'Finns' in labor camps to imprisonment in Vladimir Prison, a much harsher punishment (Appendix III, see http://www.smershbook.com). Imprisonment in this completely secret prison obviously minimized chances that rumors about Finnish prisoners might be spread and eventually reach Finland. Five 'Finns' died either in the labor camps before they were transferred to Vladimir or after the transfer. Of the twenty 'Finns' arrested, eleven survivors returned to Finland in 1954–56. Two applied for Soviet citizenship after their release, possibly because they had nowhere else to go.

After returning home, 'Leino's Prisoners' received compensation from the Finnish government of about five million Finnish marks each. However, two of the former prisoners had problems with the Finnish Security Police (SUPO). Vladimir Bastamov was put under SUPO surveillance in 1955 because of his contacts with the emigrant anti-Soviet organization NTS. Obviously, the Finns wanted no trouble with the Soviets.

The same year, Kirill Pushkarev changed his last name to Kornelius and joined the SUPO. In fact, he continued the job he had before 1945, when he had worked in the Russian Department of the Finnish Police for twenty-five years. Now he began collecting information on NTS members. In 1958, a KGB agent Grigorii Golub approached 'Kornelius' and made threats against his relatives in the Soviet Union, thus forcing 'Kornelius' to provide him with information on NTS members and former 'Leino's Prisoners.' In 1961, the Finnish police arrested 'Kornelius' as a Soviet spy. He was sentenced to a year and six months in prison.

According to the 1944 peace agreement, Finland was obliged to return Soviet citizens to the Soviet Union, and twenty-two 'Leino's Prisoners' were a small group compared to over 100,000 people that Finland, pressed by the ACC, handed over to the Soviets by January 1945.[42] Among them there were thirty-one German doctors and medical nurses who, according to international agreements, should have been released. When Finnish officials raised this question, General Savonenkov responded: 'In this case, the Red Cross and international agreements do not play any role [for us].'[43] In 1948, Yrjö Leino was dismissed from his post after a special Constitutional Commission of the Finnish Parliament concluded that he was wrong to hand over Finnish citizens to the Soviets without the official sanction of the Finnish government. Later Leino divorced Kuusinen's daughter, Hertta.

Chapter 23

Berlin and Prague Are Taken

At the end of the war, only nine fronts with their UKRs remained in Europe (Table 22-1 lists seven of them, there were also the 2nd and 3rd Ukrainian fronts). The Red Army that was moving through Germany toward Berlin looked like anything but the disciplined troops that had crossed the Soviet border in 1944. Captain Mikhail Koryakov, who served in the troops of the 1st Ukrainian Front, recalled just after the war:

> The waves of [Marshal Konev's] troops moving west out of the east had a colorful, exotic appearance. The grimy, bespattered tanks were covered with bright, brilliantly colored rugs on which sat dirty tankmen in uniforms soaked in machine oil. A soldier pulled a bottle out of his pocket, threw back his head and took a long swallow. Then he passed it to his neighbor and, trying to drown out the roar of motors and the screech of caterpillar tractors, in a hoarse, cracking voice began to shout the words of a song...
>
> The artillerymen...threatened the tankmen with their whips, and hit the horses covered with dressy horse blankets weighted down with tassels. The gun crews who jogged on the caissons had lined their seats with soft cushions embroidered with silk and made themselves comfortable. They played German mouth-organs and accordions richly inlaid with mother-of-pearl and silver.
>
> Amid the stream of tanks, guns, motor transports, and Army wagons there appeared every so often an old-fashioned, closed carriage with crystal lanterns or a large landau with a shiny folding top. These carriages were occupied by young officers and men in regulation Army coats with shoulder stripes and automatic rifles behind their shoulders, but who wore top hats and carried umbrellas. Some of them cracked long whips, played mouth-organs, and laughed; others sat very straight and with affected solemnity looked through lorgnettes at the troops moving down the highway...
>
> The Marshal established Draconian rules in an effort to restore discipline among the troops that entered Germany. The order gave a long list of officers who had been degraded and sent to disciplinary battalions. But the gory, drunken wave of debauchery rose high and swept over the dam of official orders.[1]

Finally, three fronts—the 1st and 2nd Belorussian and the 1st Ukrainian—surrounded Berlin. On April 30, units of the 1st Belorussian Front took the Reichstag, the symbol of the German government. The battle for Berlin continued until May 2, 1945, but sporadic fighting with the resisting groups, mostly SS units, continued until May 11.

Victory

The Red Army paid an enormously high price for the victory. During the Berlin Operation, Marshal Georgii Zhukov, commander of the 1st Belorussian Front, continually repeated the order 'to break through to the city's suburbs at any price and immediately inform me [so that I can] report to Comrade Stalin and release an announcement to the press.'[2] 'At any price' translated to 361,367 servicemen killed and wounded in Berlin from April 16 to May 8, 1945—an average of 15,712 men a day.[3] Compare this to casualties during the battle for Moscow (autumn 1941–winter 1942), when losses amounted to 10,910 men a day, or during the Battle of Stalingrad (1942–43): 6,392 men a day.

The war with Germany ended on May 8, 1945, after Major General Alfred Jodl signed the 'Instrument of Surrender' of the German forces in the presence of American General Walter Bedell Smith, French Major General François Sevez, and General Ivan Sousloparov, Soviet representative at the Allied Headquarters.[4] Stalin was not happy that this extremely important document was signed in Rheims (France) instead of Berlin, and that the little-known Sousloparov represented the Soviet Union instead of Marshal Zhukov, the conqueror of Berlin. Stalin telephoned Zhukov to inform him that he had ordered Deputy Foreign Commissar Andrei Vyshinsky immediately to Berlin to sign the German surrender together with Zhukov.[5]

The next day Field Marshal Wilhelm Keitel, Admiral Hans-Georg von Friedeburg, and General Horst Stumpff signed the Act of Military Surrender of Germany.[6] British General Arthur W. Tedder and Marshal Zhukov affixed their signatures on behalf of the Allies and the Soviets, respectively. When Keitel, after signing the act, removed his monocle and tried to say something, Zhukov announced: 'The German delegation may leave the hall.' From that day on, the Western Allies have celebrated V-day on May 8, and the Soviets (now Russians), on May 9. Later, in Nuremberg, Jodl and Keitel were sentenced to death and hanged on October 16, 1946.

After the signing, the Soviets threw a lavish banquet. Zhukov's personal cook recalled that to impress the Allied military leaders, delicacies such as smoked sturgeon meat, black caviar, and special Crimean wines were brought from the Soviet Union to the ruined Berlin, and trophy German wines were also served.[7] While waiting for the coming victory, on May 2 the GKO ordered the creation of a new position: Deputy Front Commander in charge of the Management of Civil Affairs.[8] These deputies also had a second title, NKVD Plenipotentiary in Charge of Combating

Spies, Saboteurs, and Other Enemies on German Territory. Ivan Serov (1st Belorussian), Lavrentii Tsanava (2nd Belorussian), and Pavel Meshik (1st Ukrainian) became Civil Affairs deputy commanders at the fronts that conquered Berlin. Operational groups of SMERSH, NKVD/NKGB officers, and units of NKVD troops were assigned to these three plenipotentiaries. They also had the right to organize their own prisons and concentration camps. Besides policing and repression, they were in charge of organizing local administrations in the occupied territory.

SMERSH in Berlin

During the Battle of Berlin all SMERSH units of the Soviet fighting troops captured and interrogated prisoners. Ivan Klimenko, head of the OKR SMERSH of the 79th Rifle Corps (3rd Shock Army, 1st Belorussian Front), later recalled that in the first days of May, SMERSH operatives captured about 800 high-ranking prisoners around the Reichstag and Hitler's Chancellery alone.[9] The most important generals and witnesses of Hitler's suicide on April 30 were caught on May 2, including SS-Gruppenführer Johann Rattenhuber, head of Hitler's personal RSD guards, Rear Admiral Hans Erich Voss, a representative of the German Navy at Hitler's Headquarters, General of Artillery Helmuth Weidling, commander of the Berlin defense; and Wilhelm Möhnke, the 33-year-old Waffen-SS General whom Hitler had appointed commander of the central area of Berlin only ten days earlier.

Rattenhuber and Möhnke participated in one of Hitler's last bizarre actions. On April 28, Hitler appointed a military tribunal, with Möhnke presiding and Rattenhuber as a member; two other members, generals Hans Krebs and Wilhelm Burgdorf, committed suicide four days later. The tribunal court-martialed Eva Braun's brother, and, therefore, Hitler's brother-in-law, Waffen-SS General Hermann Fegelein (a man close to Heinrich Himmler), as a deserter.[10] However, Hitler ordered Rattenhuber's RSD guards to execute Fegelein on the next day, after it became known that Himmler was trying to negotiate surrender to the Allies through the diplomat and head of the Swedish Red Cross, Count Folke Bernadotte. According to Traudl Junge, one of Hitler's surviving secretaries, Hitler suspected Himmler of planning to poison him, and Fegelein was allegedly part of the conspiracy. As she recalled, Fegelein 'had been shot like a dog in the park of the Foreign Office.'[11]

Escapees from Hitler's bunker in the Chancellery fled in three groups after Hitler's death.[12] Yelena Rzhevskaya, a translator of Klimenko's SMERSH group, recalled: 'The group that included...Rattenhuber and Hitler's driver [Erich] Kempke, was getting through under the cover of a tank. But a grenade thrown from a window hit the tank at the left side..."I was wounded," wrote Rattenhuber [later in his testimony], "and was taken prisoner by the Russians."'[13] Möhnke and Vice-Admiral Voss were captured in another group. SMERSH operatives additionally arrested Major Ernst Keitel, Field Marshal Keitel's son, and Hans Fritzsche, head of the Radio Department in the Propaganda Ministry and future defendant in Nuremberg.

On the same day, Colonel Klimenko and his men found the burned bodies of Paul Joseph Goebbels and his wife Magda in the garden of Hitler's Chancellery, and the bodies of their six children, poisoned by their mother, inside the bunker.[14] More exactly, a small competing SMERSH searching group of the 5th Shock Army commanded by Major Zybin found Goebbels's body first. As Zybin's superior, Leonid Ivanov, recalled later, 'Zybin was a short guy, but he stood up in front of the colonel [Miroshnichenko, Klimenko's superior] and, with his chest sticking out, pronounced: "This is my trophy, I won't give it to you!" The colonel swung his arm and struck the major [Zybin]. This is how the 3rd Army got Goebbels's corpse.'[15]

Voss, Karl Schneider, a member of Hitler's military guards, and some others identified the bodies, while Hitler's personal doctor Werner Haase testified about Hitler's suicide. Major Boris Bystrov, a member of Klimenko's SMERSH group, told Rzhevskaya about the identification of the dead Goebbels children by Voss:

> Bystrov asked Voss: 'Did you know these children?'
>
> Voss nodded positively and, exhausted, after asking permission, slipped into a chair.
>
> 'I saw them only yesterday. This is Heidi,' he pointed to the youngest girl.
>
> Before he moved into this room, he had identified [the bodies of] Goebbels and his wife...
>
> Voss was shaken; he was sitting with stooped shoulders...
>
> Suddenly he...jumped up and ran away. Bystrov rushed after him along a corridor of the dark dungeon...When he overtook Voss, [Bystrov] understood that it was Voss's gesture of desperation, without any intention or desire to escape.[16]

Voss even tried to commit suicide by cutting his veins with a small knife, but Klimenko's men interrupted his attempt.

The next day, Major General Aleksei Sidnev, deputy head of the UKR SMERSH of the 1st Belorussian Front, sent two reports to Abakumov and Beria. The first mentioned the finding and identification of the bodies of the members of the Goebbels family, and the second described testimony by Dr. Haase. Haase stated that, on April 30, he had seen Hitler for the last time, but he knew that after the meeting Hitler had poisoned himself and his body had been burned.

Possibly, both Abakumov and Beria reported the news to Stalin. SMERSH and the NKVD began competing to find out what, in fact, had happened to Hitler. Unfortunately, most of the sources published in English failed to identify two separate investigations by the two Soviet security services.[17] Here I will mention only some of SMERSH's efforts.

SMERSH operational groups began an intensive search for Hitler's body and for additional witnesses who could identify the corpse. On May 4, the captured SS-guard Harry Mengershausen provided the first detailed information that the bodies of Hitler and Eva Braun had been burned in the garden of the Chancellery.[18] The next day the badly burned bodies of a man and a woman were found by accident in a bomb crater in the Chancellery's garden. Nobody could identify them, and Klimenko ordered that they be buried again. Later he realized that the bodies could have belonged to Hitler and Eva Braun. Since now the 5th Army, and not Klimenko's 3rd Shock Army, controlled the territory of the Chancellery, Klimenko and his men stole the bodies from the site and kept them.

On May 5, Weidling gave a detailed testimony stating that 'Hitler and his wife committed suicide by taking poison, after which Hitler also shot himself.'[19] Three days later Rattenhuber said that Hitler did not shoot himself, but ordered his valet, Heinz Linge, to shoot him.

On May 8, a special medical commission of the 1st Belorussian Front headed by Lieutenant Colonel Faust Shkaravsky, chief medical forensic expert of this front, conducted an autopsy of Hitler and Braun's presumed bodies. As Rzhevskaya writes, 'it was really incredible that Doctor Faust [Shkaravsky's first name] directed an autopsy of Adolf Hitler!'[20] The commission concluded that death was caused by cyanide poisoning, and not shooting. However, the commission also noted that part of Hitler's skull was missing.

Colonel Vasilii Gorbushin, head of a SMERSH operational group, called up Rzhevskaya:

He handed me over a box and said that it contained Hitler's teeth and that I was responsible for its safety...

It was...a dark-red box with a soft lining inside made of satin...

It was a great obligation for me to have that box in my hands all the time, and I turned cold every time I thought that I might have left it somewhere...

For me...the deaths of the leaders of the [Third Reich] and the surrounding circumstances had become something ordinary.

And not only for me. When I came to the headquarters, my friend Raya, a telegraph operator, tried on Eva Braun's evening dress. Senior Lieutenant Kurashov, who was in love with her, brought her this dress from the dungeon of the Reich's Chancellery. It was long, almost down to the floor, with a deep décolleté on the front, but Raya didn't like it. And she was not interested in it as in a historical souvenir.[21]

Later the lower jaws of Hitler and Eva Braun, and both jaws of Magda Goebbels, were sent to the 2nd MGB Main Directorate (internal counter-intelligence) in Moscow and have been kept in the MGB/KGB/FSB archive since then.[22]

In the early 2000s, the German forensic scientist Mark Benecke examined Hitler's and Braun's jaws in the FSB archive.[23] The fragments were still kept in the same perfume or cigar boxes that Rzhevskaya put them in, back in 1945. Benecke wrote: 'The teeth are stored inside of large overseas travel suitcases, packed together with Hitler's uniform and the original files of the death investigation. The reports of Hitler's dentist, [Hugo] Blaschke (who had formerly studied in the U.S.), and other witnesses clearly show that the teeth in that little cigar box must indeed be the Führer's.'

In the meantime, on May 9, 1945, the Soviet Victory Day, most SMERSH arrestees and high-level generals were flown to Moscow. However, some witnesses of Hitler's death, and Fritzsche, remained in prison in Berlin and were further interrogated. Later all of them were also transported to Moscow. The witnesses were held in investigation prisons until 1951–52, when they were finally sentenced to long prison terms, and the most important of them were sent to Vladimir Prison.[24] Dr. Haase died under investigation in 1946, and Weidling died in Vladimir Prison on November 17, 1955, just before repatriation to Germany. That same year, the survivors were released and returned to Germany.

Also on May 9, Gorbushin's SMERSH operational group, which included Rzhevskaya, found and arrested Käthe Heusermann, the assistant to Dr. Blaschke, Hitler's chief dentist.[25] Heusermann's testimony concerning dental work on Hitler and Braun was crucial in identifying the bodies. Also, with her help Hitler's dental X-rays and a bridge prepared for Hitler were found in the bunker. On May 11, based on Heusermann's description and on an even more detailed description from another dentist, Fritz Echtmann, Dr. Shkaravsky concluded that the burned corpse was, in fact, Hitler.[26]

A week later, the Stavka in Moscow sent a high-level general to inspect the bodies and interrogate the witnesses again; his name remains unknown.[27] Exhumed for the general's viewing were the bodies of Hitler, Eva Braun, members of the Goebbels family, and General Hans Krebs, who also committed suicide in the bunker on May 1, after he unsuccessfully contacted General Vasilii Chuikov with Goebbels's offer of surrender. The Stavka general was perhaps in contact with Abakumov because on May 22, Abakumov complained to Beria about Ivan Serov's (NKVD Plenipotentiary at the 1st Belorussian Front) attempts to control the SMERSH investigation.[28] At the same time, in Moscow's Lubyanka Prison, Möhnke and Rattenhuber wrote detailed accounts of Hitler's last days.

On May 23, Beria received a report from Serov. Attached was the report of Aleksandr Vadis, head of the UKR SMERSH of the 1st Belorussian

Front, in which Vadis described the interrogations of additional witnesses who positively identified Hitler's body.[29]

At the end of May 1945, the 79th Rifle Corps along with the whole 3rd Shock Army was relocated to the town of Rathenau, west of Berlin. Klimenko and his OKR SMERSH took the bodies along with them, ultimately moving them several times.

On June 16, 1945, Beria forwarded all materials on the SMERSH investigation, collected by Serov, to Stalin and Molotov. Therefore, Stalin knew since the end of June 1945 that Hitler was dead. Mysteriously, he kept this information a secret from the Western Allies. In 1968, Colonel Gorbushin, former head of the SMERSH operational group, recalled that in early June 1945, Abakumov ordered him to Moscow. Instead of listening to Gorbushin's report on developing investigations in Berlin, Abakumov revealed the following order from Stalin: 'Let's be silent. Hitler's double might suddenly appear, and he could announce himself a Nazi leader. At that moment we will unmask him.'[30] In fact, on May 4, 1945, Soviet troops had already found and filmed the body of Hitler's double, Gustav Weler, in the bunker.

Strangely, in 1968 Marshal Zhukov claimed that in 1945 he had no knowledge of the results of SMERSH's investigation. When Rzhevskaya told Zhukov that Stalin knew about Hitler's death in June 1945, Zhukov was shocked and could hardly believe that Stalin had concealed Hitler's suicide from him.[31]

Colonel Klimenko expressed skepticism about Zhukov's statement: 'Although the fact that Hitler's corpse had been found was not widely announced, it was not a secret, and many people in the [79th] Corps knew about it, including [its commander] Lieutenant General S. N. Perevertkin, and Colonel I. S. Krylov, head of the Political Department. After May 13, 1945, when the autopsy report was written, the circle of persons who knew became quite wide...I personally reported on Hitler's dishonorable death to Lieutenant General Vadis...and Lieutenant General Serov...when they visited the Chancellery. They could not conceal this information from Zhukov.'[32] Klimenko may have been right because at the time Serov was very close to Zhukov.

In July 1945, when Stalin arrived in Berlin to attend the Potsdam Conference (July 17 to August 2), he refused to see Hitler's body. The writer Konstantin Simonov, who visited Berlin in 1945, recalled: 'Somebody, Beria or Serov, reported to Stalin [about Hitler], and suggested bringing the corpse for [Stalin] to see or taking Stalin to look at it. Stalin said: "OK, tomorrow morning I'll go to look at it." Then in the morning, when it was time to go, he waved his hand and said: "No, I won't go. Let Molotov and Beria go and look. I won't go."'[33] However, while talking to American Secretary of State James Byrnes in Potsdam, Stalin denied that Hitler's body had been found.[34]

In February 1946, the 3rd Army moved to the city of Magdeburg, and all fourteen bodies were reburied there. But this was not the end of the story, because the NKVD/MVD conducted its own investigation, directed by Amayak Kobulov, head of the Directorate for POWs and Interned Persons. During the Battle of Berlin, NKVD operatives arrested another group of witnesses that included Hans Baur, Hitler's personal pilot; SS-Sturmbannführer Otto Günsche, Hitler's adjutant; and Heinz Linge, Hitler's valet. They were held in NKVD/MVD prisons in Moscow, separately from SMERSH prisoners, and brutally interrogated.

In May 1946, while searching the bunker area in Berlin, a team of MVD investigators found two cranium fragments, one with a clearly visible bullet hole.[35] The investigators decided that the fragments were from Hitler's skull. Noted medical expert Pyotr Semenovsky studied the fragments and concluded that the shot was upward to the mouth or temple. In other words, it looked as if Hitler shot himself. The MVD team also found bloodstains on the sofa where Hitler was sitting during the suicide. Since 1946, the skull fragments and small pieces of bloodstained fabric and wood have been kept in secret archives along with the file on the NKVD/MVD investigation.

However, the results of a DNA study conducted in 2009 did not support the MVD's conclusion about the fragment with a bullet hole.[36] Most probably, this fragment belonged to the skull of a woman and, therefore, could not have been a fragment of Hitler's cranium. However, male DNA was identified in bloodstains on the sofa. Although this DNA study needs confirmation, it leaves open the question of whether Hitler only took poison or shot himself as well (or was shot by Linge).

Finally, from August 1948 to September 1949, Otto Günsche and Heinz Linge were held at the secret MVD Special Object no. 5, an MVD safe house in Moscow.[37] Colonel Fyodor Parparov, an intelligence officer, was in charge of overseeing them. In 1944, Parparov was awarded the Order of Patriotic War of the 1st Class for his propaganda work with captured Field Marshal Friedrich von Paulus.[38] Now, with the assistance of a group of MVD officers, Parparov translated into Russian what Günsche and Linge had written about Hitler and his death. Finally, Parparov heavily edited and altered the text in conformance with Soviet propaganda style. In December 1949, the manuscript was published as a single-copy book called *Unknown Hitler,* and was sent to Stalin as a gift for his seventieth birthday.

The manuscript was discussed again later, in 1959, at the Central Committee, but it was not until 2005 that two German historians published a German translation of it under the title *Das Buch Hitler*.[39] Writing the manuscript did not help Günsche and Linge, who, in 1950, were sentenced like the other witnesses to twenty-five years in labor camps, and released and returned to Germany only in 1955.

The story of Hitler's body ended only in March–April 1970, when on the order of KGB Chairman Yurii Andropov, the remains of Hitler, Braun, and members of the Goebbels family were exhumed again.[40] The Central Committee approved this operation under the code name *Arkhiv* (Archive), and Lieutenant General Vitalii Fedorchuk, head of the 3rd KGB Directorate, a successor of SMERSH, was in charge. According to the documents, the remains were burned to ashes and thrown into the river Ehle near Biederitz in Sachsen-Anhalt.

In 2005, Major General Vladimir Shirokov, one of the few participants in the Archive operation, briefly described it in an interview. Shirokov's superior, Nikolai Kovalenko, head of the 3rd Section of the KGB Special Department of the 3rd Shock Army (located in Magdeburg), was in command of the operation. Shirokov recalled:

> There were remains of ten individuals (four adults and six children). By the way, the information that [Hitler's] jaws are kept in an archive, is not true because they were taken only for a while for an expert evaluation... We put the bones in a new box... In the morning, we brought it to a particular place near Magdeburg, poured napalm on it, burned it and dispersed the ashes. Nikolai Grigorievich [Kovalenko] told us: 'Lads, we need to mention the place where we've dispersed the ashes. But who knows what can happen, let's write down another place.'[41]

If this is true and all the bones of the adults, including both jaws, were in place, Shirokov and Kovalenko did not destroy the bones of Hitler, Eva Braun, and Magda Goebbels, but of somebody else. Also, it would be very unusual for a KGB officer like Kovalenko to misinform KGB leaders regarding the location where the ashes were thrown away. Therefore, there are still unanswered questions about what became of Hitler's remains.

Back in 1945, SMERSH had many other problems besides finding Hitler's body, including discipline in the Soviet troops. On May 11, 1945, Meshik, deputy commander of the 1st Ukrainian Front in charge of the management of civil affairs, reported to the Soviet high command in Berlin: 'Despite Comrade Stalin's [April 20, 1945] order about the necessity of having a more lenient attitude toward the Germans, unfortunately, robberies of the local population and rapes of German women continue.'[42]

Capturing Andrei Vlasov

Unexpectedly, after the fall of Berlin, fighting with the Germans continued in Prague. On May 5, the Czech resistance broadcast a call to the Czech nation to rise up against the Germans. The next day, the radio also appealed to the American troops that were not far from Prague. The Czechs did not know that the Americans and Soviets had agreed upon a line of demarcation according to which Prague was in the Soviet zone.

On May 7, Waffen SS and SS Panzer troops stationed outside the city launched several severe attacks on the insurgents. Within a few hours the situation had become grave for the resistance. Suddenly, the uprising gained support from the 1st Division of Andrei Vlasov's Russian Liberation Army (ROA) under the command of Major General Sergei Bunyachenko.[43] A. I. Romanov, a member of the UKR SMERSH of the 1st Ukrainian Front, recalled:

> Vlasov's men took Prague by storm, took many German prisoners, SS troops in particular, and raised two flags on the town hall roof; the Czech national flag and the blue and white flag of St. Andrew, the flag of Free Russia. Vlasov was well aware that he and his men could not remain in Prague. Our [Soviet] tanks were already within a day's journey of the city. Behind the tanks came the Smersh operational groups of the First, Second, and Fourth Ukrainian Fronts.[44]

On May 7, Field Marshal Ferdinand Schörner, appointed commander in chief of the German Army by Hitler on April 27, shortly before his suicide, ordered his troops to retreat to the west and deserted the army. He tried to escape to Bavaria by plane, but the plane crashed in Austria. In Prague, the SS troops continued to fight.

On May 11, troops of the three Ukrainian fronts completed the Prague Offensive. A week later Schörner was captured by the Americans, and on May 26, they handed him over to SMERSH.[45] Schörner was sent to Moscow and became one of GUKR SMERSH's important prisoners, along with Fritzsche, Voss, and Stahel, who were interrogated as possible defendants in Nuremberg.

SMERSH operatives of the three Ukrainian fronts immediately began making arrests in the city. Nicola Sinevirsky recalled the night before the SMERSH Operational Group of the 4th Ukrainian Front moved into the city: 'The SMERSH men were preparing themselves for a big purge… Prague was…the headquarters for Russian émigrés, Ukrainian separatists, and Czech politicians of all shades and descriptions… SMERSH agents had begun to show a far greater interest in Czechs and the anti-Communist element in Russian émigré circles, than in the Germans.'[46]

Sinevirsky was right. Between the two world wars, Prague became a capital of Russian and Ukrainian émigré culture.[47] In 1925, the number of emigrants from Russia was more than 25,000, 9,000 of whom were Ukrainians. Russian periodicals, literary magazines, and numerous books were published. There were Russian departments in Charles University, the Pedagogical Institute, the Institute of Agricultural Cooperation, the Institute of Commercial Knowledge, and there were also the Russian Public

University, Archaeological Institute, the Russian Archive, the Museum of Russian Emigration, a gymnasium, and a seminary. These institutions were funded by the 'Russian Action' program of the Czechoslovak president, Tomas Masaryk, and his administration. Masaryk naively believed that the Bolshevik regime would not last long, and that after the fall of the Soviet Union the Russians from Prague would create an administration in the new democratic Russia. In 2003, the Czech government proclaimed May 11, 1945, as 'the day of the destruction of Russian intellectuals' in Prague.

Some SMERSH arrestees in Prague were immediately interrogated. Sinevirsky gave examples when he translated an interrogation that started during the day and continued through the night:

> Vlasta sat silent, motionless, quiet.
>
> 'Speak! You whore!' The Captain [Stepanov] moved toward her and caressed her hair...
>
> Vlasta wept silently.
>
> 'Look here,' Stepanov continued, 'you are a beauty and there is nobility in your whole being. But if you are not going to answer my questions, I will simply beat all the teeth out of your goddamned mouth.'
>
> [...]
>
> Without a word of warning, the Captain slugged her. His fist smacked into the girl's teeth. She reeled, but did not fall. He hit her a second time. This time she fell to the floor...The Captain kicked the prostrate girl in the face. His heavy boots left an angry mark and the blood began to flow from the cuts they left. He began trampling on her breasts in a mad dance. Blood streaked the girl's face and ran down the front of her dress...
>
> It was three o'clock the next morning before Captain Stepanov completed his preliminary questioning of Vlasta.[48]

Many arrestees were sent to Moscow, and their fates are not well known. Sergei Maslov, a leader of the emigrant Labor Agrarian Party, and Alfred Bem, a historian of Russian literature, were famous within the Russian community. SMERSH operatives arrested Maslov after he had just been released from a German concentration camp. According to rumors, the operatives executed him soon after his arrest. Bem was brought to Moscow and sentenced; he later died in a Soviet labor camp.

On June 9, SMERSH operatives arrested Prince Pyotr Dolgorukov.[49] He and his twin brother, Pavel, were among the founders of the liberal Constitutional Democratic (Cadet) Party in Czarist Russia. After the Bolshevik revolution, Pavel became one of the organizers of the White movement. In exile, Pavel Dolgorukov continued his political activity. In 1926, after illegally crossing the Soviet border with Romania, he was arrested, charged with plotting the assassination of Pyotr Voikov in Warsaw (see

Abakumov's above-mentioned accusation of Kutepov Jr.), and executed in June 1927.

On account of his brother, Pyotr Dolgorukov's fate was sealed. He was accused as follows: 'In November 1920, he organized anti-Soviet and coun-terrevolutionary formations in Czechoslovakia, and from 1939 on, chaired the "Union of Russian Emigrant Organizations in Czechoslovakia."'[50] The OSO of the NKVD sentenced Dolgorukov to five years in prison. In September 1946, he arrived in Vladimir Prison.[51] Three years later the OSO of the MGB extended his term, and on November 10, 1951, the 86-year-old prince died in the Vladimir Prison hospital.

Sergei Postnikov, founder of the Russian Archive in Prague, was also arrested in May 1945. The Gestapo had arrested him previously in 1941, but released him in 1943. SMERSH was interested in Postnikov because Soviet security services were extremely anxious to get access to the Russian Archive. It contained information about the majority of the Russian emigrants in Europe. After the war the Czechoslovak government decided to give the archive to the Soviet Academy of Sciences.[52] However, it was taken by the NKVD, and in December 1945, a train consisting of nine cars loaded with 650 boxes of documents and guarded by NKVD troops arrived in Moscow. The documents were immediately classified and the NKVD used them to compose a list of 18,000 names of wanted emigrants in Europe. On June 6, 1946, a new wave of arrests of Russians named on the list began in Prague.

The OSO sentenced Postnikov to five years in the labor camps. After his term he was exiled to the city of Nikopol in Southern Russia. Luckily, he survived, and returned to Prague in 1955.

Additionally, in May 1945, SMERSH operatives of the 1st Ukrainian Front arrested about 1,000 Ukrainian emigrants. They were brought to Kiev, where their cases were investigated by the Ukrainian NKGB. Tried by the Military Tribunal of the NKVD troops of the Kiev Military District, most of the arrestees were sentenced to terms of ten to twenty-five years in labor camps.

Thousands of ROA privates and officers became SMERSH's main target in Czechoslovakia. As Romanov wrote, on May 7, 1945, 'not far from Pibran, the Czechs [Czech partisans] seized General Vlasov's assistant, his chief of staff General [Fyodor] Trukhin, and handed him over to a SMERSH operational group. The Czechs hanged Trukhin's deputy, Colonel [Vladimir] Boyarsky, on the spot.'[53] Later, American officials handed more of Vlasov's soldiers over to SMERSH.

On May 12, Vlasov was caught near Prague in the American zone. Major Gen. Yevgenii Fominykh, Commander of the 25th Tank Corps, and Colonel Zubkov, his head of staff, reported to the Military Council of the 1st Ukrainian Front:

Intelligence reconnaissance…showed that Vlasov's 1st Division under the command of former General Buyanichenko [incorrect spelling of Bunyachenko], Vlasov, and his staff were there…

Captain [Mikhail] Yakushev [commander of a battalion in the 162nd Tank Brigade] drove to the head of the column [of the 1st ROA Division] and stopped his car across the road…

After approaching Vlasov's car, Com.[rade] Yakushev found Vlasov hiding under a blanket and shielded by a translator and a woman.

Vlasov refused to follow Yakushev's order to get out of his car and follow Yakushev to the headquarters of the 162nd Tank Brigade. His reason was that he was going to the American Army headquarters and that they were on the territory controlled by American troops.

Only after Yakushev threatened to shoot Vlasov on the spot was Vlasov forced to take a place in the car. On the way Vlasov tried to jump out of the car, but he was recaptured…

Yakushev handed Vlasov over to Colonel Mishchenko [Commander of the 162nd Tank Brigade].

In a conversation with Com.[rade] Mishchenko, Vlasov repeated that he needed to go to the American headquarters.

After a short conversation, on May 12 [1945], at 18:00, Com.[rade] Mishchenko brought Vlasov to me…

After questioning Vlasov and talking to him, I suggested that he write an order to all [his] units to give up arms and join our side.

Vlasov agreed and immediately wrote the order.

The order was typed in four copies and signed by Vlasov…[54]

On May 12, 1945, at 22:00, Vlasov was brought to the headquarters of the 13th Army. Colonel Zubkov, head of the Staff of the 25th Tank Corps, and Lieutenant Colonel Simonov, head of the OKR SMERSH, escorted him. On May 13, he was handed over to the OKR SMERSH of the 13th Army. Most probably, Fominykh and Zubkov fabricated the story that Vlasov, a man almost six feet tall, had tried to hide under a blanket in his car. It is also unclear whether Vlasov or Fominykh wrote the order to the troops because Bunyachenko's name was misspelled in it the same way as in Fominykh's report. Furthermore, knowing the Soviet treatment of traitors, it is hard to believe that Vlasov himself wrote the order's last phrase: 'The safety of everyone's life and their return to the Motherland without repercussions are guaranteed.'[55]

In a 1996 interview, Yakushev described the details of Vlasov's seizure more realistically than in his report, and the story was different.[56] In fact, there was a jeep with American officers in Vlasov's column, and a second jeep with Americans arrived after the officers in the first jeep contacted their headquarters by radio when the incident started. Yakushev claimed that to prevent an American intervention, he told them that Vlasov was a traitor and he would bring him to the American headquarters. It remains unclear how he could explain all this to the Americans in Russian. Probably, the Americans simply did not understand what was going on and did not intervene.

According to Yakushev's account, he climbed into Vlasov's car and ordered Vlasov's driver to turn around and drive to the Soviet-controlled territory instead of going to the American headquarters. Vlasov tried to escape, but Yakushev threatened to shoot him. Apparently, Vlasov was unarmed and could not resist. At 8:00 p.m. Yakushev handed Vlasov over to Major General Fominykh.

Abakumov immediately informed Beria of Vlasov's capture:

> According to the SMERSH Directorate of the 1st Ukrainian Front report, on May 12 of this year [1945], the traitor Vlasov was detained near the city of Prague. He was going by car in the direction of the Allies.
>
> On the suggestion of…Maj. Gen. Fominykh, Vlasov ordered his servicemen to join the Red Army's side. Yesterday a division of 10,000 men surrendered to our troops.
>
> I have ordered head of the SMERSH Directorate of the 1st Ukrainian Front, Lt. Gen. [Nikolai] Osetrov, to bring Vlasov under heavy guard to the Main Directorate SMERSH.
>
> Abakumov.[57]

Vlasov was transported to Moscow and placed in Lubyanka Prison as Prisoner No. 31, which meant that he was held as a secret prisoner in Cell 31. Abakumov was waiting to conduct the first interrogation by himself.

CHAPTER 24

The End of Abwehr

Hans Piekenbrock, head of Abwehr I from 1939 to March 1943, was among SMERSH's important prisoners captured in May 1945 not far from Prague. Promoted to Major General in April 1943, he commanded the 208th Infantry Division, which participated in the Kursk Battle in Russia, the biggest tank battle and the greatest German tank failure. In March 1944, Piekenbrock became Lieutenant General, and his division fought in Ukraine, Poland, Slovakia, and Silesia. While Piekenbrock was fighting, the Abwehr ceased to exist as an independent intelligence organization.

Abwehr's Decline

The Abwehr's decline occurred gradually in 1943–44. In mid-March 1943, Canaris, together with Piekenbrock, Erwin Lahousen (head of

Abwehr II) and Franz von Bentivegni (head of Abwehr III) visited the headquarters of Field Marshal Günther von Kluge, commander of the German Army Group Center, located near Smolensk. General Henning von Tresckow, chief of Kluge's General Staff, and his adjutant Fabian von Schlabrendorff, were also present at the meeting. All participants came to a mutual understanding that, as von Schlabrendorff put it, 'Only Hitler's death will put an end to this mad slaughter of people in the concentration camps and in the armies fighting this criminal war.'[1] A few days later Schlabrendorff smuggled a time bomb, disguised as bottles of cognac, onto an aircraft that carried Hitler. The bomb failed to detonate because of the extreme cold in the aircraft's cargo space. Schlabrendorff managed to retrieve the bomb. Later, on July 20, 1944 the Gestapo arrested Schlabrendorff and he was kept in a number of concentration camps. On May 5, 1945 the Fifth U.S. Army liberated Schlabrendorff along with a group of other prisoners of the Dachau concentration camp.

In the spring of 1943, Wilhelm Keitel, commander in chief of the High Command of the Armed Forces (OKW), irritated by the Abwehr's inefficiency, ordered the replacement of heads of the Abwehr I-III.[2] Soon Piekenbrock and Lahousen were sent to the Eastern Front and did not participate in the further plots to kill Hitler. From March 1943 onwards, Colonel Georg Hansen headed Abwehr I, while Colonel Wessel Freiherr von Freytag-Loringhoven headed Abwehr II. Both Hansen and Freytag-Loringhoven were also members of the anti-Hitler plot, and in July 1944 Freytag-Loringhoven even supplied Graf Claus von Stauffenberg with explosives for killing Hitler.

In February 1944, Hitler dismissed Canaris after the Gestapo arrested two high-ranking Abwehr officers on charges of treason, and Colonel Hansen replaced him.[3] In June 1944, Abwehr I and II were merged together and became the Militarisches Amt (or Mil Amt) of Walter Schellenberg's SD. Hansen headed Mil Amt until he was arrested as a member of the July 20, 1944 plot, and Schellenberg headed both the SD and Mil Amt until the end of the war. In the Mil Amt Erwin Stolze, who was previously responsible for diversions in Soviet territory, was charged with the training of terrorists sent to the rear of the Allied troops.[4]

On July 22, 1944, two days after von Stauffenberg's unsuccessful attempt on Hitler's life, the Gestapo arrested Hansen and, on the next day, Canaris.[5] Freytag-Loringhoven committed suicide on July 26, before the Gestapo could get him. Soon, on September 8, Hansen was executed in Plötenzee Prison in Berlin.

In August 1944, the Gestapo investigators found Canaris's diary in which he had written that since 1938 he headed a resistance group within the Abwehr. The diary was given to the above-mentioned Rattenhuber, head of Hitler's guards, who handed it over to Ernst Kaltenbrunner, head of the RSHA. Hitler read it on April 6, 1945, and on his order, the next day a special SS tribunal sentenced Canaris to death.

Two days later he was hanged slowly with a piano-wire noose in the Flossenbürg concentration camp. The SS-executioners were in a hurry to finish off Canaris: American troops were not far away from the camp. Before he left his cell, Canaris tapped out a message to an imprisoned Danish officer Hans Lunding, who was in the neighboring cell: 'I am dying for my country. I have a clear conscience...I did no more than my patriotic duty in trying to oppose the criminal madness of Hitler, who was leading Germany to its ruin. It was in vain, as I know now that my country will go under, as I knew already in 1942.'[6]

After Hansen and Canaris's arrests more reorganization of the former Abwehr followed. Abwehr III was divided among the SD, the Gestapo, and the OKW.[7] The latter part, known as the Truppenabwehr, included counterintelligence in the German troops, navy, and air force, as well as in the POW camps and the German Field Police (GFP). Part of the Brandenburg-800 division (within Abwehr II) joined Otto Skorzeny's special commandos unit SS-Jagdverband attached to the SD. The other part was included in the tank corps Grossdeutschland.

On December 1, 1944, Walli I and III were transferred to Schellenberg's Mil Amt and became its Branch F. Later, in April 1945, escaping the advancing Soviet troops, Walli I moved to Bavaria.

As for Bentivegni, he headed Abwehr III until March 1944, when he joined the army. In August 1944, Bentivegni was promoted to Major General, and in January 1945, to Lieutenant General. On May 15, 1945 SMERSH operatives captured Bentivegni, at the time commander of the 81st Infantry Division, among numerous prisoners taken in the Courland Pocket in Latvia.[8] The Army Group Courland of about 181,000 men was the last German unit that fought on Soviet territory until their surrender on May 9, 1945.

Bruno Streckenbach, Heydrich's former deputy in the RSHA and the Einsatzgruppen supervisor, was also captured in Courland. In September 1942, he was transferred from the RSHA to the Waffen SS, and from April 1944 onwards, Streckenbach commanded the 19th SS Waffen Grenadier Division, part of the Latvian Legion. Later promoted to Waffen-SS Lieutenant General, he was captured on May 22, 1945.[9]

On May 31, 1945 SMERSH operatives caught Erwin Stolze in Berlin in civilian clothes.[10] In 1947, he testified: 'At the beginning of April 1945...Walter Schellenberg issued an instruction that prescribed...in case the Red Army threatens to take over Berlin, to prepare false documents in advance, to destroy operational documents, to go into hiding and wait for new instructions. I followed this order.'[11] In the underground, Stolze headed a network of 800 Nazi terrorists.

In February 1946, Soviet prosecutors presented testimonies of Piek-enbrock, Bentivegni, and Stolze, written during interrogations in GUKR SMERSH, at the International Nuremberg Trial.[12] Lahousen, a rare survivor of the Abwehr resistance, personally testified in the courtroom against the Nazi defendants.

Piekenbrock, Bentivegni, Stolze, and Streckenbach remained in Moscow MGB investigation prisons until February 1952, when the Military Tribunal of the Moscow Military District sentenced Stolze to death, and Bentivegni and Streckenbach, to twenty-five years in labor camps.[13] On March 26, 1952 Stolze was executed.

However, the Military Collegium changed Bentivegni and Strecken-bach's punishment to imprisonment, and convicted Piekenbrock to the same term. After spending three years in Vladimir Prison, in October 1955 the three were released and returned to Germany.

The heads of the FHO (Foreign Armies East) and Walli met different ends. During the July 20, 1944 attempt on Hitler's life, General Reinhard Gehlen was sick, and his deputy, Gerhard Wessel, managed to destroy Gehlen's correspondence with the plotters in time.[14] As a result, Gehlen luckily escaped the Gestapo's attention, but during the last months of 1944 Hitler was outraged by the pessimistic reports of Gehlen.

At the time, Gehlen had already organized his own plot. In spring 1944, he developed a plan to save the FHO's records for the West. By February 1945, Wessel and Hermann Baun (head of Walli I), Heinz Danko Herre and Horst Hiemenz (the former and the last head of the FHO's Gruppe II), and Albert Schöller (deputy head of Gruppe II) participated in Gehlen's efforts.[15] In April 1945, Wessel succeeded Gehlen as FHO head, and the plotters safely hid the Walli I and FHO archives.

The Gehlen plotters surrendered to American military intelligence (G-2, War Department).[16] Gehlen's operation was allowed to continue using the retrieved archives. Gehlen's group, which included his immediate staff of 350 men, moved to Pullach, a suburb of Munich, and became known as the Gehlen Organization. On Gehlen's request, thousands of Abwehr, SD and SS officers were released from internment camps in violation of the de-Nazification program and joined Gehlen's staff, which reached nearly 3,000 men. Hans Schmalschläger, former head of Stab Walli and Walli III within it, headed the Nuremberg branch of the Gehlen Organization.[17]

The Organization worked under CIA control and was its main source of information on the Soviet Union and Eastern Europe. In 1956, it became the main part of the newly formed Bundesnachrichtendienst (BND or Federal Intelligence Service) of West Germany. Gehlen headed the BND until 1968.

Hermann Baun, former head of Walli I, got his own facility, and his network reached 125 agents in Western Germany.[18] Over a few years Baun completed about 800 reports on the Soviet military. In 1947, he organized a successful secret transfer of the family of Gustav Hilger, former Nazi Foreign Office official and a specialist on Russian affairs who now worked for the Americans, from the Soviet Zone to West Berlin, despite the MGB's surveillance of the family. But because Baun recruited a number of shady people and con men, he was dismissed and died in 1951. His group was included in the Gehlen Organization.

Gehlen's use of high-level Abwehr and SS war criminals as staff members compromised the BND. The hiring of Wilhelm Krichbaum, the former Field Police Chief, was especially devastating. He had already been a Soviet agent when, in 1951, he recruited another double agent, Heinz Felfe, the former SD officer who worked for both the British and the Soviets.[19] In November 1961, Felfe was arrested on spying charges, tried, and sentenced to a 14-year imprisonment. In 1969, he was exchanged for eighteen West German and three American agents imprisoned in the USSR.[20] Gehlen retired in 1968, and for the next ten years Gerhard Wessel, Gehlen's former deputy, headed the BND.

One Who Escaped SMERSH

Boris Smyslowsky, a former White Army officer, was, quite possibly, the most successful—and the luckiest—Russian who served in the Abwehr. Smyslowsky created a very efficient intelligence organization made up of Russian émigrés, and he was one of the few high-ranking Russian military collaborators not caught by SMERSH.

Smyslowsky was born in 1897 near St. Petersburg, into an officer's family.[21] After graduating from a military school in 1915, he participated in World War I and then in the Civil War, serving in the White troops under the command of General Anton Denikin. Later Smyslowsky lived in Poland and became a Polish citizen. In 1928, he moved to Germany, where he attended military courses. In 1939, after the German occupation of Poland, Smyslowsky became head of the Warsaw office of the White Russian military organization ROVS, which was called the Association of Russian Military Unions in Nazi Germany.

At the beginning of the war with the Soviet Union, Smyslowsky joined the Abwehr under the alias 'von Regenau.' In July 1941, the 1st Russian Foreign Educational Battalion attached to the Army Group North was organized under his command.[22] After a few months, it became the Northern Group that eventually comprised twelve Russian battalions. The new Russian recruits from White emigrants and new POW volunteers were trained in the Abwehr school in Warsaw.

In March 1942, the Northern Group became the Sonderstab R (Special Staff Russia) with headquarters in Warsaw under the cover name of the Eastern Construction Company 'Gilgen.' It was attached to the Referat

IX of Walli I and was supervised by Hermann Baun, head of Walli I. The Sonderstab R consisted of 20 high-ranking White Russian officers and a few hundred young men from Abwehr schools and intelligence groups. It collected intelligence mostly on partisans and the NKVD. The whole Soviet-occupied territory was divided into five (subsequently reduced to four) regions with staffs in the cities of Simferopol, Kiev, Chernigov, Minsk, and Pskov (later Vyru, in Estonia). There were also local representatives within each region. All units of the Sonderstab R's network had cover names of building and supply organizations.

The net obtained information from informers recruited among local Communist Party members, members of the Komsomol, and former Soviet functionaries. They were usually forced to work for the Sonderstab R under threat of being arrested or sent to Germany as slave laborers. Agents were sent to partisan detachments as well.

The units sent their reports to Warsaw by couriers and collaborated with the SD and the German Field Police. It wasn't until August 1944 that Soviet counterintelligence (NKGB) collected enough information to draw a general chart of the Sonderstab R organization.[23]

In 1943, Smyslowsky's intelligence net was renamed Sonderdivision R (Division for Special Task Russia) and became part of the Wehrmacht.[24] Later, regional detachments were reorganized, and the center in Warsaw became a directorate made up of the Russian, Ukrainian, and Belorussian departments, which consisted of intelligence and partisan sections. Sonderdivision R collected information on Soviet troops and the situation in both unoccupied Soviet territory and the territory liberated by the Red Army. For the latter purpose, numerous agents were left behind the front line, and in 1943, SMERSH and NKGB discovered and arrested up to 700 such agents. On the basis of information collected by the partisan sections, the FHO published a classified book, *Proceedings of the Partisan War*, detailing the organization, tactics, and propaganda work of Soviet partisans.

At the end of 1943, the Gestapo arrested Smyslowsky on charges of alleged support of the anti-Nazi Polish Home Army (Armija Krajowa) and the Ukrainian Insurgent Army (UPA), and the Sonderdivision R was disbanded.[25] Smyslowsky ended up being acquitted and even given an award after intervention on his behalf by Admiral Canaris and Reinhard Gehlen, but the Germans lost the best intelligence net they had ever had at the Eastern Front.

Later Smyslowsky headed the Staff for Special Tasks attached to the OKH, which continued doing intelligence work. Finally, in February 1945, his 1st Russian National Division was renamed first the Green Army for Special Tasks and then the 1st Russian National Army; in addition, he was promoted to Major General. To confuse Soviet intelligence and counterintelligence, Smyslowsky changed his name to Artur Holmston.

Formally, his army was an independent ally of the Wehrmacht and maintained neutrality toward the United States and England. However, it was not a real army because it consisted of only one battalion of about 600 men. Major Yevgenii Messner, a former White officer who was appointed head of the propaganda department in Smyslowsky's army, recalled that half of the battalion's men were dressed in civilian clothes and only a quarter of the battalion had rifles. He added: 'Holmston was always absent while being occupied with the intelligence work and was not involved in the organization of the corps and its HQ.'[26]

By April 1945, Smyslowsky had moved his army to the Austrian town of Feldkirch, where Grand Duke Vladimir Kirillovich, head of the Imperial Family of Russia, and his court joined Smyslowsky while escaping the Red Army. On May 2–3, Smyslowsky and a group of his 494 men and women crossed the border with Liechtenstein. This group was the only Russian unit that had fought against the Red Army that was not handed over to SMERSH or the NKVD by the Western Allies. However, neither Liechtenstein nor Switzerland issued the Grand Duke an exit visa and he went to Spain.

In Liechtenstein, Allen Dulles, the OSS representative in Switzerland, and other intelligence experts interviewed Smyslowsky about the Soviet Union.[27] On August 16, 1945, a Soviet commission representing the Directorate of the Plenipotentiary on the Repatriation headed by General Fyodor Golikov, met with Smyslowsky and other refugees. Golikov was the former head of the GRU (military intelligence), while his repatriation directorate was, in fact, an arm of SMERSH and the NKVD. The commission tried to force the authorities to extradite Smyslowsky and 59 of his officers as war criminals, but Liechtenstein's government refused to do so because the commission had no proof.[28] It is amazing that a country with a population of 12,141 and only eleven policemen dared to stand up to the Soviets. But eventually about 200 of Smyslowsky's men decided to go back to the Soviet Union.

In 1947, Smyslowsky, his wife, and about 100 Russians went to Argentina. *Time* magazine wrote in 1953: 'Pressed by the Kremlin, the tiny principality [Liechtenstein] ordered the general [Smyslowsky] to leave. With the help of the Russian Orthodox archbishop of Argentina, a friend of Juan Perón, he got permission to take the last of his men to Buenos Aires.'[29]

In Perón's Argentina, Smyslowsky's experience in the Abwehr was in demand: he taught the tactics of anti-partisan war at the military academy and became Perón's adviser on the same topic. From the mid-1960s to 1973, Smyslowsky was an adviser to the West German General Staff. During his last 13 years he lived in Liechtenstein, and he died there in 1988.

Smyslowsky always remained a Russian ultra-nationalist. In 1946, he addressed a group of young émigrés: 'You are glorious descendants of those who have been building for thousands of years the greatest Empire in the world. You are descendants not of the European, but of our own, pure Russian culture with its geniuses of state organization, unconditional loyalty, and military valor.'[30] Although these bizarre notions about Russia's exceptional role in history became popular again in the Russian society of the 2000s, Smyslowsky's prediction of the end of Soviet Communism was naive. In 1953, he told *Time*: 'The world should know that foreign armies will never conquer Russia. Only a nationalist army of Russians, fighting Communism but not Russia, can ever hope to succeed.'

There is a small 'Russian Monument' in Liechtenstein commemorating the asylum given to Smyslowsky's army. In 1993, the French film director Robert Enrico released the movie *Vent d'est* (*East Wind*) about Smyslowsky and his men's escape to Liechtenstein. The British actor Malcolm McDowell played Smyslowsky in the movie.

Part VIII. The End of WWII

CHAPTER 25

Investigations in Moscow

At the end of 1944, Stalin showed his appreciation of the SMERSH, NKVD, and NKGB operatives who worked in Moscow by considerably improving their living conditions. On September 24, 1944 the GKO issued an order 'On the Improvement of Food Supply of Operational Officers of the NKVD, NKGB, and SMERSH.'[1] Now the food rations of 119,700 high-ranking officers, including those in SMERSH, became equal to the rations of *sovpartaktiv* (Soviet and Party high-level functionaries). 11,553 officers were given the same rations as those received by Central Committee members, commissars, and their deputies, which meant being able to eat in the Kremlin's dining facilities without restriction and receiving special rations for their families. Rations were given to 27,200 officers of the second grade, and the rest, of the third grade; these were the so-called '*liter* [marked with a letter] "A" and "B" rations.'

Heads of directorates and departments (and their deputies) in commissariats were given 'A' food rations, while lower functionaries received the 'B' rations. In December 1942, the 'A' ration included the following for one person, per month: six kilograms of meat, approximately one kilogram of butter, 1.5 kilograms of buckwheat and pasta, seven kilograms of potatoes, and fifteen eggs.[2] By comparison, at that time a worker at a military plant received 800 grams of poor-quality bread and one bowl of soup per day.

Prisoners in Moscow, 1944–45

As the Red Army advanced to the west, Moscow's investigation prisons began to fill up with prisoners of war. Based on its operational lists prepared in Moscow, SMERSH field UKRs issued warrants for, and arrested, increasing numbers of important German, Hungarian, Romanian, and other foreign military figures and Russian émigrés and sent them to the capital. But most of the arrived prisoners belonged to the category of *spetskontingent* (special contingent)—that is, they were detainees held in investigation prisons without arrest warrants. Many members of the *spetskontingent* were not considered to have been formally arrested until 1950–52, when MGB investigators finally wrote arrest warrants before trials.

Nevertheless, all foreign prisoners were listed as POWs in Moscow investigation prisons. Lacking its own investigation prisons, GUKR SMERSH used two of the above-mentioned NKGB prisons: the Interior, or Lubyanka, located inside the NKGB/SMERSH building in the center of Moscow; and Lefortovo, a reconstructed palace built in the early 18th century in a remote district of Moscow. Prisoners who did not cooperate during interrogations, either by not giving the testimony that the SMERSH investigators wanted to hear, or by not admitting guilt, were transferred to the third investigation prison, Sukhanovka, where conditions were extremely harsh. SMERSH also had a section in the enormous Butyrka Prison belonging to the NKVD, which remained an NKVD/MVD investigation prison until 1950, when it was transferred to the MGB. Considered POWs, the SMERSH arrestees received the same food ration as those held in the NKVD POW camps. To encourage good behavior, investigators gave cooperative prisoners an officer's ration, which was much better than a soldier's.

Typically, Abakumov or one of his deputies would initially interrogate a newly arrived prisoner, often for several hours. Following this, a prisoner was commonly placed under the jurisdiction of Sergei Kartashov's 2nd or Aleksandr Leonov's 6th (Investigation) GUKR Department. In Kartashov's department German-speaking prisoners were questioned by investigators of its 1st Section.

Investigation of German POWs

No information about the 1st Section of the 2nd GUKR Department has ever been published. I was able to establish the names of officers of this section by studying personal files of foreign prisoners at the Russian State Military (formerly Special) Archive (RGVA). As already mentioned, two files were opened for each SMERSH, NKGB, or NKVD prisoner under investigation: the Investigation File and the Prison File.

The Investigation File contained primarily transcripts (*protokoly* in Russian) of interrogations. When the investigation was closed, the accused had to look through this file, which was also presented at the trial after the chief USSR prosecutor or his deputy concluded that the investigation was finished. After conviction, the prisoner's Investigation File went to the MGB/KGB (now FSB) Central Archive for storage. These files relevant to political cases are still essentially unavailable to researchers. Only the closest relatives of the rehabilitated former political convicts are allowed to read these files, and a researcher can examine an Investigation File at the FSB Central Archive only with notarized permission from direct relatives.

The Prison File contained documents about the prisoner's arrest and his life in investigation prisons, including orders for transfers within the same prison or to other prisons. The file also included investigators' instructions on special forms to prison personnel (a separate NKGB/MGB department not subordinate to the investigation departments) to bring the prisoner in for interrogation. The final documents in the Prison File contained the investigator's conclusion concerning the charges to be brought against the prisoner in court and the applicable punishment (before the trial!). The investigator's superiors and Abakumov or his deputy also signed the investigator's conclusion.

Most GUKR SMERSH prisoners were tried by the Special Board (OSO) of the NKVD (and, from November 1946 onwards, of the MGB), or by the Military Collegium of the Supreme Court. After the trial, the convicted person was transferred to NKVD jurisdiction. The Prison File now became a Personal File, containing copies of trial and sentencing documents as well as the investigator's recommendation as to whether the convict should be sent to a punishment prison or a labor camp. The Personal File went with the convict, and documents about his prison or camp life were added. Upon a prisoner's release the Personal File was archived. The Personal Files of foreign prisoners arrested by SMERSH, the NKGB, and NKVD ended up in the Russian State Military Archive in Moscow. If a convict died in prison, his or her Personal File went to the archive of the camp or prison's local NKVD/MVD or MGB (in the case of special prisons) branch.

According to the materials in the files, when a prisoner arrived at the 2nd GUKR SMERSH Department, at first its head Kartashov or his deputy, Nikolai Burashnikov, inspected the file and, frequently, also interrogated the detainee. Kartashov was known as an extremely capable and efficient officer.[3] No information is available on Burashnikov except his name surfaced in documents of the late 1930s, when he headed the 3rd Department (counterintelligence) of the NKVD's Moscow Branch.[4] After being interrogated by Kartashov or Burashnikov, the prisoner came under the jurisdiction of the 1st Section, headed by Lieutenant Colonel Yakov Sverchuk, or of other sections of the department. Sverchuk worked in the NKVD from 1938 onwards.

Kartashov, Burashnikov, and Sverchuk, and other investigators who did not know German, conducted interrogations through their young colleagues—Boris Solovov, Oleg Bubnov, Daniil Kopelyansky, Vladimir Smirnitsky, Anna Stesnova, and others. All of these young officers were professional German translators who had graduated just before World War II. Abakumov affectionately dubbed his favorite, Solovov, 'the teacher' because Solovov wore glasses.[5] He personally recommended Solovov as a translator for the International Nuremberg Trial. SMERSH prisoners had a different opinion of Solovov. One was the former German counselor in Ploesti (Romania), Count Ruediger Adelmann, remembered him as 'a very intelligent but mean person.'[6] Frequently, Solovov's friend Pavel Grishaev, an investigator in the 4th Department and then the 6th Department, also served as a translator at interrogations. In 1946 Grishaev, like Solovov, was sent to the International Nuremberg Trial as a translator.

Sverchuk's staff of officers was small, only about ten people. Besides the German section, other sections dealt with Finnish, Japanese, and Russian prisoners. While formally the 2nd Department was operational, meaning that it obtained intelligence from prisoners and did not investigate criminal cases, interrogations often led to the opening of a case against a prisoner. Usually interrogations took place in the offices on the fourth and sixth floors of the main Lubyanka building, or in a separate interrogation building of Lefortovo Prison. Nikolai Mesyatsev, former investigator of the 2nd SMERSH Department, described the Lefortovo offices:

> The two-story investigation building in Lefortovo Prison was big. Only a few investigators worked on the first floor, and the rest worked in the offices on the second floor, arranged along a long corridor... Every investigator usually worked in the same office. There were a stool and a small table for a prisoner under investigation located in front of the investigator's desk in the office. There was also a sofa covered with leather in front of a window where the investigator could rest between interrogations or even sleep at night.[7]

Frequently female stenographers were present during interrogations. Zinaida Kozina, Abakumov's personal stenographer, volunteered to work with investigators. She recalled the night interrogations in Lefortovo:

> The routine was the following. At 9:00 p.m. a bus was waiting at the 4th entrance [of the Lubyanka building]. It took us—me, two other women-stenographers, and investigators—to Lefortovo. There we went to offices for interrogations. At 5:00 a.m. the interrogations were over, and the bus took us to the metro station. Everybody went home... At 10:00 a.m. we were at work [in Lubyanka] again. It was necessary to immediately write down all transcripts of interrogations and to give them to the investigators.[8]

In some cases prisoners were also interrogated in Suhkanovo Prison. In many cases the 2nd and 4th or 6th GUKR SMERSH departments interrogated the same prisoners. Some of the German diplomats who arrived in Moscow from Bucharest in September 1944 were initially the responsibility of the 6th Department. For instance, Aleksandr Leonov, head of this department, personally interrogated Fritz Schellhorn, former German General Counselor, a week after his arrival. Then Schellhorn and other German diplomats were transferred to Kartashov's 2nd Department and the investigation continued by Kartashov's officers.

If a prisoner had no important intelligence information, his case was closed quickly and prepared for trial by the OSO. But the cases of important prisoners like witnesses of Hitler's death and some German diplomats turned into long-term investigations, sometimes lasting as long as eight years.

Case Example: Major Joachim Kuhn

The case of Major Joachim Kuhn, opened by the 2nd Department in mid-1944, was typical for an investigation that continued until the 1950s. Kuhn was a member of the failed military plot to assassinate Hitler on July 20, 1944. Kuhn's commander, Major General Henning von Tresckow, was a close associate of Colonel Claus von Stauffenberg, the would-be assassin.[9] Kuhn also knew von Stauffenberg well and used to visit him because Kuhn's fiancée, Maria-Gabriele, was the daughter of von Stauffenberg's cousin Clemens.[10]

Among the military plotters, Kuhn's responsibility was to supply the conspirators with explosives and handmade bombs that he kept secretly at the HQ of the German Infantry High Command in Mauerwald (now Mamerki, Poland), not far from Hitler's HQ 'Wolfschanze' (Wolf's Lair). In March 1943, the plotters made their first assassination attempt on Hitler during his visit to the Army Group Center HQ in Smolensk, in Soviet-occupied territory. As already mentioned, following the visit, before Hitler's plane took off, Fabian von Schlabrendorff, Tresckow's cousin and aide-de-camp, smuggled a concealed bomb onto the plane, while Erwin von Lahousen, head of Abwehr II, informed Admiral Canaris of the plan.[11]

The bomb did not detonate while the plane was in the air, and Kuhn and Tresckow began to plot anew. In autumn 1943, Tresckow suggested smuggling Friedrich Werner von Schulenburg through the front line in an attempt to reach Stalin for peace negotiations.[12] Von Schulenburg, a former German ambassador to Moscow who knew Molotov and Stalin well, was a high-level Foreign Ministry official and a member of the Resistance. However, Field Marshal Günther von Kluge, commander in chief of the Army Group Center and a long-time member of the military opposition, did not support this plan.

On July 21, 1944, the day after von Stauffenberg's unsuccessful assassination attempt, Tresckow drove to the 28th Rifle Division to see Major Kuhn, who had been transferred from Tresckow's HQ to this front division. After Tresckow told Kuhn everything he knew about Stauffenberg's failure, he drove into the no-man's land between the German and Soviet front lines. There Tresckow pretended to exchange fire with the enemy, and then committed suicide by blowing himself up with a grenade.[13]

Kuhn made a different choice—he went to the Soviets. His divisional commander, General Gustav von Ziehlberg, told Kuhn that he had an order to bring him to Berlin, where officials suspected Kuhn of having provided von Stauffenberg with explosives for the attack on Hitler.[14] In fact, Stauffenberg received plastic explosives from Kuhn's colleagues who also worked at the Mauerwald HQ. Apparently, von Ziehlberg expected Kuhn to commit suicide to escape arrest.

Instead, on July 27, 1944, Kuhn deserted to the Soviet troops. SMERSH operatives of the 2nd Belorussian Front arrested him and sent him to Moscow.[15] In Germany, because of Kuhn's desertion, von Ziehlberg was put on trial and sentenced to nine months in prison. His case was later reopened, and this time he was sentenced to death. On February 2, 1945, von Ziehlberg was executed.

In Moscow, Kuhn was jailed in Lubyanka Prison. On September 2, 1944, he wrote a lengthy testimony concerning his personal involvement in the German military opposition and conversations with von Stauffenberg and other opposition leaders, and provided a detailed description of German high-ranking opposition leaders whom he knew personally.[16] Investigator Daniil Kopelyansky from Kartashov's department translated Kuhn's testimony into Russian.[17] On September 23, Abakumov reported to Georgii Malenkov on the interrogation, enclosing a Russian translation of Kuhn's testimony and arriving at an unfavorable conclusion: 'Considering Kuhn's [official] denouncement in Germany as a traitor and active participant in the plot, and his testimony that he played a very important role in the plot, it is possible that the Germans sent him [to us] with a special purpose under all these covers... I have already reported this to Comrade Stalin.' A few days later, Kopelyansky's translation was on Stalin's desk and Stalin discussed the Kuhn affair with GKO members.

SMERSH investigators soon concluded that Kuhn's testimony was truthful. From August 12, 1944, until March 1, 1947, they held Kuhn under the operational alias *Joachim Malowitz,* although documents issued in Kartashov's department still listed him under his real name.[18] Twice during this period, on February 17 and 28, 1945, Abakumov ordered SMERSH operatives to take Kuhn into the forest around the village of Mauerwald, in Poland, where he helped them to find a set of plotters' documents hidden in cans and jars.[19] Among the papers, there was Stauffenberg's plan to kill Hitler in 1943 during his stay in the Wolfschanze, and draft orders to military leaders in case the assassination was successful. The Politburo rejected Abakumov's proposal to publish these documents in the press, and the documents were declassified only in the late 1990s.

From the beginning of 1947 until March 1, Kuhn was in the Butyrka Prison hospital, and from March 1, 1947 to April 22, 1948, in an 'MGB special object,' the code name for a carefully guarded MGB dacha (country house) not far from the Malakhovka train station near Moscow.[20] Abakumov ordered that Kuhn be trained for future work in the pro-Soviet East

German administration, but as MGB officers soon discovered, Kuhn had other plans. Placed with Kuhn was another German POW, an informer, who reported to MGB handlers that in private conversations Kuhn criticized the Soviet regime and said that he wanted to defect to the Americans. As a result, on April 22, 1948, Kuhn was returned to Lefortovo Prison and held there for two years. Supposedly, he was subjected to torture.[21]

On April 5, 1950, Kuhn was transferred to Butyrka Prison. Like many other important prisoners investigated by Kartashov's department, Kuhn was finally sentenced by the OSO (MGB) in the autumn of 1951. Convicted as a war criminal, he received a sentence of twenty-five years in a special prison for political prisoners.

From 1949 on, there were three such prisons under MGB supervision—Vladimir, Aleksandrovsk, and Verkhne-Uralsk; previously, they were under the NKVD/MVD jurisdiction. The most important convicts were held in Vladimir Prison not far from Moscow, where they could easily be additionally interrogated, if necessary. Kuhn was placed in Aleksandrovsk Prison near Irkutsk in Siberia. Another Aleksandrovsk inmate was the already mentioned Colonel Otto Armster, former head of the Abwehrstelle (Abwehr post) in Vienna, and also a member of the anti-Hitler plot, as well as a personal friend of Admiral Canaris. On June 21, 1945 he was brought to Moscow by plane and placed in Lefortovo Prison. In the spring of 1950, Armster was transferred to Butyrka. Like Kuhn, Armster was sentenced in 1951 and sent to Aleksandrovsk Prison. Apparently, by 1951, the MGB had already considered members of the anti-Nazi military plot to be unimportant, so these two were jailed far from Moscow.

For some time Kuhn was in solitary confinement, where he started calling himself 'Major General Graf von der Pfaltz-Zweibruecken' and hearing voices.[22] A prison-hospital psychiatrist examined Kuhn and disagreed with the administration's suspicion that he had gone insane. The doctor concluded that Kuhn 'was fit to continue serving his sentence.' Strangely, Kuhn was not transferred to the MVD Psychiatry Hospital in Kazan, as was done in similar cases of insanity.

In January 1956, Kuhn was released and returned to West Germany, where he lived in the town of Bad-Brukenau until his death in 1994. He had no desire to get together with those former plotting colleagues who had survived the Nazi persecution.[23] When two of his prewar friends finally visited him in 1980, Kuhn called himself 'Kronprinz Wilhelm von Hohenzollern.' In December 1997, Kuhn was posthumously politically rehabilitated in Russia.

Investigation of POWs in the NKVD

Important German and other foreign POWs arrested by the NKVD were investigated by the Operational Department of the previously mentioned UPVI (NKVD Directorate for POWs and Interned Persons). The

UPVI was created on Beria's order issued on September 17, 1939, after Soviet troops invaded Poland.[24] It had its own system of POW concentration camps, separate from that of the GULAG labor camps. Not only enemy POWs of various nationalities, but also civilians detained in the occupied territories were kept in these camps. Here is an example of such a camp:

By September 1, 1943, in the NKVD Camp No. 99 there were interned persons of various nationalities and citizenship,

[total of]	958 people
Of them, former Polish POWs	176
Children	94

According to nationalities, the contingent is represented by:

Jews (men, women, and children)	360 people
Poles	181
Germans	121
Spaniards	63
Hungarians	33
Romanians	30
Frenchmen, Russians, Czechs, Estonians, Danes, Finns, etc.	170.[25]

The presence of Jewish child-prisoners is the most shocking in this document. This Camp No. 99, also known as Spaso-Zavodsky Camp, was located in Kazakhstan, near the town of Karaganda—the area where prisoners were used as enslaved coal miners.[26] In 1943, captured enemy privates, not officers, were sent to this camp. Apparently, the Spaniards mentioned were soldiers of the Blue Division that fought near Leningrad in 1941–43, while the Frenchmen were soldiers drafted into the German army in Alsace-Lorraine, annexed by Nazi Germany in 1940.

Beginning in May 1943, Nikolai Ratushnyi was acting head of the UPVI. On August 3, 1943, Nikolai Mel'nikov was appointed his deputy and head of UPVI's 2nd (Operational) Department. Mel'nikov had a long NKVD career, first in foreign intelligence and then in Sudoplatov's 4th NKVD/NKGB Directorate (terrorist acts and diversions), where he headed the 1st Department in charge of foreign countries and POWs.

The Operational Department began investigating important POWs in 1944, but at first it was difficult to select these prisoners out of the general population of German POWs because of the increasing influx. In December 1943, there were about 100,000 POWs in the UPVI camps, while by December 1944, the number had increased to 680,921. Just after World War II, about 2,100,000 POWs (mostly former privates) were working in various branches of Soviet industry in all regions of the USSR.

In order to identify and select important prisoners, Mel'nikov created a net of informers among the POWs.[27] After identifying officers, the Operational Department placed them in separate POW camps for officers. Additionally, special categories of POWs were selected for transfer to a few special UPVI camps: (a) those who had committed atrocities against Soviet citizens; (b) former active fascists and members of the intelligence, counterintelligence, and repressive organs of the enemy; and (c) those POWs who tried to escape from the UPVI camps or were planning to escape.[28] On April 7, 1944, Mel'nikov committed suicide and Amayak Kobulov, former head of the NKVD *rezidentura* (network of spies) in Berlin in 1940–41, was appointed new head of the Operational Department.[29] He was 'a tall, fine-figured, handsome man from the Caucasus with a groomed moustache and black hair.'[30] Major General Il'ya Pavlov, Kobulov's deputy, was the only person on the UPVI staff who was transferred from SMERSH. In 1944, before coming to the UPVI, Pavlov was deputy head of the UKR SMERSH of the 2nd Belorussian Front.

On January 11, 1945, the UPVI was renamed the Main Directorate, becoming the GUPVI, while Ivan Petrov was appointed its head.[31] Already on February 2, Lieutenant General Mikhail Krivenko, former deputy head of the NKVD Main Directorate of the Border Guards, replaced him. His participation in the Katyn Forest massacre has already been mentioned. The 2nd (Operational) Directorate of the GUPVI staff consisted of 71 men, and the activity of its 1st Department was almost identical to that of the 1st Section of the 2nd Department of the GUKR SMERSH.

The most important war criminals and intelligence officers investigated by the Operational Directorate were kept in the NKVD/MVD investigation prisons Butyrka, Taganka, and Sretenka in Moscow. They were tried and convicted by the Military Tribunal of the Moscow Military District or the OSO (NKVD/MVD). Out of more than 400 Soviet labor camps, convicted important POWs were sent only to the camps of Vorkuta or Norilsk. Unimportant POWs were tried by POW camp tribunals and the convicts were sent to the Karlag camp (Kazakhstan) or Siblag camp (Krasnoyarsk Province in Siberia).[32] From 1949 onwards, the most important convicted POWs were held in the MVD Prison in Novocherkassk.

Camp No. 27 in Krasnogorsk

The POWs in Krasnogorsk Camp No. 27 in the Moscow suburbs were the main targets of the 1st Department of the Operational Directorate. In 1943–45, the camp's Zone No. 1 held members of the former German military elite, including Field Marshal Friedrich von Paulus, former commander of the 6th Army; Lieutenant General Arthur Schmidt, former HQ head of the same army; Lieutenant General Vincenz Müller, former commander of the German 12th Army Corps; and Hitler's personal pilot, Lieutenant General Hans Baur.[33] An Anti-Fascist School for the 're-education' of POWs ('Antifa,' in POW jargon) and barracks for its students were located in Zone No. 2. Most of the candidates selected for this school were former German and Austrian soldiers and low-level commanders.

Also held in Camp No. 27 (Zone 1) were the relatives of German political and economic leaders, including Lieutenant Heinrich von Einsiedel, a great-grandson of Chancellor Otto von Bismarck. After his release in 1948, von Einsiedel defected to the Western Zone in Berlin. Another prisoner was Lieutenant Colonel Adolf Victor von Papen, a relative of Franz von Papen, the former German Chancellor. During World War II, Franz von Papen was German envoy to Turkey, and in 1941 he was the target of an unsuccessful assassination attempt by the NKVD/GRU team led by Sudoplatov's deputy Naum Eitingon.[34] There was also Harold Bohlen und Holbach, the youngest son of Gustav Krupp (Gustav von Bohlen), the German 'cannon king,' a defendant in Nuremberg who was related to the American diplomat Charles ('Chip') Bohlen. The latter served as a Russian interpreter for President Franklin D. Roosevelt at the Tehran and Yalta conferences and for President Harry S. Truman, at the Potsdam Conference. Later, from 1953–57, he was American Ambassador to Moscow.

In August 1944, Harold Bohlen, at the time a member of the German military mission in Bucharest, was detained by the Romanian military along with other members of the mission. However, in October Bohlen, together with another officer of the mission, Major Prince Albrecht Hohenzollern, escaped from a concentration camp. Romanian King Mihai, a nephew of Prince Albrecht, organized the escape.[35] Unfortunately for him, Bohlen was caught again and ended up in Camp No. 27. Prince Albrecht managed to hide from the Soviets.

The Romanian and Hungarian generals were also held in Camp No. 27. Japanese POWs were there from August 1946 to September 1948. In 1945–47, a separate 'cottage' (barrack) of the camp held entire families of Polish aristocrats: Radziwills, Krasnickis, Zamoiskis, and Branickis. The NKVD operatives arrested the Radziwill family just after Prince Janusz Radziwill had spent several months under German arrest, suspected of participation in organizing the Warsaw Uprising.[36]

The NKVD first captured Prince Radziwill, a prominent Polish politician, in 1939, after the Soviet annexation of the Polish territory. According to Pavel Sudoplatov, in Lubyanka Prison Beria personally interrogated the prince and supposedly persuaded him to report on Hermann Goering, head of the Luftwaffe (Air Force), whom Radziwill knew well.[37] The NKVD considered Radziwill to be an 'agent of influence' rather than an 'operational agent' (i.e., a spy). An 'agent of influence' might even not have known that he was used in Soviet interests. In 1940, Prince Radziwill was released from prison and returned to Berlin, but he did not receive any instructions from Moscow.

Sudoplatov writes that at the beginning of 1945 he again used Prince Radziwill, who had been captured for the second time.[38] Sudoplatov took the prince as a translator to a dinner with W. Averell Harriman, the American Ambassador, knowing that Radziwill and Harriman were already acquainted. During the dinner Sudoplatov, who introduced himself as 'Pavel Matveyev,' tried to find out what plans for post-war Europe the Americans would bring to the conference in Yalta (February 4–11, 1945). Sudoplatov lied, saying that Radziwill was living in Moscow in exile and was free to travel to Poland and London. In fact, after the meeting Radziwill joined his family incarcerated in Camp No. 27. Both Sudoplatov's stories about Radziwill need verification.

In March 1946, British Ambassador to Moscow Archibald Clark Kerr wrote to Stalin asking him to free the Radziwill family that included two children. The release was postponed until the end of 1947, and Janusz's wife Anna Radziwill died on February 16, 1947, before the family could leave the camp.

The Operational Directorate used Camp No. 27 (Zone 1) for two main purposes: to collect information on elite prisoners through informers, and for ideological brainwashing, preparing German collaborators for future work in the Soviet-occupied zone of Germany. As von Einsiedel wrote in his memoirs, even some German generals, including Vincenz Müller, became NKVD informers and spied on their fellow prisoners.[39]

Informers and collaborators were sent back to Germany early. Thus, by September 1948, General Müller had already been repatriated to East Germany, where he became a Police General.[40] American military counter-intelligence (CIC) twice tried to organize Müller's defection to the West, but the general did not want to go.[41] In contrast, Harold Bohlen and Adolf von Papen, who refused to collaborate with the NKVD officers, were convicted only in 1950. For the alleged spying and 'aiding the international bourgeoisie' they both received sentences of twenty-five years in the labor camps. They were sent to the camps near Sverdlovsk (now Yekaterinburg) and returned to West Germany only in 1955.

In mid-1949, Camp No. 27, known as 'operational-transitional,' became one of seven GUPVI's special 'filtration' camps for vetting the most important POWs of high officer ranks before their repatriation to Germany.[42] As a result, the Operational Directorate selected forty-one generals—'military revenge-seekers'—and opened criminal cases against them.[43] For investigation they were transferred to the MVD investigation prisons in Moscow. In November 1950, Camp No. 27 was closed.

GUPVI/SMERSH Cooperation: Secret German Informers

In 1944–46, the Operational Department/Directorate frequently 'shared' German informers from Camp No. 27 with Kartashov's SMERSH/MGB department in Moscow. Paul-Erchard Hille, the former Nazi journalist and member of the editorial board of Hermann Goebbels's personal paper, *Essener National Zeitung*, is a good example.[44] As his Personal File reveals, Hille was drafted in 1943 and served in the German infantry as a lance corporal. In January 1945, he was taken prisoner in Latvia by the troops of the 3rd Baltic Front, and then held in various POW camps until March 3, 1945 when he was moved to Moscow's Lefortovo Prison. He must already have been a known informer; otherwise it would have been very unusual for SMERSH investigators to place an NKVD POW with SMERSH prisoners. From March 22 to April 4, Hille shared a cell with Vilmos Langfelder, Raoul Wallenberg's assistant and driver. Langfelder and Wallenberg arrived in Moscow on February 6, 1945, and from then on, were investigated by Kartashov's department.

After sharing a cell with Langfelder, Hille was transferred to the NKVD Butyrka Prison, where he had several cell mates. In May 1945, Yakov Schweitzer, one of the main investigators of the GUPVI's Operational Directorate, interrogated him. Interrogations continued in October of 1945 after Hille's transfer to Camp No. 27, where Schweitzer and Nikolai Lyutyi, who supervised informers, questioned him.[23] Lyutyi's interrogation or, most probably, *beseda* (a confidential conversation), points directly to Hille as a cell informer.

In January 1946, Hille was again in Butyrka Prison, where he spent from the end of February to the end of April in Cell 288 with Heinz Linge, former personal valet to Hitler. During this period, the whole Operational Directorate and Amayak Kobulov himself were preoccupied with investigating the circumstances of Hitler's death. Linge, Baur, and some other witnesses of Hitler's suicide came under intense interrogation. As Linge recalled in 1956, 'the subject of these interrogations was mainly the question [of] whether Hitler was dead or alive... During these interrogations I was always maltreated [i.e., beaten].'[46] NKVD investigators held each witness who was interrogated about Hitler's death in a cell with an informer and, moreover, these cells were bugged. The documents in Hille's file reveal that while Linge was his cell mate, Schweitzer, who was investigating Linge's case, interrogated Hille several times. Hille told Schweitzer whatever Linge tried to conceal from the investigators.[47] In May 1946, after fulfilling his role as cell spy, Hille was returned to Camp No. 27.

On October 10, 1947, Nikolai Selivanovsky (MGB deputy minister) ordered Kartashov to request Hille's transfer from Camp No. 27 to his MGB department. For an unknown reason, Amayak Kobulov did not sign the document transferring Hille to Lubyanka until January 30, 1948. In April 1951, the already mentioned officer Boris Solovov finished his interrogations of Hille. On April 14, 1951, the OSO (MGB) sentenced Hille to twenty-five years in prison for spying, and he was sent to Vladimir Prison. In July 1953, not long after Stalin's death in March that year, Hille was released, and by December 1953 he was among the first POWs repatriated to East Germany.

An Anti-Hitler Plotter in GUPVI's Hands

The GUPVI and GUKR SMERSH did not generally share information they received from prisoners during investigations. The two organizations sent separate reports to Stalin, Molotov, and other Politburo members, and only the GKO and Politburo members had full information on POWs. Abakumov and Kobulov conducted two separate investigations concerning the circumstances of Hitler's suicide and presented the Politburo with two lists of potential defendants for trial at Nuremberg. The case of Colonel Hans (Johannes) Crome, former HQ head of the 4th Army Corps, was one of those rare instances in which the NKVD shared information directly with the GRU, NKGB, and SMERSH. On September 19, 1944, Beria signed the following letter:

> September 19, 1944
> No. 997/b
>
> > To: State Committee of Defense,
> >   Comrade STALIN I.V.
> >   SNK [Sovnarkom], Comrade MOLOTOV
> >   CC VKP(b), Comrade MALENKOV
> >   Razvedupr RA, Comrade IL'ICHEV
> >   NKGB USSR, Com.[rade] MERKULOV
> >   GUKR 'SMERSH' NKO, Com.[rade] ABAKUMOV
>
> Attached to this letter is the testimony of German POW, Colonel CROME.
>
>   Hans CROME, from the family of a Lutheran priest, a professional officer of the Reichswehr, graduate of the German Academy of the General Staff, was taken prisoner near Stalingrad in January 1943, when he was in charge of the headquarters of the 4th Army Corps.
>
>   In connection with the information published in the press about the assassination attempt on Hitler, CROME reported that he was a member of an organization of military plotters created in Germany in 1941.
>
>   In his testimony CROME reported data of interest on the circumstances of organization of the plotters' group, on its members and their ideas, and on the group's goals and activity.
>
> > > PEOPLE'S COMMISSAR of INTERNAL AFFAIRS
> > > of the SOVIET UNION
> > > > (L. BERIA)
> > This is correct [a signature of a secretary]
>
> Typed in 7 copies
> [in handwriting:]

Sent to Com.[rades] Molotov, Malenkov, Il'ichev on September 22, 1944
Sent to Com.[rades] Merkulov and Abakumov on September 23, 1944.[48]

In other words, the GUPVI had a higher-level German military plotter than the SMERSH's prisoner Major Kuhn, about whom Abakumov reported to Stalin four days later. A 28-page Russian translation of Crome's testimony dated September 2, 1944 was attached to Beria's letter.

Crome claimed that the military anti-Hitler organization created in 1941 consisted of a central, leading group in Berlin, with branches in the High Command of the Armed Forces (OKW), the Army High Command (OKH), the armies at the Eastern Front, and the occupational troops in France. The central group included Colonel General Ludwig Beck, Field Marshal Erwin von Witzleben, Admiral Wilhelm Canaris, Infantry Generals Alexander Falkenhausen and Friedrich Olbricht, and Major General Hans Oster (Canaris's deputy), along with four civilians: Professor Jens Jessen; Ambassador to Rome Ulrich von Hassell (incorrectly spelled 'Gasselt' throughout the document); Oberbürgermeister Carl Goerdeler; and Prussian Staatsminister Johannes Popitz. While these names are now well known, in 1944 the Soviet leaders and heads of security services were possibly hearing about them and about the widespread German military Resistance for the first time.[49] The organization's goal was to arrest Hitler and other Nazi leaders and to try them in court. If Hitler's arrest was impossible, the plotters were prepared to assassinate him. Crome mentioned Kuhn's superior General Tresckow as the lead plotter at the Eastern Front.

Two points in Crome's testimony are most interesting. First, he claimed that Admiral Canaris was one of the leaders of the plot and that the plotters' meetings took place at his apartment in Berlin, which corresponds with some other data about Canaris.[50] Second, according to Crome, the plotters planned coups twice, in December 1941 and autumn 1942 (in fact, it turned out to be more than twice). The first attempt was cancelled, and the second was postponed. In February 1942, RSHA head Reinhard Heydrich made a sudden visit to Paris, after which came the dismissal and discharge from the army of one of the key plotters, Field Marshal von Witzleben (commander of the German Occupational Troops in France), followed by the SD's intensified oversight of Witzleben's staff officers. Obviously, Heydrich had information about the plotters' plans. Crome did not know what happened later because of his transfer to the Stalingrad Front and subsequent capture in February 1943. Unfortunately, no information is available about the reaction of the recipient of Beria's cover letter and Crome's testimony.

In 1955, Crome was repatriated to West Germany, where he continued his service and became *Brigadegeneral* of the Bundeswehr. He retired in 1961 and died in 1997. As for Field Marshal Witzleben, the Gestapo arrested him on July 21, 1944. On August 7–8, 1944 he was tried along with seven other military plotters. Witzleben was condemned to death and executed.

Interestingly, from 1963 to 1965 Crome's son Hans-Henning headed Department 85 in the BND, the West German intelligence service. This department was in charge of investigating former war criminals among the BND staff. Crome Jr. collected materials on 146 staff members, 71 of whom—former RSHA officers—resigned because their crimes had been proven. In 2010 he told an interviewer: 'My work in Department 85 is the only issue that haunts my nightmares after 40 years of my service.'[51] He was referring to the crimes committed by those staffers who had resigned. Later Crome made a successful intelligence career while being stationed in New York, Madrid, and Bern.

In May 1945, after the war in Europe, Moscow investigation prisons of both GUKR SMERSH and GUPVI's Operational Directorate were full of prisoners under investigation, and it took years to close cases and try all prisoners. But the influx of new prisoners from Europe was still coming, and in August, after the war with Japan, it increased enormously.

CHAPTER 26

War with Japan

On August 8, 1945, the Soviet Union began a war with Japan. Japan had maintained neutrality toward the Soviet Union since April 13, 1941, when Yosuke Matsuoka, the Japanese foreign minister, signed an agreement to that effect in Moscow.[1] To stress the importance of the just signed Neutrality Pact, Stalin and Molotov personally went to Moscow's Yaroslavskii Station to see off Matsuoka. Signing this pact allowed Stalin to order a month later a secret transfer of two armies from the Transbaikal and Siberian military districts to the regions near the western border for preparations for the war with Germany.[2] However, the possibility of a Japanese attack against the Soviet Union existed until the first months of 1942, and by December 1941, as a result of a new draft in Siberia, thirty-nine Soviet divisions were deployed in the Transbaikal region and the Soviet Far East. But the war with Japan was inevitable, while for the Western Allies it had started on December 8, 1941.

Preparations

On May 21, 1943, the GKO ordered the secret construction of a railroad from Komsomolsk on the Amur River to the Soviet Harbor in the Far

Eastern Pacific.[3] This railroad was crucial for the future movement of troops and military hardware to the Sea of Japan. With labor camp prisoners doing the construction work, completion was planned for August 1, 1945.

On November 1, 1943, after a dinner in the Kremlin, Stalin confidentially informed U.S. Secretary of State Cordell Hull that he planned to enter the war with Japan after the German defeat. Hull immediately cabled the news to President Franklin D. Roosevelt.[4]

In July 1944, after the Western Allies opened the Second Front in Europe, Stalin informed Marshal Aleksandr Vasilevsky, head of the General Staff, that he would be commander in chief of the war with Japan.[5] The GUKR SMERSH started preparing an operational list containing the names of Japanese intelligence members and leaders of the Russian émigré community in Manchuria, which it completed on September 15, 1944.[6] On February 11, 1945, the last day of the Yalta Conference, Stalin, Roosevelt, and Churchill signed a secret protocol, stating that after the war with Japan, the Soviet Union would acquire all of Sakhalin Island, the Kuril Islands, and a zone in Korea.[7]

On April 5, 1945, Molotov denounced the 1941 agreement in a diplomatic note to the Japanese ambassador to Moscow, Naotake Sato. The Soviet troops were already on the move to the Russian Far East. On June 28, 1945, Stalin issued an order: 'All preparations are to be carried out in the greatest secrecy. Army commanders are to be given their orders in person, orally and without any written directives.'[8] Marshal Vasilevsky was appointed commander in chief in the Far East under the alias 'Vasiliev' (previously he was 'Vladimirov,' Table 21-1), and other commanders were also given aliases.[9] All preparations were to be completed by August 1, 1945.

On May 15, 1945, Abakumov appointed his deputy, Isai Babich, and Aleksandr Misyurev, an assistant, as coordinators of SMERSH units of the Far Eastern Group of Soviet Troops.[10] They were transferred there with a staff of 150 experienced SMERSH officers. Experienced UKR SMERSH heads were put in charge of the Far Eastern fronts:

Front	SMERSH Head
Far Eastern Group of Troops	I. Ya. Babich, Deputy Head, GUKR SMERSH
Primorsk Group of Troops	D. I. Mel'nikov, Head, Karelian Front UKR SMERSH
Transbaikal Front	A. A. Vadis, Head, 1st Belorussian Front UKR SMERSH
Far Eastern Front	I. T. Saloimsky, Transbaikal Front UKR SMERSH

Later, in August 1945 the Primorsk (or Maritime) Group of Troops and Far Eastern Front became the 1st Far Eastern Front and 2nd Far Eastern Front respectively when Stalin launched his war against Japan. At the same time, GUKR SMERSH in Moscow was not idle. On June 9, 1945, it updated its operational list of Japanese intelligence members and Russian émigrés in Manchuria targeted for arrest.[11]

On July 11, 1945, Ambassador Naotake Sato tried to persuade Molotov to establish long-term friendly relations with Japan. At the time, three groups of Soviet troops totaling about 1.5 million men had already been deployed at the Manchurian border. The Japanese Kwantung Army, stationed in Manchuria since 1931, was the first to meet the Soviet offensive. In 1945, this army consisted of 713,000 men, of whom, according to the Japanese sources, about half were poorly trained teenaged recruits and old men, since the elite troops had long ago been sent to fight the Americans and British.[12] The Japanese troops had almost no fuel and as a result, during the ensuing battle with the Soviets not a single plane out of a fleet of 900 was able to take off, and all 600 Japanese tanks were seized by the Soviets before they were even used.

On July 25, 1945, Beria reported to Stalin, who was attending the Potsdam Conference in Berlin, that the construction of the railroad to the Soviet Harbor was complete.[13] The next day Harry S. Truman, Churchill, and Chinese President Chiang Kai-shek signed the Potsdam Declaration stating that if Japan did not surrender, it would be destroyed. The Japanese government did not respond.

On the morning of August 6, Truman ordered the first atomic bomb to be dropped on the city of Hiroshima. Two days later, at 5:00 p.m., Molotov officially informed Ambassador Sato that the Soviet Union would begin the war the next day. In fact, Soviet troops had already begun the offensive under the code name Operation August Storm.[14] On August 9, the Americans dropped the second atomic bomb on the city of Nagasaki.

The next day the Japanese government informed the Allies that it wished to capitulate.[15] On August 15, Japanese radio transmitted Emperor Hirohito's speech of surrender to the nation, in which he agreed to all the demands of the Potsdam Declaration. In response, U.S. commander in chief General Douglas MacArthur issued Order No. 1, stopping the advance of American troops into Japan.

But peace was not what Stalin wanted. Soviet troops had occupied only a third of the Japanese territory Stalin had agreed upon with the Allies, and on August 17, 1945, he ordered Marshal Vasilevsky to continue the offensive.[16] The next day, troops began landing on South Sakhalin and the Kuril Islands. The island of Hokkaido was not occupied only because the unexpectedly fierce Japanese defense of Sakhalin Island slowed the advancing Soviet troops.

New SMERSH Tactics

In Manchuria and other parts of China, SMERSH used new tactics. Groups of SMERSH operatives were parachuted in to Changchun,

Mukden, Port Arthur (now Lüshun), and Dairen (Dalnii in Russian). These groups consisted mostly of SMERSH officers, followed by a landing force and additional forces bearing a flag of truce. In Changchun, on August 19 a group of SMERSH operatives and truce forces compelled General Otozo Yamada to order the surrender of his Kwantung Army.[17] During this short campaign in Manchuria, Babich and Misyurev personally led two raids conducted by a group of SMERSH operatives. On September 21, 1945, Aleksandr Vadis reported to Babich:

> From August 9 to September 18, there were 35 operational-search [SMERSH] groups in Manchuria. They conducted operations along with storm troopers, taking over cities, especially those in which, according to our intelligence information, there were [enemy] intelligence and counter-intelligence organs.
>
> In total, 2,249 people were arrested by September 18, 1945. Among them:
>
> 1. Official members of the YaVM [Japanese Military Missions]317 2. YaVM agents 349
> 3. Official members of the Japanese gendarmerie 569
> 4. RFS [Russian Fascist Union] leaders and active members 305
> 5. BREM [Bureau of Russian Emigrants] leaders and active members 75
> 6. [Former] Red Army Intelligence men recruited by Japanese intelligence 10
> 7. Traitors to the Motherland 162.[18]

Officially, the number of Japanese intelligence agents captured by SMERSH operatives in the Far East and Manchuria reached 50,000, which is hard to believe.[19]

As usual, leaders of Russian émigré organizations were special targets of SMERSH operational groups. After the Civil War in Russia, many White Russian troops as well as members of the Maritime Provisional Government (May 1921–November 1922 in Vladivostok) crossed the border with China and settled there on territories later occupied by Japan. Furthermore, from 1929 to 1931, many Russian peasants crossed the Chinese border to escape enforced collectivization. In 1921–45, Grigorii Semenov was the key leader (Ataman) of all Cossacks living in nineteen large settlements in China, in charge of the 20,000-strong Cossack Union. The goal of this extremely anti-Soviet group was 'to free Russia from the power of the Comintern and to restore law and order.'[20] In August 1945, Ataman Semenov, two of his sons, and his uncle, White Lieutenant General D. F. Semenov, were captured by a SMERSH operational group parachuted into Dairen. Abakumov informed Beria:

On August 25 of the current year [1945] the operational group of the UKR SMERSH of the Transbaikal Front captured in the suburbs of the town of Dairen the leader of the White Russian Cossack Troops, head of the White Russian Guards, who had been hiding in Japan, Lieutenant General SE-MENOV, G. M., born in 1890 in the village of Durulguev in the former Transbaikal Region, a Russian, who served in the Czar's Army as a Colonel of Cossack Troops.

During the arrest, documents were taken from SEMENOV that proved his anti-Soviet activity.

SEMENOV is en route to the Main SMERSH Directorate.[21]

A month later, Abakumov reported to Beria on the arrests of leaders of the Russian Fascist Party (RFP), which was very active in Harbin in Manchuria. In the 1920s, Harbin was a Russian-émigré cultural and political center, similar to Prague and Paris.[22] The first Russian fascist organizations appeared in Manchuria in 1925, inspired by the example of Benito Mussolini. In May 1931, the first congress of Russian fascists formed the RFP, electing the charismatic Konstantin Rodzaevsky its general secretary.[23] Born in 1907 in Blagoveshchensk on the Russian left bank of the Amur River, in 1925, Rodzaevsky fled to Harbin, where he entered the Law Institute. In 1928, his father, a lawyer, and a younger brother joined him in Harbin, while the OGPU arrested Rodzaevsky's mother and two sisters who had stayed behind in Blagoveshchensk.

Rodzaevsky wrote the RFP program. The party's goal was 'to overthrow the Jewish Communist dictatorship in Russia and to create a new National-Labor Great Russia [like National Socialist Germany], Russia for the Russians.'[24] According to Rodzaevsky, Russia would achieve the highest level of prosperity and social justice, and the greatest Eurasian Empire would be created after Finland, Poland, and the neighboring Baltic countries joined Russia in that union. Rodzaevsky called Stalin 'a concubine of the American capitalists and the Jews,' and the OGPU, 'a Zionist net.'

Rodzaevsky was obsessed with the worldwide 'Jewish-Masonic plot,' which he imagined and described in Russian in a brochure, *Judas' End*, and a book, *Contemporary Judaisation of the World or the Jewish Question in the 20th Century*. The latter was republished in 2001 by the current Russian nationalists.[25] In 1934, Russian fascists formed an international organization, the Russian Far East Moscow, with its central office in Harbin and branches in twenty-six countries. But because of Rodzaevsky's extreme anti-Semitism, the leader of the American-Russian fascists, Anastase Vonsiatsky, soon broke with the RFP.[26]

The creation of the RFP coincided with the Japanese occupation of Manchuria and the creation of a puppet state, Manchukuo. The Japanese established a Bureau on the Affairs of Russian Emigrants in

Manchuria (BREM) to manage the huge Russian population in Harbin.[27] A Russian needed BREM's (i.e., Japanese) approval to be hired, to open a business, and even to visit relatives in another city. The staff of BREM consisted of Cossacks and monarchist émigrés. In 1943, Major General Lev Vlasievsky became head of BREM, while Mikhail Matkovsky, the son of another White General, Aleksei Matkovsky, was his assistant. In fact, Mikhail Matkovsky was a Soviet intelligence agent, and through him, the Soviets learned a lot about the Russian community in Harbin.[28] Despite his service, SMERSH arrested Matkovsky and later he was sentenced to a ten-year imprisonment in labor camps.

Between 4,000 and 20,000 Russians joined the RFP in Manchuria, while the total Russian population in Harbin was about 80,000.[29] In 1939, the RFP changed its name to the Russian Fascist Union or RFS. The RFS widely used terror against members of the Russian émigré community and soon became part of the Japanese-Manchurian mafia. In October 1941, Japanese security arrested Richard Sorge, head of the Soviet spy ring in Tokyo, and then started vetting the Russian population in China.[30] The Japanese detained and intensely interrogated Rodzaevsky and two other RFS leaders for a month. In 1943, the Japanese administration banned the RFS.

But in the 1930s, the Japanese enthusiastically supported the RFP's anti-Soviet terrorist activity. In 1936, the Japanese assisted a group called 'The First Fascist Unit for Saving Russia,' under the command of Rodzaevsky's bodyguard, Matvei Maslakov, in crossing the Soviet border.[31] The NKVD troops immediately discovered the group and killed forty of its members.

In 1937, General Yoshijiro Umezu, commander in chief of the Kwantung Army and, from 1939 to 1942, Japanese ambassador to Manchukuo, ordered the establishment of a special school to train Russian terrorists, appointing Rodzaevsky as its head.[32] Soviet intelligence heard about the school's activity through Ivar Lissner, a reporter for *Völkischer Beobachter* and a prominent anthropologist, who pretended to work for the Abwehr but was, in fact, a Soviet agent. In June 1940, the Japanese arrested Lissner on suspicion of espionage. He was released after the war. As for General Umezo, in July 1944 he was appointed chief of the Japanese general staff. In 1948, the International Military Tribunal in Tokyo sentenced him to life in prison and he died in prison in 1949.

The Japanese military leaders planned the active use of émigré Russian military formations in the coming war against the Soviet Union. In 1938, Ataman Semenov organized the first detachment, called the Asano Brigade after the Japanese Colonel Takashi Asano.[33] Subordinate to the HQ of the Kwantung Army, the brigade fought against Korean partisans. In 1939, a unit of 250 men from this brigade participated in the Battle of Khalkhin Gol against the Red Army. In 1943, the brigade, renamed the Russian Military Unit of the Manchukuo Army, included infantry and Cossack cavalry units. From 1944 onwards, Cossack Colonel Smirnov commanded the formation, which had grown to 4,000 men by 1945.

Another Cossack corps, 'Zakhipgapsky,' formed under the command of General A. P. Baksheev in 1943, was subordinate to Japanese Lieutenant Colonel Takashi Hishikari, the Kwantung Army ambassador to Manchukuo. Three additional small units of approximately 250 men each consisted of young Russian volunteers in three Manchurian regions. While Japanese officers commanded these units, the junior officers were Russians.

Contrary to Japanese hopes, after the first Soviet paratroopers landed in several Manchurian cities, young Russians actively assisted them in capturing Japanese military commanders. Rodzaevsky and Vlasievsky, along with several loyal men, moved to the town of Tientsin, where they met with a group of NKVD representatives. The NKVD officers told the escapees that they would be pardoned if they went to the Soviet Union voluntarily. Vlasievsky flew to Manchuria, where he met with Marshal Malinovsky. After the meeting, he was brought to the Soviet city of Chita, where SMERSH operatives arrested him and sent him to Moscow.

On September 22, 1945, Rodzaevsky wrote a letter to Marshal Vasilevsky, who handed it over to the Soviet Embassy in Beijing (then known as Peking).[34] After reading it, Soviet representatives brought Rodzaevsky to Changchun, the capital of Manchuria, where SMERSH operatives arrested him. Many other émigrés were arrested in Harbin and other cities. Prince Nikolai Ukhtomsky, a journalist and writer in Harbin, later told his fellow prisoners in the Vorkuta Labor Camp that a group of Soviet paratroopers had landed in the center of Harbin and immediately arrested him and several other White émigrés.[35] In September 1945, Abakumov reported to Beria:

The SMERSH Directorate of the Transbaikal Front has found and arrested leaders of the anti-Soviet White Guardist movement in Japan and Manchuria:

RODZAEVSKY, K. V., the ideologue and leader of the 'Russian Fascist Union,' born in 1908 in the town of Blagoveshchensk, a Russian, former member of the VLKSM [Communist Youth Union], in 1928 escaped from the Soviet Union to Manchuria;

VLASIEVSKY, L. F., head of the anti-Soviet central 'Bureau of Russian Emigrants' in Manchuria [i.e., BREM], born in 1889 in the village of Chindan (Transbaikal Region), a Russian, escaped with the rest of the gang of Ataman SEMENOV to Manchuria, Lieutenant General of the White Army.

Therefore, at present we have arrested all leaders of the White Guardists in Manchuria: SEMENOV, G. M.; RODZAEVSKY, K. V.; VLASIEVSKY, L. F.; Ataman SEMENOV's Deputy, Lieutenant General of the White

Guard Army, BAKSHEEV, A. P.; leaders of the White Cossack and anti-Soviet organizations, generals of the White Army BLOKHIN, P. I.; DRUIN, F. B.; GARMAEV, Urain; MOSKALEV, T. P.; KUKLIN, M. V.; Prince UKHTOMSKY, N. A.; and others.

RODZAEVSKY and VLASIEVSKY have already been brought to the Main SMERSH Directorate, where they will be carefully interrogated.

I have already reported the above to Comrade STALIN.[36]

More arrests, especially of the ROVS representatives in China, followed. Later most of the above-mentioned arrestees were convicted in show trials.

Also arrested was Boris Bryner, a businessman with a Swiss passport and an affiliation to the Swiss Consulate in Tientsin (Tianjin), who was the father of the famous Hollywood actor Yul Brynner. Boris Bryner was a son of Jules (Julius) Bryner, a Swiss citizen who moved to Russia and became a successful businessman, and a Buryat (Mongolian) mother.[37] Later Yul and his sister Vera added the second 'n' to the family surname after arriving in the United States. After graduating from St. Petersburg Mining Institute, Boris worked as a manager of the Tetyukhe Lead and Zinc Mines Company established by his father not far from Vladivostok. He married a Russian woman, Maria (Marousia) Blagovidova, who gave birth to Yul, the future actor (born Yulii Borisovich Bryner), and Vera. Boris maintained the rights to the family mines until 1931, which made his enterprise the longest-running private company in the Soviet Union.

In 1931, Boris was forced to leave Vladivostok for Harbin, where his wife Marousia had moved a few years earlier after Boris abandoned her and their two children; in 1934, they moved to Paris. Since the Soviets considered Boris a 'Russian capitalist,' in 1945 SMERSH operatives arrested Boris together with his second wife and their small daughter. Mr. and Mrs. Bryner were imprisoned and interrogated for six months. They were released after negotiations between the Swiss authorities and the Soviets.

SMERSH's search for Genrikh Lyushkov, possibly the most wanted enemy among the Far Eastern Russians, failed because he was already dead. Lyushkov, State Security Commissar of the 3rd Rank, was the highest NKVD officer who ever defected.[38] From 1931 to 1936, Lyushkov held high posts within the Special Political Department of the OGPU/NKVD. Later he headed the Azov-Black Sea NKVD Directorate, before Abakumov succeeded him. After this, in 1937, Lyushkov was appointed head of the NKVD Far Eastern Directorate. Stalin personally instructed Lyushkov concerning the necessity of arrests there. As a result, 250,000 people were arrested, of whom 7,000 were shot. Lyushkov also supervised the exile of 175,000 Koreans and 7,000 Chinese, considered potential Japanese spies, from that area to Central Asia.[39] In June 1938 Lyushkov was ordered to Moscow, but fearing his inevitable arrest, he defected to Japan.

In Japan, Lyushkov took the name Toshikazu Yamaguchi, became a Japanese citizen, and worked for the Japanese General Staff in Tokyo. Based on Lyushkov's information, the Japanese reorganized their army in Manchuria. Richard Sorge, the Soviet spy in Tokyo, microfilmed part of a German report on Lyushkov's interrogations by the Japanese and sent the microfilm to Moscow. Lyushkov also gave numerous interviews about ongoing terror in the Soviet Union.

Lyushkov offered Japanese intelligence a plan to assassinate Stalin at his dacha in the Caucasus. In 1939, a group of White Russian terrorists headed by Lyushkov arrived near the Turkish–Soviet border. It is possible that there was a Soviet agent in the group, because when it reached the border Soviet Border Guards were already on alert and prevented its penetration into Soviet territory.[40] Later Lyushkov made a second attempt to assassinate Stalin, but it also failed.

In July 1945, Lyushkov was transferred to the Special Intelligence Agency of the Kwantung Army in the city of Dairen. On August 19, during the Soviet offensive, Captain Yutaka Takeoka, a member of this agency, killed Lyushkov after the latter refused to commit suicide. Japanese intelligence was probably afraid that if SMERSH or the NKVD captured him, Lyushkov would release too much information.

On November 25, 1945 SMERSH operatives captured Takeoka.[41] In Moscow Abakumov personally interrogated him about Lyushkov. In April 1946, Takeoka was used as a witness at the show trial of Ataman Grigorii Semyonov, Konstantin Rodzaevsky and the others. In June 1948, Takeoka was sentenced to a 25-year imprisonment. He was kept in Vladimir Prison separately from the other Japanese prisoners, until released and repatriated in 1956.

The arrested General Yamada, commander in chief of the Kwantung Army, was sent to Kartashov's GUKR SMERSH department in Moscow. During the 1949 Khabarovsk Trial, Yamada received a prison sentence of twenty-five years for his culpability in testing biological weapons on POWs, carried out by the infamous Unit 731 that was part of the Kwantung Army.[42]

Among the other Japanese routinely sent to Kartashov's department were Colonel Saburo Asada, head of the 2nd (Intelligence) department of the staff of the Kwantung Army; his deputies, Lieutenant Colonels Tamaki Kumazaki and Hiroki Nohara; Yoshio Itagaki, a son of Seishiro Itagaki, war minister from 1938–1939; Lieutenant General Genzo Yanagita, head of the Japanese military mission in Harbin; Major Kinju Ishikawa, head of a sabotage group of that mission; and Hadjime Kanie, head of the Sakhalin military mission. Senior Lieutenant Prince Fumitaka Konoe, a son of the former Japanese Prime Minister, and Funao Miyakawa, former General Counselor in Vladivostok and then in Harbin, as well as some others, were held and interrogated for eight months in a camp for Japanese POWs in Manchuria, before being sent to Moscow.[43]

As in Europe, mass killings of Japanese and even Chinese civilians, looting, and rapes continued in Manchuria, Korea, and South Sakhalin after they were occupied by the Red Army. Corporal Hal Leith, a member of the OSS team Cardinal parachuted into a location near Mukden in Manchuria in order to rescue American POWs, recalled: 'All they [Soviet soldiers] do is loot and kill, and they don't stick to looting from the Japanese. Some soldiers wear as many as 10 watches.'[44] Another member of the same team reported that as an explanation of the atrocities, a Soviet general told the Americans that the soldiers who committed atrocities belonged to the 'shock troops' made up of men whose families had been butchered by the Germans; they were eager for revenge, he said, adding that after Germany those vengeful soldiers were dispatched to the Far East. The general claimed: 'Not being normal in their minds, they were bent on looting, killing, and rape.'[45] Even if that had been true (and it was not), the Soviet general did not explain why atrocities were not stopped by the high command, or by SMERSH.

The End of the War

On September 2, 1945, Japan signed a formal surrender in a ceremony on board the USS *Missouri*. General Douglas MacArthur, supreme commander of the Allied powers, directed the signing. The Soviet delegation of two generals and an admiral was headed by Lieutenant General Kuzma Derevyanko, the Soviet representative at MacArthur's headquarters.[46] Derevyanko spoke both English and Japanese. After the signing, Derevyanko spent several days in Hiroshima and Nagasaki, taking photos and making detailed notes about the destruction of the city. On October 5, he reported to Stalin, Molotov, Beria, Malenkov, and three military leaders in the Kremlin on Japan's capitulation and on his trip to Hiroshima and Nagasaki.[47] Nine years later, on December 30, 1954, Derevyanko died due to the effects of radiation exposure.

In the meantime, on September 3, 1945, the Soviet Union officially declared the defeat of Japan. Since then, the Western Allies and China have considered August 15 the day of the Japanese surrender, while the Russians consider September 2 the day of Japan's defeat. In 2010, September 2 became a Russian holiday to commemorate the last day of World War II.

SMERSH and NKVD operational groups continued making arrests after the end of the war. The memoirs of some arrestees reveal that in October 1945, Soviet military officials called meetings with the leaders of Russian organizations in Harbin and in other cities in Manchuria.[48] Once the émigrés had assembled, they were simply surrounded by Soviet troops and arrested.

In Mukden, an operational group arrested the last Chinese and Manchurian emperor, 39-year-old Henry Pu Yi, along with the members of his family and his court.[49] In all, 225 paratroopers landed in this city, and thirty SMERSH officers took part in arresting the former emperor. He was later held in Camp No. 27 and in a POW camp near Khabarovsk in Siberia. He wrote several letters to Stalin thanking the USSR for saving his life. Pu Yi intensively studied Marxist-Leninist philosophy as well as the history of the Soviet Communist Party, which he even wanted to join.[50] The Soviets used Pu Yi as a witness at the trials of Japanese war criminals in Khabarovsk in September 1946 and in Tokyo in May 1946–November 1948. In July 1950, on Stalin's order, officers of the GUPVI's Operational Directorate turned over Pu Yi, along with fifty-seven of his relatives and former government members, to Chinese officials. Pu Yi wrote to Stalin: 'I wish for the Soviet people to flourish forever and Generalissimo Stalin to be healthy and live for many years to come.'[51] In China, Pu Yi was held in prisons and labor camps for 'reeducation' until 1959. After his release, Pu Yi worked in the botanical gardens of the Chinese Academy of Sciences and published his memoirs.[52] He died in 1967.

In Moscow, many of the Japanese prisoners and Russian émigrés caught in China spent years in investigation prisons. In 1948–51, most of the Japanese prisoners were sentenced to twenty-five years in special prisons, where some of them died.[53] Shun Akifusa, former head of the Japanese military mission in Harbin, died in Vladimir Prison in March 1949, while Funao Miyakawa, former Japanese general counsel in Harbin, died in 1950 in Lefortovo Prison, still awaiting trial. Prince Fumitaka Konoe, a son of the former Japanese prime minister, was sentenced to twenty-five years in prison in 1951. After spending four years in Aleksandrovsk and Vladimir special prisons, he died in a transit camp en route to Japan. General Otozo Yamada survived his imprisonment and returned to Japan.

About 640,000 of the Japanese servicemen taken prisoner, including 16,000 Chinese and 10,200 Koreans, were brought to the GUPVI camps on the Soviet territory and used for slave labor.[54] This was a direct violation of the Potsdam Declaration of the western Allies, signed on July 26, 1945, the 9th point of which stated: 'The Japanese military forces, after being completely disarmed, shall be permitted to return to their homes with the opportunity to lead peaceful and productive lives.'[55] But the Soviets did not comply because Stalin did not sign this declaration. Japanese estimates reveal that approximately 250,000 Japanese POWs perished in the labor camps, while Russian officials claim that a much smaller number, 62,068 Japanese, died. It is possible that the real numbers of Japanese POWs held in Soviet captivity—and of related fatalities—will never be known.

Only on October 19, 1956, more than three years after Stalin's death, did Japan and the Soviet Union sign the agreement ending the war. A peace agreement between the two countries has never been signed due to an unresolved dispute regarding the status of the southern Kuril Islands.

Part IX. SMERSH After the War: 1945–46

CHAPTER 27

In Europe and at Home

Although SMERSH existed for only a year after World War II, this was a time of fundamental changes. In Eastern Europe, the Soviet military formations known as fronts were reorganized into four groups of occupational troops, each with its own SMERSH counterintelligence directorate. These directorates, which in mid-1946 became MGB counterintelligence directorates, played a considerable role in the Sovietization of the occupied countries, as well as in the intelligence and counterintelligence fight against the former Western Allies. Romanov, a SMERSH officer, recalled the words of Colonel Georgii Yevdokimenko, a SMERSH/MGB official in Hungary: 'For some people, perhaps, the war was over, but for us, [the] Chekists… the real war, to bring about the final destruction of the capitalist world, was only just beginning.'[1]

Demobilization

With the end of the war in Europe, the Soviet Union began the partial demobilization of its enormous 11.5-million-man army. The older soldiers were demobilized first. A veteran recalled: 'When the first soldiers were demobilized and sent back from Germany, they were put in small train cars, two persons per car… Each aged serviceman took a cow, a huge bag of sugar, a bag of flour, some clothes, and so on. The second group of demobilized servicemen…didn't have cows, but brought bags of foodstuffs. The third group brought even less.[2]

While secretly sending some of the troops to the Russian Far East in preparation for the war with Japan, the Soviets transformed the remaining troops in Europe into four groups of occupation forces (Table 27-1). SMERSH controlled the demobilization and changes. Before demobilization began, on GUKR's instructions the third OKR departments within UKRs made an evaluation of every field officer and decided which officers should be sent to the reserve, which officers should be demoted to lower posts, and so on.[3] Then special commissions, attached to the HQs of the four groups of forces in charge of demobilization, were created. Officers of the 1st OKR departments represented SMERSH in these commissions. The commissions made one of three decisions: 'demobilize from the army';

TABLE 27-1. HEADS OF COUNTERINTELLIGENCE DIRECTORATES AND INSPECTORATES IN EUROPE, 1945–46[1]

Name	Previous Position	New Position	Dates
Group of Soviet Occupation Troops in Germany (GSOVG), Commander: Marshal G. V. Zhukov (1945–1946)			
A. A. Vadis	Head, UKR SMERSH, 1st Belorussian Front	Head, Counterintelligence Directorate, GSOVG	Jun 27, 1945–Aug 12, 1945
P. V. Zelenin	Head, UKR SMERSH, 3rd Belorussian Front	Head, Counterintelligence Directorate, GSOVG	Aug 12, 1945–Apr 1, 1947
Central Group of Troops (TsGV), Austria and Hungary, Commander and Chief Commissar of Austria: Marshal I. S. Konev (1945–1946)			
N. A. Korolev	Head, UKR SMERSH, 2nd Ukrainian Front	Head, Counterintelligence Directorate, TsGV	Jun 10, 1945–Jun 9, 1947
Allied Control Commission, Vienna Chairman: Col. General A.S. Zheltov, Deputy Chief Commissar of Austria (1945–1950)			
G. S. Bolotin-Balyasnyi	Head Assistant, GUKR SMERSH (responsible for the 3rd Belorussian Front)	Head, Inspectorate	1945
N. A. Rozanov	Head Assistant, GUKR SMERSH (responsible for the Northwestern Front)	Head, Inspectorate	1945–1946
Allied Control Commission, Budapest Chairman: Marshal Voroshilov, Deputy Chairman (de facto Chairman) Lt. Gen. V. P. Sviridov (1945–1947)			
M. I. Belkin	Head, UKR SMERSH, 3rd Baltic Front	Head, Inspectorate	Jul 1945–Jun 1946

Name	Previous Position	New Position	Dates
Northern Group of Troops (SGV), Poland, Commander: Marshal K. K. Rokossovsky (1945–1949)			
Ya. A. Yedunov	Head, UKR SMERSH, 2nd Belorussian Front	Head, Counterintelligence Directorate, SGV	Jun 10, 1945–Jul 15, 1946
Southern Group of Troops (YuGV), Bulgaria and Romania, Commander: Marshal F. I. Tolbukhin (Jun 1945–Jan 1947)			
P. I. Ivashutin	Head, UKR SMERSH, 3rd Ukrainian Front	Head, Counterintelligence Directorate, YuGV	Jun 27, 1945–Nov 10, 1947
Allied Control Commission (ACC) Chairman: Marshal F. I. Tolbukhin (Jun 1945–Jan 1947) <u>Sofia Branch</u>, Deputy ACC Chairman (and Commander, 37th Army): Marshal S. S. Biryuzov (1944–1947)			
A. M. Voul	Deputy Head, UKR SMERSH, YuGV	Head, Inspectorate	Dec 1944–Dec 1947
Bucharest Branch, Deputy ACC Chairman: Lt. Gen. V. P. Vinogradov (Sep 1944–Mar 1945), Col. Gen. I. Z. Susaikin (Jan 1946–1948)			
P. P. Timofeev	Head Assistant, GUKR SMERSH (responsible for the 2nd Ukrainian Front)	Head, Inspectorate	1944–May 1946
Finland, Helsinki (did not have occupation troops)			
Allied Control Commission Chairman: Col. Gen. A. A. Zhdanov (a Politburo member) (Sep 1944–Aug 1947)			
S. F. Kozhevnikov	Head Assistant, UKR SMERSH, Leningrad Front	Head, Inspectorate	1945–1946

1. Data from N. V. Petrov, *Kto rukovodil organami gosbezopasnosti 1941–1954. Spravochnik* (Moscow: Zven'ya, 2010), 115–6 (in Russian).

'transfer to less important work'; or 'be left on active service.' All officers whose relatives were arrested in the 1930s or had participated in the ROA were demobilized into the reserve at once.

Along with checking all enlisted men, the GUKR also decided the fates of colonels, generals, and even marshals. Romanov recalled two coded messages from Moscow. One was from Abakumov: 'Refrain from demobilizing into the reserve, personnel holding the rank of general or colonels serving as acting generals, unless you receive special instructions from us. Abakumov.'[4] The second was from Nikolai Selivanovsky, Abakumov's first deputy: 'The following persons are to be demobilized either into the reserve or on to the retired list, according to the appended instructions.' For some unknown reason, Romanov called Selivanovsky 'Chernyshov' in his book. Possibly, 'Chernyshov' was Selivanovsky's alias during the war.

The changes covered also the field SMERSH units. The most capable operatives and investigators were transferred to the GUKR in Moscow, the rest were sent into reserve. Nikolai Mesyatsev, a SMERSH field operative now assigned to the 2nd GUKR Department, recalled: 'In Lubyanka... my former co-workers at the Investigation Department had already been promoted to lieutenant colonels and colonels. Some of them looked at me in a haughty matter: I had left for the front as a captain and came back as a captain.'[5]

Under these circumstances, the war of Abakumov and Beria for the total control of UKRs in Europe intensified and Beria made his final, unsuccessful, attempt to subordinate SMERSH to the NKVD.

Abakumov Regains Control

On June 22, 1945, two weeks before Stalin and Beria arrived in Berlin to attend the Potsdam Conference, Abakumov wrote a long letter to Beria, complaining about Ivan Serov, Beria's deputy and a deputy head on the matters of civilian administration of the Soviet Military Administration in Germany or SVAG headed by Marshal Georgii Zhukov.[6] Serov constantly ordered the taking under NKVD control of important detainees arrested by SMERSH operatives, which Abakumov described as 'acts of hooliganism' against SMERSH. Abakumov also informed Beria of his instruction to Aleksandr Vadis, head of the UKR SMERSH of the 1st Belorussian Front, and his deputy Grigorii Mel'nikov, not to follow Serov's orders without his (Abakumov's) approval, as a countermeasure against Serov, and asked Beria to reprimand Serov.

Instead of answering Abakumov, on that same day Beria sent Stalin a plan for the reorganization of the work of NKVD plenipotentiaries.[7] Beria proposed to keep Serov (and his staff) at Marshal Zhukov's headquarters in Berlin and to appoint Abakumov's deputy Pavel Meshik Plenipotentiary to Marshal Konev's group of troops in Austria, Hungary, and Czechoslovakia,

and Selivanovsky, Plenipotentiary to Marshal Rokossovsky's troops in Poland. Major General Aleksandr Pavlov, head of the NKVD Rear Guard
Troops at the 3rd Ukrainian Front, would be Plenipotentiary to Marshal
Fyodor Tolbukhin's troops in Romania and Bulgaria. The new plenipotentiaries would be responsible for all NKVD–NKGB–SMERSH routine
work, would command the NKVD troops in their military areas, and
would be in charge of all POWs and their transportation to the Soviet
Union.

Stalin wrote on Beria's report: 'To Com.[rade] Beria. I agree. J. Stalin.'
But something went wrong, and only Serov was reappointed Plenipotentiary. The staffs of the other plenipotentiaries were disbanded on July 4,
1945, and their members were assigned to their previous jobs.[8]

As a consequence of Serov's new appointment, the UKR SMERSH
in Germany became subordinate to Serov. The embarrassed Abakumov,
who deeply hated Serov (and the feeling was entirely mutual), ordered the
head of this directorate, Vadis, to establish a network of SMERSH operational groups in Germany.[9] Despite Serov's protest to Beria, SMERSH
departments were created under SVAG in all German counties, provinces,
regions, and cities.[10] These departments conducted surveillance of Soviet
personnel, while the NKVD units were in charge of actions against the
German population.

On July 9, 1945, the heads of all security structures received military
ranks. Beria was promoted to marshal, while Abakumov was given the rank
of colonel general, as were Beria's three deputies (Serov, Sergei Kruglov, and
Vasilii Chernyshev) and Bogdan Kobulov, NKGB first deputy Commissar.[11] Vsevolod Merkulov became an army general.

In August, Abakumov continued his attack on Serov and Beria, and
made a direct appeal to Stalin.[12] Knowing Stalin's sensitivity on the question of Party leadership, Abakumov cited a report to him from Vadis that
was strongly critical of both Zhukov and Serov. Vadis had left Germany; he
was beyond their reach and, therefore, could write openly. He claimed that
Zhukov and Serov had tried to control the political structures of SVAG,
while they should have been controlled from Moscow by the Main Political
Directorate. Vadis also reported that Zhukov had awarded Serov the Gold
Star for Hero of the Soviet Union, the highest military award, for making
him a favorite. Abakumov's statement that 'many consider Zhukov to be
the top candidate for Defense Commissar' was, of course, aimed at showing Zhukov's desire to replace Stalin as Defense Commissar, which obviously would not be well received by Stalin.

After this letter, Stalin likely spoke to Beria about Serov because the
next day Beria sent a letter to Stalin defending Serov, saying that SMERSH
operatives should be subordinate to Serov.[13] But it was too late. Apparently,
Stalin had already chosen Abakumov, and not Beria, to head state security

in the near future. On August 20, 1945, Stalin signed one of the last GKO orders (No. 9887) appointing Beria chairman of the secret State Committee No. 1, thus making him head of the Soviet atomic bomb project.[14] Later Beria was also responsible for State Committees No. 2 (jet engines) and No. 3 (radio location equipment).[15] Stalin needed Abakumov and his men as watchdogs. Soon Abakumov started collecting compromising materials on Marshal Zhukov, the conqueror of Berlin and ruler of Germany.

Marshal Zhukov and General Serov

In Germany, Marshal Georgii Zhukov became head of SVAG and commander in chief of Soviet troops.[16] The 1st and 2nd Belorussian and 1st Ukrainian fronts were reorganized as the Group of Soviet Occupation Forces in Germany or GSOVG. The UKR of GSOVG, headed by Vadis, reported not to Zhukov as commander in chief, but to Abakumov, as SMERSH's head. Vadis soon was transferred first to Bulgaria and then to the Transbaikal Front, and Pavel Zelenin, former head of the UKR of the 3rd Belorussian Front, succeeded him (Table 27-1). UKR GSOVG's headquarters were in Potsdam, a suburb of Berlin.[17]

With these reorganizations Abakumov began reporting to Stalin about Zhukov. This was not something new. Since 1939, the NKVD's OO, then UOO and SMERSH, had been collecting compromising materials involving Zhukov. The operational file was coded '*Uzel*' (Knot).[18] In 1942, Abakumov's UOO set up listening devices on the telephones at Zhukov's apartment and dacha; this action required a direct order from Stalin. But in July 1945, after arriving in Berlin, Abakumov began personally arresting Zhukov's subordinates.[19] Most likely, he was acting on Stalin's order again. However, Zhukov ordered the release of his generals and threatened to arrest Abakumov.

Abakumov first reported to Stalin on Zhukov's attempts to stop his troops' atrocities against German civilians. In June 1945, a joint order from Zhukov and his deputy, Lieutenant General Konstantin Telegin, stated: 'Local authorities, peasant communities, and individuals continue to complain about numerous acts of violence, rape, and robbery committed by men in Red Army uniforms... Women do not mow hay or work in the fields, for fear of being raped or robbed.'[20] Zhukov concluded: 'If order is not established...within three to five days... I will make serious decisions regarding all military and political personnel.'

On September 9, Zhukov issued another strong order: 'Marauding, hooliganism, and violence against the German population have not stopped; on the contrary, crimes committed by servicemen have increased. This behavior...must stop immediately at all costs.'[21] Zhukov ordered all commanders to live together with their subordinates and to completely prevent all contact with the local population.

Stalin did not support Zhukov's measures, and wrote to him eleven days later: 'Yesterday I learned from SMERSH [i.e., from Abakumov]…about the order of September 9… This order is harmful because it fails to improve discipline, and, on the contrary, breaks it and discredits commanders in the eyes of privates. Furthermore, if this order is seen by foreign army heads, they will judge the Red Army as an army of marauders. I ask that you immediately withdraw your order… I advise you to improve political work within the GSOVG troops and to use the courts of honor more frequently instead of scaring men with your orders to haul officers into the courts as common criminals.'[22] Stalin preferred covering up the atrocities to fighting against them.

Zhukov followed Stalin's order at once. Of course, measures such as courts of honor could not help, and a month later a plenum of the Supreme Court in Moscow issued a directive with the long, cumbersome title 'On the responsibility of servicemen of the Occupational Troops for Committing Crimes, According to Wartime Laws.'[23] It ordered the court martial of any serviceman who left the barracks for more than three hours without official permission. But the civilian complaints continued, and to stem the flow, a year later Serov simply ordered the organization of several show trials against complainants in each German province with the sentences published in the local press.[24] After this, Germans were afraid to report the atrocities.

Besides the atrocities, in 1945 looting in Germany by Soviet servicemen, including SMERSH operatives, became almost epidemic. Strictly speaking, Stalin's policy created this problem. In December 1944, Stalin issued the first order regulating the sending of parcels by servicemen from occupied territories.[25] A private was allowed to send parcels up to 5 kg in weight each month, while an officer could send 10 kg, and a general, 16 kg. From June 9, 1945 onwards, privates were permitted to take whatever they could carry in their arms, officers could utilize a bicycle or motorcycle, and generals could use a car to transport whatever they wanted.[26] Moreover, officers and generals could buy pianos, radios, hunting guns, watches, furs, rugs, cameras, and so on, for almost nothing. Even so, the looting continued. On September 25, 1945, Abakumov ordered:

> The Main Directorate 'SMERSH' has information that some counterintelligence units have considerable quantities of unofficially acquired vehicles and various trophy properties.
>
> These properties were not registered with and evaluated by 'SMERSH' organs. This leads to their inappropriate usage and storage and creates the conditions for violations of the law.
>
> To establish order in the keeping, accounting, and use of properties in 'SMERSH's' possession, I order:

The immediate organization of all SMERSH properties. Detailed descriptions should be reported to the Main Directorate 'SMERSH.' All properties should be sealed and their use forbidden...

Heads of 'SMERSH' organs who continue to hold unaccounted properties, or to embezzle valuables, will be court-martialed regardless of their positions.[276]

Abakumov did not apply this order to himself: a search of his two huge apartments after his arrest in 1951 yielded a long list of items stolen in Germany.

Despite a clear preference for Abakumov, Stalin did not dismiss Serov, and Serov continued to report on SMERSH in Germany. In September 1946, he described the situation during 1945 in a letter to Stalin claiming that Abakumov 'used to call Vadis or his deputy Sidnev on the phone and demand that they not report to [Serov] or follow his orders. [Abakumov] threatened them with reprimands and even arrest.'[28] Serov also complained about SMERSH's activity:

During the last period, when 'Smersh' was no longer subordinate to me in operational work, I received numerous reports about its outrageous activities, and I always informed Zelenin [head of the UKR of GSOVG] about these cases and even reported common occurrences to the Ministry [MGB]...

For instance, in the evening, drunken 'Smersh' officers went to a field near the city of Halle to carry out death sentences decreed by the Military Tribunal. Because the officers were drunk, they buried the bodies carelessly. Germans passing along on a nearby road in the morning saw two hands and a head sticking out of the ground. They dug out the corpses, saw bullet holes in the backs of their heads [a Soviet method of execution], gathered witnesses, and reported to the local police. We were forced to take urgent measures.

The same year two German women, arrested [i.e., kidnapped] in the British zone of Berlin, escaped from 'Smersh's' custody in the division commanded by General V.[asilii] Stalin [Stalin's son]. After their escape, they told the British that they had been arrested by the Russians. 'Smersh' officers tried to conceal this fact, but General V. Stalin found out and informed me about the situation. We took the necessary measures.[29]

Although Serov did not identify the particular 'urgent measures' that were taken in the first case, the Germans who found the bodies were most likely arrested and sent to a concentration camp. In the second case, since Vasilii Stalin was involved and had probably told the story to his father, the guilty SMERSH officers were most likely arrested and tried.

Zhukov Leaves Germany

Vasilii Stalin's complaints to his father about the poor quality of Soviet planes compared with American aircraft led to SMERSH's last arrests of high-ranking generals, to Zhukov's downfall and to the discrediting of Georgii Malenkov.[30] The story began in 1943 when air force commander in chief Aleksandr Novikov complained to Stalin about the undisciplined behavior of Vasilii, Stalin's 21-year-old son, who was a military pilot. Vasilii was unhappy with Novikov's order that he fly only one plane as the other pilots did, and not three planes, as he wanted.

That year Stalin promoted Vasilii from captain to colonel—two ranks higher. Soon Vasilii was appointed commander of an air force corps, but three months later the Air Force Military Council dismissed him when an officer was killed during one of his drinking parties, and eight others, including Vasilii, were wounded. Stalin approved the dismissal: 'Colonel Stalin is dismissed from the position of corps commander for drunkenness and debauchery and for corrupting the corps.'[31] Vasilii continued his service in 1944, but Stalin did not talk to him until the Potsdam Conference. Vasilii accompanied his father to Potsdam and used that opportunity to complain about Novikov.

In early December 1945, Novikov (now Chief Marshal of Aviation and Commander of the Air Force, having been twice awarded the Gold Star for Hero of the Soviet Union) did not sign a document approving the promotion of the 24-year-old Vasilii to the rank of major general. On New Year's Eve, Stalin suddenly called Novikov at home to ask why.[32] Novikov explained that Vasilii was too young and had a poor professional education, having graduated from an aviation school rather than the Zhukovsky Air Force Academy. Stalin ordered Novikov to put Vasilii's name on the general list of promotions.

After this conversation, the frustrated Novikov called Zhukov and told him of Stalin's demand. Zhukov said: 'You can't do anything, this is an order!' Since Zhukov's telephone was tapped, SMERSH now knew there was a connection between Novikov and Zhukov.

As a first step, SMERSH operatives arrested Marshal Sergei Khudyakov while he was on his way to Moscow from the Far East.[34] Khudyakov was an Armenian, and his real name was Armenak Khanferyants. During the war with Germany, he had been Novikov's deputy; then he had commanded the 12th Air Force Army that successfully fought against the Japanese. During the investigation, SMERSH operatives put Khudyakov in Sukhanovo Prison. Accused of having been a British spy, Khudyakov (under torture) signed testimony that Aviation Industry Commissar Aleksei Shakhurin and his subordinates had conducted activities to sabotage aircraft production. His statement also mentioned Novikov, Zhukov, and some others.

Stalin read the transcript of Khudyakov's interrogation, and on December 29, he instructed the Politburo to dismiss Shakhurin from his post. Shakhurin was accused of looting for bringing in seven cars from Germany, and Stalin soon ordered Abakumov to arrest Shakhurin on charges of building defective planes. On April 4, 1946, Abakumov's operatives arrested Shakhurin. The arrests of the other members of the so-called 'Aviators Case,' whose names Khudyakov was forced to mention under torture, continued through April (Appendix I, see http://www.smershbook.com). As a result, Aleksandr Repin (Chief Engineer of the Air Force and Novikov's deputy); Nikolai Seleznyov (who during the war headed the Main Directorate of the Air Force in charge of ordering military equipment); Nikolai Shimanov (a member of the Air Force Military Council); and two administrators at the Personnel Directorate of the Central Committee, A. V. Budnikov (head of the department that managed the building of airplanes) and G. M. Grigoryan (head of the department that managed the manufacture of airplane motors), ended up in Lubyanka Prison.[35]

On April 11, Stalin sent a letter to the Politburo members and the newly appointed heads of the military aviation industry, accusing Shakhurin and the other arrestees of accepting, during the war, newly built military planes that had defects in exchange for being rewarded for having a high number of new planes in the air force. The letter ended with the statement: 'Front pilots helped us to discover this affair. The guilty have already been arrested—Shakhurin, Repin, and Seleznyov, as well as a member of the Air Force Military Council, Shimanov. Testimonies of the arrested are attached. Secretary of the Central Committee J. Stalin.'[36] In fact, there were no 'front pilots' except Vasilii Stalin, who complained to his father about Novikov, while the attached 'testimonies' had been falsified by Abakumov's investigators and signed by the arrestees under torture. In support of Stalin's accusations, a special commission headed by Nikolai Bulganin concluded that the air force had accepted and used newly built military planes that had defects.

On April 22, 1946, a group of SMERSH operatives arrived in Novikov's apartment. This was the last arrest Abakumov made as head of SMERSH. Novikov's daughter Svetlana recalled:

> Abakumov himself showed up during the search [of the apartment]. Behaving like the owner of the apartment, he went through all rooms, inspecting the whole interior. Apparently, he wanted to take something. He came up to the radio-record player machine, the most advanced technological achievement of the time. He put a record on the player and listened to the music, then stepped back. Obviously, he did not like the machine: the sound was not good, and the machine did not look great. He did not

look at us [Novikov's family members]; we were useless to him. He strolled through the rooms one more time and left, clearly dissatisfied.[37]

It was common that while arresting a person and searching his room or apartment, security officers grabbed some valuables for themselves. After Novikov had been arrested, Vasilii Stalin took Novikov's dacha (country house). Novikov and all the arrested generals were deprived of their military ranks and awards.

Abakumov put Aleksandr Leonov, head of the GUKR's Investigation Department, and two of his ruthless deputies, Mikhail Likhachev and Vladimir Komarov, in charge of the investigation. Additionally, Aleksandr Chernov, head of SMERSH's Secretariat, and his deputy Yakov Brover-man, wrote falsified interrogation transcripts. Likhachev quickly reduced Novikov to 'a state of physical and moral depression.'[38] Another arrestee, Aleksandr Repin, later described Likhachev's methods: 'From the first day of my arrest I was deprived of sleep. I was interrogated day and night… After two or three days of this regime… I was reduced to a state where I would give any testimony to stop this torture.'[39]

Later Novikov told his daughter that he was interrogated during the nights until 5 a.m.[40] Then he was forced to have a drink laced with a sleeping drug. A mere hour later, at 6 a.m., all prisoners, including Novikov, were forced to get up. This treatment continued from April 22–30 and from May 4–8.

But even during that hour between 5 a.m. and 6 a.m. Novikov was not able to sleep normally, because a 500-watt light bulb was left constantly on in the cell. Prisoners were forbidden to turn over onto their bellies and hide from the light. After spending six years in prisons, for the rest of his life Novikov always covered his face with a handkerchief before going to sleep.

Soon the real target of the case was revealed: Marshal Zhukov. Abakumov personally forced Novikov to sign a false statement implicating Zhukov.[41] A letter from Novikov to Beria, dated April 2, 1953, describes this document:

In a state of deep depression, and exhausted by interrogations that continued without interruption for sleep or rest, I signed a protocol [transcript] of my interrogation, concocted by investigator Likhachev, in which I admitted being guilty of everything I was accused of…

During the investigation Abakumov interrogated me several times. Investigator Likhachev was always present. Abakumov cursed me using unprintable swear words, abused my human dignity, threatened to shoot me, to arrest my family, and so forth…

In the presence of investigator Likhachev he said I had to sign a statement addressed to I. V. Stalin that was already written and typed…

Likhachev gave me pages to sign, one by one... The statement, as I re-member it, said that I had conducted criminal actions while working in the Air Force...Then it presented various lies that implicated Malenkov, a Cen-tral Committee Politburo member, Marshal Zhukov, and Serov, deputy Interior Minister, as facts that I supposedly knew.[42]

The mention of Malenkov in the statement was no accident, as the case was part of Stalin's complicated game to reduce Malenkov's power because of his GKO coalition with Beria since 1944.[43]

The statement that Likhachev forced Novikov to sign also included a paragraph about Vasilii Stalin:

Zhukov...supposedly takes care of Vasilii Stalin like a father. However, the reality is different. Recently, before my arrest, I was in Zhukov's office. I told him that, apparently, Vasilii Stalin would soon be appointed Inspector of the Air Force. I said I didn't like this appointment and also said other bad things about Vasilii. As we were alone, Zhukov immediately responded with unprintable swearing and other disgusting remarks about Vasilii Sta-lin, much worse than anything I said.[44]

Later in Likhachev's office, Novikov 'was given some typed materi-al...and forced to rewrite it by hand, which took between five and seven hours.'[45] This way the concocted transcript would look like Novikov's 'per-sonal testimony,' and could be presented to Stalin.

Like Novikov, Shakhurin and Shimanov were also reduced to 'a state of physical and moral depression.' Shimanov's real 'guilt' may have been his participation in the Air Force Military Council meeting that dismissed Vasilii Stalin in May 1943. Abakumov forced Shakhurin and Shimanov to sign false statements addressed to Stalin. Stalin ordered copies of all state-ments and interrogation transcripts to be sent to every Politburo member. Thus a trap for Zhukov was set up.

On March 1, 1946, the Council of Commissars approved Vasilii Stalin's promotion to Major General. Vyacheslav Molotov personally called Vasilii during the night to congratulate him. However, Vasilii was so drunk that at first he could not understand the news.

The same month Stalin summoned Zhukov to Moscow, where he was appointed commander in chief of the Ground Troops, as well as deputy Defense Minister. Army General Vasilii Sokolovsky, his deputy in Germa-ny, succeeded Zhukov as Commander of GSOVG. Pavel Zelenin contin-ued as head of the Counterintelligence Directorate of GSOVG.

On March 15, Malenkov, previously deputy chairman of the Council of Commissars, was not reinstalled in the new government's Council of Min-isters. However, three days later he and Beria became full members of the

Politburo. On April 30, Novikov signed the final copy of 'his' statement in Abakumov's office. Apparently this document affected Malenkov's fate, because a week later the Politburo dismissed Malenkov from his position as a Central Committee secretary. The disgrace was not complete—two weeks later he was appointed Chairman of the Special Committee for Rocket Technology, the second most important military project after the Atomic Project headed by Beria. But Malenkov was sent out of Moscow to Kazakhstan until August 1946, when he was finally appointed Deputy Chairman of the Council of Ministers (i.e., Stalin's deputy). In 1948, he was reappointed secretary of the Central Committee. However, Malenkov never forgot Stalin's brief disfavor, and he blamed Abakumov for organizing the Aviators Case.

On Stalin's order, during April–May 1946 the Politburo members and heads of the aviation industry periodically received Abakumov's reports on the investigation entitled 'Summaries of the Results of Interrogations.'[46] Aleksandr Poskrebyshev, head of Stalin's secretariat, personally sent these 'summaries' to the addressees. For every aviation-industry addressee, the receiving of a new 'summary' was a personal threat. It was clear that if he did not please the dictator, his name would eventually appear in the records of interrogations and then he would share the fate of the previous arrestees.

On May 10–11, 1946, six days after SMERSH was merged with the MGB and Abakumov became MGB Minister, the Military Collegium chaired by Vasilii Ulrikh sentenced Novikov, Shakhurin, and the three other defendants to four to seven years, and two Party functionaries to two years in prison—an unusually lenient punishment for these crimes. All of them were charged with the 'abuse of power and negligence of duties' (Article 193-17a). Additionally, the properties of the condemned were confiscated. Immediately after the session Ulrikh sent Stalin a copy of the verdict marked 'Top Secret.'[47]

As Molotov recalled later, Novikov and Shakhurin were guilty of making technical modifications to planes 'in violation of the Politburo's decision to prohibit any unauthorized alterations in the design of aircraft already operational in the air force.'[48] In other words, specialists were forbidden to make professional adjustments in aircraft design after the Politburo had made its decision and the perpetrators were punished as criminals. Novikov was released in 1952, while those who remained imprisoned were released soon after Stalin's death.

Khudyakov was held in MGB investigation prisons until April 1950, when he was sentenced to death and shot, with Stalin's approval.[49] In January 1951, his wife and two children were arrested as family members of a traitor to the Motherland. The OSO of the MGB sentenced them to exile in the Krasnoyarsk Province in Siberia. After Stalin's death they were allowed to go back to Moscow, but their former apartment was occupied by the family of an MGB officer.

Zhukov's new appointment, shortly before his downfall, was a typical Stalin trick. Already on June 1, 1946, at a High Military Council meeting, Stalin criticized Zhukov for his behavior in Germany and accused him of attempted plotting. Zhukov was dismissed and appointed Commander of the Odessa Military District, an unimportant position. Marshal Ivan Konev replaced him as commander in chief of the Ground Troops and deputy Defense Minister. Eight days later Stalin signed an additional top-secret order denouncing Zhukov.[50] Stalin, Bulganin, and Vasilevsky prepared the text accusing Zhukov even of failure to conquer Berlin in time.

However, Stalin did not order Zhukov's arrest, possibly due to Zhukov's popularity among war veterans. The story continued two years later when Abakumov arrested Zhukov's former subordinates, including General Telegin, for looting and corruption, and presented Stalin with more material on Zhukov.

In Austria and Hungary

There were no conflicts between SMERSH and the NKVD in the other Soviet occupation zones. By the end of the war, troops of the 3rd Ukrainian Front, with its UKR under Pyotr Ivashutin, occupied most of Austria and established its HQ in Vienna. At the end of May 1945, the troops of the 1st Ukrainian Front began being relocated from Germany to Austria, Hungary, and Czechoslovakia. Five armies of the 2nd Ukrainian Front, including two Romanian armies, joined them, and on June 10, all of these troops were renamed the Central Group of Military Forces (*Tsentral'naya gruppa voisk* or TsGV).[51]

Czechoslovakia was more fortunate: by December 1, 1945, both the Soviet and American troops (the latter had occupied the western part of the country) were withdrawn from its territory. However, Czechoslovakia was not left without an oversight of Soviet security services: on April 15, 1945, Ivan Chichaev, a long-term and experienced NKVD/NKGB agent, was appointed Soviet Envoy to Prague.

The TsGV's HQ was located in the picturesque town of Baden, 26 kilometers from Vienna, while the HQ's branch was in Budapest. Marshal Ivan Konev became TsGV commander in chief and Supreme Commissar of Austria. In April 1946, Konev was called back to Moscow, and in May 1946, Army General Vasilii Urasov replaced Konev in Vienna. Nikolai Korolev, former head of the UKR of the 2nd Ukrainian Front, headed the Military Counterintelligence Directorate (UKR) of the TsGV (Table 27-1). For secrecy, until 1946 the whole TsGV was called 'Konev's outfit,' and its UKR was known as 'Korolev's outfit.'[52]

The HQ in Baden (its mailing address was 'Army Unit No. 32750') occupied a former high school building in the center of the town, while the Counterintelligence Directorate was located in several neighboring villas.

An operational NKVD battalion, attached to the UKR, was stationed in another part of the town.[53]

The basements of the UKR buildings were turned into investigation prisons. Nicholas Nagy-Talavera, a former 18-year-old prisoner who had survived previous imprisonment in Auschwitz, later recalled:

> The prison in Baden was very primitive, but very carefully done, in a former sanatorium-hotel, with a basement. Upstairs were the investigation cells with the officers, and they put you down in the basement when the examination was over...
>
> The cells were of various sizes, but always overflowing. Regardless of how big or small they were, there were always more people than there were supposed to be.[54]

During a 59-day investigation, Nagy-Talavera was mercilessly tortured. 'I still have scars from this torture—burns,' he said in 1971.[55]

In Budapest, the OKR SMERSH/MGB was located in a notorious building at 60 Andrássy Boulevard, previously occupied by the HQ of the dreadful Fascist Arrow Cross Party and then by the equally feared Communist security service, the AVO/AVH. Currently, this building houses a museum called 'House of Terror,' which reminds Hungarians of the totalitarian past of their country, and of the Soviet occupation.

In addition to the UKR of the TsGV, there were two separate operational SMERSH/MGB groups permanently based in Budapest and Vienna. These groups had names of inspectorates attached to the Allied Control Commissions (ACCs). These international commissions were established, in theory, to orchestrate the Allied control of postwar management in the defeated former Axis countries. In fact, Soviet military representatives dominated the ACCs, and the commissions became a tool of the Sovietization of the East European countries. SMERSH officers of the inspectorates were called 'inspectors.'

In Hungary the ACC was organized in March 1945 and was formally chaired by Marshal Kliment Voroshilov. However, the marshal remained in Moscow for the most part, leaving his deputy, Lieutenant General Vladimir Sviridov, in charge of all ACC affairs.[56] Mikhail Belkin, former head of the UKR of the 3rd Baltic Front, headed the Inspectorate in Budapest. Later Nikolai Velikanov, former head of the OKR SMERSH of the 52nd Army (1st Ukrainian Front), replaced Belkin. Georgii Yevdokimenko, formerly Belkin's deputy at the 3rd Baltic Front, was deputy head of the Inspectorate in Budapest. Later, from June 1947 to March 1950, Belkin headed the UKR MGB of the TsGV, and in this capacity he supervised the organization of the show trial of the prominent Hungarian Communist politician Laszlo Rajk, in Budapest in 1949.[57]

In Vienna, the ACC for Austria was established later, on July 24, 1945. Before June the Soviets simply did not allow Allied military forces to enter the city. In April, the new provisional government headed by the Austrian socialist leader Karl Renner was formed under Soviet supervision. During July 1945, the Allied governments accepted the division of Vienna and the whole of Austria into four zones: Soviet, American, British and French. The central part of Vienna became an International Zone with its Allied Commandants' Office stationed in the historical Palace of Justice. Not until October 1 did the Western Allies recognize Renner's government.

Colonel General Zheltov, deputy Supreme Commissar of Austria, headed the Soviet part of the ACC.[58] He placed his headquarters in the Hotel Imperial, while his staff lived in the requisitioned Grand Hotel. These were the most luxurious hotels in the city. Grigorii Bolotin-Balyasnyi and then Nikolai Rozanov, both continuing to be Abakumov's assistants, headed the Inspectorate of Zheltov's ACC group. This inspectorate mostly collected information from agents about the garrisons in the American and British zones of the city. Interestingly, in October 1945, Yurii Pokrovsky, head of the Legal Department of Zheltov's group, was appointed deputy Soviet Chief Prosecutor in Nuremberg.

To entertain Red Army officers in Vienna, the Soviet Officers Club (*Dom Ofitserov*) was opened in a wing of the Schönbrunn Palace. In 1830, Emperor Franz Josef I was born in this wing and he died there in 1916. The Soviet military authorities left intact the interior decoration in the wing, and used it for big parties given to impress Western diplomats and for meetings. Ernst Kolman, a Czech mathematician who became a Soviet Communist Party functionary, recalled that at the end of 1945 he gave a lecture on the political situation in Czechoslovakia to a military audience, including SMERSH officers, in Vienna.[59] The lecture took place in Franz Josef's throne hall.

Poland

At the end of the war Poland was occupied by Marshal Konstantin Rokossovsky's 2nd Belorussian Front, which on May 29, 1945 became the Northern Group of Military Forces (*Severnaya gruppa voisk* or SGV).[60] On June 24, Rokossovsky commanded the Victory Parade at Red Square in Moscow. Later, from 1949 to 1956, he was Polish Minister of Defense, Deputy Chairman of the Polish Council of Ministers, and a member of the Politburo of the Polish Communist Party. In June 1945, Yakov Yedunov, former head of the UKR of the 2nd Belorussian Front, became head of the Military Counterintelligence Directorate of the SGV. The SGV headquarters were in the town of Legnica (formerly German Liegnitz), an area soon called 'Little Moscow' by the local Poles.

Until March 1946, there were additional SMERSH and NKVD structures in Poland. Up to July 4, 1945, Abakumov's deputy Meshik was NKVD Plenipotentiary to the 1st Ukrainian Front and deputy commander in charge of civilian administration for this front in the part of Poland occupied by the 1st Ukrainian Front's troops. From March to August 1945, Meshik was also Adviser to the Ministry of Public Administration of the Provisional Polish Government. At the same time, in March–April 1945, Serov, NKVD Plenipotentiary to the 1st Belorussian Front, was also NKVD Adviser to the newly formed Polish Ministry of Public Security.[61]

On August 20, 1945, Meshik's SMERSH career ended with his appointment as deputy head of the 1st Main Directorate subordinate to the Sovnarkom.[62] This Directorate, headed by former Commissar for Munitions Boris Vannikov, was charged with building the atomic bomb.

In Poland, Nikolai Selivanovsky continued as NKVD Plenipotentiary of the 4th Ukrainian Front until July 1945, with fifteen NKVD regiments at his disposal. In addition, on April 27, he replaced Serov as NKVD Adviser to the Polish Ministry of Public Security. Selivanovsky, who was responsible for the final destruction of the Armija Krajowa, had sent Beria eighteen detailed reports about his activities up to October 1945.[63] He also helped to create a Soviet-type security service in Poland.

During Selivanovsky's presence in Poland, SMERSH and the NKVD used the infamous Auschwitz as a concentration camp for German POWs and Soviet repatriates. Nicola Sinevirsky, who in June 1945 visited the camp with a group of operatives of the 2nd Department of the UKR of the 4th Ukrainian Front, recalled:

> In the 'brick camp,' the first gas chamber was still intact… Today the 'brick camp' is the home of German war prisoners. The 'wooden camp' [with its four gas chambers] serves as the home of Russian repatriates—about twenty thousand of them. They are tightly guarded by sentries, marching day and night around the camp. SMERSH men, commanded by about fifty officers, were also working among them around the clock. The attitude of SMERSH men, which represented the real attitude of the Soviets toward these people, became worse and more degraded every day.[64]

Between October 1945 and March 1946, Selivanovsky's deputy, Semyon Davydov, signed all reports to Beria, and on March 20, 1946, Selivanovsky sent his last report from Poland. In April 1946, Selivanovsky, now back in Moscow, was reinstalled as Abakumov's deputy, while Davydov became the MVD/MGB Adviser in Poland.[65]

Bulgaria and Romania

After Marshal Fyodor Tolbukhin's 3rd Ukrainian Front was relocated from Austria to Bulgaria and Romania, it became the Southern Group of Troops (*Yuzhnaya gruppa voisk* or YuGV), with headquarters in Sofia.[66]

Tolbukhin also chaired the ACC in Bulgaria and Romania.[67] Major General Aleksei Voul, former deputy head of the UKR SMERSH of the 3rd Ukrainian Front and now deputy head of the UKR SMERSH of the YuGV, also headed the Inspectorate in Sofia (Table 27-1). The Soviet staff of the ACC included four generals, a vice admiral, and 100 officers; the rest were rank-and-file staffers—a total of 270 members.[68] By comparison, the British section consisted of 110 members; of these, 24 were officers, and the head of the section, Major General Walter Hayes Oxley, was the only general. The American ACC section consisted of 60 members with the only general, Major General John A. Crane, as its head. It arrived in Sofia in November 1944, and in March 1946, Major General Walter M. Robertson replaced General Crane.

In fact, Colonel General Sergei Biryuzov, commander of the 37th Army stationed in Bulgaria and Tolbukhin's deputy chair, was in charge of the ACC work in Bulgaria. Lieutenant General Aleksandr Cherepanov, Tolbukhin's assistant in the ACC and the Soviet military adviser to the Bulgarian Army (who later served as ACC chair from May 1947 till May 1948), wrote in his memoirs:

> Biryuzov…was a decisive, tough and demanding commander, sometimes rigorous, complementing well the restrained and gentle F. I. Tolbukhin…
>
> S. S. Biryuzov was considerably younger than Oxley, Crane, and Robertson. However, his official position was much higher than that of these generals and he was much more mature. At first General Crane tried to stress his own 'importance.' Biryuzov, on the other hand, behaved with natural dignity. This forced the Anglo-American representatives to admit that Biryuzov was the de facto ACC head.
>
> After work, the Soviet and western ACC members used to meet unofficially. S. S. Biryuzov liked to invite everybody to the concerts of our military ensemble of dancers and singers. Also, we used to watch together documentary films and movies sent from the Soviet Union, United States, and England.[69]

The American ACC members remembered Soviet receptions differently: 'Efforts were made to get an American drunk in order to pump him. The most familiar tactic was to have a Russian group at a reception insist that the American drink separately with each, or at a table a Russian might be served water in a liquor glass while the American got vodka.'[70] Undoubtedly, SMERSH officers, whom the Americans could not identify since they wore no special insignias, attended the receptions.

William Donovan, OSS Director, and other American officials conducted long negotiations with Pavel Fitin, head of the NKGB's Foreign Intelligence, on the possibility of attaching OSS teams in Bulgaria, Romania and Hungary to the American ACC delegations.[71] Biryuzov was against the presence of the American and especially British intelligence groups in Bulgaria, and in December 1944 a small new OSS team that arrived along with the ACC section a month earlier was forced to leave Sofia.

Stalin used Biryuzov and his ACC as a tool for reducing the involvement of the former Allies in Bulgarian politics, which were completely controlled by the Soviet Politburo through Bulgarian Communists.[72] In November 1944, Biryuzov wrote to the Bulgarian prime minister: 'From now on, any contact between the Allied countries and the Bulgarian government…will go only through the…[Soviet] heads of the Allied Control Commission… Any other appeal [to the Bulgarian government]…including the appeals from the other members of the Allied countries, is not allowed [to proceed].'[73] A few years later, from 1953–54, Biryuzov was appointed commander and chief Commissar of Austria.

Lieutenant General Vladislav Vinogradov, ACC deputy chair, chaired the ACC in Bucharest. Pyotr Timofeev, one of Abakumov's assistants, headed the Inspectorate of this ACC (Table 27-1). Vinogradov's deputy, Colonel General Ivan Susaikin, used to tell his Red Army subordinates about the task of the ACC: 'The world revolution is moving to the west. Our [Soviet] troops are here to help the Romanian people to follow the Socialist way of developing their country.'[74]

Unusually for a Red Army general, Vinogradov was well educated and knew several languages—German, English, French, Romanian, and even Latin and Greek—and, therefore, could easily converse with the Allied members of the ACC. Also, he was an accomplished chess master and had authored articles about the game of chess. However, like Biryuzov, Vinogradov had no problem giving orders to the local government. In December 1944, following the GKO order, he handed a draft of the decision written in the name of the Romanian government, to the Romanian prime minister.[75] In fact, this was an order to intern the whole adult population of German civilians in Romania in preparation for sending them to the Soviet Union for forced labor.

The American ACC section in Bucharest was formed in early November 1944. After the arrival on November 23 of its head, Brigade General Courtland Van Rensselaer Schuyler, the OSS team that had arrived there in September became its sub-section.[76] As in the Baltics in 1940, in 1944 American witnesses were horrified by the deportation ordered now by the intellectual Vinogradov. Many years later the widow of Frank Wisner, head of the OSS group in Bucharest, told an interviewer: 'My husband was brutally, brutally shocked. It was what probably affected his life more than any other single thing. The herding-up of those people and putting them in open boxcars to die on their way as they were going into concentration camps. While they were being hauled off as laborers by the carload in the middle of winter.'[77] Robert Bishop, a member of Wisner's OSS group, re-called in his memoirs that trains 'loaded full of human freight—thirty to a box car—[were] carrying them to slavery and death.'[78]

On the whole, 69,332 German civilians were deported from Romania, and 73 were deported from Bulgaria (the German population in Bulgaria was very small).[79] Similar deportations were conducted throughout Hungary, Czechoslovakia, and Yugoslavia, with a total number of 112,480 German men and women deported to the Soviet Union. One hundred and six specially created SMERSH operational groups assisted the NKVD troops in conducting the deportation.

Before Wisner left Bucharest in January 1945, he and Robert Bishop had for months been reading cables from Moscow to the Romanian Communist Party, which they obtained with the assistance of the Romanian Security Service, the Sigurantza.[80] Additionally, through Theodore Mannicatide (a veteran of the Romanian General Staff whom Wisner provided with the alias 'Tonsillitis'), the OSS team received copies of Soviet military orders. Robert Bishop also reported on the NKGB's and NKVD's activities in Romania, as well as on SMERSH teams in Romania, Bulgaria, Hungary, Poland, Italy, and Greece—all the countries where the ACCs or Soviet military missions were established.[81] Strangely, he called SMERSH 'GUGBZ' (*Glavnoe Upravlenie Gosudarstvennoi Bezopasnosti* or Main State Security Directorate) and mistakenly thought that it was a sub-section of the NKVD.

Apparently, Bishop's activity was noticed by the Soviet Inspectorate and in retaliation, in September 1945 the OSS sub-section of the US/ACC was closed. Additionally, the whole previous cooperation between the OSS and NKGB came to an end.[82] After this, General Van Schuyler supervised cover operations.

UKR Directorates in Action

The UKR of each of the military groups consisted of four departments.[83] The 1st was in charge of controlling the headquarters; the 2nd was in charge of finding foreign agents among the troops of the military group and checking former POWs; the 3rd was tasked with fighting against foreign agents and terrorists, as well as finding anti-Soviet elements and traitors; and the 4th was an investigation department. Romanov, who worked in the SMERSH/TsGV headquarters in Baden and Budapest, described the main goal of his directorate: spying on the secret services, military, and Western members of the ACC:

> In its internal operations Smersh took advantage of the services of Austrian civilians working for our allies... A particularly popular 'key' [for recruitment] was to promise an individual that any of his relatives who were

prisoners in the USSR would be found and released as quickly as possible…Another way was to obtain work with the western allies for persons who were known to have pro-communist views… We even recruited allied personnel themselves. Smersh took into account the strong pro-Soviet feelings which were then current among citizens of the western democracies.[84]

Romanov continued: 'For external surveillance, or spying, Smersh used…members of the Austrian Communist Party… We would provide them with documents, which would guarantee that they were left alone by both the Soviet occupation authorities and the Austrian police.' In 1945, a special political police was even formed in Austria, consisting mostly of local Communists, to help the Soviet occupational authorities.[85] However, the former Nazis were as useful as the Communists:

Smersh exploited for the same purpose former Nazis, insignificant functionaries of Hitler's NSDAP. Many of them were people, who, according to Soviet law, ought to have been in prisons and concentration camps… It's true that in this kind of case we really needed to have hostages who could be used as leverage for blackmail. An individual's wife, children or elderly parents, if they lived in the Soviet Occupation Zone, could be used for this purpose. The local Smersh bodies in the place where these relatives lived kept them under permanent secret surveillance to prevent them escaping to the west.[86]

Prostitutes were also a tool of SMERSH surveillance: 'Among the Austrian agents whom Smersh recruited, the procurers of girls for allied military personnel worked with particular success… We had in Vienna a number of "meeting houses" or brothels, which Smersh financed for the same purpose.'[87] SMERSH/MGB used these methods in all occupied countries.

In the Soviet occupational zones, the Russian Federation Criminal Code with its notorious Article 58 was introduced. Under various paragraphs of this article, not only Soviet citizens but also local citizens arrested by SMERSH were charged, mostly as spies (Article 58-6).[88] Besides investigating the arrestees locally, the UKRs sent many of those suspected of espionage to Moscow.

The fate of Gotthold Starke, a German journalist and diplomat arrested by the operatives of the UKR SMERSH of GSOVG in the town of Mulhausen in July 1945, is a good example (Appendix II, see http://www.smershbook.com). Apparently, his main 'crime' was being an attaché at the German Embassy in Moscow just before the outbreak of war. During the war, Starke served in the Press and Communication Department of the German Foreign Office, and he was chief editor of the newspaper *Deutsche Rundschau in Polen* published by the

German occupation authorities in Poland. Starke was kept in Moscow investigation prisons until October 7, 1947, when the OSO sentenced him to a 10-year imprisonment for his 'assistance to the world bourgeoisie' (Article 58-4) and spy activity (Article 58-6/1).[89] Even the length of the term shows that the case was falsified: at the time, most spies were sentenced either to no less than 15 years of imprisonment, or to death. Starke's Finnish cell mate in Vladimir Prison, Unto Parvilahti, later recalled:

> Gotthold Starke was a finely cultured man, a humanist and journalist by vocation… Starke had got terribly thin; he often had severe heart attacks; he breathed with only one lung, but it would have been hard to find a better cell-mate. If the rest of the world's diplomats were equipped with the same tact as Gotthold Starke, the world would be a more peaceful place.[90]

Starke was released in July 1955, after serving the term.

The other arrestee, Christian Ludwig of Mecklenburg, was 'guilty' of being a duke. His father, Friedrich Francis IV, was the reigning grand duke of Mecklenburg-Schwerin, but he abdicated after World War I. Christian Ludwig was his father's successor as Grand Duke due to the marriage of his elder brother Friedrich to a non-noble woman. UKR SMERSH of GSOVG arrested Duke Christian Ludwig in October 1945 at his Ludwigslust Castle. A year before that, in 1944, he was discharged from the German Army, ostensibly for being a member of a former ruling house; most probably, the real reason was that he was close to the military plotters against Hitler.

On his prisoner card in Vladimir Prison, the duke's employment status is given as 'manager of an estate.' Obviously, he personally committed no crime because later he was charged with 'the preparation and conducting of aggressive war against the Soviet Union'—a 'crime' of which any officer of the German Army could have been accused.[91] Duke Christian Ludwig was kept in Moscow investigation prisons until October 1951, when the OSO sentenced him to a 25-year imprisonment. Like Starke, the duke was sent to Vladimir Prison. The card has a handwritten note: 'He is socially dangerous due to his past.' The duke was released in June 1953.

Those arrestees who were investigated locally were tried by military tribunals of the occupation troops. The above-mentioned Nagy-Talavera described a court session of the military tribunal of the TsGV in Baden that tried him:

> The trial was a farce…
>
>   The table was covered with a red cloth and on the wall were pictures of Kalinin, Stalin, and Lenin and some slogans about Soviet justice. Two guards with machine pistols were standing in the room at all times…

[The] box where the prisoners had to be was in fact the most horrible [of all]. There were things written on it in four languages—in German 'Gott hilft mir' and 'Gott ste, mir bei,' because they were giving death sentences here also, and in Romanian and Hungarian, 'Goodbye, my mother, forever,' etc...

They sentenced me to 25 years of slave labor... Helping the Americans was the main charge. I was sentenced on Paragraph 58, Article 6 [espionage].[92]

Political convicts, including Nagy-Talavera, were transported to the Soviet Union to serve their terms. However, the OSO in Moscow made decisions on the most important cases in absentia, while prisoners were still kept in Baden or Germany. Many prisoners sentenced to death were also transported to Moscow for execution.[93]

Additionally, SMERSH operatives in all occupied countries were involved in vetting Soviet citizens brought by in the Nazis as slave laborers (*ostarbeiters*) during the war, as well as POWs. One hundred vetting camps for returning POWs and civilians, each holding 10,000 people, were created in the rear zones of the 1st and 2nd Belorussian fronts, and the 1st–4th Ukrainian fronts.[94] Vetting was performed by Vetting and Screening Commissions (PFK) that included both SMERSH officers from the staff of UKRs and officers sent from Moscow HQ.[95] SMERSH officers checked POWs, while civilians were checked by joint NKVD, NKGB and SMERSH commissions.

In Austria, the filtration camp near the town of Wiener-Neustadt, 50 kilometers from Vienna, was the biggest. Anatoly Gulin, a former Red Army sergeant who was captured by the Germans but subsequently escaped and spent the last months of the war in an Italian partisan group, recalled entering this camp with other Soviet repatriates transported from Italy:

The camp...occupied a gigantic area surrounded by a barbed-wire fence with watchtowers at the corners, manned by guards. Inside the barbed wire were the partially bombed-out buildings of a town with an aerodrome. After our companies walked into this territory, the Red Army camp administrators...insulted us with language so foul that we had almost forgotten the meaning of the words [while in captivity]. The commandant of the camp...was literally seething with hatred...It looked like if he could, he would have killed all of us...

We were put in a semi-destroyed building...

The camp was guarded by soldiers recruited in Central Asia, and they were no better than the Germans. They thought we were criminals... They used to shoot at our windows without any reason, and they wounded some of us.[96]

Gulin also briefly described the vetting procedure:

One day the *osobisty* [SMERSH officers] came to the camp, and the intense work started: one repatriate after another was called in, and some persons even twice. Finally, it was my turn. A young lieutenant interrogated me. He pretended to be important and tried to look older than he was.

After I answered his last question, he gave me permission to leave, but suddenly he stopped me at the door. He was interested in my watch and simply demanded that I give it to him. I was filled with indignation and abruptly refused. The lieutenant responded with foul language and said that if I had been clever enough to cooperate, I would have been at home in a couple of months, but now I would work for the Motherland for a few years...

The next day...I saw documents of [my] interrogation with the conclusion 'To be interned.' This is how the *osobist* took vengeance on me.

Gulin was sent to a 'labor battalion,' which was no different from being a prisoner in labor camps. He was released in December 1946.

Romanov described vetting from the point of view of a SMERSH officer:

The work of the PFKs took up a great deal of time. Camps for Soviet citizens from the west existed for several years, getting gradually smaller and closing one by one. The Chekist officers who worked in them were a sorry sight to see. They looked harassed, short on sleep, and pale, and their mood was permanently bad. There was too much work and...the entire responsibility for any persons set free after vetting lay on these officers. Their names figured in all the personal documents of the people who had passed through their hands. Those being vetted, however, were an even sorrier sight.[97]

Kidnappings were also common in the Allied occupation zones. For instance, in January 1946, General Mark Clark, commander of the American forces in Austria and head of the American delegation in the ACC, reported to Washington about one such operation. On January 23, 1946, several members of the Soviet Repatriation Mission (in fact, SMERSH officers) entered the house of a former German agent, now working for the Americans, who they wanted to kidnap. This was Richard Kauder, known also as Fritz Klatt and 'Max'. However, Clark's men had set a trap, and they arrested the entire Soviet team. One of the SMERSH officers was wearing the uniform of an American military policeman. Two others had civilian coats over their Red Army uniforms. All of them were armed. Enraged, General Clark informed TsGV Commander Marshal

Konev that the next day the offenders 'would be shoved over the line into the Russian Zone.'[98]

There was also a separate SMERSH operational group in Vienna subordinated to the 1st Department of the UKR headquarters in Baden.[99] It was responsible for the political reliability of all Soviet civilians and servicemen in Vienna, including Zheltov's group in the ACC. A small detachment of this group was also stationed in the town of Modling, not far from Vienna, where a branch (second echelon) of the TsGV's HQ was located.

This operational group had plenty of work. Any contact between Soviet servicemen and the Austrians or other foreigners was strictly forbidden, and marrying a foreigner was the worst offense of all. Vitalii Nikolsky, an intelligence officer who served in the TsGV's HQ, wrote in his memoirs:

> All contacts with the Austrian offices and private persons were strictly official and scrutinized. Personal contacts, especially with women, were prohibited. It was also forbidden to visit local restaurants, cafes and entertaining places such as cinemas, theaters, clubs, etc. The violators…were immediately sent to the country's border under a military convoy, regardless of their rank and position. Later, in the Motherland, harsh Party punishment was applied and measures at work were taken against them. Officers were commonly discharged from the army.[100]

Despite all draconian SMERSH measures, many officers risked going to restaurants and dancing halls. Colonel V. P. Babich, a signals officer who had served at the 3rd Ukrainian Front, recalled:

> A huge army of [SMERSH] operatives took care of the ideological purity of Soviet citizens and spied on them… They also involved Austrians in spying on servicemen. In one of the guesthouses I saw a notice: 'If a Soviet serviceman visits this guesthouse, please, call the Commandant's Office at this number…'
>
> One day I entered a restaurant with a girl. The waiter, who heard us speaking Russian, told us: 'The commandant of the 2nd (Soviet) Sector [in Vienna] forbids us to serve the Russians'… After this we spoke German in public places.[101]

Military service in the 'capitalistic' Austria was considered so hard that officers of the Red Army (including SMERSH) were given two vacations per year of 45 days each. However, the way home was not safe. Partisans of the Ukrainian underground army, the UPA, were constantly blowing up trains between the city of Lvov and the Soviet border in the Carpathian Mountains. It wasn't until the mid-1950s that the Soviet secret services finally liquidated the West Ukrainian partisans.

CHAPTER 28

The SMERSH Team in Nuremberg

Perhaps controlling the work of the Soviet delegation at the International Trial in Nuremberg was one of the main achievements of Abakumov's SMERSH. The role of this SMERSH team in the trial remained unknown to the Western delegations.

The London Agreement

On June 21, 1945, a series of meetings among the American, British, French, and Soviet delegations had begun at Church House, Westminster (London) to develop a protocol for the upcoming international trial of German war criminals in Nuremberg.[1] Major General of Justice Iona Nikitchenko headed the Soviet delegation at these meetings. Apparently, his Western colleagues were unaware that General Nikitchenko was no less guilty of crimes against humanity than were the future German defendants. In the 1930s, as a member of the Military Collegium, he had signed thousands of death sentences of alleged enemies of the people and received the highest Soviet awards for preparing show trials.[2] In 1937, in a single telephone conversation, Nikitchenko agreed to sentence 102 defendants to death without even seeing their case files.[3] A witness testified in 1940: 'At the session of the Military Collegium an arrestee claimed he had denied his previous testimonies because he had been beaten [by investigators]. Chairman Nikitchenko told him: "Do you want us to beat you a little bit more?"'[4]

Ongoing discussions highlighted the differences between the Western and Soviet positions since the Soviet delegation did not want to accept the concept of presumption of innocence.[5] The Soviets claimed that the future defendants were already guilty because of the decisions made by Stalin, Winston Churchill, and Franklin D. Roosevelt at the Yalta Conference on February 4–11, 1944, to 'bring all war criminals to just and swift punishment' and to 'wipe out the Nazi party, Nazi laws, organizations and institutions.'[6] In the Soviet opinion, this was enough to label all former German officials and military men as war criminals, without a trial.

Furthermore, it was not easy to overcome differences between Franco-Russian and Anglo-American criminal procedures. The American Judge Telford Taylor who participated in the trial, wrote later in his memoir:

> Under the Continental system (known to lawyers as the 'inquisitorial' system), most of the documentary and testimonial evidence is presented to an examining magistrate, who assembles all of it in a dossier... The trial proceeds with both the court and the concerned parties fully informed in

advance of the evidence for and against the defendant. If the court…decides to take further testimony, the witnesses are usually questioned by the judges, rather than the lawyers, so that cross-examinations by opposing counsel, which play so large a part in Anglo-American trials, do not often occur. The defendant is allowed to testify under oath, but may make an unsworn statement to the court.'[7]

Although the Soviet show trials of the late 1930s followed the French 'inquisitorial' system, there was a huge difference between a trial in a real French court and one in Moscow. In the Soviet system, everything was decided for the most part before the trial, and during important show trials Stalin and the Politburo edited and approved indictments and verdicts. In London, Nikitchenko admitted that he was not familiar with the Anglo-American system, and at the last meeting he asked: 'What is meant in English by "cross-examine"?'[8]

Finally a compromise was reached, and on August 8, 1945 the chief prosecutors of the four countries in charge held their first meeting. To the surprise of his Anglo-American colleagues, Nikitchenko, a prosecutor, announced that Stalin had appointed him Soviet Judge to the court, and that Lieutenant–General of Justice Roman Rudenko, Chief Prosecutor of Ukraine, who was unknown to the Western contingent, would be Soviet Chief Prosecutor.

Although he attended only a seven-year school and had no legal training, in 1937 the thirty-year-old Rudenko made a career as a prosecutor at a series of local show trials in the Donbass coal-mining region.[9] At these trials, scores of innocent defendants were sentenced to death or to ten to twenty-five years in the labor camps. In 1941, Rudenko graduated from a two-year legal course and began to work at the USSR Prosecutor's Office in Moscow.[10] In August 1942, supported by Nikita Khrushchev (then first Party secretary of Ukraine), Rudenko became Ukrainian Chief Prosecutor.

Most probably, Stalin noticed this talented demagogue in June 1945, during the show trial of sixteen members of the underground Polish government whom Ivan Serov, Beria's deputy and NKVD Plenipotentiary at the 1st Belorussian Front, secretly arrested in March 1944.[11] In fact, the entire government of Poland was kidnapped and brought to Moscow. The NKGB investigated the case.

On June 13, 1945 the Politburo ordered the Poles to be tried in an open session of the Military Collegium chaired by Vasilii Ulrikh, with Chief Military Prosecutor Nikolai Afanasiev and Rudenko as prosecutors.[12] Foreign correspondents and diplomats were invited to this show trial, and it was transmitted on the radio. The Poles were accused of collaborating with the Germans and organizing terrorist acts against the Red Army.

Brigadier General Leopold Okulicki, the last commander in chief of the Armija Krajowa and head of the underground Polish government, was sentenced to a 10-year imprisonment, and his fifteen co-defendants were sentenced to various terms. On December 24, 1946 Okulicki died in the Butyrka Prison Hospital in Moscow.[13] In the USSR, this trial of sixteen Poles made Rudenko famous.

The Politburo's Choice

In late August 1945, the Soviet leaders decided to send two high-level German prisoners to stand the International Trial in Nuremberg: Hans Fritzsche, former Radio Propaganda Chief in Goebbels's Propaganda Ministry, and Grand Admiral Erich Raeder, former commander in chief (until 1943) of the German Navy. They were second-rank officials in the Third Reich, but to Stalin's embarrassment, the Western Allies had caught all the important Nazi figures. The Politburo selected the names of Fritzsche and Raeder from two separate lists prepared by SMERSH and the NKVD.

On August 18, 1945, Andrei Vyshinsky, first deputy Commissar for foreign affairs, sent his superior, Foreign Affairs Commissar Vyacheslav Molotov, a list of proposed defendants for Nuremberg, who were in SMERSH's custody. The GUKR SMERSH supplied brief biographical data for each person listed:

Top Secret

To Comrade Molotov V. M.

I consider it necessary to include the following individuals among arrestees held in the Soviet Union in the first list of main defendants at the International Tribunal court:

1. Field Marshal SCHÖRNER Ferdinand, born 1892, former commander of the German Army groups 'South' and 'North' (Courland), and from January 1945 on, Commandant of the Army Group 'Center.'

In March 1944, SCHÖRNER headed the National Socialist Political Guidance Staff of the Armed Forces. The goal of this organization was to incite hatred among the German soldiers toward people of the anti-German coalition and especially toward nations of the Soviet Union.

In 1941, SCHÖRNER was the most reliable and trustworthy of Hitler's confidants. He rose quickly through the ranks from Lt. Colonel to General-Fieldmarshal.

Under SCHÖRNER's supervision, the German troops committed outrageous atrocities against the civilian population and POWs in the Baltic States. The Extraordinary State Commission for the Investigation of Atrocities Committed by the German-Fascist Occupants in the Baltic States concluded that SCHÖRNER was responsible for these crimes.

[Schörner] admitted that, while commanding the Army Group 'Center,' he refused to follow the order on Germany's surrender and continued fighting after May 8, 1945. When the situation of SCHÖRNER's troops became hopeless, after having ordered them to continue fighting, he dressed in civilian clothes and tried to escape.

2. <u>Goebbels's Deputy of Propaganda FRITZSCHE Hans</u>, born 1900, member of the National Socialist Party from 1933.

[Fritzsche] was one of the main organizers and leaders of Fascist propaganda.

During interrogations, FRITZSCHE pleaded guilty to being the head of Fascist propaganda efforts that slandered the Soviet Union, England, and America before and during World War II.

In speeches and using a radio service he organized, [Fritzsche] stirred up the German people against democratic countries.

In February 1945, on Goebbels's order, [Fritzsche] developed a plan to create a secret radio center to be used by the German sabotage-and-terrorism organization 'Werwolf.'

3. <u>Vice-Admiral of the German Navy VOSS Hans-Erich</u>, born 1897, German Navy representative at Hitler's headquarters.

[Voss] was among those closest to Hitler. He stayed with Hitler until the last days and was one of his confidants.

Beginning in March 1943, VOSS was informed of all German Navy actions since he represented Navy Head Admiral [Karl] Doenitz at Hitler's headquarters.

4. <u>Plenipotentiary SS-Obergruppenführer BECKERLE Adolf</u>, born 1902, German Ambassador to Bulgaria, former Polizeipresident of Frankfurt-on-Main and Lodz.

During interrogations, BECKERLE testified that Hitler had appointed him Ambassador to Bulgaria because he was an active functionary of the Fascist Party. He actively tried to involve Bulgaria in the war against the USSR and the Allies.

On BECKERLE's demand, the Bulgarian Fascist government organized provocations against Soviet diplomatic representatives in Bulgaria.

In 1943, [Beckerle] organized an anti-Soviet exhibition in Sofia for anti-Soviet propaganda purposes.

On BECKERLE's demand, the Bulgarian Fascist government intensified repressive measures against partisans.

5. <u>Lt. General STAHEL Reiner</u>, born 1892, head of the special staff at Hitler's headquarters and military commandant of Warsaw and Rome.

During interrogations, STAHEL testified that, beginning in 1918 and until 1925, while in Finland, he was among the organizers of the Schutzkorps created to fight the Red Army troops.

As one of Hitler's most reliable generals and confidants, [Stahel] was used by the German high command and personally by Hitler for special assignments.

In 1943, at the beginning of the democratic movement in Italy, [Stahel] was appointed Commandant of Rome. Using the troops under his command, [Stahel] ruthlessly suppressed democratic elements in Italy.

In 1944, on the eve of the Warsaw Uprising, Hitler personally appointed [Stahel] Commandant of Warsaw. He supervised the suppression of the Polish uprising and the destruction of the city.

In August 1944, because of Romania's departure from the war, [Stahel] was sent there to move the German troops out of Otopeni, where they were encircled.

I ask for your instructions.

A. Vyshinsky

August 18, 1945

Sent to: Beria

To file.[14]

As already mentioned, SMERSH operatives captured these prisoners in Romania and Bulgaria in September 1944 and in Berlin in May 1945. By August 1945, interrogators of the 1st Section of the 2nd GUKR Department and of the 6th GUKR Department had extracted the necessary information for the biographical sketches. Later all of them, except Fritzsche, were held in MGB investigation prisons until the end of 1951, when they were finally tried and convicted.

There is Molotov's note at the top of this letter: 'A copy should be sent to C.[omrade] Beria for his opinion. August 20, 1945.' Apparently, Beria responded quickly, because at the bottom of the first page, another handwritten note appears: 'Letter No. 992/b was sent to C.[omrade] Molotov on August 27, 1945.' This was a seven-page letter that included a list of seven German arrestees held in the GUPVI's custody who may also have been considered for trial in Nuremberg. As in the SMERSH letter, a biographical sketch accompanied each name. The handwritten note on the last page indicates that the letter was prepared by Amayak Kobulov, first deputy head of the GUPVI:

Top Secret

Copy No. 2

August 27, 1945

992/b [in handwriting]

NKID USSR [Commissariat for Foreign Affairs]

to Comrade MOLOTOV V. M.

In addition to the list of defendants at the court sent to you by Comrade Vyshinsky, I present a list of individuals (chosen from those held in our facilities) who, in my opinion, could be placed on the list of war criminals to be tried by the International Tribunal.

1. Gross-Admiral RAEDER Erich, born 1876 in the town of Wandsbeck [near Hamburg], a German, son of a Gymnasium Director, has high education, not a Party member. From 1928 to 1943, [Raeder] was Commander-in-Chief of the German Navy. After the end of the war against Poland in 1939, [Raeder] received The Knight's Cross.

While Commander-in-Chief of the Navy of Fascist Germany, RAEDER developed, planned, and carried out a sea war against the USSR. In 1941 and 1942, [Raeder] personally inspected Soviet bases in the Baltic and Black seas, taken by Germany.

On January 30, 1943, RAEDER resigned because of a dispute with Hitler on the requisite armament and equipment of large ships and their use in sea battle. After his resignation, Hitler promoted him to the rank of Admiral-Inspector of the German Navy.

[…]

In the case of a decision to send the above-mentioned persons for trial by the Nuremberg Tribunal, it is necessary, in my opinion, to create a commission under the chairmanship of Com.[rade] Vyshinsky, which should include representatives of the Military Prosecutor's Office, NKVD, 'SMERSH' NKO [Defense Commissariat], and so forth.

The commission should examine all documents that might be used for prosecution, if necessary, should organize an additional investigation to obtain documents that could be presented in court to support the indictment.

As a result, the commission should approve a verdict prepared by the Chief Military Prosecutor's Office for each person.

People's Commissar of the Interior [NKVD] of the USSR

(L. BERIA)[15]

The other eight Germans placed on the list by Amayak Kobulov were not as important as those listed by the GUKR SMERSH. They were SA-Obergruppenführer Martin Mutschmann, former Gauleiter (Governor) of Saxony, and seven Lieutenant Generals—Friedrich Gustav Bernhardt, Hilmar Moser, Johann Georg Richert, Wilhelm Robert Oksmann, Hans Julius Traut, and Günther Walter Klammt—as well as SS-Obergruppenführer and Police General Friedrich Jeckeln. All were involved in war crimes, especially the notorious Jeckeln, who was personally responsible for ordering the deaths of over 100,000 Jews, Slavs, and Gypsies in the Baltic States during the Nazi occupation.[16] Later, Bernhardt and Richert, as well as Jeckeln, were tried by Soviet military tribunals in Moscow, Minsk, and Riga respectively, in parallel with the International Nuremberg Trial. Sentenced to death, they were executed on December 30, 1945, January 30, 1946, and February 3, 1946, respectively.[17] Twenty days later, in Nuremberg, Soviet Prosecutor Mark Raginsky presented excerpts from the court-martial verdict against Bernhardt as Exhibit No. USSR-90, after Bernhard had already been executed.[18]

On September 5, 1945, the Politburo approved the governmental commission on Nuremberg proposed by Beria.[19] It had a long name: 'The Commission on the Guidance of Preparation of Indictment Materials and Activity of Soviet Representatives at the International Military Tribunal (IMT) in Nuremberg.' Two weeks later the commission was renamed the Commission on the Guidance of the Work of Soviet Representatives in the International Tribunal in Nuremberg, and in official documents it was called the Governmental Commission on the Nuremberg Trial for short.[20] I will refer to it as the Vyshinsky Commission.

Stalin suggested that Molotov supervise the commission, while Vyshinsky was appointed its chair. Its members were Vsevolod Merkulov and his deputy Bogdan Kobulov (NKGB); Abakumov (SMERSH); Konstantin Gorshenin, USSR General Prosecutor; Ivan Golyakov, Chairman of the Soviet Supreme Court; and Nikolai Rychkov, Commissar/Minister for Justice. Deputy Chief Prosecutor Grigorii Safonov and members of the Soviet Prosecution team in Nuremberg Lev Smirnov and Lev Sheinin, as well as the commission's scientific consultant, Aron Trainin, frequently took part in the meetings that followed. Decisions of the commission were sent for approval to the Politburo.[21]

The commission was in constant contact with the Soviet team in Nuremberg. In addition, Vyshinsky himself visited Nuremberg several times. The Allied delegations had no idea about Vyshinsky's supervisory role and they could only guess why he came to the trial. Lord Shawcross, the Attorney-General of England and Wales and then the United Kingdom's permanent delegate to the United Nations, told Arkadii Vaksberg, an investigative journalist, in 1988:

> We—I mean the British, French and Americans—simply could not figure out why he [Vyshinsky] kept coming to Nuremberg. In the end, not understanding much about the special features of the Soviet state structure, we decided that he was still the Procurator-General and this most likely explained why he was giving instructions during the trial to the prosecutors representing the Soviet side. Strictly speaking, there was nothing for him to do here in this capacity, instructions from Moscow could have been delivered another way, but, strangely enough, his visits somehow did not surprise us.[22]

In the absence of Vyshinsky, Rychkov chaired meetings of the Commission in Moscow. Ivan Lavrov was the Secretary of the Commission. Colonel of Justice Dmitrii Karev, a member of the Soviet team in Nuremberg, usually recorded notes of the meetings.

By August 29, the international list of the alleged major war criminals contained twenty-four names, starting with Reichsmarschall Hermann Goering.[23] To bring Fritzsche safely to Nuremberg was the job of SMERSH.

The Likhachev Team

In early September 1945, Sergei Kartashov, head of the 2nd GUKR SMERSH Department, arrived in Nuremberg.[24] He informed Nikitchenko and American officials that Fritzsche and Raeder would be presented in court. Back in Moscow, on September 10, Kartashov had written a detailed report to Abakumov giving his recommendations on how SMERSH representatives should organize their control of events at the pending trial.

A special group of investigators, culled from within GUKR SMERSH, would coordinate the preparation of materials for the trial.[25] Led by the above-mentioned deputy head of the 6th Department, Mikhail Likhachev, it also included two main subordinates (mentioned in previous chapters): Pavel Grishaev of the 4th Department and Boris Solovov of the 2nd Department. They were young but experienced interrogators.

Mikhail Likhachev, born in 1913, joined the NKVD in 1937.[26] During the war, he made his career in the Investigation Department of the UOO (by February 1942, he was already deputy head of this department) and then in the 6th Department of the GUKR SMERSH. Likhachev did not know German and spoke to the prisoners through a translator.

Pavel Grishaev, born in 1918, joined the NKVD in 1939 as a Kremlin Guard.[27] In 1942–44, he served as investigator in the OO NKVD, then UKR SMERSH of the Central/1st Belorussian Front. In December 1944, Grishaev was recalled to the GUKR SMERSH in Moscow, where he became senior investigator in the 2nd Section of the 4th Department. Nikolai Kuleshov, head of this department, was known as one of the cruelest OO investigators who interrogated the Soviet military leaders arrested in June 1941. Possibly learning by example, Grishaev also became a ruthless interrogator.

Boris Solovov, even younger, was born in 1921. In 1941, at the beginning of the war, he joined the NKVD. In 1943–46, he was an authorized officer (*operupolnomochennyi*) in the 1st Section of Kartashov's 2nd Department of the GUKR SMERSH. Both Grishaev and Solovov spoke fluent German.

In Nuremberg, the group became known as the Likhachev team. The other investigators of the 1st Section of Kartashov's department, especially those with a good knowledge of German, were also involved in the work of this team in Moscow—Captain Daniil Kopelyansky, Lieutenants Gushchin and Oleg Bubnov, Junior Lieutenant Soloviev (not to be confused with Solovov), Authorized Officer Anna Stesnova, and a translator, Maria Potapova, prepared documents for the trial.[28]

On October 12, 1945, Bogdan Kobulov, Vasilii Chernyshev (NKVD Deputy Head), and Abakumov signed a joint letter addressed to Beria requesting his order to transport Fritzsche and Raeder from Moscow to Nuremberg. Three days later the Likhachev team brought Fritzsche to Berlin.[29] Several cadets from the Military Counterintelligence School under Senior Lieutenant Gennadii Samoilov served as guards. The group also included a counterintelligence officer, Fyodor Denisov, and four female translators: Yelena Aleksandrova-Dmitrieva, Valentina Valitskaya, Olga Svidovskaya-Tabachnikova, and Elizaveta Shcheveleva-Stenina.[30] These translators later assisted Soviet prosecutors and judges.

Before Raeder was taken to Berlin, he and his wife were held at one of the special NKVD mansions near Moscow. When the NKVD officers arrived to take him to the trial, they told him he would be back in a few days. Colonel Pavel Tupikov, head of the NKVD Counterintelligence Department Smersh, along with Turaev, a military translator, escorted Raeder separately from Fritzsche.[31] After Tupikov left Nuremberg in January 1946, Grishaev continued to interrogate Raeder.

The two defendants and the Soviet security officers who held them lived in a mansion near Potsdam under the guard of military cadets who arrived with Likhachev. On October 18, 1945, Grishaev and Solovov presented the two defendants with the indictment signed by the Chief of Counsel of the International Military Tribunal. In response, Fritzsche immediately wrote the following:

> I, Hans Fritzsche, have received today, October 18, 1945, at 19:50 Berlin time, the Indictment of the Chief of Counsel of the International Military Tribunal, a statement regarding my right to defense, a list of German lawyers, and the Rules of the International Military Tribunal in the German language. The above documents have been handed to me by Red Army Officer Grishajeff, acting on orders of the International Military Tribunal, who advised me in German on the contents of the documents and on my right to defense.[32]

Later, before the trial, Fritzsche expressed his opinion of the indictment: 'It is the most terrible indictment of all time. Only one thing is more terrible: the indictment the German people will make for the abuse of their idealism.'[33]

Admiral Raeder, who, like Fritzsche, mentioned Grishaev in his statement about the indictment, later recalled in his memoirs: 'This was the first time I had heard of war crimes.'[34] After receiving the indictment, he asked for the notes he had left in Moscow. After a few days he received the notes and the text of the deposition he was supposed to sign. Raeder described the situation: 'When I examined the notes and deposition, however, I refused to sign such a statement since it was [a] fabricated jumble of excerpts from my notes, taken out of context, erroneously translated, and generally misleading.'

Raeder continued: 'A few days later Fritzsche and I were taken by auto-mobile from Berlin to Nuremberg… Like the other defendants who had preceded us or who came after us, we were incarcerated in individual cells of the Nuremberg Criminal Prison, under glaring electric lights.'[35]

For the next five months, the Likhachev team became a SMERSH watchdog that controlled the Soviet delegation. Officially Grishaev and Solovov were assigned as investigators for the Chief Prosecutor of the USSR, General Rudenko. In fact, they intervened in the work of prosecutors. On November 16, 1945, at a meeting of the Vyshinsky Commission, Kobulov announced: 'Our people, who are in Nuremberg at the moment, report to us…[that] Goering, Jodl, Keitel, and the others behave provocatively during interrogations, and that their answers frequently contain anti-Soviet declarations, while our investigator C.[omrade] [Georgii] Aleksandrov [head of the Soviet group of interrogators] responds to them weakly.'[36]

Three days later Vyshinsky rebutted: 'Neither the defendants nor witnesses attacked the USSR or me personally during interrogations… The described incident took place on October 18 [1945] in my presence during the interrogation of the defendant [Hans] Frank [former Governor-General in Poland] by the American Lieutenant Colonel Hinkel. After the interrogation, Frank, in fact, called Hinkel 'a pig'… In my opinion, this report [from Nuremberg] misinformed the government.'[37]

Colonel Thomas S. Hinkel of the Judge Advocate-General's office was one of four American lawyers who interrogated defendants before the trial. During the interrogation that Vyshinsky mentioned, the defendant Frank tried to persuade Hinkel that he was innocent of the charges: 'I want to point out that I am a believing Christian.'[38] But Hinkel did not buy Frank's sudden transformation and Frank was outraged.

Defendant Hans Fritzsche

Although Fritzsche did not belong to the highest Nazi elite, he was the highest-ranking bureaucrat captured by the Soviets. Born in 1900 in Bochum, he studied history, languages, and philosophy.[39] In 1923, he joined the nationalistic party *Deutschnationale Volkspartei*, and in 1933, the Nazi Party. From 1932, Fritzsche headed the Wireless News Service, incorporated in 1933 into Goebbels's Propaganda Ministry. In 1938, Fritzsche was appointed deputy head, and then head of the German Press Division. After this he headed the Radio Division of the Propaganda Ministry.

SMERSH operatives arrested Fritzsche in Berlin on May 2, 1945. That day he came to General Vasilii Chuikov's headquarters, where he proposed a radio broadcast calling upon the German troops to give up all resistance. He was allowed to do so. 'And then,' as Fritzsche wrote later, 'the first of many interrogations that took place in Berlin, in Lubyanka Prison in

Moscow, and in Nuremberg began.'[40] The next day he was taken to Hitler's Chancellery, where he saw about fifteen burned corpses, and on May 4, he was brought in to identify the corpse of his boss, Goebbels.

Until July 29, 1945, Fritzsche was held along with the dental technician Fritz Echtmann (who identified Hitler's dentures) in Friedrichshagen Prison in Berlin.[41] Finally, on July 29, 1945, Fritzsche and a group of other prisoners, including Vice Admiral Hans Voss, were flown to Moscow.

In Nuremberg, Fritzsche confronted Likhachev in the presence of members of the Western prosecution teams, telling of his treatment at Likhachev's hands in Moscow during the investigation:

'You know that in Moscow, you submitted me to twenty-two depositions against my present fellow-prisoners at a time when I knew nothing of an impending trial and you know that I declined to put my signature to those statements—statements which I never made. You know, too, that after three days and three nights I signed [the] twenty-third deposition, one against myself and you will remember that I did so only after some twenty alterations had been made on so-called points of honor. Curiously enough, these alterations are now missing. In addition, you know that I made the following declaration:

"I declare that no question was put to me and no answer given by me in the form in which it is set down here. I confirm the incorrectness of the wording of this deposition throughout its length. I sign solely in order that the three-man tribunal, which twice a month pronounces sentence without examining the accused...may write 'Sentence of Death' under my name by way of discharge..."

In the present circumstances, Colonel [Likhachev], I can only reaffirm the declaration which I made to you then.'

Both Li[kh]achev's hands were now fidgeting. Courteously he pressed Russian cigarettes upon everyone else present: he did not offer me any.[42]

The hearing of Fritzsche's personal responsibility for 'Crimes against Peace, War Crimes, and Crimes against Humanity' began at the morning session on January 23, 1946. A member of the American Prosecution team, Captain Drexel Sprecher, ended his presentation with the following conclusion:

Without the propaganda apparatus of the Nazi State it is clear that the world, including Germany, would not have suffered the catastrophe of these years; and it is because of Fritzsche's able role on behalf of the Nazi conspirators and their deceitful and barbarous practices in connection with the conspiracy that he is called to account before this International Tribunal.[43]

Soon after that, on February 21, 1946, Fritzsche had a breakdown after watching a Soviet documentary on the destruction of Soviet cities and cultural monuments. Fritzsche explained to the American psychiatrist Dr. G. M. Gilbert, who visited Fritzsche in his cell: 'I have had the feeling—of getting buried in a growing pile of filth—piling up week after week—up to my neck in it—and now—I am choking in it.'[44]

On June 28, 1946 Fritzsche denied all accusations. An intense dispute arose between Fritzsche and Soviet Chief Prosecutor Rudenko, whose questions consisted mostly of general accusations that had nothing to do with establishing Fritzsche's personal guilt. Fritzsche's answers revealed the sloppy work of Likhachev and other SMERSH investigators.

Rudenko stated that Fritzsche's own testimony given in September 1945 in Moscow demonstrated his guilt. To Rudenko's embarrassment, Fritzsche responded that he had been forced to sign this statement:

I signed this report but at the very moment when I signed it in Moscow I stated: 'You can do what you like with that record. If you publish it, then nobody in Germany will believe it and no intelligent person in other countries either because this is not my language...'

Not a single one of the answers in that record was given by me in that form and I signed it for reasons which I will explain to you in detail if you want me to...

Only the signature is true.[45]

After squabbling with Rudenko, Fritzsche added: 'I gave that signature after very severe solitary confinement which had lasted for several months; and...I hoped that in this manner I would at least achieve being sentenced and thus terminate my confinement.'[46]

Fritzsche continued: 'I wished to make 20 or 30 alterations [in the protocol]. Some of them were granted but passages were missing wherein I said in Nuremberg that some of the answers in that protocol contained a certain amount of truth but that none of them actually do represent my own answers.' In vain Rudenko insisted on Field Marshal Ferdinand Schörner's testimony in Moscow about Fritzsche:

Fritzsche's political activity in his function as official radio commentator... was subordinated to the main aim of National Socialism, the unleashing of the war against democratic countries, and the contributing by all possible means to the victory of German arms. Fritzsche's principal method...consisted of...the deliberate deception of the German people... The main guilt of people such as Fritzsche is that they did know the actual state of things, but despite this...fed people with lies.[47]

Obviously, a German marshal would not use such phrases as 'the unleashing of the war against democratic countries and the contributing by all possible means to the victory of German arms'; this was a typical Soviet propaganda phrase apparently written by SMERSH investigators. Fritzsche answered Rudenko: 'That is utter nonsense... I have never seen Herr Schörner... I do not know whether Schörner actually made this statement but I think it would be worthwhile to call General Field Marshal Schörner here as a witness, in order to ask him on what he based his judgment.'[48]

Rudenko did not succeed in further presenting similar excerpts from the testimonies of Vice Admiral Voss and General Reiner Stahel. Fritzsche's counsel, Dr. Heinz Fritz, made it absolutely clear that the testimonies sounded suspiciously similar:

> Mr. President, General Rudenko, during his cross examination, submitted three interrogation records... I should like to ask the High Tribunal also to compare these three records... Parts of the answers are repeated...totally, word by word... I wish to make an application that at least one of these persons who were interrogated be brought here in person for the purpose of cross-examination.[49]

Fritzsche added: 'I can only ask to have all three called.'

Rudenko's use of Vyshinsky's technique of prosecution based on generalized accusations did not work in the international court. On October 1, 1946, Fritzsche was acquitted. The Soviet prosecutors were against this decision. Nikitchenko read a long dissenting opinion before the Tribunal with the conclusion: 'I consider Fritzsche's responsibility fully proven. His activity had a most basic relation to the preparation and the conduct of aggressive warfare as well as to the other crimes of Hitler's regime.'[50]

Hungarian Countess Ingeborg Kalnoky, who ran a guesthouse in Nuremberg for trial witnesses, well remembered the day of Fritzsche's acquittal:

> Perhaps correctly the trial was dismissed by many Germans as a political one... Fritzsche, henchman of Goebbels, mouthpiece of the venal Nazi propaganda machine that had for so long suppressed all freedom of thought and speech, feeding the ignorant lies and hysteria, equally [went] free. But the nameless millions of the nation [the acquitted] had helped so industriously to discredit did not go free. Summarily judged, without benefit of trial, they served their misery and death.[51]

Four months later, on January 31, 1947, the Bavarian de-Nazification tribunal in Nuremberg sentenced Fritzsche to nine years' hard labor in a labor camp, confiscation of his main property and the permanent loss of his civil rights. He spent four years in prison until his release in September 1950. On September 27, 1953 Fritzsche, described in his obituary as 'silken-voiced radio chief in Adolf Hitler's propaganda ministry,' died in Cologne.[52]

The International Tribunal sentenced Admiral Raeder to life in prison. However, due to poor health, he was released from Spandau Prison on September 26, 1955. Four years later he died in Kiel.

The Team in Action

From time to time, members of the Likhachev team interrogated the defendants. A Soviet translator, Svidovskaya-Tabachnikova, later recalled Likhachev's interrogation of Hans Frank: 'Likhachev strictly followed a list of questions written on a piece of paper. I was shocked... In short, I could not consider the interrogation by Likhachev to be very professional.'[53]

Members of the main Soviet delegation guessed what these three men were doing in Nuremberg. Mark Raginsky, USSR Assistant Prosecutor, strongly opposed the presence of Solovov and Grishaev on the prosecutors' team, openly claiming that they 'used the work at the Tribunal only as an "umbrella" and that [they] allegedly had some other special task.'[54] Apparently, one of the group's tasks was to control the documents presented in the court. On November 26, 1945, the Vyshinsky Commission developed instructions for Soviet prosecutors. The list of issues prohibited from discussion at the trial included:

The USSR's attitude to the Versailles Treaty.

The Soviet–German Nonaggression Pact of 1939 and all questions connected with it.

Molotov's visit to Berlin and Ribbentrop's to Moscow [in 1940].

Questions concerning the social and political governance in the USSR.

The Soviet Baltic republics [annexed in June 1940].

The Soviet–German agreement regarding the exchange of the German population of Lithuania, Latvia, and Estonia with Germany [in 1940].

The foreign policy of the Soviet Union and, in particular, the [Turkish] Straits questions [discussed by Molotov in Berlin in 1940], and on the alleged territorial claims of the USSR.

The Balkan question.

The Soviet–Polish relationship (questions of the [annexed] Western Ukraine and Western Belorussia).[55]

These were sensitive issues that highlighted the differences between Stalin and the Western Allies in their approaches to international politics and emphasized Stalin's long-term goals for Soviet expansion in Europe.

Vyshinsky could rely on the Likhachev team that it would do whatever it took to avoid raising these questions in the courtroom. As Grishaev stated in 1989, in Nuremberg he used to walk 'arm in arm' with Vyshinsky.[56]

Svidovskaya-Tabachnikova recalled that Likhachev was also given the task of bringing to the Nuremberg court Field Marshal Friedrich von Paulus, former commander of the 6th German Army that surrendered at Stalingrad in February 1943, and General Erich Buschenhagen, former Commander of the 52nd Army Corps of Paulus's army. A special group conveyed the two German generals; it included five GUPVI/NKVD officers and Inver Mamedov, a translator attached to the Likhachev team.[57] The head of the group was Major General Il'ya Pavlov, deputy head of the Operational Department of the GUPVI, who, during the war, was deputy head of the SMERSH Directorate of the 2nd Belorussian Front, and thus well acquainted with Likhachev.

On February 11, 1946, the Soviet prosecutors suddenly produced von Paulus and Buschenhagen in the courtroom as witnesses. Stalin had secretly ordered this surprise for the court after Vyshinsky told him that the International Tribunal refused to accept the testimony von Paulus made outside of the courtroom.

Despite their cooperation with Soviet investigators and prosecutors, von Paulus and Buschenhagen were not released after the trial. While von Paulus's release was planned for 1950, it ended up being postponed until 1953.[58] In June 1950, the MVD Military Tribunal sentenced Buschenhagen to twenty-five years in prison for war crimes. Held in Prison No. 1 in Sverdlovsk (now Yekaterinburg), he was released in October 1955. He died in 1994.

On November 20, 1945, three more SMERSH officers from the former UKR of the 1st Belorussian Front, Leonid Kozlovtsev, Krasilnikov, and Khelipsky arrived in Nuremberg.[59] Sergei Kartashov personally approved this group, but its duties and function at the trial are unknown. The officers stayed in Nuremberg until October 1, 1946.

Undercover Confrontation

Soviet foreign intelligence also reported on events as well as on the Soviet team in Nuremberg. The secret services were convinced that American intelligence had tricked the SMERSH team and even tried to kill Likhachev. On December 8, 1945, Pavel Fitin, head of the 1st NKGB Directorate (foreign intelligence), reported to Beria:

A copy
Top Secret
To: People's Commissar of the Interior of the USSR
<u>Comrade BERIA</u>

Special Report

An NKGB officer stationed in Nuremberg described conditions of work of Soviet representatives at the International Military Tribunal.

1. American counterintelligence organized external shadowing of several members of the Soviet team in Nuremberg and is trying to provoke them. At the end of November, Major TARKHOV, who arrived in Nuremberg from the [Office of the] Political Department of the Soviet Military Administration in Berlin, was approached by a man unknown to him. The stranger said he was an illegal agent who had been discharged from Soviet counterintelligence with Romanian documents, and asked [the Major] to connect him with anybody working in Soviet counterintelligence. Major TARKHOV promised to do so.

When he told SMERSH member Colonel LIKHACHEV about this conversation, [Likhachev] approved a new meeting. He ordered that the stranger be told there was no member of Soviet counterintelligence in Nuremberg. Watching the meeting [with the stranger] from his car, Com.[rade] LIKHACHEV observed the American shadow following Com.[rade] TARKHOV.

Soon after this, on November 25, 1945, the American officer HINELY [?] sent a note to Com.[rade] TARKHOV through our communication officers, inviting him to a party of American officers that would also be attended by girls. When the Soviet communication officer answered that he could not come, HINELY told him not to tell anybody about the invitation because 'some girls' wanted to spend the evening [personally] with him.

2. It is also necessary to note the careless behavior of many of the Soviet representatives who had recently arrived for the trial. They spent a lot of time outside on the streets, and in restaurants, having friendly drinks with the Americans. Only a small proportion of the Soviet correspondents and writers who are here for the trial actually attend [sessions at] the court systematically.

Head of the 1st NKGB Directorate—Fitin

Sent to:

C.[omrade] Molotov

C.[omrade] Vyshinsky

December 8, 1945.[60]

The same day there was a strange attempt on Likhachev's life. Olga Svidovskaya-Tabachnikova recalled:

We spent many evenings in the restaurant of the Grand Hotel, which had been seriously destroyed by American bombs. There was a lobby with a revolving door and a restaurant in the part that had been somewhat restored and had lighting. Half-starved Germans entertained the Allies to the best of their abilities. The whole scene was extremely pitiful, but there was no place else [in the city] to go.

One day we—Likhachev, Grishaev, Solovov, and me—wanted to go, as usual, to the Grand Hotel, but something came up, and Likhachev could not go, so I stayed at home too. In Nuremberg, the Likhachev team was furnished with an exceptional limousine—a black and white 'Horch' with red leather upholstery. This was a unique car. There were rumors that the 'Horch' had come from Hitler's personal garage. Likhachev regularly sat to the right of the driver...

[On the evening of December 8, 1945] Grishaev and Solovov got out of the car and entered the hotel. A minute later someone opened the right-side door [of the limousine] and Buben [the driver] was shot at close range. I think Likhachev was the real target, and the shooter had assumed [Likhachev] was sitting in his usual place... The shooter escaped. Before he collapsed, Buben managed to say: 'An American shot me.' Boris Solovov claims that the Americans knew very well what, in fact, the 'Likhachev team' was about.[61]

The Horch that Svidovskaya mentioned was an eight-seat hand-made Horch 951, the dream car of all high-ranking officers of the Soviet Administration in Germany. Lieutenant General Vladimir Kryukov, one of the generals closest to Marshal Zhukov, had four cars, including two Horch 951s, one of which, the Horch 951A, was made for Hitler personally. Likhachev's Horch was possibly made for one of the defendants on trial, either Goering or Alfred Rosenberg. Apparently, Abakumov later used this Horch in Moscow to commute to the Kremlin.

Solovov was right in claiming that American intelligence was aware of the SMERSH presence in Nuremberg. A review of American military counterintelligence (CIC) reports from February 1 to June 15, 1945, reveals:

The activities of the Soviet intelligence group in Nuremberg, their previous professional experience, and their personal qualifications suggest that the members of this group were responsible to the NKGB and/or the GUKR (Counter Intelligence Administration of the Red Army) [i.e., SMERSH], despite the fact that they called themselves NKVD officers and were referred to as such by other Soviet citizens in Nuremberg. The abbreviation NKVD as used in Nuremberg was merely a general intelligence and security designation.[62]

But Richard W. Cutler, a former American counterintelligence (X-2 branch of the OSS) officer who was in Nuremberg during the trial, does not mention SMERSH and the NKGB in his memoirs.[63] He uses the acronym NKVD to describe all Soviet intelligence and counterintelligence activity. The CIC reports also did not mention the Likhachev team or the assassination attempt on Likhachev. One of the reports stated:

> Colonel Victor Staatland, alias Bendinov, aka Bimaev, appears to have been the executive or administrative officer of the NKVD Group in Nuremberg until his departure on 12 April [1946]...
>
> Staatland was in constant communication with Moscow by telephone, usually speaking from his hotel room... In court, he sat in the press section. He was always seen in civilian clothes, on which he wore several combat ribbons.
>
> Questioned about his German name, Staatland admitted that it was a 'working pseudonym' and that he is known as Bendinov in Moscow.

Another report added:

> Staatland...stopped greeting General [Lev] Smirnov, one of the [Soviet] prosecutors, after the latter had talked too openly about Russia's internal politics...
>
> Staatland...is almost certainly an NKGB man. His detailed personal knowledge of the White Russians living abroad and his preoccupation with the White Russians in Nuremberg suggest INU [NKGB foreign intelligence] connections.[64]

The CIC information about 'Colonel Staatland' makes no sense. Obviously, this was Viktor Shtatland, a famous cameraman who shot documentary films at the fronts during the war. In Nuremberg, Rudenko showed a film called *Documentary on Atrocities of the German-Fascist Occupiers*, which was made with Shtatland's participation. In the courtroom, Shtatland, as a member of the camera crew of the noted documentary filmmaker Roman Karmen, filmed the trial. After the trial, the crew produced the documentary *Sud narodov (The Judgment of Nations)*. Naturally, Shtatland talked frequently on the phone with a Moscow film studio.

The CIC report was also wrong about the other Soviet press people: 'Vsevolod Vitalievich Vishnevsky, Staatland's assistant, claimed to be a colonel but was always seen in civilian clothes decorated with combat ribbons. He has probably been in intelligence work for some time... Vishnevsky was openly a "strong-arm man," considerably lower in the administrative and social hierarchy than Staatland. He left Nuremberg on March 28... Staatland once admitted that "Vishnevsky" was not necessarily his real name.'[65] Even the description of this man, given in this report, 'stocky build; stiff black hair; narrow Kalmyk eyes; high Mongolian cheekbones; generally tough appearance,' points to Vsevolod Vishnevsky, a well-known and popular Soviet playwright who also wrote for the newspaper *Pravda*. He was neither Shtatland's assistant nor a colonel.

Prosecutor Lev Sheinin was the third person who attracted the CIC's attention: 'General Leon Sheinin, who departed from Nuremberg with Staatland on 12 April, was officially a military jurist, but unlike some of his associates appeared to have intelligence background rather than a background in military and international law. His connections with Staatland were very close.'[66] Lev Sheinin was, in fact, a jurist; he served as Vyshinsky's assistant in the 1930s, then headed the Investigation Department at the USSR Prosecutor's Office. Also, he published detective fiction stories. In 1942, Sheinin defended two Soviet agents in an Ankara court.[67] These agents had provided their Turkish adherent with a bomb in an attempt to assassinate the German Ambassador Franz von Papen, now a defendant in Nuremberg. Sheinin, a member of the team of Soviet prosecutors in Nuremberg, also headed a group of Soviet writers and journalists.[68]

The murder of Likhachev's driver on December 8, 1945 remains a mystery. In Moscow, *Pravda* published an angry article about the incident.[69] No action followed.

The Mysterious Death of General Zorya

In a March 11, 1946 letter to Robert Jackson, Rudenko openly described the issues the Soviet delegation did not want to hear in the court.[70] For some reason, this letter omitted three of the points mentioned on the above list, about the Versailles Treaty (no. 1) and about the Baltic countries (nos. 5 and 6).

Rudenko's letter and his agreement with the Allied delegations did not save the Soviet prosecution from a courtroom discussion of secret protocols that were part of the Soviet–German Non-Aggression Pact signed in August 1939. On March 25, 1946, Dr. Alfred Seidl, counsel to Rudolf Hess, presented to the court an affidavit written by the former chief of the legal department of the German Foreign Office, Dr. Friedrich Gaus.[71] Gaus had participated in negotiations with the Soviets in Moscow in 1939, and his affidavit attested to the existence of secret protocols. Then, during the cross-examination by Seidl, the defendant Joachim von Ribbentrop, former German foreign minister, and then the witness Ernst von Weizsäcker, former state secretary in the German Foreign Office, confirmed Gaus's affidavit and details of the secret protocols it contained.[72]

After a recess, the president ruled: 'The Tribunal has decided not to put the document to the witness.' Apparently, during the recess a confidential agreement was worked out with Rudenko.

For Rudenko's assistant, Major General of Justice Nikolai Zorya, Seidl's démarche ended up being fatal. On May 21, 1946, Seidl visited the Soviet prosecutors' office, wishing to discuss photocopies of the secret protocols with Rudenko. Only General Zorya was in the office, and Seidl talked to him instead. As Seidl recalled, after thinking over the matter of the photocopies, General Zorya answered: 'There is no point in having such a conversation.'[73]

The next day the American newspaper *St. Louis Post-Dispatch* published texts of the protocols. It is unknown whether Seidl had given a copy to the newspaper. The day after that, on May 23, Gennadii Samoilov, a SMERSH officer, found General Zorya dead in his hotel room with a wound to his head.

Until his own death in 1998, General Zorya's son, Yurii, was convinced that his father's death was connected with the presentation of the Katyn massacre question by Soviet prosecutors in Nuremberg, an issue tightly connected with the secret Soviet–German protocols.[74] From the beginning Rudenko and other Soviet prosecutors tried to include in the indictment the accusation that German defendants had killed 11,000 Polish officers taken as prisoners of war in 1939 by the Red Army. Despite Rudenko's objections, on March 12, 1946, the Tribunal complied with the request of Goering's counsel, Dr. Otto Stahmer, to call witnesses to rebut the Soviet version of events.[75] The cross-examination of witnesses presented by both sides took place on July 1 and 2, 1946.[76] The testimonies of German witnesses destroyed the Soviet version. Tatiana Stupnikova, the Russian translator of the German testimony, recalled that all Soviet representatives who were in the courtroom on July 1, 1946, called that day 'the black day of the Nuremberg Trial.'[77] However, the Tribunal did not make any conclusive statement on the issue, and the Soviet prosecutors made no attempt to return to the Katyn question again.

No direct evidence presented in Nuremberg connected General Zorya with the issue of the Katyn massacre. The published minutes of the meeting of the Vyshinsky Commission on May 21, 1946, containing instructions regarding Katyn, did not mention Zorya.[78] Abakumov was ordered to prepare Bulgarian witnesses, while Merkulov's duties included preparing Soviet medical experts, medical documents (which were forged), and a German witness. Vyshinsky was placed in charge of a documentary film about the massacre, and USSR Chief Prosecutor Safonov was responsible for preparing Polish witnesses. Since this was a plan involving massive falsification, it is possible that Zorya opposed it.

Prosecutors Rudenko and Gorshenin informed Stalin that Zorya had committed suicide. This is also possible if Zorya was afraid of Stalin's retaliation after the secret protocols appeared in an American newspaper.[79] In Nuremberg, Likhachev disseminated a rumor that Stalin said about Zorya: 'Bury him like a dog!'[80]

The Soviet delegation was suspiciously hasty in getting rid of the body. On the morning of the death, Rudenko went to the office of chief U.S. prosecutor Robert Jackson to ask his permission to move Zorya's body from Nuremberg in the American occupation zone to Leipzig in the Soviet zone.[81] Rudenko told Jackson that Zorya had accidentally killed himself while cleaning his gun. When Jackson sent two of his people to check out the story, they informed him that it was highly unlikely that a Soviet general would have been cleaning his own gun with the muzzle pointed between his eyes. It looked more as if somebody had shot Zorya at close range. If so, either Likhachev or his subordinate Samoilov, who supposedly found the body, would most likely have carried out the assassination.

The events that followed were even more suspicious. D. M. Reznichenko, Soviet Military Prosecutor in Leipzig, later recalled having received two phone calls from Stalin's secretariat regarding Zorya's funeral.[82] First he was ordered to bring the body to Moscow. The second order was to bury Zorya's body in an unmarked grave in Leipzig without performing an autopsy. By the next day, May 24, Prosecutor Yurii Pokrovsky had escorted Zorya's body from Nuremberg to Leipzig. The documents identify Zorya as a private instead of a major general, and later both the name of General Zorya and his photos were removed from all records and reports published in the USSR on the International Nuremberg Trial.

The circumstances of Nikolai Zorya's death remain a mystery. Since Stalin personally ordered that the body be buried secretly without an autopsy, it is most likely that Stalin gave the earlier order to kill Zorya and that the murderer was Likhachev or his subordinate. Or Stalin deeply hated Zorya for killing himself and this way escaping Stalin's punishment.

The Team Leaves Nuremberg

Soon after Zorya's death Likhachev and his team were ordered to leave Nuremberg. In 1951, the arrested Lev Sheinin testified on the reason for Likhachev's dismissal: 'Likhachev forced a young interpreter who resided in our building to live with him. After she got pregnant, Likhachev forced her to have an abortion. The operation was performed by a German doctor—unsuccessfully.'[83] Rudenko informed Chief USSR Prosecutor Gorshenin about the situation, and Gorshenin reported Likhachev's behavior to the Central Committee and Abakumov. Likhachev was ordered back to Moscow, and the team left Nuremberg.

In Nuremberg, Colonel Vsevolod Syuganov, deputy head of the 1st Department of the GUKR SMERSH, replaced Likhachev.[84] Syuganov joined the OGPU in 1927, and from 1932 on, he worked in Moscow. At the beginning of the war he served in the 3rd UOO Department (counterintelligence in armored troops and artillery), then in the 1st GUKR SMERSH Department (operational work in the NKO). Syuganov's team included five officers from GUKR in Moscow and an officer from the UKR SMERSH of the GSVOG.[85] The fact that one of the officers was from the 8th GUKR Department (ciphering) points to the possibility that the team reported directly to GUKR.

In Moscow, according to Sheinin, Likhachev was reprimanded and spent ten days under arrest as a punishment for his immoral behavior in Nuremberg. However, this brief episode did not ruin his career. He was appointed deputy head of the MGB Department for Investigation of

Especially Important Cases or OVD (former 6th GUKR SMERSH Department). Grishaev continued serving in the same department, while Solovov remained in the Investigation Division of the 4th Department of the 3rd MGB Main Directorate (military counterintelligence). All three participated in investigating prisoners from Europe and in 1947–53, of the Soviet 'enemies of the people.' Syuganov's team returned to Moscow soon after that of Likhachev.

Epilogue

The Road to the Top: Abakumov Becomes a Minister

With the end of the war, the necessity for SMERSH as a separate military counterintelligence organization disappeared and in spring of 1946, Stalin began restructuring the security services. By March, Viktor Abakumov reached the peak of his career, being appointed State Security (MGB) Minister. Many of SMERSH's high-ranking officers received key positions in the MGB, while GUKR SMERSH became the 3rd Main Directorate of the MGB. As usual, this process was a result of Stalin's planning and Politburo decisions. Here is how it happened.

On September 4, 1945, the GKO was disbanded and the Politburo returned to its routine work.[1] A month later, at the Politburo's suggestion, Stalin went on vacation to the Caucasus—his first holiday in nine years. On December 17, 1945, he was back in Moscow, and that evening he met in the Kremlin with Viktor Abakumov, who was still head of SMERSH. Also present were Nikolai Bulganin, former member of the GKO and Deputy Defense Commissar, Aleksei Antonov, head of the General Staff, and Sergei Shtemenko, head of the Operational Directorate of the General Staff. At 8:15 p.m., Abakumov left Stalin's office, while the other generals remained with Stalin for the next 40 minutes.[2] Most probably, Stalin discussed with the military leaders the changes he planned to make in the structure of the defense and state security commissariats.

On December 29, 1945, the Politburo approved Lavrentii Beria's request to be dismissed from his post as NKVD Commissar.[3] Stalin personally edited the draft of the decision and wrote the reason for the dismissal: 'Because he [Beria] is too overwhelmed with work at his other central position.' Apparently, Beria's appointment as head of the Atomic Project was so secret that Stalin did not want to mention it even in an internal Politburo document. Beria's first deputy, the colorless but dependable Sergei Kruglov (whose organization of security during the Yalta, Potsdam, and San Francisco conferences had impressed the British and American leaders), was appointed as NKVD Commissar and on January 10, 1946, he started his new job.

During the first months of 1946, Stalin was changing his policy toward former Western allies. On February 9, 1946, in a speech at a meeting at the Bolshoi Theater, Stalin stressed the economic progress in the Soviet

Union that, according to him, was the basis of the Soviet victory over Nazi Germany.[4] Stalin did not mention the role of the Western Allies in WWII and their crucial economic aid to the USSR. He did, however, discuss the inevitable clash between the two world systems of power, capitalism and Communism. This was the first step toward Soviet isolationism.

The reaction of the West was quick. On March 15, 1946, former British Prime Minister Winston Churchill delivered his famous 'iron curtain' speech in Fulton, Missouri, calling for a unified British–American response to the growing Soviet aggression.[5] The Cold War had begun, and according to Stalin, the Soviet Union needed better-organized management of its economy and tighter political control over the country.

On March 15, 1946, the same day Churchill gave his speech in Missouri, the names of all commissariats were changed to ministries on Stalin's suggestion. Stalin's reasoning was that the title 'commissar reflects the period of Civil War and revolutionary changes… The war [WWII] showed that our social organization is very strong… It is time to replace the title "commissar" with the title "minister."'[6] Four days later the Council of Commissars was renamed the Council of Ministers, and Stalin was appointed its Chairman, with Beria as one of his deputies. Kruglov became Minister of Internal Affairs or head of the MVD, and Merkulov was named State Security Minister, head of the MGB—a position he held for only a month and a half.

Before Merkulov was dismissed, on November 29, 1945, the Politburo replaced Merkulov's First Deputy Bogdan Kobulov, whom Beria brought from Georgia to Moscow in 1939, with Sergei Ogoltsov. Ogoltsov joined the CheKa in 1918 and made his career mostly in provincial special departments. Stalin chose Ogoltsov for the new MGB post because from December 1942 till March 1944, Ogoltsov headed the NKVD/NKGB regional branch in the city of Kuibyshev, the second Soviet capital during the war, where most governmental offices and foreign embassies were evacuated. Stalin considered Ogoltsov as a possible replacement of Merkulov. But for the next five years, Ogoltsov remained the second person in the MGB and became an acting minister for only a month after Abakumov's arrest in July 1951.

In April 1946, a decision to replace Merkulov with Abakumov was made. On the evening of April 24, Abakumov, Merkulov, and Ogoltsov were summoned to the meeting of 'the Six' (minus one) in Stalin's office.[7] Stalin, Beria, Zhdanov, Malenkov, and Mikoyan attended the meeting; Molotov was traveling abroad. The meeting started at 11:35 p.m. and most probably included a discussion of the reorganization of the MGB and the replacement of Merkulov with Abakumov. At 12:30 a.m., Abakumov, Merkulov, and Ogoltsov left the office, having been ordered to prepare a draft of the new MGB structure.

On May 4–7, 1946, the Politburo approved the draft.[8] Merkulov was dismissed, and Abakumov was appointed the new MGB Minister. The reasons behind Merkulov's dismissal became clear only after August 20, 1946, when Stalin dictated a Politburo resolution that stated: 'Comrade Merkulov, while holding an extremely responsible position [i.e., State Security Commissar/Minister] was dishonest and did not inform the Central Committee about a difficult situation in the CheKa [Stalin continued to call the Soviet secret service by its earliest name], and until the last moment concealed from the Central Committee the fact of the failure of the [intelligence] work abroad.'[9]

Apparently, Stalin was referring to three serious failures of the 1st NKGB Directorate (foreign intelligence). In September 1945, the cipher clerk of the Soviet Embassy in Ottawa, Igor Gouzenko, defected to the Canadian authorities.[10] He provided the Canadian, British, and American security services with detailed information on about two hundred GRU and NKGB spies in Canada and the United States who were involved in Soviet atomic espionage. Additionally, two months later, in November 1945, the former Soviet agent Elizabeth Bentley began revealing to the FBI her knowledge of NKGB operations in the United States.[11]

Finally, the NKGB deputy *rezident* (leader of a spy group) in Turkey, Konstantin Volkov, tried to defect to the British. This time the NKGB reacted immediately and a team of NKGB *agent-boeviki* (combat agents), headed by Andrei Onishchenko, was sent to Turkey without delay.[12] Onishchenko was an experienced intelligence officer and in 1943, while he was in charge of security in Tehran during the meeting of Stalin with Churchill and Franklin D. Roosevelt, Onishchenko 'overplayed' the German intelligence terrorist group headed by the legendary Otto Skorzeny. In 1945, he headed the Middle East Department within the 1st NKGB Directorate.

On September 21, 1945 the team arrived in Turkey; Onishchenko had a cover of a diplomatic courier. Three days later the team put the captured and sedated Volkov and his wife on a plane to Moscow. Volkov was secretly tried, sentenced to death, and executed. But this small triumph by the NKGB *boeviki* who prevented Volkov's defection was not enough to save Merkulov.

At Stalin's suggestion, the Politburo not only dismissed Merkulov but also demoted him to a candidate for the Central Committee membership.[13] After this, his high-level party career was over. In August 1946, Merkulov was appointed a deputy head, and from April 1947, head of the Main Directorate of Soviet Property Abroad of the Council of Ministers—an organization through which the Soviet Union managed the operation of plants, mines, and oil fields in the occupied territories of Austria, Germany, and Romania. Pavel Fitin, head of the 1st NKGB Directorate who was in charge of all operations of Soviet foreign intelligence during WWII, was also dismissed and for three months, he had no job at all.

The NKGB intelligence failures were only an excuse for the dismissals. Merkulov was a devoted ally of Beria and felt uneasy about dealing with

Stalin. After his dismissal, Merkulov wrote to Stalin: 'You, Comrade Stalin, once called me "shy." Unfortunately, this was true. I felt uncomfortable calling you on the phone and I was even more uncomfortable about writing you regarding many issues that I wrongly believed were not important enough for your attention during the war, because I knew how busy you were. The shyness I felt resulted in my making mistakes. Mainly, there were a few occasions when I didn't inform you at all, or informed you in smoothed-over terms, about issues that I should have reported to you immediately.'[14]

Stalin clearly wanted an MGB Minister who wasn't shy, and who was totally devoted and subordinated to him. And from April 1943 onwards, Abakumov was subordinated directly to and only to Stalin. Most probably, Stalin had already been planning some future trials in his mind and Abakumov, who had organized the very efficient operation of SMERSH, was the best candidate for the job.

Later Merkulov blamed Abakumov for his fall from grace, saying that Abakumov 'was no less ambitious and power-loving than Beria, but [far] more stupid.' In June 1953, Merkulov wrote to Nikita Khrushchev about the situation back in 1946: 'Abakumov stopped taking into consideration the opinion of the Politburo members... Beria was extremely afraid of Abakumov and tried to preserve a good relationship with him against all odds, although he knew that Abakumov was a dishonest man... Abakumov complained about me to Comrade Stalin and the Central Committee... For two years I did not even shake hands with Abakumov.'[15] But even if Abakumov hated Merkulov and had intrigued against him, this was not enough to prompt Stalin's decision to replace Merkulov by Abakumov. More like he was seeking, through Abakumov, to put the MGB under his direct control. In October 1950, Stalin 'pardoned' Merkulov and appointed him Minister of State Control.

However, it seems that Abakumov was fascinated with power politics. While he was still head of SMERSH, Abakumov carefully studied the Nazi hierarchy and relationships between members of Hitler's entourage. As Daniil Kopelyansky, the investigator whom Abakumov considered to be his personal translator, recalled, in 1945–46 Abakumov used to watch Nazi documentaries about Nazi leaders for hours.[16] After the war he also went to the Kremlin for a meeting with Stalin in a trophy limousine that had belonged to Heinrich Himmler. Perhaps Abakumov identified with Himmler.

In the meantime, on May 6, 1946 Abakumov presented the Politburo with a proposal regarding his new deputies:

Top Secret
USSR Council of Ministers
To: Comrade Stalin I. V.

I am sending, for your approval, a list of deputies to the USSR State Security Minister:

Ogoltsov Sergei Ivanovich, Lieutenant General, who until now worked as Deputy State Security Commissar, as [deputy] on general questions [a new title for the first deputy];

Selivanovsky Nikolai Nikolaevich, Lieutenant General, Deputy Head of the Main Directorate 'SMERSH';

Blinov Afanasii Sergeevich, Lieutenant General, Head of the Moscow Branch Directorate of the State Security Ministry;

Kovalchuk Nikolai Kuzmich, Lieutenant General, Head of the SMERSH Directorate of the Transcarpathian Military Region;

On the Cadres, Svinelupov Mikhail Georgievich, Major General, who until now worked as Deputy State Security Minister.

I am asking for your decision.

May 6, 1946.[17]

It is clear that Abakumov was ordered, probably at the previous Politburo meeting, to take only two of his future deputies from SMERSH (Selivanovsky and Kovalchuk) and the rest, from Merkulov's MGB. Abakumov's new first deputy would not be his SMERSH 'alter ego' Selivanovsky, but Ogoltsov, with whom Abakumov had never worked before. Probably Stalin wanted to keep an eye on Abakumov through Ogoltsov, who would be a candidate for Abakumov's immediate replacement, if it became necessary.

Stalin wrote in the right upper corner of Abakumov's list of proposed deputies: 'I agree. J. Stalin,' and the next day the Politburo formally approved Abakumov's deputies. Now Selivanovsky supervised military counterintelligence, and Kovalchuk controlled the interior (domestic) counterintelligence. There was no question that Kovalchuk could do his new job. Nikola Sinevirsky, who once translated the interrogation of a Hungarian POW for Kovalchuk (at that time the head of the SMERSH Directorate of the 4th Ukrainian Front), said of Kovalchuk: 'Loyal SMERSH operatives admired his [Kovalchuk's] intelligence and lived in deathly fear of his influence in high [C]hekist circles... He was a general whose conscience was stained with blood of hundreds of thousands of Russians and peoples of other countries... I observed for the first time this slim, average-sized man. His most remarkable features were his eyes, smiling, yet alarmingly sharp and piercing.'[18]

Blinov, former head of the Moscow MGB Branch (which was a very high position in the MGB hierarchy), became responsible for the Investigation Directorate for Especially Important Cases, or OVD. Very soon the OVD was involved in the investigation of all the main political cases of the late 1940s. Finally, on September 7, 1946, Lt. General Pyotr Fedotov, the new head of the 1st MGB Main Directorate (foreign intelligence) and former head of NKGB's interior counterintelligence, was also appointed Abakumov's deputy.

With the appointment of Abakumov as MGB Minister, GUKR SMERSH was absorbed into the new MGB structure. Most of it became the 3rd MGB Main Directorate (3rd GU), military counterintelligence, under Selivanovsky's command.[19] The function of the 3rd GU returned to the traditional surveillance of Soviet military forces. It consisted of three directorates controlling the Soviet Army (on February 25, 1946 the Red Army was renamed the Soviet Army), Marine Fleet, and Air Force, correspondingly. The SMERSH directorates of the Soviet troops in Germany, Austria/Hungary, Romania/Bulgaria, and Poland were renamed military counterintelligence directorates of these troops and continued their sinister activity against the civilian populations in those countries, as well as against military authorities and representatives of the secret services of the former Allies in those countries.

During the reorganization, the 6th GUKR SMERSH Department was merged with the former NKGB OVD Department, and Aleksandr Leonov, former head the 6th SMERSH Department, was appointed head of the new MGB OVD Directorate. Two of Leonov's deputies, Mikhail Likhachev and Vladimir Komarov—Abakumov's secretary from 1941 to 1946—held on to their posts in the MGB OVD Directorate. During the next five years, all three played a key role in all the major political cases of the time.

Sergei Kartashov's 2nd GUKR SMERSH Department, which investigated many important foreign prisoners, became the 4th Department of the 3rd Main MGB Directorate. It had a number of functions: (1) Counterintelligence in the zones of Germany occupied by the former allies; (2) Counterintelligence in Poland, Romania, Bulgaria, Austria, Hungary, Finland, Manchuria, and Korea against the enemy agents who had possibly penetrated Soviet offices and occupation troops in those countries; (3) Guidance of the operational activity of the Inspectorates attached to the Allied Control Commissions; (4) Work with and investigation of foreign POWs important in terms of military counterintelligence; (5) Continuation of vetting the Soviet POWs who had been in German captivity in various countries.[20] The 4th Department existed until September 1948, when most of its prisoners captured from 1944–45 had been convicted, and then it was merged with the OVD.

In August 1949, former head of the 4th Department Kartashov was sent to Hungary as Senior MGB Adviser to the State Security Directorate of the Hungarian MVD, where he stayed until May 1950. In March 1950, many of Kartashov's former investigators were transferred to the Investigation Department of the 2nd MGB Main Directorate (interior counterintelligence), where they finished cases of foreigners arrested by SMERSH during and just after the war. Interestingly, although Kartashov was not arrested along with Abakumov and his colleagues in 1951 or persecuted later, he had never been promoted to the rank of general like the other former GUKR SMERSH department heads. Kartashov continued to serve in the KGB until 1967, becoming a consultant of the head of the Foreign Intelligence (1st Main Directorate), but he remained only a colonel—the rank he was promoted to in 1943, during the creation of SMERSH.

In November 1946, Abakumov created his own MGB OSO (Special Board), and until 1953, it sentenced most of the prisoners arrested by the MGB within the country and abroad.[21] With the acquisition of the OSO, the MGB became a closed institution: it arrested people on political charges, investigated cases, tried the arrestees, and put the most important convicts into its own special prisons: Vladimir, Verkhne-Uralsk, and Aleksandrovsk.

After coming back to Moscow in May 1946, both Pavel Grishaev and Boris Solovov, watchdogs in Nuremberg, had fast-track careers. Pavel Grishaev participated in the investigation of the most important OVD cases of Andrei Vlasov (1946), the Alliluevs (relatives of Stalin's wife) (1947), the famous folk singer Lidia Ruslanova and her husband General Vladimir Kryukov (1948), members of the Jewish Anti-Fascist Committee (1951–52), and others. He became a ruthless torturer, beating both male and female prisoners.

In mid-1951, Selivanovsky, Korolev, Leonov, Likhachev, Komarov, and many other former SMERSH, then MGB, high-level officers were arrested—sharing the fate of their boss, Abakumov. This was Stalin's new wave of changes in the Party leadership and government. However, neither Grishaev, nor Solovov were arrested.

In September 1951, 33-year-old Lieutenant Colonel Grishaev was appointed Assistant to the new head of the OVD, Mikhail Ryumin, a former SMERSH investigator. In this capacity, Grishaev became one of the leading and most ruthless investigators of his former boss and patron, Abakumov.[22] Grishaev also interrogated his own former superiors, Leonov and Likhachev. In mid-1953, now arrested, Grishaev's boss Ryumin testified: 'On November 4 [1952] I, together with the assistant to the head of *sledchast'* [OVD] Grishaev, arrived in Lefortovo Prison and ordered the beating of a group of the arrested Chekists [i.e., Abakumov and his accomplices] with rubber truncheons and lashes. However, these measures did not produce any result [i.e., a false confession].'[23]

After this Grishaev participated in writing a draft proposal of the indictment of Abakumov and his nine accomplices prepared personally for Stalin. However, Stalin died before Abakumov and the other alleged leaders of the 'MGB Zionist plot' could be put on trial. Grishaev remained Assistant to the head of the OVD until March 12, 1953, after Ryumin's dismissal in November 1952 and Stalin's death on March 5, 1953. On March 17, 1953,

Ryumin was arrested, on July 7, 1954 he was sentenced to death and on July 22, he was executed.

In the meantime, in 1952, 32-year-old Boris Solovov reached the peak of his career, being appointed head of an investigation division of foreign prisoners within the 4th Department of the 2nd MGB Main Directorate. There was a lot of work for his division: new foreign prisoners, arrested by MGB counterintelligence directorates of the occupation troops, continued to arrive from the countries of Eastern Europe. Both Boris Solovov and Pavel Grishaev were discharged from the MGB in late 1953 and escaped any punishment. Amazingly, later the torturer Grishaev made a career as a law professor.

After Stalin's death and the closed trials of Beria (December 1953) and Abakumov (December 1954), many former SMERSH officers were also convicted in separate trials in the 1950s and thousands of former MGB officers were under investigation. In 1957, Ivan Serov, Abakumov's former enemy and now KGB Chairman (the KGB was created in 1954), reported to Nikita Khrushchev's Central Committee that overall, from 1954 to 1957, 18,000 former MGB officers were discharged, and of them, 2,300 were discharged due to 'violation of Soviet law', which was a KGB euphemism for torture.[24] This number included 40 generals, demoted to privates, and among them, there were generals who had served in SMERSH and the MGB and were mentioned in this book: Aleksandr Avseevich, Mikhail Belkin, Afanasii Blinov, Vasilii Blokhin, Grigorii Bolotin-Balyasnyi, Aleksandr Bystrov, Ivan Gorgonov, Nikolai Korolev, Nikolai Kovalchuk, Aleksandr Vadis, Aleksei Voul, Ivan Vradii, and Pavel Zelenin. All these measures were conducted in secrecy and the Soviet population was not aware that the Communist Party leaders of the time admitted de facto that SMERSH and the other Stalin-era secret services were involved in criminal activities.

But all this would happen later. In May 1946, the newly appointed MGB Minister, Abakumov, became one of the most powerful men in the Soviet Union and a rare favorite of his *Khozyain* (Master)—Stalin. For the next five years, Abakumov was in control of the life of almost every Soviet citizen and his MGB could arrest any citizen it chose to—without waiting for an order from Stalin. Through the MGB branches in occupied countries, Abakumov also controlled half of Europe. Those SMERSH officers who joined the MGB along with Abakumov also gained enormous power. I will describe the next five years of MGB glory and Abakumov's triumph in 1946–51, as well as his downfall, in another book.

Notes

Introduction

1. *SMERSH. Istoricheskie ocherki i dokumenty,* edited by V. S. Khristoforov, et al. (Moscow: Glavnoe arkhivnoe upravlenie, 2003; second edition 2005; and the third, 2010) (in Russian).

2. The number of divisions from Table 51 in G. F. Krivosheev et al., *Velikaya Otechestvennaya bez grifa sekretnosti. Kniga poter'* (Moscow: Veche, 2009), 206–7 (in Russian).

3. I. I. Kuznetsov, *Sud'by general'skie: Vysshie komandnye kadry Krasnoi Armii v 1940–1953 gg.* (Irkutsk: Izdatel'stvo Irkutskogo universiteta, 2000), 180 (in Russian).

4. V. N. Stepakov, *Narkom SMERSHa* (St. Petersburg: Neva, 2003), 93 (in Russian).

5. *SMERSH. Istoricheskie ocherki,* 6.

6. Ian Fleming, *Casino Royale* (first published in Great Britain by Jonathan Cape Ltd., 1953), 10.

7. Ian Fleming, *From Russia with Love* (first published in Great Britain by Jonathan Cape Ltd., 1957), 10, 28.

8. *The Library of Congress World War II Companion,* edited by David M. Kennedy (New York: Simon & Schuster, 2007).

9. Chris Bellamy, *Absolute War: Soviet Russia in the Second World War* (New York: Vantage Books, 2007), 29–30 and 644.

10. Christopher Andrew and Oleg Gordievsky, *KGB: The Inside Story of Its Foreign Operatrions from Lenin to Gorbachev* (New York: Harper Collins Publishers, 1990), 342–3.

11. Michael Parrish, *The Lesser Terror: Soviet State Security, 1939–1953* (Westport, CT: Praeger, 1996), 111–45.

12. Nicola Sinevirsky, *SMERSH* (New York: Henry Holt and Company, 1950); A. I. Romanov, *Nights Are Longest There: A Memoir of the Soviet Security Services,* translated by Gerald Brooke (Boston, MA: Little, Brown and Company, 1972). After the war, Mikhail Mondich (Sinevirsky) (1923–1969) lived in the United States, while Boris Baklanov escaped to the American sector in Vienna and went to live in London.

13. Vladimir Nikolaev, *Stalin, Gitler i my* (Moscow: Prava cheloveka, 2002), 155 (in Russian).

14. Aleksandr I. Solzhenitsyn, *The GULAG Archipelago, 1918–1956: An Experiment in Literary Investigation,* translated from the Russian by Thomas P. Whitney, Vols. I and II (New York: Harper and Row, 1973), 23.

15. Vladimir Bogomolov, *V avguste sorok chetvertogo* (Moscow: Molodaya gvardiya, 1974) (in Russian).

16. Vladimir Bogomolov, 'Ya reshil svesti do minimuma kontakty s gosudarst-vom,' *Novaya gazeta*, No. 33, May 17, 2004 (in Russian), http://www.novayaga-zeta.ru/data/2004/33/25.html, retrieved September 4, 2011.

17. Letter of the Party Central Committee, dated April 15, 1966, in A. Novikov and V. Telitsyn, 'Mertvym—ne bol'no, bol'no—zhivym,' *Voprosy literatury*, No. 6 (2004) (in Russian), http://magazines.russ.ru/voplit/2004/6/nov15.html, retrieved September 9, 2011.

18. V. V. Bykov, 'Dolgaya doroga domoi,' *Druzhba narodov*, No. 8 (2003) (in Russian), http://magazines.russ.ru/druzhba/2003/8/bykov.html, retrieved September 4, 2011.

19. 'Russia Unveils Stalin Spy Service,' *BBC News*, April 19, 2003, http://news.bbc.co.uk/2/hi/europe/2960709.stm, retrieved September 4, 2011.

20. Vadim Telitsin, *'SMERSH': Operatsii i ispolniteli* (Smolensk: Rusich, 2000) (in Russian).

21. Nikolai Poroskov, 'Voennaya kontrrazvedka vchera i segodnya,' *Voenno-promyshlennyi kur'er*, No. 48 (264), December 10-16, 2008 (in Russian), http://www.vpk-news.ru/article.asp?_sign=archive.2008.264.articles.chronicle_03, retrieved September 4, 2011

22. *SMERSH. Istoricheskie ocherki.*

23. V. N. Stepakov, *Narkom SMERSHa* (St. Petersburg: Neva, 2003), 145 (in Russian).

24. Cited in Dmitry Oreshnikov, 'Finskaya voina kak opyt sotsiologii. Chast' tret'ya,' *Yezhednevnyi zhurnal*, June 10, 2010 (in Russian), http://www.ej.ru/?a=note&id=10171, retrieved September 4, 2011.

25. Leonid Ivanov, *Pravda o 'SMERSH'* (Moscow: Yauza-Eksmo, 2009), 112 (in Russian).

26. M. B. Smirnov, *Sistema ispravitel'no-trudovykh lagerei v SSSR. 1923–1960. Spravochnik* (Moscow: Zven'ya, 1998); N. V. Petrov and K. V. Skorkin, *Kto rukovodil NKVD. 1934–1941. Spravochnik* (Moscow: Zven'ya 1999); A. I. Kokurin and N. V. Petrov, Lubyanka. *Organy VCheKa–OGPU–NKVD–NKGB–MGB–MVD–KGB. 1917–1991. Spravochnik* (Moscow: Demokratiya, 2003); N. V. Petrov, *Kto rukovodil organami gosbezopasnosti, 1941–1954. Spravochnik* (Moscow: Zven'ya, 2010). All in Russian.

27. Especially the sites http://www.sakharov-center.ru/asfcd/auth/, http://militera.lib.ru, and http://www.iremember.ru, all retrieved September 4, 2011.

28. Vyacheslav Zvyagintsev, *Voina na vesakh Femidy. Voina 1941–1945 gg. V materialakh sledstvenno-sudebnykh del* (Moscow: Terra, 2006); Aleksandr Beznasyuk and Vyacheslav Zvyagintsev, *Tribunal. Arbat, 37 (Dela i lyudi)* (Moscow: Terra, 2006).

29. Anatoli Granovsky, *I Was an NKVD Agent* (New York: The Devin-Adair Company, 1962), 235–58.

30. Recollections by Aleksander Golovanov, in F. I. Chuev, *Soldaty imperii. Besedy. Vospominaniya. Dokumenty* (Moscow: Kovcheg, 1998), 229 (in Russian).

31. Krivosheev et al., *Velikaya Otechestvennaya,* 39–43.

32. Details in Boris Sokolov, *Poteri Sovetskogo Soyuza i Germanii vo Vtoroi mirovoi voine: Metody podschetov i naibolee veroyatnye rezul'taty* (Moscow: AIRO-XXI, 2011) (in Russian).

33. Vladimir Dobryshevsky, 'Pomnit' vsekh poimenno,' *Krasnaya zvezda*, June 18, 2008 (in Russian), http://www.redstar.ru/2008/06/18_06/3_05.html, retrieved September 4, 2011.

34. Aleksandr Melenberg, 'Podachka iz arkhiva,' *Novaya gazeta*, No. 48, May 7, 2010 (in Russian), http://www.novayagazeta.ru/data/2010/048/09.html, retrieved September 4, 2011.

35. NKO orders No. 138, dated March 15, 1941 (Document No. 109 in *Russkii arkhiv: Velikaya Otechestvennaya: Prikazy Narodnogo Komissara Oborony SSSR*, 13 (2-1) (1994), 258–61), and No. 376, dated November 17, 1942 (Document No. 292 in ibid., 13 (2-2) (1997), 368), on personal lockers, and No. 330, dated October 7, 1941 (Document No. 86 in ibid., 111–2), on IDs.

36. Stepan Kashurko, 'Lezhat' smirno!,' *Novaya gazeta*, No. 33, May 12, 2005 (in Russian), http://www.novayagazeta.ru/data/2005/33/00.html, retrieved September 4, 2011.

37. Testimony of Andrei Illarionov, Senior Fellow of the Cato Institute, Washington, DC, and the President of the Institute of Economic Analysis, Moscow, before the House Committee on Foreign Affairs at the hearing 'From Competition to Collaboration: Strengthening the U.S.-Russia Relationship,' February 25, 2009, http://www.internationalrelations.house.gov/111/ill022509.pdf, retrieved September 4, 2011.

38. 'The Making of a Neo-KGB State,' *The Economist*, August 25–31, 2007, 25–28. A detailed analysis of the Russian political and business elite is given in Olga Kryshtanovskaya, *Anatomiya rossiiskoi elity* (Moscow: Zakharov, 2004) (in Russian).

39. Vladimir Ivanov and Igor Plugatarev, 'FSB menyaet orientiry,' *Nezavisimoe voennoe obozrenie*, October 29, 2004 (in Russian), http://nvo.ng.ru/spforces/2004-10-29/7_fsb.html, retrieved September 4, 2011.

40. List of published books in Russia on http://www.biblio-globus.com, retrieved September 4, 2011.

41. http://www.fsb.ru/fsb/history/author/single.htm%21id%3D10318168%2540fsbPublication.html, retrieved September 4, 2011.

42. *Istoriya Rossii. 1900–1945 gg. Kniga dly uchitelya*, edited by Aleksandr Danilov and Aleksandr Filippov (Moscow: Prosveshchenie, 2009).

43. Owen Matthews, 'Young Russians' About-Face From the West.' *Newsweek*, November 5, 2009, http://www.newsweek.com/id/221210, retrieved September 4, 2011.

44. The Soviets participated only in the Military International Tribunal and the Trial of the Major War Criminals (November 1945–October 1946). Most Russians are not aware of the twelve American Subsequent Nuremberg Proceedings that followed from 1946 to 1949.

45. Only recently were several truthful memoirs about these events published, including Nikolai I. Obryn'ba, *The Memoirs of a Soviet Resistance Fighter on the Eastern Front*, translated by Vladimir Kupnik (Dulles, VA: Potomac Books, 2007), and Vladimir Shimkevich, *Sud'ba moskovskogo opolchentsa. Front, okruzhenie, plen. 1941–1945* (Moscow: Tsentrpoligraf, 2008) (in Russian).

46. Aleksandr Melenberg, 'Pobeda. Vremya posle bedy. Chast' III. L'goty veteranam Velikoi Otechestvennoi voiny v instruktsiyakh i postanovleniyakh vlasti,'

Novaya gazeta, tsvetnoi vypusk 17 (May 11, 2007) (in Russian). http://www.novayagazeta.ru/data/2007/color17/07.html, retrieved September 4, 2011.

47. The denial intensified after the publication in 2005 of the Russian translation of Antony Beevor's *The Fall of Berlin 1945* (New York: Viking, 2002), see S. Turchenko, 'Nasilie nad faktami,' *Trud*, July 21, 2005 (in Russian). Beevor's Russian opponents ignored the fact that Beevor cited Soviet documents from the Russian military archive.

48. For instance, a discussion in Mark Solonin, *Net blaga na voine* (Moscow: Yauza-Press, 2010), 180–264 (in Russian).

49. N. N. Nikoulin, *Vospominaniya o voine* (St. Petersburg: Izdatel'stvo Gosudarstvennogo Ermitazha, 2008), 41–42 (in Russian).

Part 1. The Big Picture

Chapter 1

1. General information in Mikhail Heller and Aleksandr Nekrich, *Utopia in Power: The History of the Soviet Union from 1917 to the Present*, translated from the Russian by Phyllis B. Carlos (New York: Summit Books, 1986).

2. SNK Protocol (transcript) No. 21, dated December 20, 1917. Document No. 1, in A. I. Kokurin and N. V. Petrov, *Lubyanka. Organy VCheKa–OGPU–NKVD–NKGB–MGB–MVD–KGB. 1917–1991. Spravochnik* (Moscow: Demokratiya, 2003), 302–3 (in Russian).

3. Details in E. Rozin, *Leninskaya mifologiya gosudarstva* (Moscow: Yurist, 1996) (in Russian).

4. Robert Gellately, *Lenin, Stalin, and Hitler: The Age of Social Catastrophe* (New York: Alfred A. Knopf, 2007).

5. VCheKa Order, dated September 2, 1918. Document No. 2, in *GULAG (Glavnoe upravlenie lagerei) 1917–1960*, edited by A. I. Kokurin and N. V. Petrov (Moscow: Materik, 2000), 14–15 (in Russian).

6. SNK Decree, dated September 5, 1918. Document No. 3 in ibid., 15; on the VCheKa history see, for instance, George Legett, *The Cheka: Lenin's Political Police* (New York: Oxford University Press, 1986); Christopher Andrew and Oleg Gordievsky, *KGB: The Inside Story of Its Foreign Operatrions from Lenin to Gorbachev* (New York: HarperCollins Publishers, 1990), 38–64; changes in the VCheKa structure in 1917–21 in Kokurin and Petrov, *Lubyanka*, 14–24.

7. Nicolas Werth, 'The Red Terror in the Soviet Union,' in *The Black Book of Communism: Crimes, Terror, Repressions*, edited by Stepane Curtois et al., translated by Jonathan Murphy and Mark Kramer, 71–81 (Cambridge, MA: Harvard University Press, 1999).

8. On Dzerzhinsky's activity see, for instance, *F. E. Dzerzhinsky—predsedatel' VChK–OGPU 1917–1926*, edited by A. A. Plekhanov and A. M. Plekhanov (Moscow: Materik, 2007) (in Russian).

9. On the creation of the Red Army, see Aleksandr Melenberg, 'Krasnyi Podarok,' *Novaya Gazeta*, No. 18, February 18, 2011 (in Russian), http://www.novgaz.ru/data/2011/018/19.html, retrieved September 4, 2011.

10. Kokurin and Petrov, *Lubyanka*, 17. On the early period of the VO/OO see A. A. Zdanovich, 'Kak L. D. Trotsky i Revvoensovet Respubliki 'poteryali' kontrrazvedku,' *Voenno-istoricheskii zhurnal* (hereafter *VIZh*), no. 3 (1996): 65–73, no.

5 (1996), 75–82 (in Russian). A short overview of the OO history from 1918 to 1983 was given in Amy W. Knight, 'The KGB's Special Departments in the Soviet Armed Forces,' *ORBIS* 28, no. 2 (Summer 1984): 257–80.

11. The first network of military counterintelligence was created in the czarist army in June 1915, during World War I. Each front (a group of armies), army, and military district had its KRO or Counterintelligence Department within the headquarters, and the network reported to the KRO within the Main Directorate of the General Staff. Details in A. A. Zdanovich, *Otechestvennaya kontrrazvedka (1914–1920): Organizatsionnoe stroitel'stvo* (Moscow: Kraft+, 2004), 19–62 (in Russian). On military counterintelligence (later military intelligence) abroad see B. A. Starkov, *Okhotniki na shpionov. Kontrrazvedka Rossiiskoi imperii 1903–1914* (St. Petersburg: SiDiKom, 2006) (in Russian).

12. The czarist secret police consisted of three parts, details in Ch. A. Ruud and S. A. Stepanov, *Fontanka, 16. Politicheskii sysk pri tsaryakh* (Moscow: Mysl', 1993), 81–172 (in Russian); Z. Peregudova, *Politicheskii sysk v Rossii (1880–1917 gg.)* (Moscow: ROSSPEN, 2000).

13. Joined order of Trotsky, Dzerzhinsky and the Soviet government, dated February 3, 1919. Document No. 20, in Kokurin and Petrov, *Lubyanka*, 330–1. In 1929, *gubernii* (administration regions) were renamed *oblasti* (provinces), and the regional OGPU branches became Provincial GPUs.

14. Instruction on the Special Departments of the VCheKa, dated February 8, 1919. Document No.21, in ibid., 331–2.

15. Details in A. G.Kavtaradze, *Voennye spetsialisty na sluzhbe Respublike Sovetov* (Moscow: Nauka, 1988) (in Russian).

16. Figures from tables 69 and 70 in *Rossiya i SSSR v voinakh XX veka: Poteri vooruzhennykh sil. Statistichesloe issledovanie*, edited by G. F. Krivosheev (Moscow: Olma-Press, 2001) (in Russian).

17. On Stalin's activity during the Civil War, see, for instance, Dmitri Volkogonov, *Stalin: Triumph and Tragedy*, edited and translated from the Russian by Harold Shukman (New York: Grove Weidenfeld, 1988), 38–52, and Robert Service, *Stalin: A Biography* (Cambridge, MA: The Belknap Press, 2004), 163-74.

18. In 2004, after analyzing old medical records, a group of western neurologists concluded that most likely Lenin suffered and died of syphilis. V. Lerner, Y. Finkelstein, and E. Witztum, 'The enigma of Lenin's (1870-1924) malady,' European Journal of Neurology 11, no. 6 (June 2004), 371–6; also, Helen Rappaport, *Conspirator: Lenin in Exile* (New York: Basic Books, 2010), 306, 355.

19. In 1948, imprisoned Trotskyists who were still alive were transferred to new camps, MVD Order No. 00219, dated February 28, 1948. Document No. 41 in *GULAG (Glavnoe upravlenie lagerei)*, 135–7.

20. Detailed biography of V. P. Menzhinsky in Oleg Mozokhin and Teodor Gladkov, *Menzhinskii—intelligent s Lubyanki* (Moscow: Yauza-Eksmo, 2005) (in Russian).

21. Details in A. A. Zdanovich, *Organy gosudarstvennoi bezopasnosti i Krasnaya armiya* (Moscow: Kuchkovo pole, 2008) (in Russian).

22. Short biography of G. G. Yagoda (1891–1938) in Petrov and Skorkin, *Kto rukovodil NKVD*, 159–60, and details in Mikhail Il'insky, *Narkom Yagoda* (Moscow: Yauza-Eksmo, 2005) (in Russian). Contrary to the historical facts, the author of this book, an FSB-affiliated historian, presents Yagoda as a real plotter.

23. Artuzov headed the KRO from 1922 to 1927, and from 1931 to 1935, he headed the INO. Biography of A. A. Artuzov (1891–1937) in Petrov and Skorkin, *Kto rukovodil NKVD*, 93–94.

24. In October 1923, Ulrikh was appointed deputy chairman of the Military Collegium. Kokurin and Petrov, *Lubyanka*, 34.

25. Biography of Y. K. Olsky (1891–1938) in Vadim Abramov, *Kontrrazvedka. Shchit i mech protiv Abvera i TsRU* (Moscow: Yauza-Eksmo, 2006), 85–101 (in Russian).

26. Stalin's telegram to Menzhinsky dated June 23, 1927. Quoted in Aleksandr Yakovlev, 'Glavnokomanduyyushchii predal armiyu,' *Nezavisimaya gazeta*, No. 63, August 28, 2003 (in Russian), http://2003.novayagazeta.ru/nomer/2003/63n/n63n-s23.shtml, retrieved September, 2011.

27. L. P. Belyakov, 'Shakhtinskoe delo,' in *Repressirovannye geologi*, edited by L. P. Belikov and Ye. M. Zabolotsky, 395–8 (Moscow: Ministerctvo prirodnykh resursov, 1999) (in Russian). Recently the OGPU files of this case were declassified and the first volume of these materials was published: *Shakhtinskii protsess 1928 g. Podgotovka, provedenie,itogi. Kniga 1*, edited by S. A. Krasil'nikov et al. (Moscow: Rosspen, 2011) (in Russian).

28. On the career of Ye. G. Yevdokimov (1891–1940) and his role in the *Shakhtinskoe delo* see Stephen G. Wheatcroft, 'Agency and Terror: Evdokimov and Mass Killing in Stalin's Great Terror,' *Australian Journal of Politics and History* 53, no. 1 (March 2007), 26–43.

29. V. Goncharov and V. Nekhotin, 'Dela "Prompartii" i "Trudovoi krest'yanskoi partii (TKP)" (1930–1932)' in *Prosim osvobodit' iz tyuremnogo zaklyucheniya*, edited by V. Goncharov and V. Nekhotin (Moscow: Sovremennyi pisatel', 1998), 173–7 (in Russian).

30. Krylenko's speech on December 4, 1930. Aleksandr Solzhenitsyn discusses Krylenko's role in the promotion of confessions in political cases in *Archipelago Gulag*, Vol. 1.

31. A. Ya. Vyshinsky, *Teoriya sudebnykh dokazatel'stv v sovetskom prave* (Moscow: Yuridicheskoe izdatel'stvo, 1941), 180–1 (in Russian).

32. Details in Ya. Yu. Tinchenko, *Golgofa russkogo ofitserstva v SSSR. 1930–1931 gody* (Moscow: Moskovskii obshchestvennyi nauchnyi fond, 2000) (in Russian), N. Cherushev, *'Nevinovnykh ne byvaet…' Chekisty protiv voennykh, 1918–1953* (Moscow: Veche, 2004), 147–99 (in Russian), and a review in Degtyarev and Kolpakidi, *SMERSH*, 55–59; Zdanovich, *Organy gosudarstvennoi bezopasnosti*, 376–93.

33. Ibid., 370–2.

34. Biography of I. M. Leplevsky (1896–1938) in Petrov and Skorkin, *Kto rukovodil NKVD*, 270–1.

35. Politburo decision P55/26/3, dated August 10, 1931. Document No. 274 in *Lubyanka. Stalin i VChK–GPU–OGPU–NKVD. Yanvar'1922–dekabr' 1936*, edited by V. N. Khaustov, V. P. Naumov, and N. S. Plotnikova, 280 (Moscow: Materik, 2004) (in Russian).

36. Zdanovich, *Organy gosudarstvennoi bezopasnosti*, 507.

37. S. A. Kropachev, 'Politicheskie repressii v SSSR 1937–1938 godov: prichiny, masshtaby, posledstviya' (2007) (in Russian), http://www.kubanmemo.ru/library/Kropachev01/repress37_38.php, retrieved September 4, 2011. On the

Tukhachevsky case, see N. Cherushev, *1937 god: elita Krasnoi Armii na Golgofe* (Moscow: Veche, 2003) and Yuliya Kantor, *Voina i mir Mikhaila Tukhachevskogo* (Moscow: Vremya, 2005) (both in Russian)..

38. In 1937–38, Stalin personally ordered beatings, signing an order on January 10, 1939 to apply 'physical treatment' (torture) to the arrested 'enemies of people.' Document No. 8 in *Lubyanka. Stalin i NKVD–NKGB–GUKR 'Smersh.' 1939–mart 1946*, edited by V. N. Khaustov, V. P. Naumov, and N. S. Plotnikova, 14–15 (Moscow: Materik, 2006) (in Russian).

39. A short biography of G. G. Yagoda (1897–1938) in N. V. Petrov and K. V. Skorkin, *Kto rukovodil NKVD, 1934–1941. Spravochnik* (Moscow: Zven'ya 1999), 459–60 (in Russian). Details in Mikhail Il'insky, *Narkom Yagoda* (Moscow: Yauza-Eksmo, 2005) (in Russian). Contrary to the facts, the author, an FSB-affiliated historian, presents Yagoda as a real plotter.

40. Data from O. F. Suvenirov, *Tragediya RKKA. 1937-1938* (Moscow: Terra, 1998), 317 (in Russian). Additional information on the mechanism of repressionsions in the Red Army and Navy in Vladimir Khaustovand Lennart Samuelson, *Stalin, NKVD i repressii 1936-1938 gg.* (Moscow: ROSSPEN, 2009), 189–227 (in Russian).

41. Data from Table 2 in Michael Parrish, *Sacrifice of the Generals: Soviet Senior Officer Losses, 1939–1945* (Lanham, MD: The Scarecrow Press. Inc., 2004), xvii.

42. *Perepiska Borisa Pasternaka,* edited by Yelena V. Pasternak and Yevgenii B. Pasternak (Moscow: Khudozhestvennaya literatura, 1990), 160 (in Russian).

43. On Stalin's presumed paranoia, see, for instance, Daniel Rancour-Laferriere, *The Mind of Stalin. A Psychoanalytic Study* (Ann Arbor, MI: Ardis, 1988). In his last biography of Stalin, Robert Service cautiously characterized Stalin in the 1930s as a person with 'a deeply disordered personality' (*Stalin: A Biography* [Cambridge, MA: The Belknap Press, 2005], 344).

44. Oleg Khlevnyuk, *Khozyain. Stalin i utverzhdenie stalinskoi diktatury* (Moscow: Rosspen, 2010), 302 (in Russian).

45. Photo of this document with Stalin's editorial notes in *SMERSH. Istoricheskie ocherki i arkhivnye materialy*, edited by V. S. Khristoforov, V. K. Vinogradov, O. K. Matveev, et al. (Moscow: Glavarkhiv Moskvy, 2003), 67 (in Russian).

46. GKO (State Defense Committee) Order No. 3222ss/ov on the creation of GUKR 'SMERSH,' dated April 21, 1943. Document No. 151, in Kokurin and Petrov, *Lubyanka,* 623–6.

47. Daniil Fibikh, 'Frontovye dnevniki 1942–1943 gg.,' *Novyi Mir*, no. 5 (2010) (in Russian), http://magazines.russ.ru/novyi_mi/2010/5/fi2.html, retrieved September 4, 2011.

48. Nicola Sinevirsky, *SMERSH* (New York: Henry Holt and Company, 1950); 'Romanov,' *Nights Are Longest There*.

49. Sinevirsky, *SMERSH*, 121–6.

50. In the military history literature, a Soviet 'front' is sometimes called 'an army group.' See Mawdsley, *Thunder in the East*, 426.

51. See details in Nicholas Bethell, *The Last Secret: Forcible Repatriation to Russia, 1944–47* (London: Deutsch, 1974); Nikolai Tolstoy, *Victims of Yalta* (London: Hodder & Stoughton, 1977); J. Hoffmann, *Istoriya vlasovskoi armii* (Paris: YMCA-Press, 1990), 231–62 (in Russian, translated from the German).

52. Count Bethlen died in the Butyrka Prison Hospital in 1946, while Antonescu and several of his ministers were handed over to Romanian state security. In May 1946, they faced trial in Bucharest and were condemned to death and executed on June 1, 1946.

53. The literature on Raoul Wallenberg is vast, and many documents about his activities in Hungary have been published. See for instance Jeno Levai, *Raoul Wallenberg. His Remarkable Life, Heroic Battles and The Secret of His Mysterious Disappearance*, translated into English by Frank Vajda (Melbourne, Australia: The University of Melbourne, 1989). Unfortunately, the description of Wallenberg's captivity is given incorrectly in all his biographies in English, because the authors used old and unreliable sources.

54. For a brief discussion of Wallenberg's incarceration and death in Moscow, see V. B. Birstein, 'The Secret of Cell Number Seven,' *Nezavisimaya gazeta*, April 25, 1991, 4; 'Interrogations in Lubyanka,' *Novoe vremya*, no. 1 (1993), 42–43; and 'Raoul Wallenberg: The Story of Death,' *Evreiskie novosti*, no. 2 (July 2002), 6. All in Russian, but the English version of these articles is available at http://www.vadimbirstein.com.

55. Texts of several testimonies written by Stolze, Pieckenbrock and Bentivegni in 1945–47 while being detained by SMERSH and MGB are given in Julius Mader, *Hitlers Spionagegenerale sagen aus* (Berlin: Verlag der Nation, 1977).

56. *The Rote Kapelle: The CIA's History of Soviet Intelligence and Espionage Networks in Western Europe, 1936–1945* (Frederick, MD: University Publications of America, Inc., 1979), 110, 126–8, and others.

57. A book by Irina Bezborodova entitled *Wehrmacht Generals in Captivity*, published in Russian in 1998 (*Generaly Vermakhta v plenu* [Moscow: Rossiiskii gosudarstvennyi gumanitarnyi universitet]), unfortunately introduced some misunderstandings of the fate of a number of German general POWs in the Soviet Union.

58. Mohnke's Archival–Investigation File H-21144, FSB Central Archive, a photocopy at the USHMM Archive, RG-06.052.

59. See details in Vladimir A. Kozlov, *'Gde Gitler?' Povtornoe rassledovanie NKVD-MVD SSSR obstoyatel'st ischeznoveniya Adolfa Gitlera (1945–1949)* (Moscow: Modest Kolyarov, 2003) (in Russian).

60. Rehabilitated in 1994. *Rasstrel'nye spiski. Moskva 1935–1953*, 340.

61. Data from Shun Akifusa's Prisoner Card in the Vladimir Prison Archive.

62. Vasilevsky's order, dated August 22, 1945, and Beria's order, dated August 23, 1945, Document Nos. 474 and 475 in *Russkii arkhiv. Velikaya Otechestvennaya. Sovetsko-yaponskaya voina*, T. 18 (7-2) (Moscow: TERRA, 2000), 102–3 (in Russian).

63. L. G. Mishchenko, *Poka ya pomnyu…*(Moscow: Vozvrashchenie, 2006), 80 (in Russian).

64. The Soviets participated only in the International Military Tribunal and the Trial of the Major War Criminals (November 1945–October 1946), which I call here 'the International Nuremberg Trial.' Most Russians are not aware of the twelve American Subsequent Nuremberg Trials that followed from 1946–49.

65. The most updated description of the Katyn Forest massacre is given in *Katyn: A Crime Without Punishment*, edited by Ann M. Cienciala, Natalia S. Lebedeva, and Wojciech Materski (New Haven, CT: Yale University Press, 2007).

66. Telford Taylor, *The Anatomy of the Nuremberg Trials: A Personal Memoir* (New York: Alfred A. Knopf, 1992), 417.

67. In some Western sources, Belkin is identified with the first name 'Fyodor' or 'Fedor' instead of Mikhail. See, for instance, George H. Hodos, *Show Trials: Stalinist Purges in Eastern Europe, 1948–1954* (New York: Praeger, 1987), 30.

68. Document Nos. 41 and 42 in Kokurin and Petrov, *GULAG*, 136–41.

69. Document No. 132 in ibid., 555–67.

70. Quoted in A. S. Smykalov, ''Osobye lagerya' i 'osbye tyur'my' v sisteme ispravitel'no-trudovykh uchrezhdenii sovetskogo gosudarstva v 40–50-e gody,' *Gosudarstvo i pravo*, no. 5 (1997), 84–91 (in Russian).

71. For example, the memoir of a Soviet Nuremberg Trial translator written in the 1990s mistakenly claims that the SMERSH group in Nuremberg was supervised by Beria rather than Abakumov. T. S. Stupnikova, *'Nichego krome pravdy:' Niurenberg–Moskva. Vospominaniya* (Moscow: Russkie slovari, 1998), 60 and 101 (in Russian).

72. Thaddeus Wittlin, *Commissar: The Life and Death of Lavrenty Pavlovich Beria* (New York: Macmillan, 1972); this book, written before archival revelations, contains a lot of incorrect information. Amy Knight, *Beria: Stalin's First Lieutenant* (Princeton, NJ: Princeton University Press, 1993); also, Chapter 8 in Donald Rayfield, *Stalin and His Hangmen: The Tyrant and Those Who Killed for Him* (New York: Random House, 2004), 341–87.

73. *Arkhiv noveishei istorii Rossii, T. IV. 'Osobaya papka L. P. Berii.' Iz materialov Sekretariata NKVD–MVD SSSR 1946–1949 gg. Katalog dokumentov*, edited by V. A. Kozlov and S. V. Mironenko, 254 (Moscow: Gosudarstvennyi Arkhiv Rossiiskoi Federatsii, 1996) (in Russian).

74. A letter of V. N. Zaichikov to the Central Committee, dated July 16, 1953, quoted in Nikita Petrov, *Pervyi predsedatel' KGB Ivan Serov* (Moscow: Materik, 2005), 129 (in Russian).

75. Cited in Kirill Stolyarov *Palachi i zhertvy* (Moscow: Olma-Press, 1997), 88 (in Russian).

76. Biographies of Ya. M. Broverman (1908–?), V. I. Komarov (1916–1954), A. G. Leonov (1905–1954), M. T. Likhachev (1913–1954), and I. A. Chernov (1906–1991) in Petrov, *Kto rukovodil organami gosbezopasnosti*, 220, 479, 541–2, 548, and 906.

77. Cited in Stolyarov *Palachi i zhertvy*, 104.

78. Chernov's recollections in ibid., 98.

79. The executioner Colonel Talanov's words cited in Stolyarov, *Palachi i zhertvy*, 106.

80. V. P. Naumov, 'K istorii sekretnogo doklada N. S. Khrushcheva na XX s'ezde KPSS,' *Novaya i noveishaya istoriya*, no. 4 (1996), 147–68 (in Russian).

81. The legal aspect in V. N. Kudryavtsev and A. I. Trusov, *Politicheskaya yustitsiya v SSSR* (St. Petersburg: Yuridicheskii tsentr Press, 2002), 343–58 (in Russian) and A. G. Petrov, *Reabilitatsiya zhertv politicheskikh repressii: opyt istoricheskogo analiza* (Moscow: Izdatel'stvo INION RAN, 2005) (in Russian).

82. O. B. Mozokhin, *Pravo na repressii. Vnesudebmyepolnomochiya organov gosudarstvennoi bezopasnosti (1918-1953)* (Moscow: Kuchkovo pole, 2006), 243 (in Russian).

83. A. Muranov and V. Zavenyagin, *Sud nad sud'yami (osobaya papka Ulrikha)* (Kazan: Kazan, 1993), 60–61 (in Russian).

84 Kudryavtsev and Trusov, *Politicheskaya yustitsiya*, 329–35.

85. Leonid Mlechin, in Vladimir Kozlov, *Neizvestnyi SSSR. Protivostoyanie naroda i vlasti 1953–1985* (Moscow: Olma-Press, 2006), 13–14 (in Russian).

86. Andrei Sukhomlinov, *Kto vy, Lavrentii Beria?* (Moscow: Detektiv-Press, 2004), 449–52 (in Russian).

87. Sergei Kremlev [apparently, a pen name made up from the word 'the Kremlin'], *Beria. Luchshii menedger XX veka* (Moscow: Yauza-Eksmo, 2008) (in Russian); the second edition was published in 2011.

88. Vadim Abramov, *Abakumov—nachal'nik SMERSHa—Vzlyot i padenie lyubimtsa Stalina* (Moscow: Yauza, 2005), 205–6 (in Russian).

89. Oleg Smyslov, 'Rytsar' GB,' *Rossia*, June 9-15, 2005, 8 (in Russian).

90. Biography of S. G. Bannikov (1921-1989) in Kokurin and Petrov, *Lubyanka*, 254.

91. Stanislav Lekarev, 'Umer genii rossiiskoi kontrrazvedki,' *Argumenty nedeli*, no. 22 (56), May 31, 2007, http://www.argumenti.ru/espionage/2007/06/34624/, retrieved September 4, 2011.

92. Biography of F. D. Bobkov (b. 1925) in Kokurin and Petrov, *Lubyanka*, 256–7.

93. The current FSB structure in Andrei Soldatov and Irina Bogoraz, *The New Nobility: The Restoration of Russia's Security State and The Enduring Legacy of the KGB* (New York: Public Affairs, 2010), 243–6.

94. Molyakov's interview in Igor Korotchenko, 'Voennaya kontrrazvedka ne dopustit vooruzhennogo myatezha,' *Nezavisimaya gazeta*, June 19, 1997 (in Russian).

95. 'Obrazovan Vysshii Ofitserskii Sovet,' http://rusk.ru/st.php?idar=103107, retrieved September 4, 2011.

96. Vladimir Petrishchev, 'Rossii nuzhna svoya ideya,' *Vremya novostei*, No. 98, June 6, 2005 (in Russian).

97. 'Kadroviku prezidenta porucheno sosredotochit'sya na nagradakh,' *Pravo. ru*, October 15, 2009 (in Russian), http://www.pravo.ru/news/view/18706, retrieved September 4, 2011.

98. 'V Moskve otkryt monument slavy voennoi kontrrazvedki,' *Interfax-AVN*, May 5, 2005 (in Russian), http://www.chekist.ru/?news_id=742, retrieved March 16, 2011.

Chapter 2

1. The term 'instrument of personal rule' was coined by Yoram Gorlizki and Oleg Khlevniuk, *Cold Peace: Stalin and the Soviet Ruling Circle, 1945–1953* (Oxford: Oxford University Press, 2004), 46.

2. Three members of the Politburo, Mikhail Kalinin, Chairman of the Presidium of the Supreme Council; Andrei Andreev, Chairman of the Union Council; and Nikolai Shvernik, Chairman of the Council of Nationalities and first deputy of Kalinin, played 'decorative' roles as heads of the executive branch of the Soviet Government, the Supreme Council (consisting of the Union Council and the Council of Nationalities). The three were never members of Stalin's 'inner circle'.

3. G. Mar'yamov, *Kremlevskii tsenzor: Stalin smotrit kino* (Moscow: Kinotsentr, 1992), 11 (in Russian).

4. On the routine of the Politburo records see J. Howlett, O. Khlevniuk, L. Rogovaia, 'The CPSU's Top Bodies Under Stalin: Their Operational Records and Structure of Command,' SERAP Working Paper No. 1 (1996), http://www.uto-ronto.ca/ceres/serap/wp1.htm, retrieved September 4, 2011.

5. Recollections by Dmitrii N. Sukhanov (1904–?), former assistant to Georgii Malenkov (Politburo member and member of Stalin's inner circle), in the Russian documentary *I Worked for Stalin* (Moscow, 1990).

6. Boris Yefimov, *Desyat' desyatiletii o tom, chto videl, perezhil, zapomnil* (Moscow: Vagrius, 2000), 261 (in Russian).

7. Page 8 in A. M. Vasilevsky, 'Nakanune 22 iyunya 1941 g. (Neopublikovan-noe interv'yu marshala Sovetskogo Soyuza A. M. Vasilevskogo ot 20 avgusta 1965 g.),' *Novaya i noveishaya istoriya*, no. 6 (1994), 8–11 (in Russian).

8. Robert C. Tucker, *Stalin in Power: Revolution from Above, 1928–1941* (New York: W. W. Norton & Co., 1992), 123–4; details in I. V. Pavlova, *Mekhanizm vlasti i stroitel'stvo stalinskogo sotsializma* (Novosibirsk: Izdatel'stvo SO RAN, 2001), 151–64, 196–207 (in Russian).

9. Memoirs by I. V. Kovalev, Commissar for Railroads, in G. Kumanev, *Govoryat stalinskie narkomy* (Smolensk: Rusich, 2005), 279 (in Russian). On March 10, 1934, the Polutburo appointed Poskrebyshev head of the Special Sector (Decision P3/55/35).

10. Abdurakhman Avtorkhanov, 'Zagadka smerti Stalina,' *Novyi Mir*, no. 5 (1991), 194–233 (in Russian).

11. 'Pravyashchaya Partiya ostavalas' podpol'noi,' *Istochnik*, no. 5/6 (1993), 88–95 (in Russian).

12. Stalin's speech at the Central Committee's Plenum on March 3, 1937, page 14 in 'Materialy fevral'sko-martovskogo plenuma TsK VKP(b) 1937 goda,' *Voprosy istorii*, no. 3 (1995), 3–15 (in Russian).

13. Kaganovich's speech at the 17th Party Congress, 1934, quoted in I. V. Pavlova, *Stalinizm: stanovlenie mekhanizma vlasti* (Novosibirsk: Sibirskii khronograf, 1999), 175 (in Russian).

14. Mar'yamov, *Kremlevskii tsenzor*, 48–49.

15. Yakov Butovsky et al., in *Noveishaya istoriya otechestvennogo kino. 1986–2000. Kino i kontekst. T. 6* (St. Petersburg: Seans, 2004) (in Russian).

16. Literature on the re-evaluation of this data is vast, and growing. See, for instance, Mark Solonin, *22 iyunya, ili Kogda nachalas' Velikaya Otechestvennaya voina?* (Moscow: Yauza, 2005) (in Russian); Anatolii Tsyganok, 'K kakoi voine gotovilas' Krasnaya armiya? Chast' pervaya,' Polit.ru, June 18, 2006 (in Russian), http://www.polit.ru/analytics/2006/06/16/whichwar.html, retrieved September 4, 2011.

17. Stalin's editorial note to Timoshenko's report, dated December 1940, quoted in Vladimir Lota, *'Alta' protiv 'Barbarossy'* (Moscow: Molodaya gvardiya, 2004), 262 (in Russian).

18. Anastas Mikoyan, *Tak bylo. Razmyshleniya o munuvshem* (Moscow: Vagrius, 1999), 354 (in Russian).

19. A. I. Romanov, *Nights Are Longest There: A Memoir of the Soviet Security Services*, translated by Gerald Brooke (Boston, MA: Little, Brown and Company, 1972), 178.

20. N. A. Zen'kovich, *Tainy kremlevskikh smertei* (Moscow: Nadezhda, 1995), 383 (in Russian); Aleksei Teplyakov, 'Sibir': protsedura ispolneniya smertnykh prigovorov v 1920-kh—1930-kh godakh,' *Golosa Sibiri. Vypusk chetvertyi* (Kemerovo: Kuzbassvuzizdat, 2006), 213–77 (in Russian).

21. Merkulov's testimony in 1953 (APRF, Fond 3, Opis' 24, Delo 472, L. 57), quoted in Nikita Petrov and Marc Jansen, *'Stalinskii pitomets'—Nikolai Yezhov* (Moscow: Rosspen, 2008), 184 (in Russian).

22. 'The Hunter,' *Time*, March 22, 1948.

23. All of them are mentioned in the text or figures. Biographies in N. V. Petrov and K. V. Skorkin, *Kto rukovodil NKVD, 1934–1941. Spravochnik* (Moscow: Zven'ya 1999), 148–9, 167–8, 233–4, 289, 296–8, and 431–2 (in Russian).

24. Nikita Petrov, 'Samyi obrazovannyi palach,' *Novaya gazeta. Pravda 'GULAGa'*, no. 12 (33), August 30, 2010 (in Russian), http://www.novayagazeta.ru/data/2010/gulag12/00.html, retrieved September 4, 2011.

25. Romanov, *Nights Are Longest There*, 55.

26. Politburo decision P64/82, dated September 1938. Document No. 345, in *Lubyanka: Stalin i Glavnoe upravlenie gosudarstvennoi bezopasnosti NKVD, 1937–1938*, edited by V. N. Khaustov, V. P. Naumov, and N. S. Plotnikova, 554–55 (Moscow: Materik, 2004) (in Russian).

27. Evan Mawdsley, *Thunder in the East: The Nazi-Soviet Struggle, 1941–1945* (London: Hodder Arnold, 2005), 67.

28. Politburo decision P67/52, dated January 11, 1938. Document No. 10 in *Lubyanka. Stalin i NKVD–NKGB–GUKR 'SMERSH.' 1939–1946*, edited by V. N. Khaustov, V. P. Naumov, and N. S. Plotnikova, 16–18 (Moscow: Demokratiya, 2006) (in Russian).

29. Note on the NKVD personnel on January 1, 1940. Document No. 21, in A. I. Kokurin and N. V. Petrov, *Lubyanka. VCheKa–OGPU–NKVD–NKGB–MGB–MVD–KGB. 1917–1960. Spravochnik* (Moscow: Demokratiya, 1997), 258–60 (in Russian).

30. Biography of V. M. Bochkov (1900–1981) in Petrov and Skorkin, *Kto rukovodil NKVD*, 116.

31. Biography of A. N. Mikheev (1911–1941) in Petrov and Skorkin, *Kto rukovodil NKVD*, 306.

Chapter 3

1. A division of crimes into two groups, (a) crimes against the new political law and order, and (b) all other crimes already existed in the first Russian Federation Criminal Code of 1922 (Article 27). Criminal codes of the other Soviet republics had the same article as Article 58 but with a different article number—for instance, in the Ukrainian Criminal Code it was Article 54.

2. For an English translation of the paragraphs of Article 58 see Jacques Rossi, *The Gulag Handbook: An Encyclopedia Dictionary of Soviet Penitentiary Institutions and Terms Related to the Forced Labor Camps*, translated from the Russian by William A. Burhans (New York: Paragon House, 1989), 539–50. The main section of this volume is an invaluable dictionary of Gulag jargon and terminology.

3. Document No. 13, in *Reabilitatsiya: Kak eto bylo. Dokumenty Prezidiuma TsK KPSS i drugie materialy. Mart 1953–fevral' 1956*, edited by A. Artizov et al., 77 (Moscow: Demokratiya, 2000) (in Russian).

4. Joint decision of VTsIK (All-Russian Central Executive Committee, predecessor of the USSR Supreme Council) and Sovnarkom, dated July 20, 1934. *Sbornik zakonodatel'nykh i normativnykh aktov o repressiyakh*, edited by Ye. A. Zaitsev, 161 (Moscow: Respublika, 1993) (in Russian).

5. NKVD report to Stalin, dated October 5, 1938 (FSB Central Archive, Fond 3, Opis' 5, Delo 79, L. 281); quoted in Arsenii Roginsky and Aleksandr Daniel, 'Arestu podlezhat zheny…' *Polit.ru*, October 30, 2003 (in Russian), http://www.polit.ru/research/2003/10/30/628134.html, retrieved September 4, 2011.

6. Organizational details of persecutions of *chsiry*, including children, were given in NKVD Operational Order No. 00486, dated August 15, 1937; in *Sbornik zakonodatel'nykh i normativnykh aktov*, 86–93.

7. Quoted in Yulian Semenov, *Nenapisannye romany* (Moscow: DEM, 1989), Chapter 27 (in Russian), http://virlib.ru/read_book.php?page=31&file_path=books/9/book04207.gz, retrieved September 5, 2011.

8. Report of Yu. D. Sumbatov to Beria, dated January 29, 1939 (FSB Central Archive, Fond 3, Opis' 6, Delo 839, L. 35), quoted in Roginsky and Daniel, 'Arestu podlezhat zheny.'

9. Decree of the Presidium of the USSR Supreme Soviet, dated May 31, 1941. *Vedomosti Verkhovnogo Soveta SSSR*, no. 25 (1941) (in Russian).

10. Safonov's report to Andrei Vysinsky, dated December 22, 1941. Document No. 212 in *Deti GULAGa, 1918–1956*, edited by S. S. Vilensky, A. I. Kokurin, G. V. Atmashkina, and I. Yu. Novichenko, 376 (Moscow: Demokratiya, 2002) (in Russian).

11. Details in S. Lakoba, *Abkhazia posle dvukh imperii. XIX–XXI vv.* (Moscow, 2004), 111–22 (in Russian).

12. Politburo decision P19/277, dated August 17, 1940. Document No. 124 in *Lubyanka. Stalin i NKVD–NKGB–GUKR*, 184.

13. Victor Levenstein, *Po-nad narami tabachnyi dym…* (Moscow: Russkii put', 2008), 149 (in Russian). L. Ye. Vlodzimersky (1903–1953) headed the NKVD/NKGB/MGB Investigation Department for Especially Important Cases (OVD) until 1946.

14. Menachem Begin, *White Nights: The Story of a Prisoner in Russia*, translated from the Hebrew by Katia Kaplan (New York: Harper & Row, Publishers, 1977), 81.

15. Anna Yatskova, 'Istoriya sovetskogo suda,' *Otechestvennye zapiski*, no. 2 (2003) (in Russian), http://magazines.russ.ru/oz/2003/2/iackov.html, retrieved September 4, 2011.

16. M. Delagrammatik, 'Voennye tribunaly za rabotoi,' *Novyi Mir*, no. 6 (1997) (in Russian), http://magazines.russ.ru/novyi_mi/1997/6/delagr.htm, retrieved September 4, 2011. This source gives examples of a number of standard cases tried by military tribunals.

17. Vyacheslav V. Obukhov, *Pravovye osnovy organizatsii ideyatel'nosti voennykh tribunalov voisk NKVD SSSR v gody Velikoi Otechestvennoi voiny 1941–1945 gg.* (Moscow: MVD Moscow University, 2002). Candidate of Sciences Dissertation, 41, 96 (in Russian).

I am indebted to Professor Jeffrey Burds (Northeastern University, Boston, MA), who pointed out this source.

18. From 1943 to 1945, the USSR Supreme Court also included the Military-Railroad Collegium and the Military-Transportation Collegium. From the end of 1944 till April 1954, there was also the Collegium of Labor Camps Courts. Nikita Petrov, *GULAG*, Chapter 11, http://www.pseudology.org/GULAG/Glava11.htm, retrieved September 4, 2011.

19. Details in Obukhov, *Pravovye osnovy*, 89–101.

20. In early 1942, the Directorate of Military Tribunals was renamed the Main Directorate of Military Tribunals which consisted of the Directorate of Military Tribunals and Directorate of the Navy Tribunals. Also, the Department of Military Tribunals of the NKVD troops became the Directorate of Military Tribunals of the NKVD troops. Ibid., 42 and 96.

21. Details in ibid., 48.

22. Interview with Zyama Ioffe, former member of a divisional military tribunal, February 5, 2009 (in Russian), http://www.iremember.ru/drugie-voyska/ioffe-zyama-yakovlevich.html, retrieved September 4, 2011.

23. Delagrammatik, 'Voennye tribunaly.'

24. See whole texts of paragraphs 193-17, 193-20–23 in Vyacheslav Zvyagintsev, *Voina na vesakh Femidy. Voina 1941–1945 gg. v materialakh sledsvenno-sudebnykh del* (Moscow: Terra, 2006), 281–6 (in Russian).

25. Interview with Ioffe.

26. In 1939, the Office of the Chief Prosecutor of the Navy was established after a separate Navy Commissariat had been organized, and in 1941, it became a department within the Chief Military Prosecutor's Office.

27. The department structure from A. V. Kudryashov, "Deyatel'nost' voennoi prokuratury v gody Velikoi Otechestvennoi voiny," *Nauchnaya sessiya MIFI*, 6 (2005): 169–70 (in Russian).

28. K. F. Telegin, *Voiny neschitannye versty* (Moscow: Voenizdat, 1988), 189–90 (in Russian).

29. Zvyagintsev, *Voina na vesakh Femidy*, 382-3, 736-7.

30. Ibid.

31. In fact, on January 1, 1945 the labor camps belonged to seven NKVD directorates, including the GULAG (Main Directorate of [Labor] Camps). Kokurin and Petrov, *Lubyanka* (2003), 199.

32. On the role of prosecutors in political cases, see V. N. Kudryavtsev and A. I. Trusov, *Politicheskaya yustitsiya v SSSR* (Moscow: Nauka, 2000), 303–9 (in Russian).

33. O. F. Suvenirov, *Tragediya RKKA 1937–1938* (Moscow: Terra, 1998), 63 (in Russian).

34. GKO Order No. 460ss, dated August 11, 1941. Document No. 193, in *Lubyanka: Stalin i NKVD*, 310.

35. Delagrammatik, 'Voennye tribunaly.'

36. Sidnev's letter to Bochkov, dated March 5, 1941, in A. Muranov and V. Zvyagintsev, *Sud nad sud'yami (osobaya papka Ul'rikha)* (Kazan: Kazan, 1993), 226 (in Russian).

37. Bochkov's letter to Ulrikh, dated April 23, 1939. A photo of the letter in Muranov and Zvyagintsev, *Sud nad sud'yami*, 73–76.

38. Interview with Ioffe.

39. Delagrammatk, 'Voennye tribunaly.'

40. Ibid.

41. Zvyagintsev, *Voina na vesakh Femidy*, 736–7.

42. S. S. Zamyatin, 'Vremennye boitsy' (in Russian), http://www.proza.ru/texts/2008/05/10/375.html, retrived Septmber 4, 2011.

Chapter 4

1. Paragraph 2 in Part I of the TsIK Resolution, dated July 10, 1934. Document No. 124 in Kokurin and Petrov, *Lubyanka* (2003), 547–8.

2. A 25-year term of imprisonment was introduced by TsIK Resolution dated October 2, 1937. G. M. Ivanova, 'Zakonodatel'naya baza sovetskoi repressivnoi politiki', in *Kniga dlya uchitelya: Istoriya politicheskikh repressii i soprotivleniya nesvobode v SSSR*, edited by V. V. Shelokhaev, 39–82 (Moscow: Mosgorarkhiv, 2002) (in Russian).

3. Beria's report to Stalin, dated November 15, 1941, quoted in ibid., 56.

4. In addition to the Military Collegium, from 1923 to 1934, court sessions of three members of the OGPU Collegium that included high-level OGPU functionaries also handed down death sentences. The Collegium considered only important cases under Articles 58 and 59 in the absence of defendants whom it sentenced to long terms of imprisonment or to death. See http://www.memo.ru/memory/preface/martyr.htm (in Russian), retrieved September 4, 2011.

5. TsIK Resolution, dated September 14, 1937. *Kniga dlya uchitelya*, 70.

6. M. P. Charyev, 'Deyatel'nost' voennykh tribunalov vo vremya Velikoi Otechestvennoi voiny 1941-1945 gg.,' *Voenno-yuridicheskii zhurnal*, no. 8 (2006), 25–30 (in Russian). In 1941, there were 76 tribunals within the NKVD troops.

7. Biography of V. V. Ulrikh (1889–1951) in Zvyagintsev, *Voina na vesakh Femidy*, 52–55.

8. Ulrikh's letter to Stalin, dated April 2, 1938, quoted in Kudryavtsev and Trusov, *Politicheskaya yustitsiya*, 282.

9. Ernest Hemingway, *For Whom the Bell Tolls* (New York: Simon and Schuster, 1995), 231, 424. This novel was banned in the Soviet Union until 1968.

10. Yefimov, *Desyat' desyatiletii o tom, chto videl*, 315–7.

11. On January 17, 1940 the Politburo approved the death sentence for Koltsov as a German and French spy, and on February 2, 1940 he was executed. Koltsov's former wife, Maria Osten-Gressgener, also described by Hemingway, was executed on September 16, 1942.

12. The NKVD formed Special Departments (OOs) within the Republican Army and organized killing squads that committed numerous atrocities. Additionally, NKVD agents participated in the transfer of the Spanish gold reserve to the Soviet Union. Stéphane Courtois and Jean-Louis Panné, '17. The Shadow of the NKVD in Spain,' in Stéphane Courtois et al., *The Black Book of Communism: Crimes, Terror, Repressions* (Cambridge, MA: Harvard University Press), 333–52.

13. Beria's report to Stalin, a photo in Nikita Petrov and Marc Jansen, 'On khvastalsya rasstrelami,' *Novaya gazeta. 'Pravda GULAGa,'* no. 11, December 4, 2008 (in Russian), http://www.novayagazeta.ru/data/2008/gulag11/01.html, retrieved September 4, 2011.

14. Yakov Aizenshtat, *Zapiski sekretarya voennogo tribunala* (London: Overseas Publishing Interchange Ltd., 1991), 19–20 (in Russian).

15. Petrov and Jansen, 'On khvastalsya rasstrelami.'

16. Obukhov, *Pravovye osnovy organizatsii*, 79–81.

17. Ibid., 36, 41-43.

18. N. F. Chistyakov, *Po zakonu i sovesti* (Moscow: Voenizdat, 1979) (in Russian), http://militera.lib.ru/memo/russian/chistyakov_nf/04.html, retrieved September 5, 2011.

19. Aizenshtat, *Zapiski sekretarya*, 15–19. During the war, the Military Collegium included V. V. Ulrikh (chairman), V. V. Bukanov, A. A. Cheptsov, I. V. Detistov, L. D. Dmitriev, B. I. Ievlev, D. Ya. Kandybin, F. A. Klimin, I. O. Matulevich, A. M. Orlov, M. G. Romanychev, A. G. Souslin, V. V. Syuldin, V. A. Uspensky, and I. M. Zaryanov.

20. In these cases, the verdict usually stated: 'The sentence is final and not open to appeal. According to the TsIK decision dated December 1, 1934, it should be carried out immediately.' This decision included the following orders: terrorist acts must be investigated within 10 days; there will be no prosecution and defense representatives at the trial; convicted parties are prohibited from making appeals; and death sentences must be carried out immediately after the trial. See http://stalin.memo.ru/images/1934.htm, retrieved September 4, 2011.

21. GKO decision No. 634e-ss, dated September 6, 1941. Document No. 198 in *Lubyanka. Stalin i NKVD–NKGB–GUKR 'SMERSH.' 1939–1946*, edited by V. N. Khaustov, V. P. Naumov, and N. S. Plotnikova, 314 (Moscow: Materik, 2006) (in Russian).

22. Page 496 in A. B. Roginsky, 'Posleslovie,' in *Rasstrel'nye spiski. Moskva, 1937–1941.'Kommunarka,' Butovo. Kniga pamyati zhertv politicheskikh repressii*, edited by L. S. Yeremina and A. B. Roginsky, 485–501 (Moscow: Zven'ya, 2000) (in Russian).

23. Figures from Charyev, 'Deyatel'nost' voennykh tribunalov.'

24. For instance, documents in 'Kto utverdil smertnye prigovory N. I. Vavilovu i G. D. Karpechenko,' in *Nikolai Ivanovich Vavilov i stranitsy sovetskoi genetiki*, edited by I. A. Zakharov, 124–5 (Moscow: IOGEN RAN, 2000) (in Russian).

25. Quoted in Vladimir Pyatnitsky, 'Khronika poslednego puti,' *Novaya gazeta 'Pravda GULAGa,'* no. 3, April 3, 2008 (in Russian), http://www.novayagazeta.ru/data/2008/gulag03/05.html, retrieved September 5, 2011.

26. Olga Bobrova, 'Nado znat' vysshuyu meru,' *Novaya gazeta. 'Pravda GULAGa,'* no. 6, July 7, 2008 (in Russian), http://www.novayagazeta.ru/data/2008/gulag06/02.html, retrieved September 4, 2011.

27. Yan Rachinsky, 'Byvshii dom Voennoi kollegii Verkhovnogo suda' (in Russian), http://www.memo.ru/2011/05/17/rachinsky.htm, retrieved September 4, 2011.

28. A. B. Roginsky, 'Posleslovie,' in *Rasstrel'nye spiski. Moskva, 1937–1941*, 485–501.

29. Nikita Petrov and Marc Jansen, *'Stalinskii pitomets'—Nikolai Yezhov* (Moscow: Rosspen, 2008), 208–10 (in Russian).

30. Joint orders of the Justice Commissar and chief USSR Prosecutor, dated March 20 and May 9, 1940. A. I. Muranov and V. Ye. Zvyagintsev, *Dos'e na marshala* (Moscow: Andreevskii flag, 1996), 266 (in Russian).

31. S. Yu. Ushakov and A. A. Stukalov, *Front voennykh prokurorov (ot repressii do rasstrelov)* (Moscow: Synov'ya, 2000), 88–9 (in Russian).

32. On the OSO in 1934, see O. B. Mozokhin, *Pravo na repressii. Vnesudebnye polnomochiya organov gosudarstvennoi bezopasnosti (1918–1953)* (Moscow: Kuchkovo pole, 2006), 138–40 (in Russian).

33. Beria's report to Stalin, dated November 15, 1941. Document No. 203, in *Lubyanka: Stalin i NKVD*, 318–20.

34. GKO Order No. 903-ss, dated November 17, 1941, in Kokurin and Petrov, *Lubyanka* (2003), 77.

35. NKVD Order No. 001613 from November 21, 1941, in ibid.

36. Nikolai Mesyatsev, *Gorizonty i labirinty moei zhizni* (Moscow: Vagrius, 2005), 146–7 (in Russian).

37. On Isai Oggins, see Vadim Birstein, *The Perversion of Knowledge: The True Story of Soviet Science* (Boulder, CO: Westview Press, 2001), 132–9. Andrew Meier, the author of a detailed biography of Oggins *The Lost Spy: An American in Stalin's Secret Service* (New York: W. W. Norton and Company, 2008), gives a fictional scene of Oggins's court trial (pp. 129–32). In fact, defendants were not present at the OSO sessions.

38. The Comintern had its own international intelligence network. See Iosif Linder and Sergei Churkin, *Krasnaya pautina. Tainy razvedki Kominterna 1919–1943* (Moscow: Ripol-Klassik, 2005) (in Russian).

39. Document No. 13, in *Reabilitatsiya: Kak eto bylo. Dokumenty Prezidiuma TsK KPSS i drugie materialy. Mart 1953–fevral' 1956*, edited by A. Artizov et al., 72-74 (Moscow: Demokratiya, 2000) (in Russian).

40. Data from Zvyagintsev, *Voina na vesakh Femidy*, 736–7.

41. Page 127 in Aleksandr Kokurin and Nikita Petrov, 'NKVD–NKGB–SMERSH: struktura, funktsii, kadry. Stat'ya tret'ya (1941–1943),' *Svobodnaya mysl'*, no. 8 (1997), 118–28 (in Russian).

42. Nikita Petrov, *Istoriya imperii 'Gulag.' Glava 12* (in Russian), http://www.pseudology.org/GULAG/Glava12.htm,retrieved September 4, 2011.

43. Ibid.

44. A. S. Kuznetsov's report to Beria, dated Sepember 18, 1942, and signed by Beria on September 29, 1945. Document No. 40 in *GULAG (Glavnoe upravlenie lagerei), 1917–1960*, edited by A. I. Kokurin and N. V. Petrov, 133–4 (Moscow: Materik, 2000) (in Russian). From 1955 until 1963, all dates, places of and causes of death of the executed were falsified; see Document No. 46 in ibid., 163–4. Real information about the executions started to be released only after 1990.

45. Politburo decision P53/39, dated August 20, 1946 and MGB Order No. 00496, dated November 2, 1946. Petrov, *Kto rukovodil organami bezopasnosti*, 62.

46. Mesyatsev, *Gorizonty i labirinty*, 147.

Chapter 5

1. Details in Yevgenii Gnedin, *Vykhod iz labirinta* (Moscow: Memorial, 1994), 11–20 (in Russian). Molotov (1890–1986) headed the Foreign Affairs Commissariat from May 1939 to May 1949.

2. Details in Anthony Read and David Fisher, *The Deadly Embrace: Hitler, Stalin and the Nazi-Soviet Pact, 1939–1941* (New York: W. W. Norton and Co., 1988), 246–60.

3. 'Moscow's Week,' *Time*, October 9, 1939.

4. *Dimitrov and Stalin, 1934–1943: Letters from the Soviet Archives*, edited by Alexandr Dallin and F. I. Firsov (New Haven: Yale University Press, 2000), 151–2. Similar Stalin's political views are discussed in V. L. Doroshenko, I. V. Pavlova, and R. C. Raack, 'Ne mif: rech' Stalina 19 avgusta 1939 goda,' *Voprosy istorii* 8 (2005): 3–20 (in Russian).

5. Amnon Sella, 'Red Army Doctrine and Training on the Eve of the Second World War,' *Europe-Asia Studies* 27, no. 2 (April 1975), 245–64.

6. Cited in Aleksandr Shitov, 'Stalin khotel bol'shoi i dolgoi voiny,' *Novaya gazeta. 'Pravda Gulaga*,' no. 7, June 16, 2010 (in Russian), http://www.novayagazeta.ru/data/2010/gulag07/00.html, retrieved September 4, 2011. 2010.

7. NKVD Order No. 001064, dated September 8, 1939. Document No. 29, in *Organy gosudarstvennoi bezopasnosti*, 1 (1), 70–73. I am using the spelling 'Belorussia' and 'Belorussian,' as it was used in the Soviet Union, and not the current spelling 'Belarus' and 'Belarusian'.

8. NKVD Directive, dated September 15, 1939. Document No. 33, in ibid., 79–81.

9. Details in Mikhail Mel'tyukhov, *Sovetsko-pol'skie voiny* (Moscow: Yauza-Eksmo, 2004), 463–566 (in Russian).

10. Heinz Guderian, *Vospominaniya soldata* (Smolensk: Rusich, 1999), 114 (in Russian, translated from the German). On the cooperation of the NKVD and Gestapo see Hans Schafranek, *Zwischen NKWD und Gestapo. Die Auslieferung deutscher und osterreichischer Antifaschisten aus der Sowietunion und Nazideutschland 1937–1941* (Frankfurt/Main: ISP–Verlag, 1990).

11. Merkulov's report to Beria, dated September 28, 1939. Document No. 42, in *Organy gosudarstvennoi bezopasnosti*, 1 (1), 96.

12. NKVD Instruction No. 1042/B, dated March 20, 1940. Document No. 78, in ibid., 165–66.

13. Politburo decision P13/144, dated March 5, 1940. Document No. 1, in *Katyn. Mart 1940 g. –sentyabr' 2000 g. Rasstrel. Sud'by zhivykh. Ekho Katyni. Dokumenty*, edited by N. S. Lebedeva, N. Petrosyan, B. Woszcynski et al., 43–4 (Moscow: Ves' Mir, 2001) (in Russian).

14. Dmitrii Tokarev, former head of the Kalinin NKVD Directorate, a statement on March 20, 1991. *Katyn. Dokumenty zbrodni. Tom 2. Zagłada marzec—czerwiec 1940*, edited by W. Materski, B.Woszcyński, N. Lebiediewa, and N. Pietrosowa (Warszawa: Wydawn 'TRIO,' 1998), 432–70.

15. Nikita Petrov (Memorial, Moscow), in Igor Mel'nikov, 'Kto povinen v smerti tysyach pol'skikh grazhdan,' *Belarus' segodnya*, December 18, 2008 (in Russian), http://www.sb.by/post/78592, retrieved September 5, 2011.

16. Beria's report, dated December 12, 1940 (from the Presidential Archive), in Nataliya Lebedeva, 'Chetveryi razdel Pol'shi,' *Novaya gazeta*, no. 102, September16, 2009, http://www.novayagazeta.ru/data/2009/102/00.html, retrieved September 5, 2011.

17. NKVD report, dated January 22, 1942, in Nikita Petrov, *Istoriya imperii 'Gulag.' Glava 9* (in Russian), http://www.pseudology.org/GULAG/Glava09.htm, retrieved September 5, 2011.

18. Politburo decisions P34/332 and P34/333. Announced as the Joint Decree of the Presidium of the USSR Supreme Soviet and TsK VKP(b), dated August 17, 1941.

19. Document No. 87, in *Istoriya stalinskogo GULAGa. Konets 1920-kh—pervaya polovina 1950-kh godov. Tom 5. Spetspereselentsy v SSSR*, edited by T. V. Tsarevsaya-Dyakina, 324–5 (Moscow: ROSSPEN, 2004) (in Russian).

20. Details in Wladislaw Anders, *An Army in Exile* (London: MacMillan & Co., 1949).

21. V. M. Berezhkov, *Kak ya stal perevodchikom Stalina* (Moscow: DEM, 1993), 48 (in Russian).

22. Molotov's speech at the session of the USSR Supreme Council on October 31, 1940. *Pravda*, November 1, 1940 (in Russian).

23. Molotov's note dated November 26, 1939, published in *Izvestia*, no. 273 (7043), November 27, 1939 (in Russian).

24. Quoted in M. I. Meltyukhov, 'Ideologicheskie dokumenty maiya-iyunya 1941 goda o sobytiyakh vtoroi mirovoi voiny,' in *Drugaya voina: 1939-1945* (Moscow: RGGU, 1996), 76-105 (in Russian).

25. Page 171 in V. A. Novobranets, 'Nakanune voiny,' *Znamya*, No. 6 (1990), 165–192 (in Russian).

26. N. N. Voronov, *Na sluzhbe voennoi* (Moscow: Voenizdat, 1963), 136 (in Russian).

27. Quoted in Zvyagintsev, *Voina na vesakh Femidy*, 113.

28. Note 33 in *Lubyanka. Stalin i NKVD–NKGB–GUKR 'SMERSH.' 1939–1946*, edited by V. N. Khaustov, V. P. Naumov, and N. S. Plotnikova, 569 (Moscow: Materik, 2006) (in Russian).

29. Joint NKO and NKVD Order No. 003/0093, dated January 24, 1940, in Klim Degtyarev and Aleksandr Kolpakidi, *SMERSH* (Moscow: Eksmo, 2009), 106 (in Russian).

30. Ibid., 106–7.

31. Anatolii Tsyganok, 'Mify i pravda o Sovetsko-Finlyandskoi voine,' *Polit.ru*, February 8, 2006 (in Russian), http://www.polit.ru/analytics/2006/02/08/finn.html, retrieved September 4, 2011.

32. N. S. Khrushchev, *Vospominaniya. Kniga 1* (Moscow: Moskovskie Novosti, 1999), 258 (in Russian).

33. Quoted in Yulian Semenov, *Nenapisannye romany*, Chapter 15, http://virlib.ru/read_book.php?page=18&file_path=books/9/book04207.gz, retrieved September 5, 2011.

34. For instance, *Stalin and the Soviet-Finnish War, 1939*, translated by Tatyana Sokokina, edited by Ye. N. Kulkov (London: F. Cass, 2002).

35. Kirill Aleksandrov, *Russkie soldaty Vermakht'a: Geroi ili predateli* (Moscow: Yauza, 2005), 26–44 (in Russian).

36. Beria's letter to Stalin, dated July 29, 1940. Document No. 121, in *Lubyanka. Stalin i NKVD–NKGB–GUKR*, 181.

37. Boris Bazhanov, *Bazhanov and the Damnation of Stalin*, translation and commentary by David W. Doyle (Athens, OH: Ohio University Press, 1990), 212–4. Bazhanov was a former member of Stalin's secretariat.

38. Beria's report to Stalin, dated July 20, 1940. Document No. 118 in *Lubyanka. Stalin i NKVD–NKGB–GUKR*, 178–9.

39. Details in, for instance, M. I. Mel'tyukhov, *Upushchennyi shans Stalina. Sovetskii Soyuz i bor'ba za Evropu: 1939–1941* (Moscow: Veche, 2000), 176–211 (in Russian).

40. Timoshenko's report No. 390-ss, dated June 17, 1940, in ibid., 206.

41. Georgii Fedorov, *Bruschatka. Dokumental'nye povesti i rasskazy* (Moscow: Libr, 1997), 57 (in Russian).

42. Irena Wiley, *Around the Globe in Twenty Years* (New York: David McKay Company, Inc.: 1962), 104.

43. Prisoner cards in the Vladimir Prison Archive.

44. NKGB Report No. 1687/M, dated May 16, 1941. Document No. 207, in *Organy gosudarstvenoi bezopasnosti*, 1 (2), 144–6. Also, Document Nos. 107–108 in *Istoriya stalinskogo GULAGa. Konets 1920-kh–pervaya polovina 1950-kh godov. Tom 1. Massovye repressii v SSSR*, edited by S. V. Mironenko and N. Werth, 394–400 (Moscow: ROSSPEN, 2004) (in Russian).

45. Viktor Stepakov, *'Apostol' SMERSHa* (Moscow: Yauza-Eksmo, 2009), 75 (in Russian).

46. Politburo decision P35/407, dated January 6, 1942. By October 2, additional groups of deportees were sent to five other Siberian areas as 'fishermen'. On the whole, of the total number of 52,664 'fishermen', only 35,684 were able to work physically. NKVD reports in Yurii Bogdanov, *Ministr stalinskikh stroek. 10 let vo glave MVD* (Moscow: Veche, 2006), 106–9 (in Russian).

47. Document Nos. 2.73–2.101, in *Stalinskie deportatsii 1928–1953*, edited by N. L. Pobol' and P. M. Polyan, 215–72 (Moscow: Demokratiya, 2005) (in Russian).

48. NKGB Report No. 2288/M, dated June 17, 1941 and signed by Merkulov; Kobulov's report, dated July 13, 1941; reports of Konradov, dated June 17, 1941 and September 15, 1941. Document Nos. 110, 112–114, in *Istoriya stalinskogo GULAGa. Tom 1*, 401, 404–7. Also, Moldavian NKGB Report No. 908, dated June 19, 1941; Document No. 260, in *Organy gosudarstvennoi bezopasnost v Velikoi Otechstvennoi voine. Sbornik dokumentovi. Nakanune*, T. 1 (2) (Moscow: Kniga i bizness, 1995), 260–1 (in Russian).

49. Data from Table 1 in *The White Book: Losses Inflicted on the Estonian Nation by Occupation Regimes, 1940–1991* (Tallinn: Estoniam Encyclopedia Publishers, 2005), 37.

50. A. E. Gur'yanov, 'Pol'skie spetspereselentsy v SSSR v 1940–1941 gg.,' in *Repressii protiv polyakov i polskikh grazhdan*, edited by A. E. Guriyanov, 114–36 (Moscow: Zven'ya, 1997) (in Russian); figures for all deportations from the Baltics and other territories, in Alfred J. Rieber, 'Civil Wars in the Soviet Union,' *Kritika: Explorations in Russian and Eurasian History*, 4, no. 1 (Winter 2003), 129–62.

51. Figures from *Istoriya stalinskogo GULAGa. Tom 5*, 56.

52. Agreements between the USSR and Germany, dated January 10, 1941. Document Nos. 641 and 642, in *Dokumenty vneshnei politiki. Ministerstvo inostrannykh del Rossiiskoi Federatsii*, T. 23 (2, pt. 1) (Moscow: Mezhdunarodnye otnosheniya, 1998), 303–17 (in Russian).

53. Published in *Izvestia*, June 27, 1940. Details in Bochkov's report, dated December 16, 1940. Document No. 117, in *Istoriya stalinskogo GULAGa. Tom 1*, 411–4.

54. Figures from Document Nos. 131 and 229, in *Istoriya stalinskogo GULAGa. Tom 1*, 446–8 and 623–4.

55. However, this decree concerned mostly the workers. The majority of peasants, forced to be members of *kolkhozes* (collective farms) could not leave their villages because the administration of *kolkhozes* kept their passports.

56. Read and Fisher, *The Deadly Embrace*, 510–33.

57. Beria's reports to Stalin, dated January 1941 and February 3, 1941. Document Nos. 146 and 150, in *Lubyanka. Stalin i NKVD*, 224–6, 233.

58. The number of prisoners in 1941 from Oleg V. Khlevnyuk, *The History of the Gulag: From Collectivization to the Great Terror* (New Haven, CT: Yale University Press, 2004), 328.

59. V. I. Vernadsky, 'Korennye izmeneniya neizbezhny…Dnevnik 1941 goda,' *Novyi mir*, no. 5 (1995) (in Russian), http://victory.mil.ru/lib/books/memo/vernadsky_vi/01.html, retrieved September 5, 2011.

60. Joint Decree of the Central Committee and Council of Commissars, dated February 8, 1941. Document No. 155, in *Lubyanka. Stalin i NKVD*, 240–2.

61. NKVD/NKGB Order No. 00151/003, dated February 12, 1941. Document No. 142 in Kokurin and Petrov, *Lubyanka* (2003), 608–9.

62. Joint decision of the Central Committee and Council of Commissars, dated February 8, 1941. Document No. 155 in *Lubyanka. Stalin i NKVD*, 240–2.

63. On the Red Army structure, see Roger R. Reese, *The Soviet Military Experience: A History of the Soviet Army, 1917–1991* (London: Routledge, 2000).

64. Politburo decision P31/132, dated April 19, 1941. Document No. 162, in *Lubyanka: Stalin i NKVD*, 262–63.

65. NKVD Order No. 00232, dated February 28, 1941. Document No. 143, in Kokurin and Petrov, *Lubyanka* (2003), 609–14.

Chapter 6

1. Konstantin Simonov, *Glazami cheloveka moego pokoleniya. Razmyshleniya o I. V. Staline* (Moscow: APN, 1988), 429 (in Russian). A detailed analysis of problems in the Soviet airplane industry in 1938–42 in Mark Solonin, *Na mirno spyashchikh aerodromakh…21 iyunya 1941 goda* (Moscow: Yauza-Eksmo, 2006) (in Russian).

2. Politburo decision P31/132, dated April 19, 1941. Document No. 162, *Lubyanka. Stalin i NKVD*, 263–4.

3. A. Pechenkin, 'Chernyi den' Krasnoi Armii,' *Nezavisimoe voennoe obozrenie*, February 21, 2003 (in Russian), http://nvo.ng.ru/history/2003-02-21/5_redarmy.html, retrieved September 5, 2011.

4. L. Ye. Reshin and V. S. Stepanov, 'Sud'by general'skie,' *Voenno-istoricheskii zhurnal [hereafter, VIZh]*, no. 2 (1993), 4–15 (in Russian).

5. L. Ye. Reshin and V. S. Stepanov, 'Sud'by general'skie,' *VIZh, no.* 6 (1993), 21–28 (in Russian).

6. Pages 785–6 in Document No. 2 (appendix), in *Reabilitatsiya: Kak eto bylo. Fevral' 1956-nachalo 80-kh godov*, edited by A. Artizov et al., 671–788 (Moscow: Demokratiya, 2003) (in Russian).

7. Arkadii Vaksberg, *Neraskrytye tainy* (Moscow: Novosti, 1993), 59 (in Russian).

8. Merkulov's report to Stalin, dated May 15, 1941. Document No. 165, in *Lubyanka. Stalin i NKVD*, 285–87.

9. Oleg V. Khlevniuk, *Master of the House: Stalin and His Inner Circle*, translated by Nora Seligman Favorov (New Haven, CT: Yale University Press, 2009), 229–45.

10. Page 467 in G. A. Kumanev, *Govoryat stalinskie narkomy* (Smolensk: Rusich, 2005) (in Russian).

11. Document No. 17, in *Stalinskoe Politburo v 30-e gg.*, edited by O. V. Khlevnyuk et al., 34–35 (Moscow: AIRO-XX, 1995) (in Russian).

12. Stalin's toasts quoted in A. Pechenkin, 'Sekretnoe vystuplenie Stalina,' *Nezavisimoe voennoe obozrenie*, April 25, 2003 (in Russian), http://nvo.ng.ru/history/2003-04-25/1_stalin.html, retrieved September 5, 2011. For Stalin's speech on May 5, 1941, see Document No. 437, in *1941 god. Kinga vtoraya*, edited by L. Ye. Reshin et al., 158–61 (Moscow: Demokratiya, 1998) (in Russian).

13. On the general military events in 1941–45, see, for instance, Evan Mawdsley, *Thunder in the East: The Nazi-Soviet War 1941–1945* (London: Hodder, 2005)..

14. Notes of the meeting of Molotov with the German ambassador to Moscow, Friedrich Werner von Schullenburg, on June 22, 1941. Document No. 876, in *Dokumenty vneshnei politiki. 1940–22 iyunya 1941*. T. 23, pt. 2 (Moscow: Mezhdunarodnye otnosheniya, 1998), 753–4 (in Russian).

15. For the updated discussion, see, for instance, Mark Solonin, *22 iyunya, ili Kogda nachalas' Velikaya Otechestvennaya voina?* (Moscow: Yauza, 2005) (in Russian).

16. A. Sharavin, 'Velikaya Otechestvennaya voina 1941–1945 gg.: Sovetskie karty byli luchshe nemetskikh,' *VIZh*, no. 6 (1999): 16–25 (in Russian).

17. Report by T. Volsky to Lt. General Ya. N. Fedorenko, in ibid., page 16.

18. P. I. Ivashutin, 'Sovetskaya voennaya razvedka dokladyvala tochno,' *VIZh*, no. 5 (1990), 56–59 (in Russian).

19. Records of visitors to Stalin's office in 1941 in *1941 god. Kniga vtoraya*, edited by L. Ye. Reshin, et al. (Moscow: Materik, 1998), 298–301 (in Russian). Surprisingly, many historians ignored Vorontsov's presence at this decisive meeting and omitted or replaced his name.

20. N. G. Kuznetsov, *Kursom k pobede* (Moscow: Golos, 2000), 12–13 (in Russian). Kuznetsov did not mention that the conversation with Vorontsov occurred at the Politburo meeting in Stalin's office.

21. Draft of the Politburo decision on June 21, 1941, written by Georgii Malenkov. Document No. 596 in *1941 god. Kniga vtoraya*, 413–4.

22. Directive to the military councils of five military districts, dated June 21, 1944. Document No. 121, in *Russkii arkhiv. Velikaya Otechestvennaya. Prikazy narodnogo komissara oborony SSSR*, T. 13 (2-1) (Moscow: TERRA, 1994), 283 (in Russian).

23. Detailed biography of L. Z. Mekhlis (1889–1953) in Yurii Rubtsov, *Alter ego Stalina* (Moscow: Zvonnitsa, 1999) (in Russian).

Chapter 7

1. Text of Zhukov's speech written on May 19, 1956 (Zhukov has never made the speech). Published in Vasilii Soima, *Zapreshchennyi Stalin* (Moscow: Olma-Press, 2005), 411–28 (in Russian).

2. A. I. Mikoyan, *Tak bylo. Razmyshleniya o minuvshem* (Moscow: Vagrius, 1999), 389–90 (in Russian).

3. Joint decree of the Sovnarkom's Presidium and Central Committee, dated June 30, 1941. Details in Yurii Gor'kov, *Gosudarstvennyi Komitet Oborony postanovlyaet (1941–1945). Tsifry, dokumenty* (Moscow: Olma-Press, 2002), 30–41 (in Russian).

4. On February 3, 1942, Mikoyan and Voznesensky were added, and then Kaganovich (on February 20, 1942) and Nikolai Bulganin (on November 22, 1944). Voroshilov was expelled when Bulganin was included; Bulganin was also promoted to NKO deputy Commissar.

5. Politburo decision P34/99 and Joint decree of the Sovnarkom's Presidium and Central Committee, both dated June 23, 1941. Document No. 175 in *Lubyanka. Stalin i NKVD–NKGB–GUKR*, 289, and Document No. 8 in Gor'kov, *Gosudarstvennyi Komitet Oborony*, 494. The function and coordination of the work of the Stavka, General Staff, GKO and Stalin's control of the whole structure is described in detail in S. M. Shtemenko, *General'nyi shtab v gody voiny* (Moscow: Voenizdat, 1989), Part I, Chapter 7, and Part 2, Chapters 1 and 8 (in Russian).

6. The board of Stavka's advisers consisted of marshals Grigorii Kulik, Kirill Meretskov, Shaposhnikov, Commander of Air Forces Pavel Zhigarev, First Deputy Chief of Staff Nikolai Vatutin, Commander of Air Defense Nikolai Voronov, Mekhlis, and Politburo full and candidate members Beria, Kaganovich, Malenkov, Mikoyan, Voznesensky and Zhdanov.

7. Published in *Pravda*, July 3, 1941 (in Russian).

8. Yefimov, *Desyat' desyatiletii*, 326.

9. Decrees of the Presidium of the USSR Supreme Council, dated June 22, 1941. Texts in *Skrytaya pravda voiny: 1941 god. Neizvestnye documenty*, edited by P. N. Knyshevsky et al. (Moscow: Russkaya kniga, 1992) (in Russian), http://www.rkka.ru/docs/spv/SPV3.htm, retrieved September 5, 2011.

10. Decree of the Presidium of the USSR Supreme Council, dated June 27, 1941. Mozokhin, *Pravo na repressii*, 223.

11. Order No. 00246/00833/PR/59ss, dated June 28, 1941. Document No. 623, in *1941 god. Kniga vtoraya*, 445–6.

12. Yefimov, *Desyat' desyatiletii*, 350.

13. Novobranets, 'Nakanune voiny.'

14. In Arkadii Vaksberg, 'Taina oktyabrya 1941,' *Literaturnaya gazeta* (April 20, 1988) (in Russian).

15. Ibid.

16. Excerpt from the interrogation transcript of Merkulov in 1953, in Nikita Petrov, 'Samyi obrazovannyi palach',' *Novaya Gazeta. 'Pravda GULAGa'*, no. 12, August 30, 2010 (in Russian), http://www.novayagazeta.ru/data/2010/gulag12/00.html, retrieved September 5, 2011.

17. S. I. Vetoshkin, F. K. Charsky, V. I. Khokhlov, and Ye. A. Gul'yants were released. Vaksberg, *Neraskrytye tainy*, 57.

18. K. A. Meretskov, *Na sluzhbe narodu* (Moscow: Politizdat, 1968), 214 (in Russian).

19. Page 131 in B. L. Vannikov, 'Zapiski narkoma,' *Znamya*, no. 1 (1988), 130–60 (in Russian).

20. Memoirs by V. Filippov, quoted in Boris Sokolov, *Beria. Sud'ba vsesil'nogo narkoma* (Moscow: Veche, 2003), 214 (in Russian).

21. Page 521 in an interview with V. N. Novikov, former deputy armaments Commissar, in G. Kumanev, *Govoryat stalinskie narkomy* (Smolensk: Rusich, 2005), 512–49 (in Russian).

22. Text of Mekhlis's cable to Stalin and Stalin's answer, quoted in Vyacheslav Zvyagintsev, *Voina na vesakh Femidy. Voina 1941–1945 gg. v materialakh sledsten-no-sudebnykh del* (Moscow: Terra, 2006), 72–73 (in Russian). Also, Document Nos. 358–379, in *Organy gosudarstvennoi bezopasnosti*, 2 (1), 210–7.

23. For a description of Pavlov's case, see P. A. Pal'chikov, 'On byl obrechen,' *Moskva*, no. 5 (2006) (in Russian), http://militera.lib.ru/prose/russian/palchik-ov/01.html, retrieved September 5, 2011.

24. Interrogations of Pavlov on July 11 and 21, 1941, and Meretskov on July 12, 1941, in A. Rzheshevsky, *Pavlov. Taina rasstrelyannogo generala* (Moscow: Veche, 2005), 306–12 (in Russian).

25. Dmitri Volkogonov, *Stalin: Triumph and Tragedy*, edited and translated by Harold Shukman (London: Weidenfeld and Nicholson, 1991), 423–4.

26. Transcript of the court session of the Military Collegium, dated July 22, 1941. Page 387 in Document No. 437, in *Organy gosudarctvennoi bezopasnosti*, 2 (1), 381–92.

27. Ibid., 467.

28. Document No. 437, in ibid., 391.

29. Verdict of the Military Collegium, dated July 22, 1941. Document No. 438, in ibid., 392–3.

30. Report of Col. General N. N. Voronov, dated August 15, 1941 (from the Presidential Archive), in Aleksandr Melenberg, 'Podachka iz arkhiva,' *Novaya gazeta*, No. 48, May 7, 2010 (in Russian), http://www.novayagazeta.ru/data/2010/048/09.html, retrieved September 5, 2011.

31. Order No. 0250, dated July 28, 1941, in *Russkii arkhiv. Velikaya Otechest-vennaya. Prikazy narodnogo komissara oborony SSSR 22 iyunya 1941 g.—1942 g.*, 13 (2-2) (Moscow: Terra, 1997), 192–3 (in Russian).

32. Politburo decision P23/152, dated December 7, 1940. Document No. 140, in *Lubyanka. Stalin i NKVD*, 201–4. On Pavlov's wife, a report by Aleksandra Oseichuk (in Russian), http://memorial.krsk.ru/svidet/Maafan1.htm, retrieved September 5, 2011.

33. Zvyagintsev, *Voina na vesakh Femidy*, 80–88.

34. Quoted in B. V. Sokolov, 'Stalin i ego generally: pereklichka iz dvukh uglov,' *Znanie–sila*, no. 12 (2000) (in Russian).

35. NKO Order No. 039, dated October 4, 1941, in *Russkii Arkhiv. Velikaya Otechestvennaya. Prikazy*, 13 (2-2) (1997), 108-9.

36. Pages 524–5 in an interview with V. N. Novikov in Kumanev, *Govoryat stalinskie narkomy*, 512–49.

37. A letter of A. F. Pavlova to Nikita Khrushchev, dated April 20, 1956. Quoted on page 96 in A. P. Pal'chikov, 'On byl obrechen,' *Moskva* 5 (2006), 50–98 (in Russian).

38. Suvenirov, *Tragediya RKKA*, 334.

39. Rosamond Richardson, *Stalin's Shadow: Inside the Family of One of the World's Greatest Tyrants* (New York: St. Martin's Press, 1994), 149.

40. Vadim Birstein, *The Perversion of Knowledge: The True Story of Soviet Science* (Boulder, CO: Westview Press, 2001), 53–58, 434–5.

41. Excerpts from transcripts of interrogations in Boris Sopelnyak, *Smert' v rassrochku* (Moscow: Olma-Press, 2004), 148–9 (in Russian).

42. Details in N. S. Cherushev, *Udar po svoim. Krasnaya Armiya 1938–1941* (Moscow: Veche, 2003), 364–5 (in Russian).

43. Details in N. S. Cherushev, *'Nevinovnykh ne byvaet...' Chekisty protiv voennykh, 1918–1953* (Moscow: Veche, 2004), 421–2 (in Russian).

44. V. A. Bobrenev and V. B. Ryazantsev, *Palachi i zhertvy* (Moscow: Voenizdat, 1993), 211–3 (in Russian).

45. Details in N. A. Zen'kovich, *Tainy kremleskikh smertei* (Moscow: Nadezhda, 1995), 432–544 (in Russian).

46. Cited in Leonid Mlechin, 'Taina mogily na Donskom kladbishche' (in Russian), *Vechernyaya Moskva*, no. 100 (24145), May 7, 2005 (in Russian).

47. Quoted in Zen'kovich, *Tainy kremlevskikh smertei*, 500.

48. Text of Klykov's report in L. Ye. Reshin and V. S. Stepanov, 'Sud'by general'skie,' *VIZh*, no. 1 (1994), 15–23 (in Russian).

49. Text of Mikheev's report dated July 16, 1941, in L. Ye. Reshin and V. S. Stepanov, 'Sud'by general'skie,' *VIZh*, no. 12 (1993), 16–21 (in Russian).

50. *SMERSH. Istoricheskie ocherki i arkhivnye materialy*, edited by V. S. Khristoforov, et al. (Moscow: Glavarkhiv Moskvy, 2003), 57 (in Russian).

51. From Teplinsky's archival file, quoted in Zvyagintsev, *Voina na vesakh Femidy*, 312–3.

Chapter 8

1. GKO Order No. 187ss. Document No. 146, in A. I. Kokurin and N. V. Petrov, *Lubyanka. Organy VCheKa–OGPU–NKVD–NKGB–MGB–MVD–KGB. 1917–1991. Spravochnik* (Moscow: Demokratiya, 2003), 616–7 (in Russian).

2. NKVD Instruction No. 169, dated July 18, 1941. Quoted in *Gosudarstvennaya bezopasnost' Rossii: istoriya i sovremennost'*, edited by R. N. Baiguzin, 554 (Moscow: ROSSPEN, 2004) (in Russian).

3. NKVD Order No. 1024, cited in Aleksandr Kokurin and Nikita Petrov, 'NKVD–NKGB–SMERSH: Struktura, funktsii, kadry. Stat'ya tret'ya (1941–1943),' *Svobodnaya mysl*, no. 8 (1997), 118–28 (in Russian).

4. GKO Decision No. 1120-ss, dated January 10, 1942. Document No. 775, in *Organy gosudarstvennoi bezopasnosti SSSR v Velikoi Otechestvennoi voine. Tom 3. Kniga 1. Krushenie 'Blitskriga,' 1 yanvarya–30 iyunya 1942 goda* (Moscow: Rus', 2003), 27 (in Russian).

5. Politburo decision P34/259, dated July 21, 1941, and the decree of the Presidium of the USSR Supreme Council that followed. Document No. 186, in *Lubyanka: Stalin i NKVD*, 298–9; also, Beria's report to Stalin, dated July 30, 1941. Document No. 191, in ibid., 306–8.

6. Pages 276–8 in Document No. 27 (NKVD structure on May 20, 1942) in A. I. Kokurin and N. V. Petrov, *Lubyanka. VChK–OGPU–NKVD–NKGB–MGB–MVD–KGB. 1917–1960. Spravochnik* (Moscow: Demokratiya, 1997), 271–304 (in Russian).

7. Data from V. P. Artemiev et al., *Political Controls in the Soviet Army: A Study Based on Reports by Former Soviet Officers* (New York: Research Program on the USSR, 1954), 56.

8. See the special State Security (NKVD) ranks and their military equivalents in Appendix III.

9. Zvyagintsev, *Voina na vesakh Femidy*, 132.

10. *Istoriya sovetskikh organov gosudarstvennoi bezopasnosti* (Moscow: Vysshaya shkola KGB, 1977), edited by V. M. Chebrikov et al., 351 (in Russian), http://www.fas.harvard.edu/~hpcws/documents.htm, retrieved September 5, 2011.

11. Peter Prigov, *Why I Escaped* (London: The Harvill Press, 1950), 67.

12. Interview with Daniil El'kin, former infantryman, July 28, 2009 (in Russian), http://www.iremember.ru/pekhotintsi/elkin-daniil-arnoldovich.html, retrieved September 5, 2011.

13. Interview with Nikolai Safonov, former infantryman, April 30, 2008, http://www.iremember.ru/pekhotintsi/safonov-nikolay-ivanovich/stranitsa-4.html, retrieved September 5, 2011.

14. Directive No. 0367, Special Department, the Northwestern Front, dated July 22, 1941, in *Organy gosudarstvennoi bezopasnosti SSSR v Velikoi Otechestvennoi voine. T. 2. 'Nachalo', Kniga 1 (22 iyunya –31 avgusta 1941 goda)* (Moscow, 2000), 394–5 (in Russian).

15. *SMERSH. Istoricheskie ocherki*, 27.

16. GKO decree No. 377ss, dated August 2, 1941. Quoted in N. Ya. Komarov and G. A. Kumanyov, *Bitva pod Moskvoi. Prolog k velikoi pobede* (Moscow: Molodaya gvariya, 2005), 54 (in Russian).

17. Many servicemen from Central Asia and the Caucasus did not understand why they were fighting against the Germans because they even did not speak Russian. GKO decrees, dated October 13, 1943 and October 25, 1944, stated that men from these regions of the Soviet Union should not be drafted. A. I. Vdovin, 'Natsional'naya politika v gody Velikoi Otechestvennoi voiny,' *Doklady Akademii Voennykh Nauk. Voennaya istoriya*, no. 3 (15) (2005), 122–39 (in Russian).

18. Interview with Georgii Minin, former mortarman, July 14, 2006, http://www.iremember.ru/minometchiki/minin-georgiy-ivanovich/stranitsa-4.html, retrieved September 5, 2011.

19. Quoted in Ye. S. Senyavskaya, *1941–1945: Frontovoe pokolenie. Istoriko-psikhologicheskoe issledovanie* (Moscow: Institut Rossiiskoi Istorii RAN, 1995), 148–9 (in Russian).

20. Interview with Zyama Ioffe, former military prosecutor, February 5, 2009 (in Russian), http://www.iremember.ru/drugie-voyska/ioffe-zyama-yakovlevich/stranitsa-5.html, retrieved September 5, 2011.

21. Interview with Izo Adamsky, an artillery officer, September 12, 2006 (in Russian), http://www.iremember.ru/minometchiki/adamskiy-izo-davidovich/stranitsa-8.html, retrieved September 5, 2011.

22. A. A. Baranov, a member of the SMERSH Department of the 96th Separate Guard Mortar Regiment, quoted in Vadim Abramov, *SMERSH: Sovetskaya voennaya kontrrazvedka protiv razvedki Tret'ego Reikha* (Moscow: Yauza-Eksmo, 2005), 89.

23. Interview with Ioffe.

24. Details in Anatolii Tsyganok, 'O kollabortsionizme grazhdan SSSR vo Voroi mirovoi voine,' *Polit.ru*, May 4, 2006 (in Russian), http://polit.ru/author/2006/05/04/kollaboracionism.html; N. P. Dembitsky, 'Sud'ba plennykh,' *Skepsis* (in Russian), http://scepsis.ru/library/id_1250.html; Boris Sokolov, 'Perevy-polnenie plena,' Novaya gazeta. Spetsvypusk 'Pravda GULAGa,' no. 05 (26), April 28, 2010 (in Russian), http://www.novayagazeta.ru/data/2010/gulag05/01.html; all retrieved September 6, 2011.

25. Page 14 in B. N. Petrov, 'O strategicheskom razvertyvanii Krasnoi Armii nakanune voiny,' *VIZh*, no. 12 (1991), 10–17 (in Russian).

26. *Otkroveniya i priznaniya. Natsistskaya verkhushka o voine 'tret'ego reikha' protiv SSSR. Sekretnye rechi. Dnevniki. Vospominaniya* (translation from the German, Smolensk: Rusich, 2000), 120 (in Russian).

27. Alfred Rosenberg's letter to Field Marshal Keitel, dated February 28, 1942. Quoted in Paul Carrel and Guenther Boeddeker, *Nemetskie voennoplennye vtoroi mirivoi voiny 1939–1945* (Moscow: Izografus, 2004), 311–2 (in Russian, translated from the German). Rosenberg was sentenced to death at the International Nuremberg Trial and hanged on October 16, 1946.

28. V. P. Naumov, 'Sud'ba voennoplennykh i deportirovannykh grazhdan SSSR. Materialy Komissii po reabilitatsii zhertv politicheskikh repressii', *Novaya i noveishaya istoriya* 2 (1996), 91–112 (in Russian).

29. As given in Alexander Dallin, *German Rule in Russia, 1941–1945: A Study of Occupation* (Boulder, CO: Westview Press, 1981).

30. V. N. Zemskov, 'Repatriatsiya sovetskikh grazhdan i ikh dal'neishaya sud'ba,' *Sotsiologicheskie issledovaniya* 5 (1995), 3–13 (in Russian).

31. Directive No. 2317 by Col. Vasilii Shilin, OO head of the 16th Army, dated August 20, 1941. Quoted in I. L. Ustinov, *Na rubezhe istoricheskix peremen. Vospominaniya veterana spetsluzhb* (Moscow: Kuchkovo pole, 2008), 68–69 (in Russian).

32. 'Prikaz verkhovnogo glavnogo komandovaniya Krasnoi armii' No. 270, 16 avgusta 1941 goda,' *VIZh*, no. 9 (1988), 26–28.

33. Chris Bellamy, *Absolute War: Soviet Russia in the Second World War* (New York: Vantage Books, 2008), 257–9.

34. John Tolland, *Adolf Hitler* (Garden City, NY: Doubleday and Company, Inc., 1976), 680.

35. Valentin Runov, *1941. Pobednyi parad Gitlera. Pravda ob umanskom poboishche* (Moscow: Yauza-Eksmo, 2010) (in Russian).

36. Defense Commissar's Order No. 0321, dated August 26, 1941. Cited in N. Ya. Komarov and G. A. Kumanev, *Velikaya Bitva pod Moskvoi: Letopis'vazhneishikh sobytii. Kommentarii* (Moscow: Institut rossiiskoi istorii RAN), 76 (in Russian).

37. Yezhov's report to Stalin, dated March 4, 1938. Document No. 298, in *Lubyanka. Stalin i Glavnoe upravlenie gosbezopasnosti NKVD 1927-1938*, edited by V. N. Khaustov, V. P. Naumov, and N. S. Plotnikov, 490–6 (Moscow: materik, 2004) (in Russian).

38. F. Beck and W. Godin, *Russian Purge and the Extraction of Confession*, translated from the original German by Eric Mosbacher and David Porter (New York: The Viking Press, 1951), 136.

39. D. Ortenberg, *Iyun'-dekabr' sorok pervogo*. (Moscow: Sovetskii pisatel', 1984), 130–1 (in Russian).

40. Zhukov's cable No. 4976, dated September 28, 1941. Quoted in Boris Sokolov, 'Georgii Zhukov: narodnyi marshal ili marshal-lyudoed?' *Grani.ru*, February 23, 2001 (in Russian), http://grani.ru/Society/Myth/m.6463.html, retrieved September 6, 2011.

41. GKO Order No. 460-ss, dated August 11, 1941. Document No. 193, in *Lubyanka: Stalin i NKVD*, 310.

42. Yurii Rubtsov, *Alter ego Stalina* (Moscow: Zvonnitsa-MG, 1999), 188–91 (in Russian).

43. Mekhlis's cable to Colonel G. P. Popov, dated September 24, 1941. Quoted in ibid., 193.

44. Zvyagintsev, *Voina na vesakh Femidy*, 137–9.

45. Ibid., 137.

46. A letter by V. Koroteev, a *Red Star* correspondent, dated September 1943; quoted in Yurii Rubtsov, *Alter ego Stalina*, 242.

Part III. Military Counterintelligence:
July 1941–April 1943

Chapter 9

1. Mikhail Khodorenok and Boris Nevzorov, 'Chernyi oktyabr' 41-go. Pod Vyaz'moi i Bryanskom Krasnaya Armiya poteryala sotni tysyach boitsov,' *Nezavisimoe voennoe obozrenie* 20 (June 21–27, 2002), 5 (in Russian); details in L. Lopukhovsky, *1941. Vyazemskaya katastrofa* (Moscow: Eksmo–Press, 2008) (in Russian).

2. Details in Yu. A, Zhuk, *Neizvestnye stranitsy bitvy za Moskvu. Krakh Operatsii 'Taifun'* (Moscow: Khranitel', 2007) (in Russian).

3. Victor Kravchenko, *I Chose Freedom: The Personal and Political Life of a Soviet Official* (New York: Charles Scribbner's Sons, 1946), 374.

4. Robert Robinson with Jonathan Slevin, *Black on Red: My 44 Years Inside the Soviet Union* (Washington, DC: Acropolis Books Ltd., 1988), 161.

5. From the memoir of N. A. Sbytov. Document No. I-34, in *Moskva voennaya, 1941–1945: memuary i arkhivnye dokumenty*, edited by K. I. Bukov, M. M. Gorinov, and A. N. Ponomarev, 83–86 (Moscow: Mosgorarkhiv, 1995) (in Russian).

6. Serov's letter to Stalin, dated February 8, 1948. Document No. 29, in Nikita Petrov, *Pervyi predsedatel' KGB Ivan Serov* (Moscow: Materik, 2005), 268–73 (in Russian).

7. GKO Order No. 801ss, dated October 15, 1941. Document No. II-34, in *Moskva voennaya*, 365–6.

8. Report of K. R. Sinilov, dated August 9, 1942. Document No. III-37, in ibid., 550.

9. Kravchenko, *I Chose Freedom*, 375–6.

10. Arkadii Perventsev, 'Iskhod [iz 'dnevnikov pisatelya opervykh dnyakh Velikoi Otechestvennoi voiny],' *Moskva*, no. 1 (2005), 192–222 (in Russian).

11. During the first six months of war, there were 141 German air strikes on Moscow, and 2,196 Muscovites were killed, while 5,512 were wounded. Many

buildings were completely or partially destroyed in the center of Moscow, including the Bolshoi and Jewish theaters and Moscow University. Details in *Moskva voennaya*, 409–67.

12. An excerpt from the memoirs of V. P. Pronin, chair of Moscow Council, in ibid., 725.

13. GKO Order No. 813, dated October 19, 1941. Document No. I-55, in ibid., 124–5. Sinilov remained the commandant of Moscow until June 1953, when he participated in Beria's unsuccessful putsch.

14. Kravchenko, *I Chose Freedom*, 377. From October 20 until December 13, 1941, 121,955 people were arrested in Moscow. Of these, 23,937 were released, 4,741 were sentenced by military tribunals to imprisonment and 357 to death, while 15 were executed on the spot; the rest were tried later. Aleksandr Beznasyuk and Vyacheslav Zvyagintsev, *Tribunal. Arbat, 37 (Dela i lyudi)* (Moscow: Terra, 2006), 12 (in Russian).

15. Text of the speech at http://www.sovmusic.ru/text.php?fname=st_71141, retrieved September 6, 2011.

16. Interview with Mark Ivanikhin in Vitalii Yaroshevsky, 'Mark i katyushi,' *Novaya gazeta*, no. 41, April 19, 2010 (in Russian), http://www.novayagazeta.ru/data/2010/041/22.html, retrieved September 6, 2011.

17. Recollections by Fyodor Kiselev, the crew head, in Vladimir Batshev, '7 noyabrya 1941,' *Lebed.com*, no. 509, December 3, 2006 (in Russian), http://www.lebed.com/2006/art4815.htm, retrieved September 6, 2011.

18. Details in M. Yu. Myagkov, *Vermakht u vorot Moskvy, 1941–1942* (Moscow: RAN, 1999) (in Russian).

19. Lev Bezymensky, *Bitva za Moskvu. Proval operatsii 'Taifun'* (Moscow: Yauza, 2007), 188 (in Russian).

20. *Moskva voennaya*, 81–128.

21. Vitalii Shentalinsky, *Donos na Sokrata* (Moscow: Formica-S, 2001), 325–82 (in Russian).

22. Beria's instruction No. 2756/B, dated October 18, 1941. Document No. 617, in *Organy gosudarstvennoi bezopasnosti*, 2 (2), 215–6; also Document Nos. 650 and 675, in ibid., 260–1 and 305.

23. Stalin's resolution on the first page of the list at http://stalin.memo.ru/images/t378-196.jpg, retrieved September 6, 2011.

24. From Abakumov's report, dated December 9, 1941, in Boris Syromyatnikov, 'Neotsennyonnyi vklad,' *Nezavisimoe voennoe obozrenie*, December 1, 2006, http://nvo.ng.ru/spforces/2006-12-01/7_vklad.html, retrieved September 6, 2011.

25. Mark Solonin, *23 iyunya:"Den' M"* (Moscow: Yauza-Eksmo, 2007), 411-20 (in Russian)

26. Report of Captain Berezkin, head of the OO of the 1st Shock Army, dated February 14, 1942. Quoted in Yurii Veremeev, *Krasnaya Armiya v nachale Vtoroi mirovoi* (Moscow: Eksmo-Algoritm, 2010), 91–93 (in Russian).

27. B. V. Sokolov, 'The Role of Lend-Lease in Soviet Military Efforts, 1941–1945,' *Journal of Slavic Military Studies*, 7, no. 3 (September 1994), 567–86.

28. Quoted in Syromyatnikov, 'Neotsennyonnyi vklad.'

29. Details in Albert L. Weeks, *Russia's Life-Saver: Lend-Lease Aid to the U.S.S.R. in World War II* (Lanham, MD: Lexington Books, 2004).

30. V. F. Vorsin, 'Motor Vehicle Transport Deliveries Through "Lend-Lease",' *Journal of Slavic Military Studies*, 10, no. 2 (June 1997), 153–75.

31. N. N. Nikoulin, *Vospominaniya o voine* (St. Petersburg: Izdatel'stvo Gosudarstvennogo Ermitazha, 2008), 55–56 (in Russian).

32. Ibid., 67.

33. Dmitrii Steshin, 'Svalka na kostyakh geroev,' *Komsomol'skaya pravda*, January 27, 2009 (in Russian), http://kp.ru/daily/24233/433433/, retrieved September 6, 2011.

Chapter 10

1. OO Directive No. 003260, Southern Front, dated November 18, 1941, in *Organy gosudarstvennoi bezopasnosti*, 3 (2), 316–8.

2. NKVD Order No. 00852, dated April 28, 1942; partly quoted in Sergei Kononov, *SMERSH. Momenty istiny* (Moscow: Yauza-Eksmo, 2009), 220–2 (in Russian). Also, NKVD instruction, dated April 30, 1942. Document Nos. 1 and 2 in *Apparat NKVD-NKGB v Germanii, 1945–1953*, edited by N. Petrov and Ya. Foitsik, 54–59 (Moscow: Demokratiya, 2009) (in Russian).

3. Stakhanov's report, dated January 17, 1945, with Beria's cover letter, dated January 19, 1945. GARF, Fond R-9401, Opis' 2 (Stalin's NKVD/MVD Special Folder), Delo 92, Ll. 86–89.

4. *Na prieme u Stalina. Tetradi (zhurnaly) zapisei lits, pronyatykh I. V. Stalinym (1924–1953 gg.)*, edited by A. V. Korotkov, A. D. Chernev, and A. A. Chernobaev, 447 (Moscow: Novyi khronograf, 2008) (in Russian).

5. Bradley F. Smith, *Sharing Secrets with Stalin: How the Allies Traded Intelligence, 1941–1945* (Lawrence, KS: University Press of Kansas, 1996), 234–5.

6. Report No. 70991-sch by Belyanov, OO head of the Western Front, to Georgii Zhukov, commander of the same front, dated December 30, 1941, in *Organy gosudarstvennoi bezopasnosti*, 3 (2), 480–85.

7. Report by V. M. Kazakevich, deputy OO head of the Stalingrad Front, to the UOO, dated September 10, 1942, in ibid., 3 (2), 227–28.

8. N. V. Grekov, 'Deiatel'nost' kontrrazvedki "SMERSH" po presecheniyu izmeny i dezertirstva v voiskakh vo vremya Velikoi Otechestvennoi voiny 1941–1945 gg.,' *VIZh*, no. 2 (1996), 42–48 (in Russian).

9. Joint Directive No. 00146/004137 by Zeidin, head of the Main Directorate of Military Tribunals, and Nosov, Chief Military Prosecutor, dated November 30, 1942. Cited in Zvyagintsev, *Voina na vesakh Femidy*, 302.

10. Ye. M. Meletinsky, *Izbrannye stat'i. Vospaminaniya* (Moscow: Rossiiskii gosudarstvennyi gumanitarnyi unyiversitet, 1998), 487–8 (in Russian).

11. The above-cited report by Kazakevich, dated September 10, 1942.

12. V. P. Artemiev et al., *Political Controls in the Soviet Army: A Study Based on Reports by Former Soviet Officers* (New York: Research Program on the USSR, 1954), 60–61, 74–75.

13. Reports of political officers cited in Senyavskaya, *1941–1945*, 132–33.

14. Bykov,' Za Rodinu! Za Stalina!'

15. Decree of the Presidium of the USSR Supreme Council, dated July 16, 1941(draft edited by Stalin). Document No. 11 in 'Voina. 1941–1945,' *Vestnik Arkhiva Presidenta Rossiiskoi Federatsii* (Moscow, 2010), 37–40 (in Russian).

16. Decree of the Presidium of the USSR Supreme Council, dated October 9, 1942.

17. Pages in Artemyev et al., *Political Controls,* 9–15.

18. Georgii Arbatov, 'Nastupali po gogolevskim mestam,' *Novaya gazeta,* no. 86, November 13, 2006 (in Russian), http://www.novayagazeta.ru/data/2006/86/37.html, retrieved September 6, 2011.

19. For example, memoirs by Mikhail Baitman, former military intelligence officer, interview on September 22, 2008 (in Russian), http://www.iremember.ru/razvedchiki/baytman-mikhail-ilich.html, retrieved September 6, 2011.

20. Interview with Georgii Minin, former mortar man, July 4, 2006, http://www.iremember.ru/minometchiki/minin-georgiy-ivanovich.html, retrieved September 6, 2011.

21. Recollections of Elya Gekhtman, former infantryman, May 7, 2009 (in Russian), http://www.iremember.ru/pekhotintsi/gekhtman-elya-gershevich.html, retrieved September 6, 2011.

22. Viktor Astafiev's letter to V. Kondratiev, dated December 28, 1987, in 'Tol'ko prestupniki mogli tak sorit' svoim narodom,' *Novaya Gazeta,* no. 46, May 6, 2009 (in Russian), http://www.novayagazeta.ru/data/ 2009/046/00.html, retrieved September 6, 2011.

23. Roman Kolkowicz, *The Soviet Military and the Communist Party* (Princeton, NJ: Princeton University Press, 1967), 76–77.

24. Joint Order of the NKO and NKMF, dated July 13, 1941. From August 1941 onwards, the 2nd NKVD Special Department was responsible for censorship, but the OOs continued to perform operational censorship of army correspondence. Abramov, *SMERSH,* 64–65.

25. David Samoilov, 'Lyudi odnogo varianta. Iz voennykh zapisok,' *Avrora,* nos. 1–2 (1990), 68 (in Russian).

26. Reports in *Lubyanka v dni bitvy za Moskvu. Po rassekrechennym dokumentam FSB RF,* edited by V. K. Vinogradov et al., 291–360 (Moscow: Zvonnitsa, 2002) (in Russian).

27. Report of the OO deputy head of the Kalinin Front to Milshtein, dated February 13, 1942, in ibid., 320–3.

28. For instance, Report No. 2397/6 by the OO of the Kalinin Front to the NKVD in Moscow, dated March 4, 1942, in *Organy gosudarstvennoi bezopanosti SSSR v Velikoi Otechestvennoi voine. T. 3. Kn. 1. Krushenie 'Blitskriga.' 1 yanvarya—31 iyulya 1942 goda* (Moscow: Rus', 2003), 10–60 (in Russian).

29. Fedorenko's report to Stalin, dated October 21, 1941. Document No. 37 in 'Voina 1941–1945,' *Vestnik Arkhiva Presidenta,* 85.

30. An order to the troops of the Southwestern Front No. 0029, dated December 12, 1941, in *Skrytaya pravda voiny, Chapter 4,* http://www.rkka.ru/docs/spv/SPV4.htm, retrieved September 6, 2011.

31. GKO Decision No 562ss, dated August 22, 1941. Mentioned in NKO Order No. 0320, dated August 25, 1941. Document No. 58, in *Russkii arkhiv.*

Velikaya Otechestvennaya. Prikazy narodnogo komissara oborony SSSR (1943–1945 gg.), T. 13 (2-2) (Moscow: TERRA, 1997), 73 (in Russian).

32. GKO Order 1227s, dated May 11, 1942, cited in NKO Order No. 0373, dated May 12, 1942. Document No. 188, in ibid., 228. Also, GKO Order No. 2507s, dated November 12, 1942, cited in NKO Orders No. 0883, dated November 13, 1942, and No. 031, dated January 13, 1943, Document No. 289, in ibid., 365–6, and Document No. 16 in *Russkii arkhiv. Velikaya Otechestvennaya. Prikazy*, T. 13 (2-3), 28.

33. GKO Order No. 1889s, dated June 6, 1942, cited in NKO Order No. 0470, dated June 12, 1942. Document No. 289, in ibid., 251–2.

34. Interview with Semyon Tsvang, former sergeant in a reconnaissance company of a tank brigade, November 19, 2008 (in Russian), http://www.iremember.ru/razvedchiki/tsvang-semen-ruvimovich.html, retrieved September 6, 2011.

35. Quoted (page 763) in Frank Costigliola, '"Like Animals or Worse": Narratives of Culture and Emotion by U.S. and British POWs and Airmen behind Soviet Lines, 1944–1945,' *Diplomatic History*, 28, no. 5 (November 2004), 749–80.

36. NKO Order No. 0063, dated April 5, 1942, Document No. 161 in *Russkii arkhv: Velikaya Otechestvennaya: Prikazy*, T. 13 (2-2), 193–4.

37. Quoted in Zoya Yershok, 'My valyalis' na trave...Voina.   Svidetel'skie pokazaniya sarshego leitenanta Petra Todorovskogo,' *Novaya gazeta*, April 23, 2010 (in Russian), http://www.novayagazeta.ru/data/2010/043/19.html, retrieved September 6, 2011.

38. Interview with Nikolai Safonov, former infantryman, April 30, 2008, http://www.iremember.ru/pekhotintsi/safonov-nikolay-ivanovich.html, retrieved September 6, 2011.

39. A review of trials of the Red Army commanders in 1943 in Zvyagintsev, *Voina na vesakh Femidy*, 466–71.

40. Quoted in B. V. Sokolov, *Razvedka. Tainy Vtoroii mirovoi voiny* (Moscow: AST-Press, 2001), 432–7 (in Russian).

41. Igor Plugatarev, 'Voevat', tak s iumorom!' *Nezavisimoe voennoe obozrenie*, April 1, 2005 (in Russian), http://nvo.ng.ru/history/2005-04-01/6_humor.html, retrieved September 6, 2011.

42. Interview with Nikolai Chistiakov, former infantryman, July 14, 2006, http://www.iremember.ru/pekhotintsi/chistyakov-nikolay-aleksandrovich.html, retrieved September 6, 2011.

43. The above-cited recollections by Nikolai Safonov.

44. Serov's letter to Stalin, dated September 8, 1946, in Petrov, *Pervyi predsedatel' KGB*, 244–7.

45. Two letters: No. Sh/003778 by Sharashenidze, dated April 4, 1942, and No. 08529/4 by Isai Babich, dated July 9, 1942. Document Nos. 876 and 1006, in *Organy gosudarstvennoi bezopasnosti*, 3 (1), 321, and ibid., 3 (2), 33–40.

46. NKVD Orders No. 00988, dated May 15, 1942, and No. 001854, dated August 30, 1942 (both signed by Abakumov). Documents No. 933, in *Organy gosudarstvennoi bezopasnosti*, 3 (1), 449–51, and No. 1071, in ibid., 3 (2), 183–85.

Chapter 11

1. Zvyagintsev, *Voina na vesakh Femidy*, 558.

2. M. Delagrammatik, 'Voennye tribunaly za rabotoi,' *Novyi mir*, no. 6 (1997) (in Russian), http://magazines.russ.ru/novyi_mi/1997/6/delagr.html, retrtieved September 6, 2011.

3. NKVD report, dated January 1, 1945; quoted in Nikita Petrov, *Istoriya imperii 'GULAG.' Glava 12* (in Russian), http://www.pseudology.org/GULAG/Glava12.htm, retrieved September 6, 2011.

4. Abakumov's report to Stalin, dated December 21, 1945. Page 25 in L. Ye. Reshin and V. S, Stepanov, 'Sud'by general'skie,' *VIZh*, no. 11 (1992), 24–27 (in Russian).

5. Details of the case in Nikolai Smirnov, *Vplot' do vysshei mery* (Moscow: Moskovskii rabochii, 1997), 73–84 (in Russian).

6. Lidiya Golovkova, *Sukhanovskaya tyur'ma. Spetsob'ekt 110* (Moscow: Vozvrashchenie, 2009), 96–97 (in Russian).

7. Beria's letter to Molotov, dated November 23, 1938. Document No. 66 in *Istoriya stalinskogo GULAGa. Konets 1920-kh–pervaia polovina 1950-kh godov. Tom 2. Karatel'naia sistema: struktura i kadry*, edited by N. V. Petrov, 151–2 (in Russian).

8. Evgenii Gnedin, *Vykhod iz labirinta* (Moscow: Memorial, 1994), 70–76 (in Russian).

9. Ibid., 70.

10. Alexander Dolgun with Patrick Watson, *Alexander Dolgun's Story: An American in the Gulag* (New York: Alfred A. Knopf, 1975), 116.

11. Gnedin, *Vykhod iz labirinta*, 71.

12. Lidiya Golovkova, 'Pytochnaya tyur'ma Stalina,' *Novaya Gazeta*, no. 136, December 7, 2009 (in Russian), http://www.novayagazeta.ru/data/2009/136/23.html, retrieved September 6, 2011.

13. Gnedin, *Vykhod iz labirinta*, 76.

14. For the conditions and treatment of prisoners in this hospital, see NKVD Order No. 00913, dated July 31, 1945. Quoted in Petrov, *'Istoriya imperii "GULAG." Glava 12'*.

15. Golovkova, *Sukhanovskaya tyur'ma*, 146–50.

16. Details in Smirnov, *Vplot' do vysshei mery*, 119–26.

17. Timoshenko's words quoted in V. V. Beshanov, *God 1942—'Uchebnyi'* (Minsk: Kharvest, 2003), 220 (in Russian).

18. Recollections of Anastas Mikoyan, in G. Kumanev, *Govoryat stalinskie narkomy* (Smolensk: Rusich, 2005), 66 (in Russian).

19. From a protocol (transcript) of Levchenko's interrogation, quoted in V. A. Bobrenev and V. B. Ryazantsev, *Palachi i zhertvy* (Moscow: Voenizdat, 1993), 220 (in Russian).

20. Kuznetsov's Directive No. 621/sh, in Zvyagintsev, *Voina na vesakh Femidy*, 257–8.

21. Beria's report to Stalin No. 1066/B, dated June 18, 1942. Document No. 223, in *Lubyanka. Stalin i NKVD–NKGB–GUKR 'Smersh.' 1939–mart 1946*, edited by V. N. Khaustov, V. P. Naumov, and N. S. Plotnikova, 349–50 (Moscow: Materik, 2006) (in Russian).

22. Vasil' Bykov, 'Za Rodinu! Za Stalina!,' *Rodina*, no. 5 (1995), 30–37 (in Russian).

23. Vasil' Bykov, 'Dolgaya doroga domoi,' *Druzhba narodov*, no. 8 (2003) (in Russian), http://magazines.russ.ru/druzhba/2003/8/bykov.html, retrieved September 6, 2011.

24. Ye. S. Senyavskaya, *1941–1945: Frontovoe pokolenie. Istoriko-psikhologicheskoe issledovanie* (Moscow: Institut Rossiiskoi Istorii RAN, 1995), 112 (in Russian).

25. Stavka's Directive No. 004235, dated April 9, 1942.

26. David Samoilov, 'Lyudi odnogo varianta. Iz voennykh zapisok,' *Avrora*, no. 1–2 (1990), 66–67 (in Russian).

27. GKO Order No. 1926ss, dated June 24, 1942. Document No. 224, in *Lubyanka. Stalin i NKVD*, 350–51.

28. NKVD Instruction No. 1237, dated June 27, 1942. Document No. 994, in *Organy gosudarstvennoi bezopasnosti*, 3 (1), 577.

Chapter 12

1. Stalin's instruction to commanders of the Leningrad Front, dated November 13, 1941. Quoted in V. D. Danilin, 'Stalinskaya strategiya nachala voiny,' *Otechestveyyaya istoriya* 3 (1995).

2. Stavka's Order No. 0428, dated November 17, 1941, in *Russkii arkhiv. Velikaya Otechestvennaya. Prikazy*, 13 (2-2), 119–20.

3. Directive of the Military Council of the Western Front, dated November 9, in *Skrytaya pravda voiny: 1941 god. Neizvestnye documenty*, edited by P. N. Knyshevsky et al., 210 (Moscow: Russkaya kniga, 1992) (in Russian).

4. Photo of this order in B. M. Bim-Bad, *Stalin: issledovanie zhiznennogo stilia* (Moscow: URAO, 2002), between pages 128 and 129. Another copy is kept in the U.S. Library of Congress, Manuscript Division, 'Volkogonov Collection,' Reel 4.

5. Quoted in B. V. Sokolov, *Front za liniei fronta. Partizanskaya voina 1939–1945 gg.* (Moscow: Veche, 2008), 175 (in Russian).

6. Boris Sokolov, '43 milliona,' *Novaya gazeta*, no. 65, June 22, 2009 (in Russian), http://www.novayagazeta.ru/data/2009/065/22.html, retrieved September 6, 2011.

7. OO Instruction No. 1244/6, Southwestern Front, dated December 4, 1941. S. G. Chuev, *Spetssluzhby III Reikha. Kniga 1* (St. Petersburg: Neva, 2003), 348–51 (in Russian).

8. An order of G. N. Safonov, Acting Prosecutor, to apply the death penalty to teenagers, dated December 22, 1941. Document No. 217, in *Deti GULAGa: 1918–1956*, ed. by S. S. Vilensky et al., 376 (Moscow, Demokratiya, 2002) (in Russian).

9. GKO orders dated February 14 and October 7, 1942, quoted in M. I. Semiryaga, *Kak my upravlyali Germaniei. Politika i zhizn'* (Moscow: Rosspen, 1995), 160–61 (in Russian).

10. Instruction No. 35523, 3rd NKO Directorate, dated June 27, 1941. Document No. 327, in *Organy gosudarstvennoi bezopasnosti*, 2 (1), 90–93.

11. Milshtein's report, dated October 31, 1941. Document No. 202, in *Lubyanka. Stalin i NKVD*, 317–8.

12. Interview with Grigory Falkovsky, former infantryman, September 21, 2008 (in Russian), http://www.iremember.ru/pekhotintsi/falkovskiy-grigoriy-yak-ovlevich.html, retrieved September 6, 2011.

13. Directive to commanders and military councils of all fronts, dated September 12, 1941, dictated by Stalin. Zvyagintsev, *Voina na vesakh Femidy*, 402. Stalin repeated this order as part of NKO Order No. 227, known as 'No Step Back!'

14. P. N. Palii, 'V nemetskom plenu,' in *Nashe nedavnee*, Vol. 7 (Paris: YMCA Press, 1987), 56 (in Russian).

15. B. I. Gavrilov, *Dolina smerti. Tragediya i podvig 2-i Udarnoi Armii*, (Moscow: Dubrava, 2006), 225 (in Russian).

16. Report by Dmitrii Me'lnikov to Abakumov, dated August 6, 1942, pages 31–34 in L. Ye. Reshin and V. S. Stepanov, 'Sud'by general'skie…' *VIZh*, no. 5 (1993), 28–37 (in Russian).

17. Report of Security Major Ivanov, dated September 1942. Quoted in Zvyagintsev, *Voina na vesakh Femidy*, 448–49.

18. N. N. Nikoulin, *Vospominaniya o voine* (St. Petersburg, Izdatel'stvo Gosudarstvennogo Ermitazha, 2008), 45–46 (in Russian).

19. NKO Order No. 0321, dated August 26, 1941. Document No. 59, in *Russkii arkhiv. Velkaya Otechestvennaya. Prikazy*, 13 (2-2), 74.

20. A. F. Bichekhvost, 'K istorii sozdzniya spetsial'nykh i proverochno-fil'tratsionnykh lagerei dlya sovetckikh voennoplennykh i organizatsiya v nikh 'gosudarstvennoi proverki,' in *Voenno-istoricheskie issledovaniya v Povolzh'e. Sbornik nauchnykh trudov. Vypusk 7* (Saratov, 2006), 256-80 (in Russian), http://www.sgu.ru/files/nodes/10090/033.pdf, retrieved September 6, 2011.

21. Interview with Roman Lazebnik, former partisan, December 2, 2008 (in Russian), http://iremember.ru/partizani/lazebnik-roman-evseevich.html, retrieved September 6, 2011.

22. NKVD's 'Information on Vetting of Servicemen from the German Encirclement and Captivity by October 1, 1944', quoted in V. N. Zemskov, 'GULAG (istoriko-sotsiologicheskii aspekt)', *Sotsiologicheskie issledovaniya*, no. 6 (1991), 10-27 (in Russian).

23. Assault battalions were created on Stalin's secret directive dated August 1, 1942. Zvyagintsev, *Voina na vesakh Femidy*, 389–90.

24. In the movie *Escape From Sobibor* (1987), the actor Alan Arkin played Pecherski's role.

25. Leonid Terushkin, 'Spartak Sobibora,' *Novaya Gazeta*, No. 47, May 5, 2010 (in Russian), http://uisrussia.msu.ru/docs/nov/2010/47/nov_2010_47_02.htm, retrieved September 6, 2011.

26. Private collection, Moscow.

27. Delagrammatik, 'Voennye tribunaly za rabotoi.'

28. Beria's report No. 1066/B, dated June 18, 1942. Document No. 223, in *Lubyanka. Stalin i NKVD*, 349–50.

29. Kazakevich's report to Abakumov, dated February 17, 1943. Document 90 in *Stalingradskaya epopeya: Materialy NKVD SSSR i voennoi tsenzury iz tsentral'nogo arkhiva FSB RF*, edited by F. Pogonii et al., 403–10 (Moscow: Zvonnitsa-MG, 2000) (in Russian).

30. NKO Order No. 227, dated July 28, 1942. Document No. 1027, in *Organy gosudarstvennoi bezopasnosti*, 3 (2), 76–80. Additionally, GKO Order No. 298 entitled 'On penal detachments', dated September 28, 1942, in *Skrytaya pravda voiny*, 359–65.

31. Zvyagintsev, *Voina na vesakh Femidy*, 392.

32. Stalin's order, August 1943. Document No. 159, in *Russkii arkhiv. Velikaya otechestvennaya.Prikazy*, 13 (2-3), 198.

33. Joint Instructions of the NKVD Commissar Beria and USSR prosecutor Bochkov No. 185, dated April 29, 1942, and No. 194/17/11692/s, dated May 7, 1942. Document Nos. 910 and 918, in *Organy gosudarstvennoi bezopasnosti*, 3 (1), 387–88 and 403–4.

34. Sergei Krapivin, 'Starshina Grigorii Vlasenko: 'Ya byl radistom shtrafbata',' *Sovetskaya Belorussiya*, April 1, 2005 (in Russian), http://sb.by/post/42729, retrieved September 6, 2011.

35. Yakov Aizenstadt, *Zapiski sekretarya voennogo tribunala* (London: Overseas Publications Interchange Ltd., 1991), 62 (in Russian).

36. Zvyagintsev, *Voina na vesakh Femidy*, 394–5.

37. N. V. Petrov, 'Vnesudebnye repressii protiv voennoplennykh nemtsev v 1941–1946 gg.,' in *Problemy voennogo plena: istoriya i sovremennost':Materialy Mezhdunarodnoi nauchno-prakticheskoi konferentsii 23–25 oktyabrya 1997 g. g. Vologda. Chast' 2* (Vologda: Vologodskii institut, 1997), 77–94 (in Russian).

38. Joachim Hoffmann, *Stalin's War of Extermination, 1941–1945: Planning, Realization and Documentation*, translated by William Deist (Capshaw, AL: Theses & Dissertation Press, 2001), 244–78.

39. Stalin's telephone conversation with Zhukov on September 4, 1941 (a transcript). In Boris Sokolov, 'Pokayanie v Den' Pobedy,' *Grani.ru*, May 8, 2001 (in Russian), http://www.grani.ru/Society/History/p.3770.html, retrieved September 6, 2011.

40. Document from the Central FSB Archive (Fond 7, Opis' 1, Delo 137), cited in Petrov, 'Vnesudebnye repressii protiv voennoplennykh nemtsev v 1941–1946 gg.,' 79.

41. Ibid., 79–80.

42. For instance, a transcript of the interrogation of Otto Naumen, in *Lubyanka v dni bitvy*, 380–2.

43. Milovan Djilas, *Conversations with Stalin*, translated from Serbo-Croat by Michael B. Petrovichn (New York: Harcourt, Brace and World Co., 1962). 54.

44. For instance, Geoffrey Roberts, *Victory at Stalingrad: The Battle That Changed History* (London: Longman, 2002).

45. On 'hiwis' see, for example, Lev Kopelev, *No Jail For Thought*, translated and edited by Anthony Austin (London: Secker & Warburg, 1977), 98.

46. Report by Isai Babich, dated January 1, 1942. *Lubyanka v dni bitvy*, 302–6.

47. Sculptor N. P. Gavrilov's visit to K. K. Rokossovsky's troops in December of 1941. Document No. III-43 in *Moskva voennaya, 1941–1945: memuary i arkhivnye dokumenty*, edited by K. I. Bukov, M. M. Gorinov, and A. N. Ponomarev, 586–98 (Moscow: Mosgorarkhiv, 1995) (in Russian).

48. L. K. Brontman, 'Dnevniki 1932–1947 gg.,' *Samizdat*, 2004 (in Russian), http://militera.lib.ru/db/brontman_lk/1944.html, retrieved September 6, 2011.

Part IV. German Intelligence Services
at the Eastern Front

Chapter 13

1. Karl Heinz Abshagen, *Canaris*, translated by Alan Houghton Brodrick (London: Hutchinson, 1956), 23.

2. David Kahn, *Hitler's Spies: German Military Intelligence in World War II* (New York: Collier Books, 1978), 233.

3. Ibid., 238.

4. *SMERSH. Istoricheskie ocherki i dokumenty*, edited by V. S. Khristoforov, et al. (Moscow: Glavnoe arkhivnoe upravlenie, 2003), 75 (in Russian).

5. Details in Julius Madder, *Hitlers Spionagegenerale sagen aus* (Berlin: Verlag der Nation, 1978), 429–48.

6. Abshagen, *Canaris*, 85; Ladislav Farago, *Burn After Reading: The Espionage History of World War II* (New York: Pinnacle Books, 1972), 28; Kahn, *Hitler's Spies*, 236–7.

7. Ibid., 237.

8. A. Kolpakidi and D. Prokhorov, *Imperiya GRU. Ocherki istorii rossiiskoi voennoi razvedki. Kniga 1* (Moscow: Olma-Press, 2000), 302–4 (in Russian).

9. Reinhard Spitzy, *How We Squandered the Reich*, translated from the German by G. T. Waddington (Wilby: Michael Russell, 1997), 298.

10. Abshagen, *Canaris*, 88.

11. Mueller, *Canaris*, 233.

12. Stolze's testimony in the MGB, dated July 14, 1947. Quoted in Mader, *Hitlers Spionagegenerale*, 132.

13. S. T. Minakov, *Za otvorotom marshal'skoi shineli* (Orel: Orelizdat, 1999), 83–94 (in Russian).

14. Kirill Aleksandrov, *Armiya generala Vlasova* (Moscow: Yauza-Eksmo, 2006), 246 (in Russian).

15. Details in Franz Kurowski, *The Brandenburger Commands: Germany's Elite Spies in World War II* (Stackpole Books, 2005).

16. Details in N. N. Luzan (N. Abin), *Lubyanka: Podvigi i tragedii* (Moscow: Kuchkovo Pole, 2010), 218–358 (in Russian).

17. Michael R. D. Foot, *SOE: An Outline History of the Special Operations Executive 1940–46* (London: British Broadcasting Corporation, 1984).

18. Abshagen, *Canaris*, 86.

19. Andre Brissaud, *Canaris: The Biography of Admiral Canaris, Chief of German Military intelligence in the Second World War*, translated and edited by Ian Colvin (London: Weidenfeld and Nicolson, 1973), 274.

20. Heinz Höhne, *The Order of the Death's Head: The Story of Hitler's SS*, translated from the German by Richard Barry (New York: Ballantine Books, 1969), 289–92.

21. Detailed biography in Reinhard R. Doerries, *Hitler's Intelligence Chief Walter Schellenberg* (New York: Enigma Books, 2009).

22. Höhne, *Canaris*, 471.

23. Oscar Reile, *Tainaya voina. Sekretnye operatsii Abvera na Zapade i Vostoke (1921-1945)* (Moscow: Tsentrpoligraf, 2002), 135–36 (in Russian, translated from the German).

24. I. L. Bunich, *'Groza'. Krovavye igry diktatorov* (Ct. Petersburg: Oblik, 1997), 297 (in Russian).

25. H. Buchheit, *Abver: shchit i mech' III reikha* (Moscow: Eksmo, 2005), 247–8 (in Russian, translation from German).

26. Paul Leverkuehn, *German Military Intelligence*, translated from the German by R. H. Stevens and Constantine FitzGibbon (London: Weidensfeld and Nicolson, 1954), 156.

27. OO Directive No. 29670, dated May 25, 1941. Document No. 215 in *Organy gosudarstvennoi bezopasnosti SSSR, T. 1. Nakanune, Kn. 2* (Moscow: Kniga i bizness, 1995), 158–60 (in Russian).

28. Short descriptions of Stab Walli in Heinz Höhne and Hermann Zolling, *The General Was a Spy: The Truth About General Gehlen and His Spy Ring*, translated from the German by Richard Barry (New York: Coward, McCann & Geoghegan, Inc., 1971), 15–22; Heinz Höhne, *Canaris*, translated from the German by J. Maxwell Brownjohn (Garden City, NY: Doubleday & Co., Inc, 1979), 436–59; Kahn, *German Military Intelligence*, 248–9.

29. P. P. Stefanovsky, *Razvoroty sud'by: Avtobiograficheskaya povesti. T. 1. Abver–SMERSH* (Moscow: Izdatel'stvo RUDN, 2002), 19 (in Russian).

30. Brissaud, *Canaris*, 235.

31. Kahn, *Hitler's Spies*, 249.

32. Höhne and Zolling, *The General Was a Spy*, 18.

33. Page 208 in Arnold M. Silver, 'Memories of Oberursel: Questions, Questions, Questions,' *Intelligence and National Security* 8, No. 2 (April 1993), 199–213.

34. In 'Debriefing of Eric Waldman' on September 30, 1969, http://www.gwu.edu/~nsarchiv/NSAEBB/NSAEBB146/doc09.pdf, retrieved September 6, 2011.

35. S. G. Chuev, *Spetssluzhby III Reikha. Kniga 1 and II* (St. Petersburg: Neva, 2003), 53–54 (in Russian).

36. E. H. Cookridge, *Gehlen: Spy of the Century* (New York: Random House, 1971), 54, 369.

37. Erwin Stolze's testimony, quoted in Mader, *Hitlers Spionagegenerale*, 132.

38. Mader, *Hitlers Spionegenerale*, 259; Linda Hunt, *Secret Agenda: The United States Government, Nazi Scienticts, and Project Paperclip, 1945 to 1990* (New York: St. Martin's Press, 1991), 203.

39. Von Bentivegni's testimony during the MGB investigation, in Mader, *Hitlers Spionagegenerale*, 259–61.

40. Reile, *Tainaya voina*, 158–62; Kahn, *German Military Intelligence*, 248–9.

41. E. G. Ioffe, *Abver. Politsiya bezopasnosti i SD, tainaya polevaya politsiya, otdel 'inostrannye armii–Vostok' v zapadnykh oblastyakh SSSR. Strategiya i taktika. 1939-1945* (Minsk: Kharvest, 2007), 62, 78–79 (in Russian).

42. Kahn, *Hitler's Spies*, 249.

43 Page 208 in Silver, 'Memories of Oberursel.'

44. Abwehr I squads acquired numbers 101–106, and their groups, numbers 101–110, 114–115, 143–144, Abwehr II squads became 201–206 with groups 201–212, 214–215, 217–218, 220, and Abwehr III squads were provided with numbers 301–305, and the groups, with numbers 301–329. Details in Chuev, *Spetssluznby*, I, 56–163.

45. Mader, *Hitlers Spionage Generale*, 357–8.

46. Ioffe, *Abver. Politsiya bezopasnosti*, 56–84.

47. Höhne and Zolling, *The General Was a Spy*, 19.

48. Mader, *Hitlers Spionagegenerale*, 365.

49. Details in ibid., 368–89.

50. Reile, *Tainaya voina*, 165–6; Höhne, *Canaris*, 462–3.

51. Richard Rhodes, *Masters of Death: The SS-Einsatzgrupen and the Invention of the Holocaust* (New York: Vantage Books, 2002), 61–63.

52. Details, for instance, in Alfred J. Rieder, 'Civil Wars in the Soviet Union,' *Kritika: Explorations in Russian History*, 4, No. 1 (Winter 2003), 129–62.

53. Chuev, *Spetssluzhby*, I, 295–8.

54. David Thomas, 'Foreign Armies East and German Military Intelligence in Russia 1941–45,' *Journal of Contemporary History* 22, no. 2 (1987), 261–301. From November 1938 to March 1942, Lieutenant Colonel Eberhard Kinzel headed the FHO, then General Franz Halder (March–April 1942), and finally, Lieutenant Colonel (later Major General) Reinhard Gehlen (April 1942–April 1945).

55. Kahn, *Hitler's Spies*, 429.

56. Cited in Cookridge, *Gehlen*, 64. Chiefs of the German General Staff after Halder: Kurt Zeitzler (September 1942–June 1944), Adolf Heusinger (June 1944–July 1944), and Heinz Guderian (July 1944–March 1945).

57. Details in Thomas, 'Foreign Armies East.'

58. Höhne and Zolling, *The General Was a Spy*, 21–23.

59. Höhne, *Canaris*, 467.

Chapter 14

1. Thomas, 'German Intelligence,' 290.

2. Interrogation of Kauder on July 15, 1946, quoted in Robert W. Stephens, *Stalin's Secret War: Soviet Counterintelligence against the Nazis, 1941–1945* (Lawrence, KS: University Press of Kansas, 2004), 171.

3. Vladimir Makarov and Andrei Tyurin, *SMERSH. Gvardiya Stalina* (Moscow: Yauza-Eksmo, 2009), 258–9 (in Russian).

4. Kahn, *Hitler's Spies*, 314.

5. Reinhard Gehlen, *The Service: The Memoirs of General Reinhard Gehlen*, translated by David Irving (New York: World Publishing, 1972), 57–58.

6. MVD Report on the interrogation of K. Geisler, dated April 18, 1947. Document No. 28 in *Lubyanka, Stalin i MGB SSSR, mart 1946-mart 1953, edited by V. N. Khaustov, V. P. Naumov and N. S. Plotnikov*, 49-51 (Moscow: Materik, 2007) (in Russian).

7. Ibid.

8. Details in Nigel West and Oleg Tsarev, *The Crown Jewels: The British Secrets at the Heart of the KGB Archive* (New Haven, CT: Yale University Press, 1999), 187–203.

9. Vladimir Lotta, 'Sekretnyi front General'nogo shtaba,' *Krasnaya zvezda*, November 2, 2002 (in Russian), http://www.redstar.ru/2002/11/02_11/4_01.html, retrieved September 6, 2011.

10. Page 204 in Silver, 'Memories of Oberursel.'

11. Kahn, *Hitler's Spies*, 316–7; Stephan, *Stalin's Secret War*, 168–9.

12. Makarov and Tyurin, *SMERSH*, 260.

13. Kauder's testimony quoted in Avraham Ziv-Tal, *The Maskirovka of Max and Moritz* (Sichron-Ya'acov, Israel: Bahur Books, 2007), 222.

14. Kauder's testimony cited in Ziv-Tal, *The Maskirovka*, 222–3.

15. Ibid., 223.

16. Doerries, *Hitler's Intelligence Chief*, 118–9.

17. West and Tsarev, *The Crown Jewels*, 199–202.

18. Makarov and Tyurin, *SMERSH*, 261–81.

19. Ibid., 265–6.

20. Michael Mueller, *Canaris: The Life and Death of Hitler's Spymaster* (Annapolis, MD: Naval Institute Press, 2007), 213.

21. Makarov and Tyurin, *SMERSH*, 266.

22. Interrogation of Gerda Filitz on April 30, 1947, in ibid., 267–8.

23. Interogation of Valentina Deutsch on June 25, 1947, in ibid., 264–5.

24. Kauder's testimony in Ziv-Tal, *The Maskirovka*, 215–22.

25. Yehuda Bauer, *Jews for Sale? Nazi-Jewish Negotiations, 1933–1945* (New Haven, CTL Yale University Press, 1994), 135–40.

26. Ye. V. Popov, *'Vengerskaya rapsodiya' GRU* (Moscow: Veche, 2010), 95 (in Russian).

27. Dulles's telegram 1534-38, dated January 2, 1944. Document 2-109 in *From Hitler's Doorsteps: The Wartime Intelligence Reports of Allen Dulles, 1942-1945*, edited by Neal H. Petersen, 190–1 (University Park, PA: The Pennsylvania University Press, 1996).

28. From Hatz's Verdict pronounced by the Military Tribunal of the Moscow Military District, dated January 29, 1952, and a decision of the Plenum of the USSR Supreme Court, dated April 8, 1955. Pages 3–4 and 41–42 in Hatz's Personal File (No. UO-190819, RGVA, Moscow).

29. Hatz's statement to Commander of the 2nd Ukrainian Front, dated November 21, 1944. Document No. 31 in *Russkii Arkhiv. Velikaya Otechestvennaya* 14, No. 3 (2), 328–30 (in Russian).

30. Hatz's Personal File, 22.

31. Interrogation of Klausnitzer on June 5, 1947, in Makarov and Tyurin, *SMERSH*, 269.

32. Barry Rubin, *Istanbul Intrigues* (New York: Pharos Books, 1972), 181–6, 191–7,

33. Zvi-Tal, *Maskirovka*, 224.

34. Interrogation of Alfred Klausnitzer on July 5, 1947, in Makarov and Tyurin, *SMERSH*, 273.

35. Klausnitzer's report to SMERSH investigators, dated August 2, 1945, and quoted in ibid., 273–4.

36. Ziv-Tal, *Maskirovka*, 226.

37. Page 202 in Silver, 'Memories of Oberursel.'

38. Cited in West and Tsarev, *The Crown Jewels*, 198–200.

39. Beria's report to Stalin, dated April 13, 1944. Document No. 257 in *Lubyanka. Stalin i NKVD-NKGB-GUKR 'SMERSH.' 1939–mart 1946*, edited by V. N. Khaustov, V. P. Naumov, and N. S. Plotnikov, 420–2 (Moscow: Materik, 2006) (in Russian).

40. C. G. McKay, *From Information to Intrigue: Studies in Secret Service Based on the Swedish Experience 1939–45* (London: Frank Cass, 1993), 217.

41. Page 205 in Silver, 'Memories of Oberursel.'

42. Ibid., 204–5. Also, a review of all interrogations in Stephan, *Stalin's Secret War*, 166–73.

43. Page 203 in Silver, 'Memories of Oberursel.'

44. Memoirs by L. V. Serdakovski, 'U Khorti v Budapeshte,' *Kadetskaya pereklichka*, no. 27 (1981) (in Russian), http://www.xxl3.ru/kadeti/serdakovsky.htm, retrieved Setember 6, 2011.

45. Pavel Sudoplatov and Anatoli Sudoplatov, with Jerrold L. and Leona P. Schecter, *Special Tasks: The Memoirs of an Unwanted Witness—A Soviet Spymaster* (New York: Little, Brown and Co., 1994), 152–60.

46. V. V. Korovin, 'Poedinok s Abverom,' *VIZh*, 1995, No. 1 (in Russian); Lyudmila Ovchinnikova, 'Zheleznyi krest i Krasnuyu zvezdu on poluchil za odnu operatsiyu,' *Komsomol'skaya pravda*, August 13, 1996 (in Russian).

47. Stephan, *Stalin's Secret War*, 154,161–8.

48. The Verdict, pages 3–4 in Hatz's Personal File.

49. Bauer, *Jews for Sale*, 140.

50. Page 290 in Thomas, 'Foreign Armies East.'

51. A review of the interrogations of Gehlen and Albert Schöller (deputy head of Group I) in 'Notes on the Red Army—Intelligence and Security,' dated June 24, 1945, http://www.gwu.edu/~nsarchiv/NSAEBB/NSAEBB146/doc10.pdf, retrieved September 6, 2011.

52. Cookridge, *Gehlen*, 74.

53. B. V. Sokolov, *Okhota na Stalina, okhota na Gitlera* (Moscow: Veche, 2003), 133 (in Russian).

54. Report in Cookridge, *Gehlen*, 75.

55. A detailed discussion in Sokolov, *Okhota na Stalina*, 125-33.

56. Cookridge, *Gehlen*, 77.

57. Ibid., 81.

58. Gehlen, *The Service*, 44.

59. *SMERSH. Istoricheskie ocherki*, 87.

60. Cookridge, *Gehlen*, 84.

61. Ivan Kruzhko, 'Cherez vsyu voinu' (in Russian), http://www.clubistok.ru/kray/2006/krugkostatya06.html, retrieved September 7, 2011.

62. Details in Wilhelm Krichbaum and Antonio Munoz, *The Secret Field Police. Wehrmacht Geheime Feldpolizei Forces in World War II, 1939–1945* (Europa Books, Inc., 2008).

63. Paul B. Brown, 'The senior leadership cadre of the Geheime Feldpolizei, 1939–1945,' *Holocaust and Genocide Studies*, 17, no. 2 (Fall 2003), 278–304.

64. Pages 6–7 in Stephen Tyas, 'Allied Intelligence Agencies and the Holocaust: Information Acquired from German Prisoners of War,' *Holocaust and Genocide Studies*, 22, no. 1 (Spring 2008), 1–24.

Chapter 15

1. Perry Biddiscombe, '*Unternehmen* Zeppelin: The Development of SS Saboteurs and Spies in the Soviet Union, 1942–945,' *Europe-Asia Studies*, 52, No. 6 (2000), 1115–42; Michael Wildt, *Generation des Unbedingten. Das Fuhrungskorps des Reichssicherheitshauptamtes* (Hamburg: Hamburger Edition, 2002), 75–81.

2. Sitting at Nuremberg, Germany, 7th January to 19th January, 1946, http://www.nizkor.org/hweb/imt/tgmwc/tgmwc-04/tgmwc-04-28-06.shtml, retrieved September 7, 2011.

3. Details in *The Einsatzgruppen Reports: Selections from the Dispatches of the Nazi Death Squads' Campaign against the Jews, July 1941–January 1943*, edited by Yitzhak Arad, Shmuel Krakowski, and Shmuel Spector, v–vii (New York: Holocaust Library, 1989).

4. Telford Taylor, *The Anatomy of the Nuremberg Trials: A Personal Memoir* (New York: Knopf, 1992), 510.

5. After Reinhard Heydrich was killed by Czech partisans on May 27, 1942, Ernst Kaltenbrunner was appointed head of the RSHA in January 1943.

6. Ioffe, *Abver. Politsiya bezopasnosti i SD*, 56–57.

7. Details, for instance, in Rhodes, *Masters of Death*, 119–150.

8. Details in I. G. Starinov, *Zapiski diversanta*, Part IV, Chapters 6–8, http://militera.lib.ru/memo/russian/starinov_ig/31.html, retrieved September 7, 2011.

9. SD report to Berlin, dated October 1941. Document No. 6 in Chuev, *Spetssluzhby*, II, 42–59. Also, Alexander V. Prusin, 'A Community of Violence: The SiPo/SD and Its Role in the Nazi Terror System in Generalbezirk Kiev,' *Holocaust and Genoicide Studies*, 21, no. 1 (Spring 2007), 1–30.

10. Höhne, *Canaris*, 464–5.

11. Walter Schellenberg's testimony in Nuremberg on November 13, 1945, http://www.nizkor.org/ftp.cgi/imt/nca/supp-b/ftp.py?imt/nca/supp-b//nca-sb-02-schellenberg.02, retrieved September 7, 2011. Also, Walter Schellenberg, *The Labyrinth*, translated by Louis Hagen (New York: Harper and Brothers, 1956), 263–71.

12. Details in Perry Biddiscombe, '*Unternehmen* Zeppelin: The Development of SS Saboteurs and Spies in the Soviet Union, 1942–1945,' *Europe-Asia Studies*, 52, no. 6 (2000), 1115–42.

13. Chuev, *Spetssluzhby*, II, 192–206.

14. Ibid., 205–6.

15. Kahn, *Hitler's Spies*, 360.

16. Höhne and Zolling, *The General Was a Spy*, 42–44.

17. Details in Kirill Aleksandrov, *Russkie soldaty Vermakhta. Geroi ili predateli* (Moscow: Yauza-Eksmo, 2005), 203, 207–12, 253–6 (in Russian).

18. Chuev, *Spetssluzhby*, II, 174–6, 231-9.

19. Hitler's decree concerning the administration of the newly-occupied Eastern territories dated July 17, 1941, http://avalon.law.yale.edu/imt/1997-ps.asp, retrieved September 7, 2011.

20. Chuev, *Spetssluzhby*, I, 36–44.

21. Ibid., 45–53.

22. L. G. Ivanov, *Pravda o 'Smersh'* (Moscow: Yauza-Eksmo, 2009), 29—30 (in Russian).

23. HSSPfs: 1) Riga (Ostland): Hans-Adolf Prützmann, Jan–Nov, 1941; Friedrich Jeckeln, Nov 1941–Jan 1945; Dr. Hermann Behrends, Jan–May 1945; 2) Mogilev, later Minsk (Russland-Mitte): Erich von dem Bach-Zelewski, Jan 1941–Jan 1942; Carl Friedrich Count of Pückler-Burghauss, Jan 1942–Mar 1943; Gerrett Korsemann, Mar–Jul 1943; Curt von Gottberg, Jul 1943–Aug 1944; 3) Kiev (Russia-Süd): Friedrich Jecklen, Jun–Nov 1941; Hans-Adolf Prützmann,

Nov 1941–Mar 1944; and 4) Nikolaev (Schwartz-Meer): Ludolf von Alvensleben, Oct–Dec 1943; Richard Hildebrandt, Dec 1943–Sep 1944; Arthur Phelps, Sep 1944.

24. The Russland Ostland in Riga had branches in Estonia, Latvia, Lithuania, and Belorussia; the Russland Mitte in Minsk had branches in four Belorussian and south Russian cities, and the Russland Süd in Kiev had branches in 16 Ukrainian cities, the Caucasus and the Crimea. Details in Chuev, *Spetssluzhby*, II, 59–82, and Kovalev, *Natsistskaya okkupatsiya*, 115–38.

25. A total of 168 Russian Orthodox and two Catholic churches were opened at the German-occupied territory of the Leningrad Region; before the war, there were only five Russian Orthodox churches in that area. In N. Lomakin, *Neizvestnaya blokada* (St. Petersburg: Neva, 2004), 493 (in Russian).

26. Document No. III-43, in *Moskva voennaya, 1941–1945: memuary i arkhivnye dokumenty*, edited by K. I. Bukov, M. M. Gorinov, and A. N. Ponomarev, 591 (Moscow: Mosgorarkhiv, 1995) (in Russian).

27. GKO Decision No.1074-ss, dated December 27, 1941. Document No. 207, in *Lubyanka. Stalin i NKVD*, 324.

28. GKO Decree No. 1926-ss, dated June 24, 1942. Document No. 224 in ibid., 350–1.

29. Details, for instance, in B. N. Kovalev, *Natsistckaya okkupatsiya i kollaboratsionism v Rossii. 1941–1944* (Moscow: Tranzitkniga, 2004) (in Russian); Aleksandrov, *Russkie soldaty Vermakhta*.

30. Details in Wilfried Strik–Strikfeld, *Against Stalin and Hitler: Memoirs of the Russian Liberation Movement 1941-1945*, translated from the German by David Footman (New York: The John Day Co., 1973), 118–20.

31. Ibid., 181–6.

32. See, for instance, Christian Streit, *Keine Kameraden: Die Wehrmacht und die sowjetischen Kriegsgefangnen 1941–1945* (Bonn: Dietz, 1997).

33. On the Lokot' Republic, see B. V. Sokolov, *Okkupatsiya. Pravda i mify* (Moscow: AST-Press Kniga, 2002), 654–71 (in Russian).

34. P. N. Paliy-Vashchenko, *V nemetskom plenu. Iz zhizni voennoplennogo* (Paris: YMCA-Press, 1987), 78 (in Russian).

35. K. M. Aleksandrov, *Ofitserskii korpus armii general-leitenanta A. A. Vlasova, 1944–1945* (St Petersburg, 2001), 31 (in Russian).

36. Beria's report, dated July 27, 1944. Document No. 271 in *Lubyanka. Stalin i NKVD*, 442.

37. Figures from the German documents cited in N. M. Ramanichev, 'Vlasov i drugie,' *Istoriya*, no. 34 (2001), http://his.1september.ru/articlef.php?ID=200103403, retrieved September 7, 2011.

38. *Materialy po istorii Russkogo Osvoboditel'nogo Dvizheniya (1941–1945 gg.).* Vyp. 2 (Moscow: Arkhiv ROA, 1998), 169 (in Russian).

39. Lev Razgon, *Nepridumannoe. Biograficheskaya proza* (Moscow: Zakharov. 2007), 477–8 (in Russian).

40. Bochkov's Order No. 46-ss, dated May 15, 1942.

41. P. G. Grigorenko, *V podpol'e mozhno vstretit' tol'ko krys…*(New York: Detinets, 1981), Chapter 23 (in Russian), http://militera.lib.ru/memo/russian/grigorenko/33.html, retrieved September 7, 2011..

42. S. S. Zamyatin, 'Vremennye boitsy' (in Russian), http://www.proza.ru/texts/2008/05/10/375.html, retrieved September 7, 2011.

Part V. The Birth of SMERSH

Chapter 16

1. NKO Order No. 25, signed by Stalin and dated January 15, 1943. Document No. 18, in *Russkii arkhiv. Velikaya otechestvennaya. Prikazy Narodnogo Komissara Oborony SSSR*, 13 (2–3), 30.

2. Letter to Stalin, dated December 19, 1944, in Winston Churchill, *Triumph and Tragedy* (New York: RosettaBooks, 2002), 260–1.

3. Politburo decision P38/3, dated July 21, 1942, and Decree of the Presidium of the Supreme Soviet, dated July 29, 1942.

4. NKO Order No. 258, dated July 30, 1943. Document No. 155, in *Russkii arkhiv. Velikaya otechestvennaya. Prikazy*, 13 (2-3), 191–2.

5. A. I. Romanov's description of Merkulov in *Nights Are Longest There: A Memoir of the Soviet Security Services*, translated by Gerald Burke (Boston: Little, Brown and Company, 1972), 55.

6. Quoted in *SMERSH. Istoricheskie ocherki i dokumenty*, edited by V. S. Khristoforov et al., 64 (Moscow: Glavnoe arkhivnoe upravlenie, 2003) (in Russian).

7. *Na prieme u Stalina. Tetradi (zhurnaly) zapisei lits, pronyatykh I. V. Stalinym (1924–1953 gg.)*, edited by A. V. Korotkov, A. D. Chernev, and A. A. Chernobaev, 401 (Moscow: Novyi khronograf, 2008) (in Russian).

8. Merkulov's letters to Stalin Nos. 334/B, 340/B, and 365/B, dated April 2, 4, and 14, 1943, respectively. The last letter is Document No. 149 in A. I. Kokurin and N. V. Petrov, *Lubyanka. Organy VCheKa-OGPU-NKVD-NKGB-MGB-MVD-KGB. 1917–1991. Spravochnik* (Moscow: Demokratiya, 2003), 621–2 (in Russian).

9. *Na prieme u Stalina*, 403.

10. Politburo decisions P40/91, dated April 14, 1943. Document No. 234 in *Lubyanka. Stalin i NKVD-NKGB-GUKR 'SMERSH.' 1939–1946*, edited by V. N. Khaustov, V. P. Naumov, and N. S. Plotnikova, 371–2 (Moscow: Demokratiya, 2006) (in Russian).

11. The new NKGB structure in Merkulov's letter and the Central Committee's decision, dated April 14, 1943. Document Nos. 149 and 150 in Kokurin and Petrov, *Lubyanka*, 621–3. The NKVD structure on January 1, 1944, in ibid., 197.

12. *Na prieme u Stalina*, 404–5.

13. Photo of the document in *SMERSH. Istoricheskie ocherki*, 67.

14. *Na prieme u Stalina*, 405.

15. Document No. 151 in Kokurin and Petrov, *Lubyanka*, 623–6.

16. *Na prieme u Stalina*, 406.

17. Abakumov's letter to Stalin No. 103/A, dated April 27, 1943, and NKO Order Nos. 1/ssh and 3/ssh, dated April 29, 1943; signed by Stalin. Photos on pages 72 and 76, *SMERSH. Istoricheskie ocherki*.

18. GKO Decision No. 3399, dated May 20, 1943. Document No. 32 in Yurii Gor'kov, *Gosudarstvennyi komitet oborony postanovlyaet (1941–1945). Tsifry, dokumenty* (Moscow: Olma-Press, 2002), 527–8 (in Russian).

19. Kokurin and Petrov, *Lubyanka*, 79.

20. Page 124 in Aleksandr Kokurin and Nikita Petrov, 'NKVD–NKGB–SMERSH: Struktura, funktsii, kadry. Stat'ya tret'ya (1941–1943),' *Svobodnaya mysl* 8 (1997), 118–28 (in Russian). Details in Vadim Abramov, *Abakumov—nachal'nik SMERSHa. Vzlet igibel' lyubimtsa Stalina* (Moscow: Yauza-ksmo, 2005), 88–98 (in Russian).

21. NKVD Order, dated May 15, 1943. Kokurin and Petrov, *Lubyanka*, 79. Details in *SMERSH. Istoricheskie ocherki*, 293–310.

22. Klim Degtyarev and Aleksandr Kolpakidi, *SMERSH* (Moscow: Yauza-Eksmo, 2009), 146 (in Russian).

23. Ibid., 147.

24. Vadim Abramov, *SMERSH. Sovetskaya voennaya razvedka protiv razvedki Tret'ego Reikha* (Moscow: Yauza-Eksmo, 2005), 135 (in Russian).

25. Joint directive of the Justice Commissar and chief USSR Prosecutor, dated August 10, 1943. Vyacheslav V. Obukhov, *Pravovye osnovy organizatsii i deyatel'nosti voennykh tribunalov voisk NKVD SSSR v gody Velikoi Otechestvennoi voiny 1941–1945 gg.* Candidate of Sciences Dissertation (Moscow: MVD Moskovskii Universitet, 2002), 122 (in Russian).

26. 'Regulations on the Main Counterintelligence Directorate of the Defense Commissariat ("Smersh") and its organs,' approved by Stalin on April 21, 1943. Document No. 151 in Kokurin and Petrov, *Lubyanka*, 623–6.

27. Ibid.

28. 'Dokladnaya zapiska V. N. Merkulova na imya N. S. Khrushcheva ot 23 iyulya 1953 g.,' in *Neizvestnaya Rossiya. XX vek. Kniga tret'ya* (Moscow: Istoricheskoe nasledie, 1993), 72 (in Russian).

29. N. V. Petrov, *Kto rukovodil organami gosbezopasnosti 1941–1954. Spravochnik* (Moscow: Zven'ya, 2010), 110 (in Russian).

30. Sergei Osipov, 'SMERSH otkryvaet tainy. Interv'ev,' *Argumenty i fakty*, no. 26 (1331), June 26, 2002 (in Russian), http://gazeta.aif.ru/online/aif/1131/09_01, retrieved September 7, 2011.

31. *SMERSH. Istoricheskie ocherki*, 75.

32. Romanov, *Nights Are Longest*, 69–70.

33. *SMERSH. Istoricheskie ocherki*, 214–5.

34 Nicola Sinevirsky, *SMERSH* (New York: Henry Holt and Company, 1950), 93–94.

35. Abakumov's report to Beria No. 650/A, dated January 1945. A photo in N. V. Gubernatorov, *SMERSH protiv Bussarda (Reportazh iz akhiva tainoi voiny)* (Moscow: Kuchkovo pole, 2005) (in Russian), between pages 192 and 193.

36. Sinevirsky, *SMERSH*, 73.

37. Romanov, *Nights Are Longest There*, 70–71.

38. *SMERSH. Istoricheskie ocherki*, 150.

39. D. P. Tarasov, *Bol'shaya igra* SMERSHa (Moscow: Yauza-Eksmo, 2010), 20–21 (in Russian).

40. *SMERSH. Istoricheskie ocherki*, 166.

41. Ibid., 186–7.

42. Tarasov, *Bol'shaya igra SMERSHa*, 20.

43. NKO Order No. 0071, dated April 19, 1943. Document No. 103 in *Russkii Arkhiv. Velikaya Otechestvennaya. Prikazy*, 13 (2–3), 124–7.

44. Ibid., 242.

45. Andreas Hilger, Nikita Petrov, and Günther Wagenlehner, 'Der "Ukaz 43": Entstehung und Problematik des Dekrets des Präsidium des Obersten Sowjets vom 19. April 1943,' in *Sowjetische Militärtribunale*, vol. 1, *Die Verurteilung deutscher Kriegsgefangener 1941–1953*, edited by Andreas Hilger, Ute Schmidt, and Günther Wagenlehner, 181–5 (Cologne: Böhlau Verlag, 2001).

46. The full text of the Decree, dated April 19, 1943, was included in the NKO Order without a number. Document No. 106 in *Russkii arkhiv. Velikaya otechest-vennaya. Prikazy*, 13 (2–3) (1997), 129–30 (in Russian). An excerpt in English is on page 106 in George Ginsburgs, 'Light Shed on the Story of *Wehrmacht* Generals in Soviet Captivity,' *Criminal Law Forum* 11 (2000), 101–20.

47. NKVD Order No. 00968, dated July 11/12, 1943, and NKVD Instruction No. 311-ss, dated June 16, 1943. Document Nos. 107 and 108 in *Istoriya stalinskogo GULAGa. Konets 1920-kh –pervaya polovina 1950-kh godov. Tom 2. Karatel'naya sistema: Struktura i kadry*, ed. by N. V. Petrov (Moscow: ROSSPEN, 2004), 220–2 (in Russian).

48. Vyacheslav Zvyagintsev, *Voina na vesakh Femidy. Voina 1941–1945 gg. v materialakh sledstvenno-sudebnykh del* (Moscow: Terra, 2006), 628 (in Russian).

49. Sinevirsky, *SMERSH*, 116–7.

50. Beria and Merkulov's joint report, dated May 20, 1943. Document No. 237 in *Lubyanka. Stalin i NKVD*, 377.

51. Vyacheslav Shevchenko, '"SMERSH" opasnee smercha,' *Leninskaya smena. Ekspress-K*, no. 81 (16229), May 11, 2007 (in Russian), http://www.express-k.kz/show_article.php?art_id=8885, retrieved September 7, 2011.

52. Abramov, *SMERSH*, 264.

Chapter 17

1. Abakumov's description in a questionnaire (*anketa*) in his Investigation File. Cited in Kirill Stolyarov, *Palachi i zhertvy* (Moscow: Olma-Press, 1997), 12 (in Russian).

2. Romanov, *Nights Are Longest*, 185.

3. A photo of Abakumov's handwritten autobiography in *SMERSH. Istorich-eskie ocherki*, 108.

4. Yevgenii Tolstykh, *Agent Nikto. Iz istorii 'SMERSH'* (Moscow: Sovershenno sekretno, 2004), 150 (in Russian).

5. If Abakumov doctored information in his biography, he was not the only one. Nikolai Yezhov hid the fact that his mother was not a Russian, but a Lithuanian. Marc Jansen and Nikita Petrov, *Stalin's Loyal Executioner: People's Commissar Nikolai Ezhov, 1895-1940* (Stanford, CA: Hoover Institution Press, 2002), 2.

6. Romanov, *Nights Are Longest*, 234.

7. B. V. Sokolov, *Narkomy strakha. Yagoda, Yezhov, Beria, Abakumov* (Moscow: Ast-Press Kniga, 2001), 304–7 (in Russian).

8. Details in V. L. Krotov, '*Chonovtsy*' (Moscow: Izdatel'stvo politicheskoi literatury, 1974) (in Russian), http://www.biografia.ru/cgi-bin/quotes.pl?oaction=show&name=material73, retrieved September 7, 2011.

9. Detailed biography of N. I. Podvoisky (1880–1948) in Leonid Mlechin, *Russkaya armiya mezhdu Trotskim i Stalinym* (Moscow: Tsetropoligraf, 2002), 170–207 (in Russian).

10. Biography of M. N. Tukhachevsky (1893–1937) with new archival materials in Yuliya Kantor, *Voina i mir Mikhaila Tukhachevskogo* (Moscow: Ogonyok, 2005) (in Russian).

11. Quoted in ibid., 255.

12. Details in Boris Sokolov, *Mikhail Tukhachevsky: Zhizn' i smert' 'Krasnogo Marshala'* (Smolensk: Rusich, 1999), 206–28 (in Russian). Tukhachevsky also planned to use chemical weapons against insurgents in March 1921 during the Kronstadt anti-Bolshevik uprising.

13. Mikhail Shreider, *NKVD iznutri: zapiski chekista* (Moscow: Vozrozhdenie, 1995), 60–61 (in Russian).

14. Boris Bazhanov, *Bazhanov and the Damnation of Stalin*, translation and commentary by David W. Doyle (Athens, OH: Ohio University Press, 1990), 167.

15. I. F. Tubala (1897-1938) joined the VCheKa in 1918; in 1937, was head of the 1st Department, Main Directorate of the Border Guards. He was arrested on October 19, 1937 and executed on June 22, 1938. Klim Degtyarev and Aleksandr Kolpakidi, *Vneshnyaya razvedka SSSR* (Moscow: Eksmo, 2009), 587 (in Russian).

16. Detailed biography of M. S. Kedrov (1878–1941) in I. V. Viktorov, *Podpol'shchik, voin, chekist* (Moscow: Politizdat, 1963) (in Russian). A short biography of Nina (Antonina) Didrikil' (1882–1953) (in Russian) at http://www.oval.ru/enc/55323.html, retrieved September 7, 2011.

17. On the Frauchi family and Artuzov, see Teodor Gladkov, *Nagrada za vernost'—kazn'* (Moscow: Tsentrpoligraf, 2000) (in Russian)..

18. Oleg Mozokhin, *VCheKa–OGPU. Na zashchite ekonomicheskoi bezopasnosti gosudarstva i v bor'be s terrorizmom* (Moscow: Yauza-Eksmo, 2004), 79–80 and 264–95 (in Russian).

19. An excerpt from Abakumov's reference written by the 1st Section of the EKO in 1934; quoted in *SMERSH. Istoricheskie ocherki*, 108.

20. Shreider, *NKVD iznutri*, 60–62.

21. Yagoda's cable, dated July 16, 1924. Document No. 107, in *Genrikh Yagoda. Narkom vnutrennikh del SSSR, General'nyi komissar gosbezopasnosti. Sbornik dokumentov* (Kazan, 1997), 323 (in Russian).

22. Igor Voshchnin and Yurii Khmelnitsky, 'Jazz v Samare: vchera i segodnya' (in Russian), http://www.vkonline.ru/toprint/15015.html, retrieved September 7, 2011.

23. Already in the 1920s, guards and OGPU officers of the first Soviet labor camp for political prisoners on Solovetsky Island, the so-called *Solovki*, as well as visiting Soviet officials, used female political prisoners as prostitutes or raped them during frequently organized orgies. A. Klinger, 'Solovetskaya katorga. Zapiski bezhavshego' (first published in 1927), in *Zarya sovetskogo pravosudiya* (London: Overseas Publications Interchange Ltd., 1991), edited by Mikhail Heller, 157–262 (in Russian).

24. Testimony of Nikolai Shatalin, MVD first deputy minister, in July 1953. Pages 176–7 in Document No. II-11 in *Lavrentii Beria. 1953. Stenogramma*

iyul'skogo plenuma TsK KPSS i drugie dokumenty, edited by V. Naumov and Yu. Sigachev, 87–218 (Moscow: Demokratiya, 1999) (in Russian).

25. Cited in Yevgenii Zhirnov, 'Na doklady v Kreml' on ezdil v mashine Gimmlera,' *Kommersant-Vlast'*, no. 19 (472), May 21, 2002 (in Russian), http://www.kommersant.ru/doc.aspx?DocsID=322678&print=true, retrieved September 7, 2011.

26. A contemporary, quoted in Mikhail Tumshis, *VChK. Voina klanov* (Moscow: Yauza-Eksmo, 2004), 288–9 (in Russian).

27. Driver Buzin's testimony during an investigation, 1953, cited in Sukhomlinov, *Kto vy, Lavrentii Beria?* (Moscow: Detektiv-Press, 2004), 188 (in Russian).

28. Arkady Vaksberg, *Stalin's Prosecutor: The Life of Andrei Vyshinsky*, translated from the Russian by Jan Butler (New York: Grove Weidenfeld, 1991), 353–4.

29. Tatyana Okunevskaya, *Tat'yanin den'* (Moscow: Vagrius, 1998), 227–8, 265 (in Russian).

30. A letter of Abakumov's wife in his Investigation File, cited in Tolstykh, *Agent Nikto*, 148.

31. Christopher Andrew and Oleg Gordievsky, *KGB:The Inside Story* (New York, Harper Collins Publishers, 1990), 342.

32. Serov's letter to Stalin, dated February 8, 1948. Document No. 29 in Nikita Petrov, *Pervyi predsedatel' KGB Ivan Serov* (Moscow: Materik, 2005), 268–73 (in Russian).

33. Peter Deryabin and Frank Gibney, *The Secret World* (Garden City, NY: Doubleday & Co., Inc., 1959), 232.

34. Shreider, *NKVD iznutri*, 62.

35. Biography of Ya. A. Deich (1898–1938) in N. V. Petrov and K. V. Skorkin, *Kto rukovodil NKVD. 1934–1941. Spravochnik* (Moscow: Zven'ya 1999). 167 (in Russian).

36. The GULAG structure on April 15, 1937. Document No. II-59 in A. I. Kokurin and N. V. Petrov, *GULAG (Glavnoe upravlenie lagerei) 1917–1960* (Moscow: Demokratiya, 2000), 235–48 (in Russian). The Secret-Operational Section with Abakumov's name is on page 239.

37. Protocol No. 21 of the Sovnarkom meeting on December 20, 1917. Document No. 1 in Kokurin and Petrov, *Lubyanka*, 302.

38. Abramov, *Abakumov*, 29–30.

39.The list at http://stalin.memo.ru/spiski/pg07005.htm, retrieved Sptember 7, 2011.

40. N. S. Khrushchev, *Vospominaniya (Kniga 1)* (Moscow: Moskovskie novosti, 1999), 27 (in Russian).

41. Izabella Yakir-Belaya was sentenced to 10 years of imprisonment. Her daughter Stella was raised in an NKVD foster home and arrested in 1948. She committed suicide in 1969. Korytnyi's son, Vladimir, committed suicide in 1960, after he found out about the fate of his parents. Three brothers of Korytnyi were also arrested from 1940-43 and shot. Ye. Sokolova and E. Veniaminova, 'Ionocka, za chto?' (in Russian), http://world.lib.ru/e/ewgenija_s/yakir.shtml, retrieved September 7, 2011.

42. A letter of R. A. Rudenko to the Central Committee, dated December 9, 1954. Document No. III-42 in *Reabilitatsiya: kak eto bylo. Dokumenty Prezidiuma*

TsK KPSS i drugie materialy. Mart 1953–fevral 1956, edited by A. Artizov et al., 184–5 (Moscow: Demokratiya, 2000) (in Russian).

43. A letter of P. V. Baranov to the Central Committee, dated March 24, 1955. Document No. IV-14 in ibid., 208–9.

44. Abakumov's official biography quoted (page 87) in Vladislav Kutuzov, 'Mertvaya petlya Abakumova,' *Rodina*, No. 3 (1998), 86–90 (in Russian).

45. Quoted in A. Kolpakidi and D. Prokhorov, *KGB. Prikazano likvidirovat'. Spetsoperatsii sovetskikh cpetssluzh 1918–1941* (Moscow: Yauza-Eksmo, 2004), 437 (in Russian).

46. Pavel Sudoplatov, *Spetsoperatsii. Lubyanka i Kreml'. 1930-1950 gody* (Moscow: Olma-Press, 1998), 392 (in Russian).

47. A photo of Abakumov's handwritten autobiography in *SMERSH. Istoricheskie ocherki*, 108.

48. Biography of B. A. Dvinsky (1894–1973) in K. A. Zalessky, *Imperiya Stalina. Biograficheskii entsiklopedicheskii slovar'* (Moscow: Veche, 2000), 138 (in Russian).

49. Mikhail Frinovsky's report, dated July 20, 1937, and the Politburo decisions P51/442, dated July 31, 1937, and P61/149, dated May 13, 1938. Document Nos. 151, 152 and 325, in *Lubyanka. Stalin i Glavnoe upravlenie gosbezopasnosti NKVD. 1937–1938*, edited by V. N. Khaustov, V. P. Naumov and N. S. Plotnikova, 273–82 and 538 (Moscow: Demokratiya, 2004) (in Russian).

50. *K shesrtidesyatiletiyu so dnya rozhdeniya tovarishcha Stalina,* edited by M. I. Kalinin (Moscow: OGIZ, 1939) (in Russian).

51. Petrov and Skorkin, *Kto rukovodil NKVD*, 80.

52. V. N. Stepakov, *Narkom SMERSHa* (St. Petersburg: Neva, 2003), 32–34 (in Russian).

53. A photo of Abakumov's handwritten autobiography in *SMERSH. Istoricheskie ocherki*, 108.

54. Attachment to the Memo dated March 1, 1940. A photo on pages 197–8 in I. Linder and N. Abin, *Zagadka dlya Gimmlera. Ofitsery SMERSH v Abvere i SD* (Moscow: Ripol klassik, 2006) (in Russian). A third of the text is blacked out.

55. Ibid., 198.

56. See http://www.memo.ru/memory/DONSKOE/d40.htm, retrieved September 7, 2011.

57. Nikolai Mesyatsev, *Gorizonty i labirinty moei zhizni* (Moscow: Vagrius, 2005), 142 (in Russian).

58. Leonid Mlechin, *Predsedateli KGB. Predsedateli organov bezopasnosti. Rassekrechennye sud'by* (Moscow: Tsentrpoligraf, 2006), 270 (in Russian).

59. Fedoseev's memoirs. Document No. I-105 in *Moskva voennaya, 1941–1945: memuary i arkhivnye dokumenty*, edited by K. I. Bukov, M. M. Gorinov, and A. N. Ponomarev (Moscow: Mosgorarkhiv, 1995), 232 (in Russian).

60. Lyudmila Kafanova, 'Palach'-zhertva,' *Chaika* [*Seagull*] (Boston), no. 24, December 16 (2005), 28–42 (in Russian).

61. Page 301 in Aleksandr Liskin's memoir 'Rasskazhet ostavshiisya v zhivykh,' in Abramov, *Abakumov*, 273–329.

62. Transcript of Kochergin's interrogation on April 24, 1952. Pages 411–2 in Document No. 206 in *Lubyanka. Stalin i MGB SSSR. Mart 1946–Mart 1953,*

edited by V. N. Khaustov, V. P. Naumov, and N. S. Plotnikova, 408–23 (Moscow: Demokratiya, 2007) (in Russian).

63. Petrov, *Kto rukovodil organami gozbezopasnosti*, 777–8. For an unknown reason, 'Romanov' described Selivanovsky under the name of 'Chernyshov.' Romanov, *Nights Are Longest*, 60, 69, 165, and 192.

64. Details in V. Rogovin, *1937* (Moscow: Moskva, 1996), Chapter 39 (in Russian), http://web.mit.edu/people/fjk/Rogovin/volume4/xxxix.html, retrieved September 7, 2011; W. G. Krivitsky, *In Stalin's Secret Service* (New York: Enigma Books, 2000), 147–9.

65. Vadim Abramov, *Kontrrazvedka. Shchit i mezh protiv Abvera i TsRU* (Moscow: Yauza-Eksmo, 2006), 70–71 (in Russian).

66. Details, for instance, in Kolpakidi and Prokhorov, *KGB prikazano likvidirovat'*, 322–41.

67. N. Cherushev, *1937 god: elita Krasnoi Armii na Golgofe* (Moscow: Veche, 2003), 205–7 (in Russian).

68. Boris Syromyatnikov, *Tragediya SMERSHa. Otkroveniya ofitsera-kontrrazvedchika* (Moscow: Yauza-Eksmo, 2009), 358–9 (in Russian).

69. Quoted in ibid., 359.

70. Recollections of Mikhail Belousov, head of a department in the OO directorate of the Stalingrad Front, in ibid., 359–60.

71. Details of the case of generals Vasilii Gordov, Grigorii Kulik, and Filipp Rybal'chenko in Rudolf Pikhoya, *Moskva. Kreml'. Vlast'. Sorok let posle voiny 1945–1985* (Moscow: AST, 2007), 59–62 (in Russian).

72. Cited in Emmanuil Ioffe, 'Lichnoe delo chekista Selivanovskogo,' *Belarus' segodnya*, No. 139, July 22, 2005 (in Russian), http://www.sb.by/post/45172, retrieved September 7, 2011.

73. An interview with Meshik's son, in Irina Ivoilova, 'Smertnyi prigovor otmenit'. Posle rasstrela,' *Trud*, No. 145, August 8, 2000 (in Russian).

74. Short biography of P. Ya. Meshik (1910–1953) in Petrov and Skorkin, *Kto rukovodil NKVD*, 297.

75. Yezhov's report, dated February 8, 1938. Document No. 290 in *Lubyanka. Stalin i Glavnoe upravlenie*, 471–84.

76. Biography of S. N. Mironov (1894–1940) in Petrov and Skorkin, *Kto rukovodil NKVD*, 301–2.

77. M. M. Yakovenko, *Agnessa. Ustnye rasskazy Agnessy Ivanovny Mironovoi-Korol'* (Moscow: Zven'ya, 1997), 29–31 (in Russian).

78. Georgii Yakovlev, "'Delo' otsa i syna,' *Pravda*, no. 48 (25766), February 17, 1989 (in Russian).

79. Testimonies of P. I. Miroshnikov and N. F. Adamov, quoted in Andrei Sukhomlinov, *Kto vy, Lavrentii Beriya?* (Moscow: Detektiv-Press, 2003), 195–203 (in Russian).

80. Ibid., 197.

81. Pages 414–5 in N. Mil'chakova, 'Pisat' vsye-taki nado!' in *Reabilitirovan posmertno*, Vypusk 2, 380–433 (in Russian).

82. Page 58 in B. S. Popov and V. T. Oppokov, 'Berievshchina,' *ViZh*, no. 10 (1991), 56–62 (in Russian).

83. Simon Sebag Montefiore, *Stalin: The Court of the Red Tsar* (New York: Alfred A. Knopf, 2004), 151.

84. Nikita Petrov, in Igor Mel'nikov, 'Kto povinen v smerti tysyach pol'skikh grazhdan,' *Belarus' segodnya*, December 18, 2008 (in Russian), http://www.sb.by/post/78592, retrieved September 8, 2011.

85. Meshik's Instruction No. A-1282, dated April 10, 1941; a report to Nikita Khrushchev, Ukrainian Party Secretary, dated April 15, 1941, and Instruction No. A-1760, dated May 31, 1941; Reports to the Ukrainian Central Committee Nos. A-1250/sn and A-1292/sn, dated April 9 and 12, 1941. Document Nos. 180-181, 184-185 and 223 in *Organy gosudarstvennoi bezopasnost v Velikoi Otechstvennoi voine. Sbornik dokumentovi. Nakanune*, T. 1 (2) (Moscow: Kniga i bizness, 1995), 82–85, 95–100, 188–92 (in Russian).

86. Excerpts cited in Genrikh Sikorsky, 'Kak eto bylo. Nachalo ispytanii,' *Kievskie vedomosti*, no. 127 (3513), June 22, 2005 (in Russian).

87. Ibid.

88. The new NKVD structure in Kokurin and Petrov, *Lubyanka*, 74–77.

89. The above-mentioned letter from Serov to Stalin regarding Abakumov, dated February 8, 1948. Page 270 in Document No. 29 in Petrov, *Pervyi predsedatel' KGB*, 268–73.

90. Page 59 in Popov and Oppokov, 'Berievshchina,' *ViZh*, no. 10 (1991).

91. A short biography of I. Ya. Babich (1902-1948) in Petrov and Skorkin, *Kto rukovodil NKVD*, 95–96.

92. Joachim Hoffmann, *Stalin's War of Extermination, 1941–1945: Planning, Realization and Documentation*, translated by William Deist (Capshaw, AL: Theses & Dissertation Press, 2001), 197.

93. *SMERSH. Istoricheskie ocherki*, 75. Biography of I. I. Vradii (1906–1984) in Petrov, *Kto rukovodil organami bezopasnosti*, 267–8; also, Yevgenii Zhirnov, 'Chisto chekistskaia chistka,' *Kommersant-Vlast'*, no. 36 (690), September 11, 2006 (in Russian).

94 . A photo of this order in *SMERSH. Istoricheskie ocherki*, 75.

95. On September 25, 1955, Ivan Vradii was promoted to Lieutenant General.

96. I. M. Leplevsky (1896–1938) headed the 5th GUGB department from December 25, 1936 till July 14, 1937. He was arrested on April 26, 1938, sentenced to death by the Military Collegium on July 28, 1938, and shot the same day. Petrov and Skorkin, *Kto rukovodil NKVD*, 270–1.

97. N. S. Cherushev, *Udar po svoim. Krasnaya Armiya 1938–1941* (Moscow: Veche, 2003), 417–23 (in Russian); Abramov, *SMERSH*, 591.

98. Sinevirsky, *SMERSH*, 140.

99. Quoted in Cherushev, *Udar po svoim*, 423.

100. In the 4th Department, Kazakevich participated, for instance, in the falsification of the case against high-level Party members who allegedly planned terrorist acts against Stalin. V. A. Agranovsky, *Poslednii dolg: Zhizn' i sud'ba zhurnalistskoi dinastii Agranovskikh* (Moscow: Academia, 1994), 19–22 (in Russian).

101. Testimony of V. I. Budarev, former OO investigator, in Cherushev, *Udar po svoim*, 191.

102. Cited in ibid., 421.

103. Ibid., 422.

104. An excerpt from the transcript of an interrogation of Sergei Goglidze, 1953, quoted in Sukhomlinov, *Kto vy, Lavrentii Beria*, 175. A short biography of N.K. Kovalchuk (1902–1972) in Abramov, *SMERSH*, 504–5.

105. Details in *SMERSH. Istoricheskie ocherki*, 78–80.

106. GKO Order dated June 15, 1943, in ibid., 78.

107. Mesyatsev, *Gorizonty i labirinty*, 126.

108. Sinevirsky, *SMERSH*, 57.

109. NKO Order No. 1-ssh, signed by Stalin and dated April 29, 1943. A photo in *SMERSH*, 72.

110. Romanov, *Nights Are Longest There*, 67.

Part VI. SMERSH in Action: 1943–1944

Chapter 18

1. Directive of GUKR SMERSH No. 49519, dated September, 1943. Appendix 1 in Klim Degtyarev and Aleksandr Kolpakidi, *SMERSH* (Moscow: Eksmo, 2009), 527–33 (in Russian).

2. NKO Order No. 319, dated December 16, 1943. Document No. 185 in *Russkii Arkhiv: Velikaya Otechestvennaya: Prikazy Narodnogo komissara oboroyy SSSR (1943–1945 gg.)*, T. 13 (2-3) (Moscow: TERRA, 1997), 233–4 (in Russian).

3. These tactics are described in Vladimir Bogomolov, *V avguste sorok chetvertogo* (Moscow: Molodaya gvardiya, 1974) (in Russian).

4. Biography of P. K. Ponomarenko (1902–1984) in K. A. Zalessky, *Imperiya Stalina. Biograficheskii entsiklopedicheskii slovar'* (Moscow: Veche, 2000), 365 (in Russian). After the war, Ponomarenko was a Central Committee secretary, then he became Soviet Ambassador to Poland, India, and the Netherlands. In 1961, Ponomarenko was deemed *persona non grata* after he participated in the kidnapping attempt of a Soviet female defector in Amsterdam and fought with Dutch police.

5. A. Yu. Popov, *Diversanty Stalina: Deyatel'nost' organov gosbezopasnosti na okkupirovannoi sovetskoi territorii v gody Velikoi Otechestvennoi voiny* (Moscow: Yauza, 2004), 34–54 (in Russian). Later, the 5th Department of the General Staff became the RU and then the GRU.

6. Literature on the Soviet partisan movement in English is vast; for instance, A. Hill, *The War Behind the Eastern Front: The Soviet Partisan Movement in North-West Russia 1941–44* (London: Frank Cass, 2005).

7. See the structure of Sudoplatov's department (later directorate), in A. I. Kokurin and N. V. Petrov, *Lubyanka. VCheKa–OGPU–NKVD–NKGB–MGB–MVD–KGB. 1917–1960. Spravochnik* (Moscow: Demokratiya, 1997), 275–76 (in Russian). and Aleksandr Kolpakidi, *Likvidatory KGB. Spetsoperatsii sovetskikh spetssluzhb 1941–2004* (Moscow: Yauza-Eksmo, 2004), 10–13 (in Russian).

8. Report by Ivan Syromolotnyi, head of the 8th Department of the Political Directorate of the Southern Front, dated March 6, 1942; quoted in Aleksandr Gogun and Anatolii Kentii, '...Sozdavat' nevynosimye usloviya dlya vraga i vsekh ego posobnikov...' *Krasnye partizany Ukrainy, 1941–1944* (Kiev: Ukrainskii izdatel'skii soyuz, 2006), 12–13 (in Russian).

9. V. I. Pyatnitsky, *Razvedshkola No. 005* (Moscow: AST, 2005) (in Russian), Chapter 1, http://militera.lib.ru/memo/russian/pyatnitsky_va/01.htmlm retrieved September 8, 2011.

10. Mentioned in NKO Order No. 00125, dated June 16, 1942. Document No. 208 in *Russkii arkhiv. Velikaya otechestvennaya. Prikazy,* 13 (2-2), 254.

11. Popov, *Diversanty Stalina,* 183–6.

12. Ibid., 91.

13. An excerpt cited in B. V. Sokolov, *Okkupatsiya. Pravda i mify* (Moscow: AST-Press, 2002), 291 (in Russian).

14. Kenneth Slepyan, 'The Soviet Partisan Movement and the Holocaust,' *Holocaust and Genocide Studies* 14, no. 1 (Spring 2000), 1–27; Leonid Smilovitsky, 'Antisemitism in the Soviet Partisan Movement, 1941–1944: The Case of Belorussia,' *Holocaust and Genocide Studies* 20, no. 2 (Fall 2006), 207–234.

15. S. G. Chuev, *Spetssluzhby III Reikha. Kniga 1* (St. Petersburg: Neva, 2003), 234–50 (in Russian).

16. V. I. Boyarsky, *Partizany i armiya. Istoriya upushchennykh vozmozhnostei* (Moscow: AST, 2001), 149 (in Russian).

17. Vyacheslav Zvyagintsev, *Voina na vesakh Femidy. Voina 1941–1945 gg. v materialakh sledstvenno-sudebnykh del* (Moscow: Terra, 2006), 498–509 (in Russian).

18. Quoted in Sokolov, *Okkupatsiya,* 291–2.

19. *The New York Times,* July 13, 1941. Reports on Czaplinski from Berlin and Philadelphia.

20. Quoted in Sokolov, *Okkupatsiya,* 292.

21. An excerpt quoted in Popov, *Diversanty Stalina,* 199.

22. Ibid., 199–200.

23. Kirill Stolyarov, *Palachi i zhertvy* (Moscow: Olma-Press), 117 (in Russian).

24. This SMERSH activity has been detailed in a series of books in Russian, including *Lubyanka 2. Iz istorii otechestvennoi kontrrazvedki,* edited by Ya. F. Pogonyi et al., 238–53 (Moscow: Mosarkhiv, 1999) (in Russian) and Vadim Telitsin, 'SMERSH': operatsii i ispolniteli (Smolensk: Rusich, 2000), 34–238 (in Russian).

25. Detailed biography of P. V. Fedotov (1901–1963) in Vadim Abramov, *Kontrrazvedka. Shchit i mech protiv Abvera i TsRU* (Moscow: Yauza-Eksmo, 2006, an electronic version), 101–30 (in Russian).

26. Memoirs by Sergei Fedoseev. Document No.106 in *Moskva voennaya, 1941–1945: memuary i arkhivnye dokumenty,* ed. by K. I. Bukov, M. M. Gorinov, and A. N. Ponomarev, 223–32 (Moscow: Mosgorarkhiv, 1995).

27. D. P. Tarasov, *Bol'shaya igra* SMERSHa (Moscow: Yauza-Eksmo, 2010), 33 (in Russian).

28 Directive of GUKR SMERSH No. 38288, dated July 16, 1943. Appendix 2 in Degtyarev and Kolpakidi, *SMERSH,* 533–5.

29. A photo of Baryshnikov's report to Abakumov, dated June 25, 1943, on page 372 in I. Linder and N. Abin, *Zagadka dlya Gimmlera. Ofitsery SMERSH v Abvere i SD* (Moscow: Ripol klassik, 2006) (in Russian).

30. *SMERSH. Istoricheskie ocherki,* 194.

31. Tarasov, *Bol'shaya igra,* 40.

32. Ibid. Photos of examples of radio messages approved by Kuznetsov in Linder and Abin, *Zagadka dlya Gimmlera,* 384 and 399.

33. Pavel Sudoplatov and Anatoli Sudoplatov, with Jerrold L. and Leona P. Schecter. *Special Tasks: The Memoirs of an Unwanted Witness—A Soviet Spymaster* (New York: Little, Brown, and Company 1994), 160.

34. Quoted in Abramov, *Abakumov*, 104. Examples of disinformation texts approved by Abakumov are given in photos of documents on pages 241–3 in *Lubyanka 2*.

35. Boris Sokolov discusses in detail Sudoplatov's inconsistencies and, apparently, inventions regarding the Operation Monastyr' by comparing Sudoplatov's memoirs with the memoirs of two other participants in the operation. B. V. Sokolov, *Okhota na Stalina, okhota na Gitlera* (Moscow: Veche, 2003) (in Russian), 121–211.

36. Telitsyn, *'SMERSH,'* 224–38.

37. Otto Skorzeny, *Skorzeny's Special Missions. The Memoirs of 'the Most Dangerous Man in Europe'* (London: Greenhill Books, 1997), 125–6.

38. Telitsyn, *'SMERSH,'* 207–14.

39. J. Otto Pohl, *Ethnic Cleansing in the USSR, 1937–1949* (Westport, CT: Greenwood Press, 1999), 63–64.

40. Politburo decision P42/235, dated December 27, 1943, in *Politburo TsK RKP(b)–VKP(b). Povestki dnya zasedanii. Tom III. 1940–1952. Katalog*, edited by Z. N. Tikhonova, 330 (Moscow: ROSSPEN, 2001) (in Russian). On the deportation of Kalmyks, see Document Nos. 152–155 in *Istoriya Stalinskogo GULAGa. Konets 1920-kh–pervaya polovina 1950-kh godov. Tom 1. Massovye repressii v SSSR*, edited by N. Werth and S. V. Mironenko, 477–81 (Moscow: ROSSPEN, 2004) (in Russian).

41. Pyatnitsky, *Razvedshkola No. 005*, Chapter 1.

42. Details, for instance, in Pohl, *Ethnic Cleansing*, 61–73.

43. A photo of a translation of part of this statement in *SMERSH. Istoricheskie ocherki*, 198. The complete text in Vladimir Galaiko, '"SMERSH" igral na korotkoi volne,' *Trud*, October 30, 2003 (in Russian).

44. Ibid.

45. Telitsin, *'SMERSH,'* 238–62.

46. E. H. Cookridge, *Gehlen: Spy of the Century* (New York: Random House, 1971), 85.

47. Ibid.

48. *Lubyanka 2*, 253–6.

49. Tarasov, *Bol'shaya igra*, 170-3.

50. On several FSB versions, see Boris Sokolov, 'Kak ubivali Stalina,' *Grani. ru*, May 12, 2009 (in Russian), http://www.grani.ru/opinion/sokolov/m.151001. html, retrieved September 8, 2011.

51. Merkulov's report No. 4126/M. quoted in Vladimir Makarov and Andrei Tyurin, '"Delo Tavrina" i radioigra "Tuman",' *Voenno-promyshlennyi kur'er*, No. 32 (248), August 13–19, 2008 (in Russian), http://vpk-news.ru/articles/5210, retrieved September 8, 2011.

52. A transcript of the interrogation in S. G. Chuev, *Spetssluzhby III Reikha. Kniga II* (St. Petersburg: Neva, 2003), 286–314 (in Russian).

53. The biography of G. N. Zhilenkov (1907–1947) in Kirill Aleksandrov, *Russkie soldaty Vermakhta. Gerio ili predateli* (Moscow: Yauza-Eksmo, 2005), 244–6 (in Russian).

54. Tarasov, *Bol'shaya igra*, 171. Alfred Backhaus worked in RSHA VI C/Z until April 1945. After the war he served in the police in Western Germany.

55. Tarasov, *Bol'shaya igra*, 172.

56. Quoted in Telitsin, *'SMERSH,'* 256.

57. Tarasov, *Bol'shaya igra*, 173.

58. Quoted in Makarov and Tyurin, 'Do poslednego.'

59. Quoted in Oleg Matveev and Sergei Turchenko, 'On dolzhen byl ubit' Stalina,' *Trud*, No. 147, August 10, 2000 (in Russian), http://www.trud.ru/issue/article.php?id=200008101470801, retrieved September 8, 2011.

60. Christer Jörgenson, *Hitler's Espionage Machine: The True Story Behind One of the World's Most Ruthless Spy Networks* (Guilford, CT: The Lyons Press, 2004), 126.

61. Aleksandr Mikhailov, 'Ubit' Stalina,' *Aeroport*, no. 8 (37), October 2007 (in Russian), http://www.rimv.ru/aeroport/37/predatel.htm, retrieved September 8, 2011.

62. These methods were described in the document written by Ukrainian nationalists in 1945 and published in Jeffrey Burds, *Sovetskaya agentura. Ocherki istorii SSSR v poslevoennye gody (1945–1948)* (Moscow: Sovremennaya istoriya, 2006), 206–38 (in Russian).

63. Zhilenkov's statement quoted in Mikhailov, 'Ubit' Stalina.' I. M. Vareikis (1894–1939) was the 1st Secretary of the the Voronezh Province Party Committee (June 1934–March 1935), then the 1st Secretary of the Stalingrad and after that, of the Far Eastern Province. On October 10, 1937 he was arrested and executed on July 29, 1939 See Zalessky, *Imperiya Stalina*, 82.

64. Recollections by Dmitrii Tarasov in Yevgenii Zhirnov, 'Na doklady v Kreml' on ezdil v mashine Gimmlera,' *Kommersant-Vlast'*, no. 19 (472), May 21, 2002 (in Russian), http://www.kommersant.ru/doc.aspx?DocsID=322678&print=true, retrieved September 8, 2011.

65. Memoirs by P. P. Stefanovsky, *Razvoroty sud'by. Kniga pervaya: Abver–SMERSH* (Moscow, 2002), 288–336 (in Russian).

66. Photos of the Coupon for Arrest No. 293 and of other documents from Gälfe's file in *Lubyanka 2*, 251–2. Also, a photo of the report on capturing Gälfe on page 437 in Linder and Abin, *Zagadkia dlya Gimmlera*.

67. Quoted in Mlechin, *KGB. Predsedateli organov bezopasnosti. Rassekrechennye sud'by* (Moscow: Tsentrpoligraf, 2006), 290 (in Russian).

68. Aleksandr Petrushin, 'Rozysk ili sysk,' *Tyumenskii kurier*, no. 1444 (2041), October 24, 2006 (in Russian), http://www.a-pesni.golosa.info/ww2/oficial/tyumen/a-rozysk.htm, retrieved September 8, 2011.

69. Ignatiev's handwritten report to Stalin, dated November 15, 1952, in Nikita Petrov, 'Pytki ot Stalina: 'Bit' smertnym boem," *Novaya gazeta. 'Pravda GULAGa,'* no. 9, October 16, 2008 (in Russian), http://www.novayagazeta.ru/data/2008/gulag09/00.html, retrieved September 8, 2011.

70. Valentin Kodachigov, 'Smert' shpionam,' *Nezavisimoe voennnoe obozrenie*, no. 15, April 25, 2004 (in Russian), http://nvo.ng.ru/spforces/2003-04-25/7_smersh.html, retrieved September 8, 2011.

71. *SMERSH. Istoricheskie ocherki*, 167.

72. Ibid., 169.

73. Quoted in V. A. Bobrenev and V. B. Ryazantsev, *Palachi i zhertvy* (Moscow: Voenizdat, 1993), 297–9 (in Russian).

74. Ibid., 268–94.

75. Cited in ibid., 314.

76. Cited in Igor Kuznetsov, 'Oplacheno krov'yu,' *Belorusskaya delovaya gazeta*, no. 1440, June 29, 2004 (in Russian).

77. An instruction quoted in Vladimir Bogomolov, 'Sram imut i zhivye, i mertvye, i Rossiya…' *Svobodnaya mysl'*—XXI, no. 7 (1995), 79–103 (in Russian), http://vivovoco.rsl.ru/vv/papers/history/bogomolov.htm, retrieved September 8, 2011.

78. Rokossovsky's order, dated January 27, 1945, cited in ibid.

79. Reports to Abakumov, dated October 30 and November 1, 1943, and Abakumov's report to Stalin, dated November 1, 1943, in N. V. Gubernatorov, *SMERSH protiv Bussarda (Reportazh z arkhiva tainoi voiny)* (Moscow: Kuchkovo pole, 2005), 143–56 (in Russian).

Chapter 19

1. *'Ognennaya duga': Kurskaya bitva glazami Lubyanki*, edited by A. T. Zhadobin, V. V. Markovchin, and V. S. Khristoforov, 25 (Moscow: Moskovskie uchebniki, 2003) (in Russian).

2. Zvyagintsev, *Voina na vesakh Femidy*, 558.

3. Report of A. S. Shcherbakov to Stalin, dated May 22, 1943. Document No. 238 in *Lubyanka. Stalin i NKVD–NKGB–GUKR 'Smersh.' 1939–March 1946*, edited by V. N. Khaustov, V. P. Naumov, and N. S. Plotnikova, 377–85 (Moscow: 2006) (in Russian).

4. Ibid., 382–3.

5. Yakov Aizenstadt, *Zapiski sekretarya voennogo tribunala* (London: Overseas Publication Interchange Ltd., 1991), 69 (in Russian).

6. The above-cited Shcherbakov's report, 383.

7. Ibid., 384.

8. NKO Order No. 0089-ss, dated May 31, 1943. Document No. 240 in *Lubyanka. Stalin i NKVD*, 385–6.

9. Ibid., 384.

10. Zvyagintsev, *Voina na vesakh Femidy*, 294.

11. Lidiya Golovkova, *Sukhanovskaya tyur'ma. Spetsob'ekt 110* (Moscow: Vozvrashchenie, 2009), 96–97 (in Russian).

12. Details of Paulus's surrender in I. A. Laskin, *Na puti k perelomu* (Moscow: Voenizdat, 1977), 322–34 (in Russian).

13. From unpublished memoirs by Ivan Laskin, quoted in Aleksandr Rud', 'Moi general,' *Literaturnyi Krym*, no. 17–18 (164–165), May 27, 2005 (in Russian), http://lit-crimea.narod.ru/164-167/rud17-20.html, retrieved September 8, 2011.

14. 'Ivan Laskin' (in Russian), http://militarytimes.com/citations-medals-awards/recipient.php?recipientid=22918, retrieved September 8, 2011.

15. Aleksei Teplyakov, 'Chekist dlya Soyuza pisatelei,' *Politicheskii zhurnal*, no. 11-12 (154-155), April 2, 2007 (in Russian).

16. An excerpt from Teplinsky's letter to Marshal Aleksandr Vasilevsky, dated June 4, 1953. Quoted in Vyacheslav Zvyagintsev, *Tribunal dlya 'stalinskikh sokolov'* (Moscow: Terra, 2008), 356 (in Russian).

17. Abakumov's report, dated April 1, 1944. Quoted in B. V. Sokolov, *Razvedka. Tainy Vtoroi mirovoi voiny* (Moscow: Ast-Press, 2001), 196–201 (in Russian).

18. Quoted in ibid., 202–3.

19. Quoted in ibid., 180.

20. Soviet biographers of Marshal Vasilii Sokolovsky do not mention Sokolovsky's failure. See M. Cherednichenko, 'Marshal Sovetskogo Soyuza Vasilii Sokolovskii,' in *Polkovodtsy i voennonachal'niki Velikoi Otechestvennoi. Vypusk 1* (Moscow: Molodaya gvardiya, 1971), 331–71 (in Russian), http://militera.lib.ru/bio/commanders1/10.html, retrieved September 8, 20011.

21. NKO Order No. 0379, dated November 23, 1944. Document No. 268, in *Russkii arkhiv. Velikaya Otechestvennaya. Prikazy*, 13 (2-3), 332 (in Russian).

22. P. G. Grigorenko., *V podpol'e mozhno vstretit' tol'ko krys...*(New York: Detinets, 1981), 294–306 (in Russian).

23. V. M. Shatilov, *A do Berlina bylo tak daleko...*(Moscow: Voenizdat, 1987), 324 (in Russian).

24. Page 741 in Mikhail Shmulev, 'Pochemu ya ne prazdnuyu Den' pobedy,' *Golosa Sibiri. Vypusk vtoroi* (Kemerovo: Kuzbassvuzizdat, 2005), 738–49 (in Russian).

25. Pages 299–300 in Anna Timofeeva-Yegorova, *Nebo, 'shturmovik,' devushka. 'Ya—"Beryoza"! Kak slyshite menya?...'* (Moscow: Yauza-Eksmo, 2007) (in Russian).

26. Zvyagintsev, *Tribunal dlya 'stalinskikh sokolov,'* 130.

27. Recolections by Nikolai Bogdanov, in M. I. Veller, *Kavaleriiskii marsh* (St. Petersburg: Lan', 1996) (in Russian), Chapter 7, http://militera.lib.ru/prose/russian/veller1/01.html, retrieved September 8, 2011.

28. Zvyagintsev, *Tribunal dlya 'stalinskikh sokolov,'* 136–8. A. I. Pokryshkin (1913–1985) was the only pilot who became a Hero of the Soviet Union three times.

29. V. N. Stepakov, *Narkom SMERSHa* (St. Petersburg: Neva, 2003), 95.

30. *SMERSH. Istoricheskie ocherki*, 6.

31. A. Kokurin and N. Petrov, 'NKVD–NKGB–SMERSH: struktura, funktsii, kadry. Stat'ya chetvertaya (1944-1945),' *Svobodnaya mysl'*, No. 9 (1997), 97–101 (in Russian).

32. B. V. Sokolov, *Beria. Sud'ba vsesil'nogo narkoma* (Moscow: Veche, 2003), 167–70 (in Russian).

33. Valerii Yaremenko, '"I kolesa stuchat, i telegarmmy letyat..." K godovshchune deportatsii chechenskogo naroda,' *Polit.ru*, February 23, 2006 (in Russian), http://www.polit.ru/article/2006/02/23/checheviza/, retrieved Septmber 8, 2011.

34. Eduard Abramyan, *Kavkaztsy v Abvere* (Moscow: Yauza, 2006), 116 (in Russian).

35. Details in Yaremenko, 'I kolesa stuchat, i telegarmmy letyat...'

36. Abramyan, *Kavkaztsy v Abvere*, 118–28.

37. Details in Hans von Herwarth and Frederick Starr, *Against Two Evils* (New York: Rawson & Wade, 1981), 228–39.

38. Sokolov, *Beria*, 152–64.

39. Quoted in ibid., 162.

40. Document Nos. 156–165 in *Istoriya Stalinskogo GULAGa. Tom 1*, 481–94, and Nos. 3.111-3.136 in *Stalinskie deportatsii*, 443–76.

41. GKO Order Nos. 5073-ss and 5074-ss dated January 31, 1944. Document Nos. 3.111 and 3.112 in ibid., 443–7.

42. Interview with Nikolai Tolkachev, former NKVD officer, on May 25, 2009, http://www.iremember.ru/drugie-voyska/tolkachev-nikolay-fomich.html, retrieved September 8, 2011.

43. Excerpts from various NKVD reports in Yurii Stetsovsky, *Istoriya sovetskikh repressii*, T. 1 (Moscow: Znak-SP, 1997), 460–4 (in Russian).

44. Sokolov, *Beria*, 165–6.

45. Document Nos. 156–169 in *Istoriya Stalinskogo GULAGa. Tom 1*, 481–6, and Nos. 3.136–3.145 in *Stalinskie deportatsii*, 477–91.

46. Document Nos. 166–174 in *Istoriya Stalinskogo GULAGa. Tom 1*, 494–505, and Nos. 3.146–3.170 in *Stalinskie deportatsii*, 494–522.

47. Herwarth and Starr, *Against Two Evils*, 238.

48. Document Nos. 3.172–3.183 in *Istoriya Stalinskogo GULAGa. Tom 1*, 525–40.

Chapter 20

1. Lawrence D. Stokes, 'From Law Student to Einsatzgruppe Commander: The Career of a Gestapo Officer,' *Canadian Journal of History* 37, no. 1 (April 2002), 41–73. Details about the activity of Einsatzgruppe D in Andrej Angrick, *Besatzungspolitik und Massenmord. Die Einsatzgruppe D in der südlichen Sowjetunion 1941–1943* (Hamburg: Hamburger Edition 2003).

2. *SMERSH.Istoricheskie ocherki*, 315. The ChGK was created on November 2, 1942 and consisted of Shvernik (Chairman); Andrei Zhdanov, a Politburo member; Academicians Nikolai Burdenko, Boris Vedeneev, Trofim Lysenko, Yevgenii Tarle, and Ivan Trainin; the writer Aleksei Tolstoi; a female pilot, Valentina Grizodubova; and the clergyman Metropolitan Nikolai of Kiev. The ChGK played mostly the propaganda role and concealed the anti-Jewish Nazi racial policy and falsely ascribed the Katyn massacre to the Nazis. Marina Sorokina, 'People and Procedures: Towards a History of the Investigation of Nazi Crimes in the USSR,' *Kritika: Explorations in Russian and Eurasian History* 6, no. 4 (Fall 2005), 797–831.

3. *The People's Verdict: A Full Report of the Proceedings of the Krasnodar and Kharkov German Atrocity Trials* (London: Hutchinson & Co., 1944), 7–44. Also, Ilya Bourtman, '"Blood for Blood, Death for Death": The Soviet Military Tribunal in Krasnodar, 1943,' *Holocaust and Genocide Studies* 23, no. 2 (Fall 2008), 246–65.

4. The defendants: I. F. Kladov, I. F. Kotomtsev, M. P. Lastovina, G. N. Misan, Y. M. Naptsok, V. S. Pavlov, I. I. Paramonov, N. S. Pushkarev, I. A.Rechkalov, V. P. Tishchenko, and G. P. Tuchkov.

5. *The People's Verdict*, 21.

6. Executed: Kladov, Kotomtsev, Lastovina, Misan, Naptsok, Pushkarev, Rechkalov, and Tishchenko. See two Soviet documentaries about the trial and execution at http://www.history-vision.de/detail/2702.html and http://www.history-vision.de/detail/3164.html, retrieved September 8, 2011.

7. Alexander Werth, *Russia at War, 1941–1945* (New York: E. P. Dutton & Co., 1964), 732.

8. For instance, the memoir by the American prosecutor Benjamin B. Ferencz, *A Visionary for World Peace, Chapter 4. Story 33. The Biggest Murder Trial in History*, http://www.benferencz.org/index.php?id=8&story=32, retrieved September 8, 2011.

9. *Nazi Mass Murder: A Documentary History of the Use of Poison Gas*, edited by Eugen Kogon, Hermann Langbein, and Adalbert Ruckerl, 69–71 (New Haven, CT: Yale University Press, 1993).

10. Bernie Farber, 'Painfully slow court system gives war criminals free pass,' *The Star*, February 16, 2010, http://www.thestar.com/Article/764817, retrieved September 8, 2011.

11. On January 31, 1943, Lieutenant General Arthur Kurt Schmidt was taken prisoner along with Field Marshal von Paulus and his other generals. On June 24, 1950 the Military Tribunal of the Moscow Military District sentenced him as a war criminal to 25 years' imprisonment. On September 25, 1953 he was repatriated to Germany. Schmidt's MVD card in I. V. Bezborodova, *Generaly Vermakhta v plenu* (Moscow: Rossiiskii gosudarstvennyi gumanitarnyi universitet, 1998), 172 (in Russian).

12. Document No. 80 in *Stalingradskaya epopeya: Vpervye publikuemye dokumenty, rassekrechennye FSB* (Moscow: Zvonnitsa, 2000), 354–63 (in Russian).

13. *Moscow Conference, October 1943. Joint Four-Nation Declaration*, http://www.yale.edu/lawweb/avalon/imt/moscow.htm, retrieved January 5, 2011.

14. *SMERSH. Istoricheskie ocherki*, 316–7.

15. Ibid., 317.

16. The English translation of the document UK-81 in *Nazi Conspiracy and Aggressio*. Vol. VIII (USGPO: Washington, 1946), 572–82; http://www.ess.uwe.ac.uk/genocide/USSR2.htm, retrieved September 8, 2011.

17. Details in George M. Nipe, Jr., *Last Victory in Russia: The SS–Panzer–Korps and Manstein's Kharkov Counteroffensive, February–March 1943* (Atglen, PA: Schiffer Publishing, 2000).

18. Charles W. Sydnor, Jr., *Soldiers of Destruction: The SS Death's Head Division 1933–1945* (8 ed.) (Princeton: Princeton University Press, 1990), 269.

19. Curzio Malaparte, *Kaputt*, translated from the Italian by Cesare Foligno (New York: E. P. Dutton and Company, 1946), 19–20.

20. Gerald Reitlinger, *The SS: The Alibi of a Nation, 1922–1945* (New York: Viking Press, 1957), 196.

21. *SMERSH. Istoricheskie ocherki*, 317–8.

22. Soviet documentaries on the trial and execution of the condemned at http://www.history-vision.de/detail/1705.html, http://www.history-vision.de/detail/3162.html, and http://www.history-vision.de/detail/3163.html, retrieved September 8, 2011.

23. *The People's Verdict*, 48–49.

24. Ibid., 65–66.

25. Ibid., 68–69.

26. Ibid., 78.

27. Ibid., 85–86.

28. For instance, Yitzhak Arad, *Belzec, Sobibor, Treblinka—The Operation Reinhard Death Camps.* (Bloomington, ID: Indiana University Press, 1987).

29. Karl Pfeifer, 'Zum Feifer- und Bedenkjahr 2005: Patriotische Einleitung,' http://www.hagalil.com/archiv/2005/01/einleitung.htm, retrieved September 8, 2011.

30. *The People's Verdict*, 89.

31. Ibid., 90.

32. Arthur Koestler, *The Yogi and the Commissar* (New York: Macmillan, 1945), 143.

33. 'Pattern of Hanging,' *Time*, December 27, 1943. The American and British officials were cautious about the information on the trial because of the Nazi threat to retaliate against the Allied POWs. Arieh J. Kochavi, *Prelude to Nuremberg: Allied War Crimes Policy and the Question of Punishment* (Chapel Hill, NC: The University of North Carolina Press, 1998), 69–73.

34. 'On the mass shooting of Jews by the German murderers in the Drobitzki Valley. Protocol. September 5, 1943,' http://www.jewishvirtuallibrary.org/jsource/Holocaust/Kharkov.html, retrieved September 8, 2011.

35. Report of Major General I. M. Grishaev, commander of the Political Department of the 60th Army, dated January 29, 1945. Cited in Pavel Polyan, 'Otvet na evreiskii vopros,' *Novaya gazeta*, no. 6, January 28, 2008 (in Russian), http://www.novayagazeta.ru/data/2008/06/17.html, retrieved September 8, 2011.

36. *The People's Verdict*, 95–99.

37. Ibid., 121.

38. Yurii Zainochkovsky, 'Kharkovskii prolog Nyurenberga,' *Sobytie*, No. 52, December 25–31, 2003 (in Russian), http://www.interami.com/2003-213.html, retrieved January 5, 2011.

39. NKO Order No. 74, dated May 29, 1944. Document No. 221 in *Russkii arkhiv. Velikaya Otechestvennaya. Prikazy*, 13 (2-3), 282.

40. Recollections by Nikolai Belov, who defended Mikhail Bulanov, in Zinovii Sagalov, 'Protsess v Kharkove—prelyudiya k Nurenbergu,' http://z-sagalov.narod.ru/publi_process.html, retrieved September 8, 2011.

41. Birstein, *The Perversion of Knowledge*, 88–92.

42. A. N. Trainin, *The Criminal Responsibility of the Hitlerites* (Moscow: Yuridicheskoe izdatel'stvo, 1944), discussed in George Ginsburgs, *Moscow's Road to Nuremberg: The Soviet Background of the Trial* (The Hague: Kluwer Law International, 1996), 71–90, and Francine Hirsch, 'The Soviets at Nuremberg: International Law, Propaganda, and the Making of the Postwar Order,' *American Historical Review* 113, no. 3 (June 2008), 701–30.

43. 'Kharkov Trial. First Pictures From Russian Movie Show Legal Trial and Death of Nazi War Criminals,' *Life*, July 10, 1944, p. 94.

44. Producer Irvin Shapiro, commentary written by John Bright and naarated by Everett Sloane. See 'At the Little Carnegie,' *New York Times*, June 4, 1945; 'The New Pictures,' *Time*, June 4, 1945, http://www.time.com/time/magazine/article/0,9171,775791,00.html, retrieved September 8, 2011.

45. The archive of the US Holocaust Memorial Museum has a copy of Heinisch's SMERSH Investigation File from the FSB Central Archive, RG-06.025*02 Kiev, 1945–1946 (N-18762, tom 4), Georg Josef Heinisch.

46. Jantschi's Personal File, RGVA, Moscow. Also, Jantschi's and Karl Kosch's prisoner cards in Vladimir Prison Archive.

47. *SMERSH. Istoricheskie ocherki*, 318–20.

48. The Burdenko report falsely stated that German troops were responsible for the Katyn massacre. Details in *Katyn: A Crime Without Punishment*, edited by Anna M. Cienciala, Natalia S. Lebedeva, and Wojcech Materski (New Haven, CT: Yale University Press, 2007), 226–9.

49. Frank Ellis, 'Dulag-205: The German Army's Death camp for Soviet Prisoners at Stalingrad,' *The Journal of Slavic Military Studies* 19, no. 1 (March 2006), 123–48.

50. Special report by N. G. Khannikov to Abakumov, dated December 20, 1944. Document No. 25 in *Tragediya Litvy: 1941–1944 gody. Sbornik arkhivnykh dokumentov o prestupleniyakh litovskikh kollabortsionistov v gody Vtoroi mirovoi voiny* (Moscow: Evropa, 2006), 122–4 (in Russian).

51. Ibid., 321.

52. Poliburo decisions P47/107 snd P47/132, dated November 10 and 21, 1945. Document Nos. 330 and 332 in *Lubyanka. Stalin i NKVD*, 543–4 (in Russian). The commission consisted of Andrei Vyshinsky (chairman), deputy Foreign Minister; Nikolai Rychkov (deputy chairman); Konstantin Gorshenin, USSR Prosecutor; Ivan Golyakov, chair of the Supreme Court; Sergei Kruglov, first deputy NKVD Commissar; Abakumov; and Nikolai Afanasiev, Chief Military Prosecutor.

53. Alexander Victor Prusin, '"Fascist Criminals to the Gallows!": The Holocaust and Soviet War Crimes Trials, December 1945–February 1946,' *Holocaust and Genocide Studies* 17 (2003), no. 1, 1–30.

54. On the Remlinger Trial see Chapter 5 in I. S. Jažbovskaja, A. Yu. Yablokov, and V. S. Parasadanova, *Katynskii syndrome v sovetsko-pol'skikh otnosheniyakh* (Moscow: Materik, 2005) (in Russian); Diere's 'testimony' was mentioned in 'Two Nazi Generals Hanged by Russians,' *The New York Times*, December 31, 1945.

55. The other condemned to death were Karl Hermann Strüfling, Ernst Böhm, Fritz Engel, Eduard Sonnenfeld, Gerhard Jahnicke, Erwin Skotki, and Ernst Gehrer. Soviet documentaries about the trial and execution of the condemned at http://www.history-vision.de/detail/3177.html and http://www.history-vision.de/detail/3178.html, retrieved January 6, 2011.

56. Politburo decision P59/200, dated September 10, 1947. *Politburo TsK RKP(b)*, 489; Nikita Petrov, 'Prestupnyi kharakter stalinskogo rēgima: yuridicheskie osnovaniya,' *Polit.ru,* November 19, 2009 (in Russian), http://www.polit.ru/lectures/2009/11/19/stalin.html#pin16, retrieved September 8, 2011.

57. Report of N. Rychkov, K. Gorshenin and S. Kruglov to Molotov and Stalin, dated November 4, 1947. GARF, Fond R-9401, Opis' 2 (Molotov's NKVD/MVD Special Folder), Delo 174, Ll. 234–7.

Part VII. Toward Berlin

Chapter 21

1. Stalin's Order No. 70, dated May 1, 1944, page 187 in I. V. Stalin, *Sochineniya*, T. 15 (Moscow: Pisatel', 1997), 185–8 (in Russian).

2. Nicola Sinevirsky, *SMERSH* (New York: Henry Holt & Co., 1950), 62–63.

3. Wilhelm Hoettl, *The Secret Front: The Story of Nazi Political Espionage* (New York: Frederick A. Praeger, 1954), 182. On Ion Antonescu (1882–1946), see Dennis Deletant, *Hitler's Forgotten Ally: Ion Antonescu and His Regime, Romania 1940–1944* (New York: Palgrave Macmillan, 2006).

4. Details in transcripts of Stahel's interrogations in GUKR SMERSH on April 28 and August 25, 1945. Document Nos. 79 and 80 in *Generaly i ofitsery Vermakhta rasskazyvayut…Dokumenty iz sledstvennykh del nenetskikh voennoplennykh. 1944–1951*, edited by V. G. Makarov and V. S. Khristoforov (Moscow: Demokratiya, 2009), 387–402 (in Russian).

5. Hoettl, *The Secret Front*, 188; Michael Bloch, *Ribbentrop* (London: Bantam Press, 1992), 411.

6. Quoted in 'German Diplomats in Bucharest after 23 August, 1944,' *Radio Romania International*, July 8, 2009, http://www.rri.ro/arh-art. shtml?lang=1&sec=9&art=22271, retrieved September 8, 2011.

7. 'Turkey: Advance Man's Retreat,' *Time*, October 13, 1941.

8. Elizabeth W. Hazard, *Cold War Crubicle: United States Foreign Policy and the Conflict in Romania. 1943–1953* (Boulder, CO: East European Monographs, 1996), 40–81.

9. Later Frank Wisner became CIA station chief in London, chief of the CIA's Office of Policy Coordination, and the CIA's deputy director of plans. In 1965, he suffered a nervous breakdown and committed suicide.

10. Hazard, *Cold War Crubicle*, 44–45.

11. Shlomo Aronson, *Hitler, the Allies, and the Jews* (New York: Cambridge University Press, 2004), 162–6.

12. *The Secret War Report of the OSS*, edited by Anthony Cave Brown, 286 (New York: Berkley Publishing Corporation, 1976).

13. Hazard, *Cold War Crubicle*, 60.

14. An interview with Lawrence Houston, cited in ibid., 196, and a speech by Allen Dulles on May 4, 1959, quoted in Richard Harris Smith, *The OSS: The Secret History of America's First Central Intelligence Agency* (Berkeley, CA: University of California Press, 1972), 118.

15. On SOE operations in Romania see Alan Ogden, *Through Hitler's Back Door: SOE Operations in Hungary, Slovakia, Romania and Bulgaria 1939–1945* (Barnsley, South Yorkshire: Pen & Sword Military, 2010), 197–263.

16. Bradley F. Smith, *Sharing Secrets with Stalin: How the Allies Traded Intelligence, 1941–1945* (Lawrence, KS: University Press of Kansas, 1996), 20–26; Martin Kitchen, 'SOE's Man in Moscow,' *Intelligence and National Security* 12, No. 3 (July 1997), 95–109.

17. Smith, *Sharing Secrets with Stalin*, 254.

18. Quoted (page 395) in B. D. Yurinov, "Ternistyi put' sotrudnichestva," in *Ocherki istorii rossiiskoi vneshnei razvedki. T. 4. 1941–1945 gody* (Moscow: Mezhdunarodnye otnosheniya, 1999), 385–98 (in Russian).

19. Testimony of Max Braun on September 10, 1947. Page 324 in Document No. 43 in *Generaly i ofitsery Vermakhta*, 217–20.

20. The Romanians handed over several members of the mission, including Colonel Hans Schwickert, to the NKVD—not SMERSH—operatives. Yevgenii Zhirnov, 'Prints skryl svoyu nastoyashchiuiu familiyu,' *Kommersant-Vlast'*, no. 14 (668), April 10, 2006 (in Russian), http://www.kommersant.ru/doc. aspx?DocsID=664971, retrieved September 8, 2011.

21. Stavka's directive No. 220218, dated September 17, 1944. Document No. 24 in *Russkii Arkhiv. Velikaya Otechestvennaya* 14, no. 3 (2), 107–8 (in Russian).

22. Interrogation of Max Braun, dated September 10, 1947. Page 220 in Document No. 43 in *Generaly i ofitsery Vermakhta rasskazyvayut.*

23. Marie Vassilchikov, *Berlin Diaries, 1941–1945* (New York: Vintage Books, 1988), 25–27, 46, 54, 82–88, 95, 150, and Giles MacDonogh, *A Good German: Adam von Trott zu Solz* (Woodstock, NY: The Overlook Press, 1992), 26, 97, 127, 164, 168, 170, 182, 215, 283.

24. Kurt Welkisch and his wife Margarita (alias *LZL*) belonged to the Alta group that also included Ilse Stebe, Gerhard Kegel, and Rudolf von Scheliha (alias *Ariets*). Details in Vladimir Lota, *'Alta' protiv 'Barbarossa'* (Moscow: Molodaya gvardiya, 2004) (in Russian).

25. In 2001, recollections of Gerhard Stelzer translated into Romanian were published: Rolf Pusch and Gerhard Steltzer, *Diplomati Germani la Bucuresti, 1937–1944* (Bucharest: Editura All Educational, 2001).

26. Shtemenko, *General'nyi shtab*, 359.

27. Report of Malinovsky and Susaikov, dated September 2, 1944, Document No. 29 in *Russkii arkhiv. Velikaya Otechestvennaya. Krasnaya Armiya v stranah tsentral'noi, severnoi Evropy i na Balkanakh' 1944–1945. Dokumenty i materialy,* T. 14 (3–2) (Moscow: Terra, 2000), 38–39 (in Russian).

28. Boris Syromyatnikov, 'Sorok shest' chasov s rumynskim diktatorom,' *Voenno-promyshlennyi kur'er,* No. 40 (October 17–23, 2007) (in Russian). Also, a photo of the first page of Abakumov's report No. 753/A to Beria, dated June 1945, in *SMERSH. Istoricheskie ocherki*, 90.

29. Transcripts of interrogations in the Romanian File, RG–05.025, US Holocaust Memorial Museum (a photocopy of the File H–19767, three volumes, kept in the FSB Central Archive in Moscow).

30. Page 146 in ibid.

31. Details in Radu Ioanid, *The Holocaust in Romania: The Destruction of Jews and Gypsies under the Antonescu Regime, 1940–1944* (Chicago, IL: Ivan R. Dee, 2000).

32. Page 526 in the File H–19767 and Hugh Seton-Watson, *The East European Revolution* (New York: Frederick A. Praeger, 1951), 205.

33. 'Razboiul anti-URSS a fost legitim,' *Ziua*, 20 February 2007 (in Romanian).

34. During WWI, Baron Sergei N. Delvig (1866–1944?) commanded an artillery unit. From 1917–20, he served in the Ukrainian Army. In 1920, Delvig emigrated to Romania.

35. Abakumov's report to Beria No. 606/A, dated November 22, 1944. A photo of the report in *SMERSH. Istoricheskie ocherki*, 142.

36. Cited in Dmitri Volkogonov, *Triumf i tragedia. Politicheskii portret I. V. Stalina.* Kniga 2 (Moscow: Agenstvo pechati Novosti, 1989), 24 (in Russian). This cable was not included in the English version of Volkogonov's book.

37. Unto Parvilahti, *Beria's Gardens: Ten Years' Captivity in Russia and Siberia,* translated from the Finnish by Alan Blair (London: Hutchinson & Co., 1959), 54.

38. Shtemenko, *General'nyi shtab*, 360.

39. The awarded Soviet military leaders: I. S. Stalin (twice), A. M. Vasilevsky (twice), G. K. Zhukov (twice), A. I. Antonov, L. A. Govorov, I. S. Konev, R. Ya. Malinovsky, K. A. Meretskov, K. K. Rokossovsky, S. K. Timoshenko, and F. I. Tolbukhin. Additionally,

on February 20, 1978, Leonid Brezhnev received this award; however, on September 21, 1989 Mikhail Gorbachev abolished the decision to award Brezhnev.

40. The awarded foreigners: US Army General Dwight D. Eisenhower (June 5, 1945), British Field Marshal Bernard Montgomery (June 5, 1945), King Mihai I (July 6, 1945), Polish Marshal Michał Rola-Żymierski (August 9, 1945), and Yugoslavian Marshal Josip Broz Tito (September 9, 1945).

41. Cited in Craig S. Smith. 'Romania's King Without a Throne Outlives Foes and Setbacks,' *The New York Times*, January 27, 2007.

42. Robert Lee Wolff, *The Balkans in Our Time* (Cambridge, MA: Harvard University Press, 1974), 242–8.

43. Michael Bar-Zohar, *Beyond Hitler's Grasp: The Heroic Rescue of Bulgaria's Jews* (Holbrook, MA: Adams Media Company, 1998), 46–48.

44. Vojtech Mastny, *Russia's Road to the Cold War: Diplomacy, Warfare, and the Politics of Communism, 1941–1945* (New York: Columbia University Press, 1979), 202–3.

45. Details in Yelena Valeva, 'Politicheskie protsessy v Bolgarii, 1944–1948 gg.,' '*Karta*,' no. 36-37 (2003), 48-59 (in Russian), http://www.hro.org/node/10845, retrieved September 8, 2011.

46. In September 1944, the Communist authorities liquidated about 18,000 arrestees without trial. *Vostochnaya Evropa v dokumentakh rossiiskikh arkhivov, 1944–1953 gg. Tom 1. 1944–1948 gg.*, edited by T. V. Volokitina et al., 150–1 (Moscow: Sibirskii khronograf, 1997) (in Russian).

47. Document Nos. 28 and 30, in *Vostochnaya Evropa*, 101, 104–5.

48. Bogdana Lazorova, 'Cherveniyat teror 1944–1949 g.,' *DARIK News*, May 6, 2006 (in Bulgarian), http://www.dariknews.bg/view_article.php?article_id=63793, retrieved September 8, 2011. Overall, from December 20, 1944 until the end of April 1945, the Bulgarian people's courts tried 11,122 political defendants, and of these, 2,730 were sentenced to death, 1,305 were convicted to life imprisonment, and the rest, to various terms of imprisonment.

49. Nadezhda and Maiya Ulanovskie, *Istoriya sem'i* (New York: Chalidze Publications, 1982), 212 (in Russian).

50. Report by Claudio de Mohr, former Italian Cultural Counselor, in Agne Hamrin, 'Ännu en Moskgafänge vittnar om Wallenberg: Svenskarna kränktes om skyddsuppdrag,' *Dagens Nyheter*, September 1, 1953. Also, a statement by Adolf Heinz Beckerle, former German Minister to Sofia, to the Swedish authorities, dated April 15, 1957. I am grateful to Susanne Berger for these references.

51. Shtemenko, *General'nyi shtab*, 375–6.

52. *The Secret War Report of the OSS*, edited by Anthony Cave Brown, 290–1 (New York: Berkley Publishing Corporation, 1976) 1.

53. Vladimir Antonov, 'Syn protiv otsa,' *Nezavisimoe voennoe obozrenie*, September 16, 2005 (in Russian), http://nvo.ng.ru/spforces/2005-09-16/7_syn.html, retrieved September 8, 2011.

54. V. G. Chicheryukin-Meingardt, *Drozdovtsy posle Gallipoli* (Moscow: Reittar, 2002), 66–79 (in Russian).

55. A. V. Okorokov, *Russkaya emigratsiya. Politicheskie, voenno-politicheskie i voinskie organizatsii, 1920–1990 gg.* (Moscow: Azuar Consulting, 2003), 81–82 (in Russian).

56. Vadim Abramov, *SMERSH. Sovetskaya voennaya razvedka protiv razvedki Tret'ego Reikha* (Moscow: Yauza-Eksmo, 2005), 213 (in Russian).

57. Details in Stanislav J. Kirschbaum, *History of Slovakia: The Struggle for Survival* (New York: Palgrave Macmillan, 2005), 205–25.

58. Vladimir Lota, *Informatory Stalina. Neizvestnye operatsii sovetskoi voennoi razvedki. 1944–1945* (Moscow: Tsetrpolitgraf, 2009), 216-27 (in Russian).

59. On SOE involvement in the Uprising, see Ogden, *Through Hitler's Back Door*, 62–84.

60. Report about Šmidke's mission to Stalin, dated August 10, 1944, and a Russian translation of Čatloš's letter to the Soviet leaders. Document No. 1 in *Russkii Arkhiv. Velikaya Otechestvennaya*, 14 (3–2), 478–82.

61. Details in Ján Stanislav, 'Mocnosti protifašisickej koalície a ozbrojený zápas v SNP,' in *Humanisické tradície v literárnom odkaze Slovenskeho národého povstania* (Banská Bystrica, Slovakia: Štátna vedecká knižnica, 2004), 18–42 (in Slovakian), http://www.snp.sk/docs/zbornik.pdf, retrieved September 8, 2011.

62. Jan Loyda's letter to the commandant of Vladimir Prison, dated January 28, 1953, from his personal file (page 78). A copy in the *Riksarkivet Utrikesdepartementet* (RA UD, Archive of the Swedish Ministry for Foreign Affairs), Stockholm.

63. On January 8, 1947, representatives of the 3rd MGB Main Directorate handed Čatloš in Prague over to the Czechoslovak authorities. From Čatloš's prisoner card at the Military Archive in Moscow.

64. 'Jozef Turanec' (in Czech), http://forum.valka.cz/viewtopic.php/p/186621#186621, retrieved September 8, 2011.

65. Peter B. Vlčko and Ryan P. Vlčko, 'The Soviet Union's Role in the Slovak National Uprising. The Talsky Affair: Incompetent, Traitor or Pawn?' (2005), 34, http://sitemaker.umich.edu/ryanvlcko/files/soviet_role_in_the_slovak_national_uprising__snp_.pdf, retrieved September 8, 2011.

66. Parvilahti, *Beria's Gardens*, 75.

67. On the NSNP see Boris Pryanishnikov, *Novopokolentsy* (Silver Spring, MD: Multilingual Typesetting, 1986) (in Russian).

68. Aleksandr Kolpakidi, *Likvidatory KGB. Spetsoperatsii soverskikh spetssluzhb, 1941–2004* (Moscow: Yauza-Eksmo, 2004), 286 (in Russian).

69. Shulgin published a series of memoirs in Russian, but only one was translated into English: V. V. Shulgin, *The Years: Memoirs of a Member of the Russian Duma, 1906–1917*, translated by Tanya Davis (New York: Hippocrene Books, 1984).

70. See SMERSH's documents on Shulgin's arrest in *Tyuremnaya odisseya Vasiliya Shulgina. Materialy sledstvennogo dela i dela zaklyuchennogo*, edited by V. G. Makarov, A. V. Epnikov, and V. S. Khristoforov, 135–42 (Moscow: Knizhnitsa, 2010) (in Russian).

71. Details in A. Kolpakidi and D. Prokhorov, *KGB: Prikazano likvidirovat'. Spetsoperatsii sovetskikh spetssluzhb 1918–1941* (Moscow: Yauza, 2004), 215–28 (in Russian).

72. Boris Koverda (1907–1987), a Russian emigrant, targeted Pyotr Voikov (1888–1927) for assassination because in 1917, Voikov participated in the decision to liquidate Nicholas II and his family. The Polish Extraordinary Court sentenced Koverda to life in prison, but in 1937 he was amnestied. After

WWII, Koverda emigrated to the United States, where he lived and died near Washington, DC.

73. A photo of Abakumov's report No. 759/A dated June 1945. *SMERSH*, 90.

74. Yu. B. Mordvinov, *Belogvardeitsy. Avtobiograficheskaya povest'* (2001), 95–109 (in Russian).

75. Pavel Kutepov was released in 1954. He was not permitted to live in Moscow and settled down in the city of Ivanovo. In 1960, he was hired by the Moscow Patriarchate as a translator and moved to Moscow. In 1967, Kutepov was promoted to head of the Translation Bureau of the Foreign Affairs Church Department of the Moscow Patriarchate. He died in 1983. Shulgin was released on September 14, 1956, but he was allowed to live only in Vladimir. His wife came from abroad to join him. He died on February 15, 1976 and was rehabilitated on November 12, 2001.

76. A photo of the first page of Abakumov's report to Beria No. 684/A dated March 1945, *SMERSH. Istoricheskie ocherki*, 150.

77. Memoirs by Yevgenii Popov, former RU translator, cited in Vladimir Lota, *Informatory Stalina. Neizvestnye operatsii sovetskoi voennoi razvedki. 1944–1945* (Moscow: Tsentrpoligraf, 2009), 317–20 (in Russian).

78. Atzel's statement to the officers of the Political Directorate of the 46th Army, dated November 27, 1944. Document No. 33 in *Russkii Arkhiv. Velikaya Otechestvennaya*, 14 (3–2), 331–5.

79. On van der Waals's story in Budapest see Karoly Kapronczay, *Refugees in Hungary: Shelters from Storm During World War II*, translated by Eva Barcza-Bessenyey (Toronto: Matthias Corvinus Publishing, 1999), 198–203; on SOE in Hungary see Ogden *Through Hitler's Back Door*, 23–61, 90–93.

80. Report by Folke Persson, Swedish Consul in New York, to the Swedish Foreign Ministry about a conversation with Karl Schandl, dated February 7, 1958. In *Raoul Wallenberg—A Collection of Documents* (Stockholm: Utrikesdepartement), Vol. 42 (the collection does not include a year of publication or page numbers).

81. Sinevirsky, *SMERSH*, 183.

82. Report of Major Petrovsky, assistant head of the 2nd Department, UKR SMERSH, 2nd Ukrainian Front, dated January 23, 1945. Raoul Wallenberg's Document Database (RWDD), *Riksarkivet Utrikesdepartementet* (RA UD, Archive of the Swedish Ministry for Foreign Affairs), Stockholm.

83. On Raoul Wallenberg's background and his work in Budapest, see Jenö Lévai, *Raoul Wallenberg: His Remarkable Life, Heroic Battles and the Secret of His Mysterious Disappearance*, translated into English by Frank Vajda (Melbourne: University of Melbourne, 1989) and Paul A. Levine, *Raoul Wallenberg in Budapest: Myth, History and Holocaust* (London: Valentine Mitchell, 2010).

84. T. Kushner, 'Rules of the Game: Britain, America and the Holocaust in 1944,' *Holocaust and Genocide Studies* 5, no. 4 (1990), 381–402.

85. Document Nos. 18 and 74 in *Dokumenty vneshnei politiki. 1940–22 iyunya 1941*, Tom 23, Kniga 1 (Moscow: Mezhdunarodnye otnosheniya, 1998) (in Russian), and Document No. 804 in ibid., Tom 23, Kniga 2 (2) (Moscow: Mezhdunarodnye otnosheniya, 1998), 634–6 (in Russian).

86. Copies of military reports and orders regarding Raoul Wallenberg and Jan Spišjak, Max Meier and Harald Feller (RWDD, RA UD, Stockholm).

87. Cable to Commander of the 30th Rifle Corps, dated January 14, 1945 (RWDD, RA UD, Stockholm).

88. Ibid.

89. Zakharov's cable No. 987 to Bulganin (RWDD, RA UD, Stockholm).

90. Bulganin's order to Zakharov and Abakumov (cable No. 5533/sh), dated January 17, 1945 (RWDD, RA UD, Stockholm).

91. Wallenberg's prisoner card from the FSB Central Archive (RWDD, RA UD, Stockholm).

92. Note to Lt. Colonel Ryndin, head of the Operational Group of the 2nd Ukrainian Front in Budapest, dated January 22, 1945 (RWDD, RA UD, Stockholm).

93. Zakharov's cable No. 1619 to Bulganin, dated January 25, 1945 (RWDD, RA UD, Stockholm).

94. Special Annex to *Bulletin No. XXXII* (1945), 8. Courtesy by Lovice Maria Ullein-Reviczky, Antal Ullein-Reviczky Foundation (Hungary).

95. Bulganin's cable to Zakharov No. 1367/sh, dated January 27, 1945 (RWDD, RA UD, Stockholm).

96. Information released by the Russian participants of the Swedish-Russian Working Group on Raoul Wallenberg on April 14–15, 1993.

97. Nicholas Nyaradi, *My Ringside Seat in Moscow* (New York: Thomas Y. Crowell Co., 1952), 221.

98. Details in Krisztián Ungváry, *The Siege of Budapest: One Hundred Days in World War II*, translated from the Hungarian by Ladislaus Löb (New Haven, CT: Yale University Press, 2003), 339–63;

99. Nyaradi, *My Ringside Seat*, 222. An analysis of atrocities in James Mark, 'Remembering Rape: Divided Social Memory and the Red Army in Hungary 1944–1945,' *Past and Present*, no. 188 (August 2005), 133–61.

100. Report of the Swiss Legation in Budapest in the spring of 1945. Appendix III in John Flournoy Montgomery, *Hungary—The Unwilling Satellite* (New York: Devin-Adair Co., 1947), http://www.hungarianhistory.com/lib/montgo/montgo21.htm, retrieved September 8, 2011.

101. Letter of Mikhail Vetrov to Vladimir Dekanozov, dated May 24, 1945 (RWDD, RA UD, Stockholm).

102. Special Annex to *Bulletin No. XXXII* (1945), 8.

103. *SMERSH. Istoricheskie ocherki*, 159.

104. Cable to 'Director' (Ivan Il'ichev, head of the GRU), dated March 2, 1943, quoted in Shandor Rado, *Pod psevdonimom Dora* (Moscow: Voenizdat, 1973), 203–4 (in Russian).

105. Quoted in Ignác Romsics, *István Bethlen: A Great Conservative Statesman of Hungary, 1974-1946* (Boulder, CO: Social Science Monographs, 1995), 385.

106. A report by G. S. Zhukov to the Central Committee, dated April 17, 1944. Document No. 5 in *Sovetskii factor v Vostochnoi Evrope. 1944–1963. Tom 1. 1944–1948. Dokumenty*, edited by T. V. Volokitina, G. P. Murashko, and A. F. Noskova (Moscow: Rosspen, 1999), 56–58 (in Russian).

107. See Wlodzimierz Borodziej, *The Warsaw Uprising of 1944*, translated by Barbara Harshow (Madison, WI: University of Wisconsin Press, 2006).

108. Directive of the HQ of the NKVD rear guard troops of the 3rd Belorussian Front, dated August 25, 1944. Quoted on page 198 in P. A. Aptekar', 'Vnutrennie voiska NKVD protiv pol'skogo podpol'ya (Po dokumentam Rossiiskogo gosudarstvennogo voennogo arkhiva),' in *Repressii protiv polyakov i pol'skikh grazhdan*, edited by A. E. Gur'yanov (Moscow: Zven'ya, 1997), 197–206 (in Russian).

109. Stavka's directive, dated August 2, 1944. Document No. 9, Chapter 4 in *Russkii Arkhiv. Velikaya otechestvennaya. SSSR i Pol'sha: 1941–1945. K istorii voennogo soyuza. Dokumenty i materialy*, T. 14 (3–1), edited by V. A. Zolotarev, 334–35 (Moscow: TERRA, 1994) (in Russian).

110. GKO Order on Poland, dated July 31, 1944. Quoted in *NKVD i pol'skoe podpol'e (Po 'Osobym papkam' I. V. Stalina)*, edited by A. F. Noskova, 12 (Moscow: Institut slavyanovedeniya, 1994) (in Russian).

111. Nikita Petrov, *Pervyi predsedatel' KGB Ivan Serov* (Moscow: Materik, 2005), 21–31 (in Russian).

112. Serov's report to Beria, dated October 16, 1944. Forwarded to Stalin and Molotov. Document No. 5 in *NKVD i pol'skoe podpol'e*, 37–42.

113. An excerpt cited as a note to Document No. 5 in ibid., 38.

114. Serov's report to Beria, dated October 26, 1946. Document No. 9 in *NKVD i pol'skoe podpol'e*, 55–58.

115. Quoted in Andrei Blinushov, 'Takikh lagerei predstoit mnogo...,' '*Karta*,' no. 2, 5–6 (in Russian), http://www.hro.org/files/karta/02/p05.jpg, retrieved September 8, 2011. A detailed examination of the torture methods used by the Soviet and Polish investigators in Marek Jan Chodakiewicz, 'The Dialectics of Pain: The Interrogation Methods of the Communist Secret Police in Poland, 1944–1955,' *Glaukopis*, 2/3 (2004–2005). One of the victims described 39 methods of torture that he was subjected to.

116. Beria's report to Stalin, dated October 29, 1944. Document No. 10 in *NKVD i pol'skoe podpol'e*, 58–59.

117. Document Nos. 16, 104, and 128 in N. S. Lebedeva, N. A. Petrosova, B. Woszcynski et al., *Katyn. Mart 1940 g.—sentyabr 2000 g. Rasstrel. Sud'by zhivykh. Ekho Katyni. Dokumenty*, 66, 219–21 and 275–9 (Moscow: Ves' Mir, 2001) (in Russian).

118. Cable to Beria, dated September 3, 1944, and Document No. 11 in *NKVD i pol'skoe podpol'e*, 59–65.

119. The same cable to Beria, dated September 3, 1944.

120. Cable to Beria, dated November 8, 1944. Document No. 12 in *NKVD i pol'skoe podpol'e*, 65–71.

121. N. Ye. Yeliseeva et al., 'Katalog eshelonov s internirovannymi polyakami, otpravlennymi v glub' SSSR,' in *Repressii protiv polyakov*, 215–25.

122. Cable to Beria, dated approximately November 13, 1944. Document No. 15 in *NKVD i pol'skoe podpol'e*, 77–81.

123. Yeliseeva et al., 'Katalog eshelonov.'

124. O. A. Zaitseva and A. E. Gur'yanov, 'Dokumenty TsKhIDK ob internirovanii pol'skikh grazhdan v SSSR v 1944–1949 gg.,' in *Repressii protiv polyakov*, 226–47.

125. Beria's cover letter to Abakumov and Tsanava's report, dated November 14, 1944. Document No. 16 in *NKVD i pol'skoe podpol'e*, 82–83.

Chapter 22

1. NKVD Order No. 0016, dated January 11, 1945. Document No. 1 in *Spetsial'nye lagerya NKVD/MVD SSSR v Germanii. 1945–1950 gg. Sbornik dokumentov i stsatei*, edited by S. V. Mironenko, 11–14 (Moscow: ROSSPEN, 2001) (in Russian).

2. N. V. Petrov, 'Apparat upolnomochennogo NKVD–MGB SSSR v Germanii (1945–1953 gg.),' in *Spetsial'nye lagerya NKVD/MVD*, 349–66.

3. On the Nazi underground resistance see Perry Biddiscombe, *The SS Hunter Battalions: The Hidden History of the Nazi Resistance Movement 1944–45* (Tempus, 2006).

4. Quoted on page 311 in V. A. Kozlov, 'Deyatel'nost' upolnomochennykh i operativnykh grupp NKVD SSSR v Germanii v 1945–1946 gg.,' in *Spetsial'nye lagerya NKVD/MVD*, 311–30.

5. Abakumov's report, dated January 15, 1945, quoted in Kozlov, 'Deyatel'nost' upolnomochennykh,' 315.

6. According to the above-cited NKVD Order No. 0016, dated January 11, 1945.

7. Tsanava's Order No. 10ss, dated January 22, 1945. Document No. 4 in *Apparat NKVD-NKGB v Germanii, 1945–1953*, edited by N. Petrov and Ya. Foitsekh, 62–63 (Moscow: Demokratiya, 2009) (in Russian).

8. Abakumov's report, dated February 15, 1944, cited in Antony Beevor, *The Fall of Berlin 1945* (New York: Viking, 2002), 96–98.

9. Quoted in ibid., 98.

10. Paul Born, *Smertnik Vostochnogo fronta, 1945. Agoniya III Reikha* (Moscow: Yauza-Press, 2009), 79–80 (in Russian, translated from the German).

11. Leonid Rabichev, 'Voina vse spishet,' *Znamya*, no. 2 (2005) (in Russian), http://magazines.russ.ru/znamia/2005/2/ra8-pr.html, retrieved September 8, 2011.

12. Quoted in Petrov, *Pervyi predsedatel' KGB*, 44.

13. Stavka's directive No. 11072, dated April 20, 1945. Quoted in Mark Solonin, *Net blaga na voine* (Moscow: Yauza-Press, 2010), 242–3 (in Russian).

14. Details of the Solzhenitsyn case, including a number of documents from his file, in Kirill Stolyarov, *Palachi i zhertvy* (Moscow: Olma-Press, 1997), 333–49 (in Russian).

15. Aleksandr I. Solzhenitsyn, *The Gulag Archipelago, 1918–1956: An Experiment in Literary Investigation, Volumes One and Two*, translated from the Russian by Thomas P. Whitney (New York: Harper & Row, 1973), 164.

16. Details in Pavel Polyan, *Ne po svoei vole…Istoriya i geografiya prinuditel'nykh migratsii v SSSR* (Moscow: OGI-Memorial, 2001), 191–216 (in Russian).

17. Details in ibid., 189–90.

18. GKO Order No. 7467-ss, dated February 3, 1945. An excerpt quoted in ibid., 211.

19. Ibid., 213–6.

20. A photo of Abakumov's report to Beria, dated March 10, 1945 in *SMERSH*, 91.

21. Tkachenko's report to Beria, dated March 17, 1945. Document No. 301 in *Lubyanka. Stalin i NKVD–NKGB–GUKR 'Smersh.' 1939–mart 1946*, edited by

V. N. Khaustov, V. P. Naumov, and N. S. Plotnikova, 502–4 (Moscow: Materik, 2006) (in Russian).

22. NKVD Order No. 00453, dated May 5, 1945. Document No. 4 in *Spetsial'nye lagerya NKVD/MVD*, 18–19.

23. M. I. Semiryaga, *Kak my upravlyali Germaniei: politika i zhizn'* (Moscow: ROSSPEN, 1995), 161–2 (in Russian).

24. Beria's report No. 438/b, dated April 17, 1945. Document No. 2 in *Spetsial'nye lagerya NKVD/MVD*, 14–16.

25. V. A. Kozlov, 'Deyatel'nost' upolnomochennykh i operativnykh grupp NKVD SSSR v Germanii v 1945–1946 gg.,' in *Spetsial'nye lagerya NKVD/MVD*, 321.

26. NKVD Order No. 00315, dated April 18, 1945. Document No. 3 in *Spetsial'nye lagerya NKVD/MVD*, 16–18.

27. A. Von Plato (253–254), 'Sovetskie spetslagerya v Germanii,' in *Spetsial'nye lagerya NKVD/MVD*, 245–87.

28. NKVD Order No. 00461, dated May 10, 1945. Document No. 5 in *Spetsial'nye lagerya NKVD/MVD*, 19–25.

29. The above-cited NKVD Order No. 00315.

30. Alfred J. Reiber, 'Zhdanov in Finland,' *The Carl Beck Papers*, no. 1107 (1995), 1–81.

31. Edvard Hamalainen, 'Uzniki Leino,' *Russkaya mysl'* (Paris), no. 4371, July 5, 2001 (in Russian), http://www.kolumbus.fi/edvard.hamalainen/docs/uzniki. htm, retrieved September 8, 2011. From 1948 to 1951, G. M. Savonenkov (1898–1975) was Soviet Ambassador to Finland.

32. Major General Sergei Kozhevnikov was Abakumov's assistant in charge of the Leningrad Front and head of the Inspection (SMERSH group) at the Allied Control Commission in Finland. N. V. Petrov, *Kto rukovodil organami gosbezopasnosti 1941–1954* (Moscow: Zven'ya, 2010), 471–2 (in Russian). Possibly, Kolesnikov was Kozhevnikov's operational name.

33. Abakumov's report to Beria, dated May 1945; a photo of the letter in *SMERSH. Istoricheskie ocherki*, 143.

34. Kirill Aleksandrov, *Russkie soldaty Vermakhta. Geroi ili predateli* (Moscow: Yauza/Eksmo, 2005), 31 and 37 (in Russian). Aleksandrov refers to numerous documents from the Military Archive in Helsinki.

35. Abramov, *SMERSH*, 219–20.

36. Parvilahti, *Beria's Gardens*, 21.

37. Eleonora Ioffe-Kemppainen, 'Karl Gustav Emil Mannerheim—marshal i prezident,' *Zvezda*, no. 9 (1999) (in Russian), http://karelkurs.narod.ru/files/kgm. en.html, retrieved September 8, 2011.

38. Quoted in Hamalainen, 'Uzniki Leino.'

39. Dmitrii Prokhorov, 'Tragediya kronshtadtskogo "myatezhnika",' *Sovershenno sekretno—versiya v Pitere*, no. 8 (March 3, 2002) (in Russian).

40. P. Bazanov, 'Prokuror i ruka s ruporom,' *Rodina*, no. 4 (2009) (in Russian), http://www.istrodina.com/rodina_articul.php3?id=2976&n=141, retrieved January 24, 2011.

41. W. G. Krivitsky, *In Stalin's Secret Service* (New York: Enigma Books, 2000), 209.

42. Jussi Pekkarinen and Juha Pohjonen, *Poshchady ne budet. Peredacha voennoplennykh i bezhentsev iz Finlyandii v SSSR, 1944–1981* (Moscow: ROSSPEN, 2010), 39 (in Russian).

43. Ibid., 29.

Chapter 23

1. Mikhail Koryakov, *I'll Never Go Back*, translated from the Russian by Nicholas Wreden (London: George G. Harrap & Co., 1948), 59–61.

2. Zhukov's orders to the 1st and 2nd Tank Armies on April 20), quoited in O. A. Rzheshevsky, 'Poslednii shturm: Zhukov ili Konev,' *Mir istorii*, no. 5 (2001) (in Russian), http://militera.lib.ru/research/rzheshevsky1/02.html, retrieved September 9, 2011.

3. Table on page 171 in G. F. Krivosheev et al., *Velikaya Otechestvennaya bez grifa sekretnosti. Kniga poter'* (Moscow: Veche, 2009) (in Russian).

4. Shtemenko, *General'nyi shtab*, 424–6, 436

5. G. K. Zhukov, *Vospominaniya i razmyshleniya* Vol. 2 (Moscow: OLMA-Press, 2002), 330–2 (in Russian).

6. Antony Beevor, *The Fall of Berlin 1945* (New York: Viking, 2002), 403–5.

7. Memoirs by Lyushen'ka Glushkova, the NKVD cook (the NKVD had its own schools for cooks) in Tat'yana Romashenkova, 'Lichnyi povar Zhukova,' *Rossiiskaya gazeta*, no. 3768, May 13, 2005 (in Russian), http://www.rg.ru/2005/05/13/povar.html, retrieved September 9, 2011.

8. GKO Order No. 8377ss, dated May 2, 1945. Document No. 306 in *Lubyanka. Stalin i NKVD*, 511.

9. An interview with Colonel Ivan Klimenko in Yekaterina Sazheneva and Yurii Rabotin, 'Ispoved' posle smerti,' *Moskovskii komsomolets*, May 7, 2005 (in Russian).

10. Details in James P. O'Donnell, *The Bunker: The History of the Reich Chancellery Group* (New York: Da Capo Press, 2001), 177–215.

11. Traudl Junge, *Until the Final Hour: Hitler's Last Secretary*, translated from the German by Anthea Bell (New York: Arcade Publishing, 2004), 180–1.

12. Details in ibid. and Joachim Fest, *Inside Hitler's Bunker: The Last Days of the Third Reich* (Farrar, Straus and Giroux, 2004).

13. Ye. M. Rzhevskaya, *Berlin, mai 1945: Zapiski voennogo perevodchika* (Moscow: Voennaya literatura, 1986), 146 (in Russian).

14. Details in Martyn Merzhanov, *Tak eto bylo (poslednie dni fashistskogo Berlina)* (Moscow: Izdatel'stvo politicheskoi literatury, 1975) (in Russian), http://lib.ru/MEMUARY/WEGER/merzhanow.txt, retrieved September 9, 2011.

15. An interview with L. G. Ivanov in Il'ya Zubko, 'Tovarishch polkovnik, ya Gebbelsa nashel!', *Samara segodnya*, May 8, 2005, http://news.samaratoday.ru/news/57530/, retrieved September 9, 2011.

16. Rzhevskaya, *Berlin*, 73–75.

17. For instance, Ada Petrova and Peter Watson, *The Death of Hitler: The Full Story with New Evidence from Secret Russian Archives* (New York: W. W.Norton and Company, 1995).

18. Rzhevskaya, *Berlin*, 86–156.

19. Weidling's testimony on May 8, quoted in Vladimir A. Kozlov, *'Gde Gitler?'* *Povtornoe rassledovanie NKVD–MVD SSSR obstoyatel'stv ischeznoveniya Adolfa Gitlera* (1945–1949) (Moscow: Tri kvadrata, 2003), 48 (in Russian).

20. Rzhevskaya, *Berlin*, 154.

21. Ibid., 158–9.

22. Photos of fragments of Hitler's and Braun's jaws in *Hitler's Death: Russia's Last Great Secret from the Files of the KGB*, edited by J. E. Pogonyi et al., 97–98 (London: Chaucer Press, 2005).

23. Mark Benecke, 'Hitler's Skull and Teeth,' *Annals of Improbable Research* 9 (2003), no. 2, 9–10; http://wiki.benecke.com/index.php?title=2003_AIR:_Hitler%C2%B4s_Skull_%26_Teeth, retrieved September 9, 2011.

24. This group included Rattenhuber, Voss, Weidling, Möhnke, and Wilhelm Eckhold, head of Goebbels's guards.

25. Rzhevskaya, *Berlin*, 171–2. Dr. Hugo Blaschke was captured by the Americans and released in 1948.

26. Shkaravsky's medical report in Lev Bezymensky, *Operatsiya 'Mif,' ili skol'ko raz khoronili Gitlera* (Moscow: Mezhdunarodnye otnosheniya, 1995), 92–98, 121 (in Russian).

27. Rzhevskaya, *Berlin*, 173–4.

28. Abakumov's letter to Beria, dated June 22, 1945, quoted in Petrov, *Pervyi predsedatel' KGB*, 60–61.

29. Kozlov, *Gde Gitler?*, 66–67; the report by Vadis, in Bezymensky, *Operatsiya 'Mif,'* 111–7.

30. An interview with Vasilii Gorbushin in ibid., 121.

31. Rzhevskaya, *Berlin*, 453–4.

32. Klimenko's recollections quoted in Boris Sokolov, *Neizvestnyi Zhukov: Portret bez retushi v zerkale epokhi* (Minsk: Rodiola-Plus, 2000), 545–6 (in Russian).

33. K. Simonov, *Glazami cheloveka moego pokoleniya* (Moscow: Izdatel'stvo APN, 1988), 414 (in Russian).

34. R. C. Raack, 'With Smersh in Berlin: New Light on the Incomplete Histories of the Führer and the Vozhd',' *World Affairs* 154, no. 2 (1991), 47–55.

35. Photos on pages 114–5 in *Hitler's Death*. Also, reports in Bezymensky, *Operatsiya 'Mif,'* 162–7.

36. Uki Gonui, 'Tests on Skull Fragment Cast Doubt on Adolf Hitler Suicide Story,' *The Observer*, September 27, 2009, http://www.guardian.co.uk/world/2009/sep/27/adolf-hitler-suicide-skull-fragment, retrieved September 8, 2011.

37. Details in Kozlov, *Gde Gitler?*, 168–76.

38. Boris Khavkin, '"Satrap" i general "Prezus",' *Nezavisimoe voennoe obozrenie*, February 4, 2006 (in Russian), http://nvo.ng.ru/history/2006-02-03/5_paulus.html, retrieved September 9, 2011.

39. The English version: *The Hitler Book: The Secret Dossier Prepared for Stalin from Interrogations of Otto Guensche and Heinz Linge, Hitler's Personal Aides*, edited by Henrik Ederle and Matthias Uhl, translated from German by Giles MacDonogh (New York: PublicAffairs, 2005).

40. Documents on the Operation 'Archive' in *Hitler's Death*, 331–7.

41. Vladislav Kramar, 'Gruppa v Drezdene byla nebol'shaya, no moshchnaya,' *Voenno-promyshlennyi kur'er*, no. 47 (114), December 14–20 (2005), 7 (in Rus-

sian), http://vpk-news.ru/site_media/pdf/issue_114.pdf, retrieved September 9, 2011.

42. Quoted in Petrov, *Pervyi predsedatel' KGB*, 49.

43. Details in Aleksandrov, *Russkie soldaty Vermakhta,* 319–56. c

44. Romanov, *Nights Are Longest There,* 150.

45. The date of Schörner's arrest on his prisoner card in Vladimir Prison Archive.

46. Nicola Sinevirsky, *SMERSH* (New York: Henry Holt and Company, 1950), 141–2.

47. For instance, Catherine Andreyev and Ivan Savicky, *Russia Abroad: Prague and the Russian Diaspora, 1928–1939* (New Haven, CT: Yale University Press, 2004).

48. Sinevirsky, *SMERSH,* 163.

49. Dolgorukov's prisoner card from Vladimir Prison Archive.

50. Quoted in Tatiyana Galanshina, Igor Zakurdaev and Sergei Loginov, *Vladimirskii tsentral* (Moscow: Eksmo, 2007), 74 (in Russian).

51. A note on Pyotr Dolgorukov's prisoner card, the Vladimir Prison Archive.

52. Lyudmila Bobrovskaya, 'Rozhdenie i gibel' Russkogo Arkhiva v Prage,' *Russkii zhurnal,* October 3 (2003) (in Russian), http://old.russ.ru/ist_sovr/20031003_bobrov.html, retrieved September 9, 2011.

53. Romanov, *Nights Are Longest,* 150.

54. Report to the Military Council of the 1st Ukrainian Front signed by Major General Fominykh and Colonel Zubkov. Document No. 129 in *Russkii Arkhiv. Velikaya Otechestvennaya. Bitva za Berlin. Dokumenty i materially,* T. 15 (4–5) (Moscow: Terra, 1995), 170–2 (in Russian).

55. Document No. 128 in *Russkii Arkhiv. Velikaya Otechestvennaya. Bitva za Berlin,* T. 15 (4–5) (Moscow, Terra, 1995), 170.

56. M. I. Yakushev, 'Kak ya vykral generala Vlasova,' *Argumenty i fakty,* No. 19 (May 1996) (in Russian).

57. Cited in O. S. Smyslov, *General Abakumov. Vsesil'nyi khozyain SMERSHa* (Moscow: Veche, 2005), 273 (in Russian).

Chapter 24

1. André Brissaud, *Canaris* (Garden City, NY: Grosset & Dunlap, 1974), 297.

2. Heinz Hohne, *Canaris,* translated from the German by J. Maxwell Brownjohn (Garden City, NY: Doubleday & Co., Inc., 1970), 528–30.

3. David Kahn, *Hitler's Spies: German Military Intelligence in World War II* (New York: Collier Books, 1978), 268–71.

4. Stolze's statement during an interrogation in the MGB, dated July 14, 1947, quoted in Julius Madder, *Hitlers Spionagegenerale sagen aus* (Berlin: Verlag der Nation, 1977), 419, 441–8.

5. Hohne, *Canaris,* 555–99; Michael Mueller, *Canaris: The Life and Death of Hitler's Spymaster,* translated by Geoffrey Brooks (Annapolis, MD: Naval Institute Press, 2007), 251–8.

6. Quoted in André Brissaud, *Canaris,* translated and edited by Ian Colvin (London: Weidenfeld and Nicolson, 1973), 331.

7. S. G. Chuev, *Spetssluzhby tret'ego reikha* (St. Petersburg: Neva, 2003), Kniga I, 21–22 (in Russian).

8. Bentivegni's personal card in the Vladimir Prison Archive.

9. Streckenbach's prisoner card in the Vladimir Prison Archive.

10. Julius Madder, *Hitlers Spionagegenerale* (Berlin: Verlag der Nation, 1979), 131–3.

11. Quoted in Aleksandr Beznasyuk and Vyacheslav Zvyagintsev, *Tribunal. Arbat, 37 (dela i lyudi)* (Moscow: Terra, 2006), 111–2 (in Russian).

12. Madder, *Hitlers Spionagegenerale*, 419, 441–8. Also, sitting at Nuremberg, Fifty-Sixth Day: Monday, 11th February, 1946, http://www.nizkor.org/hweb/imt/tgmwc/tgmwc-06/tgmwc-06-56-12.html, retrieved September 9, 2011.

13. Prisoner cards of Piekenbrock, Bentivegni and Streckenbach in the Vladimir Prison archive.

14. *The Service: The Memoirs of General Reinhard Gehlen*, translated by David Irving (New York: World Publishing, 1972), 98.

15. Details in James H. Critchfield, *Partners at the Creation: The Men Behind Postwar Germany's Defense and Intelligence Establishments* (Annapolis, MD: Naval Institute Press, 2003), 28–32.

16. Documents in *The CIA and Nazi War Criminals*, edited by Tamara Feinstein, February 4, 2005, http://www.gwu.edu/~nsarchiv/NSAEBB/NSAEBB146/index.htm, retrieved September 9, 2011.

17. Linda Hunt, *Secret Agenda: The United States Government, Nazi Scientists, and Project Paperclip, 1945 to 1990* (New York: St. Martin's Press, 1991), 205.

18. Critchfield, *Partners at the Creation*, 33, 116–8.

19. Paul B. Brown, 'Analysis of the Name File of Wilhelm Krichbaum,' http://www.archives.gov/iwg/declassified-records/rg-263-cia-records/rg-263-krichbaum.html; Norman J. W. Goda, 'CIA Files Relating to Heinz Felfe, SS Officer and KGB Spy,' http://www.fas.org/sgp/eprint/goda.pdf, both retrieved on September 9, 2011.

20. Dmitrii Ivanov, 'Veteran razvedki Vitalii Korotkov: "Kurta" obmenyali na tselyi avtobus zapadnykh shpionov,' *Izvesiya*, December 20, 2007 (in Russian).

21. Kirill Aleksandrov, *Russkie soldaty Vermakhta. Geroi ili predateli* (Moscow: Yauza-EKSMO, 2005), 195–9 (in Russian).

22. Chuev, *Spetssluzhby*, I, 254–73.

23. Photo on page 121 in *SMERSH. Istoricheskie ocherki*.

24. Chuev, *Spetssluzhby*, I, 263–4.

25. Aleksandrov, *Russkie soldaty*, 236–9.

26. Quoted in ibid., 237.

27. N. Tolstoi, *Zhertvy Yalty* (Paris: YMCA-Press, 1988), 435 (in Russian).

28. Yefim Barban, 'Russkii soyuznik nemtsev,' *Ogonyok*, no. 21, May 19–25, 2009 (in Russian).

29. 'Argentina: Last of the Wehrmacht,' *Time*, April 13, 1953.

30. General Holmston-Smyslowsky, 'Lichnye vospominaniya o generale Vlasove,' *Suvorovets*, nos. 30–38, August–October 1949, http://m.shkuro.webnode.com/products/gjen-kholmston-smyslovskij-lichnyje-vospominanija-o-gjenjeralje-vlasovje-/, retrieved September 9, 2011.

Part VIII. The End of the Wor

Chapter 25

1. GKO Order No. 6594, dated September 24, 1944. Quoted in Viktor Cherepanov, *Vlast' i voina. Stalinskii mekhanizm gosudarstvennogo upravleniya v Velikoi Otechestvennoi voine* (Moscow: Izvestia, 2006), 329 (in Russian).

2. Ibid., 435.

3. *SMERSH. Istoricheskie ocherki i dokumenty,* edited by V. S. Khristoforov et al., 214–5 (Moscow: Glavnoe arkhivnoe upravlenie, 2003) (in Russian).

4. Document 6 (Indictment of the Austrian composer, Hans Hauska) in *'Vernite mne svobodu!' Deyateli literatury i iskusstva Rossii i Germanii—zhertvy stalinskogo terrora,* edited by V. F. Kolyazin and V. A. Goncharov, 118–9 (Moscow: Medium, 1997) (in Russian).

5. Vladimir Abarinov, 'A report of Doctor Smoltsov,' *Novoe vremya,* No. 1 (1993), 40–41 (in Russian).

6. A notarized testimony of Count Adelmann about Raoul Wallenberg given to the Swedish authorities on February 6, 1956 (in German) (RWDD, RA UD, Stockholm).

7. Nikolai Mesyatsev, *Gorizonty i labirinty moei zhizni* (Moscow: Vagrius, 2005), 141 (in Russian).

8. Page 123 in Dmitrii Dontsov, 'Stenografistka generala Abakumova,' in *Voennaya kontrrazvedka of 'Smersha' do kontrterroristicheskikh operatsii* (Moscow: Kuchkovo pole, 2010), 112–31 (in Russian).

9. Roger Moorhouse, *Killing Hitler: The Plots, the Assassins, and the Dictator Who Cheated Death* (New York: Bantam Books, 2006), 236–41.

10. Peter Hoffmann, *Stauffenberg: A Family History, 1905–1944* (New York: Cambridge University Press, 1995), 181.

11. Michael Mueller, *Canaris: The Life and Death of Hitler's Spymaster,* translated by Geoffrey Brooks (Annapolis, MD: Naval Institute Press, 2007), 224–5.

12. Klemens von Klemperer, *German Resistance Against Hitler: The Search for Allies Abroad, 1938–1945* (New York: Oxford University Press, 1992), 374–5.

13. Fabian von Schlabrendorff, *The Secret War Against Hitler,* translated by Hilda Simon (London: Hodder and Stoughton, 1966), 295.

14. Peter Hoffmann, *The History of the German Resistance 1933–1945,* translated from the German by Richard Barry (Cambridge, MA: The MIT Press, 1979), 334–5.

15. Boris Chavkin and Aleksandr Kalganov, 'Neue Quallen zur Geschichte des 20. Juli 1944 aus dem Archiv des Foederalen Sicherheitsdienstes der Russischen Foederation (FSB). "Eigenhaendige Aussagen" von Major i.G. Joachim Kuhn,' in *Forum für osteuropäische Ideen- und Zeitgeschichte,* 5. Jahrgang, 2001, Heft 2, 355–402.

16. Kuhn's statement, dated September 2, 1944. Document No. 1 in ibid., 374–98.

17. Kopelyansky's Russian translation in Boris Khavkin, 'Zagovor protiv Gitlera. Iz "Sobstennoruchnykh pokazanii" Kyuna,' *Rodina,* no. 6 (2004) (in Russian), http://istrodina.com/rodina_articul.php3?id=1199&n=67, retrieved July 23, 2008.

18. Ibid.

19. Photos of these documents in Peter Hoffmann, 'Oberst i. G. Hennig von Tresckow und die Staatsstreichpläne im Jahr 1943,' *Vierteljahrshefte für Zeitgeschichte* 55, No. 2 (2007), 331–64.

20. Khavkin, 'Zagovor protiv Gitlera.'

21. Peter Hoffmann, 'Major Joachim Kuhn: Explosives purveyor to Stauffenberg and Stalin's prisoner,' *German Studies Review*, Vol. 28, No. 3 (October 2005), 519–46. Unfortunately, this article contains inaccurate details.

22. Kuhn's letter dated February 15, 1952, in Chavkin und Kalganov, 'Neue Quellen zur Geschichte,' 369–70; Hoffmann, 'Major Joachim Kuhn,' 537–8.

23. Von Herwarth, *Against Two Evils*, 261.

24. NKVD Order No. 0308, dated September 19, 1939. Document No. 2–1 *Voennoplennye v SSSR 1939–1956. Dokumenty i materialy* (Moscow: Logos, 2000), edited by M. M. Zagorul'ko, 72–74 (in Russian). An overview of the UPVI/GUPVI activity is given in Stefan Karner, *Im Archipel GUPVI. Kriegsgefangenschaft in der Internierung in der Sowjetunion. 1941–1956* (Wien: R. Oldenbourg Verlag, 1995).

25. A GUPVI's report, RGVA, Fond I/p, Opis' 07e, Delo 136, L. 747.

26. NKVD Order No. 00398, dated March 1, 1943. Document No. 2.12 in *Voennoplennye v SSSR*, 100–5.

27. NKVD Instruction No. 489, dated October 7, 1943. Document 7.3 in ibid., 729–32.

28. NKVD Order No. 00130, dated September 9, 1944. Document 7.4 in ibid., 732–5.

29. NKVD Order No. 00100, dated February 20, 1945. Document 2.23 in ibid., 122–3.

30. V. M. Berezhkov, *Stranitsy diplomaticheskoi istorii* (Moscow: Mezhdunarodnye otnoshenoya, 1987), 208 (in Russian).

31. NKVD Order No. 0014, dated January 11, 1945. Document 2.22 in *Voennoplennye v SSSR*, 120–2.

32. MVD Directive No. 219, dated August 31, 1946. Document 7.6 in ibid., 739.

33. V. A. Vsevolodov, *'Srok khraneniya—postoyanno!' Kratkaya istoriya lagerya voennoplennykh i internirovannykh UPVI NKVD-MVD No. 27 (1942–1950 gg.)* (Moscow: LOK-motiv, 2003), 53–58 (in Russian).

34. Details in Aleksandr Kolpakidi, *Likvidatory KGB. Spetsoperatsii sovetskikh spetssluzhb. 1941–2004* (Moscow: Yauza-Eksmo, 2004), 20–25 (in Russian).

35. Yevgenii Zhirnov, 'Prints skryl svoyu nastoyashchuyu familiyu,' *Kommersant-Vlast'*, no. 14 (668), April 10, 2006 (in Russian), http://www.kommersant.ru/doc.aspx?DocsID=664971, retrieved September 9, 2011.

36. Kruglov's report to Molotov, dated March 16, 1946. GARF, Fond R-9401, Opis' 2 (Molotov's NKVD/MVD Special Folder), Delo 142. L. 56–58.

37. Pavel Sudoplatov and Anatoli Sudoplatov, with Jerrold L. and Leona P. Schecter, *Special Tasks: The Memoirs of an Unwanted Witness—A Soviet Spymaster* (New York: Little, Brown and Co., 1994), 112–5.

38. Ibid., 223–7.

39. Heinrich Graf von Einsiedel, *I Joined the Russians: A Captured German Flier's Diary of the Communist Temptation* (New Haven (CT): Yale University Press, 1953), 225–7.

40. Details in Peter J. Lapp, *General bei Hitler und Ulbricht. Vincenz Müller— Eine deutsche Karrier* (Berlin: Christoph Links Verlag, 2003).

41. Alaric Searle, '"Vopo"-General Vincenz Müller and Western Intelligence, 1948–54: CIC, the Gehlen Organization and Two Cold War Covert Operations,' *Intelligence and National Security* 17 (2002), no. 2, 27–50.

42. Document Nos. 7.23 and 7.25 in *Voennoplennye v SSSR*, 768–9, 772–3.

43. Document No. 54 in Vsevolodov, *Srok khraneniya*, 246–8.

44. Data from Hille's personal file, Military Archive, Moscow; Hille's prisoner card in Vladimir Prison; and Hille's interview given on September 1, 1954 to the Swedish journalist, Rudolph Phillipp.

45. From February till August 1946, N. V. Liutyi-Shestakovskii (1899–?) was deputy head, and from August 1946 till February 1948, head of the 2nd Department (supervision of secret agents) of the GUPVI Operational Directorate. *Voennoplennye v SSSR*, 1077.

46. Joachimsthaler, *The Last Days of Hitler*, 254.

47. V. A. Kozlov, *'Gde Gitler?' Povtornoe rassledovanie NKVD–MVD SSSR obstoyatel'stva ischeznoveiya Adolfa Gitlera (1945–1949)* (Moscow: Modest Kolyarov, 2003), 123 (in Russian).

48. GARF, Fond R-940, Opis' 2 (Stalin's Special NKVD/MVD Folder), Delo 66, L. 293–323.

49. For all these people see, for instance, von Klemperer, *German Resistance Against Hitler*.

50. John H. Waller, 'The Double Life of Admiral Canaris,' *The International Journal of Intelligence and Counterintelligence* 9, no. 3 (Fall 1996), 271–89.

51. Peter Carstens, 'Eime "zweite Entnazifizierung,"' *FAZ.net*, March 18, 2010, http://www.faz.net/s/Rub594835B672714A1DB1A121534F010EE1/Do c-EA65AAB2D1C2048249EAD3E3BC2FA6BAA-ATpl-Ecommon-Scontent. html, retrieved September 9, 2011.

Chapter 26

1. Details of negotiations and of the agreement in Boris Slavinsky, *The Japanese-Soviet Neutrality Pact: A Diplomatic History, 1941–1945*, translated by Geoffrey Jukes (New York: RoutledgeCurson, 2004), 32–60.

2. I. P. Makar, 'Iz opyta planirovaniya strategicheskiogo razvertyvaniya Vooruzhennykh Sil SSSR na sluchai voiny s Germaniei i neposredstennoi podgotovki k otrazheniyu agressii,' *VIZh*, no. 6 (2006), 3–9 (in Russian).

3. GKO Decision No. 3407ss, 'The NKVD Construction Site No. 500,' dated May 21, 1943.

4. *Foreign Relations of the United States Diplomatic Papers. The Conferences at Cairo and Tehran, 1943* (Washington, DC: U.S. Government Printing Office, 1943), 147.

5. Vasilevsky was summoned to Stalin's office on July 9, 26, 28, and 29. *Na prieme u Stalina. Tetradi (zhurnaly) zapisei lits, pronyatykh I. V. Stalinym (1924– 1953 gg.)*, edited by A. V. Korotkov, A. D. Chernev, and A. A. Chernobaev, 437–8

(Moscow: Novyi khronograf, 2008) (in Russian); A. M. Vasilevsky, *Delo vsei zhizni* (Moscow: Politizdat, 1978), 507 (in Russian).

6. *SMERSH, Istoricheskie ocherki*, 246.

1283. The text of the protocol at http://avalon.law.yale.edu/wwii/yalta.asp, retrieved September 9, 2011.

8. Cited in Volkogonov, *Stalin*, 493.

9. Ibid., 419–20.

10. Abakumov's report to Beria, dated June 30, 1945, in *SMERSH.Istoricheskie ocherki*, 246.

11. Ibid., 246.

12. Takashi Nakayama, 'Invasion of the Soviet forces," Chapter 1 in *The Japanese Internees and Forced Labor in the USSR after the Second WorldWar; The Excerpt Version*, 1-49, http://www.heiwa.go.jp/en/pdf/10/chapter_01.pdf, retrieved September 9, 2011.

13. Beria's report to Stalin, dated July 27, 1945. Document No. 85 in *Stalinskie stroiki GULAGa 1930–1953*, edited by A. I. Kokurin, and Yu. N. Morukov (Moscow: Demokratiya, 2005), 250 (in Russian).

14. Details, for instance, in David M. Glantz, *The Soviet Strategic Offensive in Manchuria, 1945: 'August Storm'* (London: Frank Cass Publishers, 2003).

15. On the events in Tokyo see, for instance, Christopher Andrew, *For the President's Eyes Only: Secret Intelligence and the American Presidency from Washington to Bush* (New York: Harper Perennial, 1996), 152–5.

16. Details in Tsuyoshi Heasegava, *Racing the Enemy: Stalin, Truman, and the Surrender of Japan* (Cambridge, MA: Belknap Press, 2005), 252–89.

17. Vladimir Vereshchagin and Nikolai Gordeev, 'Voennaya kontrrazvedka Zabaikal'ya v razgrome Kvantungskoi armii i osvobozhdenie severo-vostoka Kitaya,' *Istoriko-ekonomicheskii zhurnal*, no. 4 (1998) (in Russian), http://www.chekist.ru/print/1217, retrieved September 9, 2011; A. Doshlov, 'Zabaikal'tsy za Khinganom,' *VIZh*, no. 5 (2005), 24–25 (in Russian).

18. Report of Vadis to Babich, dated September 21, 1945, quoted in *SMERSH. Istoricheskie ocherki*, 248.

19. Ibid., 249.

20. Cited in Yurii Tsurganov, 'I na Tikhom okeane svoi zakonchili pokhod,' *Posev*, n. 9 (2005), 34–39 (in Russian).

21. A photo of Abakumov's report to Beria, dated August 28, 1945, in *SMERSH*, 248.

22. Details, for instance, in N. I. Dubinina and Yu. N. Tsipkin, 'Ob osobennostyakh dal'nevostochnoi vetvi rossiiskoi emigratsii (na materialakh Harbinskogo komiteta pomoshchi russkim bezhentsam),' *Otechestvennaya istoriya*, No. 1 (1996), 70–84 (in Russian); G. Melikhov, *Belyi Harbin. Seredina 20-kh* (Moscow: Russkii put', 2003) (in Russian).

23. On the Russian fascist movement see John J. Stephan, *The Russian Fascists: Tragedy and Farce in Exile, 1925–1945* (New York: Harper & Row, 1978).

24. Cited in Anton Utkin, 'Duche iz Blagoveshchenska,' *Sovershenno sekretno*, No. 47 (2003) (in Russian).

25. K. Rodzaevsky, *Zaveshchanie russkogo fashista* (Moscow: FERI-V, 2001) (in Russian).

26. In June–August 1942, A. A. Vonsiatsky (1898–1965) and five of his co-defendants were convicted in a federal court in Connecticut (USA) on the charge of espionage for Germany. Vonsiatsky was sentenced to a five-year term in a federal penitentiary and assessed a fine of $5,000. Details at http://www.fbi.gov/about-us/history/famous-cases/vonsiatsky-espionage, retrieved September 9, 2011.

27. S. Onegina, 'Buro po delam rossiiskoi emigratsii v Manchzhurii,' *Problemy Dal'nego Vostoka*, No. 5 (1996), 141–6 (in Russian).

28. Vadim Abramov, *Abakumov—nachal'nik SMERSHa. Vzlet i gibel' lyubimtsa Stalina* (Moscow: Yauza-ksmo, 2005), 150–1 (in Russian).

29. N. A. Ablova, *Istoriya KVZhD i rossiiskoi emigratsii v Kitae (pervaya polovina XX veka)* (Moscow: Russkaya panorama, 2004), Chapter 4 (in Russian), http://asiapacific.narod.ru/countries/china/n_e_ablova/4.4.htm, retrieved September 9, 2011.

30. Utkin, 'Duche iz Blagoveshchenska.'

31. S. Onegina, 'Pis'mo K. V. Rodzaevskogo I. V. Stalinu: Vstupitel'naya stat'ya,' *Otechestvennaya istoriya*, No. 3 (1992), 92–96 (in Russian).

32. Chapter 4 in Ye. A. Gorbunov, *Skhvatka s Chernym Drakonom. Tainaya voina na Dal'nem Vostoke* (Moscow: Veche, 2002), http://militera.lib.ru/research/gorbunov_ea/index.html, retrieved September 9, 2011.

33. Viktor Usov, *Poslednii imperator Kitaya Pu I (1906–1967)* (Moscow: Olma-Press, 2003), 193–200 (in Russian).

34. Onegina, 'Pis'mo K. V. Rodzaevskogo.'

35. On the imprisonment of N. A. Ukhtomsky in Rechlag (Vorkuta) see L. P. Markizov, *Do i posle 1945: Glazami ochevidtsa* (Syktyvkar, 2003 [no publisher]), 101–12 (in Russian).

36. A photo of Abakumov's report, dated September 28, 1945, in *SMERSH. Istoricheskie ocherki*, 248.

37. On the Bryner/Brynner family and its enterprises, see Rock Brynner [son of Yul], *Empire & Odyssey: The Brynners in Far East Russia and Beyond* (Hanover, NH: Steerforth Press, 2006).

38. Alvin D. Coox, 'L'Affaire Lyushkov: Anatomy of a Defector,' *Soviet Studies* 19, no. 3 (January 1968), 405–20; Alvin D. Coox, 'An Intelligence Case Study: The Lesser of Two Hells: NKVD G. S. Lyushkov's Defection to Japan, 1938–1945. Part I,' *The Journal of Slavic Military Studies* 11 (1998), no. 3, 145–86; Alvin D. Coox, 'An Intelligence Case Study: The Lesser Two Hells: NKVD G. S. Lyushkov's Defection to Japan, 1938–1945, Part 2,' ibid., 11 (1998), no. 4, 72–110.

39. Details in N. L. Pobol' and P. M. Polian, *Stalinskie deportatsii 1928–1953* (Moscow: Demokratiya, 2005), 80–97, and 101–4 (in Russian).

40. Yoshiaki Hiyama, 'Plany pokusheniya na Stalina,' *Problemy Dal'nego Vostoka*, No. 5 (1990), 109–11 (in Russian).

41. Boris Sokolov, *Okhota na Gitlera, okhta na Stalina. Tainaya bor'ba spetssluzhb* (Moscow: Veche, 2000), 22–23 (in Russian).

42. On the trial, see, for instance, Boris G. Yudin, 'Research on humans at the Khabarovsk War Crimes Trial: A historical and ethical examination,' in *Japan's Wartime Medical Atrocities: Comparative Inquiries in Science, History, and Ethics*, edited by Jing-Bao Nie et al., 59–78 (NY: Routledge, 2010).

43. V. A. Bobrenev and V. B. Ryazantsev, *Palachi i zhertvy* (Moscow: Voenizdat, 1993), 146–69 (in Russian).

44. Hal Leith, *POWs of Japanese Rescued!: General J. M. Wainwright* (Trafford Publishing, 2004), 76.

45 Major R. Lamar, 'Survey of the Mukden Area Situation,' September 11, 1945, quoted in Ronald H. Spector, *In the Ruins of Empire: The Japanese Surrender and the Battle for Postwar Asia* (New York: Random House, 2007), 33.

46. Vice Admiral Andrei Stetsenko and Major General of Aviation Nikolai Voronov were the other two Soviet representatives. L. Poritsky, 'Na bortu linkol'na "Missuri",' *Zerkalo nedeli*, No. 36 (309), September 16–22, 2000 (in Russian).

47. *Na prieme u Stalina*, 463.

48. Innokentii Pasynkov, 'Stalinskie "nabory" za granitsei,' '*Karta,*' no. 22–23 (1999) (in Russian), http://www.hro.org/files/karta/22-23/p66.jpg, retrieved September 9, 2011.

49. Usov, *Poslednii imperator*, 257–65; Vereshchagin and Gordeev, 'Voennaya kontrrazvedka Zabaikal'ya.'

50. Usov, *Poslednii imperator*, 266–99.

51. Ibid., 297.

52. Pu Yi, *The Last Manchu: The Autobiography of Henry Pu Yi, Last Emperor of China*, translated by Kuo Ying Paul Tsai (London: A. Barker, 1967).

53. Bobrenev and Ryazantsev, *Palachi i zhertvy*, 137–69. Also, prisoner cards from Vladimir Prison of the Japanese diplomats Yoshio Higashi, Kumasaburo Nakamura, Toshio Hoshiko, and Saburo Asada, head of the 2nd Department, HQ of the Kwantung Army.

54. V. P. Galitsky, 'Yaponskie voennoplennye i internirovannye v SSSR,' *Novaya i noveishaya istoriya*, no. 3 (1999), 18–33 (in Russian).

55. See text at http://www.ndl.go.jp/constitution/e/etc/c06.html, retrieved September 9, 2011.

Part IX. SMERSH after the War: 1945-46
Chapter 27

1. A. I. Romanov, *Nights Are Longest There: A Memoir of the Soviet Security Services,* translated by Gerald Brooke (Boston, MA: Little, Brown and Company, 1972), 144. From July 1945 to October 1947, G. S. Yevdokimenko (1914–1996) was deputy head of the Inspection (SMERSH/MGB operational group) at the Allied Control Commission in Budapest.

2. Interview with Yevgenii Agapov, former intelligence officer, on Aprrill 6, 2009, http://iremember.ru/razvedchiki/agapov-evgeniy-fedorovich.html, retrieved September 9, 2011.

3. Romanov, *Nights Are Longest*, 163–5.

4. Ibid., 165.

5. Nikolai Mesyatsev, *Gorizonty i labirinty moei zhizni* (Moscow: Vagrius, 2005), 212 (in Russian).

6. Abakumov's letter to Beria, dated June 22, 1945, quoted in Nikita Petrov, *Pervyi predsedatel' KGB Ivan Serov* (Moscow: Materik, 2005), 60–61 (in Russian).

7. Beria's report to Stalin No. 718/b dated June 22, 1945. Document No. 7 in *Spetsial'nye lagerya NKVD/MVD SSSR v Germanii. 1945–1950 gg. Sbornik dokumentov i stsatei*, edited by S. V. Mironenko, 27–28 (Moscow: ROSSPEN, 2001) (in Russian).

8. NKVD Order No. 00780, dated July 4, 1945. Document No. 8 in ibid., 28–30; Beria's report No. 1023/b, dated August 30, 1945. Document No. 319 in *Lubyanka. Stalin i NKVD-NKGB-GUKR 'SMERSH.' 1939–mart 1946*, edited by V. N. Khaustov, V. P. Naumov, and N. S. Plotnikova (Moscow: Materik, 2006), 533–4 (in Russian).

9. Page 353 in N. V. Petrov, 'Apparat upolnomochenogo NKVD-MGB SSSR v Germanii (1945–1953 gg.),' in *Spetsial'nye lagerya NKVD/MVD SSSR v Germanii*, 349–66.

10. Serov's report to Beria, dated July 22, 1945. Document No. 12 in Petrov, *Pervyi predsedael' KGB*, 227.

11. Decree of the Presidium of the USSR Supreme Council, dated July 9, 1945, cited on page 99 in Aleksandr Kokurin and Nikita Petrov, 'NKVD-NKGB-SMERSH: Struktura, funktsii, kadry. Stat'ya chetvertaya,' *Svobodnaya mysl'*, no. 9 (1997), 93–101 (in Russian).

12 Abakumov's report No. 824/A, dated August 28, 1945, quoted in Petrov, *Pervyi predsedatel' KGB*, 61.

13. Beria's letter to Stalin No. 1023/b, dated August 29, 1945, quoted in ibid., 61–62.

14. David Holloway, *Stalin and the Bomb: The Soviet Union and Atomic Energy, 1939–1956* (New Haven: Yale University Press, 1994), 129.

15. I. V. Bystrova, 'Voenno-promyshlennyi kompleks SSSR,' in *Sovetskoe obshchestvo: vozniknovenie, razvitie, istoricheskii final* (Moscow, 1997). T. 1, 150–89 (in Russian).

16. Stavka's Directive No. 11095, dated May 29, 1945. Document No. 267 in *Russkii Arkhiv. Velikaya Otechestvennaya*, 15 (4–5), 420–1.

17. David E. Murphy, Sergei A. Kondrashev, and George Bailey, *Battleground Berlin: CIA vs. KGB in the Cold War* (New Haven, CT: Yale University Press, 1997), 31.

18. Rudolf Pikhoya, *Moskva. Kreml'. Vlast'. Sorok let posle voiny 1945–1985* (Moscow: AST, 2007), 47–50 (in Russian).

19. A. N. Buchin, *170,000 kilometrov s G. K. Zhukovym* (Moscow: Molodaya gvardiya, 1994), 184–5 (in Russian).

20. Zhukov and Telegin's telegram to the GSOVG troops, dated June 30, 1945, quoted in Petrov, *Pervyi predsedatel' KGB*, 49–50.

21. Zhukov's Order No. 00138/op, dated September 9, 1945, and quoted in ibid., 54.

22. Stalin's directive to the Military Council of GSOVG, dated September 20, 1945, published in *Voenno-istoricheskii arkhiv*, no. 10 (2000), 146–8 (in Russian).

23. Directive of the Plenum of the USSR Supreme Court No. 13/14/V, dated November 27, 1945, cited in Petrov, *Pervyi predsedatel' KGB*, 56.

24. Serov's note to General S. F. Gorokhov and Colonel S. I. Tyulpanov, dated December 1946, quoted in ibid., 57.

25. Order No. 0409, dated December 26, 1944. Document No. 281 in *Russkii Arkhiv. Velikaya Otechestvennaya. Prikazy Narodnogo komissara Oborony SSSR (1943–1945)*, Tom 13 (2-3) (Moscow: Terra, 1997), 343–7 (in Russian).

26. P. Knyshevsky, *Dobycha. Tainy germanskikh reparatsii* (Moscow: Soratnik, 1994), 120, 137 (in Russian).

27. Abakumov's Order No. 00170, dated September 27, 1945. Quoted in Yevgenii Tolstykh, *Agent Nikto. Iz istorii 'Smersh'* (Moscow: Sovershenno sekretno, 2004), 149–50 (in Russian).

28. An excerpt from Serov's report to Stalin about Abakumov, dated September 8, 1946. Page 245 in Document No. 19 in Petrov, *Pervyi predsedatel' KGB*, 244–7.

29. Pages 245–6 in ibid.

30. On the 'Aviators Case' see I. N. Kosenko, 'Taina "Aviatsionnogo dela,"' *VIZh*, nos. 6 & 8 (1994); Pikhoya, *Moskva. Kreml'. Vlast'*, 50–55.

31. Text of Stalin's order, dated May 26, 1943, in O. S. Smyslov, *Vasilii Stalin. Zalozhnik imeni* (Moscow: Veche, 2003), 153 (in Russian).

33. Recollection by Svetlana Novikova, a daughter of Aleksandr Novikov, in Larisa Goryacheva, 'Interview no. 28,' 2000 (in Russian), http://www.peoples.ru/military/aviation/novikov/, retrieved September 9, 2011.

34. On the case of S. A. Khudyakov (1902–1950) see Nikolai Smirnov, *Vplot' do vysshei mery* (Moscow: Moskovskii rabochii, 1997), 132–6 (in Russian).

35. Vyacheslav Zvyagintsev, *Tribunal dlya 'stalinskikh sokolov'* (Moscow: Terra, 2008), 339–49 (in Russian).

36. Text of the letter in Pikhoya, Pikhoya, *Moskva. Kreml'. Vlast'*, 53.

37. Quoted in Aleksandr Vais, 'Dolgozhitel'. 'Aviatsionnoe' delo, *Argumenty i fakty*, 8 (92), April 21, 2006 (in Russian), http://gazeta.aif.ru/online/longliver/92/23_01, retrieved September 9, 2011.

38. Decision of the Presidium of the Central Committee on rehabilitation of A. I. Shakhurin, A. A. Novikov, and others, dated June 12, 1953. Document No. I-28 in *Reabilitatsiya: Kak eto bylo. Dokumenty Prezidiuma TsK KPSS i drugie materially. Mart 1953–fevral' 1956*, edited by A. Artizov et al., 50–51 (Moscow: Demokratiya, 2000) (in Russian).

39. Quoted in A. A. Lyovin, *Perebitye kryl'ya: dokumental'naya povest'* (Moscow: [no publisher], 1996), 238 (in Russian).

40. Yelena Loria, 'Svetlana Novikova: "Ottsa nazyvali 'letayushchim krylom Zhukova",' *Izvestia*, February 3, 2003 (in Russian).

41. Abakumov's short cover letter addressed to Stalin, dated April 30, 1946, with Novikov's statement from the same date. Document No. 3 in *Lubyanka. Stalin i MGB SSSR. Mart 1946–mart 1953*, edited by V. N. Khaustov, V. P. Naumov, and N. S. Plotnikova, 11–16 (Moscow: Materik: 2007) (in Russian).

42. Quoted in Lyovin, *Perebitye kryl'ya*, 235–6.

43. Gennadii Kostyrchenko, 'Malenkov protiv Zhdanova. Igry stalinskikh favoritov,' *Rodina*, No. 9 (2000), 85–92 (in Russian).

44. Quoted in Smyslov, *Vasilii Stalin*, 196.

45. Quoted in Lyovin, *Perebitye kryl'ya*, 237.

46. Pikhoya, *Moskva. Kreml'. Vlast'*, 54.

47. Zvyagintsev, *Tribunal dlya 'stalinskikh sokolov,'* 346–7.

48. *Molotov Remembers: Inside Kremlin Politics* (Chicago: Ivan R. Dee, 1993), 309.

49. Smirnov, *Vplot' do vysshei mery*, 134, 136.

50. The text in *Georgii Zhukov. Stenogramma oktyabr'skogo (1957 g.) plenuma TsK KPSS i drugie dokumenty*, edited by V. Naumov, 16–17 (Moscow: Demokratiya, 2001) (in Russian).

51. Stavka's Directive No. 11096, dated May 29, 1945. Document No. 268 in *Russkii Arkhiv. Velikaya Otechestvennaya*, 15 (4-5), 421–2.

52. Romanov, *Nights Are Longest There*, 153.

53. Ibid., 149.

54. Nicholas M. Nagy-Talavera, *Recollections of Soviet Labor Camps, 1949-1955. An Interview Conducted by Richard A. Pierce*, 1971. University of California at Berkeley, Bancroft Library, Regional Oral History Office (a typed manuscript), 7.

55. Ibid., 5.

56. S. Kertesz, 'Soviet and Western Politics in Hungary, 1944–1947,' *The Review of Politics* 1, no. 1 (January 1952), 47–74.

57. Contrary to the opinion of many western historians [for instance, R. J. Crampton, *Eastern Europe in the Twentieth Century and After* (London: Routledge, 1997), 263], Abakumov and his MGB, especially Belkin—and not the NKVD/MVD –supervised the preparation of the Rajk Trial. Biography of M. I. Belkin (1901-1980) in N. V. Petrov, *Kto rukovodil organami gosbezopasnosti 1941–1954* (Moscow: Zven'ya, 2010), 188–9 (in Russian).

58. G. M. Savenok, *Venskie vstrechi* (Moscow: Voenizdat, 1961), 156–66 (in Russian).

59. E. Ya. Kolman, *My ne dolzhmy byli tak zhit'* (New York: Chalidze Publications, 1982), 230 (in Russian).

60. Stavka's Directive No. 11097, dated May 29, 1945. Document No. 269 in *Russkii Arkhiv. Velikaya Otechestvennaya*, 15 (4–5), 422–4.

61. Beria's letter to Stalin and Molotov dated March 1, 1945. Document No. 30 in *Iz Varshavy. Moskva, tovarishchu Beria...Dokumenty NKVD SSSR o pol'skom podpol'e 1944-1945 gg.*, edited by A. F. Noskova, 115 (Moscow: Sibirskii khronograf, 2001) (in Russian).

62. Meshik's biography in N. V. Petrov and K. V. Skorkin, *Kto rukovodil NKVD. 1939–1941. Spravochnik* (Moscow: Zven'ya, 1999), 297 (in Russian).

63. Document Nos. 66–72 and 76 in *Iz Varshavy. Moskva* , 230–44, 254–5.

64. Nicola Sinevirsky, *SMERSH* (New York: Henry Holt and Co., 1950), 205.

65. Biography of S. P. Davydov (1909–1959) in Petrov, *Kto rukovodil organami gosbezopasnosti*, 325–6.

66. Stavka's Directive No. 11098, dated May 29, 1945, in *Russkii arkhiv: Velikaya Otechestvennaya. Stavka VKG: Dokumenty i materially 1944–1945*, T. 16 (5–4) (Moscow: Terra, 1999), 243 (in Russian).

67. The structure and staff of the ACC in Bulgaria approved by the Politburo on November 13, 1944 (Decision 44/169). Document Nos. 53 and 54 in *Russkii Arkhiv. Velikaya Otechestvennaya*, 14 (3–2), 144–7 (in Russian).

68. A. I. Cherepanov, *Pole ratnoe moe* (Moscow: Voenizdat, 1984), 272–3 (in Russian).

69. Cherepanov, ibid., 271–2.

70. Roy M. Melbourne, *Conflict and Crisis: A Foreign Service Story* (Lanham, MD: University Press of America, 1997), 96.

71. Donovan's final report on activities of the OSS units in Romania and Bulgaria, dated November18, 1944. Documents 93–94 in *The OSS–NKVD Relationship, 1943–1945 (Covert Warfare series, Volume 8)* (New York: Garland Publishing, Inc., 1989). Biryuzov is mentioned as 'Berezov' in Document 72 in ibid.

72. Yelena Valeva, 'Politicheskie protsessy v Bolgarii, 1944–1948 gg.,' '*Karta,*' no. 36-37 (2003), 48-59 (in Russian), http://www.hro.org/node/10845, retrieved September 8, 2011.

73. Biryuzov's letter to Kimon Georgiev, dated November 28, 1944, in Cherepanov, *Pole ratnoe moe,* 272.

74. Memoirs by Vladimir Skorodumov, 'Rusaika,' *Neva,* no. 10 (2006) (in Russian), http://magazines.russ.ru/neva/2006/10/sk15-pr.html, retrieved September 9, 2011.

75. GKO Decision No. 7161-ss, dated December 16, 1944. Details in V. B. Konasov and A. V. Tereshchuk, '"Budut nemedlenno predany sudu Voennogo Tribunala..." Iz istorii internirovaniya grazhdanskogo naseleniya Avstrii, Bolgarii, Vengrii, Germanii, Rumynii, Chekhslovakii i Yugoslavii v 1944–1945 gg,' *Russkoe proshloe,* no. 5 (1994), 318–37 (in Russian).

76. Elizabeth W. Hazard, *Cold War Crubicle: United States Foreign Policy and the Conflict in Romania. 1943–1953* (Boulder, CO: East European Monographs, 1996), 64–72.

77. Interview with Mrs. Polly Wisner Fritchey in Burton Hersh, *The Old Boys: The American Elite and the Origins of the CIA* (New York: Charles Scribner's Sons, 1992), 208.

78. Robert Bishop and E. S. Crayfield, *Russia Astride the Balkans* (New York: Robert McBride, 1948), 123.

79. Polyan, *Ne po svoei vole,* 210.

80. Hersh, *The Old Boys,* 208.

81. Hazard, *Cold War Crubicle,* 96–98. In October 1946, Mannicatide, who had joined the OSS staff, and his family were smuggled out of Romania under General Schuyler's supervision, and they ended up in the United States.

82. B. D. Yurinov, 'Vzaimodeistvie razvedok SSSR i SshA v gody voiny,' *Ocherki istorii rossiiskoi vneshnei razvedki. T. 4. 1941–1945 gody* (Moscow: Mezhdunarodnye otnosheniya, 1999), 399–415 (in Russian).

83. Nikita Petrov, 'Die militärische Spionageabwehr in Österreich und die Todesstrafe. Struktur, Funktionen, Praxis,' in *Stalins letzte Opfer: Verschleppte und erschossenen Österreicher in Moscau 1950–1953,* edited by Stefan Karner and Barbara Stelzl-Marx, 79–96 (Wien: Böhlau Verlag, 2009).

84. Romanov, *Nights Are Longest There,* 158.

85. Report No. 3067 by Lieutenant Colonel Bogdanov, head of the Inspectorate in Austria, to deputy MGB Minister Selivanovsky, dated September 9, 1947. Document No. 104 in *Die Rote Armee in Osterreich: Sovjetische Besatzung 1945-1955. Dokumente,* edited by Stefan Karner, Barbara Stelzl-Marx, and Alexander O. Tschubarian, 478–84 (München: Oldenbourg Verlag, 2005).

86. Romanov, *Nights Are Longest There,* 158-9.

87. Ibid., 160.

88. Pages 31–34 in N. Petrov and Ya. Foitsik, 'Vvedenie. Apparat upolnomochennogo NKVD-MGB SSSR v Germanii, politichesrie repressii i formirovanie nemetskikh organov bezopasnosti v GDR 1945–1953 gg.,' in *Apparat NKVD-NKGB v Germanii, 1945–1953*, edited by N. Petrov and Ya. Foitsik, 5–53 (Moscow: Demokratiya, 2009) (in Russian).

89. Gotthold Starke's prisoner card in the Vladimir Prison Archive.

90. Unto Parvilahti, *Beria's Garden: Ten Years' Captivity in Russia and Siberia*, translated from the Finnish by Alan Blair (London: Hutchinson and Company, 1959), 141. Starke briefly described his imprisonment in Gotthold Starke, 'Archbishop Reins in the Prison of Vladimir,' *Modern Age*, no. 2 (Spring 1958), 182-5.

91. According to Duke Christian Ludwig's prisoner card in Vladimir Prison, he was tried under the Control Council Law No. 10 (Punishment of Persons Guilty of War Crimes, Crimes Against Peace and Against Humanity adopted at the Nuremberg Trials), Article 2-1a (crimes against peace).

92. Nagy-Talavera, *Recollections*, 8.

93. List of the Austrians executed in 1945–47, in *Stalins letzte Opfer*, 631–2.

94. Stavka's Directive No. 11086, dated May 11, 1945. Document No. 266 in *Russkii Arkhiv. Velikaya Otechestvennaya*, 15 (4–5), 418–9.

95. Romanov, *Nights Are Longest There*, 172.

96. Anatoly Gulin, 'I ne komissar, i ne evrei…Moya nevolya,' *Novyi Mir*, no. 7 (2003) (in Russian), http://magazines.russ.ru/novyi_mi/2005/7/gu4.html, retrieved September 9, 2011.

97. Romanov, *Nights Are Longest There*, 173–4.

98. Mark W. Clark, *Calculated Risk* (New York: Harper & Brothers, 1950), 476–7.

99. Romanov, *Nights Are Longest There*, 159.

100. V. N. Nikolsky, *GRU v gody Velikoi Otechestvennoi voiny* (Moscow: Yauza-Eksmo, 2005) (in Russian), http://militera.lib.ru/h/nikolsky_va01/index.html, retrieved September 9, 2011.

101. V. P. Babich, *Velikaya Otechestvennaya voina: Vospominaniya V. P. Babicha, Chapter 1. Dlinnyi put' domoi* (in Russian), http://vsbabich.narod.ru/dolgoe1.htm, retrieved September 9, 2011.

Chapter 28

1. Joseph E. Persico, *Nuremberg: Infamy on Trial* (New York: Viking, 1994), 32–34.

2. Arkadii Vaksberg, *Stalin's Prosecutor: The Life of Andrei Vyshinsky*, translated from the Russian by Jan Butler (New York: Grove Weidenfeld, 1991), 101 and 134.

3. A report of the Commission of the Central Committee of the Communist Party to the Presidium of the Central Committee, signed by P. Pospelov and A. Aristov and dated February 9, 1956. Document No. V-15 in *Reabilitatsiya: Kak eto bylo. Mart 1953–fevral' 1956 gg. Dokumenty Presidiuma TsK KPSS i drugie materially*, edited by A. Artizov et al., 317–65 (Moscow: Demokratiya, 2000) (in Russian).

4. Ibid., 343–4.

5. George Ginsburgs, *Moscow's Road to Nuremberg: The Soviet Background to the Trial* (The Hague: Martinus Nujhoff Publishers, 1996), 95–115.

6. Edward R. Stettinius, Jr., *Roosevelt and the Russians: The Yalta Conference* (Garden City, NY: Doubleday & Co., Inc., 1949), 334.

7. Telford Taylor, *The Anatomy of the Nuremberg Trials: A Personal Memoir* (New York: Alfred A. Knopf, 1992), 63.

8. Ibid., 64.

9. Yurii Shcheglov, 'Pered Nurenbergom...' *Kontinent*, no. 120 (2004) (in Russian), http://magazines.russ.ru/continent/2004/120/shegl14-pr.html, retrieved September 9, 2011.

10. Aleksandr Zvyiagintsev and Yurii Orlov, *Prokurory dvukh epoch. Andrei Vyshinsky i Roman Rudenko* (Moscow: Olma-Press, 2001), 208–12 (in Russian).

11. On the arrest of the sixteen Polish leaders see Document Nos. 42-44 in *Iz Varshavy. Moskva*, 148–59.

12. Politburo decision P45/277, dated June 13, 1945. See text in ibid., 216.

13. Although many sources claim that General Okulicki was killed, medical documents in his prison file (a copy of the file was handed over to Polish officials in 1990) point to death from natural causes.

14. 'On the inclusion in the list of main defendants,' dated August 18, 1945. GARF, Fond R-9401, Opis' 2 (Molotov's NKVD/ MVD Special Folder), Delo 103, L. 356–7.

15. 'A list of War Criminals Who Should Be Tried by the International Tribunal,' dated August 27, 1945. GARF, Fond R-9401, Opis' 2 (Molotov's NKVD/ MVD Special Folder), Delo 103, L. 330–6.

16. See, for instance, a transcript of Friedrich Jeckeln's interrogation on December 14, 1945, http://www.nizkor.org/ftp.cgi/people/ftp.py?people//j/jeckeln.friedrich/jeckeln-interrogation.1245, retrieved September 9, 2011.

17. GUPVI's registration cards of Bernhardt and Richert in I. V. Bezborodova, *Generaly Vermakhta v plenu* (Moscow: Rossiiskii gosudarstvemmyi gumanitarnyi universitet, 1998), 61 and 140 (in Russian). In 1947, Generals Klammt and Traut were sentenced to a 25-year imprisonment in labor camps; in October 1955, they were repatriated to Germany. Their cards in ibid., 99 and 146.

18. I will cite the *Trial of the Major War Criminals Before the International Military Tribunal, Nuremberg, 14 November 1945 –1 October 1946* (Buffalo, NY: William S. Hein & Co., Inc.) as *The Nuremberg Trial. The Nuremberg Trial*, Vol. 8, 105, http://avalon.law.yale.edu/imt/02-22-46.asp, retrieved September 9, 2011.

19. Politburo decisions P46/238 and P46/240, dated September 5 and 6, 1945. *Politburo TsK RKP(b)-VKP9b). Povestki dnya zasedanii.* T. 3, 1940–1953, edited by G. M. Adibekov, 399 (Moscow: ROSSPEN, 2001) (in Russian). In April 1946, the new MVD Minister Sergei Kruglov replaced Merkulov in the Commission.

20. Politburo decision P47/131, dated September 21, 1945. *Politburo*, 409.

21. Yu. Zorya, '"Prokurorskaya diplomatiya" Vyshinskogo,' in *Inkvizitor. Stalinskii prokuror Vyshinskii* (Moscow: Respublika, 1992), 208-88 (in Russian); N. Lebedeva, 'Kak gotovilsya Nurenbergskii protsess,' *Mezhdunarodnaya zhizn'*, No. 8 (1996), 99–108 (in Russian).

22. Vaksberg, *Stalin's Prosecutor*, 260.

23. Details, for instance, in Richard Overy, *Interrogations: The Nazi Elite in Allied Hands, 1945* (New York: Viking, 2001), 41–42.

24. *SMERSH. Istoricheskie ocherki i arkhivnye dokumenty*, edited by V. S. Khristoforov et al., 322 (Moscow: Glavarkhiv Moskvy, 2003) (in Russian).

25. Vladimir Abarinov, 'V kuluarakh dvortsa yustitsii,' *Gorizont*, no. 5 (1990), 61–70 (in Russian).

26. Biography of M. T. Likhachev (1913–1954) in Petrov, *Kto rukovodil organzmi gosbezopasnosti*, 548.

27. *SMERSH. Istoricheskie ocherki*, 271.

28. Ibid., 325.

29. P. I. Grishaev and B. A. Solovov, 'Domyslami nel'zya snyat' 'khrestomatiinyi glyanets' s istorii Nyurenbergskogo protsessa,' *Gorizont*, No. 5 (1990), 38–43 (in Russian).

30. Communication by Vladimir Abarinov, 1990.

31. Tupikov was in Nuremberg until January 1946. He left for Moscow and then escorted the Japanese arrestees to the trial in Tokyo.

32. Declarations written by Fritzsche and Raeder on October 18, 1945. *The Nuremberg Trial*, Vol. 1, http://www.yale.edu/lawweb/avalon/imt/proc/v1-08. htm, retrieved September 9, 2011.

33. G. M. Gilbert, *Nuremberg Diary* (New York: Da Capo Press, 1995), 7.

34. Erich Raeder, *My Life*, translated from the German by Henry W. Drexel (Annapolis, MD: US Naval Institute, 1960), 386.

35. Ibid., 386–7.

36. Minutes of the Vyshinsky Commission meeting on November 16, 1945, in Nataliya Lebedeva, 'Neizvestnyi Nurenberg,' *Rodina*, no. 6-7 (1991) (in Russian).

37. Vyshinsky's telegram to Gorshenin, dated November 19, 1945, in ibid.

38. Cited in Overy, *Interrogations*, 204.

39. Anton Joachimsthaler, T*he Last Days of Hitler: Legend, Evidence and Truth*, English translation by Helmut Bogler (London: Cassell & Co., 2000), 288; 'Hans Fritzsche' in *Nazi Conspiracy and Aggression*. Vol. II, Chapter XVI, 1035–52, http://www.nizkor.org/hweb/imt/nca/nca-02/nca-02-16-21-index.html, retrieved September 9, 2011.

40. Document No. 193 in *Russkii Arkhiv*, 15 (4/5), 281–2.

41. Echtmann's testimony on April 27, 1953, quoted in Joachimsthaler, *The Last Days*, 238–9.

42. Hans Fritzsche, *The Sword in the Scales*, as told to Hildegard Springer, translated by Diana Pyke and Heinrich Fraenkel (London: Allan Wingate, 1953), 41.

43. *The Nuremberg Trial*, Vol. 6, 72, http://avalon.law.yale.edu/imt/01-23-46. asp, retrieved February 20, 2011.

44. Gilbert, *Nuremberg Diary*, 163–4.

45. *The Nuremberg Trial*, Vol. 17, 202, http://avalon.law.yale.edu/imt/06-28-46.asp, retrieved September 9, 2011.

46. Ibid., 203.

47. Ibid., 215.

48. Ibid., 215–6.

49. Ibid., 231.

50. Nikitchenko's speech, http://avalon.law.yale.edu/imt/juddiss.asp, retrieved September 9, 2011.

51. Ingeborg Kalnoky and Ilona Herisko, *The Witness House* (Indianapolis: Bobbs-Merrill Company, Inc., 1974), 228–9.

52. *Ellensburg Daily Record*, September 26, 1953, 14.

53. Quoted in Abarinov, 'V kuluarakh.'

54. Grishaev and Solovov, 'Domyslami nel'zya snyat' 'khrestomatiinyi gly-anets', 41.

55. Quoted in Abarinov, 'V kuluarakh,' 68–69, and discussed in Francine Hirsch, 'The Soviets at Nuremberg: International Law, Propaganda, and the Making of the Postwar Order,' *The American Historical Review* 113, no. 3 (June 2008), 701–30.

56. Arkadii Vaksberg, 'Zasluzhennyi deyatel,' *Literaturnaya Gazeta*, March 13 (1989), 13 (in Russian).

57. I. F. Finyaev, 'General-feldmarshal F. Paulus svidetel'stvuet,' *VIZh*, no. 5 (1990), 52–54 (in Russian).

58. Report by Vyshinsky and Kruglov with an attached draft of Decision of the USSR Council of Ministers, dated March 29, 1950. Cited in *Arkhiv noveishei istorii Rossii. T. 1.'Osobaya papka' I. V. Stalina*, edited by V. A. Kozlov and S. V. Mironenkom 307 (Moscow: Blagovest, 1994) (in Russian).

59. Anatrolii Tereshchenko, *SMERSH v boyu* (Moscow: Yuza-Eksmo, 2010), 187 (in Russian).

60. Fitin's report, dated December 8, 1945. GARF, Fond R-9401, Opis' 2 (Molotov's NKVD/ MVD Special Folder), Delo 105, L. 354–5.

61. Quoted in Abarinov, 'V kuluarakh.'

62. Drafts (LX-1 and LX-2) and the final version of the report 'General Observations on the Soviet Intelligence Mission in Nuremberg' dated October 16, 1946 (February 1—June 15, 1946). NARA (Washington), RG 226, Entry 213, Box 2.

63. Richard W. Cutler, *Counterspy: Memoirs of a Counterintelligence Officer in World War II and the Cold War* (Washington, DC: Brassey's, Inc., 2004), 125—31.

64. The final report, NARA, RG 226, Entry 213, Box 2.

65. Report LX-1 dated February 1–June 15, 1946, NARA, RG 226, Entry 213, Box 2.

66. Ibid.

67. Vaksberg, *Stalin's Prosecutor*, 232–3.

68. Boris Yefimov, *Desyat' desyatiletii. O tom,chto videl, perezhil, zapomnil* (Moscow: Vagrius, 2000) , 416–7, 428 (in Russian).

69. *Pravda*, December 12, 1945.

70. Abarinov, 'V kuluarakh,' 69–70.

71. Details in Zorya, 'Prokurorskaya diplomatiya,' 279–82.

72. *The Nuremberg Trial*, Vol. 10, 310–4, http://avalon.law.yale.edu/imt/04-01-46.asp; Vol. 14, 285, http://avalon.law.yale.edu/imt/05-21-46.asp, retrieved September 9, 2011.

73. Alfred Seidl, *Der Fall Rudolf Hess 1941—1987: Dokumentation des Verteidigers* (München: Universitas, 1988), 170.

74. Krystyna Kurczab-Redlich, 'Doklad Zori,' *Russkii Zhurnal*, November 24, 2000 (in Russian), http://old.russ.ru/ist_sovr/other_lang/20001124.html, retrieved September 9, 2011.

75. Application of Dr. Otto Stahmer on March 8, 1946, in *The Nuremberg Trial*, Vol. 9, 2–3, http://avalon.law.yale.edu/imt/03-08-46.asp, retrieved September 9, 2011.

76. Ibid., Vol. 17, http://avalon.law.yale.edu/imt/07-01-46.asp; http://avalon.law.yale.edu/imt/07-02-46.asp, retrieved September 9, 2011. More information in Taylor, The Anatomy of Nuremberg, 466–72.

77. T. S. Stupnikova, '...*Nichego, krome pravdy...*' *Nurnberg—Moskva: Vospominaniya* (Moscow: Russkie slovari, 1998), 104 (in Russian).

78. Transcript of the meeting on March 21, 1946. Document No. 222 in *Katyn. Mart 1940 g.—sentyabr' 2000 g. Rasstrel. Sud'by zhivykh. Ekho Katyni. Dokumenty,* edited by N. S. Lebedeva, N. A. Petrasova, B. Voshchinski, et al. (Moscow: Ves' Mir, 2001), 555–6 (in Russian).

79. An interview with the historian Nataliya Lebedeva, in Yekaterina Latartseva, 'Nepriyatnaya pravda Nyurnberg', *Trud*, no. 149, August 31, 2011 (in Russian), http://luke.trud.ru/index.php/article/31-08-2011/267017_neprijatnaja_pravda_njurnberga.html, retrieved September 9, 2011.

80. Stupnikova, '...*Nichego krome pravdy...*' 104.

81. Persico, *Nuremberg*, 343–4.

82. A letter of D. M. Reznichenko to Yu. N. Zorya, quoted in Abarinov, 'V kuluarakh,' page 68.

83. Sheinin's testimony quoted in Aleksandr Zvyagintsev and Yurii Orlov, *Prokurory dvukh epokh. Abdrei Vyshinsky i Roman Rudenko* (Moscow:Olma-Press), 215 (in Russian).

84. Grishaev and Solovov, 'Domyslami nel'zya snyat.'

85. *SMERSH. Istoricheskie ocherki*, 324.

Epilogue

1. Politburo decision P46/232, dated September 4, 1945. Document No. 1 in *Politburo TsK VKP(b) i Sovet Ministrov SSSR 1945–1953,* edited by O. V. Khlevnyuk et al., 21 (Moscow: ROSSPEN, 2002) (in Russian).

2. *Na prieme u Stalina. Tetradi (zhurnaly) zapisei lits, pronyatykh I. V. Stalinym (1924–1953 gg.),* edited by A. V. Korotkov, A. D. Chernev, and A. A. Chernobaev, 464 (Moscow: Novyi khronograf, 2008) (in Russian).

3. Politburo decision P47/111, dated December 29, 1945. Document No. 3, in *Politburo TsK VKP(b)*, 24.

4. Hugh Thomas, *Armed Truce: The Beginning of the Cold War, 1945–46* (New York: Atheneum, 1987), 4, 7–15.

5. Ibid., 503–14.

6. Decree of the USSR Supreme Council, dated March 15, 1946. Document No. 5, in *Politburo TsK VKP(b)*, 25–26.

7. *Na prieme u Stalina,* 472.

8. Politburo decisions P51/V, P52/2, and P52/8, dated May 4, 5, and 7, 1946. Document Nos. 184–186 in *Politburo TsK VKP(b)*, 207–8.

9. A footnote to Document No. 187 in *Politburo TsK VKP(b)*, 208–9.

10. Amy Knight, *How the Cold War Began: The Igor Gouzenko Affair and the Hunt for Soviet Spies* (New York: Carrol & Graf Publishers, 2006).

11. Details in Kathryn S. Olmsted, *Red Spy Queen: A Biography of Elizabeth Bentley* (Chapel Hill, NC: University of North Carolina Press, 2002).

12. Aleksandr Kolpakidi, *Likvidatory KGB. Spetsoperatsii sovetskikh spetssluzhb 1941–2004* (Moscow: Yauza-Eksmo, 2004), 407–8 (in Russian). A report of Kim Philby on Volkov's attempted defection to Philby's handler, the NKGB *rezident* Boris Krotov, played a key role in capturing Volkov and his wife. See details in Andrew and Gordievsky, *KGB*, 371–2. Supposedly, in 1947 Volkov was sentenced to a 25-year imprisonment.

13. Decision of the Central Committee's Plenum P9/2, dated August 21–23, 1946. Document No. 187 in *Politburo TsK VKP(b)*, 208–9.

14. Merkulov's letter, June 1946. Quoted in Nikita Petrov, 'Samyi obrazovannyi palach,' *Novaya gazeta. 'Pravda Gulaga,'* No. 12 (33), August 30, 2010 (in Russian), http://www.novayagazeta.ru/data/2010/gulag12/00.html, retrieved September 8, 2011.

15. Merkulov's letter to Khrushchev, dated August 23, 1953. Document No. 5 in O. Marinin, '"Dokladyvayu o soderzhanii razgovorov, kotorye u menya byli s vragom naroda Beria...",' in *Neizvestnaya Rossiya: XX vek* , Vol. 3 (Moscow: Istoricheskoe nasledie, 1993), 43–84 (in Russian).

16. In Yevgenii Zhirnov, 'Na doklady v Kreml' on ezdil v mashine Gimmlera,' *Kommersant-Vlast'*, no. 19 (472), May 21, 2002 (in Russian), http://www.kommersant.ru/doc/322678, retrieved September 9, 2011.

17. The report in *Politburo TsK VKP(b)*, 208.

18. Nicola Sinevirsky, *SMERSH* (New York: Henry Holt and Company, 1950), 82.

19. Detailed new MGB structure in N. V. Petrov, *Kto rukovodil organami bezopasnosti 1941–1954. Spravochnik* (Moscow: Zven'ya, 2010), 35–64 (in Russian).

20. Ibid., 51.

21. MGB Order No. 00496, dated November 2-4, 1946. Details in O. B. Mozokhin, *Pravo na repressii* (Moscow: Kuchkovo pole, 2006), 331 (in Russian).

22. Grishaev's report on Abakumov, dated November 15, 1952, in Kirill Stolyarov, *Palachi i zhertvy* (Moscow: Olma-Press, 1997), 66–67 (in Russian).

23. Quoted in Nikita Petrov, 'Bukhgalter—takoi prostoi,' *Novaya gazeta. Pravda 'GULAGa'*, no. 18, October 27, 2010, http://www.novayagazeta.ru/data/2010/gulag18/01.html, retrieved September 9, 2011..

24. Cited in Nikita Petrov, *Pervyi predsedatel' KGB Ivan Serov* (Moscow: Materik, 2005), 151 (in Russian).

INDEX

Also available from Biteback

OPERATION GARBO

THE PERSONAL STORY OF THE MOST
SUCCESSFUL SPY OF WORLD WAR II

NIGEL WEST & JUAN PUJOL GARCÍA

Garbo was the British codename of Juan Pujol García, perhaps the
most influential spy of the Second World War. By feeding false
information to the Germans on the eve of the D-Day landings he
ensured Hitler held troops back that might otherwise have defeated
the Normandy landings. Amazingly, Garbo's cover was never
broken and he remains the only person ever to have been awarded
both the British MBE and the German Iron Cross. After the war
Garbo faked his own death and fled to Venezuela. Ironically, his
family in Spain only found out he was still alive when this book
was published, Garbo having failed to realise it would also be
translated into Spanish.

288pp paperback, £9.99

Available from all good bookshops or to order from
www.bitebackpublishing.com

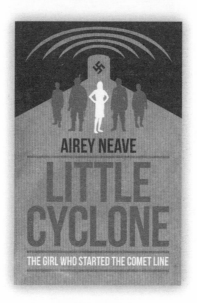